P9-DHT-029

## DATE DUE

1978

OCT 24 1990

GAYLORD     PRINTED IN U.S.A.

# Three Faces of Marxism

**Wolfgang Leonhard**
*Translated by Ewald Osers*

# Three
## Faces
# of Marxism

## The Political Concepts
## of Soviet Ideology, Maoism,
## and Humanist Marxism

HOLT, RINEHART AND WINSTON

*New York*

Published simultaneously in Canada by Holt, Rinehart and
Winston of Canada, Limited.

Library of Congress Cataloging in Publication Data

Leonhard, Wolfgang.
Three faces of Marxism.

Translation of Die Dreispaltung des Marxismus.
Bibliography: p.
1. Communism—1945–        2. Communism—Russia.
3. Communism—China (People's Republic of China, 1949–        )
4. Communist strategy.   I.   Title.
HX44.L39813        335.43        71–182771
ISBN 0–03–088620–1

10   9   8   7   6   5   4   3   2

Designer: Winston Potter

Printed in the United States of America

# Contents

□the Transition to Communism□the Future Communist Society□from World Revolution to Great-Russian Chauvinism□Peaceful Coexistence and the Inevitability of Wars□the Changes from Marx to Stalin□Marxist-Leninist Critique of Stalinism.

**A Few Conclusions** *355*

**Notes** *371*

**Selected Bibliography** *429*

**Index** *481*

# Preface

This book deals with the political ideas of Marxism from 1848 to 1968. It attempts to present in comprehensive form the changes undergone by the political concepts of Marx and Engels as they developed first into Leninism, later into Stalinism, and finally into the three main trends that exist today: Soviet Marxism-Leninism, Maoism, and humanist Marxism.

The theme of the political concepts of Marxism is limited in a three-fold way. First, it means that this book is concerned exclusively with the *political* aims and concepts of Marxism in the narrow sense of the word, not with philosophical, economic, historical, or legal problems or considerations, interesting and important as these often are.

Second, the book concentrates on the political *concepts and aims* of Marxism but not on the development of the Marxist or Communist movement in general, let alone on any practical political measures of organization or parties professing Marxism. Third, the book confines itself to the political concepts and theories of Marxism developed by Marx and Engels and subsequently supplemented, amended, or transformed in the world Communist movement, but not with Left-wing, socialist, or revolutionary doctrines in general.

At the heart of the political concepts of Marxism, from Marx to the present day, are a few central issues which fall into two major groups. The first group concerns the *social* (or "socialist") *revolution* in the broadest sense of the term. This group embraces the following problems: what class is to perform the transformation of society? To what extent are other classes or strata necessary as allies? What forms of struggle are to be used? How should the Party, the political instrument, be structured and what are its characteristic features? What tasks does the Party have to fulfill, and with what tactical means is the struggle to be waged? What part is played by the national liberation movements in the world-wide conflict? How are the problems of war, peace, and disarmament to be assessed, and what attitude should be adopted toward them? What are the social and political prerequisites necessary for the social (or "socialist") revolution? Can the revolution be accomplished only in several countries simultaneously, or in one country alone? Is a peaceful transformation of society possible and, if so, under what conditions?

The second group of problems is concerned with the *future class-*

*less society*—again in the broadest sense of the term. Is a dictatorship of the proletariat necessary after a revolution and, if so, what are its characteristic features? What transitional measures are necessary after a revolution in order to achieve socialism? What are the economic and political features characteristic of a socialist society? How does the first stage, socialism, differ from the final objective, the Communist society? Can the new social order be established only in several countries simultaneously or also in one single country? What sort of relations will exist between capitalist and socialist countries, and among the socialist countries themselves? How long will it take to establish socialism and later Communism? By what path can these goals be attained? What are the fundamental features and characteristics of a future Communist society?

In the course of the development of the political concepts of Marxism from the 1840's to the present these questions in both groups have been answered not only in several totally different ways—with widely diverging interpretations of Marx's and Engels' original ideas—but, as a result of a multitude of newly emerging problems, a great number of new doctrines and entire theories have been added to them.

*Four major periods* may be distinguished in the development of the political concept of Marxism. The first embraces the period from the 1840's to the 1890's. That period of *Marxism,* or original Marxism (incidentally, Marx and Engels never used this term but invariably referred to "scientific socialism"), is characterized by the development, exposition, and dissemination of Marx's and Engels' theories. That period also saw the emergence of organizations and parties, principally in Europe, which professed scientific socialism and based their policies entirely or predominantly on this theory.

The second period, during the first quarter of the twentieth century, embraces the work of *Lenin* who adapted the concepts of Marx and Engels to the conditions of the revolutionary movement in czarist Russia and added a large number of new doctrines and theses to the political theory of Marxism. After the October Revolution of 1917 *Leninism* (even though Lenin himself warned against any excessive export of Russian experiences) gained international validity for the world Communist movement.

Leninism was succeeded by *Stalinism.* It was during this period, from the mid-1920's to the early 1950's, that Leninism was subjected to further major alterations, with Stalin habitually proclaiming the "ultimate wisdom" on all problems of Marxism, and of political theory in particular. The political doctrine of Stalinism—soon to become ossified into complete dogma—was designed to justify the hardships and privations of Soviet industrialization, but above all Stalin's dictatorial bureaucratic centralized regime of terror.

The changes undergone by the political concepts of Marxism in these three periods from the *Communist Manifesto* (spring 1848) to Stalin's last pamphlet, *Economic Problems of Socialism in the U.S.S.R.* (October 1952), are discussed in the first part of the book.

This span of just over one hundred years (from 1848 to 1952) has seen a large number of additions to and adaptations of Marxism, many of the original objectives of the theory have changed almost beyond recognition. These changes—both from Marxism to Leninism and from Leninism to Stalinism—repeatedly encountered opposition within the Marxist and, subsequently, Communist movement. Thus, during the first quarter of this century, important exponents of Marxism opposed many of Lenin's new interpretations. Even greater was the opposition within the Communist movement to Stalin's doctrinal changes. But these theoretical analyses, critiques, and warnings remained without appreciable political effect; the prevailing trend, supported and enforced by an apparatus that pretended to speak on behalf of millions, was still too powerful.

The first change came when Stalin's Soviet Union ceased to be the only country ruled by a Communist Party. In the wake of World War II, as other socialist states emerged—especially those which accomplished their social transformations not through the occupation by Soviet troops but by their own revolution—the Soviet Union was no longer able to maintain its leading role in the accustomed manner. Yugoslavia's break with the Stalin leadership in the summer of 1948 was a clear signal. For the first time the monolithic character of Stalin-type world Communism was broken and the Stalinist interpretation of Marxism-Leninism was no longer sacrosanct.

The death of Stalin in March 1953 and, even more, the Twentieth Congress of the Communist Party of the Soviet Union (February 1956) marked the beginning of the process of differentiation within the world Communist movement which found expression in the "Polish October," the Hungarian Revolution of 1956, the Sino-Soviet conflict, Rumania's growing independence (since spring 1962), and the great reform process in Czechoslovakia in the spring and summer of 1968.

Certainly, in this process of differentiation within world Communism the national traditions of the various countries, the different stages of development as well as a large number of practical political and state conflicts of interest played an important part. But I believe it would be wrong to see the increasing trend toward independence within world Communism solely and exclusively from this point of view, or to regard disputes or ideological and political theory as a mere cover for national differences. The differentiation in the world Communist movement was and is accompanied by a multiplicity of political and ideological arguments, polemics, discussions, and controversies. Within the relatively short span of two decades totally divergent interpretations of the political principles of Marxism have emerged.

Thus, within the world Communist movement—and this is the subject of the second part of this book—there occurred a three-way split in Marxism. *Three main currents* emerged, differing from one another fundamentally on all vital theoretical political issues, and it is this difference that has dominated the political, ideological, and intellectual life of world Communism.

Of the three present-day trends the Soviet interpretation still holds the leading place, though admittedly only due to the power behind it. The political concepts of Soviet ideology have been officially described by Moscow since the early 1960's as "scientific communism." *Soviet Marxism-Leninism* reflects the endeavor of the Soviet leadership, on the one hand, to maintain the ruling bureaucratic, centralized system in an emerging Soviet industrialized society, and, on the other, to consolidate and ideologically justify the U.S.S.R.'s leading role vis-à-vis the rest of the socialist countries.

Soviet Marxism-Leninism is opposed by the second current: the political theory of the Chinese Communists, invariably described by Peking for the past few years as "the great thought of Mao Tse-tung." Maoism is marked by the tendency to declare the lessons and conclusions of the Chinese civil war and of the revolution conducted by the Chinese Communist Party as generally valid for Communists all over the world. This has led to the development of a large number of new doctrines and theories which are scarcely based any longer on Marx, Engels, and Lenin but almost exclusively on Mao Tse-tung himself.

Independently of these two trends, the Soviet and the Chinese, there has arisen over the past two decades, chiefly in Europe, a third current in the political theory of Marxism: "associationist socialism," "intellectual Marxism," "humanist socialism," "self-management socialism," and "socialism with a human face"—these are the labels the followers of this trend have given themselves. In this book their concepts will be described under the collective term of "humanist Marxism." The champions of humanist Marxism hope to emphasize once more the original ideas of Marxism and to free the Marxist political concepts from later falsifications and deformations. They support a more humane development toward socialism, as well as a new model of the socialist society, in which the emphasis would be on democratic freedom, social self-management, and human dignity.

This book attempts to convey objective information—both on the changes of political aims and concepts from Marx to Stalin and on the three chief interpretations of Marxism in the present-day world Communist movement. It is concerned not so much with a critique as with the attempt at presentation, with the intention of allowing Marx, Engels, Lenin, and their very heterogeneous successors to speak, as far as possible, for themselves. In view of the fact that both Moscow and Peking give publicity only to those observations of Marx, Engels, and Lenin that are in line with their own objectives, it seemed important to recall, above all, those concepts that are being at present suppressed by both these "centers." In all those instances in which Marx, Engels, and Lenin expressed different or contradictory views on a particular issue, these divergent ideas are noted. Since all extraneous criticism was avoided, it seemed desirable to make at least a brief reference to the most important critical analyses and observations made in the course of this development by the followers of Marxism themselves—the more so as an acquaintance with these internal criticisms will promote an understanding of the present three-way split of Marxism into Soviet, Chinese, and humanist-Marxist trends.

The *Communist Manifesto* of 1848 is separated from the Chinese cultural revolution, the "Prague Spring," and Soviet neo-Stalinism by a span of 120 years. In view of the vast quantity of writings and other documents on the political concepts of Marxism during that period it is obvious that this book must confine itself to the central issues and give only main outlines. Thus the account goes straight from Marxism to Leninism without dealing with such figures as Karl Kautsky and Eduard Bernstein, Georgi Plekhanov and Franz Mehring; similarly, the numerous and often important arguments during the transformation from Leninism to Stalinism (those, for example of Trotsky and Bukharin) are not discussed here. As for the political concepts of Marxism during the past twenty years—i.e., since Yugoslavia's break with Moscow in 1948—this account confines itself to Soviet Marxism—Leninism, Maoism, and humanist Marxism. Ho Chi Minh and Castro, Régis Debray, and Che Guevara, as well as the political concepts of the "New Left" are outside the scope of this book. It is hoped that the exposition of the main lines of the political concepts of Marxism will provide a sufficient framework for locating the positions of various additional trends without much difficulty.

In accordance with my aims of giving a descriptive analysis of the changes in the political concepts of Marxism from Marx to Stalin, and of the three mainstreams of Marxism existing today, this book is based almost entirely on original sources. The chapter on Marx and Engels is based on the new East Berlin edition of the collected works of Marx and Engels (thirty-nine volumes and four supplementary volumes, 1961–68); whenever possible English translations of individual works of Marx and Engels have been used, since the complete works have not yet appeared in English. The chapter on Lenin is based on the official forty-four-volume English edition of the collected works of Lenin (Moscow: Progress Publishers, 1960–70), and the chapter on Stalin on the prematurely discontinued thirteen-volume English-language edition of his collected writings (up to 1934) published in Moscow and for the later period on other individual works written by Stalin. For the developments since Stalin's death official ideological textbooks, the program of the Communist Party of the Soviet Union, and statements of the Central Committee have been used.

The chapter on Maoism is based on the writings of Mao Tse-tung and documents published by the Central Committee of the Communist Party of China. The chapter on humanist Marxism is based on books and articles published by humanist Marxists in various countries during the last two decades.

The preliminary work for the German original of this book (published in the spring of 1970) was done during my one-year stay as a senior research fellow at the Russian Institute of Columbia University in New York City. I would like to thank Professor Alexander Dallin, who was director of the institute at that time, for providing me with the opportunity to do the groundwork for this book. My special thanks go to Yale University, where I have been teaching courses on international Communism and on the history of the Soviet Union since 1966, and where I had a chance for frequent conversations with experts, students, and friends, especially with Professor Leon Lipson with whom I had many fruitful discussions. I am also grateful to Richard Bosley, a Yale student, and Michael Fire, who helped me a great deal with the problems involved in producing the English edition.

*Wolfgang Leonhard*

*New Haven, Connecticut*
*April 1973*

# Part I

---

# The Background:
## From Marx
### to Stalin

---

# 1

## The Political Aims of Marx and Engels

In his first political article Marx discussed a question as topical today as it was then: the freedom of the press. "The essence of a free press is the principled, reasonable, moral essence of freedom. The character of a censored press is the unprincipled aberration of unfreedom, it is a civilized abomination, a perfumed monster," Marx wrote in early May 1842. According to Marx, censorship is based on the principle that the end justifies the means, "but an end which requires unjustifiable means is not a justifiable end." This first political article by Marx is not readily quoted nowadays, either in Soviet or in Chinese publications, possibly because Marx sharply condemned government control of the press: "A censored press has a demoralizing effect. . . . The government only hears its own voice, it knows that it only hears its own voice, yet it persists in the delusion that it hears the voice of the people and in turn demands of the people that they should persist in this delusion."[1]

Marx was only twenty-four years old when he wrote these lines. Born in Trier (Trèves) on May 5, 1818, the second of eight children of Heinrich Marx, an attorney, he first attended the Friedrich-Wilhelm Gymnasium in Trier (1830–35), and in October 1835, at the age of seventeen, began his studies at the University of Bonn, later continuing them at the Faculty of Law of Berlin University. "My special subject was law, but in fact I pursued this only as a subordinate discipline alongside philosophy and history," Marx was to remark later.[2] Having received his doctor's degree from the Faculty of Philosophy in Jena in April 1841—with a thesis on the difference between the natural phi-

*3*

losophy of Democritus and Epicurus—Marx moved to Bonn, and there, in April 1842, began working for the newly founded liberal *Rheinische Zeitung* in Cologne.

Following his article on the freedom of the press, Marx, in the autumn of 1842, covered the discussions in the Rhenish Parliament about timber theft and the parceling of land. Those debates, Marx later recalled, "provided the first occasions for occupying myself with economic questions."[3] He wrote two extensive reports on the economic position of the Eifel peasants and the Moselle vinegrowers, and from then on economic and social problems increasingly engaged his interest —alongside his philosophical studies—stimulated above all by the first steps of the labor movement, which were just then becoming perceptible.

The dramatic growth of the industrial labor force was not to be overlooked at that time. The first major actions of the working class— such as the uprisings in Lyons in 1831 and 1834 and the Chartist movement in England—raised not only political but also social problems and were a clear sign that labor was beginning to form itself into a class and to put forward its own demands. The "social problem" was on everybody's lips, and socialist and Communist ideas, proposals, and patterns for a more just social order were being discussed more than ever before. At first Marx was reserved, even critical. He was unable, as he wrote in October 1842, "to concede theoretical reality to Communist ideas, let alone desire their practical realization." Marx announced that he would "subject these ideas to a thorough critique."[4]

Having moved to Cologne in mid-October 1842 and assumed the editorship of the *Rheinische Zeitung,* Marx now zealously and seriously studied the contemporary French literature on socialism and Communism, including the writings of Charles Fourier, Étienne Cabet, and Pierre-Joseph Proudhon. While he was engaged in this work, the *Rheinische Zeitung,* which had been severely censored before, was finally banned. Marx could see no possibility for effective political work in Germany: "I am tired of hypocrisy, stupidity, crude authority, and of our yielding, bending, tergiversation and picking of words," he wrote at the beginning of 1843. "I can no longer do anything in Germany. One becomes dishonest toward oneself here."[5]

In the autumn of 1843 Marx moved to Paris—then the heart of the revolutionary movement. Alongside his philosophical studies and a series of philosophical essays (which lie outside the framework of this book) Marx continued his study of socialist writings, repeatedly attended workers' meetings, and made the personal acquaintance of the radicals, democrats, and socialists then living in Paris—among them Proudhon, Louis Blanc, Heinrich Heine, Georg Herwegh, and Mikhail

Bakunin. Although he was impressed by some socialist ideas of the day, the fact did not escape him that the new just social order was here being described, often in detail, without any indication of the road that would lead to it. The whole project of constructing the future, Marx wrote in the autumn of 1843, was of no concern. What mattered at the moment was the "uncompromising critique of everything that exists—uncompromising in the sense that the critique must be afraid neither of its own results nor of conflict with the prevailing powers."[6]

However, the most important event of Marx's stay in Paris (November 1843 to March 1845) was his encounter with Friedrich Engels. In their extensive discussions both declared "our complete agreement in all theoretical fields."[7] This was the beginning of the lifelong friendship and collaboration of the founders of scientific socialism.

Friedrich Engels, born in Barmen on November 28, 1820, the son of a textile manufacturer, had first attended the Gymnasium in Elberfeld (1834–37). On his father's insistence young Engels, though by no means delighted at the prospect, was sent to a large business firm in Bremen to receive some commercial training; his free time, however, was spent almost exclusively with literature and philosophy. After his military service in the Guards Artillery in Berlin (1841–42) he was sent to Manchester to complete his commercial training (1842–44)—an opportunity Engels used to study the social and political conditions in Britain and, above all, the living and working conditions of the English workers. "While I was in Manchester, it was tangibly brought home to me," Engels was to write later,

that the economic facts, which have so far played no role, or only a contemptible one, in the writing of history, are, at least in the modern world, a decisive historical force; that they form the basis of the organization of the present-day class antagonisms; that these class antagonisms, in the countries where they have become fully developed, thanks to large-scale industry, hence especially in England, are in their turn the basis of the formation of political parties and of party struggles, and thus of all political history.[8]

These ideas were expressed in Engels' book *The Condition of the Working Class in England,* which he published in Leipzig as early as May 1845. Shortly afterward Marx and Engels, both of whom had been living in Brussels since the spring of 1845, embarked on their joint work *The German Ideology* and on other writings. Their aim was "to work out our newly gained way of looking at things in the most varied directions and in detail."

Of decisive importance for the political concept was Marx's and Engels' emphasis on the close connection of socialist aims with economic and social reality and with the struggle of the working class. Communism, Engels wrote, "no longer meant the concoction, by means of imagination, of an ideal society as perfect as possible, but insight into the nature, the conditions and the consequent general aims of the struggle waged by the proletariat." Communism was now seen as

a movement of the modern oppressed class, the proletariat, as the more or less developed forms of its historically necessary struggle against the ruling class, the bourgeoisie; as forms of the class struggle, but distinguished from all earlier class struggles by this one thing, that the present-day oppressed class, the proletariat, cannot achieve its emancipation without at the same time emancipating society as a whole from division into classes and, therefore, from class struggles.[9]

## ☐ The Political Writings of Marx and Engels

Marx and Engels, however, did not wish to bury their discoveries in large tomes published exclusively for the learned world; they wanted above all "to win over the European, and in the first place the German, proletariat to our convictions."[10] As early as 1836, German refugee artisans in Paris founded the secret "League of the Just," which was at first equally devoted to propaganda and to conspiracy, but gradually moved away from utopian socialism and acquired international character.

At the beginning of 1847 Marx and Engels, both then in Brussels, were invited to join the League so that they would have the opportunity to expound their view of Communism at a congress, and to have it later published as the manifesto of the League.[11] At the League's congress in London (in June 1847), in which Friedrich Engels participated, the "League of the Just" was renamed the "Communist League," the old slogan "All men are brothers" replaced by the new slogan "Workers of the world, unite," and the former conspiratorial secret society transformed into a political organization. At Marx's and Engels' suggestion the League adopted a new statute, the first article of which read: "The aim of the League is the overthrow of the bourgeoisie, the rule of the proletariat, the abolition of the old bourgeois society based on class antagonisms and the foundation of a new society without classes and without private property."[12]

At the Second Congress of the Communist League in London, in December 1847, which both Marx and Engels attended, the statute was not only confirmed, Marx and Engels were instructed to work out a political program. Friedrich Engels, in the autumn of 1847, had already sketched a draft in the form of questions and answers (later to be known as the *Principles of Communism*) which, however, did not entirely satisfy him. "Think over the confession of faith a bit," he wrote to Marx. "I believe we had better drop the catechism form and call the thing: *Communist Manifesto*. I am bringing you what I have done here with me, it is simply a narrative, but miserably put together in fearful haste."[13]

Having been reworked by Marx—who adopted all the principal arguments of Engels' draft but gave the *Manifesto* its final shape—the *Communist Manifesto* was published in London during the second half of February 1848. Here, for the first time, the fundamental ideas of scientific socialism were summed up in the form of a program.

The basic idea of the *Communist Manifesto*, according to Friedrich Engels, was that

economic production and the structure of society at every historical epoch necessarily arising therefrom, constitute the foundation for the political and intellectual history of that epoch; that consequently (ever since the dissolution of the primeval communal ownership of land) all history has been a history of class struggles, of struggles between exploited and exploiting, between dominated and dominating classes at various stages of social development; that this struggle, however, has now reached a stage where the exploited and oppressed class (the proletariat) can no longer emancipate itself from the class which exploits and oppresses it (the bourgeoisie) without at the same time forever freeing the whole of society from exploitation, oppression, and class struggles.[14]

Although Marx and Engels in their own lifetime repeatedly and very readily admitted that certain passages would have to be phrased differently in many respects, and that the *Communist Manifesto* was outdated in places, nevertheless "the general principles laid down in this *Manifesto* are, on the whole, as correct today as ever."[15]

Almost to the day that the *Communist Manifesto* appeared in London, the February Revolution of 1848 broke out in France; it was soon to spread to Vienna, Berlin, and other parts of Europe. Having set up in Paris the new headquarters of the Communist League, which proclaimed the "demands of the Communist Party in Germany," Marx together with Engels returned to Cologne in April 1848 and there published the *Neue Rheinische Zeitung*. Marx was its editor. Entirely in the spirit of the *Communist Manifesto*, Marx and Engels were trying to promote the revolutionary movement as it existed at that time. They did not want to lecture on Communism in a small obscure paper or to found a small sect. Instead, it was their intention to work through the *Neue Rheinische*

*Zeitung* in the interests of a great party of action, to advocate a democracy that would emphasize its specific proletarian character and would further promote the revolution.[16]

The *Neue Rheinische Zeitung* appeared for barely a year; yet during that short period Marx wrote over eighty articles and Engels over forty. After the defeat of the 1848 revolution its last number, printed in red type, appeared on May 18, 1849. Once more Marx and Engels went into exile, this time for life—Marx to London, Engels (until 1870) to Manchester. Their original intention was to publish the *Neue Rheinische Zeitung* from abroad, in the form of a monthly "political-economic review"; but this did not survive beyond the first five issues. Nevertheless, in these few issues Marx published his historical analysis "The Class Struggles in France, 1848 to 1850" and Engels his essay "The Peasant War in Germany." As late as the spring of 1850—as can be seen in his "Address of the Central Committee to the Communist League," in which, incidentally, he proclaimed the famous slogan of "permanent revolution"—Marx entertained hopes of a revival of the revolution. But by the time of the second address (June 1850) Marx and Engels had lost that hope; for the first time they spoke of a longer period, extending over ten, fifteen, or twenty years.

This meant both the need and the opportunity for using this period of relative calm for important theoretical analyses. Engels wrote his *Revolution and Counter-Revolution in Germany* (August 1851 to September 1852) and Marx *The Eighteenth Brumaire of Louis Bonaparte* (December 1851 to March 1852). It was about that time—in November 1851—that Engels made a rarely mentioned but important proposal to Marx. He suggested that Marx should sum up scientific socialism in four volumes. The first two volumes were to contain a critique of political economy, the third would critically discuss the various socialist currents and their theories, and the fourth would finally present "the much-vaunted 'positive features,' the things you 'really' want." This, Engels pointed out, would "have the advantage that the much-coveted secret is revealed only at the very end," only when the curiosity of the reader has been "kept alive throughout three volumes."[17]

This project, unfortunately, was never realized, even though Marx was at that time fully concentrating on the study of economics with the aim of writing a critique of political economy. At first, as he himself wrote, he believed he would complete this task in a few weeks. But it was not until 1859 that his *Critique of Political Economy* was published (and not until 1867 that the first volume of *Capital* appeared). The long delay was due to Marx's poor state of health—since 1849 he had been suffering from a gall-bladder and liver complaint, aggravated later by furunculosis, as well as insomnia brought on by excessive night work. His exceedingly straitened financial circumstances, moreover, continually compelled him to take on other work which kept him from his researches.

For nearly a decade Marx was predominantly engaged in journalism, mainly for the *New York Daily Tribune*. Interesting and important though many of his articles were—on the Crimean War of 1854–55, on British colonial policy in India, on the development of China (Marx wrote about the then current Russo-Chinese border conflict), and on the American Civil War—it was this preoccupation that prevented him from compiling a comprehensive study of scientific socialism of the kind that Engels had envisioned. Yet even these journalistic activities did not relieve Marx of his financial worries. Often he was without money "even to pay the most pressing baker's and butcher's bills,"[18] and at the beginning of 1852 he wrote that he no longer left the house since all his clothes were pawned and he had nothing to eat because he had no money.[19] At that time Marx also suffered two tragic personal losses: his year-old daughter Franziska died in 1852 and Jenny, Marx's wife, had to borrow £2 from a French refugee to pay for the coffin. In the spring of 1855 Marx's only son, Edgar, known in the family as "Mush," died at the age of nine. "The house of course is quite deserted and orphaned since the death of the dear child who was the soul that gave it life. It is indescribable how we miss the child everywhere. I have had all kinds of bad luck before, but only now do I know what real misfortune is," Marx wrote to Engels. "Amidst all the terrible sufferings I have been through in these days it was always the thought of you and your friendship that supported me and the hope that we may still have something sensible to do together in this world."[20]

Under these difficult circumstances, with permanent financial support from Engels, Marx completed his *Critique of Political Economy* at the beginning of 1859. Even so he lacked the money to mail the manuscript to the publisher. "I do not believe," he wrote, "that anyone has ever written about 'money' while suffering from such a shortage of money himself."[21]

It is here, in the preface to his *Critique of Political Economy,* that we find those famous sentences which Marx himself described as his "principal theme":

In the social production of their life men enter into definite relations that are indispensable and independent of their will, relations of production which correspond to a definite stage in the development of their material productive forces. The sum total of these relations of production constitutes the economic structure of society, the real foundation, on which rises a legal and political superstructure and to which correspond definite forms of social consciousness. The mode of production of material life conditions the social, political and intellectual life process in general. It is not the consciousness of men that determines their being, but, on the contrary, their social being that determines their consciousness. At a certain stage of their development, the material productive forces of society come in conflict with the existing relations of production, or—what is but a legal expression for the same thing—with the property relations within which they have been at work hitherto. From forms of development of the productive forces these relations turn into their fetters. Then begins an epoch of social revolution. . . . No social order ever perishes before all the productive forces for which there is room in it have developed; and new, higher relations of production never appear before the material conditions of their existence have matured in the womb of the old society itself.[22]

When Marx wrote these lines the European labor movement was experiencing a new upsurge. In 1862, at the World Exhibition in London, the first contacts took place between British, French, and German workers' delegations and this co-operation was strengthened at a big protest meeting in London on the occasion of the crushing of the Polish uprising in 1863. At a mass rally in St. Martin's Hall in London on September 28, 1864, the International Workingmen's Association was founded, later to be known as the First International. Marx, as the representative of the German workers' movement, was elected to the managing committee that was charged with drafting the statutes, and he soon emerged as the leading figure of the International. He wrote not only the "Inaugural Address of the International Workingmen's Association" (September 1864), which established the organization's program, but also the statutes of the International, which proceeded from the principle that "the emancipation of the working classes must be achieved by the working classes themselves"; "the struggle for the emancipation of the working classes means not a struggle for class privileges or monopolies, but for equal rights and duties and for the abolition of all class-rule"; and that "the emancipation of labor is neither a local nor a national, but a social problem embracing all countries in which modern society exists."[23]

The International Workingmen's Association was an alliance of independent workers' organizations from various countries, jealous of their independence and representing the multifarious political currents of the labor movement of the day—followers of Fourier, Cabet, Proudhon, Blanqui, Bakunin, and Mazzini, as well as the advocates of Marx's and Engels' scientific socialism. The International Workingmen's Association, Marx emphasized, "is not the hothouse plant of a sect or a theory. It is a naturally grown product of the proletarian movement which in turn springs from the normal and irresistible tendencies of modern society."[24] Under these conditions, as he wrote to Engels, he had to remain impartial between the various organized workers' groups,[25] the more so "as I am in fact the head of the business."[26]

The International Workingmen's Association, as Marx saw it, was a living movement, not a centrally directed organization. "The Association does not dictate the form of political movements; it only requires a pledge as to their end," Marx wrote. "In each part of the world some special aspect of the problem presents itself, and the workingmen there address themselves to its consideration in their own way. Combinations among workingmen cannot be absolutely identical down to the last detail in Newcastle and in Barcelona, in London and in Berlin." Even the question of whether in a particular country the social transformation should take place in a peaceful or a violent manner "is the affair of the working classes of that country. The International does not presume to dictate in the matter and hardly to advise. But to every movement it accords its sympathy and its aid, within the limits assigned by its own laws."[27] Moreover, as Marx expressly pointed out, each organization and group "has the right to leave the International; whenever this happens the General Council has simply to take official notice of such a resignation but on no account to adjourn it."[28] Finally—a point hardly ever mentioned in Soviet writings—Marx warned against organizing the labor movement in a centralized and conspiratorial manner as this "runs counter to the development of the proletarian movement" and because such organizational forms subject the workers "to authoritarian and mystical laws which impair their independence and guide their consciousness in a wrong direction."[29]

For several years—from 1864 to 1872—Marx devoted his efforts mainly to the International, including the preparation of the most important congresses—in Geneva (September 1866), Lausanne (September 1867), Brussels (September 1868), and Basle (September 1869). In the midst of all this work the first volume of *Capital* appeared at the beginning of September 1867. Gratefully Marx wrote to Engels: "Without you I should have never completed the work,"[30] adding, when he sent him the galley proofs: "At any rate, I hope the bourgeoisie will remember my carbuncles all the rest of their lives."[31]

The Franco-Prussian War of 1870–71 confronted the International —and hence also Marx—with a new task. Marx drafted his two "Addresses on the Franco-Prussian War" (July and September 1870) and, after the French defeat, at first warned the workers of Paris against unpremeditated and precipitate actions. But when the Paris Commune was proclaimed (March 18, 1871), the General Council of the International, upon Marx's proposal, decided on a campaign of demonstrations that would show its solidarity. Even at the time of the Paris Commune Marx praised the "historical initiative . . . of our heroic Party comrades" and referred to them as "these Parisians storming heaven." The Paris Commune had shown, he wrote, that what mattered was not to transfer the bureaucratic-military machine from one hand to another, but to smash it."[32] With the Paris Commune the struggle of the working class had entered a new phase.[33] Marx set forth the theoretical and political conclusions he had drawn from the Paris Commune in his publication *The Civil War in France* (May 1871). Only a year later, in his addresses and statements at the Hague congress (September 1872) Marx, more clearly than before, supported a differentiated road of social transformation in different countries and stressed the possibility of a peaceful transformation of society.[34]

Because of the intensification of repressive measures and also because of internal arguments within the First International—notably the conflict with the Bakuninists—the Hague congress in September 1872, upon Marx's proposal, decided to move the General Council of the International to New York. "As I view European conditions," Marx wrote, "it is quite useful to let the formal organization of the International recede into the background for the time being. . . . Events and the inevitable development and complication of things will of themselves see to it that the International shall rise again, improved in form."[35]

From 1872 on Marx again devoted most of his time to theoretical research, though increasingly troubled by his steadily deteriorating health. Particularly important for its political concepts was his *Critique of the Gotha Program* (March 1875) in which he discussed a number of fundamental questions concerning the future classless society. Marx's main preoccupation, however, was his work on the second and third volumes of *Capital* (which he did not complete and which were published after his death, by Engels); Marx was particularly interested in the Russian agrarian question and, in fact, began to teach himself Russian.

The main concepts of scientific socialism became known mostly during the 1870's and 1880's, through the writings of Friedrich Engels, such as *The Housing Question* (1873), *The Bakuninists at Work* (late 1873), *Social News from Russia* (1875), and especially through *Herr Eugen Dühring's Revolution of Science,* known as *Anti-Dühring* (1878).

A few chapters of this book, with a new introduction, were published by Engels in 1880 under the title *Socialism: Utopian and Scientific*—probably the most important comprehensive presentation of scientific socialism.

About that time Marx considered the completion of the second and third volumes of his *Capital* as the main task of his life. More and more frequently, however, he had to undergo treatment at some spa—in England, in France, and, repeatedly, at Karlsbad. In the spring of 1882 Marx left Europe for the first time, to spend a few weeks in Algeria, where he was appalled by the methods of some French colonial authorities, such as, for instance, the use of torture to extract confessions from Arabs.[36]

The state of his health deteriorated perceptibly, especially after his return to London. On March 14, 1883, Friedrich Engels visited him for the last time: "Come in, he is half asleep," Engels was told. "When we came back we found him in his armchair, peacefully gone to sleep—but for ever."[37]

Only a few people attended his interment at Highgate Cemetery on March 17, 1883. Jean Longuet read, in French, the message of the Russian, French, and Spanish socialists; Karl Liebknecht spoke on behalf of the German Social Democrats, and Engels, in English, for the international movement:

On the 14th of March, at a quarter to three in the afternoon, the greatest living thinker ceased to think. . . .

Just as Darwin discovered the law of development of organic nature, so Marx discovered the law of development of human history: the simple fact, hitherto concealed by an overgrowth of ideology, that mankind must first of all eat, drink, have shelter and clothing before it can pursue politics, science, art, religion, etc.; that therefore the production of the immediate material means of subsistence, and consequently the degree of economic development attained by a given people or during a given epoch form the foundation upon which state institutions, the legal conceptions, arts, and even the ideas on religion of the people concerned have evolved, and in and from the light of which they must, therefore, be explained, instead of vice versa, as had hitherto been the case.

But that is not all. Marx also discovered the special law of motion governing the present-day capitalist mode of production and the bourgeois society that this mode of production has created. . . . Such was the man of science. But this was not even half the man. . . . For Marx was before all else a revolutionist. His real mission in life was to contribute, in one way or another, to the overthrow of capitalist society and of the state institutions which it had brought into being, to contribute to the liberation of the modern proletariat, which he was the first to make conscious of its own position and its needs, conscious of the conditions of its emancipation. . . . And, consequently, Marx was the best-hated and most calumniated man of his time. Governments, both absolutist and republican, deported him from their territories. Bourgeois, whether conservative or ultra-democratic, vied with one another in heaping slanders upon him. All this he brushed aside as though it were cobwebs, ignoring it, answering only when extreme necessity compelled him. And he died beloved, revered, and mourned by millions of revolutionary fellow workers—from the mines in Siberia to California, in all parts of Europe and America—and I make bold to say that though he may have had many opponents he had barely one personal enemy.

His name will endure through the ages and so will also his work.[38]

After Marx's death Friedrich Engels regarded it as his foremost task to publish the second and third volumes of *Capital* from the papers left by Marx (1885 and 1894, respectively). In addition to a few philosophical studies and a large number of lesser articles, Engels' publications after Marx's death included *The Origin of the Family, Private Property and the State* (1884), a work of importance for the Marxist concept of the state; *The Role of Force in History* (1888); *The Foreign Policy of Russian Czarism* (1890); *Critique of the Social Democratic Draft Program* (1891); *Can Europe Disarm?* (1893), which for the first time argued the possibility and necessity of disarmament from a Marxist point of view; *The Peasant Question in France and Germany* (end of 1894), which contained the first thoughts on how agriculture should transform itself in the process of social revolution; and, finally, a few months before his death on August 5, 1895, his introduction—which was later much debated—to Marx's *The Class Struggle in France 1848 to 1850*. In this introduction Engels emphasized more than ever before the possibility of a peaceful transformation of society.

The new East German edition of the collected works of Marx and Engels comprises thirty-nine volumes and four supplementary volumes. The writings covered a multiplicity of fields: They include studies of historical events, philosophical and economic works, a great number of articles on international relations of their day, writings on military problems (chiefly by Engels) and observations, scattered for the most part, on the arts, philology, and the natural sciences. The sum total of Marx's and Engels' observations and expositions concerned with the political concepts of scientific socialism in the narrow meaning of the words would probably barely fill two volumes. But since Marx and Engels almost invariably mentioned their political concepts in connection with philosophical and economic problems or with historical events, these are scattered throughout a vast number of writings; it is interesting that Engels discussed these problems more frequently and often also more extensively than Marx.

## ☐  The Working Class as the Gravedigger of Capitalism

Marx and Engels regarded the history of mankind as a history of class struggle: In different social systems different classes faced each other antagonistically. The class struggle was seen as the driving force of history. Capitalist society, based on private ownership of the means of production, is characterized by the class struggle between the bourgeoisie (the capitalist entrepreneurs) and the proletariat (the working class).

Capitalism, however, is characterized not only by economic exploitation and political oppression but also—and this idea has been pushed more and more into the background in the further development of Soviet Marxism—by the alienation and self-alienation of man. In the social order based on division of labor and private property, the product produced by the working man and his own knowledge become the private property of another. The more goods and values the worker produces, the more insubstantial and poorer he himself becomes, and the more powerful grows the hostile world of capital confronting him.

In this alienation of man from the product of his work Marx saw the most fundamental form of all human alienation. It is reflected in the fact that his work, which as a process of self-realization should be his prime requirement of life, is felt by him, under the prevailing conditions, a crushing burden. The increasing division of labor changes work from being a means of man's development to a means of his degradation. The worker is increasingly alienated from the product of his labor, since he no longer controls it; he is alienated from work itself, which to him becomes servitude; in consequence he is alienated from himself, from his true nature; and he is finally alienated from his fellow humans.[39] The result is that "machinery, gifted with the wonderful power of shortening and fructifying human labor, we behold starving and overworking it. The new-fangled sources of wealth, by some strange, weird spell, are turned into sources of want. The victories of art seem bought by the loss of character. At the same pace that mankind masters nature, man seems to become enslaved to other men or to his own infamy."[40]

The working class, described by Marx as the class of the proletariat, thus "feels annihilated in its alienation and in it sees its own impotence and the reality of an inhuman existence."[41] In order to overcome alienation, whose roots Marx believed to be in private ownership, social conditions had to be fundamentally changed—by means of the proletarian revolution, through the realization of the Communist classless society. Communism to Marx, therefore, meant not only the abolition of the exploitation of man by man, but also the overcoming of all kinds of alienation of man. "To be radical means to grasp things by the root. But the root for man is man himself"; it was therefore necessary "to overthrow all conditions in which man is a humiliated, enslaved, forsaken and contemptible being."[42]

The overcoming of alienation and self-alienation, the liberation of the human personality, were connected for Marx and Engels with the real trends of the development of capitalist society. The inevitable class struggle of capitalism, between entrepreneurs (the bourgeoisie) and industrial workers (the proletariat), must inevitably lead to the decline of capitalism and the emergence of a new classless society. The decisive force of this revolution is the working class, the proletariat.

The further development of capitalism means, in Marx's and Engels' view, that capitalist society is doomed to perish for two reasons —first, as a result of the inherent contradictions of capitalism itself (which are analyzed in their economic writings, especially in *Capital*), and, second, because the working class continues to grow with further industrial development (both numerically and in its political and organizational strength) so that capitalist society produces its own gravediggers.[43] Capitalism is doomed to perish, its judge, history, and "its executioner, the proletariat."[44] The term "proletariat" (the working class) meant to Marx and Engels the industrial workers, the "class of modern wage laborers who, having no means of production of their own, are reduced to selling their labor power in order to live."[45]

There were three decisive reasons why Marx and Engels regarded the working class (the proletariat) as the social force that would bring about the fall of capitalism and effect the social revolution of society.

First, because the working class under capitalism—an entirely realistic conclusion in light of the conditions of that period—was the most exploited class and, therefore, most revolutionary-minded; "Of all the classes that stand face-to-face with the bourgeoisie today, the proletariat alone is a really revolutionary class."[46]

Second, because in the course of industrial development the working class would become the numerically strongest class and eventually form the majority of the population. In contrast to all previous revolutionary movements, which had sprung from a minority of the population, the proletarian movement was the "independent movement of the immense majority in the interest of the immense majority."[47]

Third, because the working class was least affected by nationalism or permeated by national prejudices, but was marked by an international class consciousness: "The proletarians in all countries have one and the same interest, one and the same enemy, one and the same battle to fight; the proletarians in their great majority are, by nature, free from national prejudices."[48] The working class is "international in its innermost nature."[49]

Since Marx and Engels regarded the labor movement as a movement of the immense majority, they only rarely concerned themselves with whether the working class had to seek allies for its struggle from other social strata. Indeed, in the *Communist Manifesto* they even believed that the middle class, the small manufacturers, the artisans, and the peasants would perish in the course of further industrial evolution. All these forces are "reactionary, for they try to roll back the wheel of history." If they do emerge in a revolutionary role, then it is only because they are abandoning their own standpoint "to place themselves at that of the proletariat."[50]

After the 1848 Revolution, however, Marx and Engels wrote several times about a possible alliance between workers and peasants. "The peasantry find their natural ally and leader in the urban proletariat."[51] Even greater importance was attached to the peasantry by Marx in his remark (now continually quoted by Soviet ideologists): "The whole thing in Germany will depend on the possibility of covering the rear of the proletarian revolution by a second edition of the *Peasants' War*."[52] Two decades later Engels was referring to the "approaching alliance between the workers in the towns and the peasants in the countryside."[53] In order to capture political power the Party must first go from the towns to the countryside and become a power in the countryside."[54]

Of decisive importance for Marx and Engels was the conclusion that in its struggle for liberation the working class represents the interests of society as a whole. By liberating itself and abandoning its own oppressed and exploited position, the working class liberates society from inhuman living conditions.[55] The working class cannot "achieve its emancipation without at the same time emancipating society as a whole from division into classes and, therefore, from class struggles."[56]

## ☐   The Party and Its Tasks

In order to realize these aims the working class needs its own political party. The working class must not confine itself to "serving the
bourgeois democrats as an applauding chorus" but should form an independent workers' party "in which the position and the interests of the
proletariat can be discussed independently of bourgeois influences."[57]
This workers' party, however, was not conceived by Marx and Engels
as an elite organization that would "lead" the working class, but as
part of the labor movement itself:

> The Communists do not form a separate party opposed to other work-
> ing-class parties. They have no interests separate and apart from those of
> the proletariat as a whole. They do not set up any sectarian principles of
> their own by which to shape and mold the proletarian movement.
> The Communists are distinguished from other working-class parties by
> this only: (1) In the national struggles of the proletarians of the different
> countries, they point out and bring to the front the common interests of
> the entire proletariat, independently of nationality. (2) In the various
> stages of development which the struggle of the working class against the
> bourgeoisie has to pass through, they always and everywhere represent the
> interests of the movement as a whole.
> The Communists therefore are, on the one hand, practically, the most
> advanced and resolute section of the working-class parties of every country,
> that section which pushes forward all others; on the other hand, theoretically,
> they have over the great mass of the proletariat the advantage of clearly
> understanding the line of march, the conditions, and the ultimate general
> results of the proletarian movement.[58]

To Marx and Engels the Party was never an end in itself, let
alone an instrument that would have to be artificially created and organized from outside. Thus Marx declared that the workers' party
"grows naturally from the soil of modern society everywhere"; to him
the concept "party" invariably meant "the party in the great historical
sense."[59] Marx therefore also warned against turning the concept of the
party into an absolute. All that the political movement of the working
class needs is "a previous organization . . . developed up to a certain
point"; what matters is "a movement of the class," which merely requires "a certain degree of previous organization."[60]

Marx and Engels advocated a workers' party that would be free of
all personality cult and authoritarian superstition. "When Engels and I
first joined the secret Communist Society we made it a condition that
everything tending to encourage superstitious belief in authority was to

be removed from the statutes."[61] Engels shared this view: "Both Marx and I have always opposed all public demonstrations connected with individual personalities."[62]

The workers' party was to be democratic in its shape and structure: "The looser the organization is now in appearance, the stronger it is in reality," Engels wrote. He was against a system whereby the Party leader would make final decisions on everything and where "anybody who attacks one of them is a heretic."[63] The workers' party was to make "no claims to dogmatic orthodoxy or doctrinaire supremacy."[64] Any unity of thought and action, of the kind demanded by present-day Soviet Party doctrine, was rejected by Marx and Engels: "Unity of thought and action is merely another name for orthodoxy and blind obedience."[65]

It was with obvious approval, and indeed as an example, that Engels in 1885 described the Communist League of the 1840's: "The organization itself was thoroughly democratic, with elective and always removable boards. This alone barred all hankering after conspiracy, which requires dictatorship." The labor movement no longer needed "any official organization, either public or secret. The simple, self-evident interconnection of like-minded class comrades" was entirely sufficient. The labor movement had meanwhile so grown in strength that "the simple feeling of solidarity based on the understanding of the identity of class position suffices to create and to hold together one and the same great party of the proletariat among the workers of all countries and tongues."[66]

Marx and Engels rejected any superior position for Party bureaucrats. Party members should "stop handling the Party officials—their own servants—with perpetual kid-gloves." They should be critical and not "obediently stand to attention as if before infallible bureaucrats."[67] Moreover: "The Party is so great that absolute freedom of debate within it is a necessity," Engels wrote. Newly joined Party members "cannot be drilled like schoolboys; there must be discussion and also a little shouting." Above all he warned against "the folly of throwing people out," since the Party "cannot exist unless all shades of opinion are allowed free expression in it."[68]

The Party papers must likewise be independent of the Party leadership and freely practice the right of criticism. "It is absolutely essential to have a free press in the Party, independent of the Executive and even the Party Congress, i.e., it must be in the position, within the framework of the program and the tactics adopted, to make unashamed opposition against individual Party measures and also, within the limits of Party propriety, freely to criticize program and tactics."[69] Engels rejected any "capture" of the press by the Party, since this would impede the further development of socialist theory. "You—the Party—*need* the socialist science, and this cannot thrive without freedom of movement."[70]

This was to apply in even greater measure to literature and the arts. The idea that a "Marxist" Party could one day direct and control literary and artistic activity never entered Marx's or Engels' head. Engels even rejected any excessively politically oriented literature. The tendentious character must spring "from the situation and the action themselves without being expressly pointed out and the author is not obliged to serve the reader on a platter the future historical resolution of the social conflicts which he describes." A socialist author fully discharges his task "if, by a faithful portrayal of the real relations . . . he inevitably instills doubt as to the eternal validity of that which exists, without himself offering a direct solution of the problem involved, even without at times ostensibly taking sides."[71] Three years later he expressed the same thought even more clearly in a letter to a socialist woman author: "I am far from finding fault with your not having written a point-blank socialist novel—a *Tendenzroman* (problem novel) as we Germans call it—to glorify the social and political views of the author. That is not at all what I mean. The more the opinions of the author remain hidden the better for the work of art."[72]

Marx and Engels—unlike their successors—thus quite clearly regarded the Party not as an elite organization which was to "lead" the working class, but as part of the working class itself. The Party was to be democratically organized, free from all personality cult and authoritarian superstition, and its members were to be critical toward Party officials. Within the Party there was to be absolute freedom of debate in which all shades of opinion must be heard. The Party press was to be independent of the leadership in order to vouchsafe the free and independent further development of political theory, and the independence of socialist writers and authors was to be a matter of course.

Between themselves, in their private correspondence, Marx and Engels sometimes expressed themselves rather frivolously about "the Party": "We have an opportunity once again—the first for a long time —of showing that we need no popularity, no support from any party of any country, and that our position is totally independent of that kind of trickery," Engels wrote to Marx. "How can people like ourselves, who shun official position like the plague, fit into a 'party'? What use to us, who spit on popularity, who doubt ourselves the moment we begin to be popular, is a 'party,' in other words, a pack of asses who swear by us because they believe us to be their kind?"[73]

For Marx and Engels there was no such thing as a detailed political strategy and tactics of the Party, of the kind that forms part and parcel of doctrine and practice today. They confined themselves to the basic idea that the Communists should support "every revolutionary movement against the existing social and political order of things," while at the same time preserving a critical attitude toward their allies.[74] The most progressive grouping in any country in question was to be supported against the common opponent; at the same time one's own position should be clearly defined: "The relation of the revolutionary workers' party to the petty-bourgeois democrats is this: it marches together with them against the faction which it aims at overthrowing, it opposes them in everything whereby they seek to consolidate their position in their own interests."[75] It was intended that the labor movement should wage a theoretical (in present-day Communist Party parlance "ideological"), political, and practical economic struggle, and, moreover, "in harmony and in its interconnections, and in a systematic way."[76]

## ☐  War, Peace, and Disarmament

Marx and Engels repeatedly dealt with the wars fought in their day. Foremost in their considerations were the general international situation and the interests of the international labor movement. Their attitude to the wars of their time depended on whether the military conflict in question served reaction or progress, in other words, whether, in the long term, it would be in the interests of the labor movement.

Marx and Engels most sharply rejected reactionary and dynastic wars. The working class must oppose "squandering in piratical wars the people's blood and treasure"; the proletarians have the duty "to master themselves the mysteries of international politics" in order to "assert the simple laws of morals and justice, which ought to govern the relations of private individuals, as the paramount rules of the intercourse of nations."[77] Marx hoped that "the alliance of the working classes of all countries will ultimately kill war."[78]

After the 1870's Marx and Engels also repeatedly expressed their hope that the further development of military techniques—both the growth of military expenditure and the increasingly high risks—would bring about a situation in which no one would any longer dare unleash a war. Armaments production had "become a branch of modern large-scale industry"; the state now had "to pay for one ship as much as a whole small fleet used to cost," and each new weapon was obsolete, and therefore worthless, before it was even brought into use. If, Engels pointed out, the armaments race is pursued "to a pitch of perfection," then weapons will become outrageously costly and unusable in war, until eventually "militarism, as any other historical phenomenon, is being brought to its doom in consequence of its own development."[79]

In a later publication Engels also pointed out that "the incredibly rapid progress of weapons technology" had resulted in "new inventions being overtaken" even before they were "introduced in a single army." Added to this was "the absolute unpredictability of the chances, the total uncertainty as to who will eventually emerge victorious from this giant struggle." Under these circumstances, "all pretexts for the lunatic rearmament which is turning the whole of Europe into an armed camp" had lost their validity, and even the German Reichstag must soon "erect a dam against the ceaselessly growing demands for money for military purposes."[80]

The militarist system had been so exacerbated and had reached such a degree that "it must either ruin the nations economically through their military burden or else degenerate into a general war of extermination." As a way out of this impasse Engels proposed disarmament: "I maintain that disarmament and hence the guarantee of peace is possible, that it is even relatively easy to accomplish, and that Germany, more than any other civilized state, has both the power and the duty to carry it out."[81]

☐    **Internationalism and National Liberation Movements**

Marx and Engels were internationalists. All their lives they invariably championed international co-operation by the working-class movement. "It is one of the great purposes of the Association," Marx declared, "to make the workmen of different countries not only *feel* but *act* as brethren and comrades in the army of emancipation."[82] Engels similarly declared that the working-class movement must preserve "the true international spirit which allows no patriotic chauvinism to arise and which readily welcomes every new advance of the proletarian movement, no matter from which nation it comes."[83]

International co-operation, however, can be realized only on a voluntary basis and under conditions of equal rights. At the time of the First International, when a few Russian representatives were trying to achieve unity by pressure from above, Engels wrote: "A priceless imputation that, in order to bring unity to the European proletariat, it must be commanded in Russian!"[84] Marx and Engels denied the existence of a "leading party" in the international working-class movement: "It is not at all in the interest of this movement that the workers of any particular country should march at its head."[85]

An internationalist attitude was altogether typical of Marx and Engels, which of course does not mean that they denied the existence of a national question. Although the sentences from the *Communist Manifesto,* "The workingmen have no country. We cannot take from them what they do not have." are frequently quoted, they are very rarely followed by the next sentence: "Since the proletariat must first of all acquire political supremacy, must rise to be the leading class of the nation, must constitute itself the nation, it is, so far, itself national, though not in the bourgeois sense of the word."[86]

Marx and Engels viewed national liberation struggles in conjunction with the interests and the struggle of the international workers' movement. Moreover, and for this particular reason, they repeatedly and most emphatically demanded the right of self-determination of nations. "A nation which oppresses others cannot emancipate itself"[87] was their motto. "A nation cannot become free while it continues to oppress other nations."[88] In nationally mixed regions—Engels here chose Russo-Polish and Franco-German border areas as examples—measures must be taken to ensure that "the population in question can itself decide its fate."[89] Marx and Engels rejected anti-Semitism on principle. "Anti-Semitism is the hallmark of a retarded civilization," Engels wrote, "a reaction of medieval, declining social strata against modern society."[90]

The independence and sovereignty of a nation were to Marx and Engels the prerequisites of peace and international co-operation. "If international peace is to be ensured, then avoidable national frictions must first be eliminated, and every people must be independent and master in its own house."[91] Engels elsewhere stated this demand similarly: "A sincere international collaboration of the European nations is possible only if each of these nations is fully autonomous in its own house."[92]

Their personal attitude to the national liberation movements of their day depended on their international objectives. Thus Marx and Engels supported the national movements in Ireland[93] and in Poland,[94] whereas—at least at the time—they feared that the national movements of the Czechs, Moravians, and Southern Slavs might be exploited by Russian Czarism, in which they saw their principal enemy and the bulwark of reaction.

It is interesting that even at that time Marx and Engels reflected on the possibility of national liberation movements in the colonies, i.e., in the dependent countries of Asia and the Arab world. As early as the beginning of 1850 Marx prophesied that China was on the eve of a mighty revolution; "The oldest and most imperturbable empire on the earth" is now on "the threshold of a social upheaval, one that will in any case hold most significant consequences for civilization."[95] In India Marx predicted that, thanks to the economic activity of the British colonial rulers, the material conditions for an Indian liberation struggle were being created until "the Hindus themselves shall have grown strong enough to throw off the English yoke altogether."[96]

Engels even prophesied in 1882 that all colonies would become independent and that, in achieving this independence, there would be revolutions in India, Egypt, and Algeria; admittedly, he was wrong in assuming that by then the socialist revolution would have long been victorious in Europe and North America:

> In my opinion the colonies proper, i.e., the countries occupied by a European population, such as Canada, the Cape, Australia, will all become independent; the countries inhabited by a native population, who are simply subjugated—India, Algeria, the Dutch, Portuguese and Spanish possessions —must be taken over, for the time being, by the proletariat and led as rapidly as possible toward independence. How this process will develop is difficult to say. India will progress, indeed very probably produce a revolution. . . . The same might also take place elsewhere, e.g., in Algeria and Egypt. . . . But as to what social and political phases these countries will then have to pass through before they likewise arrive at socialist organization—we today can only advance rather idle hypotheses, I think.[97]

## ☐ The Social Revolution

Of all political themes it is—naturally enough—the problem of the social revolution that occupies most space in Marx's and Engels' writings. What strikes one first of all is that the term "socialist revolution," as invariably used in the Communist world today, was hardly ever used by Marx and Engels; they preferred such terms as "social revolution," "liberation of labor," "abolition of class distinctions," and "reorganization of society."

The most concise definition of social revolution was given by Engels in 1875:

> The revolution which modern socialism strives to achieve is, briefly, the victory of the proletariat over the bourgeoisie, and the establishment of a

new organization of society by the destruction of all class distinctions. This requires not only a proletariat that carries out this revolution, but also a bourgeoisie in whose hands the productive forces of society developed so far that they allow the final destruction of class distinctions.[98]

This definition alone makes it clear that Marx and Engels were far from regarding a social revolution as possible everywhere or at any time, but only under certain conditions. One of the first of these was that capitalism must have reached a high economic level and that the material conditions must exist for its replacement by socialism. Second, the contradictions between the economic and technological state of development (the productive forces), on the one hand, and the social relationships (production relations), on the other, must have become exacerbated to such a degree that a radical transformation of the economic, social, and political system has become indispensable. Third, the industrial workers must account for the majority of the population, or at least occupy an important position. A social revolution, therefore, cannot be propagated or "made" at will but becomes possible only under conditions that are totally independent of the will of individual political parties, classes, or persons. "A radical social revolution is connected with definite historical conditions of economic development; the latter are its prerequisite. Therefore, it is possible only where, alongside capitalist production, the industrial proletariat accounts for at least a considerable portion of the people."[99] This fundamental idea was developed by Marx more particularly in his famous preface to the *Critique of Political Economy:* "No social order ever perishes before all the productive forces for which there is room in it have developed; and new, higher relations of production never appear before the material conditions of their existence have matured in the womb of the old society itself."[100]

From the 1840's to the 1890's Marx and Engels reiterated this crucial thesis without ever changing or modifying their view. The conditions for a social revolution consist, "on the one hand, of a class whose conditions of life necessarily drive it to social revolution" and, on the other, a state of productive forces "which, having grown beyond the framework of capitalist society, must necessarily burst that framework and which at the same time offer the means of abolishing class distinctions once and for all in the interest of social progress itself."[101] Social revolution presupposes, therefore, "the development of production carried out to a degree at which appropriation of the means of production and of the products, and, with this, of political domination, of the monopoly of culture and of intellectual leadership by a particular class, of society, has become not only superfluous but economically, politically and intellectually a hindrance to development."[102]

A high level of economic and technological development was seen by Marx and Engels—and this thesis is of special importance in view of later developments—not only as the necessary condition for a social revolution, but above all as the necessary condition for the classless society to be realized after the revolution. Thus Marx and Engels declared—and it is certainly no accident that this important remark is not being quoted by today's Soviet ideologists—that a high development of productive forces is "absolutely necessary as a practical premise; for the reason that without it only *want* is made general, and with *want* the struggle for necessities and all the old filthy business would necessarily be reproduced."[103]

In the absence of the economic conditions necessary for a social revolution, the abolition of class distinctions is unlikely to be permanent: "Only at a certain level of development of the productive forces of society, a very high level even for our modern conditions, does it become possible to raise production to such an extent that the abolition of class distinctions can be real progress, can be lasting without bringing about stagnation or even a decline in the mode of social production."[104] Marx and Engels therefore warn against "anticipating the revolutionary process of development, artificially driving it toward a crisis, or extemporizing a revolution without the conditions for revolution."[105]

Any attempt to accomplish a social revolution without the economic preconditions (a high level of economic development) and the social preconditions (the working class representing the majority of the population) must, Engels warned, lead to a new dictatorship. It is wrong to see a "revolution as a *coup de main* of a small revolutionary minority" because in such an event "it automatically follows that its success must inevitably be followed by the establishment of a dictatorship—not, it should be noted, of the entire revolutionary class, the proletariat, but of the small number of those who accomplished the insurrection and who themselves are at first organized under the dictatorship of one or several persons."[106]

There can, therefore, be no doubt that Marx and Engels linked a social revolution to definite economic and social prerequisites. Only under the condition of a high level of economic and technological development can the abolition of class distinctions be permanent. If these preconditions do not exist—and one cannot help thinking of the October Revolution in Russia in 1917—only the privations are shared out; under those conditions a new social stratification, a new ruling layer or class will arise. A process will take place that is politically accompanied by a new dictatorship—not the rule of the working class but that of a small group or even a few individuals.


☐   **The "Universal Revolution"**

Marx and Engels never used the term "world revolution," which became so familiar in the later development of the theory of Communism. They laid the foundations for this concept, however, by repeatedly expressing the view that a social revolution cannot take place in isolation in one country, but only simultaneously in several countries. The social revolution "is only possible as the act of the dominant peoples 'all at once' or simultaneously."[107] This idea is also emphasized in the *Communist Manifesto:* "United action, of the civilized countries at least, is one of the first conditions for the emancipation of the proletariat."[108] The social revolution "will be not only a national one; it will take place in all civilized countries, that is, at least simultaneously in England, America, France and Germany."[109] Thus it is impossible "to consummate a proletarian revolution within the national walls of France"; a social revolution must "leave its national soil forthwith and conquer the European terrain on which alone the social revolution of the nineteenth century can be accomplished."[110] The revolution means the emancipation of the working class all over the world and is therefore "as universal as capital rule and wage slavery."[111]

In later publications Marx and Engels repeatedly emphasized that "the emancipation of the working classes requires the fraternal concurrence of different nations."[112] Only when the life-giving principle of international solidarity is ensured in a future social revolution "we shall achieve the great goal we have set ourselves. The revolution needs solidarity; and we have a great example of it in the Paris Commune, which fell because a great revolutionary movement corresponding to that supreme rising of the Paris proletariat did not arise in all centers, in Berlin, Madrid, and elsewhere."[113]

The revolution was to be accomplished by the internal forces in each separate country, and on no account imposed upon a nation from outside. "One thing is certain: the victorious proletariat can force no blessings of any kind upon any foreign nation without undermining its own victory by so doing."[114]

Although Marx and Engels supported a simultaneous revolution in the developed industrial countries, they never expressed the opinion that such a revolution would take the same course in all countries. On the contrary, they repeatedly pointed to the tradition, the national peculiarities, the economic, political, and cultural conditions of the country concerned. "In each of these countries"—the reference is to Britain, America, France, and Germany—the social revolution "will take a longer or shorter time to develop, depending on which has a more developed industry, more wealth, and a greater mass of the productive forces."[115] True, the workers must assume political rule in all countries in order to establish the new society, "but we have by no means affirmed that this goal would be achieved by identical means. We know of the allowances we must make for the institutions, customs and traditions of the various countries."[116]

□   **Revolution: Violent or Peaceful?**

But how would the social revolution be accomplished? By violent armed revolution or by peaceful means? This crucial question—which was subsequently to lead to fierce argument within the Marxist movement—was not consistently answered by Marx and Engels. They repeatedly emphasized that this must depend on the situation prevailing at the time in the country concerned. A comparison of their observations on this point, however, permits the conclusion that initially they put their emphasis on violent revolution, whereas later (roughly after the 1870's) they tended to stress peaceful transformation.

Engels observed in 1847 that it would be desirable to accomplish the social revolution by peaceful means, "and the Communists would surely be the last people to object to this." But it was an unmistakable fact that "the advancement of the proletariat is in nearly every civilized country forcibly suppressed and that thereby the opponents of the Communists are tending in every way to promote revolution."[117] The *Communist Manifesto* of 1848 refers to the "more or less veiled civil war, raging within existing society, up to the point where that war breaks out into open revolution, and where the violent overthrow of the bourgeoisie lays the foundation for the sway of the proletariat." The Communists declare openly that "their ends can only be attained by the forcible overthrow of all existing social conditions."[118] Force had always played a revolutionary role in history; it is "the midwife of every old society pregnant with a new one,"[119] and "the instrument with the aid of which social movement forces its way through and shatters the dead, fossilized political forms."[120] The same view was expressed by Marx in 1871 in his now famous letter to Kugelmann, a letter invariably quoted by Lenin and by the present-day Soviet ideologists. In a social revolution it is the duty of the working class not only to "transfer the bureaucratic and military machine from one hand to another, but also to smash it," and that is "essential for every real people's revolution on the Continent."[121] A year later Marx again emphasized that "in most of the Continental countries it is force that will be the lever of our revolutions; it is force that we shall someday resort to in order to establish a reign of labor."[122]

What strikes one in the last two remarks is the fact that Marx speaks expressly of the European Continent, in other words, that he excludes Britain and America. In point of fact, he and Engels believed that in these two countries (where bureaucracy and militarism were not greatly developed at the time) it might be possible to accomplish the social transformation without violent revolution. After the early 1870's —by which time an independent working-class movement had come into existence in nearly all European countries—Marx and Engels increasingly stressed the peaceful transition to the new classless society. "We do not deny that there are countries, such as America, England and I would add Holland, if I knew your institutions better, where the working people achieve their goal by peaceful means."[123] The importance of Parliament, and the hope of achieving a labor majority in it, were now becoming more and more important to Marx and Engels: "If, for instance, in Britain or the United States the working class should win majority in Parliament or in Congress, then it could in a constitutional manner abolish the laws and institutions obstructing its advancement."[124]

After Marx's death, Engels added France to the list of these countries, and indeed spoke of the old society peacefully growing into the new one:

One can picture the old society growing into the new one peacefully in countries where the National Assembly concentrates all power in its hands, where anything one wishes may be done constitutionally as soon as one is backed by the majority of the nation—in democratic republics such as France and America, in monarchies like Britain where the dynasty is powerless against the will of the people.[125]

Even for Germany—Engels believed in 1893—it was possible to calculate the time "when we shall have the majority of the population on our side," to which he added: "We have no ultimate aim. We are *evolutionists,* we have no intention of dictating definitive laws to mankind."[126]

☐   **The Dictatorship of the Proletariat**

The *Communist Manifesto* described the "conquest of political power by the proletariat" as the objective of the Communists.[127] Ever since, the concept of the "dictatorship of the proletariat" has been part and parcel of the political theory of Marxism. No concept has undergone so many changes in the course of further development, and no other subject has given rise to such a multiplicity of polemics, discussions, and even sharp clashes.

What, then, did Marx and Engels understand by the "dictatorship of the proletariat"?

They proceeded from the thesis that the rule of the working class (sometimes described as the "dictatorship of the proletariat") was a short step, a "transitional period," in the establishment of the classless society. Thus Marx declared in 1850: "The class dictatorship of the proletariat is the necessary transit point along the road to the abolition of class distinctions."[128] Shortly afterward he remarked that it was not his achievement to have discovered the existence of classes and of the class struggle, but rather that "the class struggle necessarily leads to the *dictatorship of the proletariat*" and that this "dictatorship itself represents only the transition of the *abolition of all classes* and to a *classless society*."[129] Engels, too, spoke of the "necessity of political action by the proletariat and its dictatorship as the transition to the abolition of classes and, with them, of the state."[130] The following statement by Karl Marx has become particularly famous and is frequently quoted: "Between capitalists and Communist society lies the period of the revolutionary transformation of the one into the other. There corresponds to this also a political transition period in which the state can be nothing but the *revolutionary dictatorship of the proletariat*."[131]

The concept of the "dictatorship of the proletariat" is understood by quite a few people today—partly because of the subsequent application of this term and partly because of our experience in the last few decades—to mean a dictatorial or even totalitarian system. But nothing of the kind was in Marx's or Engels' mind. On the contrary, they believed that the realization of a democratic political system and of universal franchise would almost automatically lead to a majority of workers' representatives in Parliament, and therefore to the political rule of the working class; indeed, they sometimes equated the concept of "democratic constitution" with that of the role of the working class. This may seem incredible but is confirmed time and again in Marx's and Engels' writings. "Democracy in all civilized countries has as its necessary consequence the political rule of the proletariat, and the political rule of the proletariat is the first prerequisite of all Communist measures."[132]

In 1847, in his famous brochure *Principles of Communism* Engels declared that the future social revolution "will inaugurate a *democratic constitution* and thereby, directly or indirectly, the political rule of the proletariat." He justified this view by pointing out that in Britain the workers already accounted for the majority of the people and that this would soon also be the case in other countries.[133] Three years later Engels wrote that the working class must first of all capture political power and that it must do so through universal franchise, which would enable it to introduce a majority of workers into the House of Commons.[134] Marx in 1852 similarly identified the dictatorship of the proletariat with such a majority: "For the British working-class universal franchise is synonymous with political power since the proletariat there represents the great majority of the population." If universal franchise was successfully applied in Britain, then "its inevitable outcome will be the political rule of the working class."[135]

All these remarks date from the period between 1847 and 1852. After that, something exceedingly strange happened. For nearly twenty years, from August 1852 until April 1871, Marx and Engels never once mentioned either the dictatorship of the proletariat or the rule of the working class. This strange twenty years' silence was broken only in the spring of 1871, after the demise of the short-lived Paris Commune (March 18 to May 28, 1871) which had come into being as a result of a revolt following France's defeat in the war of 1870–71. Marx and Engels not only followed the heroic struggle of the revolutionary workers of Paris with great sympathy, but they also saw in the Paris Commune the first example of the dictatorship of the proletariat: Marx praised the Paris Commune as an "essentially working-class government" and as "the political form, at last discovered, under which to work out the economic emancipation of labor."[136] Engels expressed himself similarly: "Do you want to know what this dictatorship looks like? Look at the Paris Commune. That was the dictatorship of the proletariat."[137]

The decisive characteristics of the Paris Commune—and therefore of the dictatorship of the proletariat—are described by Marx as follows:

The first decree of the Commune therefore was the suppression of the standing army, and the substitution for it of the armed people. The Commune was formed of the municipal councillors chosen by universal suffrage in the various wards of the town, responsible and revocable at short terms. The majority of its members were naturally working men, or acknowledged representatives of the working class. The Commune was to be a working, not a parliamentary, body, executive and legislative at the same time. Instead of continuing to be the agent of the Central Government, the police was at once stripped of its political attributes, and turned into the responsible and at all times revocable agent of the Commune. So were the officials of all other branches of the Administration. From the members of the Commune downward, the public service had to be done at workmen's wages. . . . The whole of the educational institutions were opened to the people gratuitously, and at the same time cleared of all interference of church and state.[138]

Engels similarly put great emphasis on the fact that the Paris Commune had overcome "the oppressing power of the former centralized government, army, political police, bureaucracy."[139]

However, Engels added the point—which is particularly interesting and significant in the light of the subsequent development of Communism—that it was not enough to abolish the instruments of power of the old order. The important thing was to make sure that, after a socialist transformation, the state organs do not once more turn from the servants of society into its masters, and that a new "socialist" bureaucracy does not emerge: "From the very outset the Commune was compelled to recognize that the working class . . . in order not to lose again its only just conquered supremacy . . . must safeguard itself against its own deputies and officials, by declaring them all, without exception, subject to recall at any moment." In order to prevent the transformation of the state organs "from the servants of society into the masters of society" the Paris Commune applied

two infallible means: In the first place, it filled all posts—administrative, judicial, and educational—by election on the basis of universal suffrage of all concerned, subject to the right of recall at any time by the same electors. And, in second place, all officials, high or low, were paid only the wages received by other workers. In this way an effective barrier to place-hunting and careerism was set up.[140]

To Marx and Engels, therefore, the concept of the dictatorship of the proletariat meant the following: (1) The oppressive power of a centralized government, army, and bureaucracy are abolished, and the police is stripped of its political functions; (2) public affairs are in the hands of a body elected by universal secret ballot, and this body simultaneously performs legislative and executive functions; (3) to prevent the working class from losing its newly captured rule, and to prevent the state organs from once more transforming themselves into the masters of society, all representatives and officials must be subject to recall at any time—such recall being the right of those who elected them—and receive a remuneration not exceeding a worker's wages.

## ☐ The Transition to a Classless Society

According to Marx and Engels, it is the purpose of the dictatorship of the proletariat to carry out the necessary transitional measures for the establishment of the new society. They repeatedly emphasized that these transitional measures will be different in different countries[141] and "will everywhere have to be in accordance with the relations existing at the moment."[142] Under the conditions of the mid-nineteenth century Marx and Engels proposed the following transitional measures for the most advanced countries: limitation of private property by means of progressive taxes and high inheritance taxes, the gradual expropriation of the holdings of big landowners and entrepreneurs, "partly through the competition of state-owned industry, partly against direct compensation"; the organization of state farms and factories with high wages for the workers (so that the private property owners "are compelled to pay the same increased wages as the state"); the nationalization of transport and banking; the free education of the children; the demolition of all unhealthy and ill-built dwellings and urban districts; as well as measures designed to overcome the differences between town and country and aimed at "combining the advantages of urban and rural life without the citizens having to suffer from the one-sidedness and the disadvantages of either."[143]

Marx and Engels repeatedly reflected on whether it was possible in an economically backward country to achieve a socialist reorganization of society by means of a series of transitional measures. They were thinking mainly of czarist Russia. Provided the socialist revolution had been victorious in Western Europe, they concluded, it would be possible, by "leaping over the entire capitalist period," to transfer Russia into a socialist society. It was obvious, however, that the "initiative for such an eventual transformation of the Russian community can never come from itself but only from the industrial proletariat of the West."[144]

Whether, during the transfer of the means of production into the hands of society, the former private owners should be compensated or not must depend on specific circumstances. It was possible that the working class may "simply seize by force the instruments of production" or that "it will pay immediate compensation for them," or that "it will redeem the property therein by small installment payments."[145] Marx and Engels certainly preferred compensation: "We by no means consider compensation as impermissible in any event; Marx told me (and how many times!) that in his opinion we would get off cheapest if we could buy out the whole lot of them."[146]

In agriculture, the transition of the farms of individual peasants into co-operatives was to take place slowly and circumspectly. It was a matter of course that

> when we are in possession of state power, we shall not even think of forcibly expropriating the small peasants (regardless of whether with or without compensation) as we shall have to do in the case of the big land-owners. Our task relative to the small peasants consists, in the first place, in effecting a transition of his private enterprise and private possession into co-operating ones, not forcibly but by dint of example and the proffer of social assistance for this purpose.[147]

By means of such transitional measures the class distinctions were to be gradually eliminated and the transfer of the means of production into the hands of society accomplished. This would result in the abolition of the political oppression of one class by another; public power, the state, would lose its political character, and the new classless society would arise, "an association in which the free development of each is the condition for the free development of all."[148]

Marx and Engels in the 1840's appear to have envisaged initially a protracted transitional period. The proletariat would "only be able gradually to transform existing society, and will abolish private owner-ship only when the necessary quantity of means of production has been created."[149] More than forty years later—when industrialization had meanwhile made enormous strides—Engels declared that a new social order would emerge "after a short transitional period involving some privation, but at any rate of great value morally"[150]—a statement which, naturally enough, is not being quoted by today's Soviet ideologists since it is too much in conflict with the various "periods of transition" in the Soviet Union, which by now have gone on for half a century.

☐ **The Future Classless Communist Society**

The widespread belief that Marx and Engels said nothing at all or only very little about the classless society of the future is incorrect. True, they did not define the details of their hoped-for social order because they rejected such predictions as utopian. Likewise there is no single work by them exclusively concerned with the classless society. However, they have recorded a number of reflections and important suggestions in more than thirty works, which, taken together, outline the decisive economic, social, and political characteristics of the new society, and even speculate about the family life and education in that new society.

First, Marx and Engels made a number of attempts to define the classless society of the future. The final objective of the Communists is "the abolition of classes, the inauguration of a society in which there will be no private ownership of land and means of production."[151] The classless society is "a situation in which every member of society will be enabled to participate not only in the production but also in the distribution and administration of social wealth, and which so increases the social productive forces and their yield by planned operation of the whole of production that the satisfaction of all reasonable needs will be assured to everyone in an ever-increasing measure."[152] The association of the future was to unite the sober approach of capitalist commercial companies with the care shown for the common social welfare by the *polis* of antiquity, the communities of ancient Greece.[153]

Engels sums up the chief characteristics of the classless social order of the future as follows:

The general association of all members of society for the common and planned exploitation of the productive forces, the expansion of production to a degree where it suffices to provide for the needs of all, the cessation of the condition when the satisfaction of the needs of some is effected at the expense of others, the complete abolition of classes and their antithesis, the all-round development of the abilities of all the members of society through the abolition of the hitherto prevalent division of labor, through industrial education, through the change of activity, through the participation of all in the blessings produced by all, through the fusion of town and country.[154]

Marx and Engels, however, did not confine themselves to a definition of the future classless society, but repeatedly—even if sporadically, in a number of separate writings—described certain characteristic features of this hoped-for society.

Economically the new society was to be based on the social ownership of the means of production. But this did not mean a nationalized economy: "State ownership of the productive forces is not the solution of the conflict, but concealed within it are the technical conditions that form the elements of that solution. This solution can only consist in . . . society openly and directly taking possession of the productive forces which have outgrown all control except that of society as a whole."[155] By the formulation of "society's taking possession, openly and without subterfuge, of the productive forces," Marx and Engels did not mean a centralized state economy but rather a co-operative economic system, the association of free producers. Thus Marx spoke of a "co-operative society based on common ownership of the means of production."[156]

The means of production will be "in the hands of the associated producers"[157] and therefore be their social property.[158] Society will be "composed of associations of free and equal producers."[159] Like Marx, Engels described the classless society of the future as a society that will "recognize production on the basis of a free and equal association of the producers."[160] Society will not only "be based on the association of the workers in each factory, but also combine all these associations in one great big union."[161] Agriculture, too, will be under the control of associated producers.[162] All land was to be nationalized.[163] The big estates were to be handed over to the co-operatives, and co-operative operation was to be applied on an extensive scale.[164]

In contrast to Marx's and Engels' continuous reference to the association of free producers and the co-operative economic system—references that are hardly ever mentioned in the present-day writings of Soviet ideologists—the founders of scientific socialism were relatively rarely concerned with economic planning, a subject that has since received so much emphasis. We find only a few statements on this subject. "The social anarchy of production gives place to a social regulation of production upon a definite plan according to the needs of the community and of each individual."[165] In the classless society of the future it will be "possible for its productive forces to dovetail harmoniously into each other on the basis of one single vast plan."[166]

Society's acquisition of the means of production, Marx and Engels believed, would eliminate the wastage of productive forces, which culminates in economic crises. A large quantity of the means of production and products would become available through the abolition of luxury spending by the ruling classes and their political representatives. "Anarchy in social production is replaced by systematic, definite organization."[167] Socialist production will be possible "on the account of society as a whole and in accordance with a previously determined plan."[168]

The planned organization of the economy means that "the regulation of the labor time and the distribution of the social labor among the various groups of production, also the keeping of accounts in connection with this, become more essential than ever."[169] But the new society would need not only more accountants but above all "doctors, engineers, chemists, agronomists and other specialists; so the point is that we must seize control not only of the political machinery but equally of all social production—and this requires not high-sounding phrases but solid knowledge."[170]

The classless Communist society would reach such a high state of economic production that the gratuitous distribution of all products to the members of the society would become possible. In this connection Marx and Engels frequently referred to the realization of the principle "to each according to his needs."[171] The question of how the new society would be able to realize this principle was answered by Friedrich Engels as follows:

The expropriation by society of the private capitalists of the use of all productive forces and means of communication, as well as of the exchange and distribution of products, and their management by society according to a plan based on the available means and the requirements of society as a whole, will eliminate first of all the bad consequences large-scale industry entails at present. Crises will cease to be. . . . Instead of bringing misery in its wake, over-production exceeding the immediate needs of society will satisfy the needs of all, will create new needs and simultaneously the means for their gratification. . . . Once liberated from the yoke of private ownership, large-scale industry . . . will provide society with a quantity of products sufficient to satisfy the needs of all. Agriculture, too, hindered by the pressure of private ownership and the parcelation of land from introducing available improvements and scientific achievements, will mark a new advance and place at the disposal of society an ample mass of products. Thus society will produce sufficient products to arrange a distribution that will satisfy the requirements of all its members.[172]

The future classless society—this was a decisive idea of Marx and Engels—will no longer require a state. The state, necessary before the social revolution as an organ for the suppression of one class by another, will no longer be required after the transformation of society and will, therefore, wither away. Hardly any subject was discussed so often and so emphatically by Marx and Engels as the withering away of the state. As early as 1846—before the *Communist Manifesto*—Marx observed that the working class would replace present society with "an association which precludes classes and their conflict; there will be no political power proper because this political power is the official expression of the class conflict within bourgeois society." In this society, "in which there are no more classes and class antagonisms, *social evolutions* will cease to be *political revolutions*.[173] With the abolition of class distinctions "the public power will lose its political character."[174] It is inevitable that "with the introduction of the socialist order of society the state will dissolve of itself and disappear."[175]

This process, however, should not be viewed as the abolition of the state, but as its gradual withering away: "State interference in social relations becomes, in one domain after another, superfluous and then dies out of itself; the government of persons is replaced by the administration of things, and by the conduct of processes of production." The state is not "abolished; it dies out."[176] "Once the aim of the proletarian movement, i.e., the abolition of classes, is attained, the power of the state which serves to keep the great majority of producers in bondage to a very small exploiter minority disappears, and the functions of government become simple administrative functions."[177]

Even in his brief obituary for Marx in 1883 Engels did not omit to point out expressly that since 1845 Marx and he had consistently held the view that the coming proletarian revolution "will result in the gradual dissolution of the political organization designated as the state."[178]

Along with the abolition of the classes, "the state will inevitably fall. Society, which will reorganize production on the basis of a free and equal association of the producers, will put the whole machinery of state where it will then belong: into the museum of antiquities, by the side of the spinning wheel and the bronze axe."[179] The victorious proletariat will endeavor to curtail the state, which, after all, "is nothing but a machine for the oppression of one class by another . . . until such time as a generation reared in new, free social conditions is able to throw the entire lumber of the state on the scrap heap."[180]

Another characteristic of the new classless society would be the elimination of the differences between town and country. This thesis, too, was persistently stressed by Marx and Engels, from the 1840's to the end of their lives. The result of the abolition of classes and class distinctions would be that "the antithesis between town and country will likewise disappear. The carrying on of agriculture and industrial production by the same people, instead of by two different classes, is even for purely material reasons an essential condition of communistic association."[181] Marx and Engels regarded the abolition of the antithesis between town and country as one of the most fundamental questions which a future social revolution would solve.[182]

The elimination of the contrast between town and country is necessary for two reasons. First, it is the only way to overcome the pollution of cities. "Only by the fusion of town and country [can] the present poisoning of the air, water and land be put to an end," and this requires as a condition "the most equal distribution possible of modern industry over the whole country." This is not only possible but "has become a direct necessity of industrial production itself, just as it has become a necessity of agricultural production and, besides, of public health."[183] Second, the elimination of the contrast between town and country is necessary in order to involve the rural population in the life of the population as a whole:

Only as uniform a distribution as possible of the population over the whole country, only an intimate connection between industrial and agricultural production together with the extension of the means of communication made necessary thereby—granted the abolition of the capitalist mode of production—will be able to deliver the rural population from the isolation and stupor in which it has vegetated almost unchanged for thousands of years.[184]

The demand for the elimination of the contrast between town and country was inseparably linked for Marx and Engels with the abolition of the division of labor and the liberation of the human personality. "The abolition of the antagonism between town and country is one of the first conditions of communal life" because this contrast is "the most crass expression of the subjection of the individual under the division of labor, under a definite activity forced upon him which makes one man into a restricted town-animal, the other into a restricted country-animal, and daily creates anew the conflict between their interests."[185]

The liberation of the human personality from the enslaving division of labor, from alienation and oppression, was always a vital aim of Marx and Engels. In one of his first articles Marx had stated: "The critical danger for each individual consists in losing himself. Loss of freedom is therefore man's real mortal danger."[186] In the view of Marx and Engels the division of labor results in "man's own activity becoming an alien power opposing him and subjecting him, instead of his dominating it. The moment labor begins to be divided, each person has a circumscribed and exclusive sphere of activity which is forced upon him and from which he cannot escape: he is a hunter, a fisherman or a herdsman, or a critic, and must remain that unless he wants to lose his means of subsistence." Matters will be different

in Communist society, where nobody has one exclusive sphere of activity but each can become accomplished in any branch he wishes, society regulates the general production and thus makes it possible for me to do one thing today and another tomorrow, to hunt in the morning, fish in the afternoon, raise cattle in the evening, criticize after dinner, just as I have a mind, without ever becoming a hunter, fisherman, shepherd or critic.[187]

The elimination of the division of labor will make it possible to replace "the detail-worker of today, reduced to the mere fragment of a man, by the fully developed individual . . . to whom the different social functions he performs are but so many modes of giving free scope to his own natural and acquired powers."[188]

The educational system was to prepare the young people of this future society for that goal of continually changing occupational activity —a goal that is difficult to visualize in a highly industrialized country.

Education will enable young people quickly to acquaint themselves with the whole system of production, it will enable them to pass in turn from one branch of industry to another according to social needs or the bidding of their own inclinations. It will therefore abolish one-sidedness in development imposed on all by the present division of labor. Thus a communistically organized society will be able to provide its members with the opportunity to utilize their comprehensively developed abilities in a comprehensive way.[189]

This demanded first of all that intellectual and physical work should be fused, and that schooling should be combined with practical work through polytechnical education. The Communist society of the future would introduce in the schools "technical instruction, both theoretical and practical"[190] and "combine productive labor with instruction and physical training . . . in the case of every child over a given age," as the only method for the development of "fully developed human beings."[191] In this way all members of society will be guaranteed "the greatest possible development of his varied aptitudes."[192]

Man's liberation from the division of labor, his new education and the opportunity of choosing his own activity and occupation, and changing it continually—all these would lead also to a new attitude to work. Owing to the division of labor under capitalism, people were forced into one particular kind of work; but "man knows no more degrading or unbearable misery than forced labor," because it forced man "to work every day from morning to night against his will at a job that he abhors." Conversely, "man knows no greater happiness than that which is derived from productive work voluntarily undertaken."[193]

In the new classless society the old division of labor will disappear and productive work, therefore, will no longer be viewed as a means of enslavement; from a burden it would become a pleasure "by offering each individual the opportunity to develop all his faculties, physical and mental, in all directions and exercise them to the full."[194]

The establishment of a classless society would also change the conditions of marriage and family life. The Communist society of the future would

make the relations between the sexes a purely private affair which concerns only the persons involved, and calls for no interference by society. It is able to do this because it abolishes private property and educates children communally, destroying thereby the two foundation stones of hitherto existing marriage—the dependence of the wife upon her husband and of the children upon the parents conditioned by private property.[195]

The transition to the new social order would mean "the abolition of prostitution both public and private"[196] in the new society. In marriage "the hitherto existing economic foundations of monogamy will disappear." The only remaining motive would be mutual affection. Prostitution would disappear and "monogamy, instead of declining, finally becomes a reality."[197]

Finally, Marx and Engels pointed out that in the new classless society religions would gradually disappear:

When society, by taking possession of all the means of production, and using them on a planned basis, has freed itself and all its members from the bondage in which they are now held by these means of production which they themselves have produced but which confront them as an irresistible alien force; when therefore man no longer merely proposes but also disposes—only then will the last alien force which is still reflected in religion vanish; and with it will also vanish the religious reflection itself, for the simple reason that then there will be nothing left to reflect.[198]

Admittedly, this would be a gradual process, not to be achieved by administrative measures, since "persecution is the best means of strengthening undesirable convictions. This much is certain: The only service that can still be rendered to God today is to make atheism a compulsory dogma."[199]

In nearly all their writings Marx and Engels described the typical features of the classless society of the future without distinguishing between phases of social development. Only once did Marx refer to such phases in the society of the future:

What we have to deal with here is a Communist society, not as it has developed on its own foundation, but, on the contrary, just as it emerges from capitalist society; which is thus in every respect, economically, morally, intellectually, still stamped with birth marks of the old society from whose womb it emerges. . . . But these defects are inevitable in the first phase of Communist society as it is when it has just emerged after prolonged birth pangs from capitalist society. . . . In a higher phase of Communist society, after the enslaving subordination of the individual to the division of labor, and therewith also the antithesis between mental and physical labor, has vanished; after labor has become not only a means of life but life's prime want; after the productive forces have also increased, the all-round development of the individual and all the springs of co-operative wealth flow more abundantly—only then can . . . society inscribe on its banners: From each according to his abilities, to each according to his needs![200]

As for the detailed development of these phases and the solutions that would have to be found for individual practical questions, Marx and Engels declined all discussion, since they regarded this as utopian speculation. "The working class [has] . . . no ready-made Utopias to introduce *par décret du peuple*," Marx declared. They have "no ideals to realize but to set free the elements of the new society with which the old collapsing bourgeois society already is pregnant."[201] It is not the task of Communists "to create utopian systems for the organization of the future society,"[202] least of all in questions of detail: "To speculate on how a future society might organize the distribution of food and dwellings leads directly to *Utopia*."[203] The people of the Communist society of the future "will not care a rap about what we today think they should do."[204]

There is one more issue to which Marx and Engels repeatedly referred, one they believed would result from the abolition of class distinctions and the establishment of the new society: the elimination of national conflicts and quarrels, and the establishment of peaceful coexistence among nations.

As early as November 1847 Marx wrote: "The victory of the proletariat over the bourgeoisie is simultaneously the victory over the national and industrial conflicts which today lead the different nations to confront each other in hostility. The victory of the proletariat over the bourgeoisie is therefore at the same time the signal of liberation for all oppressed nations."[205] The *Communist Manifesto* also emphasizes that the abolition of the exploitation of man by man will mean that "the exploitation of one nation by another will also be put to an end."[206] The old society will be replaced by a new society "whose International rule will be *Peace* because its national ruler will be everywhere the same—*Labor!*"[207] Since the working class has common international interests, "as soon as the working class attains political rule all pretexts for national enmity will be removed."[208] The triumph of the working class will "abolish the struggles between the nations and make peace and happiness a reality in the civilized countries."[209]

Finally, there is one point of crucial importance: the political life in the Communist society based on the association of free producers. Marx and Engels never went into details of what political life would be like after the abolition of class rule and the withering away of the state. But there is one important remark by Engels—never quoted by the Soviet ideologists—which clearly emphasizes political freedom. When a few utopian socialists tried to set up isolated communes as the germ cells of a new society, Engels gave them this advice: "Show them . . . that your communes will not subject mankind to any 'iron despotism.' . . . Show them that true freedom and true equality are possible only under the conditions of a commune, show them that *justice* requires such conditions—and then you will have them all on your side."[210]

In conclusion, it is worth pointing out one surprising and significant omission by Marx and Engels: Nowhere in their writings is there any mention, or even a hint, of the existence of a political party in the class-less society of the future, let alone a party that would play a leading role. The classless society, to Marx and Engels, was a society without exploitation and oppression, without classes, without state, and without parties.

☐  **Important Conclusions for Today**

This brief summary of Marx's and Engels' political views enables us to draw a few important conclusions for the further development of the political theory of Marxism, in particular for the present-day Soviet version of Marxism-Leninism.

Marx and Engels proceeded from the thesis that, with the progressive development of capitalism, the working class would form the largest class of society and eventually the majority of the population. The working-class movement, as the movement of the majority in the interest of the majority, would, by liberating itself, liberate society as a whole from oppression and exploitation. For the realization of its aims the working class needed a working-class party, but this was envisaged not as a leading elite but as the representative of the interests of the working class as a whole. The Party was to have a democratic structure and avoid all authoritarian beliefs. Moreover, the Party press was to be independent of the Party to ensure free discussion and the further development of the political theory of scientific socialism.

The social revolution presupposes a high level of economic and technological development, as well as a working class comprising the majority of the population. Only in this way can the elimination of class distinctions be permanent. In the absence of this prerequisite, a transition to the classless society would not be possible, since at a lower level of economic development a social struggle would again break out and with it a new class stratification, a new ruling class. The social revolution would be possible only by a simultaneous victory in several industrially developed countries; the colonial and dependent countries would first of all be taken over by the working class after its victory in the industrially developed countries and then guided to independence as rapidly as possible. The social revolution would have different forms in various countries; whereas at first Marx and Engels stressed revolution by force, after the 1870's they regarded a peaceful transformation by means of a labor majority in Parliament as desirable and probable.

The social revolution would lead to the political rule of the working class (dictatorship of the proletariat), through the destruction of the power of bureaucracy, army, and police, and their replacement with a body elected by general secret ballot, exercising legislative and executive power. Office workers and officials in public life would receive a remuneration not exceeding a worker's pay and would be liable to recall by their electors at any time.

The dictatorship of the proletariat would, during a short transitional period, put into effect the measures necessary for the transformation of society, including the transfer of the decisive means of production to the ownership of society—compensation to their former owners being desirable but not mandatory. Through this transformation the classless Communist society would emerge, and this would be characterized by the following features: (1) social ownership of the means of production in the form of associations of free producers or a union of co-operatives; (2) a planned development which would so increase the co-operative wealth that the distribution of all products would become possible according to the individual's requirements ("to each according to his needs"); (3) the elimination of class rule and of class distinctions, resulting in the abolition of state power and the emergence of a society without state or classes; (4) the elimination of the contrast between town and country; (5) the abolition of the enslaving division of labor and the chance of unimpeded development of a person's full mental and physical potential, so that his personality could unfold fully; (6) the elimination of national conflicts and quarrels, and the achievement of peace and friendship among nations.

These, in short, are Marx's and Engels' political concepts, which decisively influenced the socialist and social-democratic parties of many countries.

Marx and Engels, however, were far from regarding their views and theories as infallible political doctrine. "I am not in favor of our planting a dogmatic flag. On the contrary," Marx wrote. What mattered was to link up with actual struggles and to identify with them. "Then we do not face the world in doctrinaire fashion with a new principle, declaring: here is the truth, kneel here!"[211] Engels shared this opinion: "Communism is not a doctrine but a movement; it proceeds not from principles but from facts."[212] Marx and Engels held this view all their lives: "Our theory is not a dogma but the exposition of a process of evolution, and that process involves successive phases."[213] The rejection of any kind of dogmatism was rooted also in their personal attitudes. In reply to a question in the mid-1860's Marx stated that his favorite motto was: *De omnibus dubitandum* (Everything should be doubted).[214]

From the 1870's Marx and Engels feared more and more that some of their followers, who noisily proclaimed themselves "Marxists," would falsify the basic concept of scientific socialism and turn it into a dogma. By the end of the 1870's Marx had dissociated himself from such "Marxists" with his famous reply: *"Tout ce que je sais, c'est que moi, je ne suis pas marxiste"* ("All I know is that I am no 'Marxist' ").[215] This was not, as is sometimes assumed, a casual remark, but a statement frequently repeated by Marx,[216] expressing his growing misgivings about the "Marxists" appearing at that time. Engels, too, was uneasy about these followers. Thus he criticized some followers who were trying "to make of their imported and not always understood theory a kind of dogma necessary to salvation and to keep aloof from any movement which did not accept that dogma."[217] Many of these "Marxists" were "people whose incompetence is matched only by their arrogance."[218]

Engels was especially worried about the possible future misinterpretations of Marx's fundamental concepts. After Marx's death, Engels feared, "everybody will guess more into . . . than read correctly from"[219] the manuscripts left behind by Marx. Engels, therefore, asked most emphatically "to study this theory further from its original sources and not at second-hand," since it happened "only too often that people think they have fully understood a theory and can apply it without more ado from the moment they have mastered its main principles, and those even not always correctly. And I cannot exempt many of the more recent 'Marxists' from this reproach, for the most wonderful rubbish has been produced from this quarter too."[220]

Prophetically, yet full of profound skepticism, Engels wrote on March 15, 1883, two days after Marx's death: "The local lights and lesser minds, if not the humbugs, will now have a free hand. The final victory is certain, but circuitous paths, temporary and local errors—things which even now are unavoidable—will become more common than ever."[221]

Marx's and Engels' gloomy premonitions toward the end of their lives were only too justified—indeed, they were left far behind by the reality of subsequent developments. A crucial reason for this was the geographical and political shift of Marxism from Western Europe to Russia. The subsequent political development did not entirely follow the lines anticipated by Marx and Engels. Instead of the hoped for and often predicted social revolution in the industrially developed countries of Western Europe and North America, an evolutionary development—a gradual improvement of the economic and social situation of the working class—took place, brought about largely by the rapid growth of socialist parties and organizations which increasingly succeeded in making their influence felt in municipal administrations, co-operatives, and parliaments. As a result, the socialist parties gained a growing influence on practical politics, including social policy and legislation, and the opportunity, even within the existing society, of increasingly and successfully championing the necessary reforms desired by labor. This, of course, meant that the ultimate objective, the social revolution and the establishment of the classless society of the future, was relegated more and more to the background.

All this is reflected also in the debates and arguments about the political concepts of Marx and Engels after the deaths of these two founders of scientific socialism. An account of this discussion would go beyond the scope of this book. Let the following observation suffice. The statements of Marx and Engels, which were sometimes contradictory, including those on the vital question of whether the social revolution should be accomplished by peaceful or violent means, enabled people of the most varied political views to produce whatever passages of Marx and Engels they needed to support their own views. The reformists referred to Marx's and Engels' remarks about the peaceful growth of one society into another, while the revolutionary Left stressed their remarks about a revolutionary transformation and the establishment of the dictatorship of the proletariat.

In the Western European countries, where the socialist working-class movement was, as a rule, operating legally, and where big social-democratic mass parties were increasingly able to influence social policy and legislation in the interests of labor, the reformist trend gradually gained the upper hand. Matters were different in most countries of Eastern and Southeastern Europe, and especially in czarist Russia. In these economically backward countries, where the workers lived under poor and often catastrophical economic and social conditions, and where the socialist workers' organizations were usually suppressed, operating only illegally and without any chance of promoting reforms within the existing society, the revolutionary interpretation of Marx's and Engels' concepts gained the upper hand.

It was, above all, Russia that was of decisive importance for the subsequent development of the political doctrine of Communism. Marx died in 1883 and Engels in 1895. A mere seven years later, in 1902, Vladimir Ulyanov, then known as Ilyin and later as Lenin, proclaimed an entirely new doctrine of the Party and thereby inaugurated the transition from Marxism to Leninism.

# 2

## The First Transformation: Leninism

"Give us an organization of revolutionaries, and we will overturn Russia."
These words of Lenin's, from his book *What Is to Be Done?*, published in
1902, herald the transition from Marxism to Leninism. Vladimir Ulyanov,
born in 1870 and known to the world under his Party name of Lenin, had
been endeavoring since the beginning of this century to adapt the political
theory of Marxism to the conditions of the socialist workers' movement in
the czarist Russia of his day, i.e., an economically backward country
where the industrial workers represented an infinitesimal part of the
population, a country with strong elements of feudalism, a country that
had not yet passed through the period of a bourgeois revolution.

Under the conditions of autocratic czarism, the Social Democratic
Workers' Party of Russia, founded in Minsk in 1898, was forced from
the start to operate illegally. Its members and functionaries were under
constant threat of arrest and deportation; from the very outset there was
little hope of legally instituting reforms in the interests of the workers. It
was within this Party, which at its Second Congress in the summer of 1903
split into a moderate wing, the Mensheviks, and an extremist wing, the
Bolsheviks, that Lenin had been playing an increasingly important role
since the turn of the century.

Lenin's very first writings reveal a certain conflict between the
Marxist theoretician and the active revolutionary. Marxist theory stated
that the social transformation of society was possible only in an economically advanced country, where the industrial workers constituted
the majority of the population. This was not the case in czarist Russia

at the turn of the century. Did one really—this is the feeling one reads between the lines of Lenin's writings of those years—have to wait that long? Would this not, under Russian conditions, mean an excessively long postponement of the revolution?

Lenin, the practical revolutionary, rebelled against the theory to which he had committed himself. His revolutionary impatience and energy were not to be overlooked. In 1901–2 while he was living in Munich, Lenin wrote his book *What Is to Be Done?,* which contained the new concept of a Party composed of professional revolutionaries, centrally organized and disciplined, and designed to lead the workers. This efficient elite Party proposed by Lenin would make it possible to attach greater importance to problems of political tactics, including the skillful use of conflicts within the ranks of its opponents and the winning of allies. The idea of the working class was gradually being replaced by the concept of the "alliance of workers and peasants." Instead of a social revolution of the working class, Lenin, as early as 1905, postulated for the Russia of his day that, first of all, a bourgeois-democratic revolution was to be aimed at which would then, under the leadership of the working class and its Party, gradually grow into a socialist revolution. The Russian Revolution of 1905 provided an opportunity to test the new concept and to acquire new experience; indeed it became, as Lenin later put it, the "dress rehearsal for 1917."

But Lenin did not stop at the adaptation of Marxism to Russian conditions and the theoretical-political discussion of Russian revolutionary problems. The momentum gained by the national revolutionary movements in the colonial and dependent countries—whose importance he was quick to realize—led him to the conclusion, even before World War I, that these movements represented allies of the socialist workers' movement in Europe. World War I led Lenin to a searching examination of the social-democratic countries of Western Europe and the problems of war generally. He developed a new doctrine of the war (including the inevitability of wars), and from his economic analyses of imperialism and the uneven development of capitalism drew the conclusion (in 1915–16) that a social revolution did not necessarily have to take place simultaneously in all industrial countries but was possible in one single country.

At the same time, he shifted the emphasis from the social and economic prerequisites of revolution, as stressed by Marx and Engels, to political factors ("a revolutionary situation"). Lenin replaced the "social revolution" championed by Marx and Engels with the concept of the "socialist revolution"—to be led by a revolutionary party. In contrast to Marx and Engels, Lenin regarded the possibility of peaceful transition as the exception, the forcible overthrow in the form of an armed uprising as the rule.

All these ideas had been developed by Lenin before the 1917 Revolution in Russia. In 1917 he was to put them into practice. To begin with, however, Lenin—who was then living in Zurich, Spiegelgasse 13— was taken by surprise by the Russian February Revolution of 1917. It was only in January 1917, just a month earlier, that Lenin in a lecture given in German had declared: "We of the older generation may not live to see the decisive battles of this coming revolution."[1]

Very soon, however, in April 1917, came Lenin's celebrated journey in a sealed train through Germany to Russia, together with leading Bolsheviks (including his wife, Nadezhda Krupskaya, G. J. Zinoviev, L. P. Serebriakov, Grigory Sokolnikov, Karl Radek, and Mieczislav Bronsky, as well as the Swiss socialist Fritz Platten. After his arrival in Petrograd (now Leningrad), Lenin, at a Bolshevik conference at the end of April 1917, put forth, as part of the immediate action program, the demand (the "April theses") that the bourgeois-democratic revolution must be further developed into a socialist revolution. At first, however, he encountered opposition among his own party activists, who were reluctant to endorse his far-reaching demands.

After the reverse of July 1917—when Lenin had to go into hiding, and Trotsky and other Bolshevik leaders were arrested and the Party outlawed—Lenin used his forced exile in that autumn to write his programmatic work *State and Revolution*. However, political developments soon pulled him away from this work. The failure of Kornilov's reactionary *coup d'état* at the end of August and the growing revolutionary ferment throughout the country soon began to benefit the Bolsheviks. They gained the majority in the soviets of the large cities, including Petrograd, where on August 31 (according to the old Russian calendar [O.S.] still valid at the time, but September 13 by ours and the modern Russian calendar [N.S.] Trotsky was elected chairman of the Petrograd soviet.

From his hiding place, but supported in Petrograd by Trotsky, Lenin with increasing persistence urged the preparation of an armed uprising. "History will not forgive us if we do not assume power now."[2] The majority of the members of the Bolshevik Central Committee were, at that time, not yet prepared to follow his instructions. They were hoping to become the main force at the Second All-Russian Congress of Soviets, scheduled for November 2, and perhaps even to gain a majority. But Lenin kept bombarding the Central Committee with his demands.

"The Bolsheviks have no right to wait for the Congress of Soviets; they must take power at once. . . . To wait for the Congress of Soviets would be a childish game of formalities . . . a betrayal of the revolution."[3]

Following Lenin's illegal return to Petrograd in disguise on October 7 (20), the question of the armed uprising was discussed at two illegal meetings of the Central Committee on October 10 (23) and 16 (29). Lenin succeeded, supported mainly by Trotsky, in imposing his point of view. By ten votes to two (Zinoviev and Kamenev), and at the second meeting by nineteen votes to two with four abstentions, the Central Committee decided in favor of an armed uprising.

At the same time, the Revolutionary Military Committee of the Petrograd Soviet was set up on October 12 (25). Headed by Trotsky, and with the particularly active participation of the Bolsheviks Vladimir Antonov-Ovseyenko, Nicolai Podvoisky, Officer Candidate N. V. Krylenko (after the October Revolution temporarily Commander-in-Chief of the Army), and the sailor Pavel Dybenko of the Baltic Fleet, the Committee functioned as a kind of improvised general staff for the impending uprising. The Committee had its headquarters in the Smolny Institute. Through hundreds of commissars and plenipotentiaries it was linked with the armed combat groups in the factories (most of whom strongly sympathized with the Bolsheviks) and with the "Red Guards," who numbered about 20,000.

During the night of October 24–25 (November 6–7) the October Revolution, which was to bring to power the first Marxist government in history, erupted in Petrograd. Only Stalin and Zinoviev kept aloof during this decisive night; Lev Kamenev, though at first against the uprising, took an active part at headquarters in the Smolny Institute. Bridges, telegraph offices, telephone exchanges, and other strategically vital points were seized, and all key positions in the city were in Bolshevik hands by the morning of November 7. The uprising had taken place so smoothly that it had hardly been noticed by the public. That morning, at 10 o'clock, leaflets printed by the Revolutionary Military Committee of the Petrograd Soviet announced the victory of the uprising and the overthrow of the Provisional Government, which had its seat in the Winter Palace.

Late at night on November 7, the Second All-Russian Congress of Soviets was opened under Kamenev's chairmanship in the Smolny Institute. The Bolsheviks, with 390 supporters, had a bare majority of the 650 (according to other sources 670) delegates. While the Congress met throughout the night, sailors, workers, and soldiers under Bolshevik leadership stormed the Winter Palace. In the early hours of November

8, at 2:10 A.M., they penetrated to the Hall of Mirrors where the Provisional Government was assembled. "I declare you, the members of the Provisional Government, under arrest," Antonov-Ovseyenko announced on behalf of the Revolutionary Military Committee. "The members of the Provisional Government yield to force and surrender to avoid bloodshed," replied A. I. Konovalov, the Deputy Premier of the Kerensky Government, the last non-Communist government of Russia.

In the course of November 8, a few members of the Bolshevik Central Committee, in a corner of the Smolny Institute and without regard to formality, decided to call the new government the "Council of People's Commissars." Lenin first proposed Trotsky as chairman, but he declined. The first Soviet Government included only Bolsheviks—eleven intellectuals and four workers—most of whom had lived through many years of prison and exile. Only one of them, Lenin himself, who accepted the chairmanship of the government, was over forty. All the other People's Commissars—Trotsky (Foreign Affairs), Alexei Rykov (Interior), V. P. Miliutin (Agriculture), Alexander Shliapnikov (Labor), Viktor Nogin (Trade and Industry), I. A. Teodorovich (Food), Stalin (Nationalities), G. J. Oppokov-Lomov (Justice), I. I. Skvorzov-Stepanov (Finance), Anatoly Lunacharsky (Public Education), N. P. Glebov (Post and Telegraph), Antonov-Ovseyenka, and Krylenko (Army Affairs)—were in their thirties, and the sailor Dybenko (Navy) was only twenty-eight.

In the evening of November 8, the Second Congress of Soviets continued its meeting and declared that the Provisional Government had been deposed. Then Lenin stepped up to the rostrum.

"Dressed in shabby clothes, his trousers much too long for him" —this is how the American journalist John Reed, a Bolshevik sympathizer, described this historic moment—"Lenin, gripping the edge of the reading stand, letting his little winking eyes travel over the crowd as he stood there waiting, apparently oblivious to the long, rolling ovation, which lasted several minutes. When it finished, he said simply: 'We shall now proceed to construct the socialist order!' "[4]

The Bolsheviks now held power—but in an economically backward country of not quite 140 million inhabitants, five-sixths of whom were peasants and more than 70 per cent illiterate; a country in which the industrial workers made up only an infinitesimal part of the population; a country whose economy had been wrecked by war, in which famine, misery, and need were rampant.

"The worst thing that can befall a leader of an extreme party," Engels had written in 1850,

is to be compelled to take over a government in an epoch when the movement is not yet ripe for the domination of the class which he represents and
for the realization of the measures which that domination would imply. . . .
Thus he necessarily finds himself in a dilemma. What he *can* do is in contrast
to all his actions as hitherto practiced, to all his principles and to the present interests of his party; what he *ought* to do cannot be achieved.[5]

This was the situation in which the Bolsheviks found themselves.
On the one hand, inspired by the theory of Marxism, they sincerely
and unselfishly hoped to create a classless Communist society; on the
other, they were compelled to work in a country and at a time when the
prerequisites for the realization of this objective were lacking—and that
in the midst of a struggle against a rapidly reorganizing counterrevolution. In November 1917, within a few weeks of the victory at Petrograd,
the Bolsheviks suffered their greatest blow. In the elections to the Constituent Assembly, which the Bolsheviks had always demanded, they
received only one-quarter of the votes, while the Social Revolutionaries,
a moderate socialist peasant party, achieved an overwhelming majority.
When the Constituent Assembly was convened on January 18, 1918, 370
of the 707 deputies were Social Revolutionaries, 175 Bolsheviks, 40
Left Social Revolutionaries, 17 KD's ( a bourgeois party), and 16
Mensheviks; there was also a substantial group of deputies without
party affiliation. The Constituent Assembly refused to approve the
measures so far taken by the Bolshevik Government. Thereupon the
Bolsheviks resorted to force: A detachment of Bolshevik Red Guards
forced its way into the Hall, dissolved the Constituent Assembly, and
arrested many of its members.

The Bolsheviks, a minority party, now determined the course of
events. The Social Revolutionaries and Mensheviks, the two socialist
parties which represented the absolute majority of the population, were
removed from power, and their newspapers were banned. Moreover,
the Cheka ("Extraordinary Commission for the Struggle Against Counterrevolution, Speculation, and Sabotage"), set up by the Bolsheviks
on December 7 (20), 1917, directed its activity not only against the
declared opponents of the revolution but also against members of the
socialist parties, even though they were in favor of Soviet rule and
socialism, and merely opposed a one-party government by the Bolsheviks.

In the years of the Civil War, from 1918 to 1921, the dictatorial
element of Bolshevism grew stronger. As a minority party at the head
of a ruined country, fighting against a multiplicity of enemies, the
Bolsheviks distinguished themselves by courage, dedication, self-sacri-
fice, and heroism. At the same time, however, in their struggle for

victory in the Civil War, they centralized all economic, political, and military power in the country and suppressed the democratic freedoms. At the Tenth Party Congress in March 1921, even the freedom of opinion within the Party was curtailed; the "unity of the Party" and the ban on factions within it was proclaimed. True, Lenin and his fellow-fighters, undoubtedly from honest motives, viewed all these measures as no more than temporary necessities, forced upon them by particularly difficult circumstances. They were also far from presenting these measures as examples or models for Communists in other countries. Nevertheless, certain realities were created in those years which were difficult to undo later. Lenin's writings during the last few years of his life testify that he suspected and perhaps even realized this. By then gravely ill, full of doubts and gloomy premonitions, he tried to change course. But it was too late.

Lenin's collected works (forty-four volumes) include both his pre-1917 ideas and the conclusions drawn from the 1917 October Revolution and the first few years of Soviet rule. For his political concepts before the October Revolution, the most important writings are: *What Is to Be Done?* (1902), *Two Tactics of Social Democracy in the Democratic Revolution* (November 1905), *The Awakening of Asia* (May 1913), *On the Right of Self-Determination of Nations* (spring 1914), *Karl Marx* (July–November 1914), *The Collapse of the Second International* (June 1915), *Socialism and War* (July–August 1915), *The Revolutionary Proletariat and the Right of Nations to Self-Determination* (early 1916), *On the Junius Pamphlet* (summer 1916), *On a Caricature of Marxism and on "Imperialist Economism"* (August–October 1916), *The Military Program of the Proletarian Revolution* (September 1916), *State and Revolution* (August–September 1917), *Marxism and Insurrection* (mid-September 1917), *Will the Bolsheviks Maintain State Power?* (end of September 1917), *On the Revision of the Party Program* (early October 1917), and *Advice of an Onlooker* (also early October 1917).

Lenin's most important writings after the October Revolution include: *The Immediate Tasks of the Soviet Government* (April 1918), *The Proletarian Revolution and the Renegade Kautsky* (autumn 1918), *The Great Beginning* (June 1919), *Economics and Politics in the Era of the Dictatorship of the Proletariat* (October 1919), *"Left-Wing" Communism—an Infantile Disorder* (April–May 1920), and *On Co-operation* (January 1923). Of importance for the Soviet period are also a large number of Lenin's speeches, including those to the Seventh Party Congress (March 1918), the Eighth Party Congress (March 1919), the Ninth Party Congress (March 1920), to the Party Conference of the

Moscow Guberniya (November 1920), to the membership of the Moscow Party organization (December 1920), to the Tenth Party Congress (March 1921), on the fourth anniversary of the October Revolution (October 1921), to the Eleventh Party Congress (March 1922), speeches and draft resolutions for the Second, Third, and Fourth Congresses of the Communist International (June 1920, June 1921, and November 1922) and, above all, his "Letter to the Party Congress" (December 1922 to January 1923), which has become known as his "Testament."

## ☐ The New Doctrine of the Party

Whereas Marx and Engels had regarded the workers' party as the representative of the interests of the workers as a whole, and had visualized that party as a loosely structured democratic organization with a largely independent party press—an auxiliary tool of a powerful working-class movement—Lenin proclaimed the doctrine of a militant elite party whose nucleus must consist of disciplined professional revolutionaries and which must lead and direct the working-class movement.

Lenin proceeded from the view that the workers cannot develop any socialist consciousness of their own. The most they can possibly develop by themselves is a trade-union kind of awareness, to organize themselves in associations and fight for economic demands. Their political awareness, on the other hand, can be awakened only from the outside, and this was the task of the revolutionary socialist intelligentsia.[6]

In order to accomplish this task, a special type of Party was needed, an organization of revolutionaries, capable of conducting the political struggle with energy, toughness, and continuity.[7] This organization of revolutionaries must be distinguished by a "stable organization of leaders, maintaining continuity" and must consist chiefly of people "professionally engaged in revolutionary activity."[8] The nucleus of the Party must be composed of people "whose profession is revolutionary work." This meant that "all distinctions as between workers and intellectuals, not to speak of distinctions of trade and profession, in both categories, must be effaced."[9] A professional revolutionary must not spend the whole day working in a factory. He must receive enough financial support from the Party to make it possible for him to go underground if necessary, to change his place of work as often as necessary, to acquire organizational experience, and in general to widen his horizon.[10] Without such professional revolutionaries, who had to be equipped with the requisite knowledge, to have undergone a thorough schooling and to be capable of co-operating superbly with one another, no successful struggle was possible.[11]

All functions of the Party must be concentrated "in the hands of the smallest possible number of professional revolutionaries." Centralization of the conspiratorial functions of the organization should be combined with the enlistment of the broadest masses within the movement.[12] A firm organization of tested revolutionaries would give Party members "confidence in its strength."[13] Only such a disciplined Party, led by professional revolutionaries, could, in Lenin's view, ensure victory. "Give us an organization of revolutionaries and we will overturn Russia!"[14]

This doctrine, formulated in 1901–2, remained one of Lenin's lifelong guiding principles. When, at the Second Congress of the Social Democratic Workers' Party of Russia in the summer of 1903, the question of who could be a member of the Party was discussed (the famous debate about Article 1 of the Statute), Lenin demanded that only one who endorsed the Party program, supported the Party materially, and— this was the vital point—"is regularly active under the direction of one of its organizations" could become a Party member. Thus, Lenin wanted to reserve Party membership for members actively engaged in the work of a Party organization: "It is our task to safeguard the firmness, consistency, and purity of our Party. We must strive to raise the calling and importance of a Party member."[15]

Two years later, in the autumn of 1905, Lenin supplemented his doctrine of the Party by the thesis that the Party press must be subordinate to the Party. The literary and journalistic activity of Party members must become part and parcel of organized systematic Party work. True, Lenin declared that "literary work bears to a lesser extent than anything else a mechanical equalization, a leveling, a rule of the majority over the minority," and for that reason, "it is absolutely necessary to ensure wide scope for personal initiative and individual leanings, scope for ideas and fantasy, form and content." But he held to the view that literary activity must be an inseparable part of Party work: "Newspapers must become the organs of the various Party organizations, and their writers must by all means become members of these organizations. Publishing and distributing centers, bookshops and reading-rooms, libraries and similar establishments must all be under Party control."[16] Instead of Engels' demand for the independence of the Party press from Party authorities and for the independent advancement of socialist writing and theory, Lenin now demanded its subordination to the Party.

Proceeding from this principle, Lenin as early as 1905 proclaimed the ideological unity of the Party and the ban on the propagation of views running counter to the Party:

Anybody is free to write and speak as he likes, without the least limitation. But any free association (and this includes the Party) is similarly free to throw out such members as use the shield of the Party for preaching views running counter to the Party. . . . The Party is a voluntary association which would inevitably disintegrate, first ideologically and then also materially, if it did not rid itself of those members who preach anti-Party views.

All those who were "not completely Marxist and not altogether correct," must be removed from the Party by "periodical cleansings."[17]

The Party, according to Lenin, was to be based on the organizational principle of "democratic centralism." This principle meant "freedom to criticize, so long as this does not disturb the unity of a definite action; it rules out all criticism that disrupts or makes difficult the unity of an action decided upon by the Party."[18] At the Sixth Party Congress of the Bolsheviks, in August 1917, the principle of "democratic centralism" was incorporated in the Party Statute, and at the Second Congress of the Communist International, in the summer of 1920, Lenin demanded the acceptance of this principle for all Communist parties in the world by a declaration that "parties belonging to the Communist International must be organized on the principle of 'democratic centralism.' "[19] Even after the Revolution of 1917, when the Bolshevik Party was functioning no longer in conspiratorial illegality but legally, and even after it was in fact in power, Lenin adhered to the thesis that the working class must be led by the Party. It was the Party that was to be able "to assume power and to lead the whole community to socialism, to direct and to organize the new order, and to be the teacher, guide, and leader of all the toiling and the exploited."[20] This required "the most rigorous and truly iron discipline in our Party."[21]

Lenin's doctrine of the Party culminated in his demand for "Party unity" and the ban on the formation of any factions. Upon Lenin's proposal, "unity and closing of their ranks" was imposed as a duty upon all Party members at the Tenth Party Congress in March 1921. At the same time the "harmful nature and inadmissibility of the formation of any kind of faction whatever" were proclaimed, even if "the representatives of the various groups have the best intention to preserve Party unity." True, criticism was still to be permitted, but within narrow boundaries: as for the form of such criticism, anyone practicing it must take account "of the position of the Party, surrounded as it is by enemies."[22]

Even allowing for the historical circumstances—the fact that the

Bolshevik Party had been predominantly illegal until 1917, compelled to work under continuous harassment, and that from late 1921 to 1922 it determined the fate of Soviet Russia under the conditions of a blockade and of civil war—it remains an undeniable fact that Lenin made a substantial change in the original political ideas of Marx and Engels. Instead of a democratically organized body representing the interests of all workers who engaged in free discussion, Lenin's doctrine of the Party now envisaged an elite led by professional revolutionaries, organized on the principle of democratic centralism, with restricted freedom of discussion, and making great demands on Party members, who must operate in unity and with closed ranks in order to lead the working class.

□ **Political Tactics**

One result of the new doctrine of the Party was the fact that questions of political tactics now began to play an increasingly important and at times predominant part. The more all members and functionaries within the Party were ideologically streamlined and welded together by unified Party discipline, the greater the opportunity for the Party leadership to veer in its outward activities, to maneuver, to enter into political alliances, to switch instantly from one method of struggle to another, to enter into compromises and to go over from the offensive to the defensive. Lenin formulated the following definition of Party tactics as early as 1905: "By the Party's tactics we mean its political conduct or the character, direction, and methods of its political activity. Tactical resolutions are adopted by Party congresses in order to accurately define the political conduct of the Party as a whole with regard to new tasks or in view of a new political situation."[23]

The large number of Lenin's tactical instructions may be reduced to the following six principal ones:

The first is the demand to gain political allies and, for that purpose, to exploit all conflicts in the ranks of the opponent: "Only those who are not sure of themselves can fear to enter into temporary alliances even with unreliable people; not a single political party could exist without such alliances."[24] In order to acquire such allies it was important to exploit most carefully all clashes of interest among one's opponents:

The more powerful enemy can be vanquished only by exerting the utmost effort, and by the most thorough, careful, attentive, skillful and obligatory use of any, even the smallest, rift between the enemies, any conflict of interests among the bourgeoisie of the various countries, and also by taking advantage of any, even the smallest, opportunity of winning a mass ally, even though this ally is temporary, vacillating, unstable, unreliable and conditional. Those who do not understand this reveal a failure to understand even the smallest grain of Marxism, of scientific, modern socialism.[25]

To achieve this objective one must be prepared for anything: "If you are unable to adapt yourself, if you are not inclined to crawl on your belly through the mud, you are not a revolutionary but a chatterbox; and I propose this, not because I like it, but because we have no other road."[26]

In order to gain allies, the Party must be prepared to make compromises, to make concessions—without losing sight of the realization of its ultimate aim: "The task of a truly revolutionary party does not consist in proclaiming some impossible renunciation of all compromise, but in knowing how to remain true to its principles, to its class, to its revolutionary task of preparing for the revolution and guiding the people's masses to victory in the revolution, in spite of all compromises that may be unavoidable."[27]

On the relationship between the objectives of Communism and political compromise Lenin observed: "It is necessary to link the strictest devotion to the ideas of Communism with the ability to effect all the necessary practical compromises, tacks, conciliatory maneuvers, zigzags, retreats, and so on . . . [so that] the proletariat will defeat them all and capture political power."[28]

A distinction must be made between compromises necessary for the attainment of the ultimate objective and compromises that are impermissible because they would mean the abandonment of the ultimate objective. Lenin illustrated this distinction by the following example:

Imagine that your car is held up by armed bandits. You hand them over your money, passport, revolver, and car. In turn you are rid of the pleasant company of the bandits. That is unquestionably a compromise. "*Do ut des*" ("I give you money, firearms, and a car, so that you give me the opportunity to get away with a whole skin"). It would, however, be difficult to find a sane man who would declare such a compromise to be "inadmissible on principle," or who would call the compromiser an accomplice of the bandits (even though the bandits might use the car and the firearms for further robberies). There are different kinds of compromises. One must be able to analyze the situation and the concrete conditions of each compromise, or of each variety of compromise. One must learn to distinguish between a man who has given up his money and firearms to bandits so as to lessen the evil they can do and to facilitate their capture and execution, and a man who gives his money and firearms to bandits so as to share in the loot.[29]

Closely linked with this idea is Lenin's third tactical directive: Communists must strive everywhere, in all organizations, associations, and parliaments, to influence the working people and win them over for the objective of the Party. Thus Lenin demanded that "one had absolutely to learn how to work legally in the most reactionary of parliaments, in the most reactionary of trade unions, co-operative and insurance societies and similar organizations."[30] To achieve this end, one must be capable of any sacrifice, of overcoming the greatest obstacles, for it is important "to carry on agitation and propaganda systematically, perseveringly, persistently and patiently in those institutions, societies and associations—even the most reactionary—in which proletarian or semi-proletarian masses are to be found."[31] If necessary, Communists must be prepared "to resort to stratagems, artifices and illegal methods, to evasions and subterfuges, as long as we get into the trade unions, remain in them and carry on Communist work within them at all costs."[32] This applies also to the activities of Communists in parliaments: "While you lack the strength to do away with bourgeois parliaments and every other type of reactionary institution, you *must* work within them."[33] Communists must "not stew in their own juice but must learn" to penetrate into "prohibited premises where the representatives of the bourgeoisie are influencing the workers."[34]

Fourth, Lenin in his tactical directives again and again pointed out that all fighting methods must be mastered—not only attack and advance but also an orderly retreat. The Party must be able to "master all forms or aspects of social activity without exception," and it "must be prepared for the most rapid and brusque replacement of one form by another." In politics, even more than in warfare, "all the weapons, all the means and methods of warfare that the enemy possesses, or may possess" must be mastered.[35] It must be remembered that "victory is impossible unless one has learned how to attack and retreat properly."[36]

Fifth, Lenin demanded that the Party's policy must always take account of the experience of the masses, i.e., the working people. "Millions of people will never listen to the advice of parties if that advice does not fall in with their own experience."[37] Above all, the opponent must not be underrated: "The most dangerous thing . . . is to underrate the enemy and to reassure ourselves with the thought that we are stronger."[38]

Finally, Lenin called for concentration on the main task, the "main link in the chain," for an emphasis on the most important task, in order to lead the masses forward to the decisive struggle:

It is not enough to be a revolutionary and an adherent of socialism or a Communist in general. You must be able, at each particular moment, to find the particular link in the chain which you must grasp with all your might in order to hold the whole chain and to prepare firmly for the transition to the next link—the order of the links, their form, the manner in which they are linked together, the way they differ from each other in the historical chain of events, are not as simple and not as meaningless as those in an ordinary chain made by a smith.[39]

The aim must be to "search after forms of the *transition* or the *approach* to the proletarian revolution"[40] as well as discovering, isolating, and correctly identifying the concrete road or the particular turn of events that will bring about "the victory of Soviet power and the dictatorship of the proletariat on a world-wide scale."[41]

□ **The National Liberation Movements**

At the beginning of the century Lenin recognized the importance of the revolutionary movements in the colonial and dependent countries. He welcomed the Persian Revolution of 1907, the Revolution of the Young Turks of 1908, and the national revolutionary movements in India and China.[42] Several years before World War I Lenin spoke of "the political awakening of the Asian peoples."[43] The revolution of 1911 in China was evidence for him that there too "the social movement and a democratic upswing are now vigorously" developing; he also welcomed the revolutionary democratic movement in the Dutch East Indies (Indonesia) and declared that "the awakening of Asia" marked "the new phase in world history that began early this century."[44]

Even before World War I Lenin regarded the national revolutionary movement in the colonial countries as an ally of the socialist workers' movement in Europe: "The fact that Asia, with its population of 800 million, has been drawn into the struggle for the same European ideals should inspire us with optimism and not despair."[45] Lenin predicted that the national liberation movements in those countries would lead "to the creation of nationally independent and nationally unified states."[46]

Like Marx and Engels, Lenin supported sovereignty and independence, the right of self-determination of nations. By this he meant "the political separation . . . from alien national bodies," and the formation of an independent national state.[47] By the autumn of 1915 he was more definite: "We demand freedom of self-determination, i.e., independence, i.e., freedom of secession for the oppressed nations."[48] In this connection Lenin was fond of quoting Marx's and Engels' dictum: "No nation can ever be free if it oppresses other nations."[49]

The more powerfully the national revolutionary movements were developing in the colonial countries, the more emphatically Lenin supported the view that the socialist workers' movements in Europe must ally themselves with these national liberation movements. The socialist revolution in the advanced countries could only succeed in alliance with the "national liberation movements of the undeveloped, backward, and oppressed nations."[50] The socialist workers' movement must not only "demand the unconditional and immediate liberation of the colonies" but must also decisively support "the more revolutionary elements in the bourgeois-democratic movements for national liberation in these countries."[51]

After the victory of the October Revolution in 1917, Lenin, at the Second Congress of the Communist International (1920), announced special directives for the work of Communists in the national liberation movements of colonial and dependent countries. Support for these movements was imposed as a duty on all Communist parties; in detail, the Communists were to oppose the clergy and other reactionary elements, pan-Islamism, and similar endeavors; they were to give their particular support to peasant movements against landowners; and they were finally to wage a "determined struggle against attempts to give a Communist coloring to the bourgeois-democratic liberation trends in the backward countries." The Communist parties were to support the national movements in the colonial and dependent countries and "enter into a temporary alliance with bourgeois democracy in the colonial and backward countries." They must not, however, fuse with that movement but "under all circumstances uphold the independence of the proletarian movement, even if it is in its most embryonic form." It was the duty of Communists "to regard with particular caution and attention the survivals of national sentiments in the countries and among nationalities which have been oppressed the longest."[52]

Lenin appealed to the Communist parties to "give effective support" to the peasant movements, for otherwise the Communist parties would never be in a position to "pursue Communist tactics" in the backward countries. Although Lenin admitted that in many of these countries there can be no question of a purely proletarian movement, the Communists should nevertheless endeavor to assume the leadership of the movement: "There is practically no industrial proletariat in these countries. Nevertheless, we have assumed, we must assume the role of leaders even there."[53]

Lenin of course realized that it would be impossible, after a victorious revolution in the colonial and dependent countries, to pass on immediately to a socialist society. He therefore proposed that this objective should be reached by way of a number of intermediate stages, and thereby laid the foundation for the present-day Soviet doctrine of the "non-capitalist road of development." In the summer of 1920 Lenin declared that the objective in those countries must be to enable the backward countries to attain the Soviet order "with the aid of the proletariat of the advanced countries," and "through certain stages of development, to [achieve] Communism without having to pass through the capitalist stage."[54] Lenin so confidently hoped that this was possible that he proposed that the slogan "Workers of all countries, unite!" change to "Workers of all countries and all oppressed peoples, unite!"[55]

□ **War and Peace**

Unlike Marx and Engels, who concerned themselves only with the "limited" wars of their own time, Lenin—largely influenced by World War I—introduced an entire doctrine of war into the theory of Communism. This doctrine included the criteria for judging a war, the distinction between just and unjust wars, and finally the thesis of the "inevitability of wars" in the era of imperialism.

To Lenin, wars were "the direct and inevitable outcome" of the private ownership of the means of production. "Under capitalism there are no other means of restoring the periodically disturbed equilibrium than crises in industry and wars in politics."[56]

In assessing a war, according to Lenin, it did not matter who started it, who was the aggressor and who the defender. "The question of which group dealt the first military blow or first declared war is immaterial in any determination of the tactics of socialists."[57] To a Marxist it was of no importance at all *"where* the armies stand"; what mattered was *"what issues* are at stake."[58]

Lenin, who was very fond of Clausewitz' well-known dictum: "War is the continuation of policy" and frequently quoted it, regarded it also as the decisive criterion in assessing a war:

War is the continuation of policy. Consequently, we must examine the policy pursued prior to the war, the policy that led to and brought about the war. If it was an imperialist policy, i.e., one designed to safeguard the interests of finance capital and rob and oppress colonies and foreign countries, then the war stemming from that policy is imperialist. If it was a national liberation policy, i.e., one expressive of the mass movement against national oppression, then the war stemming from that policy is a war of national liberation.[59]

It did not matter who the aggressor was: "The character of the war (whether it is reactionary or revolutionary) does not depend on who the attacker was, or in whose country the 'enemy' is stationed; it depends *on what class* is waging the war, and on what policy this war is a continuation of."[60]

Lenin used this criterion to distinguish between just and unjust wars: "War is the continuation of the politics of this or that class; and in every class society, slave-holding, feudal or capitalist, there have been wars which continued the politics of the oppressor classes, and also wars which continued the politics of the oppressed classes."[61]

Just wars, according to Lenin, were wars "by an oppressed class against the oppressor class, by slaves against slave-holders, by serfs against landowners, and by wage-workers against the bourgeoisie," as well as all wars "which, despite all the horrors, atrocities, distress and suffering that inevitably accompany all wars, were progressive, i.e., benefited the development of mankind by helping to destroy most harmful and reactionary institutions (e.g., an autocracy or serfdom) and the most barbarous despotisms in Europe (the Turkish and the Russian)."[62]

Examples of just wars quoted by Lenin were the Spartacus Rising in ancient Rome (73–71 B.C.),[63] the wars of the French Revolution,[64] the American War of Independence (1775–83), which Lenin called one of those rare "great and genuine liberation wars," and the American Civil War (1861–65), which he said had attained "such world-historic, progressive and revolutionary importance."[65] Among possible just wars in the future Lenin referred to liberation wars by the colonial people against the colonial powers, even if they should be wars of aggression:

For example, if tomorrow Morocco were to declare war on France, or India on Britain, or Persia or China on Russia, and so on, these would be "just," and "defensive" wars, irrespective of who would be the first to attack, and any socialist would wish the oppressed, dependent, unequal states victory over the oppressor, slave-holding and predatory "Great" Powers.[66]

Unjust, imperialist wars were wars which either aimed at the oppression of other nations or wars between imperialist powers. "A war is certainly imperialist if both warring sides oppress foreign countries or nationalities, and are fighting for their share of the loot and for the right to 'oppress and rob' more than the others."[67] As examples of unjust wars Lenin quoted the Punic Wars between Rome and Carthage in classical antiquity,[68] the Seven Years' War (1756–63),[69] the war of the United States against the Philippines (1899–1901), and World War I (1914–18), which had been an imperialist war on both sides.[71]

Admittedly, wars could change their character in the course of the fighting:

A national war *might* be transformed into an imperialist war and vice versa. Here is an example: The wars of the Great French Revolution began as national wars and indeed were such. They were revolutionary wars—the defense of the great revolution against a coalition of counterrevolutionary monarchies. But when Napoleon founded the French Empire and subjugated a number of big, viable, and long-established national European states, these national wars of the French became imperialist wars and, in turn, led to wars of national liberation against Napoleonic imperialism.[72]

According to Lenin, the uneven development of capitalism means that "imperialist wars are absolutely inevitable."[73] Imperialism, he said, was characterized by endeavors to annex both agricultural and developed industrial territories and by reaching out "for *any kind* of territory"[74] in this new share-out of the world. In the event of two or three imperialist countries getting into conflict with one another, they would drag "the whole world into *their* war over the division of *their* booty."[75] Second, one of the fundamental features of imperialism consists in conquering colonies, accelerating economic development in those colonies, and thereby strengthening the social and political forces that must rise against national oppression; "and from this it follows inevitably that imperialism must often give rise to national wars."[76] Third, imperialism exacerbates the internal contradictions and hence also the class struggle, which could turn into civil war. "He who accepts the class struggle cannot fail to accept civil wars, which, in every class society are the natural, and under certain circumstances inevitable, continuation, development and intensification of the class struggle."[77]

For all these reasons, wars are unavoidable under imperialism, since imperialism inescapably produces "the inevitability, first, of revolutionary national rebellions and wars; second, of proletarian wars and rebellions *against* the bourgeoisie; and, third, of a combination of both kinds of revolutionary war."[78]

These are Lenin's tenets, which subsequently became known (and still are known) as his doctrine of the inevitability of wars.

☐ **World Revolution or Coexistence?**

The concept of the inevitability of wars had been developed by Lenin in 1915–16, i.e., before the October Revolution. After the victory of the Bolshevik Revolution in 1917, however, a new problem arose: Soviet Russia's relations with the Western capitalist countries.

The present-day claim of Soviet ideologists that Lenin had always favored coexistence is factually incorrect. To begin with, he invariably viewed the Russian Revolution and Soviet Russia as part of the world revolution: "If we, the Bolshevik Party, have undertaken this task single-handed, then we have done so in the conviction that the revolution was ripening in all countries," Lenin declared at the Seventh Congress in March 1918. "Our salvation from all these difficulties is an all-European revolution."[79] Again and again he pointed to the inseparable link between Soviet Russia and international revolution: "We are now, as it were, in a besieged fortress, waiting for the other detachments of the world socialist revolution to come to our relief."[80] In the summer of 1921 Lenin again declared that from the very outset the Bolsheviks had regarded their revolution as part of the international revolution:

When we started the international revolution, we did so not because we were convinced that we could forestall its development, but because a number of circumstances compelled us to start it. We thought: either the international revolution comes to our assistance, and in that case our victory will be fully assured, or we shall do our modest revolutionary work in the conviction that even in the event of defeat we shall have served the cause of the revolution and that our experience will benefit other revolutions. It was clear to us that without the support of the international world revolution the victory of the proletarian revolution was impossible.[81]

Only occasionally, in connection with topical or practical issues, did Lenin make any observations about relations with the Western capitalist countries—and these varied according to the situation or the issue. Lenin declared, for instance, that as long as Soviet Russia was weaker than the capitalist world "we must be able to take advantage of the antagonisms and contradictions existing among the imperialists." With astonishing frankness Lenin added:

At present, we stand between two foes. If we are unable to defeat both of them, we must be able to dispose our forces in such a way as to make them fall out among themselves; whenever thieves fall out, honest men come into their own. However, as soon as we are strong enough to overcome capitalism as a whole, we shall immediately seize it by the scruff of the neck. . . . The practical task of Communist policy is to take advantage of this hostility and to play one side off against the other.[82]

Elsewhere Lenin similarly stated: "Our policy" consists in "utilizing the discord among the imperialist powers."[83]

The crucial question whether wars between Soviet Russia and the capitalist countries were unavoidable, or whether peaceful coexistence was possible, was answered by Lenin differently at different times. On the one hand, he declared that military clashes between the Soviet Republic and the capitalist countries were inevitable: "We are living not merely in a state but in a system of states, and it is inconceivable for the Soviet Republic to exist alongside of the imperialist states for any length of time. One or the other must triumph in the end. And before that end comes, there will have to be a series of frightful collisions between the Soviet Republic and the bourgeois states."[84] In 1920 he observed similarly: "While capitalism and socialism exist side by side, they cannot live in peace: one or the other will ultimately triumph— the last obsequies will be observed either for the Soviet Republic or for world capitalism."[85] These remarks suggest that Lenin always believed in the inevitability of wars between Russia and the capitalist countries.

Yet on the other hand—and the Soviet Communists are nowadays fond of quoting these remarks—he repeatedly came out in favor of a predominantly economic co-operation between Soviet Russia and the capitalist countries: "We are decidedly in favor of an economic understanding with America—with all countries, but *especially* with America."[86] He even proposed a kind of truce: "Let the American capitalists leave us alone. We shall not touch them."[87]

In connection with America, Lenin expressed the hope that besides concessions, steps would be taken toward "the normal development of reciprocal economic assistance."[88] On one occasion he spoke of a period when socialist and capitalist states will coexist side by side.[89]

In December 1920 Lenin stated: "All our politics and propaganda . . . are directed toward putting an end to war, and in no way toward driving nations to war."[90] A year later he again emphasized that "we shall endeavor with all our strength to continue to preserve peace, and we shall not shrink from major concessions and sacrifices in order to preserve this peace," since "our workers and peasants prize above all the blessings of peace."[91]

□  **The Socialist Revolution**

Unlike Marx and Engels, who envisaged a universal revolution, Lenin proclaimed that revolution was possible in one single country. In his view, imperialism inevitably led to an uneven economic and political development: "Hence, the victory of socialism is possible first in several or even in one capitalist country alone."[92] A year later, in

1916, he formulated this thesis more precisely: "The development of capitalism proceeds extremely unevenly in different countries. This cannot be otherwise in view of their commodity production. From this fact it follows irrefutably that socialism cannot achieve victory in *all* countries simultaneously. It will achieve victory first in one or several countries, while the others will for some time remain bourgeois or pre-bourgeois."[93]

Whereas Marx and Engels invariably declared that the prerequisite for a socialist revolution was a high level of social and economic development of capitalism, as well as the need for the working class to represent the majority of the population, Lenin as early as 1905 put forward the thesis that a socialist revolution was possible even in an economically backward country, such as czarist Russia. It would take place when a bourgeois-democratic revolution (aimed at abolishing feudalism and the big landowners, and at establishing a democratic republic) was actively supported by the working class and the Marxist Party. Provided the working class and the Marxist Party succeeded in playing a decisive part in this revolution, or indeed in taking over its leadership, it would then be possible, following the completion of the bourgeois-democratic revolution, to advance it further, and to go on directly to a socialist revolution.[94] "From the democratic revolution we shall immediately, in accordance with our strength, with the strength of the class-conscious and organized proletariat, embark upon the transition to the socialist revolution."[95]

By transforming a bourgeois-democratic revolution into a socialist revolution Lenin believed the Marxist parties could accomplish the hoped-for revolution also in countries where the prerequisites stipulated by Marx and Engels were absent. Under these circumstances, what mattered were no longer the economic and social prerequisites, but solely a favorable political situation that must be utilized by the Marxist Party. Lenin coined the concept of the "revolutionary situation," characterized by the following three features:

1. When it is impossible for the ruling classes to maintain their rule without any change; when there is a crisis, in one form or another, among the "upper classes," a crisis in the policy of the ruling class, leading to a fissure through which the discontent and indignation of the oppressed classes burst forth. For a revolution to take place, it is usually insufficient for "the lower classes not to want" to live in the old way; it is also necessary that the "upper classes should be unable" to live in the old way.
2. When the suffering and the want of the oppressed classes have grown more acute than usual.

3. When, as a consequence of the above causes, there is a considerable increase in the activity of the masses, who uncomplainingly allow themselves to be robbed in "peacetime" but, in turbulent times, are drawn both by all the circumstances of the crisis and by the "upper classes" themselves into independent historical action.[96]

This revolutionary situation ensured merely the objective pre-requisite of a socialist revolution; a revolution, however, could be successful only provided "the above-mentioned objective changes are accompanied by a subjective change, namely, the ability of the revolutionary *class* to take revolutionary mass action strong enough to break (or to dislocate) the old government which never, not even in a period of crisis, 'falls,' if it is not overthrown."[97]

Later, after the October Revolution, Lenin repeatedly returned to this "revolutionary situation":

For a revolution to take place it is not enough for the exploited and op-pressed masses to realize the impossibility of living in the old way, and demand changes; for a revolution to take place it is essential that the ex-ploiters should not be able to live and rule in the old way. It is only when the "lower classes" do not want to live in the old way and the "upper classes" cannot carry on in *the old way* that the revolution can triumph. This truth can be expressed in other words: revolution is impossible without a nation-wide crisis (affecting both the exploited and the exploiters). It follows that, for a revolution to take place, it is essential, first, that a majority of the workers (or at least a majority of the class-conscious, thinking, and po-litically active workers) should fully realize that revolution is necessary, and that they should be prepared to die for it; second, that the ruling classes should be going through a governmental crisis, which draws even the most backward masses into politics . . . weakens the government and makes it possible for the revolutionaries to rapidly overthrow it.[98]

## ☐  The Armed Uprising

In contrast to Marx and Engels, who, after the 1870's, had stressed the peaceful transition to socialism, Lenin emphasized violent revolution. "The working class would, of course, prefer to take power *peacefully*," but to renounce the revolutionary seizure of power was madness and would merely represent "a disgraceful retreat in face of the bourgeoisie and all other propertied classes." It was to the highest de-gree improbable that the ruling classes would make concessions peace-fully; hence, "the working class is left no other way to realize its objective but revolution."[99] Subsequently, Lenin spoke of the "inevitability of violent revolution" and declared that "the substitution of a proletarian for a capitalist state is impossible without violent revolution."[100]

Only once—in the autumn of 1917—and then only for a few days, did Lenin see a possibility for Russia to advance from the existing parliamentary form of government to Soviet rule by a peaceful road. "By seizing full power the Soviets could still today—and this is probably their last chance—ensure the peaceful development of the revolution . . . and power could pass peacefully from one party to another." Lenin was in favor of using this "chance to secure a peaceful development of the revolution," since otherwise "the fiercest civil war between bourgeoisie and proletariat is inevitable."[101] But eleven days later he no longer saw this possibility and declared that "the transfer of power to the Soviets now means armed uprising."[102]

In this situation, immediately before the Bolshevik October Revolution, Lenin issued his directives for an armed uprising, directives that have since remained unchanged as part of Soviet political theory:

To be successful, insurrection must rely not upon conspiracy and not upon a party but upon the most advanced class. That is the first point. Insurrection must rely upon a revolutionary upsurge of the people. That is the second point. Insurrection must rely upon a turning-point in the history of the growing revolution when the activity of the advanced ranks of the people is at its height and when the vacillations in the ranks of the enemy and in the ranks of the weak, half-hearted and irresolute friends of the revolution are strongest. That is the third point.[103]

The successful accomplishment of an armed uprising, according to Lenin, requires the following:

1. Never play with insurrection, but when beginning it, realize firmly that you must go all the way.
2. Concentrate a great superiority of forces at the decisive point and at the decisive moment, otherwise the enemy, who has the advantage of better preparation and organization, will destroy the insurgents.
3. Once the insurrection has begun, you must act with the greatest determination and by all means, without fail, take the offensive. "The defensive is the death of every armed rising."
4. You must try to take the enemy by surprise and seize the moment when his forces are scattered.
5. You must strive for daily successes, however small (one might say hourly, if it is the case of one town), and at all costs retain "moral superiority."[104]

The October Revolution confirmed Lenin in his concept of violent revolution. "Every great revolution, and a socialist revolution in particular," he said, was "inconceivable without internal war, i.e., civil war."[105]

Lenin, therefore, changed Marx's and Engels' concepts of the social revolution in three vital aspects. First, instead of the simultaneous victory of the revolution in several countries, he proclaimed the possibility of a socialist revolution in a single country. Second, instead of the economic and social prerequisites stressed by Marx and Engels (a high level of economic development and the working class as the majority of the population), he postulated certain political conditions (the "revolutionary situation") as well as the Party's ability to exploit it. The social revolution of the working class was transformed into a political revolution under the leadership of a Party. Third, in contrast to Marx and Engels, who had emphasized a peaceful transformation after the 1870's, Lenin proclaimed violent revolution and civil war as the decisive method of the socialist revolution.

☐  **Changes in the "Dictatorship of the Proletariat"**

Marx and Engels regarded the dictatorship of the proletariat as a transitional phase on the road to a classless society. The dictatorship of the proletariat was to be characterized by the existence of an elected organ, which would exercise legislative and executive power simultaneously, and in which all elected representatives and employees of the public service would receive a remuneration not exceeding a worker's wages and be subject to recall at any time. The police was to be stripped of its political power, and the organs of the state were no longer to be the masters of society but its servants. Lenin, too, initially spoke of the rule of the working class as "a state *without* a standing army, *without* a police opposed to the people, *without* an officialdom placed above the people."[106] At the same time, however, Lenin promoted the concept of the dictatorship of the proletariat, only sporadically used by Marx and Engels, to the key feature of Marxism altogether. Only he who works for "the recognition of the dictatorship of the proletariat" is a Marxist.[107] More important still was the change in the meaning of the term "dictatorship of the proletariat." Since Marx and Engels made the social revolution dependent on the condition that the working class would represent the majority of the population, the existence of an elected organ was to them entirely sufficient for carrying out the desired changes in society. Lenin, on the other hand, proceeded from the idea that a socialist revolution must be led by an elite Party. For that reason the suppression of the opponent, the application of dictatorial means of force were for him at the very center of his concept of the "dictatorship of the proletariat." By late 1916 Lenin spoke of the dictatorship of the proletariat as a rule that "rests directly on coercion," necessary "to overthrow the bourgeoisie and repel its attempts at counterrevolution."[108] The dictatorship of the proletariat, while achieving "democracy for the poor, democracy for the people," at the same time required "a series of restrictions of liberty in the case of the oppressors, exploiters, and capitalists. We must crush them in order to free humanity from wage-slavery; their resistance must be broken by force. It is clear that where there is suppression there must also be violence, and there cannot be liberty or democracy."[109] In the same study Lenin spoke of the dictatorship of the proletariat as "an authority shared with none else and relying directly upon the armed force of the masses."[110]

After the victory of the October Revolution Lenin proclaimed Bolshevik rule in Russia as the realization of the dictatorship of the proletariat. It would be "extremely stupid" to assume that "the transition from capitalism to socialism is possible without coercion and without dictatorship." The dictatorship is necessary since "capitalism cannot be defeated and eradicated without the ruthless suppression of the resistance of the exploiters," who would always try to overthrow the new power. Second, a socialist revolution is "inconceivable without internal war, i.e., civil war." To solve these problems, "an iron hand" is needed. The dictatorship of the proletariat demands "absolute and strict unity of will."[111] The dictatorship of the proletariat presupposes a "revolutionary government that is really firm and ruthless"; indeed Lenin complained that the Bolshevik Soviet rule was still "too mild."[112] The dictatorship of the proletariat is "a rule that is unrestricted by any laws."[113] However, Lenin repeatedly pointed out that the dictatorship of the proletariat was a special form of class alliance between the proletariat, the vanguard of the working people, and the numerous nonproletarian strata of working people (the petty bourgeoisie, small property owners, the peasantry, the intelligentsia, etc.)[114] The aim of the dictatorship of the proletariat was to raise "tens of millions of working and exploited people" to a "new democracy and independent participation in the administration of the state."[115] Subsequently, Lenin spoke of the vital task of "drawing the mass of people into administrative work."[116]

Yet the need for the use of force was to Lenin beyond all doubt: "This dictatorship presupposes the ruthlessly severe, swift and resolute use of force to crush the resistance of the exploiters, the capitalists, landowners and their underlings. Whoever does not understand this is not a revolutionary, and must be removed from the post of leader or adviser of the proletariat."[117] By way of explanation, Lenin added: "The will of tens and hundreds of thousands of people can be expressed by one person. This composite will is achieved in the Soviet way."[118]

In this connection Lenin made it clear beyond all doubt—unlike Marx and Engels who never touched upon this issue—that the dictatorship of the proletariat must be under the leadership of the Party. It was the Party's task "to direct and organize the new order, to be the teacher, guide, leader of all the toiling and exploited,"[119] since the dictatorship of the proletariat was "a persistent struggle, bloody and bloodless, violent and peaceful, military and economic, educational and administrative—against the forces and traditions of the old society." It was impossible to wage such a struggle successfully "without a Party of iron that has been tempered in the struggle." Especially during the dictatorship of the proletariat must the Party be united and disciplined: "Whoever brings about even the slightest weakening of the iron discipline of the Party of the proletariat (especially during its dictatorship), is actually aiding the bourgeoisie against the proletariat."[120] On one occasion Lenin even mentioned (though subsequently he toned this point down) the leading role of the Bolshevik Party in the Soviet state: "No important political or organizational question is decided by any state institution in our republic without the guidance of the Party's Central Committee."[121] The dictatorship of the proletariat was "a period of struggle between dying capitalism and nascent Communism or, in other words, between capitalism which has been defeated but not destroyed and Communism which has been born but is still very feeble."[122] Unlike Marx and Engels, Lenin believed that classes would continue to exist throughout the duration of the dictatorship of the proletariat; although they would undergo changes, "the class struggle does not disappear under the dictatorship of the proletariat; it merely assumes different forms."[123] What mattered during this period of transition was who would prove victorious, who would outstrip whom, the capitalist elements or the proletarian state power—a confrontation which Lenin summed up in his famous formula "Who Whom?"[124]

## ☐   The Transition to Socialism

Like Marx and Engels—though with the important differences mentioned above—Lenin viewed the dictatorship of the proletariat as a period of transition leading to the establishment of the Communist classless society. But whereas Engels had referred to a short transitional period, Lenin, proceeding from the conditions in Soviet Russia, declared that the realization of a socialist society would require "a fairly long period of transition," if only because "the reorganization of production is a difficult matter, because radical changes in all spheres of life need time, and because the enormous force of habit of running things in a petty-bourgeois and bourgeois way can only be overcome by a long and stubborn struggle."[125] Lenin even remarked that the transition to the classless society would cover "an entire historical epoch."[126] In March 1919 he pointed out that it was "still a long way" to the realization of the socialist society: "The bricks of which socialism will be composed have not yet been made."[127] In April 1920 Lenin again observed: "Socialism has not yet been built; and it will take a long time to build."[128] To create new forms of social order and discipline requires decades.[129] Lenin even thought in terms of whole generations: "We know that we cannot establish a socialist order now—God grant that it may be established in our country in our children's time, or perhaps in our grandchildren's time."[130]

Marx and Engels had always proceeded from the assumption that a social revolution would take place in economically developed and industrialized countries. Their own transitional measures were based on this assumption. However, the socialist revolution in Russia, in an economically backward country with a predominantly peasant population and a rather low proportion of industrial workers, created an entirely different situation. This was reflected in Lenin's new concept of industrial development, of the creation of the economic foundations of the future socialist society. It was necessary, Lenin declared within a few months of the October Revolution, to "lay the firm foundation of socialist society stone by stone."[131]

In November 1920 Lenin came out in favor of the electrification of Russia as a necessary prerequisite for the establishment of Communism: "There can be no question of rehabilitating the national economy or of Communism unless Russia is put on a different and a higher technical basis than that which has existed up to now. Communism is Soviet power plus the electrification of the whole country, since industry cannot be developed without electrification."[132] In December 1920, addressing the Congress of Soviets, Lenin once more repeated his famous formula: "Communism means Soviet power plus electrification of the whole country." It was important to "see to it that the economic basis is transformed from a small-peasant basis into a large-scale industrial basis. Only when the country has been electrified, and industry, agriculture and transport have been placed on the technical basis of modern large-scale industry, only then shall we be fully victorious."[133]

Lenin singled out three political tasks for the period of transition.

First, he consistently urged the winning over of the bourgeois intelligentsia, the specialists. It was necessary to transform "specialists from servants of capitalism into servants of the working people, into their advisers,"[134] and to "take all that is valuable from capitalism, take all its science and culture."[135] The new society, Lenin observed in November 1919, "cannot be built without knowledge, technique, and culture, and this knowledge is in possession of bourgeois specialists. Most of them do not sympathize with Soviet power, yet without them we cannot build Communism. They must be surrounded with an atmosphere of comradeship."[136]

In March 1920 Lenin uttered this warning: "With management in the hands of incompetent people . . . the very existence of Soviet Russia is at stake." For that reason, "everyone with a knowledge of bourgeois culture, bourgeois science, and bourgeois technology must be treasured," because "without them we shall be unable to build Communism."[137] In January 1922 he went so far as to assert the Communist Party and the Soviet Government must "guard as the apple of their eye every specialist who does his work conscientiously and knows and loves it—even though the ideas of Communism are totally alien to him."[138]

The second decisive problem of the period of transition was the socialist transformation of agriculture. Like Marx and Engels, Lenin called for a cautious and sensitive approach. Any coercion of the peasants, let alone any collectivization decreed from above, was rejected by him on principle.

As early as January 1918 Lenin declared that "socialism cannot be imposed upon the peasants by force."[139] In February 1919 he added: "No Communist, no intelligent socialist, has even entertained the idea of violence against the middle peasants. All socialists have always spoken of agreement with them and of their gradual and voluntary transition to socialism."[140] At the Eighth Party Congress in March 1919 Lenin demanded that the socialist transformation of agriculture should be effected cautiously and slowly. The Bolsheviks must "stress the truth that here, by the very nature of the case, nothing is to be achieved with forcible methods." It was important "to make allowance for the specific living conditions of the peasants and to learn from the peasants how a transition can be made to a better system—but *don't you dare to give orders!*" It was not correct to force agricultural decrees about cooperatives upon the peasants.[141]

In November 1919 Lenin again urged to give "the greatest attention and most serious thought to the issue . . . that cannot be solved at one blow . . . there can be no question of forcibly imposing socialism on anyone." But "we must render every support to the working peasant, treat him as an equal, without the slightest attempt to impose anything upon him by force."[142] A few weeks later he explained: "We have millions of individual farms in our country, scattered and dispersed throughout remote rural districts. It would be absolutely absurd to attempt to reshape these farms in any rapid way, by issuing an order or bringing pressure to bear from without." Unfortunately, a number of "stupid attempts" had been made "to drive the peasants into the communes by force." Lenin expressed the hope that "if isolated examples of such coercion are to be met with now, they are very few," and demanded that "the last trace of this outrage" be "swept from the face of the Soviet Republic."[143] Any attempt to apply pressure on the peasants, Lenin believed, should in fact be punished: "In organizing peasants in communes, artels, etc., the Party policy must be strictly adhered to, which in this respect does not permit any coercion, leaving it to the peasants to decide freely for themselves and penalizing all attempts to introduce the principle of coercion."[144]

The third task for the period of transition, according to Lenin, was the overcoming of Russian great-power chauvinism and the establishment of friendly and equal relations between the major and minor nationalities living on the territory of the Soviet Republic.

Any Russian nationalism was not only totally alien to Lenin, he opposed it wherever he encountered its symptoms. Thus, at the Eighth Party Congress in March 1919, Lenin complained about "chauvinist objections" following certain territorial concessions made to Finland by Soviet Russia: "Scratch some Communists and you will find a Great-Russian chauvinist."

When a few Russian Communists demanded obligatory Russian-language teaching in all schools throughout the country, Lenin declared: "In my opinion such a Communist is a Great-Russian chauvinist. Many of us harbor such sentiments and they must be combated."[145] In November 1919 Lenin called on the Communists active in Turkestan to "wipe out all traces of Great-Russian imperialism."[146] During the same month he reminded the Party members working in the Ukraine of their duty to "use every means to help remove all barriers in the way of the free development of the Ukrainian language and culture." As a result of centuries of oppression nationalist tendencies, although undesirable, were understandable among the Ukrainian population, and the Russian Communists, therefore, had a duty to meet them and oppose them with all possible tact, avoiding needless Russification. They must "counteract attempts at Russification that push the Ukrainian language into the background."[147]

The Bolsheviks, according to Lenin, had a duty "to combat very vigorously the survivals (sometimes unconscious) of Great-Russian imperialism and chauvinism among 'Russian' Communists." What mattered was always the trend toward a socialist development since "for an internationalist the question of state frontiers is a secondary, if not tenth-rate question." It was therefore entirely possible and by no means alarming to find "the Ukrainian workers and peasants trying out different systems, and in the course of, say, several years, testing by practice union with the R.S.F.S.R., or seceding from the latter and forming an independent Ukrainian Soviet Socialist Republic."[148]

The Russian Communists, Lenin insisted, must always be "very cautious and patient, and make concessions to the survivals of national distrust," and at the same time persecute "with the utmost severity the slightest manifestation in our midst of Great-Russian nationalism," because such manifestations were "a betrayal of Communism."[149] Also in dealings with the nationalities living in the Caucasus Lenin insistently urged "caution and maximum good will toward the Moslems" as well as "sympathy for the Moslems, their autonomy, and independence, etc."[150] In his very last writings Lenin observed that the solution of the nationalities question required "not merely formal equality." It was important, especially for a Russian Communist, "by one's attitude or by concessions . . . to compensate the non-Russians for the lack of trust, for the suspicion and the insults to which the government of the 'dominant' nation subjected them in the past. . . . That is why in this case it is better to overdo rather than underdo the corrections and leniency toward the national minorities."[151] Lenin proposed that in the Central Executive Committee of the Union, then the highest state body of the U.S.S.R., the chairmanship should "at all costs" rotate between a Russian, a Ukrainian, a Georgian, etc. "I declare war to the death on dominant nation chauvinism. I shall eat it with all my healthy teeth as soon as I get rid of this accursed bad tooth."[152]

Without ever changing or modifying his view from 1917 until his death, Lenin quite unequivocally laid down three crucial directives for the period of transition to socialism: First, the establishment of a good comradely relationship with the intelligentsia, with the bourgeois specialists—even if, and particularly if, they hold totally different political and ideological positions. Second, in full agreement with Marx and Engels, Lenin opposed all pressure or the application of any compulsion against the peasants, whose conversion to a co-operative form of economy could take place only on an absolutely voluntary basis. Third, again in complete agreement with Marx and Engels, Lenin opposed any manifestation of nationalism or chauvinism and supported an internationalist attitude toward the non-Russian nationalities, the numerous small national groups that had previously been oppressed by Russian czarism.

☐   **Inconsistencies in Lenin's Views**

In addition to the unequivocal attitude listed above, there are a number of important economic and political issues connected with the development toward socialism that were never systematically formulated by Lenin in a fundamental theoretical concept, but on which he would from time to time express views in accordance with the situation of the moment. These views therefore differed a good deal, reflecting clearly the conclusions he drew from Soviet developments. These inconsistent and at times contradictory observations subsequently enabled the most varied currents of Communism to cite Lenin as their authority.

These issues include the system of economic management (centralized or decentralized? state-owned or co-operative?), the incentives in a socialist economy (moral or material incentives?), the role of trade unions, the extent and limit of the freedom of the press, the extent and limit of terror during the period of revolutionary transition, and finally —and most important of all—the role of the Communist Party in the transition to socialism.

Of particular importance, especially in view of later, and even present-day, discussions within the world Communist movement, was the question whether the economy should be centralized or decentralized. Initially, shortly before the October Revolution, Lenin was in favor of centralized state planning of the economy. He called for "the strictest control, by society and by the state, of the quantity of labor and the quantity of consumption." He spoke of the transformation of "*all* the citizens" into "employees and workers of *one* national state 'syndicate,' " and declared: "All citizens are here transformed into the hired employees of the state, which is formed by the armed workers. . . . It simply resolves itself into a question of all working to an equal extent . . . and of all receiving equal pay."[153] In October 1917 Lenin added: "We are in favor of centralism and of a 'plan,' but of the centralism and plan of the *proletarian* state."[154] In the spring of 1918 Lenin again observed that the solution of the economic tasks "calls for absolute and strict *unity of will,* which directs the joint labors of hundreds, thousands and tens of thousands of people." "That the people *unquestionably obey the single will* of the leaders of labor" was in the interest of socialism.[155]

These and similar observations have repeatedly been quoted since Lenin's death—especially under Stalin. On the other hand, particularly in his later years, Lenin supported the autonomy of local economic authorities. At the Eleventh Party Congress, in March 1922, he declared the necessity of "extending and developing the autonomy and activities of the regional economic conferences."[156] A few months later he even remarked that the successes achieved had been possible only "due to our having always devoted most of our attention to the local government bodies and to local experiences."[157] In the final years of his life—and this was (and still is) a particularly delicate problem for the Soviet ideologists—Lenin seemed to have doubts about the state-owned economy altogether. In line with Marx's and Engels' original ideas about the association of free producers, Lenin then emphasized the co-operatives. He announced the "task of uniting the whole population in co-operatives." He proposed that "all types" of co-operatives, i.e., consumer, credit, and producer co-operatives "should, by appropriate stages and with due care, be amalgamated into a Central Union of Consumer's Societies."[158] Shortly before his death, Lenin, in an article devoted exclusively to this problem, claimed that there "was not enough attention" devoted to co-operatives in the Soviet Union. It is important "to organize the population in co-operative societies." Once that is achieved, Lenin argued, "is this not all that is necessary to build a complete socialist society?" This would have to be a co-operative system in which "really large masses of the population actually take part." Indeed, Lenin described the socialist society as "the system of civilized co-operators" with "social ownership of the means of production."[159]

There was a similar change in Lenin's attitude on the question whether, in an emerging socialist society, moral incentives or material incentives, i.e., personal interest, played the decisive part. At first he believed that economic problems could largely be solved by moral incentives, revolutionary enthusiasm, and competitions. Later, after 1921, he stressed the importance of material incentives and personal interest. Alongside "the enthusiasm engendered by the great revolution," it was necessary to stress the component "of personal interest, personal incentive," since "personal interest increases production."[160] For that reason, Lenin remarked in the autumn of 1921, "every important branch of the economy must be built upon the principle of personal incentive."[161]

On the subject of the role of the trade unions after the victory of the socialist revolution, Lenin described the unions as "a school of Communism" and "a school in the art of managing socialist industry." But alongside this statement, which is continually being quoted in the Soviet Union, Lenin also pointed out that the trade unions—even, and especially, during the transition to socialism—must champion the satisfaction of the "lawful and practicable demands of the masses" and "protect the interests of the masses of the working people."[162]

Of particular importance for subsequent developments have been Lenin's inconsistent observations, made in response to particular conditions, on the political situation during the transition to socialism.

On the subject of the freedom of the press Lenin made such contradictory remarks that both dictatorial and democratic Communists were subsequently able to refer to his authority. Lenin's dictum: "Freedom of the press will help the force of the world bourgeoisie" and "be a weapon in the hands of this world bourgeoisie,"[163] has been quoted repeatedly by dictatorial elements among the Communists. On the other hand, Lenin also advocated freedom of the press: "Freedom of the press means that all opinions of all citizens can be disseminated freely." Lenin proposed the "publication of big newspapers by the Soviets"—not by the Party—in order "to give a guarantee to a much larger number of citizens that they can air their views—let us say, any group that can raise a certain number of signatures. Such a reform would make the freedom of the press much more democratic in practice and incomparably more complete."[164]

On the crucial question of the extent and limits of terror during the transitional period—and one should not overlook here the particular conditions of Russia throughout four years of stubborn and savage civil war—Lenin's views underwent a clear change. At first, shortly after the founding of the Cheka (the "Extraordinary Commission for the Struggle Against Counterrevolution, Speculation, and Sabotage"), Lenin praised and defended this instrument of power, observing that the "Cheka is directly exercising the dictatorship of the proletariat, and in that respect its services are invaluable."[165] The Cheka, moreover, was "magnificently organized."[166] At the same time, however, Lenin also voiced some critical misgivings that "alien elements are infiltrating into the Cheka."[167]

But by February 1920, even before the conclusion of the Civil War, Lenin was trying to restrict the terror and the organs of oppression:

We were forced to use terror in response to the terror employed by the Entente, when the mighty powers of the world flung their hordes against us, stopping at nothing. We could not have lasted two days had we not replied to these attempts of officers and white guardists in a merciless fashion. This meant the use of terror. . . . But as soon as we had gained a decisive victory, even before the end of the war, immediately after the capture of Rostov, we renounced capital punishment. . . . We say that the use of violence arises from the need to crush the exploiters, the landowners and capitalists. When this is accomplished we shall renounce all extraordinary measures.

Lenin voiced his hope that the Soviet Government would decide to make it impossible "to apply the death penalty in Russia."[168]

Immediately after the conclusion of the Civil War in December 1921, Lenin declared that "it is essential to reform the Cheka, define its functions and powers. . . . The closer we approach conditions of unshakable and lasting power and the more trade develops, the more imperative it is to put forward the firm slogan of greater revolutionary legality."[169] In March 1922 Lenin proposed to replace the Cheka with state-political courts.[170] Lenin therefore—a point only rarely and reluctantly mentioned by later Soviet writers—as early as 1920 and 1921 viewed terror, the death penalty, and the Cheka as merely temporary measures in the struggle and as institutions of the Civil War, to be abolished immediately upon its conclusion.

Of particular importance, however, are his conflicting attitudes on the role of the Communist Party during the transition to socialism—the question of whether a one-party system should exist and, if so, by what methods and means. Soviet ideologists most frequently quote those remarks in which Lenin refers to rule by the Bolshevik Party, such as that "240,000 members of the Bolshevik Party" were entirely capable to "govern Russia,"[171] or his dictum after the victory of October 1917: "Power is in the hands of our Party, which enjoys the confidence of the broad masses."[172]

On the other hand—and this is a point not mentioned in Soviet writings—Lenin also regarded a true multi-party system as possible under Soviet conditions. In an interesting (and unfortunately little-known) article of December 1917 Lenin supported the proportional representation system for elections in Soviet Russia, as this was "in fact the most democratic type of election." Moreover, the public should enjoy the democratic right of being able to recall any elected person at any time. He quoted as positive examples that "in some cantons of Switzerland and in some states of America . . . the democratic right of recall" had "been preserved." The system of proportional representation and the right of recall should, Lenin believed, be introduced also in Soviet Russia: "The direct, consistent and immediate democratic principle, namely, the right of recall, must be introduced. . . . The transfer of power from one party to another may then take place peacefully, by mere re-election."[173]

Generally speaking, however, Lenin regarded the Bolshevik Party as the decisive power in the Soviet system—though certainly not in the sense of the subsequently proclaimed "leading role of the Party." To him, the advance toward socialism was primarily a task for the people themselves: "Socialism cannot be decreed from above. Its spirit rejects the mechanical bureaucratic approach; living, creative socialism is the product of the masses themselves."[174] Lenin also repeatedly warned against reliance on force: "Nothing can be done here by force alone, organization and moral authority are all that is needed." Only through "the moral authority and strength of the people who have sacrificed themselves for the victory of socialism" can socialism be established in practice.[175] A few months later Lenin coined the formula: "Socialism has the force of example." Force was, at best, "effective against those who want to restore their rule. But at this stage the significance of force ends, and after that only influence and example are effective. We must show the significance of Communism in practice, by example."[176] He therefore also demanded that the Party apparatus should be distinct from the state apparatus.[177] He warned against the view that the socialist society could be established by the Communist Party: "Socialism cannot be implemented by a minority, by the Party. It can be implemented by tens of millions when they have learned to do it themselves."[178] At the Eleventh Party Congress, in March 1922 Lenin once more restated this important point of view: "The idea of building Communist society exclusively with the hands of the Communists is childish, absolutely childish. We Communists are but a drop in the ocean, a drop in the ocean of the people."[179]

□   **Differentiation Between Socialism and Communism**

Like Marx and Engels, Lenin regarded "social ownership of the means of production"[180] and "abolishment of the classes" as decisive characteristics of the new society. "Our aim is to abolish classes."[181] The objective of the new society is to "abolish the division of society into classes, make all members of society working people, and remove the basis for all exploitation of man by man."[182]

At this point Lenin introduced an important change into the

characterization of the future classless Communist society. Proceeding from a single remark by Karl Marx in his *Critique of the Gotha Program* (March 1875) about distinct phases in the classless society of the future, Lenin now differentiated between a first phase, which he called socialism and a higher phase, Communism. For the first time he declared—and this has since become part of the political theory of Communism—that the earlier phase, socialism, would be characterized by a "distribution of the products in accordance with the work done by each individual" ("to each according to his work"). Only in the higher phase, Communism, would the principle of "from each according to his abilities, to each according to his needs" be realized.[183] Shortly afterward Lenin referred to a "scientific distinction between socialism and Communism."[184]

If we were to ask ourselves in what way Communism differs from socialism, we should have to say that socialism is the society that grows directly out of capitalism; it is the first form of the new society. Communism is a higher form of society, and can only develop when socialism has become fully established. Socialism implies work without the aid of the capitalists, socialized labor with strict accounting, control and supervision by the organized vanguard, the advanced section of the working people; the measure of labor and remuneration for it must be fixed. . . . We give the name of Communism to the system under which the people form the habit of performing their social duties without any special apparatus of coercion, and when unpaid work for the public good becomes a general phenomenon. It stands to reason that the concept of "Communism" is a far too distant one for those who are taking the first steps toward complete victory over capitalism.[185]

During the first phase, now always described as "socialism" by Lenin, the means of production would already become common property but society would neither be economically equal nor yet free from the traditions and survivals of capitalism. Moreover, during that first phase, the state would continue to exist. The withering away of the state was "a prolonged process." The state could only wither away completely "when people have become accustomed to observing the fundamental principles of social life and their labor is so productive that they will voluntarily work according to their abilities."[186] True, even socialism would lead to the participation of the majority of the population in all spheres of public life. But not until "all, or be it only the greater part of society, have learned how to govern the state," and until the observance of all basic rules of human coexistence have become a habit, would the transition to "the higher phase, and along with it to the complete withering away of the state" take place.[187]

The higher phase of the Communist society would be characterized —and here Lenin followed Marx's and Engels' original ideas—by the total abolishment of classes and the withering away of state power: "The economic basis for the complete withering away of the state is that high stage of development of Communism when the distinction between brain and manual work disappears, consequently, when one of the principal sources of modern *social inequalities* will have vanished." The advance toward Communism would result in "breaking away from the division of labor, of the destruction of the antagonism between brain and manual work, of the transformation of work into 'a first necessity of life.' "[188]

However, the association of free producers which was central to Marx's and Engels' concepts, the elimination of alienation and the liberation of the human personality played only a subordinate role in Lenin's thinking. Instead, he particularly stressed that the classless society was characterized by "Communist labor," meaning "labor performed gratis for the benefit of society, labor performed not as a definite duty, not for the purpose of obtaining a right to certain products, not according to previously established and legally fixed quotas, but voluntary labor, irrespective of quotas; it is labor performed without expectation of reward."[189] Like Marx and Engels, Lenin repeatedly pointed out that under Communism there would be a gratuitous sharing out of products on the basis of the principle "to each according to his needs." He even believed that after the eventual victory of Communism on a world scale it would be possible to use gold for "building public lavatories in the streets of some of the largest cities of the world."[190]

☐ **Against the Glorification of Russian Bolshevism**

In spite of the victorious October Revolution, Lenin—in contrast to his successors and the present-day Soviet leadership—opposed any glorification of Russian Bolshevism. Again and again he criticized not only public authorities and institutions but the entire work of the Party, including the directives proclaimed by himself. "I say once again," he declared in 1919, "that we have never regarded our activity in general and our Constitution in particular as models of perfection."[191]

Whereas today's Soviet historians glorify in a downright mythical way the first few weeks after the October Revolution, when the Bolsheviks were still sitting in the Smolny Institute (the "Smolny period"),

Lenin stated: "We committed follies enough in and around the Smolny period."[192] The October Revolution had taken place not only "at the price of incredible difficulties and hardships" but had also been accompanied by "serious reverses and mistakes."[193] Lenin repeatedly and with obvious approval quoted Engels' dictum: "A lot of mistakes are unavoidably made in any revolution, as they are indeed at all other times."[194]

Lenin went even further in his statement at the Eighth Party Congress, in March 1919, a statement naturally not quoted in the Soviet Union:

It would be absurd to set up our revolution as the ideal for all countries, to imagine that it has made a number of brilliant discoveries and has introduced a heap of socialist innovations. I have not heard anybody make this claim and I assert that we shall not hear anybody make it. . . . If we behave like the frog in the fable and become puffed up with conceit, we shall only make ourselves the laughing-stock of the world, we shall be mere braggarts.[195]

In much the same spirit was Lenin's dislike of all jubilee celebrations—both for himself and for various "anniversaries." In April 1920, when an assembly was held in honor of his fiftieth birthday, he expressed his thanks for having been spared "congratulatory speeches" and proposed that "a more suitable method of celebrating anniversaries" should be discovered "than the one hitherto in vogue, which has sometimes formed the subject of remarkably good caricatures." Lenin hoped to be "saved in future such jubilee celebrations altogether."[196] Later he added: "The best way to celebrate the anniversary of a great revolution is to concentrate attention on its unsolved problems."[197]

With astonishing frankness—and modesty—Lenin criticized the activity of the Bolshevik Party. He attacked "the mistake of transferring the experience we had gained in the political and war periods to economic problems," and called it "an important, a fundamental mistake which, comrades, we still repeat at every step."[198] In an official speech to the Congress of Soviets, Lenin said, "for every ten faults that any of you can point out to me, I can immediately point out a hundred more."[199] He also repeatedly castigated the practical working methods of the Bolshevik Party: "We are indeed in the position, and it must be said that it is a very absurd position, of people sitting endlessly at meetings, setting up commissions and drawing up plans without end."[200] Shortly afterward Lenin remarked: "Not five Party committees out of a hundred can show practical results."[201] At one point he exclaimed: "Nobody knows what is going on, who is responsible; everything is mixed up."[202] Even at a Congress of the Communist International, before a large number of foreign delegates, Lenin most readily admitted, "we have done a host of foolish things."[203]

☐ **Different Roads to Socialism**

Lenin did not only confine himself to disclaiming any kind of "infallibility" for the Soviet Communists or to a critical examination of his own policy in a manner unthinkable to the present Soviet leadership; he also kept emphasizing that he did not in any way regard Soviet rule in Russia as an example or a model for Communists of other countries. Communists in each country have to take their own road to socialism, Lenin declared, adding the hope that they would manage better than the Russian Bolsheviks.

At the Seventh Party Congress, in March 1918, Lenin pointed out that the transition to socialism was greatly complicated "by features that are specific to Russia and do not exist in most civilized countries. And so it is not only possible but inevitable that the stages of transition will be different in Europe; it would be theoretically incorrect to turn all attention to specific national stages of transition that are essential to us but may not be essential in Europe." This is the reason that the Russian Bolsheviks "are confident that the European workers . . . will do what we are doing, but do it better."[204]

Lenin never ceased to emphasize the different roads to socialism. Thus, "the measures of transition to socialism cannot be identical in countries with large-scale and those with small-scale farming."[205] This applied also to the countries directly bordering on Soviet Russia: "It goes without saying that the transition to socialism in Estland [Estonia], that small country in which the whole population is literate, and which consists of large-scale farms, cannot be the same as the transition to socialism in Russia, which is mainly a petty-bourgeois country."[206] Lenin also advised the Communists of the Caucasus to understand "the singularity of their position" in contrast to conditions in Russia (the R.S.F.S.R.) and therefore to "refrain from copying our tactics, but thoughtfully vary them in adaptation to the differing concrete conditions." Lenin, above all, stressed the need "to practice more moderation and caution, and show more readiness to make concessions to the petty bourgeoisie, the intelligentsia, and particularly the peasantry," because "a slower, more cautious and more systematic transition to socialism" was necessary for the republics of the Caucasus in contrast to the R.S.F.S.R.[207] Lenin repeatedly warned against copying the Russian Revolution. He explained that "the subsequent revolutions in Oriental countries, which possess much vaster populations and a much vaster diversity of social conditions, will undoubtedly display even greater distinctions than the Russian Revolution."[208]

Other countries—Lenin hoped—would, once they embarked on the road of the dictatorship of the proletariat, manage things better and outstrip Soviet Russia:

> When I said to one of the best comrades among the Polish Communists, "You will do it in a different way," he replied, "No, we shall do the same things but better than you." To such an argument I had absolutely no objections. They must be given the opportunity of fulfilling a modest wish— to create a better Soviet power than ours. We cannot help reckoning with the fact that things are proceeding in rather a peculiar way . . . and while foreseeing every stage of development in other countries, we must decree nothing from Moscow.[209]

Lenin time and again placed his hope in social revolutions in Europe, in the prospect of a socialist development in the highly developed countries: "Soviet Republics in more developed countries, where the proletariat has greater weight and influence, have every chance of surpassing Russia once they take the path of the dictatorship of the proletariat."[210] On the subject of the Soviet Republic in Hungary in 1919, Lenin was quoted as having remarked: "The people of that cultured country were taking into account the entire experience of the Russian Revolution," and for that reason "the edifice of socialism was being built more systematically and successfully."[211] After the victory of the socialist revolution in an advanced country, Lenin believed, there would probably be "a sharp change" in that "Russia will cease to be the model and will once again become a backward country (in the 'Soviet' and the socialist sense)."[212]

There was no doubt in Lenin's mind that any future socialist revolutions in the countries of Western Europe would take a different course. "The revolution in Italy will run a different course from that in Russia," Lenin declared in the summer of 1921 and, turning to the foreign Communist delegates, added that the Communist International "will never call upon you slavishly to imitate the Russians."[213] A year later Lenin criticized a Russian resolution about the structure, methods, and activity of foreign Communist parties on the grounds that it was "too Russian," reflected only Russian experience and "no foreigner can read it." Hanging Russian resolutions "in a corner like an icon" and "praying" to them should not be expected of foreign Communists.[214]

## ☐ The New Political Elements of Leninism

There is no doubt that Lenin and his comrades-in-arms regarded themselves as Marxists and indeed as having helped Marxism to victory in one country, Russia. There is also no doubt that many of the political concepts of Marx and Engels can be found in the works and writings of Lenin, in Leninism. Lenin's internationalism, his opposition to nationalism and chauvinism—even, and especially, in his own nation—his abhorrence of all sycophancy and of the glorification of Russian experience (and of his own person), his support of an evolutionary, voluntary socialist transformation of agriculture, and, most of all, his most emphatic support of the different roads to socialism in different countries—all this and much more proves that Lenin adopted many fundamental tenets of Marxism and developed them further. Side by side with this continuity, however, we immediately find six important changes from Marx's and Engels' original political concepts.

The first change concerns the Party. For Marx and Engels the emphasis was on the working class, the proletariat, as the decisive force charged with the social transformation of society. Lenin shifted this emphasis to the Party, an organization of professional revolutionaries, based on a common ideology, with the Party press subordinate to it, organized on the principle of democratic centralism and prohibiting the dissemination of anti-Party views—a united, disciplined, elite Party designed to lead and guide the workers.

The second point is the importance of political tactics. While Marx and Engels touched on this problem only rarely and casually, for Lenin, who proceeded from the idea of the elite Party, tactical problems were of major importance. His numerous tactical directives concerning alliances, compromises, concessions, forms of struggle, and, above all, the methods of working within other organizations and institutions, undoubtedly affected the way of thinking and possibly also the moral attitude of Party members and functionaries.

The third area of change concerns the socialist revolution. Marx and Engels had invariably linked the social revolution to certain prerequisites (high level of economic development, workers representing the majority of the population), of a simultaneous revolution in the major industrial countries, and had increasingly stressed the possibility of a peaceful transformation of society. Lenin changed this concept fundamentally. In his view the prerequisites listed by Marx and Engels were no longer decisive; instead, a socialist revolution would take place at "the weakest link in the chain" of imperialism, under conditions of certain pronounced political contradictions (the "revolutionary situation"). Such a revolution could succeed even in a single country and would as a rule take the form of a violent overthrow, an armed uprising. The social transformation, to be accomplished by the industrial workers, was thus replaced by a socialist revolution led by an elite Party—and that was precisely the pattern of the Russian October Revolution of 1917.

A fourth major change was the new interpretation of the dictatorship of the proletariat. The political rule of the working class, as envisaged by Marx and Engels, was modified by Lenin by his emphasis on the application of forcible dictatorial measures against the overthrown exploiting class, a power based directly upon force, practiced by a Party which, in order to discharge its tasks, must be disciplined and united, and must not tolerate any factions ("Party unity"). The Bolshevik rule in Russia after 1917, consisting of the power of the soviets, was thus proclaimed by Lenin to be the realization of the dictatorship of the proletariat, and this interpretation was merely toned down by repeated reminders that other countries would in the future realize the dictatorship of the proletariat differently and in a better way.

Lenin's concept of the transitional measures on the road to socialism similarly reflected specific Russian conditions. Instead of the short transition envisaged by Engels, Lenin supported the view of a very prolonged transitional period, in the course of which not only the transformation of society would be achieved but also the economic foundations laid for socialism ("Communism is Soviet power plus electrification"). Lenin's often rather contradictory remarks about property relations, economic management, the role of trade unions, economic incentives, the extent and limits of pressure and terror, as well as on the role, function, and working methods of the Party were subsequently to enable the most varied trends within Communism to refer to his authority.

Lenin finally made some important changes in the concept of the classless Communist society of the future. Starting with a single hint by Marx, Lenin now differentiated between a first stage, socialism, and a higher stage, Communism. Under socialism, remuneration was to be in accordance with the work done ("to each according to his work") and the state was to continue to exist for the time being; not until the higher phase of Communism was reached would it wither away. Likewise, the ideas of the association of free producers, the elimination of alienation, and the liberation of the human personality, all of them emphasized by Marx and Engels, receded almost totally into the background in Lenin's concept of the classless Communist society.

All these changes wrought by Lenin in the political doctrine of Communism reflected his endeavor to adapt the original political concepts of Marx and Engels to the tasks and objectives of the Russian Marxist movement. The state of society in czarist Russia and the fact that industrial workers there represented only a minority of the population led him to his new concept of the Party. The absence of the prerequisites for a social revolution led to his completely new interpretation of the socialist revolution. The victory of the Bolshevik Revolution in Russia in October 1917—for which, according to Marx and Engels, the prerequisites were totally lacking—was reflected in the changes made by Lenin in the concepts of the dictatorship of the proletariat and of the classless society of the future.

## ☐  Marxist Critique of Leninism

Even among Marxists, and indeed within the Bolsheviks' own ranks, some of the changes made by Lenin in the political theory of Marxism were by no means accepted without contradiction. Rosa Luxemburg raised the following objection to Lenin's new doctrine of the Party as early as 1904: "The ultra-centralism which Lenin demands seems to us, however, not at all positive and creative, but essentially sterile and domineering. Lenin's concern is essentially the control of the activity of the Party and not its fruition, the narrowing and not the development, the harassment and not the unification of the movement." In contrast to Lenin, Rosa Luxemburg demanded the unlimited right of criticism of higher Party organs as a means to avoid all fossilization. She emphasized the need for a creative development: "Errors made by a truly revolutionary labor movement are historically infinitely more fruitful and more valuable than the infallibility of the best of all possible 'central committees.' "[215] About the same time Trotsky wrote the following prophetic words about Lenin's doctrine of the Party: "These methods lead, as we shall yet see, to this: The Party organization is substituted for the Party, the Central Committee is substituted for the Party organization, and finally a 'dictator' is substituted for the Central Committee."[216]

In 1917, when Lenin called for the bourgeois-democratic revolution in Russia to be transformed into the socialist revolution, Alexei Rykov, a leading Bolshevik, uttered this warning: "I think that under present conditions, with our standard of living, the initiation of the socialist overturn does not belong to us. We have not the strength, the objective conditions, for this."[217] Lenin's call for an armed uprising in October 1917 similarly met with opposition.

Two of the most prominent Bolshevik leaders—Kamenev and Zinoviev—voted against it and declared: "We are deeply convinced that to call at present for an armed uprising means to stake on one card not only the fate of our Party, but also the fate of the Russian and international revolution."[218]

Instead of the Bolshevik one-party government postulated by Lenin after the October Revolution, many Bolsheviks, including a powerful group within the Central Committee, demanded the formation of a socialist coalition government of the three leading socialist parties: the Bolsheviks, the Mensheviks, and the Social Revolutionaries. Of the fifteen members of the first Bolshevik Government of November 1917 (the "Council of People's Commissars"), five People's Commissars—Rykov (Interior), Milyutin (Agriculture), Nogin (Trade and Industry), Teodorovich (Food), and Shliapnikov (Labor)—resigned and, together with a number of other Bolsheviks, issued a declaration: "We take the stand that it is necessary to form a socialist government of all parties in the Soviet. . . . We assert that other than this there is only one path: the preservation of a purely Bolshevik government by means of political terror. We cannot and will not accept this. We see that this will lead . . . to the establishment of an irresponsible regime and to the ruin of the revolution."[219]

What gave rise to particularly strong opposition was Lenin's equation of Bolshevik rule in Russia with the dictatorship of the proletariat proclaimed by Marx and Engels, as well as the methods of Bolshevik rule, the oppression of other socialist forces. Karl Kautsky voiced his anxieties as follows:

The motives of the Bolsheviks were certainly of the best. Right from the beginning of their supremacy they showed themselves to be filled with human ideals, which had their origin in the conditions of the proletariat as a class. . . . Their culpability comes to light at the time when they proclaimed the "immediate and complete emancipation of the working classes" in spite of the backward state of Russia; and with this end in view, since the democracy had not fulfilled their expectations, established their own dictatorship in the name of "the dictatorship of the proletariat."[220]

Even Rosa Luxemburg, that champion of revolutionary Marxism, while commending the Bolsheviks for their resolute revolutionary attitude, warned against their disregard of democratic freedoms and against the increasingly dictatorial elements in Bolshevism. "It is a well-known and indisputable fact that without a free and untrammeled press, without the unlimited right of association and assemblage, the rule of the broad mass of the people is entirely unthinkable. . . . Freedom only for the supporters of the government, only for the members of one Party— however numerous they may be—is no freedom at all. Freedom is always and exclusively freedom for the one who thinks differently."[221]

In the autumn of 1918 Rosa Luxemburg criticized Lenin's and Trotsky's theory of the dictatorship of the proletariat as follows:

> The tacit assumption underlying the Lenin-Trotsky theory of the dictatorship is this: that the socialist transformation is something for which a ready-made formula lies completed in the pocket of the revolutionary party, which needs only to be carried out energetically in practice. This is, unfortunately—or perhaps fortunately—not the case. . . . The socialist system of society should only be, and can only be, a historical product, born out of the school of its own experiences, born in the course of its realization, as a result of the developments of living history. . . . The negative, the tearing down, can be decreed; the building up, the positive, cannot. . . . Only unobstructed, effervescing life falls into a thousand new forms and improvisations, brings to light creative force, itself corrects all mistaken attempts. . . . The only way to a rebirth is the school of public life itself, the most unlimited, the broadest democracy and public opinion. It is rule by terror which demoralizes.[222]

On the basis of these views Rosa Luxemburg predicted that Bolshevik rule would lead to the emergence of a new bureaucracy:

> With the repression of political life in the land as a whole, life in the soviets must also become more and more crippled. Without general elections, without unrestricted freedom of the press and assembly, without a free struggle of opinion, life dies out in any public institution, becomes a mere semblance of life, in which only the bureaucracy remains as the active element. Public life gradually falls asleep . . . only a dozen outstanding heads do the leading and an elite of the working class is invited from time to time to meetings where they are to applaud the speeches of the leaders, and to approve proposed resolutions unanimously.[223]

The dictatorship of the proletariat, according to Rosa Luxemburg, "must be the work of the *class* and not that of a little leading minority." It must be subject to the control of complete public activity; it must arise out of the growing political training of the mass of the people.[224]

Above all, she warned against putting off the realization of socialist democracy to some distant time ahead:

> It is the historical task of the proletariat, when it seizes power, to create a socialist democracy to replace bourgeois democracy—not to eliminate democracy altogether. But socialist democracy is not something which begins

only in the promised land after the foundations of socialist economy are created; it does not come as some sort of Christmas present for the worthy people who, in the interim, have loyally supported a handful of socialist dictators. Socialist democracy begins simultaneously with the destruction of class rule and of the construction of socialism.[225]

## The Transition to Stalinism

The further development of Bolshevism fully justified Rosa Luxemburg's criticisms and warnings. During the years of the Civil War, military and economic power was more and more centralized, in the economy the elected workers' control committees were abolished and enterprises placed under state managers. Not only counterrevolutionary forces but also critical opinions and trends within the revolutionary camp were silenced by the Cheka.

With the Bolsheviks' successes in the Civil War the composition and character of the Party underwent a change. The many years of civil war, famine, and privations had paralyzed revolutionary enthusiasm while the Bolshevik apparatus, on the other hand, had been gaining in strength and size. The Party was increasingly filled with the kind of people who invariably join the winning side. Within the Party, now functioning as the only government party, a new privileged stratum developed.

"When the tension relaxed and the nomads of the revolutions passed on to settled living, the traits of the man in the street, the sympathies and tastes of self-satisfied officials, revived in them." This is how Trotsky later described this transformation. At the meetings of the Central Committee, Trotsky observed "the attitude of moral relaxation, of self-content and triviality," as well as "philistine gossip." Joint drinking parties with the inevitable talk about those absent were, according to Trotsky, "amusements that were becoming more and more common in the lives of the new governing stratum."[226]

This development was viewed with anxiety and alarm by many Bolsheviks at the time—especially by the "workers' opposition" headed by Shliapnikov, and by the opposition group of the "democratic centralists." Both sharply opposed the centralization and bureaucratization of the Party, and the suppression of the freedom of opinion. The "workers' opposition" also opposed the centralized management of the economy and the appointment of industrial managers from the top, and instead demanded—entirely in agreement with Marx's and Engels' ideas —that economic enterprises should be run by elected workers' councils.

"We do not stand for the point of view of 'construction of socialism by the organizers of the trusts.' We stand for the point of view of the construction of the proletarian society by the class creativity of the workers themselves, not by ukase of 'captains of industry,' " declared the opposition Bolshevik Valerian Osinsky. "Socialism and socialist organizations must be set up by the proletariat itself, or they will not be set up at all; something else will be set up—state capitalism."[227]

Sapronov, the spokesman for the group of "democratic centralists," warned against the increasing centralization and bureaucratization in the Party: "You transform the members of the Party into an obedient gramophone, with leaders who give orders." If this development continued, the Central Committee itself would be replaced by a leader: "Here also a single commander can be appointed," and then "the revolution will have been gambled away."[228]

At the beginning of 1923, the "workers' group" made the last stand of this kind against the new trend in the Party: "The central leadership of the Russian Communist Party refuses to tolerate criticism since it considers itself as infallible as the Pope of Rome."[229] This "workers' group" predicted that a new ruling stratum would emerge in the Soviet Union.

The greatest danger springs from the fact that the style of living of a very considerable proportion of the commanding top people has rapidly begun to undergo a change. If conditions persist for any length of time whereby the members of the board of some trust—say the sugar trust, for example— receive a salary of 200 gold rubles a month, and in addition a good cheap flat, and the free use of a motor car,

while a worker, "apart from the modest ration allocated to him by the state, receives on an average four to five rubles a month," a new class stratification was inevitable. "If such conditions do not disappear soon but remain effective for ten or twenty years, the material conditions of the ones as much as the others will determine their outlook and they will confront each other like two protagonists in opposite camps." There was, therefore, a danger of the proletarian power turning into an oligarchy. The Party was beginning to "change into a group of rulers who hold in their hands the economic resources and the government of the country" and would transform themselves "into a closed caste."[230]

Although Lenin regarded these views as exaggerated and opposed their exponents and indeed took "administrative measures" against them, or at least allowed such measures to be taken, he himself viewed this development with anxiety—even though he certainly underrated the danger. In December 1920 Lenin complained "that our state is a workers' state *with a bureaucratic twist to it.*"[231] By February 1921 he was referring to "Soviet bureaucrats"[232] and complained that "in our apparatus . . . a very great number of bureaucratic practices have seeped in."[233] In March 1921 he observed that the "bureaucratic ulcer" had "to be treated in earnest,"[234] criticized the "inadequate democracy,"[235] and complained that "the bureaucratic machine is so enormous."[236]

Not until the end of 1922, however, did Lenin realize the full extent of the threat represented by the bureaucratic apparatus. The Soviet apparatus, he wrote, was in fact the old "Russian apparatus" which the Bolsheviks "took over from czarism and slightly anointed with Soviet oil." The Bolsheviks could not vouch "for our apparatus as our own." Lenin began to see the apparatus as an alien menacing power. "We must, in all conscience, admit . . . the apparatus we call ours is, in fact, still quite alien to us; it is a bourgeois and czarist hodge-podge." He was also seriously worried about the growing Russian nationalism: "There is no doubt that the infinitesimal percentage of Soviet and sovietized workers will drown in that tide of chauvinist Great-Russian riffraff like a fly in milk."[237]

Moreover, the Bolsheviks' hopes of world revolution had proved illusory. Soviet Russia remained alone. The place of internationally minded intellectual revolutionaries, inspired by revolutionary Marxism and socialist aims, was increasingly taken by narrow-minded *apparatchiks* with a provincial outlook, men who found their fulfillment in wielding power. They rallied around the Organizational Bureau and the Secretariat of the Party, where Stalin, General Secretary of the Party since March 1922, held court. In March 1922 Lenin complained that Soviet developments had come to be determined by "the enormous undivided prestige enjoyed by the small group which might be called the Old Guard of the Party." A slight internal struggle could result in a situation that would weaken the group to such a degree as to rob it of its power to determine policy."[238]

Lenin died on January 21, 1924. His warnings against Stalin were disregarded; his urgent proposal that Stalin should be deposed[239] was not implemented. Developments in the Soviet Union, as Lenin had foreseen, now no longer depended on the Old Guard of Bolsheviks but on the new bureaucratic *apparatchiks* whose spokesman and leader was Stalin.

The future development not only of the Soviet Union but also of the political theory of Communism was thenceforward to be determined by the son of a Georgian cobbler, the man whose name was Iosif Vissarionovich Dzhugashvili, who was first active in the Bolshevik Party under the name of Koba and later gained world-wide renown under the name of Stalin.

# 3

## The Second Transformation: Stalinism

Comrades! We Communists are people of a special mold. We are made of a special stuff. We are those who form the army of the great proletarian strategist, the army of Comrade Lenin. . . . There is nothing higher than the title of member of the Party whose founder and leader was Comrade Lenin. It is not given to everyone to be a member of such a party. It is not given to everyone to withstand the stresses and storms that accompany membership in such a party.[1]

These words were spoken by Stalin on January 26, 1924, in his oath at Lenin's graveside. Even this first major political statement contains, though in embryonic form, a good deal of what was to become typical of the Stalinist doctrine: the comparison of the Party with an army, the marked emphasis on the leading role of the Party whose members were of a "special type" and molded "of special stuff," the indirect though perceptible claim to infallibility, and the glorification of one person (at this point still Lenin) as the "leader."

Lenin's death provided Stalin with the opportunity to introduce a cult of "Leninism." While Lenin had declined all glorification of his person, there were now bombastic declarations of loyalty to his memory, his body was embalmed in a mausoleum, and within three months of his death Stalin gave a series of lectures under the title "Foundations of Leninism," lectures that for the next quarter of a century were regarded as a great theoretical study and were intended to establish Stalin's reputation as "continuer of Lenin's cause."

All revolutionary enthusiasm had meanwhile evaporated; hopes of world revolution had been finally disappointed. The public (including many Party members), paralyzed and weakened by many years of war and civil war, by hardships, misery, and privations, lapsed into passivity. The bureaucratic apparatus now moved more markedly into the foreground and, on Stalin's orders, a "Lenin enrollment" was launched. The Party's doors, until then carefully locked, were thrown wide open. Within a few months, hundreds of thousands joined the Party—mostly people who had neither taken part in the illegal revolutionary struggle under czarism nor in the revolution, and who could, therefore, be readily molded and manipulated by the apparatus. The old Bolsheviks of the years of the revolution became a minority.

True enough, immediately after Lenin's death his closest companions—Trotsky, Bukharin, Rykov, Kamenev, Zinoviev, and Tomsky —continued to hold what seemed to be controlling positions in the Politburo. But the real power progressively shifted into the hands of Stalin's Secretariat, which increasingly managed and controlled the local Party organizations, chose the delegates to Party congresses, promoted the obedient and malleable, and eliminated those who were disobedient or in opposition. Having successfully prevented the publication of Lenin's "Testament," which would have been highly dangerous to him, Stalin celebrated his triumph at the Fourteenth Party Congress in December 1925. The Congress delegates had been carefully chosen by Stalin's apparatus. In vain did Nadezhda Krupskaya, Lenin's widow, protest against the concealment of the "Testament," in vain did Kamenev call from the Congress rostrum: "Back to Lenin! We are against creating a theory of the 'Leader,' we are against making a 'Leader.' " The delegates selected by Stalin's apparatus shouted Kamenev down. When Kamenev openly voiced his doubts of Stalin's ability to assume the leadership of the Party, the unrest grew. Amid an uproar Kamenev once more exclaimed: "We are against the theory of one-man rule, we are against creating a 'Leader.' "[2]

But his final warnings were drowned by the repeated shouts of the delegates: "We want Stalin!"

The die was cast. One after another, Stalin's opponents and Lenin's former companions were removed from their positions, expelled from the Party, banished, or even arrested. By December 21, 1929—his fiftieth birthday—Stalin had succeeded in eliminating all of Lenin's comrades-in-arms from the leadership and in elevating himself to the position of "*Vozhd*" or "Leader." The course of the Soviet Union was now determined by Stalin and his obedient bureaucratic *apparatchiks*.

Although the first Five-Year Plan (1928–33) did lay the foundations for the industrial power of the Soviet Union, the social and political system underwent far-reaching changes. The rights of the workers were curtailed; the trade unions were entirely eliminated; the peasants were pressed into collective farms in a forcible collectivization campaign. As a result of an increasing differentiation of wages and salaries, the social privileges of the ruling bureaucracy were extended.

Since the construction of new factories, plants, and enterprises was not accompanied by a widening of the influence of manual or office workers but, on the contrary, destroyed it entirely, the growth of the Soviet economic potential simultaneously led to a considerable strengthening of the power of the new ruling stratum. The coercive machinery of Stalin's dictatorship was further developed, oppression and terror became an inseparable part of the system, and all intellectual and cultural life was subordinated to the Stalin dictatorship. The transition from Leninism to Stalinism was first reflected in the ideological field by Stalin's thesis, put forward between 1924 and 1926, of the possibility of the victory of socialism in one country. The public was to be prepared for the "building of socialism," and the privations and hardships produced by industrialization and collectivization were to be justified as passing difficulties.

Stalin's rejection of the socialist ideal of equality—as early as 1925 —served to justify the increasingly marked social differences within the Soviet Union and the privileges of the new ruling stratum. Stalin's theses of the "intensified class struggle" and the "capitalist encirclement" during the building of socialism were designed to give the population the impression of living in a beleaguered fortress which, it was argued, required iron discipline and terror. The same objective was served by Stalin's new concept of the Party: self-criticism, purges, vigilance, and the "struggle against deviations" and "conciliatoriness" were introduced by Stalin not only into practical politics but also into political doctrine.

Lenin's revolutionary internationalism, which had been relegated to the background by Stalin ever since the end of the 1920's, was replaced in early 1934 by the new concept of "Soviet patriotism." When the remaining old Bolsheviks and Lenin's comrades-in-arms had been removed from the Party by continuous "Party purges," Stalin, in May 1935, without any further ado dissolved altogether the Society of Old Bolsheviks.

Suddenly, in November 1936, the "Leader" proclaimed the "victory of Socialism" in the Soviet Union. Socialism was to be politically characterized chiefly by the "moral-political unity" and the "leading role of the Party." But the solemn proclamation of socialism had hardly died away when Stalin's great purge began. In the course of a few months millions of people were arrested—including the flower of the Soviet intelligentsia, and over 70 per cent of senior Party, state, and economic functionaries, and of the officer corps. Especially hard hit were Lenin's former companions. The leaders of the October Revolution of 1917 were now defamed as "agents," "murderers," "rabid dogs," "fascist lackeys," "monsters," the "scum of humanity," and a "gang of people's enemies"; they were sentenced on grotesque charges and shot.

Following the show trial of August 1936, Zinoviev and Kamenev were shot; Tomsky, a Politburo member under Lenin, committed suicide in the notorious Lubyanka prison in Moscow. In January 1937—after the second great show trial—Serebriakov, Sokolnikov, and Radek, who had traveled in the sealed train with Lenin across Germany, shared the same fate. Serebriakov was shot, and Sokolnikov and Radek detained; they died in Stalin's prisons. In March 1938 followed a show trial of twenty-one of Lenin's closest comrades-in-arms. Eighteen of them were shot, including Bukharin, for many years a member of the Politburo and described by Lenin in his "Testament" as "a most valuable and major theorist" and "the favorite of the whole Party."[3]

As for the fifteen members of the first Soviet Government of 1917, Rykov, at first People's Commissar of the Interior and after Lenin's death appointed to succeed him as Chairman of the Council of People's Commissars, was arrested in February 1937 and shot after the show trial of March 1938. Eight other People's Commissars of the first Soviet Government, which had been headed by Lenin, were arrested in the course of the great purge of 1936–38 and died in Stalin's forced-labor camps: Miliutin (Agriculture), Shliapnikov (Labor), Oppokov-Lomov (Justice), Teodorovich (Food), Glebov (Post and Telegraph), Antonov-Ovseyenko, Krylenko, and Dybenko (Army and Navy).

After this extermination campaign, the further bureaucratic development progressed with greater speed and fewer restrictions than ever before. Whereas in the past the bureaucracy had endeavored to conceal its effective power, it now came out into the open with the proud display of epaulettes, service grades, and badges of rank. The huge social differences were no longer concealed; on the contrary, the "Soviet millionaires" were given praise and publicity in the press. The equality of nations was abolished by Stalin not only in practice but quite openly by his declaration about the hegemony of the "leading Russian nation."

To justify this trend, Stalin evolved a large number of new political doctrines and concepts. He explained the great purge and mass arrests as the "intensification of the class struggle with the further development of socialism"; to justify the existence of a huge bureaucratic, terror, and power apparatus Stalin quite simply replaced Marx's concept of the withering away of the state with a new thesis of the "strengthening of the state." The *Short Course* of Soviet Party history, published in the autumn of 1938, was designed to wipe out the last memories of the real history of the Bolshevik Party. Great Russian nationalism, fostered since the end of the 1930's, was to provide a new ideological bond, and the new cult of Stalin, which exceeded anything previously known, was to silence all criticism before it was even uttered. Finally, Stalin had to make sure that his bureaucratic-terrorist system was perpetuated in the future. To that end he proclaimed in the spring of 1939 that the state would continue to exist even under Communism. The concept of the classless Communist society was changed by Stalin during the last years of his life, when it was decreed that even under Communism the social distinctions between the "leading personnel" and the simple workers would continue to exist.

Consequently, ideology was degraded to an ex-post-facto "justification" of measures already taken, and the original concepts of Marx, Engels, and Lenin were arbitrarily changed and even turned into their very opposite.

Stalin's rule did not bring only conceptual changes in political doctrine. He was totally different from Marx, Engels, and Lenin as a personality. While these were fluent in several languages and had spent many years of exile in a wide range of European countries, Stalin only spoke Georgian and Russian and, with very few exceptions, did not leave Russia or, later, the Soviet Union. Marx and Engels, and to a lesser extent Lenin, were the authors not only of purely political articles but also of a large number of writings on economic, sociological, and political subjects; Stalin, by contrast, confined himself to the field of practical politics. While the authority of Marx and Engels and, largely, also of Lenin rested mainly on their superiority as political theorists, this was not the case with Stalin. Only after Stalin had achieved supreme political power did people accept his political doctrines as directives. In contrast to Marx, Engels, and Lenin, who had to engage in theoretical and political discussions, often among their own ranks, this was rarely the case with Stalin—or only on a very limited scale during the early years, roughly from 1925 to 1929. After 1929, when Stalin had raised himself to the position of sole leader of the Soviet Union, his remarks, at least within his own sphere of power, were not only accepted without contradiction but indeed regarded as "inspired statements" of the "wise leader and teacher" and the "coryphaeus of learning."

This was reflected also in Stalin's style. The writings of Marx, Engels, and Lenin were pervaded with lively and often sparkling polemics; Stalin, on the other hand, pronounced his political theorems in dogmatically simple sentences, often in the form of a question he proceeded to answer—and that repetitiously. To elucidate political problems and processes, Stalin frequently used similes from the military or technical spheres. Thus he compared the Party to an army; the senior, medium, and lower Party functionaries to generals, officers, and NCO's; political strategy to a war; political tactics to a battle. He likened Soviet society to a great machine, with the leaders sitting at the control levers while the ordinary citizens were tiny cogs. He described writers as "engineers of the human soul."[4]

Stalin's principal writings on problems of political doctrine include: *The Foundations of Leninism* (April 1924), *The October Revolution and the Tactics of the Russian Communists* (December 1924), *Concerning Questions of Leninism* (January 1926), *The Possibility of Building Socialism in our Country* (February 1926), and *The International Character of the October Revolution* (November 1927). Of importance also are his speeches at the Fourteenth Party Congress (December 1925), the Fifteenth Party Congress (December 1927), on "The Right Deviation in the Communist Party of the Soviet Union" (April 1929), on questions of agrarian policy (December 1929), at the Sixteenth Party Congress (July 1930), to senior economic officials (February and June 1931), at the Seventeenth Party Congress (January 1934), on the draft constitution of the Soviet Union (November 1936), on "Defects in Party Work and Measures for Liquidating Trotskyite and Other Double-Dealers" (March 1937—called in English: "Mastering Bolshevism"), and, finally, his Report to the Eighteenth Party Congress (March 1939). Questions of political doctrine are dealt with also in his *Marxism and Linguistics* (summer 1950) and *Economic Problems of Socialism in the U.S.S.R.* (autumn 1952).

☐　**The New Doctrine of "Socialism in One Country"**

Less than a year after Lenin's death, in December 1924, Stalin announced his first major change in the political theory of Communism. Until then it had been accepted by Communists, as a matter of course, that the establishment of a socialist society in the Soviet Union would be possible only after successful revolutions in the major industrial countries; but now Stalin drew these conclusions from the uneven development of capitalism: "In view of this, the victory of socialism in one country, even if that country is less developed in the capitalistic sense, while capitalism remains in other countries, even if those countries are more highly developed in the capitalistic sense—is quite possible and probable."[5] Only the complete victory of socialism, Stalin argued, "requires the united efforts of the proletarians of several countries."[6]

For the first time, therefore, Stalin proclaimed his new doctrine of "socialism in one country"—though still in a rather cautious formulation. A few months later, in June 1925, Stalin formally announced that the Soviet Union had long possessed "all that is needed to build a complete socialist society."[7] The "working class" (by which term Stalin meant the Party) could use its power "to build a complete socialist society in our country . . . without the preliminary victory of the proletarian revolution in other countries."[8] In February 1926 Stalin again declared that "we are capable of completely building a socialist society by our own efforts and without the victory of the revolution in the West."[9] By the end of 1926 he felt sufficiently strong to declare openly that "the old formula of Engels" (Marx, who had said the same thing, was not mentioned) had become "incorrect." It had "inevitably to be replaced by another formula, one that affirms the possibility of the victory of socialism in one country"[10] since "if there is no certainty that the building of socialism can be completed, there can be no will to build socialism."[11]

These few short statements mark the abandonment of Lenin's revolutionary internationalism. Its place was taken by a concentration on Soviet internal problems. Though Stalin's new doctrine about "socialism in one country" was diametrically opposed to Leninism, it was entirely in keeping with the regionally and nationally limited views of the practical Party functionaries who formed Stalin's support. They now had one task: "to build socialism." It was the first major step in the transition from a revolutionary doctrine to a doctrine of industrialization. It was a step that was important not only in its content, but also in its form. It was the first time that a new doctrine was not ideologically, theoretically, or historically expounded but quite simply pronounced *ex cathedra* —a method that was to become typical of Stalinism.

☐  **The "Building of Socialism"**

From 1925 on, Stalin introduced the concept of the "building of socialism" into the political theory of Communism. He described the Soviet Union as the country "that is building socialism" and spoke of "the fight for the victory of socialist construction."[12] By this concept Stalin understood the objective of creating "the economic basis of socialism."[13] While Marx and Engels had seen a high level of economic and technical development in a country as the prerequisite for a social revolution, Stalin now proclaimed a new thesis—that the economic prerequisites for the new order of society were not to be established until after the victory of a socialist revolution. The building of socialism, however, was taking place in a "capitalist encirclement." This "capitalist encirclement"—which he kept emphasizing—served Stalin as the justification of oppression.

The organs of suppression, the army and other organizations, are as necessary now, at the time of construction, as they were during the period of the Civil War. Without these organs, constructive work by the dictatorship with any degree of security would be impossible. It should not be forgotten that for the time being the revolution has been victorious in only one country. It should not be forgotten that as long as capitalist encirclement exists the danger of intervention, with all the consequences resulting from this danger, will also exist.[14]

In his later writings and statements Stalin similarly kept referring to the "capitalist encirclement" as a decisive factor of "socialist construction" in the Soviet Union.[15]

A second change was Stalin's public abandonment of Marx's original ideal of equality. At the end of 1925 Stalin declared: "One must not play with phrases about equality, because that means playing with fire."[16] Stalin maintained that "the difference between skilled and unskilled labor would exist even under socialism, even after classes had been abolished." In consequence he demanded, "We must abolish wage equalization"[17] and "organize wages properly."[18] Later he added pontifically: "The kind of socialism under which everybody would get the same pay . . . is unknown to Marxism."[19] This abandonment of the Marxian ideal of equality and the fight against "leveling" (a concept introduced by Stalin and part and parcel of Soviet political doctrine to this day) was designed to justify the social differentiation that had arisen in the Soviet Union, and the growing caste of the socially privileged.

Naturally, Stalin never directly mentioned the emergence of a new privileged class in his speeches or writings. But he was certainly aware of it, since in the spring of 1925 he spoke of the emergence of "new commanders of the work of building the new economy and the new culture." Specialists in the various fields were "commanders of the work of building the new society." "The new society cannot be built without new commanders, just as a new army cannot be built without new commanders."[20] The new classless society was now to be established by commanders and commanding cadres—an idea that would certainly have astonished Marx and Engels.

The third change in political theory consisted in Stalin's proclamation of the collectivization of agriculture. Marx, Engels, and also Lenin had favored a gradual transition from individual farmsteads to co-operatives. But Stalin now proclaimed the "socialist way" in agriculture, "which is to introduce collective farms and state farms," the road leading to "uniting the small-peasant farms into large collective farms."[21] In direct contrast to Marx, Engels, and Lenin, who had merely demanded the expropriation of the big landowners (with Marx and Engels not even ruling out compensation), Stalin now declared that the wealthy peasants (the "kulaks") must likewise not only be resolutely fought but even eliminated as a class. At the end of 1929 Stalin announced: "We have passed from the policy of restricting the exploiting tendencies of the kulaks to the policy of eliminating the kulaks as a class."[22] For Stalin, the expropriation of the kulaks' holdings was a matter of course: "It is now ridiculous and foolish to discourse at length on dekulakization. When the head is off, one does not mourn for the hair." The kulaks must not be admitted into collective farms because "they are sworn enemies of the collective-farm movement."[23] The struggle against the kulaks (who, it should be remembered, were not rich landowners but merely wealthy peasants—and that only in a relative sense) was described by Stalin as follows: "In order to oust the kulaks as a class, the resistance of this class must be *smashed* in open battle and it must be *deprived* of the productive sources of its existence and development (free use of land, instruments of production, land-renting, right to hire labor, etc.)."[24] The collectivization, it was later declared, had been "accomplished *from above,* on the initiative of the state, and directly supported *from below* by the millions of peasants."[25]

The fourth change was Stalin's new doctrine about the class struggle in the period of socialist construction. Marx and Engels had envisioned the social revolution as the immediate prelude to the classless society and had never mentioned any class struggle after a social revolution. Lenin had declared that after a socialist revolution the class struggle would continue in a different form. In the spring of 1929 Stalin now actually spoke of an "intensification of the class struggle" and of an "increase in the resistance of the capitalist elements of town and country," with "wrecking activities of the bourgeois intellectuals" being a typical phenomenon of the class struggle.[26] This frequent emphasis on an intensified class struggle during the period of socialist construction (when big landowners and capitalist entrepreneurs had long ceased to exist )was a clear admission of the resistance of the working population to the measures of the Stalin leadership. Stalin subsequently even described the intensification of the class struggle as necessary in order to attain the classless society: "The abolition of classes is not achieved by the extinction of the class struggle, but by its intensification."[27]

With this statement Stalin laid the foundation stone for another significant change—his new doctrine about the strengthening of the state:

We stand for the withering away of the state. At the same time we stand for the strengthening of the dictatorship of the proletariat, which is the mightiest and strongest state power that has ever existed. The highest development of state power with the object of preparing the conditions for the withering away of state power—such is the Marxist formula. Is this "contradictory"? Yes, it is "contradictory." But this contradiction is bound up with life, and it fully reflects Marx's dialectics.[28]

At the end of 1931 Stalin again called for the "consolidation" of the "socialist state."[29]

Two years later he provided the following explanation of why the state could not wither away but had to be strengthened as much as possible:

The state will wither away, not as a result of weakening the state power but as a result of strengthening it to the utmost, which is necessary for finally crushing the remnants of the dying classes, for organizing the defense against the capitalist encirclement, which is far from having been done away with as yet, and will not soon be done away with.[30]

By the mid-1930's, therefore, Stalin had made a series of important changes in Lenin's doctrine: his new thesis of "socialism in one country"; the replacement of a gradual transformation of agriculture by collectivization involving the annihilation of the class of wealthy peasants; the abandonment of Marx's ideal of equality and the call for a struggle against "leveling"; the concept of an elite of "commanding cadres" which would set up a new socialist society; and finally the "capitalist encirclement" and the "intensified class struggle" during the period of "socialist construction," leading not to the withering away of the state but, on the contrary, to its strengthening.

☐ **Stalin's New Doctrine of the Party**

Lenin's concept of an elite Party, based on democratic centralism, internally solid and united, charged with the leadership of the working class, was not only adopted by Stalin but given much sharper outlines both in practice and in political doctrine.

At the end of 1924 Stalin formulated his "six features of the Party" which throughout three decades remained at the center of the political doctrine of Communism. According to this new teaching, the Party is, first of all, the "advanced detachment of the working class" and, second, the "organized detachment of the working class." More important, however, is the third feature, according to which the Party is the "highest form of class organization of the proletariat"—for the reason that the Party determines the political line of all other organizations, including trade unions, co-operatives, factory organizations, etc., and co-ordinates and directs their activity.[31] The Party, therefore, must be the "directing force" while the other organizations are "levers" and "transmission belts." Stalin's concept of "levers" and "transmission belts" was not only politically important but also reflected the style that was increasingly gaining ground:

> What are these "transmission belts" or "levers" in the system of the dictatorship of the proletariat? What is this "directing force"? Why are they needed?
>
> The levers or transmission belts are those very mass organizations of the proletariat without the aid of which the dictatorship cannot be realized.
>
> The directing force is the most advanced detachment of the proletariat, its vanguard, which is the main guiding force of the dictatorship of the proletariat.[32]

According to Stalin's fourth feature, the Party must be the instrument of the dictatorship of the proletariat. It is necessary not only for the socialist revolution; it must be further consolidated and developed after the dictatorship of the proletariat has been established.

Stalin's fifth feature determined the internal structure of the Party. According to Stalin, it represented a "unity of will, unity incompatible with the existence of factions," because the Party was characterized by the "unity of will" and the "complete and absolute unity of action on the part of all members of the Party"; this precluded "all factionalism." The Party, therefore, could be strengthened only "by purging itself of opportunist elements." There was a steady influx into the Party—and this was how Stalin explained his sixth feature—of elements of the peasantry, the petty bourgeoisie, and the intelligentsia, introducing into it "the spirit of hesitancy and opportunism, the spirit of demoralization and uncertainty." The Party, therefore, must learn "in good time to purge itself of the opportunist pollution."[33]

Stalin's "six features" (proclaimed first in the spring of 1924) served to justify centralization and the subjugation of Party members. Thus he went a good way beyond Lenin in his emphasis on the leading role of the Party in the Soviet state: "The Party is the guiding force in our state. . . . The Political Bureau is the supreme organ not of the state but of the Party, while the Party is the supreme guiding force in the state." From this Stalin concluded that "in all fundamental questions of our internal and foreign policy, the Party has played the leading role."[34] Elsewhere Stalin declared: "In our country the Party guides the government"[35]; indeed, he expressly referred to "our Party's monopoly."[36] The slogans of the Soviet Party were "not mere agitational slogans," they "have the force of practical decision, the force of law, and must be carried out immediately."[37]

The stricter subjugation of Party members was clearly reflected in Stalin's demand "that the decisions of the Party should be unquestioningly carried out by all members of the Party, once these decisions have been adopted and approved by the leading Party bodies."[38] Regular Party purges were described by Stalin as "the essential condition" for improving the Party's work and lending the Party "a sharp edge."[39] The Party, according to Stalin, must oppose not only deviations but also "conciliation," which meant a liberal, conciliatory attitude toward deviations. By the spring of 1929 Stalin demanded "a determined fight against the Right deviation and conciliation toward it."[40] From that date on, a "conciliatory attitude" was regarded as equally dangerous as the deviation itself.

Under Stalin, finally, self-criticism was introduced not only into political practice but also into political doctrine. Stalin defined the concept of "self-criticism" as a "Bolshevik method of training the forces of the Party"[41] and "an indispensable and permanent weapon in the arsenal of Bolshevism."[42] The objective of self-criticism was the elimination of certain mistakes and shortcomings in the Party, in order "to *promote* the Party spirit" and "to *consolidate* the Soviet regime."[43] Stalin later added that without self-criticism "we cannot advance the cause of building socialism and of curbing the wrecking activities of the bourgeoisie."[44]

Early in 1934 Stalin declared that any deviation one had ceased to fight could develop into a "danger to the state."[45] Hence political views that diverged from the Party's general line were officially labeled criminal offenses against the state. Under these circumstances vigilance became not only a feature of practical Party life but also part of the ideology, of the Party doctrine: "We must not lull the Party but sharpen its vigilance; we must not lull it to sleep, but keep it ready for action;

not disarm it, but arm it; not demobilize it, but hold it in a state of mobilization."[46]

These reflections eventually, in the spring of 1937, led Stalin to compare the Soviet Communist Party to an army:

> In our Party, if we have in mind its leading strata, there are about 3,000 to 4,000 first-rank leaders whom I would call our Party's corps of generals.
>
> Then there are 30,000 to 40,000 middle-rank leaders who are our Party's corps of officers.
>
> Then there are about 100,000 to 150,000 of the lower-rank Party command staff who are, so to speak, our Party's non-commissioned officers.[47]

## ☐ Strategy and Tactics

Simultaneously with his new doctrine of the Party, Stalin also announced new concepts of political tactics. It was in the spring of 1924 that he first introduced the distinction between long-term strategy and short-term tactics. As he had done in his observations on the Party, he again used largely military terminology. He defined strategy as "determination of the direction of the main blow of the proletariat at a given stage of the revolution"; strategy sought "to win the war against czarism, let us say, or against the bourgeoisie, to carry through the struggle against czarism or against the bourgeoisie to its end." By contrast, tactics are "the determination of the line of conduct of the proletariat in the comparatively short period of the flow or ebb of the movement, of the rise or decline of the revolution." Tactics were concerned "not with the winning of the war as a whole" but with "winning of some particular engagements or some particular battles, the carrying through successfully of some particular campaigns or actions." Tactics, therefore, were part of strategy and subordinate to it.[48]

According to Stalin it was the task of strategy to assess correctly the ratio between the revolutionary forces and the direct reserves (peasantry and middle strata of one's own country, workers' movements of other countries, and revolutionary movements in the colonial and dependent countries), and also to utilize the indirect reserves (antagonisms and conflicts in the ranks of opponents) in the interests of one's own movement.

The most important strategic tasks, according to Stalin, were, first, the concentration of one's main forces at the crucial moment against the most vulnerable spot of the enemy; second, the correct choice of the moment for the decisive blow; third, consistent pursuit of the course adopted, regardless of all possible difficulties; and, fourth, such maneuvering of one's reserves that an orderly retreat could be executed should retreat become unavoidable.[49]

Tactics were concerned chiefly "with the forms of struggle and the forms of organization of the proletariat, with their changes and combinations."[50] It was the task of the tactical leadership "to master all forms of struggle and organization of the proletariat and to ensure that they are used properly in order to achieve, with the given ratio of forces, the maximum results necessary to prepare for strategic success."[51] It was the task of political tactics, first, to concentrate on those forms of struggle and organization which, in the given circumstances, were most likely to lead the workers "to the revolutionary front" and, second, to discover the particular "link in the chain," that particularly topical task whose solution would enable the accomplishment of all other topical tasks.[52]

## ☐   "The Victory of Socialism"

On the evening of November 25, 1936, the radio was turned on in all factories and plants, in all collective and state farms, in all schools and universities, offices and institutions, and in all clubs. The entire population of the Soviet Union had been enjoined to listen to Stalin's speech at the Eighth Extraordinary Congress of Soviets in Moscow.

After a historical survey of the development of the Soviet Union, Stalin suddenly announced: "Our Soviet society has already, in the main, succeeded in achieving socialism; it has created a Socialist system, i.e., it has brought about what Marxists in other words call the first, or lower, phase of Communism. Hence, in the main, we have already achieved the first phase of Communism, socialism."[53]

The thunderous applause of the Congress delegates was carried by radio into the remotest village. But even loyal Party members—at least in the first moments after that statement—had some doubts. Socialism realized? Stalin's justification failed to convince many. He declared that capitalism had been expelled from the sphere of Soviet industry, and the "socialist form of production now holds undivided sway in the sphere of our industry." In agriculture there was "an all-embracing system of collective farms and state farms," while "the kulak class . . . has been eliminated." Speculators and merchants had been driven out of trade and a "Soviet trade—a trade without profiteers, trade without capitalists," had been established. Hence, Stalin declared, "the complete victory of the socialist system in all spheres of the national economy is now a fact" and "exploitation of man by man has been abolished."[54]

The Soviet Union, Stalin continued, was characterized by the fact that the exploiting classes (big landowners, capitalist entrepreneurs, and kulaks) had ceased to exist. There were only two classes (the working class and the peasantry), and a social stratum (the intelligentsia). But these classes, according to Stalin, were of a character totally different from those under capitalism. The place of the proletariat had been assumed by the working class of the Soviet Union, which was leading Soviet society. The former individual peasants had been replaced by a collective peasantry based upon collective property and collective work; and in place of the "old hidebound intelligentsia" a totally new intelligentsia had emerged, one that was "bound up by its very roots with the working class and the peasantry."[55]

As for the political structure of the socialist society, Stalin proclaimed that in it "only one party can exist, the Communist Party."[56] A few years later he added that Soviet socialist society was distinguished by a number of new motive forces, including "the moral and political unity of Soviet society" and "Soviet patriotism."[57] Finally, in 1952, Stalin formulated the so-called economic basic law of socialism, which forms part of Soviet political doctrine to this day: "The securing of the maximum satisfaction of the constantly rising material and cultural requirements of the whole of society through the continuous expansion and perfection of socialist production on the basis of higher techniques."[58]

The crucial characteristics attached by Marx and Engels to a classless society of the future, including the absence of classes and the withering away of the state, the association of free producers, the elimination of the differences between town and country, the attainment of communal wealth and the realization of the principle "to each according to his needs," the abolition of the division of labor and a free choice of occupation and field of activity as the prerequisite for the liberation of the human personality—none of these were even mentioned by Stalin in his announcement of socialism in the Soviet Union. The absence of wealthy landowners, capitalist entrepreneurs, and rich peasants, as well as the nationalization of industry (which Marx and Engels had envisaged as a brief transitional stage) now became the decisive criteria of a socialist society that was to be led by a Communist Party never mentioned by Marx and Engels in this context.

## ☐   The Intensification of the Class Struggle Under Socialism

Just when Stalin had proclaimed the "victory of socialism" and declared that the exploiting classes had ceased to exist in the Soviet Union, the Great Purge began. Millions of people were arrested and sent to forced-labor camps. The percentage of Party members arrested was higher than of non-Party people, while the percentage of Party functionaries arrested was higher than that of rank and file Party members. The highest percentages were among senior Party, state, and economic functionaries and managers—from 70 to 90 per cent.

This campaign of annihilation had continued for six months before Stalin, in March 1937, attempted to justify it. Under the peculiar title —unique in the history of Marxism—of "Defects in Party Work and Measures for Liquidating Trotskyite and Other Double-Dealers," Stalin proclaimed his new doctrine of the "intensification of the class struggle with the further development of socialism." This doctrine, which under Stalin was an integral part of ideology (suspended only after Stalin's death), runs as follows:

It is necessary to smash and sweep away the rotten theory that the class struggle must progressively die down in our country with every step that we advance, or that the class enemy is growing increasingly tame in the measure in which we score our successes. This is not only a rotten theory but also a dangerous theory, for it lulls our people to sleep and lures them into a trap while giving the class enemy a chance to rally his forces for a struggle against Soviet power.

On the contrary, the further forward we advance, the greater the successes we achieve, the greater will be the fury of the remnants of the broken exploiting classes, the sooner will they resort to sharper forms of struggle, the more will they seek to harm the Soviet state and the more will they clutch at the most desperate means of struggle, as the last resort of doomed people.[59]

Thus, in March 1937, four months after his announcement of the victory of socialism and the abolition of all exploiting classes in the Soviet Union, Stalin proclaimed the intensification of the class struggle.

## ☐   The Transition to Communism

On November 25, 1936, Stalin had declared the victory of socialism. That meant that the transition to the higher phase, to Communism, had become an immediate task. In the speech in which he referred to the victory of socialism he also declared that the Party was now setting itself "the aim of achieving the higher phase of Communism in the future."[60] At the Eighteenth Party Congress in March 1939, Stalin was even more definite: "We are going ahead, toward Communism."[61]

How was this transition to Communism to be accomplished? On this important political question Stalin announced two new concepts. First, he proclaimed the thesis that Communism, at least in its essential features, could be achieved in one country. This required, however, that the Western capitalist countries must be equaled and surpassed in economic matters, a thesis that remains in force unchanged to this day, after nearly three decades:

> We have outstripped the principal capitalist countries as regards technique of production and rate of industrial development. That is very good, but it is not enough. We must also overtake them in an economic respect. We can do it, and we must do it. Only if we outstrip the principal capitalist countries economically can we reckon upon our country being fully saturated with consumer goods, of having an abundance of products, and on being able to make the transition from the first phase of Communism to its second phase.[62]

Elsewhere in the same report Stalin said the overtaking of the capitalist nations was a "cardinal economic task."[63]

Stalin's second new concept concerned the withering away of the state. He did not believe that the state would wither away even now, in the period of transition to Communism. In his speech at the Eighteenth Party Congress in March 1939 he declared that "Engels' formula" about the withering away of the state was only conditionally correct. It was correct only, Stalin explained, on condition that socialism had already been victorious in all, or in most, countries and that there was therefore no danger "from outside any longer and the strengthening of the army and the state is no longer necessary." This, however, did not apply in the case of the Soviet Union; the Soviet Union is "a totally new socialist state such as history has not known." Stalin then announced his new thesis in his favorite question-and-answer style: "We are going ahead, toward Communism. Will our state remain in the period of Communism also? Yes, it will, unless the capitalist encirclement is liquidated, and unless the danger of foreign military attack has disappeared. . . . No, it will not remain and will atrophy if the capitalist encirclement is liquidated and a socialist encirclement takes its place."[64]

In the summer of 1950 Stalin once more justified the maintenance and strengthening of the state by referring to the capitalist encirclement:

The Soviet Marxists, on the basis of the study of the world situation in our time, came to the conclusion that, under conditions of capitalist encirclement, when the victory of the socialist revolution has taken place in only one country, while capitalism rules in all other countries, the country of the victorious revolution must not weaken, but in every way strengthen, its state, the state institutions, the intelligence organs, and the army, if this country does not wish to be crushed by the capitalist encirclement.[65]

The replacement of the withering away of the state—a particularly important thesis in the political theory of Marx and Engels—by the strengthening of the state, which moreover was to continue to exist even under Communism, very clearly reflects Stalin's turning away from the original ideas of Marxism. His continuous reference to the "capitalist encirclement" might at best justify the necessity of outward-oriented instruments of power but certainly not the huge centralized bureaucratic state machine and the terror apparatus within the country, which in fact reflect the social and political conflicts of Stalin's system. From the viewpoint of political doctrine it is interesting that Stalin several times described the withering away of the state as "Engels' formula," referring merely to *Anti-Dühring* without once mentioning that Marx and Engels had supported this concept a dozen times, from the 1840's to the 1880's, in all their important writings.

In his last work, *Economic Problems of Socialism in the U.S.S.R.,* in the autumn of 1952, Stalin once more dealt with the transition to Communism. He formulated "three main preliminary conditions" for the advent of the Communist society:

First, the "continuous expansion of all social production, with a relatively higher rate of expansion of the production of the means of production"—i.e., the priority given to heavy industry was to be maintained further until the final Communist objectives were achieved.

Second, he demanded that collective farm property should be raised "to the level of public property" and the circulation of merchandise gradually replaced "by a system of products exchange, under which the central government or some other social center might control the whole output of social production in the interests of society." This meant that any kind of trade was to be abolished and the entire economy further centralized.

Third, the working day was to be shortened to six and later to five hours, housing conditions were to be improved, the real wages of workers and office workers were to be at least doubled, the prices of mass consumer goods were to be further reduced and, finally, general polytechnical schooling was to be introduced "so that the members of society are in a position to freely choose their occupations and not be tied all their lives . . . to some one occupation." After the fulfillment of these three preliminary conditions it would be possible to go over from the socialist formula: "from each according to his ability, to each according to his work" to the Communist formula: "from each according to his ability, to each according to his needs."[66]

## ☐ The Future Communist Society

Throughout the nearly twenty-five years of his rule Stalin dealt only twice in detail with the future Communist society—the first time in the autumn of 1927, at the beginning of Stalinism. In reply to a question from an American labor delegation as to the decisive characteristics of the future Communist society, he made the following statement which is still strongly reminiscent of Marx and Engels:

Briefly, the anatomy of Communist society may be described as follows: It is a society in which (a) there will be no private ownership of the instruments and means of production, but social, collective ownership; (b) there will be no classes or state power, but there will be working people in industry and agriculture who manage economic affairs as a free association of working people; (c) the national economy, organized according to plan, will be based on the highest level of technique, both in industry and agriculture; (d) there will be no antithesis between town and country, between industry and agriculture; (e) products will be distributed according to the principle of the old French Communists: "from each according to his ability, to each according to his needs"; (f) science and art will enjoy conditions sufficiently favorable for them to attain full flowering; (g) the individual, freed from concern about his daily bread and from the necessity of adapting himself to the "powers that be," will become really free.[67]

This characterization was given by Stalin in 1927, i.e., at a time when the transition to Communism and to a Communist society seemed to him to lie in the distant future. But as the "building of socialism" progressed, Stalin's characterization was mentioned less and less. After the announcement of the "victory of socialism" in the autumn of 1936, this characterization became highly uncomfortable. It was no longer quoted and not even dealt with in Party schools. By then all questions about the Communist society of the future had come to be regarded as a "utopian deviation." In the 1930's and 1940's Stalin confined himself to quite short references, such as that in the higher phase of Communism "everyone will work according to his ability and be rewarded for his work according to his needs," and that the principle "from each according to his ability, to each according to his needs" would be realized.[68]

Not until the autumn of 1952—in his last work, *Economic Problems of Socialism in the U.S.S.R.*—did Stalin again refer to the ultimate aim of Communism.

Of the seven decisive characteristics of the Communist society, listed by Stalin himself in the autumn of 1927, only one survived: the realization of the principle "from each according to his ability, to each according to his needs."

Four of the decisive characteristics listed in 1927 were now, a quarter of a century later, no longer mentioned at all—neither the free association of workers nor the absence of state power, neither the liberation of the human personality nor the free development of science and art to full flower.

The remaining two characteristics were considerably curtailed. In 1927—entirely in line with Marx and Engels—Stalin had referred to the abolition of the contrast between town and country, between industry and agriculture. In October 1952, however, he announced that Communism would not abolish all but merely the essential differences. Even under Communism the big cities would continue to exist and indeed "further new great cities will come into being." Moreover, "certain differences" between agriculture and industry would continue to exist even under Communism.

The characteristics of the classless society and the abolition of the differences between intellectual and physical work were likewise minimized by Stalin. True, the essential difference between intellectual and physical work, in the sense of a major inequality, would disappear. "But some distinction, even if inessential, will remain, if only because the conditions of labor of the managerial staffs and those of the workers are not identical." Hence, according to Stalin's new definition, even the Communist society of the future would be marked by differences between "leading personnel" and rank-and-file workers.[69]

☐ **From World Revolution to Great-Russian Chauvinism**

The Stalin era finally witnessed—in practice as much as in political theory—a gradual transition from Lenin's internationalist ideas of world revolution to Soviet patriotism and later even to Great-Russian chauvinism.

This transition began as early as 1924, immediately after Stalin had proclaimed his doctrine of "socialism in one country." This doctrine—a point that is sometimes overlooked—was accompanied by a reinterpretation of the concept of "world revolution." Whereas Lenin had seen the world revolution as the coalescence of revolutionary movements in the industrialized countries of Europe with the national liberation movements in the colonial and dependent countries, Stalin announced his new doctrine of world revolution in terms of "two centers" and the "struggle between two systems." Accordingly, two centers would emerge "in the course of the development of the world revolution"—a center of imperialism, rallying around it the capitalist countries, and a center of socialism, consisting of Soviet Republics—and "the struggle between these two systems will fill the history of the unfolding of the world revolution."[70] The further development of world revolution no longer depended—as it did for Lenin—on the revolutionary movements in the various countries of the world, but primarily on the further development of the Soviet Union, on its political, economic, and military strength. The relationship between the Soviet Union and world revolution had thus been reversed. While in Lenin's view the destiny of Soviet Russia depended on the world revolution, under Stalin's new thesis the destiny of world revolution depended on the development of the Soviet state.

Stalin now proclaimed more and more emphatically that the Soviet Union was the example and model for Communists in all countries, and, proceeding from this point of view, he demanded that foreign Communists subordinate themselves, both in practice and in theory, to the directives of the Soviet Union. Even in 1925 he took the view that "the revolutionary part of the working proletariat of Europe . . . regarding [the Soviet state] as its child, is ready to defend it and to fight for it if need be."[71] Less than two years later, in August 1927, Stalin made it the duty of Communists in all countries to put the interests of the Soviet state above all else:

A *revolutionary* is one who is ready to protect, to defend the U.S.S.R. without reservation, without qualification, openly and honestly, without secret military conferences; for the U.S.S.R. is the first proletarian, revolutionary state in the world, a state which is building socialism. An *internationalist* is one who is ready to defend the U.S.S.R. without reservation, without wavering, unconditionally; for the U.S.S.R. is the base of the world revolutionary movement, and this revolutionary movement cannot be defended and promoted unless the U.S.S.R. is defended. For whoever thinks of defending the world revolutionary movement apart from, or against the U.S.S.R. goes against the revolution and must inevitably slide into the camp of the enemies of the revolution.[72]

Unlike Lenin, who most readily spoke of the mistakes and short-comings of the Bolsheviks and by no means regarded the October Rev-olution as an infallible model for other countries, Stalin now described the October Revolution of 1917 as "of an international world order" and as "a radical turn in the world history of mankind."[73] The Soviet Union was no longer part of the revolutionary movement—as it had been to Lenin—but "the *motherland* of the world proletariat."[74] Two years later Stalin went even further: "The revolutionaries of all coun-tries look with hope to the U.S.S.R. as the center of the liberation struggle of the working people throughout the world and recognize it as their only motherland." The revolutionary workers of all countries re-garded the Soviet working class "and first and foremost the *Russian* working class" (thus emphasized by Stalin!) as their "recognized leader." This, he said, filled "the hearts of the Russian workers with a feeling of revolutionary national pride that can move mountains and perform miracles."[75]

This marked the beginning of the second phase of the transition to nationalism. Not only was the Soviet Union proclaimed the mother-land of the proletariat and all working people, but Russia's past was being emphasized more and more. In 1931 Stalin for the first time re-sorted to patriotic Russian justifications for the U.S.S.R.'s industrializa-tion:

One feature of the history of old Russia was the continual beatings she suffered because of her backwardness. She was beaten by the Mongol khans. She was beaten by the Turkish beys. She was beaten by the Swedish feudal lords. She was beaten by the Polish and Lithuanian gentry. She was beaten by the British and French capitalists. She was beaten by the Japanese barons. All beat her—because of her backwardness, because of her military back-wardness, cultural backwardness, political backwardness, industrial back-wardness, agricultural backwardness. They beat her because to do so was profitable and could be done with impunity. . . . Such is the law of the ex-ploiters—to beat the backward and the weak. . . . You are backward, you are weak—therefore you are wrong, hence you can be beaten and enslaved. You are mighty—therefore you are right, hence we must be wary of you. That is why we must no longer lag behind."[76]

The tenor of this speech which, incidentally, according to the official announcement, was made to "business executives," reflected the change of mood. The new ruling stratum was not greatly in-spired by revolutionary internationalism but rather by pride in the country's economic achievements and the power of the state. It was interested less in the fate of foreign Communists than in their own privileged ruling position. Soviet patriotism and national pride were much more in tune with their philosophy of life than the aims of world revolution as proclaimed by Lenin. Stalin's public abandonment of world revolution reflected this trend. On March 7, 1936, in an interview given to the American newspaper publisher Roy Howard, Stalin renounced world revolution.

ROY HOWARD: "What about the plans and intentions concerning world revolution?"
STALIN: "We never had such plans or intentions."
ROY HOWARD: "Yes, but . . ."
STALIN: "They are due to a misunderstanding."
ROY HOWARD: "A tragic misunderstanding?"
STALIN: "No, a comical one—or, if you like, a tragi-comical one."[77]

After that interview, which was published in all Soviet papers, the concept of world revolution came to be considered "Trotskyite" and was no longer used. Since then, it has always been implied, indirectly perhaps but clearly, that the success of international Communism is identical with strengthening the U.S.S.R.'s power and extending Soviet influence. The emphasis is not on the international revolutionary movement but on the Soviet motherland.

But even the concept of "motherland" was soon to undergo a change. In his above-mentioned speech of 1931 Stalin had declared that, following the overthrow of capitalism, "we have a motherland and will uphold its independence."[78] By "motherland" he still understood the entire Soviet Union, a multi-national state in which the Russians accounted for only slightly more than half the population. At the beginning of the war, however, in November 1941, Stalin already referred to "the great Russian nation" without mentioning the other nationalities of the U.S.S.R. The great examples he quoted were all Russians, including the czarist generals Suvorov and Kutuzov.[79] At the end of the war, in a thanksgiving toast on May 24, 1945, Stalin described the Russian people as the most outstanding nation and the leading force among the nations of the Soviet Union:

I should like to propose a toast to the health of our Soviet people, and in the first place, the Russian people. (Loud and prolonged applause and shouts of "Hurrah.")

I drink in the first place to the health of the Russian people because it is the most outstanding nation of all the nations forming the Soviet Union.

I propose a toast to the health of the Russian people because it has won in this war universal recognition as the leading force of the Soviet Union among all the peoples of our country.

I propose a toast to the health of the Russian people, not only because it is the leading people but also because it possesses a clear mind, a staunch character, and patience.[80]

Stalin's identification with Russia's czarist past went so far that on the occasion of Japan's surrender in September 1945 he declared that czarist Russia's defeat in the Russo-Japanese War of 1904–5 (which had largely triggered off the Revolution of 1905 and had repeatedly been welcomed by Lenin) had "left grave memories in the minds of our peoples. It was as a dark stain on our country." He continued: "Our people trusted and awaited the day when Japan would be routed and the stain wiped out. For forty years have we, men of the older generation . . . waited for this day. And now this day has come."[81]

□ **Peaceful Coexistence and the Inevitability of Wars**

By the end of the Lenin era it had become clear that the hoped-for world revolution had failed to materialize and that the Soviet Communists would have to accommodate themselves to a prolonged co-existence between the Soviet Union and the capitalist countries. This was reflected in Stalin's new foreign policy concepts. In December 1925 he referred for the first time to an "equilibrium which has determined the present period of 'peaceful coexistence' between the land of the Soviets and the capitalist countries."[82] The period of war had been replaced by "a period of 'peaceful coexistence.' "[83]

The existence of two opposite systems—the capitalist and the socialist—did not, according to Stalin, rule out "temporary agreements with capitalist states in the field of industry, in the field of commerce, and perhaps in the field of diplomatic relations." These were "possible and expedient" and indeed could "be of a more or less lasting character." Naturally, such agreements were limited "by the opposite natures of the two systems, between which there is rivalry, struggle."[84] Three months later, in December 1927, Stalin went a good deal further: "Our relations with the capitalist countries are based on the assumption that the coexistence of two opposite systems is possible. Practice has fully confirmed this."[85]

These statements were still rather vague. Following Hitler's rise to power in 1933 and the Soviet Union's entry into the League of Nations in the autumn of 1934, Stalin expressed himself more definitely, with particular stress on coexistence between the United States and the Soviet Union. "American democracy and the Soviet system can coexist and compete peacefully . . . provided we do not indulge too much in carping about trivialities,"[86] Stalin declared in the spring of 1936.

After the end of World War II Stalin, invariably in the form of interviews with foreign correspondents, politicians, or statesmen, repeatedly made similar statements. In reply to the question whether amicable and lasting co-operation was possible between the Soviet Union and the Western democracies, in spite of the existence of ideological differences, Stalin stated in the autumn of 1946: "I believe so absolutely."[87] When Elliott Roosevelt asked him whether coexistence between the United States and the Soviet Union was possible, he replied: "Undoubtedly, yes."[88] The difference between the American and the Soviet systems was "not of decisive importance insofar as co-operation is concerned," he declared in a conversation with Harold Stassen on April 9, 1947. The United States and the Soviet Union had been allies in the war, although they had totally different systems. "The idea of co-operation between the two systems was first expressed by Lenin." He "shared Lenin's point of view on the possibility and desirability of collaboration between the two economic systems."[89]

Even after the beginning of the Cold War Stalin continued to support coexistence, at least in his foreign-policy statements, such as his reply to an open letter from Henry Wallace: "The government of the U.S.S.R. is of the opinion that, in spite of the difference of economic systems and ideologies, the coexistence of these systems and the peaceful resolution of differences of opinion between the U.S.S.R. and the U.S.A. are not only possible but also absolutely necessary in the interest of universal peace."[90] In April 1952, barely a year before his death, Stalin again answered the question of a group of American editors about the basis on which the coexistence of capitalism and Communism was possible: "Peaceful coexistence of capitalism and Communism is entirely possible, provided there is a wish on both sides for collaboration and a readiness to discharge obligations undertaken, and provided the principle of equality and non-interference in the internal affairs of other states is observed."[91]

However, Stalin considered all these coexistence statements as part of practical foreign policy, not as fundamental principles of ideology. This was clearly reflected in Party schools where coexistence was dealt with—if at all—only in current-policy seminars.

The thesis of the inevitability of new imperialist wars, taken over from Lenin, on the other hand, remained valid throughout the Stalin era. Following his endorsement, in 1927, of the "inevitability of wars,"[92] it continued to be upheld in all instructional material and ideological publications of the 1930's and 1940's.

After the end of World War II, however, the question whether this thesis could still be valid under the changed conditions was being asked more and more often. Moreover, doubts were frequently expressed whether the world peace movement, inspired and directed by the Stalin leadership in Moscow, could fulfill its tasks if his own ideology continued to maintain that wars were inevitable.

However, in his last publication, in October 1952, Stalin still clung to the concept of the inevitability of wars. His repeated polemics against "some comrades"—in Party parlance invariably an indication of a strong current—clearly showed that he was informed about the critical views on this point:

Some comrades hold that, owing to the development of new international conditions since the Second World War, wars between the capitalist countries have ceased to be inevitable. They consider . . . that the policy-shaping minds have been sufficiently taught by the two world wars and the severe damage they caused to the whole capitalist world, not to venture to involve the capitalist countries in war with one another again—and that, because of all this, wars between capitalist countries are no longer inevitable. These comrades are mistaken.[93]

The antagonisms between the capitalist countries, according to Stalin, continued to exist and "it follows from this that the inevitability of wars between capitalist countries remains in force." As an explanation he added: "It is said that Lenin's thesis that imperialism inevitably generates war must now be regarded as obsolete, since powerful popular forces have come forward today in defense of peace and against another world war. That is not true. . . . To eliminate the inevitability of wars, it is necessary to abolish imperialism."[94]

## ☐ The Changes from Marx to Stalin

Stalin died on March 5, 1953. More than a century had passed since Marx's and Engels' first published writings. During that century their original political concepts had been changed almost beyond recognition. No doubt Stalin himself was aware of it, and that is why he tried to gloss over it with the claim that Marxism had been "creatively developed" on a few questions and issues.

To this end, the publication of Marx's and Engels' collected works was suspended in the 1930's. Instead, the Party's Directorate for Ideological Training published short brochures on the principal works of Marx, Engels, and Lenin, confined to those of their statements that were still valid, and accompanied by a suitable commentary. In November 1938 the Central Committee in a resolution condemned the "harmful separation . . . of Marxism and Leninism" and introduced the obligatory concept of Marxism-Leninism[95]—though this was in fact reduced to a recital of Stalin's interpretations and only occasionally contained a few "suitable" quotations from Marx, Engels, and Lenin.

The vast schism between Marx's and Engels' original concepts and the Stalinist doctrine of a century later becomes obvious if we recall the changes undergone by the principal ideas.

The liberation of the human personality from the enslaving division of labor—for Marx and Engels the starting point of their political concepts—had almost entirely receded into the background. On the extremely rare occasions when alienation, an important concept to Marx and Engels, was mentioned at all it was represented as already eliminated under Stalin's type of socialism.

Marx's and Engels' idea that the working class was the social force that would overcome capitalism, and that the working class— as the movement of the vast majority in the interest of the vast majority—would with its own liberation liberate society as a whole from oppression and exploitation, had in the course of a century become the object of mere lip service. The concept of "the working class" was used, partially under Lenin and fully under Stalin, as a synonym for the Party; under Stalin the much-used phrase "loyalty to the working class" meant nothing other than loyalty to the Party, an individual's readiness and resolve to subordinate himself totally to the Party's decisions, and to implement them. Anyone beginning to question a certain Party line or to oppose it was instantly charged with "treason to the working class." The working class, for Marx still the decisive social force for the transformation of society, had been reduced to a mythical concept in order to justify the existence of the Communist Party and to guarantee discipline and authority within the Party.

Marx's and Engels' idea of the workers' party as the representative of the interests of the working class as a whole, a Party democratically structured, free from all authoritarianism, with an independent Party press and an autonomous development of socialist theory, had already been changed by Lenin's concept of a homogeneous, closed, disciplined elite organization, a Party controlling its own press, with a common ideology, a Party that must lead and guide the working class. Under Stalin —and this was entirely in line with practice—the Party was now likened to the hierarchical structure of an army, the unconditional subordination of Party members to the leadership was proclaimed, and deviations were declared to be dangerous to the state.

From the few references of Marx and Engels to the attitude of the workers' party to other political forces Lenin had developed an entire doctrine about its tactics, with full details on the forms of the struggle and their change, on work within other institutions and organizations, permissible and impermissible compromises, and the conclusion of the most varied political alliances. Stalin finally, with his concept of the "main blow," his "direct and indirect reserves," the long-term strategic objectives of a war and the short-term tactical objectives of a battle, altogether likened the Party's external activity to a military plan of attack.

In contrast to Marx and Engels, who only occasionally referred to the working-class movement's attitude to war, a detailed concept of the causes and the nature of wars had come into existence, with a distinction between "just" and "unjust" wars and, above all, with the thesis that wars were inevitable. This thesis, proclaimed by Lenin in World War I, remained in force unchanged until Stalin's death. Simultaneously, however, peaceful coexistence between the Soviet Union and the Western countries was said to be possible; indeed, after the early 1950's the same Stalin who regarded wars as inevitable created a world peace movement in order to prevent war.

Marx's and Engels' theory about the conditions necessary for a social revolution (high level of development and the workers forming the majority of the population) had been replaced by the doctrine of a "socialist revolution," to be led and accomplished by a small elite Party of professional revolutionaries. The decisive prerequisite was no longer the economic and social conditions but the extent of political antagonisms. The social revolution, seen by Marx and Engels after the 1870's as a peaceful transformation, was replaced by the concept of violent revolution, mainly in the form of an armed uprising under the leadership of the Party, complete with detailed directives for its execution.

Marx's and Engels' concept of universal revolution, the simultaneous victory of the revolution in the principal industrialized countries, was first weakened by the new concept of the socialist revolution in one country; before long, Stalin was to describe the whole objective of world revolution as a "comical misunderstanding"—with the obvious intention of ascribing the victory of Communism not to its own revolutionary transformation in the various countries but to the extension and further growth of the U.S.S.R.'s power. The equality of the workers' parties of the different countries, as postulated by Marx, Engels, and Lenin, who rejected any leading role by the working-class movement of any one country, was replaced—both in practice and in official doctrines—by the total subordination of the world Communist movement to the interests of the U.S.S.R.

The dictatorship of the proletariat, envisaged by Marx and Engels as a necessary, short-lived transitional stage, with the concentration of political power in the hands of an elected organ that would simultaneously exercise legislative and executive power, with all officials and employees receiving salaries not exceeding a worker's wages and subject to recall at any time, a political system without a standing army, without bureaucracy, and without a political police, had been supplanted by the concept of a "state of the dictatorship of the proletariat" which would continue to exist for decades even after the socialist revolution, a power not restricted by any laws, marked by the ruthless and strict application of force, and led by a Party never mentioned by Marx and Engels. Under Stalin, the concept of the "dictatorship of the proletariat" was eventually used to justify a bureaucratic-administrative system characterized by the existence of a new hierarchically ramified ruling stratum exercising its rule by pressure, violence, and terror.

Marx and Engels always spoke of a reshaping, a reorganization or reconstruction of society, to be performed only after the necessary economic and social conditions had been achieved. From this transformation of society the emphasis was now completely shifted—since the revolution took place in a country where, according to Marx and Engels, its prerequisites were absent—to the "building of socialism." This meant that not until after the victory of the revolution would that economic basis be created which Marx and Engels had seen as the precondition of revolution. From an idea about the transformation of society, Marxism was turned into a doctrine of industrialization.

According to Marx and Engels, a number of transitional measures would be carried out in the course of a social revolution, including the transfer of the vital means of production into the hands of society, preferably with compensation to their former owners; other features would be the abolishment of the contrast between town and country, the withering away of the state, and in agriculture a slow, gradual transition to co-operatives, without pressure, compulsion, or incursions into the private property of the peasants. Instead of this concept, however, the social distinctions were now by no means narrowed; they were magnified. The withering away of the state was replaced by the strengthening of the state. A slow evolutionary development toward agricultural co-operatives was replaced, both in practice and in theory, by a collectivization decreed from above and executed with all means of pressure and terror, with expropriation and the elimination of a large portion of the peasantry and the forcible amalgamation of peasants to form collective farms. This "building of socialism" took place under the absolute leadership, guidance, and control of a ruling Party that had never even been mentioned by Marx and Engels in connection with the transition to the Communist classless society of the future.

All these changes in political theory led logically to a total reinterpretation of the ultimate aim, the classless Communist society. Step by step, the attainment of this objective was put off further and further, and was subdivided by Lenin into a first phase, "socialism" (a term never used in this sense by Marx and Engels), and a second, higher phase, "Communism." Socialism was subsequently defined by Stalin as an order of society that was, in its essential features, economically based on state ownership (which Marx and Engels had envisaged merely as a temporary expedient during the social revolution), whose citizens would be remunerated according to their work ("to each according to his work"), and which would be politically led, guided, and directed by a Party (never mentioned by Marx and Engels). The "withering away of the state," a central feature of Marx's and Engels' view of the transformation of society, was postponed to the distant future by Lenin and subsequently replaced by Stalin with the concept of the "strengthening of the socialist state"—a concept that would have made Marx's and Engels' hair stand on end.

Marx's and Engels' vision of the Communist society of the future was a society based on the association of free producers, a society without class or state, which would so increase its social wealth that the distribution of all products could be performed on the principle "to each according to his needs," a society in which the differences between town and country, between intellectual and physical work, had disappeared, and in which, as a result of the elimination of the enslaving division of labor, the human personality was free to develop—all this had been totally changed. The association of free producers, for Marx and Engels a key feature of the new society, was no longer mentioned at all; instead, Stalin spoke of a "central power" that was to direct and embrace all production. The state, it was now argued, would continue to exist even under Communism; as for the liquidation of the differences between town and country, and between intellectual and physical labor, only the "essential" differences were to be abolished, while others would continue to exist; instead of the classless society, differences between "leading personnel" on the one hand and workers on the other would continue to exist even under Communism.

Internationalism, the typical and overriding feature of Marx's and Engels' thinking, while taken over by Lenin, was turned into its opposite by Stalin. The concept of "internationalism" was now degraded to an obligation of foreign Communists to subordinate themselves to Moscow. Subsequently "Soviet patriotism" was introduced, and finally the Russian nation extolled as the leading nation, czarist military leaders presented as examples, and even a military defeat of czarist Russia described as a "black stain" that had to be expunged.

While Marx and Engels had rejected any cult of personality or adulation of authority and had wanted scientific socialism to be understood not as a dogma representing an exclusive path to salvation but rather as the exposition of an evolutionary process, this was turned into its very opposite in the course of a century. Marxism-Leninism of the Stalinist mold, as laid down in the *Short Course* of the history of the Soviet Communist Party and in Stalin's writings, was regarded as infallible. Within its own sphere of power all criticism, even if only of a single sentence of these writings, was punished with arrest. Stalin himself was glorified—usually as the "great genius of leader and teacher," the "coryphaeus of learning," the "wise teacher," and the "leader of progressive humanity." On the title page of *Pravda* Stalin's name used to appear, on an average, forty to fifty times a day; for many years not a single lead article was published in *Pravda* without Stalin being named at least twice and quoted at least once—regardless of the subject matter.

## ☐ Marxist-Leninist Critique of Stalinism

Under the Stalinist system, critical views of the differences between Marxism and Leninism, or (of more immediate concern) between Leninism and Stalinism, could be exchanged only secretly and in whispers. Only outside the Soviet Union could some critical voices be publicly heard, voices that criticized and politically challenged Stalin's centralized bureaucratic system from the point of view of Marxism and Leninism. Such a critique came especially from the followers of Trotsky and Bukharin, usually scattered but occasionally associated in small groups, although the details of their critiques were based on different points of view.

A typical and perhaps the best-known example among many such writings is Trotsky's critique of Stalinism in his book *The Revolution Betrayed,* published in 1936. Trotsky saw the emergence of Stalinism as the result of the "bureaucratic degeneration" of Lenin's revolutionary party:

Together with the theory of socialism in one country there was put into circulation by the bureaucracy a theory that in Bolshevism the Central Committee is everything and the party nothing. . . . Availing itself of the death of Lenin, the ruling group announced a "Leninist levy." The gates of the party, always carefully guarded, were now thrown wide open. Workers, clerks, petty officials, flocked through in crowds. The political aim of this maneuver was to dissolve the revolutionary vanguard in raw human material, without experience, without independence, and yet with the old habit of submitting to the authorities. The scheme was successful. By freeing the bureaucracy from the control of the proletarian vanguard, the "Leninist levy" dealt a death blow to the party of Lenin. The machine had won the necessary independence. Democratic centralism gave place to bureaucratic centralism. In the party apparatus itself there now took place a radical reshuffling of personnel from top to bottom. The chief merit of a Bolshevik was declared to be obedience. Under the guise of a struggle with the opposition there occurred a sweeping replacement of revolutionists with *chinovniks* [professional governmental functionaries]. The history of the Bolshevik Party became a history of its rapid degeneration. . . . Of party democracy there remained only recollections in the memory of the older generation. And together with it had disappeared the democracy of the soviets, the trade unions, the co-operatives, the cultural and athletic organizations. Above each and every one of them there reigns an unlimited hierarchy of party secretaries. The regime had become "totalitarian" in character several years before this word arrived from Germany.[96]

As a result of this development, according to Trotsky, a system emerged in the mid-1930's that had nothing in common with Marx's, Engels', or Lenin's original ideas:

However you may interpret the nature of the present Soviet state, one thing is indubitable: at the end of its second decade of existence it has not only not died away, but not begun to "die away." Worse than that, it has grown into a hitherto unheard of apparatus of compulsion. The bureaucracy not only has not disappeared, yielding its place to the masses, but has turned into an uncontrolled force dominating the masses. . . . With the utmost stretch of fancy it would be difficult to imagine a contrast more striking than that which exists between the schema of the workers' state according to Marx, Engels, and Lenin, and the actual state now headed by Stalin.[97]

In his book *Stalin's Crimes,* published a year later, Trotsky contrasted Stalinism with a socialist society:

The OGPU barracks are not the ideal that the working class is fighting for. Socialism means an absolutely lucid social order based on the self-administration of the working people. Stalin's regime is based on a conspiracy of the rulers against the ruled. Socialism means a steady growth of equality of all. Stalin has established a system of atrocious privileges. Socialism aims at the all-sided development of the human personality. Where and when has the human personality been so humiliated as in the U.S.S.R.? Socialism would be pointless outside a society marked by unselfish, honest, humane relations between people. Stalin's regime has permeated social and personal relations with lies, careerism and betrayal.[98]

Soviet bureaucracy, as Trotsky called the new ruling stratum, was wielding almost unlimited economic power. "It has in its hands such levers as wages, prices, taxes, the budget, and credit. . . . The exploitation of certain strata of the population by other strata has not disappeared, but has been disguised."[99] However, the Soviet bureaucracy was not a new ruling class. It had not yet "created special types of property," and for that reason the description of the Stalinist system as state capitalism was incorrect: "The bureaucracy has neither stocks nor bonds. It is recruited, supplemented, and renewed in the manner of an administrative hierarchy, independently of any special property relations of its own. The individual bureaucrat cannot transmit to his heirs his rights in the exploitation of the state apparatus."[100]

The effects of Stalinism on the theoretical development of Marxism were summed up by Trotsky as follows:

In spite of the fact that Marxism is formally a state doctrine in the Soviet Union there has not appeared during the last twelve years one Marxian investigation—in economics, sociology, history, or philosophy—which deserves attention and translation into foreign languages. The Marxian works do not transcend the limit of scholastic compilations which say over the same old ideas, endorsed in advance, and shuffle over the same old quotations according to the demands of the current administrative conjuncture. Millions of copies are distributed through the state channels of books and brochures that are of no use to anybody, put together with the help of mucilage, flattery, and other sticky substances. Marxists who might say something valuable and independent are sitting in prison, or forced into silence, and this in spite of the fact that the evolution of social forms is raising gigantic scientific problems at every step![101]

But the effect of this critique and discussion at first remained limited. Groups criticizing and politically opposing Stalin's ideology and system from the positions of Leninism could not become a serious force so long as not only the Soviet Union but the entire world Communist movement was totally dominated and ruled by the Stalin leadership; any discussion of such a theme would instantly be labeled "treason against the working class" and jeopardize the personal safety of anyone trying to discuss these issues with Communists.

Not until the 1940's did this situation begin to change. Whereas in most countries of Eastern and Central Europe a pro-Soviet system was set up during 1945–47 by the bayonets of the Red Army, in Yugoslavia partisan armies had fought under Communist leadership without appreciable Soviet help. Their victory offered them the opportunity of embarking on their own road not only in practice but also in political theory. This opportunity became a reality after Yugoslavia's break with the Moscow leadership in 1948. Yugoslavia's independent development meant not only the first rupture of the monolithic unity of world Communism under Stalin's leadership, but also an end to Stalin's interpretation of Communism as being the only valid one. Soon after the break with the Stalin leadership the Yugoslav Communists began to criticize certain features of Stalinism in theory and practice. As an inevitable result of this critique of Stalinism they moved further and further along their own road, independent of Moscow, gaining new experience all the time, and consequently extending their critique of Stalinism.

Thus, by the end of May 1949, Edvard Kardelj in his book *On People's Democracy in Yugoslavia* pointed out that the development in the Soviet Union and other socialist countries was leading "to bureaucracy, to aloofness of the bureaucratic apparatus from the masses of the people, to subordination of these masses to the bureaucratic apparatus." This had led to a multiplicity of negative features, such as the "strangling of creative initiative from below, education of bureaucrats without backbones, stagnation of ideas," as well as "superstitious awe of the state," and efforts to solve "all phenomena in the light of ready-made prescriptions." Socialism, however, Kardelj declared, could be realized only by the initiative of the working people themselves, of people "unfettered by bureaucratic centralism." The state apparatus must be "the servant of the people and not a force above them."[102]

Proceeding from these views, Milovan Djilas, then still a member of the Yugoslav Communist leadership, in March 1950 expounded his concept of the "two directions" in the development of the dictatorship of the proletariat:

> Marx and Engels, on the basis of the economic laws of the development toward Communism, predicted that the victorious working class and socialism would be threatened by two dangers—the defeated bourgeoisie on the one hand and its own bureaucracy on the other. It was not for nothing that Marx demanded that officials should be elected, and only for a certain period of time, after which they would have to return to production. . . . The dictatorship of the proletariat, so-called socialist democracy, can therefore develop in two directions—in the direction of its own withering away as socialism itself grows stronger, or in the direction of a strengthening

of bureaucracy and its transformation into a privileged class living at the expense of society as a whole.[103]

In the Soviet Union the development had followed the latter direction. Because of a number of special circumstances, including "the fact that the Soviet Union for a long time was the only socialist country, and moreover a backward country surrounded by capitalism, with a relatively slight conscious part played by the masses in the struggle for the building of socialism and relatively weak external and internal revolutionary forces," there had "arisen a privileged bureaucratic layer, a bureaucratic centralism, a temporary transformation of the state into a power above society."[104]

A detailed explanation of the transformation of Leninism into Stalinism in the Soviet Union was given by Edvard Kardelj in April 1952, in his brochure *Socialist Democracy*. In view of the "exceptionally great general backwardness of the social-economic structure of Russia" and the "weakness of the proletariat," the "executive apparatus acquired extraordinary power and authority and began to produce an independent bureaucratic caste with special social interests."

This process, Kardelj asserted, began with the transformation of the Bolshevik Party:

The history of Soviet authority has shown us that the workers' party, grown from the revolution, began to turn into an organ of the bureaucratic caste from the moment it began to rule "in place of" or "in the name of" the working class. By merging and identifying itself with the apparatus of the State's executive authority, by concentrating absolute power over the whole social life within the apparatus, that is, in its own hands, it became an authority over both the working class and the working masses in general. It thereby ceased to be a workers' party, and the working class ceased to be the ruling class.[105]

The further development, chiefly during the first and second five-year plans (i.e., the period from 1929 to 1937), was decisive for the emergence of the Stalinist system:

This system received its final affirmation in the period of the first Five-Year Plan, and that not by chance just at that time. For the fulfillment of the Plan the Soviet system required a tremendous concentration of power in the executive organs of authority, among which I count the leading core of the Communist Party of the U.S.S.R., which means in the organs that had already been bureaucratized and which were therefore bound to become, by absolute authority, a closed artificial caste.

To be sure, the first and second Five-Year Plans were on the whole successful. For Russian conditions, a great economic victory was achieved, which to a considerable extent wrested the Soviet Union from the fetters of backwardness. But this success was accompanied by yet another victory—that of a state-capitalist bureaucratic despotism. . . . The apparatus of republican, regional, and district soviets became the apparatus of central, federal organs, with the soviets themselves as a mere decoration, devoid of any rights or authority. Absolutely subordinated—in the factory to the board and the chief economic administration; on the collective farm to a professional president appointed from above; and in the soviet to a civil service apparatus which itself lacks rights or, rather, is only "entitled" to carry out blindly the orders of the central administrative authority—the Soviet working man lost every means of influencing state authority. Decorated with medals and corrupted by privileges, but frozen with fear before the Pharaonic heights of the central executive authority, Soviet bureaucracy naturally had ever-improving economic rewards conferred on it for discharging this kind of role—to the detriment of workers and working peasants.[106]

A similar observation was made by Tito at the Sixth Congress of the Yugoslav Communists in November 1952:

The Soviet Union in its internal development has long deviated from a socialist development to the road of state capitalism with an unprecedented system of bureaucracy. Bureaucracy has become an end in itself in the Soviet Union. It is increasingly turning into an exploiting power that has placed itself above society, that not only obstructs all further development of the revolution and of revolutionary thought but also progressively liquidates the achievements of the October Revolution.[107]

Stalin's claims about the realization of socialism in the U.S.S.R. were described by Tito as "empty phrases" and "juggling with Marxist terms." Practice, he said, instead showed "that the exploitation of the workers has not been liquidated in the Soviet Union, since they do not manage production but are poorly paid wage-workers; they have no share in the distribution of the surplus value which is instead seized in its entirety by the state bureaucracy in the form of gigantic salaries and bonuses." The Stalinist Soviet Union was "increasingly assuming the hideous shape of a state-capitalist bureaucratic system."[108]

To describe such a system as the "dictatorship of the proletariat," Kardelj pointed out, was an utter contradiction:

For Soviet Stalinist theory and practice the "dictatorship of the proletariat" means the complete subordination of the working class and the masses to the monopolist authority of an elite of the "wisest," the absolute identifying and merging of the instruments of that "elite"—that is, of the Party— with the state executive and administrative apparatus, the total concentration of all social functions in the hands of that apparatus, the maximum centralization within that system—that is, the concentration of all authority in the hands of a central few—and the subjection of the whole field of science and ideas to the interests of the system's survival.[109]

In these circumstances, Kardelj explained, the Stalinist ideology was not the legitimate heir of the revolution but an instrument for the justification of the ruling bureaucracy:

Let the high priests of the Cominformist Stalinist cult quote Marx and Lenin to exhaustion, yet they are daily finding it more difficult to conceal the gods and the ends they serve in converting today the already ancient stories of the origin of their power, which allegedly sprang from the flames of the revolution like a phoenix from the ashes, into a modern divine-metaphysical and petty-profiteering Stalinist rigmarole about how the fires of the Russian Revolution not only bestowed infallibility on the present Soviet state leadership, but even blessed it with the right and duty of proclaiming the "eternal truths" of socialism and "dialectical materialism." In point of fact, by protecting the untenable material and political privileges of one caste, which has become a fateful obstruction on the path to social-ism, they are compelled to declare as "solely socialist" precisely that which is not socialist, which has even become the greatest impediment to the continued progress of socialism.[110]

These and quite a few other critical analyses by Yugoslav Com-munists of the theory and practice of Stalinism were made in Stalin's lifetime, during the Stalin era. They testified to the fact that Stalinism had lost its monopoly on the interpretation of Marxism not only in practice but also in theory. Indeed, its methods of government and many crucial features of the Stalinist system, as well as the Stalin doctrine proclaimed to justify it, had long become shackles not only for the world Communist movement but for the further development of the Soviet Union itself.

"Tomorrow Stalin will be an embarrassment for the ruling stratum," Trotsky had prophesied in the mid-1930's. "Stalin is near the conclusion of his tragic mission. The more it seems that he needs no one else, the nearer the moment approaches when no one will need him. Moreover, Stalin will receive scarcely a word of thanks for the work he has done. . . . Stalin will leave the stage loaded with all the crimes he has committed."[111]

Stalin's death marked the opening of a new phase in the develop-ment of the Soviet Union and of world Communism. The monolithic character of world Communism belonged to the past. The differentia-tion of world Communism was shown in the emergence of three currents, three different interpretations of Marxism. De-Stalinization in the Soviet Union, though proceeding hesitantly and inconsistently, found its ideological expression in the Soviet political doctrine of scientific Communism. Chinese Communism dissociated itself totally from Moscow, not only in its political practice but also in its ideology—a process eventually leading to the development of the great teaching of Mao Tse-tung, hailed by the Chinese Communists as the "culmination of Marxism-Leninism." Finally, proceeding from Yugoslavia's own development after 1948, there arose the trend known as humanist Marxism, which found supporters on an increasing scale in the different Communist countries and parties. The aim of the humanist Marxists was the realization of a new, freer, and more humane model of socialism, the stripping of Marxist political theory of all later falsifications and deformations, the re-examination of the fundamental concepts and humanistic origins of Marx and Engels and their placement in the framework of our present-day problems.

It is with these currents in present-day world Communism that the second part of this book is concerned.

# Part II

## The Three Mainstreams of Contemporary Marxism

# 4

## Soviet Political Doctrines Since Stalin

"The heart of Lenin's comrade-in-arms and the inspired continuer of his work, the heart of the wise leader and teacher of the Communist Party and the Soviet people, Iosif Vissarionovich Stalin, has ceased to beat."

With these words Moscow radio announced the death of Stalin on the morning of March 6, 1953. At once a dissociation from Stalin became noticeable. The obsequies were confined to a minimum. Of the top leaders, who until then had invariably praised Stalin in the most extravagant terms, not one wrote a commemorative article. By the end of March 1953, Stalin's name appeared less and less often in the Soviet press. *Pravda* proclaimed collectivity as "one of the fundamental principles of Party leadership" since "individual decisions are always or almost always one-sided decisions."[1] The Party leadership declared that "a feeling for what is new" was "the most important characteristic of a Party member"[2]—a clear hint of imminent changes and reforms. The wave of purges was suspended, the principle of "socialist legality" was proclaimed,[3] and Soviet citizens already detained were released.

Thus, within a few weeks of Stalin's death, there began a change of course, a de-Stalinization, an attempt by the Soviet leadership by means of reforms controlled and directed from above to move away step by step from many aspects of Stalinism and to adapt the Soviet system to the changed conditions and requirements.

Even the higher echelons of the Kremlin leadership realized that the problems of the emerging Soviet industrial society could no longer be solved by Stalinist methods—by police terror, slave labor, and the centralized bureaucratic regulation of all spheres of life. During the Stalin era (1929–53) the foundations of a modern industrial society had been laid with brutal terror and coercion. During that quarter of a century the number of industrial workers and office workers had more than trebled. The social structure had changed completely. Millions of skilled workers, hundreds of thousands of technicians and engineers had been trained in professional schools, colleges, and universities. The industrial workers, technicians and engineers, managers and scientists, writers and artists had all gained in importance. The Soviet Union had meanwhile reached an industrial level which required differentiated methods of direction, and people able to tackle the complex new problems because of their own motives and interest, people who could show initiative and freely develop their abilities. Economic managers in the cities and in the country, workers and collective farmers had to be freed from their paralyzing fear and given a measure of personal security and a few basic rights which they had been denied under Stalin.

Moreover, after Stalin's death the Soviet leaders were faced with a large number of foreign political problems that required new solutions. The onset of the atomic age, the new military and political situation created by nuclear armaments, the massive progress of national liberation movements in the developing countries, the emergence of dozens of new independent states in Asia and Africa, the growing importance of international organizations, and many other new phenomena called for new political ideas that would take account of the changed circumstances—especially as the Soviet Union was changing more and more from a continental empire into a world power.

Added to this were the new problems of the world Communist movement. The Soviet Union was no longer the only Communist-ruled country in the world. Until the early 1950's the Soviet Union managed to keep the people's democracies of Eastern and Southeastern Europe in the status of satellites; subsequently this became increasingly difficult. With the Soviet-Yugoslav conflict in the summer of 1948 and socialist Yugoslavia's independent posture, a Marxist alternative to Stalinist-type Soviet Communism had come into being. After the victory of the Chinese Revolution in 1949, a new power factor arose in the Communist world, one which in the long run could not be overlooked. But other socialist countries, thanks to their increasing economic and political strength, also began to extend their specific influence. Under these circumstances the Soviet leadership could no longer maintain its monopolistic position in its former Stalinist form. Here, too, it had to adapt to new circumstances, take account of new forces, and realize the Soviet Union's "leading role" in world Communism in a more flexible form.

The retreat from Stalin's outdated doctrines and methods of government became necessary in order to adapt to new circumstances and also to the leadership's own objectives. The Soviet leadership viewed (and still views) as one of its main tasks the fastest possible economic advance of the U.S.S.R., the introduction of the most modern technology, and the full automation of entire industries, in order to catch up with and outstrip the U.S.A. in the shortest time. To achieve this it was (and is) necessary to allow economic managers, technicians, and engineers greater flexibility, to free the economy and research from the fetters of state, Party, and ideological tutelage, to increase material incentives, and to enable representatives of the workers to participate in the management of enterprises.

However, the modernization of the economic system was in turn inseparably linked with a multitude of reforms in the social, political, administrative, and cultural spheres. The development of Soviet society urgently demanded the abandonment of Stalin's centralized bureaucratic, terrorist dictatorship and a change to more modern, more efficient, more flexible, and more liberal methods of government. Such a development, however, implied not only the elimination of the terrorist components of the system but also the abandonment, or at least the extensive curtailment, of the all-embracing dictatorship of the Party machine. Terror would have to be replaced by legal guarantees, decrees, and pressure from above by participation and initiative from the society. The necessary reforms thus were (and are) permanently at variance with the political power interests of the apparatus and the leadership, whose members will invariably oppose all "excessive" reforms, endeavoring to confine them to the smallest possible measure, or to obstruct them altogether.

Soviet developments since Stalin's death have, therefore, clearly reflected two trends: on the one hand the necessity to abandon outdated forms and methods of government and to adapt the system to the requirements of a developed industrial society, and on the other hand the attempts of the leadership and the Party apparatus to contain the necessary changes within the framework of the system, so as not to lose control over it. The operation of these two factors explains both the extent and the limitations of the changes since Stalin's death.

Whereas the first eleven years after Stalin's death (the so-called Khrushchev period, from 1953 to 1964) were characterized—even though on a continual zigzag course and with many oscillations—by de-Stalinization, the period since Khrushchev's overthrow (October 1964) has been marked by a harder course and by neo-Stalinist trends.

All this was clearly reflected in ideology, especially in political concepts. During the post-Stalinist period, ideology was reduced, more than ever before, to serve practical politics—sometimes to psychologically prepare a planned reform, more often to justify a certain political action of the leadership. Never before had political concepts been changed so frequently; never before had new doctrines been produced so rapidly—only to be presently reinforced or weakened in accordance with the changing practical situation. This ideological zigzag was also clearly reflected in the principal ideological publications after Stalin's death— the speeches and resolutions of the Twentieth Party Congress (February 1956), the textbook *Fundamentals of Marxism-Leninism* (October 1959), the Declaration of the Eighty-one Communist Parties (December 1960), the new Soviet Party program (October 1961), and *Foundations of Scientific Communism* (1967), the official ideological textbook after Khrushchev's fall.

Three areas of Soviet ideology have been at the center of attention since Stalin's death: the doctrines justifying de-Stalinization and adaptation to the conditions and tasks of a modern Soviet industrial society; a multiplicity of doctrines reflecting the Soviet Union's foreign and international objectives (which, in view of the U.S.S.R.'s increasing role in world politics, were gaining importance); and political doctrines concerned with internal Soviet developments in the future (i.e., the problems of transition to Communism and to the future Communist society).

## ☐ The First Steps to de-Stalinization (1953–56)

The widespread view that de-Stalinization began, both in practice and in ideology, with the Twentieth Party Congress in February 1956 is incorrect. The very first three years after Stalin's death witnessed a "silent de-Stalinization" which considerably changed the political atmosphere of the Soviet Union.

A dictator enjoying Byzantine adulation had been replaced by a collective leadership whose members were not perhaps equals but who were at least strong enough to prevent the emergence of a new leader. The methods of leadership, too, began to change. Under Stalin the top leaders had resided in the Kremlin, hermetically sealed off from the people, but they moved out at the beginning of 1954. The Kremlin was thrown open—something inconceivable under Stalin—at first for a few special events and later, in May 1955, to all visitors. The Soviet leaders—Khrushchev, Malenkov, Molotov, Bulganin, and Mikoyan—frequently visited different regions of the Soviet Union, meeting medium and lower functionaries, visiting local Party conferences, factories, and collective farms. Visits to foreign countries and meetings with foreign diplomats and journalists became more frequent.

The secret police, the feared, all-powerful institution of terror of the Stalin era, was first publicly criticized shortly after Stalin's death. The wave of arrests initiated by Stalin was suspended, "socialist legality" was proclaimed, and for May Day, 1953, the Central Committee announced a new and rather unusual slogan: "The Soviet citizens' rights, as guaranteed by the Constitution, are inalienable and are protected by the Soviet Government." Beria's overthrow in the summer of 1953 was followed by a significant reduction in the powers of the terror apparatus. The "special courts" introduced in 1934, which had played such a disastrous role in the purges from 1936 to 1938, were dissolved. Hundreds of thousands of inmates were released from the camps and the living conditions of the prisoners who remained in the camps and places of detention were improved. Public trials were held, including the Abakumov trial in December 1954, in which the former top state security officials were indicted for having arrested innocent people on the pretext of fictitious (but in fact non-existent) conspiracies and having forced them, by criminal methods of interrogation, to make false statements and confessions.[4] The suspension of mass arrests, the curtailment of the powers of the secret police, and the promise of a new penal code encouraged large groups of the population to hope that a liberalization of the system had begun.

In the field of economic policy Premier Malenkov in August 1953 announced the new consumer goods program and thereby abandoned Stalin's doctrine of the priority of heavy industry. For more than a year the emphasis was on increased production of consumer goods. Even though this was again reversed in early 1955—when Malenkov lost his post of Premier—the departure from Stalinism was nonetheless noticeable in other areas of economic policy. A decentralization of the economic system was begun; factory directors and collective farm chairmen received new, somewhat more extensive, powers. Stalin's theses, set forth in his *Economic Problems of Socialism in the U.S.S.R.,* were publicly criticized. Financial alleviations for collective farmers, the announcement of a reform of industrial wages, and the active role given to the trade unions—which, at the Twelfth Trade Union Congress in March 1954 and at the July 1955 Plenum of the Party were at long last granted the right of championing the social interests of manual and office workers—seemed to herald an improvement in the position of workers and peasants.

The sphere of cultural policy was marked by the "Thaw." In spite of repeated zigzags, a certain relaxation was unmistakable. Writers and poets produced works whose publication would have been unthinkable under Stalin. His ostentatious architecture was officially condemned and the demand made that energy should be concentrated on erecting housing for the population rather than magnificent public buildings. Soviet architecture should be "distinguished by simplicity, severity of form, and efficiency."[5]

Stalin's isolationism was replaced by the slogan "learning from abroad." Sessions of the Central Committee were openly told about those industries and products in which the Soviet Union was still lagging far behind foreign countries, and from which countries and in what areas there was much to be learned.

A change was also beginning to take place in the Soviet Union's relations with the other socialist countries. The number of overseers and "advisers" was reduced, the so-called "mixed companies" (which granted huge privileges to the Soviet Union) were described as outdated and dissolved.[6] In the autumn of 1954, *Pravda* for the first time stated that the experiences of the Soviet Union could not be "mechanically applied" to the socialist countries of Eastern Europe. Instead, the economic policy of those countries must be worked out "with regard for the specific features of the given country's historical development, the level of productive forces, and the specific features of class relationships."[7] Stalin's anti-Yugoslav campaign was toned down and eventually stopped altogether. On November 29, 1954, at a Yugoslav Embassy reception in Moscow, Khrushchev and Malenkov raised their glasses "to the health of Comrade Tito and the Communist Party of Yugoslavia." At the beginning of May 1955, Marshal Zhukov urged that the Soviet-Yugoslav conflict be "rapidly liquidated and amicable relations between our countries restored."[8] Following this psychological and political preparation, Khrushchev's famous journey to Belgrade took place toward the end of May 1955. "The grave accusations and insults," directed against Yugoslav Communists in the past, Khrushchev said on his arrival at Belgrade airport, had been wrong; they had been "fabricated by agents of imperialism who fraudulently infiltrated the ranks of our Party."[9] The conclusion of the Soviet-Yugoslav talks was the first occasion ever for Soviet leaders to declare that "questions of the internal order" and differences in "the concrete forms of development of socialism are exclusively matters for the people of the countries concerned."[10]

In the ideological field it was noted that Stalin and the *Short Course of the History of the Communist Party of the Soviet Union* were being pushed into the background. Publication of Stalin's collected works—the first thirteen volumes had appeared by the time of his death—was suspended. The new theses of the Central Committee, *Fifty Years of the Communist Party of the Soviet Union,* published in July 1953, mentioned Stalin only five times as against more than forty references to Lenin; moreover, the charges against Trotsky, Bukharin, Kamenev, and Zinoviev, until then defamed as "enemies of the people" and "agents," were considerably toned down.[11] A new edition of the Resolutions and Decisions of the Soviet Communist Party from 1898 to 1953 appeared at the beginning of 1954; this contained a number of documents not included in earlier collections published during the Stalin era. The new collection was clearly designed to replace Stalin's *Short Course.*[12]

Apart from the diminution of Stalin's role and the incipient revision of Party history, the period of "silent de-Stalinization" was marked also by a turning away from Stalinist isolationism. Under Stalin, and in particular during his last years, Soviet historians had been made to concentrate on the country's own history, with any serious study of other countries being labeled "cosmopolitanism." They were now criticized because they "poorly follow foreign historical literature and the state of historiography in the capitalist countries." The history of the Western countries, it was said, had been neglected, and it was regrettable that only one major work on the history of the U.S.A. was available. Major historical figures of other countries had frequently been judged one-sidedly and it was a mistake—it was now asserted—that "the outstanding scholar and public figure of the eighteenth century, Benjamin Franklin," had been described as "an exponent of the idea of world rule by the American bourgeoisie." The traditions of other nations must not be underrated, and Soviet historians should in future devote more attention to the history of the capitalist countries.[13]

For the first time Soviet historians were being encouraged to strengthen their contacts with foreign scholars. The isolationist and nationalist Russian historiography was criticized. It was the duty of Soviet historians to "uncover as fully as possible" the history of all nations of the world, great and small alike.[14]

The new features of capitalism were to be studied more earnestly and objectively. "Many scholars are adopting a dogmatic and over-simplified attitude to the economic situation of present-day capitalism. This is reflected in an unfounded rejection or in the concealment of achievements attained in the capitalist countries as a result of the development of production, science, and technology."[15] In 1954 even the official Party periodical warned against "over-simplified ideas about the rotting of capitalism, such as are bandied about in our own propaganda." Such views resulted in "the achievements of the capitalist countries in the fields of production, science, and technology being denied or passed over in silence." It was important "to assess correctly the forces and potentialities of capitalism, without belittling or exaggerating."[16]

This incipient de-Stalinization in ideology, however, could take place only if Soviet ideologists, historians, and economists were, to some extent at least, relieved of the paralyzing fear of committing "a mistake," if discussion and exchanges of views were encouraged. In point of fact, Soviet periodicals repeatedly criticized "dogmatism" and "book learning" after 1954, demanding instead the "development of a clash of opinions and scientific criticism, with free discussion of controversial issues."[17] In the autumn of 1954, a Soviet periodical reproached the publishers of theoretical writings with showing excessive caution and a tendency to play it safe. "Many manuscripts are re-edited countless times. In consequence, one and the same essay is continuously rewritten, put up for discussion once more, again worked over and once more discussed, as a result of which its value is by no means enhanced."[18] Similarly, there was not enough free, creative discussion among academic economists: "This state of affairs is due partly to the wish to play it safe and the fear of certain directors of putting controversial questions up for discussion." Under these circumstances the economists would confine themselves to quotations from the classics of Marxism-Leninism and to the assembly of facts "which merely serve to illustrate and confirm the tenets expressed in the quotations."[19]

Any independent and creative work by historians or academic economists, however, was possible only if they were given access to archives—but the archives were in the hands of the Ministry of the Interior (MVD). "The central MVD archives contain much larger quantities of material than other archives," a historical periodical complained in the autumn of 1954.

Every bit of manuscript that is sent to the reader's hall is examined by an archive worker to see whether it corresponds to the researcher's topic and whether he may be permitted to see it. Each document copied by the researcher, whether material of the 1917 Revolutionary Committee or a *prikaz* of the seventeenth century, is again examined by the archive worker.

The checking of the reader's notes and permission to copy material usually drags on for a very long time.[20]

At the beginning of 1955 Soviet historians were enjoined to engage in a "creative examination" of Soviet history. They were not to confine themselves to quotations from the classics of Marxism-Leninism but were to draw "independent conclusions" and not hush up the difficulties encountered in the building of socialism: "Mistakes and shortcomings which occurred in the practice of socialist construction were often passed over in silence. The development of Soviet society was represented as one triumphal progress. In the writings of some historians, this resulted in a touched-up and hence distorted picture of history."[21] Stalin's *Short Course* was no longer to be a model for Soviet historiography, since it was wrong "to transfer mechanically the pattern of Party history to the history of Soviet society by dividing it into corresponding periods."[22] At the beginning of January 1955 the post-Stalinist leadership decided that the annual Lenin commemorations would no longer take place, as before, on the anniversary of his death (January 21), but on that of his birth (April 22). Instead of the glorification of Stalin and the Stalin era, Lenin was now moved into the center in order, as the decision of January 4, 1955, put it, "to lend this day a significance that would reflect to a greater measure the whole spirit of Leninism as an eternally living, life-asserting teaching."[23]

By the autumn of 1955, a Party periodical was warning against the "political harmfulness of the cult of personality," demanding the abolishment of dogmatism and announcing that Stalin's *Short Course* would be replaced by new publications, since the reader expected "fundamental studies of Party history."[24] Early in January 1956, at a conference of 600 historians, the well-known Soviet historian Anna Pankratova and E. N. Burdzhalov, the deputy editor of the periodical *Voprosi Istorii,* in particular, called for a re-examination of Party history. It was impossible, they said, that historians, as had been the practice until then, should write about Party congresses without using the shorthand records. Party history must be cleansed of falsifications.[25]

All these changes in domestic, economic, and cultural policy— the methods of leadership, the attitudes to the other socialist countries— and in ideology testified to the change of direction that had been taking place in the Soviet Union between 1953 and 1956. The departure from Stalinism had begun. But so far Stalin had not been criticized directly. Now, at the beginning of 1956, the moment had come to change from indirect criticism of Stalin to open criticism—both in order to justify the dissociation from Stalin that had already begun and in order to prepare

the ground for further de-Stalinization. This happened at the Twentieth
Party Congress.

☐   **The New Concepts of the Twentieth Party Congress**

The Twentieth Congress of the Communist Party of the Soviet
Union was held in Moscow, February 14–25, 1956. Mikoyan rightly
declared that "the Twentieth Party Congress is the most important
Congress in the history of our Party since Lenin."[26] This is no exaggeration, as the Twentieth Congress brought important changes in Soviet
policy and ideology.

The first thing to strike the delegates was the dissociation from
Stalinism. Stalin's portrait was missing from the Congress hall. In his
seven-hour report Khrushchev mentioned Stalin only once—and that
was a reference to his death. Stalin's terrorist despotism—always
described at the Party Congress as "the cult of personality"—was condemned by nearly all the top Soviet leaders. Malenkov observed that
the personality cult had led to "the suppression of the creative activity
of the Party masses," to "peremptory one-man decisions," and hence
"to arbitrariness."[27] Mikhail Suslov, the Party ideologist, criticized the
dogmatism and stagnation of Marxist theory. All that was left to the
ordinary mortal, he said, was to "assimilate and popularize" Stalin's
directives.[28] Khrushchev declared that during the Stalin era the secret
police had placed itself "above the Party and the government" and that
"an atmosphere of lawlessness and arbitrariness" had reigned. The
secret police had "fabricated false charges against honest leading officials
and rank-and-file Soviet citizens." For the elimination of the personality
cult Khrushchev proclaimed the "restoration of justice." The rehabilitation of innocently condemned people was to be continued, and the
secret police to be placed under "the proper control by the Party and the
government." Party organs must "unmask . . . anyone who violates
socialist law and order and the rights of Soviet citizens, and sternly call
a halt to the slightest manifestation of lawlessness and arbitrariness."[29]
Khrushchev further urged that the history of the Party be cleansed of
Stalinist falsifications: "During the past seventeen years our propaganda
was based mainly on the *History of the Communist Party of the Soviet
Union (Short Course)*." It was now necessary to produce a "Marxist
textbook on the history of the Party, based on historical fact"—a clear
hint by Khrushchev that he did not regard the *Short Course,* generally
ascribed to Stalin, as a book founded on historical fact.[30]

Mikoyan, who went further than any other of the Soviet leaders in his criticism of Stalin, observed that "for about twenty years we had in fact no collective leadership; the cult of the individual flourished." As for a "capitalist encirclement"—one of Stalin's crucial doctrines—there could be, Mikoyan said, "no question of this now." Soviet foreign policy, he said, had made "mistakes" in the past, and in some cases the Soviets "were to blame for the aggravation of relations." Mikoyan also criticized "the isolation of Soviet public and state organizations from the outside world." The thesis, current under Stalin, of "capitalism's complete stagnation" was wrong, and Stalin's *Economic Problems of Socialism* was "hardly correct" since it "does not explain the complex and contradictory phenomena of contemporary capitalism and the fact that capitalist production has grown in many countries since the war." Other tenets of Stalin also needed "critical revision." The new phenomena in capitalism needed to be "strictly scrutinized." Much historical research of the Stalin era "stretched the facts, arbitrarily exalted some people and failed even to mention others, exaggerated secondary events and belittled other, more important events." Complex and contradictory events were being "explained by some historians not as changes in the correlations of class forces at a specific period of time but as alleged sabotage by some of the Party leaders of the time, who were wrongly declared enemies of the people many years after the events described." Such "historical nonsense" had nothing in common with a Marxist view of history. Mikoyan called on historians to see not only the facade "without embellishment" but to describe the many facets of life in the Soviet Union. He used plain words about the stagnation of Marxist-Leninist theory: "We do not experience profound Marxist-Leninist creative work. The majority of our theoreticians are engaged in repeating and paraphrasing old quotations, formulas and precepts." All this would have to change because it was important "that we not only swear by Lenin's name but are exerting all our efforts to put Lenin's ideas into practice."[31] This critique of the Stalin era provided the prerequisites also for abandoning Stalin's doctrines in the international sphere and proclaiming new ideological concepts in tune with the changed conditions of the Soviet Union.

The Soviet Union's growing role in world politics within the framework of the atomic age made it necessarry for the doctrine of the "inevitability of wars," elaborated by Lenin and adopted by Stalin, to be declared invalid. On February 14, 1956, in his report to the Twentieth Party Congress, Khrushchev announced the new thesis of the noninevitability of wars. Lenin's ideas about the inevitability of wars, Khrushchev explained, had been worked out at a time when imperialism was still an all-embracing world system. At that time no one had been able to compel the imperialist forces to renounce wars. Lenin's thesis had been valid for World War I and partially still for World War II, but meanwhile "a world camp of socialism" had arisen and grown into a "mighty force." Moreover, there was a group of other countries— Khrushchev evidently referred to the neutral countries of Asia and Africa—which was likewise not interested in war. Finally, the workers' movement and the peace movement had become powerful factors. At present, therefore, there were powerful forces in existence capable of preventing the imperialists from unleashing a war. True, Khrushchev admitted, so long as imperialism existed, "the economic base giving rise to wars will also remain," and there were still reactionary forces eager for warlike adventures and aggression, "but war is not a fatalistic inevitability."[32]

The new concept of the non-inevitability of wars—attacked by the Chinese Communists in the 1960's—formed the cornerstone of the foreign policy doctrine of coexistence. Although Stalin, as mentioned earlier, had referred to coexistence with Western (capitalist) countries in interviews with foreign correspondents, it was only at the Twentieth Party Congress that coexistence was proclaimed as an ideological doctrine of the Soviet Communist Party.

Khrushchev declared that countries with different social problems could not only coexist side by side but must aim at an improvement of relations and a strengthening of confidence and mutual co-operation. Peaceful coexistence implied also economic competition between the two systems. This was now raised to the supreme ideological principle. "The Leninist principle of peaceful coexistence of states with different social systems has always been and remains the general line of our country's foreign policy." Coexistence was "not a tactical move, but a fundamental principle of Soviet foreign policy. . . . Indeed, there are only two ways—either peaceful coexistence or the most destructive war in history. There is no third way." Peaceful coexistence, however, was not to be transferred to ideology. He said that from the fact that the U.S.S.R. supports peaceful coexistence and economic competition with capitalism it must on no account be deduced that the struggle against bourgeois ideology, against the remnants of capitalism in the consciousness of people may be weakened. It was to continue to be the Party's task to unmask bourgeois ideology, its anti-popular character, its reactionary nature.[33]

The Twentieth Party Congress also proclaimed new ideological concepts for the world Communist movement. While under Stalin Soviet development was praised as the only example for Communists in all countries, the Twentieth Congress for the first time reverted to the concept (previously supported by Marx, Engels, and Lenin) of different roads to socialism in different countries. Khrushchev declared that "the forms of transition to socialism are getting more and more varied."[34] Otto Kuusinen, a long-time leader of international Communism, regarded the thesis of the different roads to socialism as "of great theoretical importance" for the policy of Communist parties in capitalist countries. It must be realized "that the path of transition to socialism is not the same wide street . . . for all countries."[35]

In this connection the Twentieth Party Congress, also for the first time, stressed the possibility of peaceful socialist transformation. Under Stalin, as mentioned earlier, the thesis had been held that a revolution could be accomplished only by violence. Khrushchev now declared that, although the Soviet Communists continued to be convinced of the "revolutionary transformation of capitalist society into socialist society," the transition to socialism was not necessarily "associated with civil war under all circumstances." Since the Russian Revolution of 1917, "fundamental changes have taken place, permitting a new approach to the issue." The forces of socialism had grown stronger, while those of capitalism had become weaker. In a number of capitalist countries there existed, therefore, a realistic possibility of "inflicting a defeat upon the reactionary anti-people's forces, capturing a stable majority in parliament and converting it from an organ of bourgeois democracy into a tool of the real will of the people" with a view to "implementing fundamental social transformation."[36]

A decisive turnabout had therefore taken place even before the meetings of the Twentieth Party Congress were over. The Soviet leadership had dissociated itself from Stalin and the Stalin era and had criticized the Party history valid until 1956. Simultaneously the Twentieth Party Congress had announced important new theses—about the non-inevitability of wars, about coexistence as the general line and fundamental principle of Soviet foreign policy, about each country's right to its own road to socialism, and about the possibility of the socialist revolution having a peaceful character.

However, this new political and ideological line encountered the opposition of conservative and dogmatic circles and could be forced through only after a tough battle. In order to break the opposition of these circles and (as Khrushchev recalled on a later occasion) to apply a "shock" to the conservative and dogmatic circles, the Khrushchev wing in the leadership had decided on a much more far-reaching step—an open and sharp condemnation of Stalin. Thus, at the morning session of February 25, 1956, there was made what is probably the most important report in the history of the Bolshevik Party. At a closed session, to which only the regular Congress delegates were invited, Khrushchev read a forty-three page manuscript entitled "The Personality Cult and Its Consequences," which has become known outside the Soviet Union as "Khrushchev's secret speech."

## ☐ Khrushchev's Secret Speech

Less than three years after the death of Stalin—who during his lifetime was praised and glorified in the Soviet Union and in the world Communist movement more than any other Communist leader ever had been—Khrushchev in his secret speech now presented a totally different and undoubtedly much more truthful picture. Khrushchev's observations clearly revealed his intention of dissociating himself from the past by underlining the negative and criminal aspects of Stalinism, while at the same time so limiting his criticism that the authority and power of the Soviet Communist Party and its apparatus were not threatened.

In his secret speech Khrushchev proceeded from the observations of Marx and Engels which opposed the glorification of individuals. Khrushchev reminded his audience of Lenin's personal modesty and of the fact that in his day Party congresses and Plenary meetings of the Central Committee were held regularly. Of particular importance was the fact that Khrushchev quoted from Lenin's "Testament"—until then kept strictly secret—and disclosed Lenin's decision to break with Stalin. In view of subsequent developments, Khrushchev observed, "Lenin's anxiety was justified."

In his characterization of Stalin, Khrushchev emphasized, above all, his "despotic character":

Stalin acted not through persuasion, explanation, and patient co-operation with people, but by imposing his concepts and demanding absolute sub-mission to his opinion. Whoever opposed this concept or tried to prove his viewpoint and the correctness of his position was doomed to removal from the leading collective and to subsequent moral and physical annihilation. This was especially true during the period following the Seventeenth Party Congress, when many prominent Party leaders and rank-and-file Party workers, honest and dedicated to the cause of Communism, fell victim to Stalin's despotism.[37]

During the period from Lenin's death to the Seventeenth Party Congress in January 1934, during the country's industrialization and the struggle against Trotskyites and Bukharinites—Khrushchev explained—Stalin had played a "positive role." The turning point had come at the time of the Seventeenth Congress. At that time, "when the ideological opponents of the Party were long since defeated politically—then the repression directed against them began."

The great purge of 1936–38 was described by Khrushchev as "mass repression," justified by the term "enemies of the people," introduced by Stalin.

This term automatically rendered it unnecessary that the ideological errors of a man or men engaged in a controversy be proven; this term made possible the usage of the most cruel repression, violating all norms of revolutionary legality, against anyone who in any way disagreed with Stalin, against those who were only suspected of hostile intent, against those who had bad reputations. . . . The only proof of guilt used, against all norms of current legal science, was the "confession" of the accused himself; and, as subsequent probing proved, "confessions" were acquired through physical pressure against the accused.

The great purge, as Khrushchev now openly informed his audience, had led to the liquidation of loyal and devoted Communists. "It became apparent that many Party, Soviet, and economic activists, who were branded in 1937–38 as 'enemies,' were actually never enemies, spies, wreckers, etc., but were always honest Communists; they were only so stigmatized and, often, no longer able to bear barbaric tortures, they accused themselves."

The result of the great purge had been disastrous. "It was determined," Khrushchev stated, "that of the 139 members and candidates of the Party's Central Committee who were elected at the Seventeenth Congress, ninety-eight persons, i.e., 70 per cent, were arrested and shot ( mostly in 1937–38 )." The mass arrests had entailed also grave moral consequences in the Party; they "created a situation of uncertainty, contributed to the spreading of unhealthy suspicion, and sowed distrust among Communists. All sorts of slanderers and careerists were active." The Soviet armed forces had likewise been weakened by the great purge: "During these years repressions were instituted against certain parts of military cadres beginning literally at the company and battalion commander level and extending to the higher military centers; during this time the cadre of leaders who had gained military experience in Spain and in the Far East was almost completely liquidated."

The mass arrests in the army, according to Khrushchev, had been a decisive cause of the Soviet defeats at the beginning of the war in 1941. Khrushchev—quite rightly—accused Stalin of having dismissed the numerous warnings, both from Western and from Soviet sources, about

Hitler's impending attack on June 22, 1941. In contrast to the version of Soviet history valid until then, which praised Stalin's courage and resolution and his military genius, Khrushchev disclosed that "after the first severe disaster and defeat at the front, Stalin thought that this was the end. In one of his speeches at the time he said: 'All that Lenin created we have lost forever.' " As for the military operations, Stalin had no longer taken any part in them at all during the first few months of the war. When the members of the Central Committee were summoned to Moscow to a meeting in October 1941, they had waited "two days for the opening of the Plenum, but in vain. Stalin did not even want to meet with and talk to the Central Committee members." Khrushchev emphasized that during the first few months of the war Stalin had been "demoralized" and had shown "symptoms of nervousness and hysteria."

Throughout the whole war Stalin had "never visited any section of the front or any liberated city except for one short ride along the Mozhaisk highway during a stabilized situation at the front. To this incident were later dedicated many literary works, full of fantasies of all sorts, and so many paintings."

Stalin's interference in military operations had inflicted "serious damage," especially since Stalin would frequently issue orders "which did not take into consideration the real situation at a given section of the front and which could not help but result in huge losses of personnel." As a particularly serious example Khrushchev quoted Stalin's directive for the Soviet counteroffensive at the end of 1941, when Stalin "instead of great operational maneuvers flanking the opponent and penetrating behind his back . . . demanded incessant frontal attacks and the capture of one village after another. Because of this, we paid with great losses." More disastrous still had been Stalin's refusal, in the early summer of 1942, to allow the Soviet troops in the Kharkov area to be pulled back in good time: "Contrary to common sense, Stalin rejected our suggestion and issued the order to continue the operation aimed at the encirclement of Kharkov, despite the fact that at this time many army concentrations were themselves actually threatened with encirclement and annihilation." As a result of Stalin's interference the Soviet troops had been encircled, "and we lost hundreds of thousands of our soldiers."

Khrushchev further accused Stalin—also quite rightly—of having deported entire nations, including the Karachai and Kalmucks (late 1943), the Chechens and Ingush (March 1944), and the Balkars (April 1944). He did not, however, mention the Volga Germans or the Crimean Tartars who had also been deported. The "mass deportations . . . of whole nations, together with all Communists and Komsomols," Khrushchev declared, were "not dictated by any military considerations. . . . The Ukrainians avoided meeting this fate only because there were too many of them and there was no place to which to deport them. Otherwise, he would have deported them also."

By the end of the war the situation had become "even more complicated." Stalin had become "even more capricious, irritable and brutal; in particular, his suspicion grew. His persecution mania reached unbelievable dimensions." While the Soviet people and the Party were faced with the task of rebuilding their war-ravaged country, Stalin had staged imaginary conspiracies, such as the "Leningrad affair" (the Leningrad secret trial, in the spring of 1949, of the Politburo member Voznesensky, the Central Committee Secretary Kuznetsov, and others), the "Mingrelian affair" (the purge of the Party apparatus in Georgia in 1951–52), the "affair of the Kremlin doctors" (the arrest and investigation of thirteen Kremlin doctors in January 1953). These "affairs" had served the purpose of precipitating the Soviet Union into a new great purge. Khrushchev disclosed that, at the time of the affair of the Kremlin doctors toward the end of 1952, Stalin had threatened S. D. Ignatyev, then Minister of State Security: "If you do not obtain confessions from the doctors we will shorten you by a head." Stalin had summoned the investigating judge to his presence and given him detailed instructions on the investigation methods to be applied. "These methods were very simple—beat, beat and, once again, beat."

Khrushchev—again quite rightly—held Stalin responsible for the Soviet-Yugoslav conflict. Although, according to Khrushchev, it would have been "completely possible" to avoid a conflict with Yugoslavia, Stalin had begun to inflate the affair artificially. Khrushchev himself had been summoned from Kiev to Moscow, where Stalin had told him: "I will shake my little finger—and there will be no more Tito. He will fall." This remark had been typical of Stalin's "mania for greatness." Stalin "had completely lost consciousness of reality; he demonstrated his suspicion and haughtiness not only in relation to individuals in the U.S.S.R., but in relation to whole parties and nations."

Khrushchev's critical examination also dealt with Stalin's self-adulation. He called the official *Short Biography of Stalin,* published in 1948, "an example of how a man is made into an idol, how he is turned into an infallible sage—into the 'greatest leader,' into a 'sublime strategist of all times and nations.' Finally, no new words could be found with which to lift Stalin up to the heavens." Khrushchev quoted a few concrete examples of how Stalin himself supplemented and magnified the praise bestowed on his person. Not even the czars had endowed prizes in their own names—but Stalin had introduced "Stalin prizes," he had personally chosen as the best text for the new Soviet national anthem (introduced in 1944) the version that contained the words: "Stalin brought us up in loyalty to the people. He inspired us to great toil and acts." On June 2, 1951, Stalin had signed the decree concerning "the erection on the Volga-Don canal of an impressive monument to Stalin" and had personally authorized the allocation of thirty-three tons of copper for this gigantic monument. At the same time he had obstructed the endowment of Lenin prizes, decided upon in August 1925, and prevented the erection of an already authorized Lenin memorial on top of the Palace of Soviets.

The principal results of Stalin's rule, Khrushchev continued, had been not only mass terror but also "crude violations of internal Party and Soviet democracy, sterile administration, deviations of all sorts, covering up the shortcomings, and varnishing of reality." Under the conditions of Stalin's rule "flatterers" and "specialists in false optimism" had come to the fore while most of the functionaries in the Party, the economy, and the state "began to work uncertainly, showed over-cautiousness, feared all which was new, feared their own shadows and began to show less initiative in their work."

Even the Soviet leaders in Stalin's immediate entourage had lived under a permanent threat. "It has happened sometimes that a man went to Stalin on his invitation as a friend," Bulganin had told Khrushchev after the end of the war, "and when he sat with Stalin, he did not know where he would be sent next—home or to jail." During the final months of Stalin's rule even the top Kremlin leaders and his closest collaborators had been in danger from Stalin's paranoia. Voroshilov had no longer been invited to Politburo meetings; Stalin had suspected him of being a British agent and had had a listening device installed in his flat. Molotov and Mikoyan had also been on Stalin's liquidation list. "It is not excluded," Khrushchev said in his report, "that had Stalin remained at the helm for another several months, Comrades Molotov and Mikoyan would probably have not delivered any speeches at this Congress."

But how had it been possible for Stalin to commit all these crimes unimpeded, in the name of the Party? Why had the other leaders not opposed Stalin's personality cult earlier? Khrushchev tried to explain this by the fact that the Politburo members had assessed Stalin's measures variously at various times. To begin with, during the first few years after Lenin's death and during the collectivization and industrialization drives, they had supported Stalin because his struggle against Trotskyites, Zinovievites, and Right-wing deviationists had, according to Khrushchev, been substantially correct. Later, however, when Stalin had begun to misuse his power more and more, conditions in the leadership had been such as to rule out all opposition. Plenary sessions of the Central Committee had no longer been called at all, and Politburo meetings only occasionally. It had thus been exceedingly difficult for the Politburo members to oppose the injustices and the grave mistakes and short-comings in the practice of leadership. Besides, since the end of the war, Stalin had begun to split up the Politburo into various committees of five, six, or seven, and in this way even Politburo members were "kept away from participation in reaching the most important state matters." Finally, Khrushchev pointed out—and here the limitations of his critique of Stalin are particularly clear—it was wrong to say that Stalin's measures had been "deeds of a giddy despot." Instead, according to Khrushchev, Stalin had believed his actions to be "in the interest of the party, of the working masses, in the name of the defense of the Revolution's gains. In this lies the whole tragedy!"

In conclusion, Khrushchev demanded the resolute abolition of the personality cult, in both "ideological-theoretical and practical work." In the ideological field he demanded that the "widespread erroneous views" in historiography, philosophy, economics, literature, and art should be critically examined from a "Marxist-Leninist viewpoint" and rectified. The Soviet national anthem was to be given a new text; Lenin prizes were to be introduced; cities, factories, and collective farms were no longer to be named after living persons. The rules of the Party statutes were to be rigorously observed and collective leadership firmly estab-lished. Particularly significant was Khrushchev's point that the principles of socialist democracy, "expressed in the Constitution of the Soviet Union" were to receive full validity. Arbitrariness and abuse of power were to be opposed, and infringements of "socialist legality" eliminated without exception."[38]

The Twentieth Party Congress has become the symbol of de-Stalinization. There is scarcely a reformist movement in the Communist world that has not since referred to the Twentieth Party Congress as its authority. Khrushchev's critique of Stalin, his dissociation from vital features of the Stalinist system, and his new concepts of de-Stalinization in domestic developments (collective leadership, socialist legality), in foreign policy (non-inevitability of wars, coexistence), and in the world Communist movement (different roads to socialism, possibility of peace-ful socialist transformation) all demonstrated his determination to find new ways.

At the same time, however, it is important to realize the limits of this critique of Stalinism. For one thing, Khrushchev's critique in his secret speech was concerned almost exclusively with Soviet develop-ments after 1934. Stalin's rise to power and the emergence of Stalinism were not included by him—no doubt deliberately. The shared responsibility of the top leaders then in office (including Khrushchev himself) was hardly touched upon in the secret speech. Even more important was the fact that Khrushchev's criticism almost exclusively concerned Stalin's person, his traits of character and methods of leadership, without any analysis of the Stalinist system. From this it followed almost logically that Khrushchev did not propose any fundamental measures for overcoming Stalinism. He confined himself almost entirely to organizational rectifications to reduce the excesses of the system. There was no mention of any fundamental changes, such as guarantees for personal safety under the law, freedom of the press, separation of the Party from the state, internal democratization of the Party, independence of the trade unions, or introduction of workers' councils and self-management of producers.

It is clear, therefore, that what the Soviet leadership wanted at that time was controlled de-Stalinization from above, and not a breakthrough to socialist democracy. In spite of these important reservations the significance of the Twentieth Party Congress is enormous: for the first time the leadership itself had provided an opportunity for dissociation from Stalinism in the most various spheres of public life.

## ☐  The Struggle for de-Stalinization

Immediately after the Twentieth Party Congress the customary meetings were held in all factories, collective farms, organizations, administrative offices, and army units. At closed Party meetings Khrushchev's secret report was read aloud, even though in a somewhat shortened and toned-down version. But even at public meetings the "personality cult" was sharply criticized. This criticism of Stalin and his rule of terror, the declarations in favor of collective leadership and socialist legality, as well as the large number of new political and ideological concepts made the public prick up its ears.

To many Soviet citizens, who had until then faithfully looked up to Stalin, the new line came as a shock. Many bureaucratic and dogmatic functionaries accepted de-Stalinization in a disciplined manner but most reluctantly. Yet most people welcomed the Twentieth Party Congress with relief and hope. It was as if a load had been taken off the minds of many people—that is how a Yugoslav correspondent working in Moscow at the time described the atmosphere. Political remarks were again heard in the streets of Moscow. In the Mausoleum visitors were heard uttering words of respect and sympathy at Lenin's sarcophagus while uttering curses at Stalin's. Remarks were beginning to be heard in Moscow attributing the mistakes of the past not to Stalin's person but to the system that had made his autocracy possible.[39] The Soviet writer Olga Bergholz wrote that the decisions of the Twentieth Party Congress had "brought us, alongside with very complicated and indeed difficult psychological experiences, also a profound moral satisfaction and an unsuspected confidence in the future." She hoped that Soviet writers would now be given that scope "in which one can breathe freely and which stimulates one's strength and one's wish to work for the good of the people."[40]

From March until June 1956 the Soviet Union underwent a considerable degree of de-Stalinization, embracing both political practice and ideology. New measures followed each other in rapid succession. Working hours on days preceding Sundays and holidays were limited to six hours (March 8, 1956), monthly advances were introduced for members of collective farms (March 10), leave for expectant and nursing mothers was extended from 77 to 112 days (March 28), and the much-feared special courts of the Ministry of the Interior were officially disbanded (April 9). In the Caucasus a trial was held of former functionaries of the secret police (April 12–26). The hated Stalin decree of June 26, 1940, was rescinded under which workers were sentenced to six weeks of obligatory educational work at their place of employment for having once been twenty minutes late. On the same day (April 25) workers were granted the right to leave their jobs and the freedom of choice of employment. Working hours for young people were reduced from eight to six hours, and a new law was issued increasing old-age pensions (May 9). The decentralization of the economy was vigorously promoted by the transfer of all enterprises of the light and textile industries, as well as shipping, to the Union Republics (May 31), a juridical commission was set up to revise the penal code (end of May), and school fees for high schools and tuition fees for universities (introduced by Stalin in 1940) were once more abolished (June 9, 1956).

These and many other practical political measures were accompanied by a significant de-Stalinization in the intellectual and ideological sphere, such as the Soviet Union never experienced before or since. In many articles the history of the Soviet Union and of the Soviet Communist Party was cleansed of various Stalinist falsifications and presented a little more truthfully. Well-known Soviet leaders who had lost their lives or been murdered during the Stalin era, and who had until then been regarded as "enemies of the people" and "spies," were now rehabilitated—among them the Politburo members Jan Rudsutak, Pavel

Postyshev, and Vlas Chubar, the old Bolshevik Andrei Bubnov, the former Komsomol General Secretary Kosarev, as well as Nikolai Skrypnik, who had committed suicide in 1933.[41] Through the publication of a letter from Lenin to Rykov,[42] that well-known leading Bolshevik, who had been sentenced to death in March 1938 as an alleged "enemy of the people" and "spy," was at least indirectly rehabilitated. The Revolution of 1917 was also reanalyzed[43]; it was frankly admitted that "the revolutionary struggle of the Party in 1917" had until then been "treated one-sidedly and in a number of instances incorrectly,"[44] and the great Russian Marxist Georgi Plekhanov, who had died in 1918, was reassessed more positively.[45] Soviet periodicals demanded that the earlier history of Russia should be cleansed of a one-sided nationalistic presentation, since an objective examination of history was incompatible with "a glossing over of the past or the hushing up of generally accepted facts."[46]

But the main emphasis was on a critical examination of the Stalin era. In the sphere of justice the usual practice (until then) of sentencing defendants merely on the strength of a personal confession was described as "a flagrant violation of the principles of socialist justice and jurisprudence."[47] Stalin's agricultural policy was now being openly criticized,[48] as was his role during the Civil War and World War II; the demand was made that historical accounts should be rectified and Soviet military science cleansed of the cult of Stalin.[49] Not even press policy was exempted from criticism: "The elements of scholasticism, political mumbo jumbo, and Talmudic 'paeans of praise' must be mercilessly eradicated from our papers."[50] The "spirit of monotony in the papers" was criticized: "A lively, interesting paper will be free from the bureaucratic tone of command."[51]

All these individual critical remarks and statements together represented a co-ordinated integral critique of the Stalinist past, intended to produce conclusions for the present and the future. "The struggle against the personality cult now being boldly waged by our Party has a profound meaning," an official Party periodical declared in the spring of 1956. "Its essence lies in a penetrating analysis of the mistakes permitted in Party and administrative work, with a view to preventing their repetition."[52] Directives from above were to be replaced by creative discussion: "Elimination of the personality cult is not a matter of banning quotations or expunging names. What matters is a truthful Marxist illumination of the process of history." Such a reorganization could "not be accomplished with the 'panacea' of the directives to which our cadres have become so accustomed, nor with 'directives' in the form of articles," but only in the form of "a free exchange of opinion, of creative discussion."[53]

In these decisive months the relations of the U.S.S.R. with the world Communist movement were also changed. Mid-April 1956 saw the dissolution of the Information Bureau of Communist and Workers' Parties (Cominform), the Stalinist control instrument for the subordination of other Communist parties. In connection with the dissolution of the Cominform, *Pravda* observed that "more than ever" the Communist parties must now be asked to carefully take into account "the specific and national characteristics of their countries," and to develop a policy of their own which would best meet the "characteristics and traditions of each people."[54]

A mere six weeks later President Tito of Yugoslavia, insulted as a "fascist" by the Soviet press only three years before, arrived in the Soviet Union on an official state visit. While he was touring the Soviet Union, accompanied by Khrushchev and Mikoyan, and enthusiastically welcomed by the Soviet population, the official Party periodical *Kommunist* published a large number of previously secret documents of Lenin, including his famous "Letter to the Party Congress," known to the world as Lenin's "Testament." For the first time, the Soviet public was now being informed not only about Lenin's demand for Stalin's dismissal but also about Lenin's fairly positive remarks about Trotsky, Bukharin, Kamenev, and Zinoviev. In an editorial statement *Kommunist* condemned not only Stalin's crimes but also Stalin's serious mistakes in agriculture, in military matters, and in the field of foreign policy, and defined the Party line as the restoration of legality, of intra-Party democracy, a new nationalities policy, and the promotion of socialist democracy.[55]

The Soviet-Yugoslav declaration signed in June 1956, at the end of Tito's visit, emphasized the independence and equality of the socialist countries and their different roads to socialism more strongly than ever before. The Soviet leaders now confirmed with their signatures that "the roads of socialist development in different countries and under different conditions differ from one another," that "the variety of forms in the development of socialism contributes to its strengthening," and that "neither the one side nor the other has any intention whatever of imposing its own views on the definition of the forms and roads of socialist development."[56] The publication of Lenin's "Testament" and the Soviet-Yugoslav declaration marked the climax of the Soviet de-Stalinization of 1956. From the beginning of July 1956 on, a deceleration from above became noticeable. The increasing tendencies toward liberalization and independence in some of the countries of Eastern Europe (principally in Poland and Hungary) and in a few Communist parties of Western Europe (Togliatti in Italy had already proclaimed "polycentrism" and demanded that criticism should not be confined to Stalin's person but extend to an investigation of the social causes of Stalinism) had clearly alarmed the Soviet leadership. There was a risk that de-Stalinization might burst the bounds assigned to it.

Under these circumstances the conservative and bureaucratic forces in the leadership gained strength. We know from subsequent statements by Soviet leaders themselves that the de-Stalinization course had to be forced through "under conditions of stubborn opposition." For more than a year—the year 1956—"a fierce struggle was waged in the Central Committee against the realization of the decisions of the Twentieth Party Congress," especially "against any rehabilitation of persons who had suffered innocently." Influential forces in the Party leadership—chiefly Molotov, Kaganovich, and Voroshilov—were trying to "push" the Party "back into the period of the personality cult." When the mass persecution measures of the Stalin era were discussed at a Plenary Meeting of the Central Committee, Voroshilov suddenly leaped to his feet and shouted: "You are still too young; we will have to straighten you out!" When the new textbook of Party history was being drafted (as decided at the Twentieth Party Congress), Molotov and Kaganovich, "frothing with wrath," resisted any criticism of the Stalin era and demanded that "everything that happened in the past—hence also during 1937–38—should be acknowledged as correct."[57]

Fear that de-Stalinization might go too far and pressure by conservative and dogmatic forces resulted in a change of course in the summer of 1956. De-Stalinization was considerably curtailed. In an important resolution, "The Personality Cult and Its Consequences," published in early July 1956, the Central Committee continued to criticize Stalin, to mention Lenin's criticism of Stalin, and to condemn the great purge as "mass persecution," but Trotskyites and Bukharin's followers were once more described as "enemies of Leninism" whose policies would have led to a "restoration of capitalism in the U.S.S.R." Stalin's mistakes, it was alleged, had nothing to do with the social order in the U.S.S.R., and the consequences of the personality cult had already been eliminated. The different roads to socialism were circumscribed by the reservation that "ideological unity" and "the ideological closing of ranks" of all Communist parties were equally necessary.[58] Within a few days *Pravda* declared that Stalin's terror had been necessary within certain limits, in order to conduct "a merciless struggle" against "the enemies of Leninism."[59] At the end of July 1956, *Pravda* warned against "the chimeras of some theoreticians who want to reach socialism not like the others but by their own road." "Homogeneity from the same mold" was as necessary as "irreconcilable opposition to all manifestations of revisionism."[60]

The more strongly the reform movement came out into the open in the autumn of 1956 (especially in Poland and Hungary), the more the Soviet leadership applied the brakes to de-Stalinization. In September 1956 progressive Soviet historians were publicly reproved because in the spring of the same year they had demanded excessive de-Stalinization.[61] The emphasis was now once more on the allegedly indispensable "monolithic unity" of the world Communist movement, and this entailed the demand "to defend jointly one's own achievements against the intrigues of international imperialism."[62]

Immediately after the bloody suppression of the Hungarian uprising (described by the Soviet press as a "counterrevolution"), Suslov, in November 1956, proclaimed four "common features and laws" allegedly existing in all socialist countries, including "the resolute defense of the achievements of the socialist revolution against the intrigues of the former exploiting ruling classes," in an attempt to justify Soviet military intervention in Hungary.[63] At the end of December 1956 *Pravda* denied that there had ever been any such thing as Stalinism in the Soviet Union: "Above all, it must be said that any such doctrine as 'Stalinism' is unknown to us." Stalin, the paper said, had been a remarkable Marxist and had been guided in his doctrines by Marxism. Stalin's mistakes had been criticized by the Communist Party of the Soviet Union. The campaign against Stalinism, it was alleged, represented an "offensive of imperialist reaction against the achievements of the Soviet Union." Instead of advocating different roads to socialism, *Pravda* now called on all Communist parties in all countries "to rally even more closely around the banner of proletarian internationalism."[64]

This change of course went so far that in mid-January 1957—less than a year after the Twentieth Party Congress—Khrushchev paid a tribute to Stalin. At a Chinese Embassy reception in Moscow (certainly not an accidental occasion) Khrushchev declared "the term 'Stalinist,' like Stalin himself, is inseparable from the great title of 'Communist.' " Both in defending the Revolution and "in the revolutionary struggle against our class enemies" Stalin had "courageously and unyieldingly defended the cause of Marxism-Leninism." Khrushchev actually concluded with these words: "May God grant that every Communist will be able to fight as Stalin fought."[65]

## ☐ Khrushchev on Coexistence and World Revolution

De-Stalinization suffered a serious setback in the autumn and winter of 1956. However, this soon proved to have been a temporary check. Khrushchev, First Party Secretary since September 1953, succeeded in June 1957 in displacing his political opponents from the Soviet leadership. In March 1958 he also assumed the office of Premier and thus combined in his hand the decisive functions of power. De-Stalinization was continued, albeit more cautiously. Terror was curtailed, more people were released and rehabilitated, new, somewhat more moderate, criminal laws were promulgated, and reforms were carried out in the economy and in social policy. There was an economic upswing in those first years following Stalin's death, the Soviet populace was once more hopeful, and Khrushchev became popular. In the international field sputniks, rockets, and summit conferences testified to the rise of the Soviet Union to the rank of a world power. All this was reflected in new international concepts.

The doctrine of coexistence, formulated by Khrushchev at the Twentieth Party Congress only as a brief authoritative statement, was considerably developed during 1957–59. At the Twenty-first Party Congress (January 27–February 5, 1959) Khrushchev declared that it was possible even before the world-wide victory of socialism to force the warmongering circles to desist from unleashing new world wars. "Thus, there will arise a real possibility of excluding world war from the life of society even before the complete triumph of socialism, even with capitalism existing in part of the world."[66] At the same time he declared the new concepts of the non-inevitability of wars and the doctrine of coexistence to be the "general line" of Soviet foreign policy. This was also reflected in the titles under which Khrushchev's speeches and articles on international issues were published: *For Victory in Peaceful Competition with Capitalism* and *World Without Arms, World Without War.*[67]

The Khrushchev leadership propagated the Soviet doctrine of coexistence in the form of three linked theses: (1) the peaceful coexistence of states with different social systems, (2) economic competition between capitalism and socialism, (3) continuation of the ideological struggle. This was justified by Soviet ideologists by what might be described as a three-level theory. In the Soviet view, relations between socialist and capitalist countries developed on three separate levels, necessitating different relations on each of them:

In the field of politics it is possible and necessary within reasonable limits to take into account the point of view of the opponent (otherwise negotiations would be out of the question since the object of the latter is to find points of contact, and rapprochement between the standpoints). . . . In the economic sphere concessions are likewise natural (on a mutual basis, of course), concessions which in the final analysis benefit the two parties. . . . In the ideological sphere there has been no peaceful coexistence between socialism and capitalism, nor can there be any.[68]

On the subject of political relations between capitalist and socialist countries Khrushchev stated that the policy of peaceful coexistence implied

repudiation of war as a means of solving controversial issues. However, this does not cover the entire concept of peaceful coexistence. Apart from the commitment to non-aggression, it also presupposes an obligation on the part of all states to desist from violating each other's territorial integrity and sovereignty in any form and under any pretext whatsoever. The principle of peaceful coexistence signifies a renunciation of interference in the internal affairs of other countries with the object of altering their system of government or mode of life or for any other motives. The doctrine of peaceful coexistence also presupposes that political and economic relations between countries are to be based on complete equality of the parties concerned, and on mutual benefit.[69]

The second component of the doctrine of coexistence—economic competition between the camp of socialism and the camp of capitalism —was designed, according to Khrushchev, to show "which system is more viable, which accords more with the aspirations of the peoples and can satisfy more fully both the material and spiritual requirements of the people."[70] This competition consisted in "building more houses, schools, and hospitals," producing "more grain, milk, meat, clothes, and other consumer goods"[71] and demonstrating who "produces more per head of population, who provides a higher material and cultural standard for the people."[72]

Khrushchev compared this economic competition with a horse race in which "the capitalist horse of the United States" was making only slow headway while "our socialist horse" was in full flight and would soon catch up with the U.S.A.[73] The distance between the Soviet Union and the United States, Khrushchev believed optimistically, would shortly narrow down in favor of the Soviet Union: "The U.S.A. is still running ahead of us. That is not surprising. It started before us. Figuratively speaking, however, it is already under great pressure and breathing heavily. As a young and stronger runner the socialist Soviet Union is now slowly catching up and will soon leave the United States behind."[74] The socialist countries, Khrushchev remarked in the spring of 1960, would be victorious in this economic competition and "outstrip the most highly developed capitalist countries in terms of productivity."[75] The Soviet Union would "considerably annoy the capitalist world by ensuring that Soviet people will have the shortest working day, the highest wages, the best housing conditions, and better cultural services."[76]

The third component of the Soviet doctrine of coexistence—the ideological struggle—was again and again emphasized by Khrushchev. "The ideological differences are unbridgeable, and they will continue to exist."[77] An ideological struggle would exist "as long as capitalism exists in the world," for ideological clashes were "inevitable because an ideological, political struggle is being waged."[78] In the policy of coexistence there must be no concessions on principles: "Mutual concessions in the interest of peaceful coexistence must not be confused with concessions on principles, in matters affecting the nature of our socialist system, in our ideology. Here there can be no question of concessions or changes."[79] Leonid Ilyichev, the chief Soviet ideologist of the Khrushchev era, declared even more emphatically: "Peaceful coexistence between ideologies, about which some muddlers speak, is as unthinkable as a reconciliation between light and darkness."[80]

The Soviet doctrine of coexistence has always been expressly confined to the foreign policy sphere, to state relations between socialist and capitalist countries, but has never applied to the sphere of the "international class struggle." The increased power and strength of the Soviet Union, its growing influence on world politics, the rapid growth of national liberation movements—all these led the Soviet leadership, and no doubt Khrushchev himself, to expect the world-wide victory of Communism with renewed confidence. Khrushchev's remark "We shall bury you," often quoted in the West, has never been published in the Soviet press—nevertheless, Khrushchev frequently, though in different words, emphasized his aims of world revolution.

"Our ideas will conquer the minds of all men," he declared in the spring of 1957. "We affirm that the ideas of Communism are incomparably stronger, that these ideas will ultimately prevail."[81] The world-wide victory of Communism was inevitable: "When we speak of the triumph of Communism all over the world, we have in mind, first and foremost, the inevitable victory of Communist ideas," Khrushchev explained; "the development of countries in accordance with objective laws that are independent of our will, laws which Marx and Lenin discovered."[82] The Soviet Communists "are convinced that the peoples of all countries will come to socialism, to Communism,"[83] and "we can already see our ultimate goal appearing on the horizon—the victory of the working class throughout the whole world, the victory of the ideas of Communism."[84]

Khrushchev even prophesied the victory of Communism in individual countries—a thing never done since the Lenin era. Thus, referring to the United States, he remarked: "And your grandchildren will live under socialism in America too."[85] The same would happen in Japan: "I believe that Communism will be victorious in Japan. I am convinced of this because I am a Communist."[86] The "inevitable victory of the ideas of Communism" would also engulf Britain: "We do not have to teach the British, for example, to effect a revolution and establish the socialist system in their country. They will do it themselves."[87] In the summer of 1958 he predicted the victory of Soviet-type Communism in West Germany: "If today it is only the German Democratic Republic that is socialist, the time will come when all Germany will follow the socialist path, and not just Germany, but the entire world."[88]

At the same time, Khrushchev repeatedly emphasized that a world-wide victory of Communism was not to be brought about by military means, not by military intervention, let alone by war. The Soviet Union would "never take up arms to force the ideas of Communism upon anybody."[89] The victory of a revolution depends upon the conditions in the country concerned and "comes with the domestic affairs of the given country; there must be no interference from without,"[90] since "we can manage without bombs and are convinced that our cause will be victorious."[91] In the spring of 1958 Khrushchev even asserted that the Soviet Communists had "never imposed on other countries by force of arms the socialist way of life and our ideology, nor do we intend to."[92] At the beginning of 1960 he declared in the Supreme Soviet that Communism would be victorious, "but not in the sense of other countries being conquered by the socialist countries."[93]

The rejection of military means for spreading Communism was linked by Khrushchev with a concept that might be called the example theory. According to this new theory, the ruling class of the capitalist countries has so far been able to point to the difficulties and shortcomings in the building of socialism. However, with the further economic progress of these countries this would no longer be possible, since the time was not distant "when the citizens of the Soviet Union, and of all socialist countries, will have much higher living standards than the working people of any capitalist country."[94] This, in turn, would increase the attraction of Communism in the capitalist countries and strengthen all those forces supporting the victory of a Soviet-type socialism:

At present our country is approaching a level of development when our economic achievements will enable us to create an abundance of consumer goods. The ideas of Communism will then reach the minds of many people not only through the study of Marxism-Leninism, but also by way of our example. The working people of all countries will see that only Communism provides material and spiritual benefits in abundance. That is why victory will be ours.

Even those who now opposed Communism, Khrushchev believed, would "take our path without even being aware of it."[95]

## ☐ The New Concepts for the World Communist Movement

The ideological changes effected during the years 1953–58, especially in practical political concepts, implied a certain departure from Stalin. The Soviet leadership, therefore, regarded a systematic summing-up of post-Stalinist ideology as necessary. In August 1956 the Soviet Central Committee had decided on the preparation of a new ideological textbook, which would include not only dialectical and historical materialism and political economy, but above all the political concepts. The Party leadership granted a group of well-known Soviet ideologists, under the chairmanship of Otto Kuusinen, "nine months' creative leave at full salary" to enable them to produce the required work.[96] Instead of nine months, however, more than three years elapsed (even Soviet ideologists do not always stick to their delivery dates) before the textbook, *Fundamentals of Marxism-Leninism,* running to about 800 pages, appeared at the end of October 1959. Of the twenty-seven chapters of this textbook, seventeen were devoted to political theory, with a systematic exposition of its individual doctrines, including (in this order) the tasks of the working class; the doctrine of the Party (including political strategy and tactics); the policy of political alliances; the national liberation movements; the problems of war, peace, and coexistence; the socialist revolution; the dictatorship of the proletariat; the period of transition to socialism; the economic and political characteristics of a socialist society; the "world socialist system" (i.e., relations between socialist countries); the transition from socialism to Communism; and, finally, the Communist society of the future.

The second ideological key document of that period was the "Declaration of Eighty-one Communist Parties" of December 1960. This declaration was to be valid for all Communist parties; it was worked out amid tough and sharp arguments at the Moscow World Conference of eighty-one Communist parties from November 10 to December 5, 1960. The Yugoslav Communists were not represented at this conference; as for the Chinese and Albanian Communists, it was the last time they participated in any conference convened by Moscow. Since the "Chinese wing" rejected the Soviet concepts of the non-inevitability of wars, of peaceful coexistence, and of a peaceful transition to socialism, and since the Italian Communist Party delegation (supported on a few issues by other Communist Party delegations) was particularly emphatic in favor of these concepts and opposed any centralized direction of the world Communist movement, as well as any condemnation of Yugoslavia, the "Declaration of the Eighty-one Communist Parties" contained a number of compromise formulas. Nevertheless, the key concepts betrayed Soviet drafting.

A few months later, on July 30, 1961, the New Soviet Party Program was finally published—initially as a draft and eventually, following official endorsement at the Twenty-second Party Congress, on October 31, 1961, in its final version.

Although the three ideological documents mentioned above—the *Fundamentals of Marxism-Leninism,* the "Declaration of the Eighty-one Communist Parties," and the New Soviet Party Program—differed from each other in certain details, they nevertheless had important features in common. They reflected the Soviet aims of the early 1960's —continuation along the road taken at the Twentieth Party Congress (although in some respects in a slightly toned-down version), and the Soviet leadership's increasing concern with foreign political and international problems, including its endeavors to maintain or restore, in a somewhat "modernized" form, the Soviet Union's leading role in the "world socialist system" and in the world Communist movement. Finally they expressed the (largely over-optimistic) hopes of the Soviet leadership at that time in the future course of Soviet domestic developments— mainly with regard to the transition to Communism and the Communist society of the future.

Of particular importance was the assessment of the contemporary world situation (in Soviet Party parlance, the "character of the epoch"), which was defined as follows:

> Our time, the main content of which is the transition from capitalism to socialism initiated by the Great October Socialist Revolution, is a time of struggle between the two opposing social systems, a time of socialist revolutions and national liberation revolutions, a time of the breakdown of imperialism, of the abolition of the colonial system, a time of transition of more peoples to the socialist path, of the triumph of socialism and Communism on a world-wide scale. It is the principal characteristic of our time

that the world socialist system is becoming the decisive factor in the development of society.[97]

The transition from capitalism to socialism on a world scale, which henceforth was to be greatly emphasized, was envisaged as resulting from the amalgamation of several revolutionary currents: "the peoples who are building socialism and Communism, the revolutionary movement of the working class in the capitalist countries, the national liberation struggle of the oppressed peoples and the general democratic movement—these great forces of our time are merging into one powerful current that undermines and destroys the world imperialist system." Simultaneously, "the world socialist system" was one of "the central factors of the day."[98] The revolutionary currents were joining up "in a single world-wide revolutionary process." Revolution in every country was being conducted as "part of the world socialist revolution," but must rely on its own forces: "The revolution is not made to order. It cannot be imposed on the people from without."[99]

Proceeding from this increasingly international approach, the emphasis was now no longer, as under Stalin, on the "doctrine of the Party" but on the relations in the world Communist movement. Stalin's previously much-emphasized "six features of the Party" were now replaced by the considerably more elastically phrased "three characteristics" which were clearly intended to be valid for all Communist parties in the world.[100] These were: (1) the irreconcilability to capitalism; (2) adherence to the revolutionary theory of Marxism-Leninism; and (3) unity, identity of action, and flexibility of tactics. True, the Communist parties of the various countries were to be "independent and have equal rights" and to base their policies on "the specific conditions in their respective countries," but at the same time they were to support an "internationalist solidarity of all Marxist-Leninist parties." The Communist parties of all countries were to distinguish themselves by "elaborating a common attitude." Continuous joint consultations were to ensure the working out of concerted positions in the struggle for common objectives, and the strengthening of the unity of the world Communist movement was, in fact, laid down as the highest international duty of every Marxist-Leninist Party. As under Stalin, reference was once more made to the "experience which the CPSU has gained," and the Soviet Party was proclaimed the leading force in the world movement: "The Communist Party of the Soviet Union has been, and remains, the universally recognized vanguard of the world Communist movement, being the most experienced and steeled contingent of the international Communist movement."[101]

Finally, it was made the duty of all Communists parties to fight against "deviations," against revisionism on the one hand and dogmatism and sectarianism on the other. The term "revisionism" meant primarily the views of the Yugoslav Communists and their followers in other countries (who supported a fresh examination of the problems of the Party, of revolution, of the dictatorship of the proletariat, and of the economic and political features of a socialist society), while the terms "dogmatism" and "sectarianism" were meant to describe the efforts of the Chinese Communists and of neo-Stalinist elements within the Soviet Union and other Communist parties who opposed the reforms and changes. The declaration even maintained that in this "struggle on two fronts" revisionism remained "the main danger," and described the "further exposure" of the Yugoslav Communists as "an essential task of the Marxist-Leninist parties"—even though dogmatism and sectarianism "can also become the main danger at some stage of the development of individual parties."[102]

In the discussion of political strategy and tactics Stalin's formulations, above all his analogies with military operations (main thrust, main and secondary reserves, comparison of strategy with a war and tactics with a battle), were openly criticized "because political strategy radically differs from military strategy." The political struggle was concerned "not with ready-formed armies but with social classes and forces . . . some of which act consciously while others act spontaneously." Several other factors greatly complicated "the task of political leadership compared with military leadership."[103] Doctrine on political strategy and tactics was reformulated in a more flexible manner and supplemented by extensive expositions of the policy of alliances, above all the creation of a narrower "unity of action" (collaboration of workers' organizations of different types) and a broader "democratic unity" (unity of action and co-operation of Communists with national and democratic forces).

The national liberation movements were described as "a development ranking second in historic importance only to the formation of the world socialist system,"[104] and the doctrine about them was further developed. The national liberation movements, it was explained, passed through two phases. With the beginning of the second phase, i.e., following the national liberation of the former colonial countries, the social antagonisms became exacerbated, with the "national bourgeoisie" (a term understood by Soviet ideologists to cover the leading non-Communist forces in the developing countries) inclining toward "deals with reaction and imperialism." In these conditions the Communists must support non-capitalist development. This meant a road enabling the countries of Africa and Asia, still largely at a feudal stage, to "skip" capitalism and approach, step by step and through a series of intermediate phases, a Soviet-type socialism. This non-capitalist road of development was the only road for these nations to free themselves from exploitation, poverty, and starvation.[105] The non-capitalist road was to be "ensured by the struggles of the working class and the masses of the people, by the general democratic movement, and meet the interests of the absolute majority of the nation."[106]

In the course of this non-capitalist development a state of national democracy was to be aimed at as an intermediate stage. National democracy was defined as a state which, in foreign policy, "fights against imperialism and its military blocs, against military bases on its territory," and "against the new forms of colonialism and the penetration of imperialist capital." In terms of domestic politics the state of national democracy was characterized, for instance, by the fact that it "rejects dictatorial and despotic methods of government," and that the population enjoys "broad democratic rights and freedoms (freedom of speech, press, assembly, demonstration, establishment of political parties and social organizations), the opportunity to work for the enactment of agrarian reform, and other democratic and social changes, and for participation in shaping government policy."[107] The national democratic state was the political foundation on which to "consummate the anti-imperialist, antifeudal, democratic revolution."[108]

Other concepts to be further developed and supplemented were those of war, peace, and coexistence. While under Stalin this doctrine had been described as "attitude toward war" or "war and peace," it was now called "the danger of war and the struggle of the peoples for peace."[109] The distinction between "just wars" and "unjust wars," which under Stalin occupied the central place in the doctrine, was supplanted by the new doctrine, first proclaimed at the Twentieth Party Congress, of the non-inevitability of wars. There was "no task more pressing than that of safeguarding humanity against a global thermonuclear disaster."[110] The possibility of avoiding wars was strongly emphasized and supplemented by the demand for general and total disarmament.

The doctrine of coexistence was regarded not only as "the firm foundation" of the foreign policy of the socialist countries, but also as an obligatory general line for "Communists of the whole world"; however, the connection between this foreign policy doctrine and the international class struggle was being more strongly emphasized. The policy of peaceful coexistence did not imply "renunciation of the class struggle" but indeed represented "a form of class struggle between socialism and capitalism." The policy of peaceful coexistence was not only necessary to prevent wars but also "strengthens the positions of socialism" and increases "the prestige and influence of the Communist parties in the capitalist countries." Coexistence gives rise to favorable opportunities for "the development of the class struggle in the capitalist countries and the national liberation movement." The policy of coexistence did not imply any "conciliation of the socialist and bourgeois ideologies" but rather "intensification of the struggle of the working class, of all the Communist parties, for the triumph of socialist ideas."[111]

## ☐ Socialist Revolution and Socialist Society

The ideological changes after Stalin's death were reflected also in the concept of socialist revolution. In complete agreement with Lenin the *Fundamentals* stipulated a revolutionary situation as the prerequisite of a socialist revolution. The decisive features of a revolutionary situation in the capitalist countries at present are "an unusual increase in exploitation, mass unemployment, a rapid rise in the cost of living," and "an economic slump which robs the masses of their confidence in the future," as well as a few political factors including an intensified danger of war, the danger of a new fascism, the danger that the country in question might be drawn into "an atomic catastrophe," or "unbridled political reaction," or "the danger that the country might be occupied by foreign troops."[112] In the present conditions, according to the *Fundamentals,* an immediate socialist revolution would not take place in the Western ("capitalist") industrial countries, but instead there would at first be an anti-monopolist people's revolution with the aim of liquidating the capitalist monopolies. An "anti-monopolist people's revolution" would, first, "remove the henchmen of the big monopolies from power." Power would pass into the hands of a "coalition of democratic forces," with the result that "the main forces of reaction" would be isolated and overthrown during "the very first, democratic stage." Second, such a revolution would make it possible to nationalize the property of the large trusts and concerns. "In the developed capitalist countries this would result in the creation of a powerful state-owned sector of the national economy with about 60 to 80 per cent of the industrial capacity." In consequence, the anti-monopolistic democratic revolution in the highly-developed capitalist countries would at its very outset lay solid foundations for the transition to socialism.[113] However, in many capitalist countries it was equally possible that "the socialist transformation will take place directly, bypassing the general democratic stage."

All three ideological documents emphasized the new thesis of the Twentieth Party Congress on the possibility of a peaceful transition to socialism, i.e., the capture of state power without civil war, of winning a stable parliamentary majority in order to "transform parliament from an instrument serving the class interests of the bourgeoisie into an instrument serving the working people."[114] A peaceful transition to socialism has "a number of advantages." The transformation of public life could be performed with a minimum of sacrifices and a minimum of destruction to the production process. "The working class takes over the production machine from the capitalist monopolies almost intact and, after the necessary reorganization, immediately puts it into operation in order that all sections of the population may rapidly convince themselves of the advantages of the new mode of production and distribution." Moreover, the peaceful transition to socialism offered an opportunity to make use of "so traditional an institution as Parliament." In consequence, the power of the working class instantly acquires the necessary authority, facilitating the subsequent socialist transformations. "Any resistance to the socialist revolution would in this case be illegal, not only *de facto* but also *de jure,* and aimed against the will of the nation expressed by Parliament."[115] The peaceful realization of the socialist revolution, however, was impossible without "an extra-parliamentarian mass struggle." For in the event of "the exploiting classes resorting to violence against the people," the Communists must not lose sight of the possibility of a "non-peaceful transition to socialism."[116]

A victorious socialist revolution, in the view of the Soviet ideologists, would lead to the establishment of the dictatorship of the proletariat. In contrast to Stalin's concept of the dictatorship of the proletariat, it was noticeable that the use of force against the former exploiting classes, though emphasized, was no longer at the center of the concept. The dictatorship of the proletariat, it was held, had so far emerged in two forms (Soviet power in Russia and people's democracies in the countries of Eastern and Southeastern Europe), but new forms of a dictatorship of the proletariat were conceivable in the future, and these might manage with less use of force.

The period of transition to socialism was to be marked for all countries—as in the Soviet Union—by nationalization, by socialist industrialization, and by a collectivization of agriculture (now usually described as "co-operativization"). However, a certain variation in the forms, methods, and speed of transition was conceded for the realization of these measures. In future nationalization the "interests of the small share-owners are to be protected," including "the owners of small pensions" and "the holders of insurance policies." Provided the capitalists loyally supported the new order and co-operated in its construction, the dictatorship of the proletariat would endeavor "to make the transition to a life of work as easy and painless as possible"; indeed, over a certain period of time, sums of money might be paid out to the former owners and "appropriate positions at the enterprises" given to them. If, however, the capitalist elements should take active measures against the state power, committing sabotage or causing difficulties, then "the bourgeoisie will bring reprisals upon itself."[117] Collectivization, too, might be effected in the most varied forms. Provided the wealthy peasants "are sensible" in this transformation, "they have the prospect of becoming equal members of socialist society." Future collectivization in the "highly developed capitalist countries" with their mechanized agriculture would "undoubtedly contribute much that is new to the forms and methods of co-operation."[118]

The outline of the socialist society kept to Stalin's assertion of 1936 that socialism had been victorious in the Soviet Union and maintained his thesis of the two allied classes (workers and peasants) and the intermediate stratum (the intelligentsia). On the other hand, Stalin's thesis of March 1937, on an alleged intensification of the class struggle with the further development of socialism, was severely criticized. This thesis was "wrong in principle" and "particularly dangerous because it justified crude infringements of the principles of socialist democracy and legality."[119]

The Stalinist doctrine of "capitalist encirclement" (scrapped in 1956) was now replaced by the entirely new doctrine of the world socialist system which—at first rather optimistically—characterized economic and political co-operation between the socialist countries as enabling "the national interests of each country to be harmoniously combined with the interests of the world socialist system as a whole." The world socialist system was "a community of free and equal states," and not "an ordinary coalition of states bound by interests that temporarily coincide." In the atmosphere of fraternal co-operation, "the hotbeds of nationalist discord and former enmity are swiftly stamped out, nationalist prejudices are obliterated and disappear." Of possible difficulties or antagonisms there was no mention whatever.

Economic co-operation between the socialist countries was to be based on the principle of the international socialist division of labor. According to this Soviet concept (which was criticized by both the Yugoslav and the Chinese Communists, and subsequently also by the Rumanian Communists) no socialist country was able to view its economy in isolation but only as part of the world socialist system. Bilateral agreements between socialist countries were "inadequate"; what was necessary was "a wider and many-sided co-ordination of economic activity." A socialist country did not need a complete system of economic branches; instead, there should be among socialist countries "a specialization and co-operation of production," and a close "co-ordination of plans."[120]

The line of "socialist construction in isolation, detached from the world community of socialist countries" was "theoretically untenable," "harmful economically," and finally "dangerous politically" since, allegedly, it "nourishes bourgeois nationalist tendencies and may ultimately lead to the loss of the socialist gains."[121] This assertion was even at the time challenged with particular vehemence by the Yugoslav Communists who declared (and were to be proved right by the Soviet intervention in Czechoslovakia in 1968): "In this way it seems that any action that might be taken in the name of 'true socialism' for 'saving' some country from such 'degeneration' is to be justified ideologically and politically in advance."[122]

□ **The Transition to Communism**

The over-optimistic hopes of the Party leadership—and presumably of Khrushchev himself—were reflected in the assumption that the Soviet Union would be able to enter the phase of Communism as early as 1980. "The party solemnly proclaims: the present generation of Soviet people shall live in Communism!" ran the final sentence of the Party Program, prominently printed in italics.[123] The first prerequisite was the establishment of the material and technological foundations of Communism. During the very first decade, i.e., from 1961 to 1970, the Soviet Union was to outstrip the U.S.A. in per-capita production; all working people were to enjoy "a good standard of living" and have comfortable homes; collective and state farms would be "transformed into highly productive enterprises with high incomes"; heavy physical work would disappear, and the Soviet Union would become the country with the shortest working day in the world. In the following decade, from 1970 to 1980, the material and technological basis of Communism would have been established and the entire population would receive an abundance of material and cultural goods. Immediately afterward, the transition to the principle of distribution according to need would be accomplished, as well as the transition to one universal people's property, so that "the

Communist society will have been established in its principal features" in the U.S.S.R. This Communist society would then receive its finishing touches in a subsequent period.

To achieve this objective it was envisaged that industrial production would increase 2.5 times between 1960 and 1970, and at least 6 times by 1980. Agricultural production was to increase 2.5 times by 1970 and 3.5 times by 1980. This would mean that the Soviet Union would have far outstripped the U.S.A. in per-capita production, both in industry and in agriculture. In the social sphere the real income per head of population was to rise more than 3.5 times by 1980. By 1970 a 35-hour working week would have been introduced, and by 1980 the Soviet Union would be the country with the shortest, most productive, and best paid working day.[124]

In order to accomplish the transition to the principle of "to each according to his needs" the Party Program promised to satisfy the following needs of the population, free of charge, by 1980: accommodation of children in boarding schools (if desired by their parents); education in all teaching establishments; medical care for all citizens (including supply of medicines and in-patient treatment); use of housing (i.e., abolition of rents) and all major communal services (water, gas, and heating); use of communal public transport; and eventually the principal daily meal in factories, offices, and for collective farmers engaged in production. Recreation homes, holiday accommodations, and tourist hostels were to be partially free of charge.[125]

The differences between town and country were to be abolished by transforming the collective-farm villages into bigger localities of an urban type, with the most up-to-date facilities, so that gradually the differences between the living conditions of the rural and the urban population would disappear. By reducing the differences between "low-paid and high-paid personnel," social equality was gradually to be achieved. With the transition to Communism the cash-commodity relationship would become economically pointless and would wither away.[126]

In the political sphere, the Party Program proclaimed the new doctrine of the transformation of the dictatorship of the proletariat into the state of the entire people. According to this doctrine (which was at once sharply attacked by the Chinese Communists), the dictatorship of the proletariat had fulfilled its historical mission in the Soviet Union and was no longer necessary from the point of view of internal Soviet developments. The socialist state was beginning to transform itself into a "nation-wide organization of the working people of socialist society." The state, which had arisen as a state of the dictatorship of the proletariat, had become "a state of the entire people, an organ expressing the interests and will of the entire people."[127] Even though the transformation of the dictatorship of the proletariat into a "state of the entire people" was rather questionable in terms of ideology, and even though *Pravda* itself had to admit that "some comrades do not quite correctly understand the thesis of the draft program concerning the dictatorship of the proletariat,"[128] the new doctrine nevertheless played a certain positive part: it served as the ideological justification for certain, though limited, reforms in Soviet political life. Thus, the membership of the soviets was to be renewed by at least one-third at each election, and functionaries at all levels were not, as a rule, to hold office for more than three consecutive terms. Regular accounts were to be presented by the soviets, the state apparatus was to be reduced in size, and socialist legality was to be strictly observed. The social organizations were to be given the right of proposing draft legislation. Draft laws and other important decisions were to be submitted to the public for discussion prior to enactment, and important laws were to be subject to a referendum. These and other measures were gradually to bring the state to "Communist self-government." However, the complete withering away of the state would not take place until after the establishment of a "developed Communist society" and the consolidation of socialism in the international arena.[129]

This building of Communism was to be accompanied by a rapprochement of nations. The boundaries of the union republics would lose "their former significance," and Soviet citizens of different nationalities would develop "common Communist traits," as well as their own culture, morality, and style of life.[130]

Analogous to the new concept of the "state of the entire people" the Party Program proclaimed that the Communist Party had developed from a Party of the working class into a Party of the entire people. The Party, officially described as "the brain, the honor, and the conscience of our epoch," was to acquire even greater importance during the transition to Communism. In the Party, too, the rotation system was to be introduced, which meant that after each election (i.e., every four years) the Central Committee and the Party Praesidium (since April 1966 the "Politburo") were to have at least one-quarter of their membership replaced. Members of the Praesidium (Politburo) were not, as a rule, to be elected for more than three consecutive terms (i.e., to hold office for more than twelve years). At the middle and lower levels of the Party apparatus the Party functionaries were to be exchanged even more frequently in accordance with a laid down formula.[131]

All these directives, however, were concerned only with the transition to Communism in the Soviet Union. How the other socialist countries were to accomplish their transition to Communism remained somewhat vague. On the one hand, the Party Program stated that the transition of the socialist countries "into the period of the full-scale construction of Communism" would be "non-simultaneous," while on the other it referred to the prospect of "effecting the transition to Communism more or less simultaneously, within one and the same historical epoch."[132]

☐ **The Future Communist Society**

In contrast to the Stalin era, when precise descriptions of the Communist society of the future were regarded as utopian, the future Communist society was now described in detail. The term Communism was defined in the Party Program as follows:

Communism is a classless social system with one form of public ownership of the means of production and full social equality of all members of society; under it, the all-round development of people will be accompanied by the growth of the productive forces through continuous progress in science and technology; all the springs of co-operative wealth will flow more abundantly, and the great principle "From each according to his ability, to each according to his needs" will be implemented. Communism is a highly organized society of free, socially conscious working people, in which public self-government will be established, a society in which labor for the good of society will become the prime, vital requirement of everyone, a necessity recognized by one and all, and the ability of each person will be employed to the greatest benefit of the people.[133]

In addition to this general definition of the Communist society of the future, the Party Program and the *Fundamentals of Marxism-Leninism* also described several of its specific characteristics. The character of work would change as a result of highly organized production. The division of labor would disappear, and people would have the opportunity of freely developing all their abilities. Everybody would be able to choose an activity in line with his inclinations and skills, and would be free to change his place of work. In the Communist society people would only spend 20 to 25 hours a week—and later even less—on their specific work.[134] Under those circumstances, they would have a high labor consciousness and "develop a deep-felt need to work voluntarily and according to their inclinations for the common benefit." Work would cease to be a burden or a mere means of subsistence: "It will be a genuinely creative process and a source of joy."[135] Recreation and leisure would no longer be associated with the idea of idleness. Besides their professional activity, which would take up only a few hours a day, many people would want to engage in scientific pursuits, invention, art, or literature in their spare time. The cultural and scientific level would then be so high that this free activity would contribute to the advancement and flowering of the whole of society.[136]

Under Communism, the principle "to each according to his needs" would become reality: "People's requirements will be satisfied from public sources. Articles of personal use will be in the full ownership of each member of society and will be at his disposal."[137] The *Fundamentals* pointed out that this would also have moral and psychological consequences. With the gratuitous distribution of all goods, the people of the future Communist age would be freed from anxiety about the morrow. The quest after profit and private property would disappear, and people would turn to higher interests. Answering possible objections by opponents of Communism as to what would happen if a man in the Communist society were to express eccentric wishes, such as a new suit every day, or a new car every so often, or a palace, the *Fundamentals* state: "People themselves will be sufficiently cultured and conscious not to make obviously unreasonable demands on society." Should even under Communism some people make unjustifiably high demands, they would only put themselves "in a ridiculous light before public opinion. After that, hardly anyone would want to repeat such an experiment."[138]

The description of the future Communist self-administration no longer emphasized the "association of free producers"—as Marx and Engels saw it; in fact, this was not mentioned at all. There was, instead, mention of "high standards of organization, precision, and discipline" and a "planned economy." The Communist society, according to the Program, was "a highly organized society of free, socially conscious working people."[139] The Communist self-administration, the *Fundamentals* declared, was a system of organization, "embracing the entire population, which will directly administer its own affairs with the help of this system." The main task of self-administration, which was to consist of a widely ramified system of mass reorganizations and collectives, was the establishment of voluntary associations and the collaboration between various production collectives and economic areas. Social self-administration under Communism would be distinguished by the fact that the problems of society would be publicly discussed, that all members were informed about them, and would display "a very high degree of civic activity" and "deep interest in these affairs." Naturally, the public discussion of the affairs of society "will involve disputes," but this was no obstacle; on the contrary, it would ensure "the most correct solution of problems." In view of the "deep-seated community of interests, aims, and world outlook," it would not be difficult to overcome such differences of opinion.[140]

Other ideological writings of 1960–61 described the Communist self-administration of the future as "the organization of a harmonious system of bodies elected by the population—bodies which are no longer political organizations but which enjoy the natural authority commanded by the oldest and most experienced members of any collective." This system would embrace all members and have a center at its disposal.[141]

As for the role of the Party under Communism, it was pointed out that the Party would at first continue to exist even under Communism, in order to co-ordinate the work of the various organizations of Communist self-administration. Only when the entire population had reached the ideological awareness of the vanguard (i.e., the Party) would the Party cease to be necessary. But this was a difficult task to achieve and would take some time.[142] Another ideological article also pointed out that the withering away of the state did "not automatically entail the Party's exit from the stage of society's life." Only when the Party had fully discharged its tasks would it vanish from the social scene. This process, however, could not be described as a withering away or elimination; the Party would instead "dissolve" in the Communist society, though "only after the victory of Communism on a whole world scale, under the conditions of the mature Communist society."[143]

Science under Communism would have a multitude of new problems to solve, such as predicting and preventing all natural disasters, making the forces of nature subservient to man, opening up all inhospitable regions—perhaps even the ocean bed—extending the life span of man to an average of 150 to 200 years, conquering old age and fatigue, and learning "to restore life in case of untimely, accidental death."[144]

Another subject discussed in Soviet ideological writings in the 1960's was the human being under Communism. The Party Program confined itself to the statement that under Communism man would be distinguished by "a high degree of Communist consciousness, industry, discipline and devotion to the public interest." The high development of technology and science would greatly increase "his power over nature." Since Communism achieved the unity of personal and social interests, "harmonious relations will be established between the individual and society." Under Communism, "the abilities and talents of free man, his best moral qualities, blossom forth and reveal themselves in full."[145] The *Fundamentals* pointed out that Communism would enable character and emotions to reach the summit of perfection. New moral impulses—solidarity, friendship, a sense of closest community with other people—would emerge, and there would be relationships of "solidarity, mutual good will, a deep sense of community." The Communist society would be free from all phenomena of inhumanity, injustice, uncivilized behavior, ignorance, crime, and vice. "Violence and self-interest, hypocrisy and egotism, perfidy and vain glory," would "vanish forever" from relations between human beings.[146]

The disappearance of crime was mentioned also in other ideological articles at the time. Above all, offenses against property—which accounted for 95 per cent of all criminal offenses—would disappear. Murder, bodily injury, forgery and other forms of fraud would become things of the past.[147] The people of the Communist future would be distinguished by "humanism, a developed sense of freedom, a creative attitude toward life, personal initiative and comradeship,"[148] and in particular by their high level of education. Under Communism about half the population would "possess medium-level vocational training and the remainder university-standard education."[149] Man would command not only "the scientific and technological knowledge of his day" but would "also be familiar with the problems of the social sciences and with the achievements of literature and art."[150]

Living conditions under Communism were to be distinguished by the fact that, instead of the present type of houses, people would live in "communal palaces," each for about 2,000 to 2,500 people with a residential floor space of up to 40,000 square meters. In these communal palaces, which were described in great detail, people would, as a rule, have their midday and evening meals together in dining halls, but they would also have adequate opportunity for privacy.[151] Cities would consist of "micro-districts," each of 8,000 to 10,000 inhabitants, with a social center, and with buildings serving cultural purposes accounting for 60 to 70 per cent (instead of the present 30 per cent) of the over-all built-up area.[152]

The description of marital and family relationships under Communism emphasized that Communism would mark the beginning of "a period of consistent monogamy." The family would attain its proper purpose under Communism: as a bulwark of love and personal happiness and to raise the future generation. At the same time, it should

not be thought that Communism would eliminate all clashes and conflicts in the family, since "social harmony is by no means commensu-
rately reflected in harmony in love."[153] Extra-marital contacts would
not exist under Communism. Communist morality opposes on principle
extra-marital contacts "out of immoral or frivolous motives. . . . Those
who are ready to go from embrace to embrace are to be pitied, for they
do not know the deep and all-embracing feeling of the attraction of
two hearts, of individual love. . . . Real love requires only two
partners."[154]

As for the upbringing of the children under Communism, a certain
controversy arose in the early 1960's. In the summer of 1960 a well-
known Soviet ideologist had declared the education of children to be
"a public matter" and to be assumed by society, which would "leave to
the family only those functions which may be readily entrusted to it
without harm to the children." The experienced educator could "do far
more for a child than the most sensitive and loving mother." Education
was to be in the hands of society: "Every Soviet citizen will be assigned
to a crèche immediately upon leaving the maternity home; from there
he will pass to a kindergarten or a children's home, then to boarding
school, and from there into independent life, i.e., production, or else to
the study of his chosen special subject."[155] However, this view was opposed by A. Kharchev, the official expert on family matters under
Communism. The function of the parents, he declared, would continue
to exist as far as bringing up children was concerned, as "parental influence on children is unique and cannot be replaced by any other influence." For that reason, direct contact between parents and their
children under domestic conditions would continue to be no less
necessary in the future than it was at present."[156] The Party Program
itself, however, did not discuss these details but confined itself merely
to the statement: "Family relationships will be free once and for all
from material calculations and will be based solely on mutual love and
friendship."[157]

This ideological outline of the Communist future was confined to
the Soviet Union itself. The situation following the world-wide victory
of Communism was mentioned in ideological articles only briefly and
by implication. It would mean that the economy and culture of all nations would approximate one another and that everything would disappear from international relations "that gives even the least pretext
for enmity and discord, isolation and estrangement, national egoism and
exclusiveness."[158]

The world-wide victory of Communism would gradually result also
in a unified Communist world economy. On this point the Soviet ideolo-

gists repeatedly referred to Lenin who once mentioned "a single world economy, regulated by the proletariat of all nations as an integrated whole and according to a common plan."[159] In a similar vein, the Soviet Party Program referred to "the future creation of a world Communist economy regulated by the victorious working people according to one single plan."[160] In due course, moreover, a Communist world culture would arise. "It will be the culture of a classless society, a culture of the entire people, of all mankind."[161] With the world-wide victory of Communism the national cultures of the different nations "will be increasingly imbued with a single Communist content" and this would "lead to the formation of a single, deeply international culture which will be truly the culture of all mankind."[162]

Finally—although this point was not mentioned in the Party Program—a world language of Communism would arise in the future. This idea was first alluded to by Stalin in 1930[163]; in 1950 he again declared that after world-wide victory "the zonal languages will fuse into one common international language, which will of course be neither German, nor Russian, nor English, but a new language."[164] Present-day Soviet ideologists similarly declare that the Communist world language of the future would be "neither Russian nor Chinese, nor English, nor any other of the languages at present existing" but that "a new language will emerge which will unite in itself the worthy achievements of the present languages but will be more perfect and richer."[165] "On the basis of a unified Communist world economy," after the victory of Communism there would also emerge "a unified world language as a means of communication between the nations." In 1962 a Soviet ideologist suggested that the "conditions for the emergence, the spread, and the enrichment of the future unified world language" should theoretically be studied today.[166]

One final question remained: what, in the view of the Soviet ideologists, would happen once the Communist society had become reality? How would the development continue, once all people were joyfully working for but a few hours a day, freed from all anxieties and vices? Once people were distinguished by an invariably noble character, once they were administering themselves, once the state, the courts of law, the prisons had all withered away, once family life and the human personality were in full flower? What then? What mainsprings would be operative then, once the ideals of brotherhood, peace, and equality were realized throughout the world?

The *Fundamentals* state that, even after the realization of Communism, progress would not halt. "Even after attaining that summit, people will not stop, will not be idle, will not give themselves over to passive contemplation. On the contrary, their energies will multiply tenfold. Solved problems will be replaced by new ones; in place of the attained goals, new ones, still more entrancing, will arise." Mankind will be confronted by ever new problems "whose solution will require the creative effort of each succeeding generation."[167]

☐   **The Twenty-second Party Congress (October 1961)**

The Twenty-second Party Congress (October 14–31, 1961) had originally been convened in order to adopt the new Party Program and thus to popularize the prospect of an early realization of Communism in the Soviet Union. The entire preparatory campaign had served this aim. Immediately after the publication of the draft Program at the end of July 1961, a so-called "people's discussion" was organized by the Party leadership. By mid-October 1961, according to official reports, more than 500,000 meetings had been held at which 73 million people were said to have participated. Some 4,600,000 people took part in the discussion of the draft Party Program, and 300,000 Soviet citizens wrote letters or articles on the subject.[168] For months on end all Soviet papers and periodicals published comment and suggested additions, but these were nearly all concerned with practical questions of detail. The Party Program was hailed and celebrated as the "Communist manifesto of the twentieth century," and there was no sign of any serious opposition to it.

The Party Congress, however, showed that this impression was far from the truth. Both Khrushchev's de-Stalinization policy in general and the Party Program in particular had been opposed by conservative dogmatists. At the Party Congress Khrushchev announced that "some comrades" (invariably a term denoting strong opposition) had declared that the dictatorship of the proletariat must be preserved until the final victory of Communism (as demanded also by the Chinese Communist Party). Others had suggested "prohibiting collective farm trade" and "generally dispensing with trade and replacing it by direct distribution" (which was in line with Stalin's proposals in his *Economic Problems of Socialism in the U.S.S.R.*). A downright sensation, however, was caused by repeated statements at the Twenty-second Party Congress that Molotov, who had been removed from the Party leadership in the summer of 1957, had sharply criticized the Party Program in a letter to the Central Committee. Molotov maintained that "the new program is anti-revolutionary in spirit," since it makes "no connection between the building of Communism in the U.S.S.R. and the long-term prospects of the revolutionary struggle of the working class in the capitalist coun-' tries, the prospects of socialist revolution on an international scale." The draft Program, according to Molotov, "gives rise to illusions that the further advance toward Communism by the countries of the so- cialist community" could "take place without revolutionary struggle." He described the draft program as "pacifist" and "revisionist" and de- clared that its final passage was "in profound contradiction to the revolutionary character of Marxist and Leninist teaching."[169]

Even these few observations published in the Soviet press testified to the growing resistance of Stalinist forces. In these circumstances it was not surprising that the Twenty-second Party Congress no longer focused its attention on the optimistic visions of the future, as repre- sented by the Party Program, but on argument with conservative dog- matists within the Soviet Union (generally described as "anti-Party") and with the Chinese-Albanian line in world Communism. As both these forces opposed de-Stalinization, the Twenty-second Congress was marked by a general settling of accounts with Stalinism which surpassed even the Twentieth Congress.

At the very beginning of his opening speech Khrushchev referred to "crudest violations of socialist legality," to "abuse of power," "arbi- trariness," and "persecution of many honest people" during the Stalin era and defended the policy of de-Stalinization. The speakers who fol- lowed him almost vied with each other in their revelations of mis- demeanors and crimes committed during that period. The Uzbek Mukhitdinov reminded the delegates that many loyal functionaries and representatives of the intelligentsia in the non-Russian Union Republics had "been ruined." Defense Minister Malinovsky remarked: "I see in this hall senior military commanders who were innocently imprisoned."[170] Nikolai Podgorny reported that in the Ukraine "leading writers of the Republic, as well as a number of executive Party officials" had been accused "of nationalism, literally without any grounds."[171] Leonid Ilychev, at that time the chief ideologist, reported how Stalin had de- layed the preparation of a textbook of political economy because "the 'Stalinist stage in the development of the political economy of Marxism' was poorly elucidated." Stalin had forbidden the old Bolsheviks to publish their recollections of meetings with Lenin and had blocked any initiative by the ideologists. "There was a suspicious attitude toward any attempt to look into the phenomena of life somehow in a new way, toward any attempt to understand new facts and draw new conclu- sions," Ilychev declared. "The cult of the individual in the sphere of theory is in essence an attempt to solve theoretical problems by fiat, through administrative means. This is abuse of authority in the sphere of theory."[172]

However, all earlier accounts paled into insignificance when the aged Nikolai Shvernik stepped up to the rostrum at the afternoon sitting of October 26. Quoting a wealth of detail, Shvernik described how in Stalin's closest circle proscription lists had been compiled, nonexistent conspiracies staged, and how a minor automobile accident of Molotov's had been dressed up as an attempt on his life, to serve as a pretext for new, far-reaching arrests.[173] After that all restraint was abandoned. Alexander Shelepin (at that time Chairman of the State Security Committee) used the strongest terms and considerable detail to condemn the terror of Stalin and of the leaders responsible for the crimes of the past: "You sometimes wonder how these people can calmly walk the earth, how they can get a quiet night's sleep," Shelepin declared. "They should be haunted by nightmares, they should hear the sobs and curses of the mothers, wives, and children of comrades who perished innocently."[174]

On October 27, Khrushchev once more addressed the Congress— this time with far sharper accusations than in his report on the opening day. Precise details concerning the murder of Kirov in December 1934, the suicide of Ordjonikidze in March 1937, and Stalin's mistrust of even his closest collaborators were now frankly revealed. Stalin, Khrushchev reported, might look at a comrade with whom he was sharing a table and say: "Your eyes are shifty today," and at once one could assume that the comrade with the allegedly unsteady eyes was under suspicion. Khrushchev relentlessly demanded that the terror of the Stalin era should be investigated down to the last detail: "It is now too late to bring the dead back to life, as the saying goes. But it is necessary that all this be recorded truthfully in the history of the Party. This must be done so that phenomena of this sort can never be repeated in the future." Khrushchev then proceeded to make the astonishing (though not implemented) proposal that a memorial for the victims of Stalin's terror should be erected in Moscow, "a monument to the memory of the comrades who fell victim to arbitrariness."[175]

This proposal evidently went too far for most of the Party functionaries, and a compromise was therefore reached to remove Stalin's body from the Mausoleum in Red Square—a proposal made by I. V. Spiridonov, then Leningrad Party Secretary. Spiridonov justified his motion by speaking of the great purge of 1936–38:

Throughout a period of four years an incessant wave of persecution swept over Leningrad, a persecution of honest people who had committed no crime whatever. Promotion to a responsible post often was the first step to the brink of the abyss. Many people were then killed without trial and on the strength of mendacious, hurriedly fabricated accusations. Not only functionaries were exposed to these persecutions, but also their families and even totally innocent children. . . . . The atrocities both during 1935–37 and again during 1949–50 were committed either at Stalin's direct orders or with his knowledge and approval. . . . On behalf of the Leningrad Party organization and the working people of Leningrad I propose to the Twenty-second Party Congress that the mortal remains of Stalin be removed as quickly as possible from Vladimir Ilyich Lenin's Mausoleum and taken to some other place.[176]

Spiridonov's proposal was supported by other Party secretaries with similar condemnations of Stalin's terror. Then, on October 30, 1961, came what was probably the most astonishing scene at a Soviet Party Congress ever. The Old Bolshevik Lazurkina, a member of the Party since 1902 and a comrade-in-arms of Lenin from the days of World War I, who had spent nineteen years of the Stalin era in prisons and camps, now stepped up to the rostrum. Hers was no longer the customary cold and dry Party jargon, but a lively personal account of the horrors of Stalin's rule:

The great injustice committed by Stalin consists not only in that many of our best people lost their lives, that arbitrariness reigned supreme and that numerous innocent people were shot or sent to prison without trial. No, that is not all. The entire atmosphere which then arose in the Party was in no way compatible with the spirit of Lenin. . . . Comrade Zhdanov was secretary of the Oblast Party Committee of Leningrad in May 1937. One day he summoned us, the leading functionaries of the Oblast Committee, to a meeting and announced: two enemies of the Party have been unmasked within the ranks of the Leningrad Party organization—Chudov and Kadatsky. They have been arrested in Moscow. We were unable to utter a word. We were virtually speechless. But when the conference was over and Zhdanov was about to leave the hall I said to him: "Comrade Zhdanov, I don't know Chudov. He has not been in our Leningrad organization long. But I can vouch for Kadatsky. He has been a Party member since 1913 and I have known him for many years. He is a loyal Party member and took part in the struggle against all opposition groups. His arrest is unbelievable! I must get to the bottom of this business." Zhdanov looked at me angrily and said: "Lazurkina, you'd better stop talking like this or you will have to bear the consequences. . . ." We, Lenin's followers, were in the grip of a fear we had not previously known. One person denounced another, mutual confidence had vanished, and one no longer even trusted oneself. Lists for the arrests of innocent people were being compiled. We were tortured so we should denounce others. We were given the lists and forced to sign them; they promised us freedom and threatened:

"If you don't sign we'll torture you." But many remained steadfast, preserving their Bolshevik soul and never signing anything![177]

The roughly 5,000 Party delegates gave Lazurkina an ovation. It seemed hardly credible but it was true: they were frantically applauding an old Bolshevik who had stood up to the tortures of Stalinist functionaries and had never signed a fake confession. Lazurkina's speech was the climax and grand finale of this anti-Stalinist Party Congress, which not only endorsed the de-Stalinization policy of the Twentieth Congress but further confirmed and extended the condemnation of Stalinism. The dissociation from Stalin and the adoption of a reformed line in the Soviet Union seemed now more likely. Immediately after the conclusion of the Party Congress, the coffin with Stalin's body was removed from the Mausoleum and transferred to the Kremlin wall.[178]

Towns and villages that had until then borne Stalin's name (including Stalingrad) were renamed. The trends and decisions of the Twenty-second Party Congress lent a tremendous impetus to reformist Communist forces outside the Soviet Union.[179] In the Soviet Union itself the Party Congress gave rise to lively discussions.[180] During the following few months a number of publications described the negative and tragic consequences of Stalin's rule.[181] But the effects of the Twenty-second Party Congress fell far short of what might have been expected. Neither were any fundamental reforms of the system announced, nor did Soviet ideologists investigate the causes of Stalinism or proceed to analyze the Stalinist system with a view to deriving the necessary lessons or working out a coherent program of reforms. There were many indications that soon after the Congress the opposition of conservative and dogmatic forces was gaining in strength. This was reflected, for instance, in the fact that the Soviet ideologists were made to concentrate on quite a different subject.

## ☐   Suslov Proclaims "Scientific Communism"

Within a few months after the Twenty-second Party Congress Suslov, at a big ideological conference in Moscow (January 30–February 2, 1962) announced an important change in the structure of Soviet Marxism-Leninism. Whereas until then philosophy (dialectical and historical materialism), political economy, and Party history had long been established as independent ideological disciplines with their own appropriate official Party textbooks, the status of the political doctrine of Soviet ideology was still unclear. True, it had been systematically presented in *Fundamentals of Marxism-Leninism,* but it had not yet been recognized as an independent discipline. A few Soviet ideologists had proposed in 1960–61 that the political theory of Soviet ideology should be denoted as "scientific Communism" and regarded as an independent part of Marxism-Leninism.[182]

But it was only now, at the ideological conference of 1962, that these proposals were endorsed in the highest official quarters. Suslov announced that the political concepts of Soviet ideology were to be regarded, under the name "scientific Communism," as an independent part of Marxism-Leninism. Scientific Communism, according to Suslov, was to concern itself with the "main stages in the history and theory of the international workers' movement" and the "practice of building socialism"; however, "the central issues of the course must be the problems of the building of Communism."[183] The new discipline was to be introduced as an independent course in all universities and colleges in the Soviet Union. Within the framework of Marxism-Leninism the subjects studied were to be first dialectical and historical materialism, then political economy, and finally the "foundations of scientific Communism."

The official proclamation of scientific Communism confronted the Soviet ideologists not only with the task of preparing the appropriate instructional materials and textbooks, but also of clarifying a number of ideological questions. A great many articles, therefore, debated in detail how the concept of scientific Communism was to be defined, and how overlapping with other ideological disciplines (above all historical materialism, Party history, and political economy) was to be avoided.[184]

Although all ideologists agreed that scientific Communism was to concern itself with the conditions of the transition from capitalism to socialism and the further evolution to Communism, many attempts were made (some of them rather dogmatic) to define this. Increasing emphasis was now being placed on the early history of present-day scientific Communism, including the role and significance of the utopian socialists;[185] indeed, the history of socialist and Communist ideas was described as "one of the most responsible sectors of the ideological front."[186] This was reflected in V. Roshin's book *Introduction to the Theory of Scientific Communism* (1963). The author devoted about one-fifth of his 164 pages to the origins of scientific Communism. As "precursors" Roshin described the utopian socialists Sir Thomas More (1478–1535), Thomas Campanella (1568–1639), Denis Veiras (especially his *History of the Sevarambs*), the Abbé Morelly (*Shipwreck of the Floating Islands*), Gabriel Mably (1709–85), *François-*

Noël Babeuf (1760–97), Saint-Simon (1760–1825), Charles Fourier (1772–1837), Robert Owen (1771–1858), Etienne Cabet (1788–1856), and Wilhelm Weitling (1808–71), as well as the Russian "revolutionary democrats" Vissarion Belinsky (1811–48), Nikolai Dobrolyubov (1836–61), Alexander Herzen (1812–74), and N. G. Chernyshevsky (1828–89).

Obligatory courses in scientific Communism (usually amounting to 60–70 hours) were introduced in all universities and colleges in 1963. Scientific Communism was also taught as an independent discipline at the two-year and four-year Party colleges.[187]

Just as the ideologists were busy preparing appropriate textbooks of scientific Communism, collections of documents and curricula, a new problem suddenly emerged in January 1965. The well-known Soviet ideologist Fyodor Burlatsky proposed in *Pravda* that political science should be introduced in the Soviet Union as an independent subject within the framework of the social sciences.[188] Just as, a few years earlier, sociology had become "respectable" in the Soviet Union, so Burlatsky now believed the moment had come to introduce political science also. Both in his article and at the subsequent meeting of the Soviet Association of Political Sciences Burlatsky proposed that political science should concern itself with four main subjects. The most important of these, according to him, was the study and investigation of the political system of the socialist countries (including such problems as the role of the state and Party), the methods of scientific guidance of society and the possibility of forecasting the selection, promotion, and replacement of leading functionaries, and public opinion and the forms and methods of propaganda. Political science should, moreover, examine political conditions in the capitalist countries and in the developing countries of Asia and Africa, as well as the problems of international relations and foreign policy, and finally the present political theories, movements, and ideologies.

To cope with these tasks, Burlatsky proposed that special institutes of political science should be set up in the Soviet Union, closely tied to Party and state organs, and with the requisite information at their disposal to enable them not only to examine theoretical problems and train experts in political science, but also to solve immediate practical tasks for Party and state bodies. Sociological research was to be applied to this end on the widest possible scale.

It was clear that Burlatsky's proposal concerning political science cut across the ideological discipline of scientific Communism, and he himself declared that the delineation was "particularly complicated." He therefore suggested that scientific Communism should concentrate on political, economic, and philosophical problems connected with the building of socialism and Communism. A number of other questions, including the national liberation movements, relations between socialist and capitalist states on the one hand and developing countries on the other, the principles of international politics, and the problems of the struggle for peace and coexistence were to be dealt with by political science. Although, even according to the official report,[189] a number of Soviet ideologists supported the introduction of political science, Burlatsky's proposal was turned down. Scientific Communism, it was stated, was the Marxist-Leninist science of politics and there was no need to introduce any special political science in the Soviet Union.

The rejection of Burlatsky's proposal put the final seal of authorization on scientific Communism. The ensuing problems were discussed in detail at three ideological conferences in the spring of 1965. Of particular importance was the conference convened at the end of February 1965 by the periodical *Voprosi Filosofii,* at which a report by Stepanyan was followed by a lengthy discussion on scientific Communism.[190] In March 1965 there followed a conference of university teachers of scientific Communism in Leningrad, and in May 1965 a meeting of the Academic Council of the Faculty of Scientific Communism of the Academy of Social Sciences under the Party Central Committee.[191]

Although the discussion of certain controversial questions continued even after these conferences,[192] the vital problems were now "clarified" for the Soviet ideologists, who were now able to concentrate on the compilation of the new textbooks. By the end of 1965 the publishing house of the Ministry of Defense produced a series of lectures of the Military Political Academy, entitled *Foundations of Scientific Communism* (in three volumes), under the general editorship of Colonel Sulimov. This was followed in the summer of 1966 by an extensive two-volume *Collection of Texts on Scientific Socialism,* whose first volume contained exclusively selections from the utopian socialists; indeed, under the heading "Utopian Theories of the Ancient World," the collection started with excerpts from the writings of Plato and Aristotle. In addition to the utopian socialists listed above, this collection also introduced Gerard Winstanley (1608–57) and Jean Meslier (1664–1729) as "precursors."[193] In the late summer of 1966 followed V. G. Afanasyev's book *Scientific Communism—A Popular Outline,*[194] which appeared in an English translation a few months later.[195]

These preliminary works were followed toward the end of 1966 by the official Party textbook *Foundations of Scientific Communism* in a first printing of 600,000 copies.[196] For the first time in Soviet history the political theory of Communism was here presented as an independent subject, ranking "equal" with dialectical and historical materialism, with political economy, and with the history of the Party. There was, however, one important difference between this textbook and the *Fundamentals of Marxism-Leninism,* for which Otto Kuusinen had been responsible: the new *Foundations* were exclusively the work of professional ideologists. The publication of the new textbook, as was to be expected, was appropriately celebrated but, somewhat surprisingly, also slightly criticized on the grounds that the problems of the future Communist society were described in it in excessive detail.[197] The new textbook at long last contained the "official" definition: "Scientific Communism is the study of the laws of the class struggle of the proletariat and of the socialist revolution, of the building of socialism and Communism. . . . The principles of Scientific Communism represent the theoretical foundations for the practical work of the Marxist-Leninist parties."[198]

Far more important than this definition, however, was the fact that the *Foundations of Scientific Communism* of 1967 differed very extensively from all the ideological documents of the Khrushchev era mentioned so far. Criticism of Stalin had disappeared and the de-Stalinization doctrines had been either considerably toned down or else replaced by neo-Stalinist doctrines—in line with the political changes that had taken place in the Soviet Union since the fall of Khrushchev in October 1964.

☐ **Khrushchev's Fall and the End of de-Stalinization**

On October 15, 1964, the world (but above all the Soviet public itself) was startled by the news that the First Secretary of the Central Committee and Premier of the U.S.S.R. had been relieved of all his functions. The first explanation, that Khrushchev had resigned for "reasons of health," was not believed by anyone and was not even repeated in the Soviet press.

There can be no doubt that an important part in Khrushchev's overthrow was played by his widely unpopular methods of leadership: his over-optimism, the large number of his often ill-prepared reorganizations and reforms, his frequently changed and usually grandiose plans, and his attempts to pronounce and implement new directives without informing the leading bodies. These methods of leadership had been tolerated by Party, state, and army officials as long as Khrushchev had successes to show, but they encountered increasing and indeed open resistance as his serious setbacks became more and more marked during the last years of his rule—reverses in his foreign policy (withdrawal of missiles from Cuba), in the economy (falling short of his own grandiloquently proclaimed targets by ever wider margins), in agriculture (the harvest failure of 1963 and the need to import vast quantities of grain from abroad), and finally in the sphere of international Communism (Peking's increasing influence and the impossibility of convening a representative world conference).

But important as dissatisfaction with Khrushchev's methods of leadership and his setbacks had been during the final years of his rule, more important, and possibly decisive, had been the growing opposition of dogmatic and conservative forces against Khrushchev's general line of de-Stalinization. The sharp critique of Stalin and his crimes, the propagation of socialist legality, the curbing of the secret police, the releases of prisoners and the rehabilitations, the policy of coexistence (however contradictory), and the evident preparation of further reforms —all this had aroused increasing opposition among dogmatic and bureaucratic forces, especially in the Party apparatus and the secret police.

The speed and ease with which Khrushchev was overthrown suggests a temporary "common front" of a number of forces and groups which conspired against Khrushchev for totally different reasons. Whereas some circles (predominantly in the economy and in the state apparatus) merely opposed Khrushchev's methods of leadership while wishing to continue his de-Stalinization reforms—though perhaps in a somewhat more orderly fashion, a kind of "Khrushchevism without Khrushchev"—the conservative dogmatists saw the overthrow of Khrushchev as their long awaited chance to halt de-Stalinization, to revalue Stalin and Stalinism, and to go over to a tougher and harder line in all fields of social life.

During the first few months after Khrushchev's fall it seemed as if the new Soviet leadership under Brezhnev and Kosygin would continue Khrushchev's policy. The changes were so far confined almost exclusively to the methods of leadership. The new Party leadership expressly endorsed the de-Stalinization resolutions of the Twentieth and Twenty-second Party Congresses and merely criticized—a clear allusion to Khrushchev without his name being mentioned—"harebrained scheming," "hasty decisions and actions divorced from reality," as well as "bragging and bluster." The new leadership promised "to appraise soberly the successes achieved," "to concentrate efforts on those tasks which have to be solved in the immediate future," and to take decisions "corresponding to objective regularities and real requirements."[199]

The fall of Lysenko, who was (rightly) extremely unpopular in academic circles, in February 1965, the discussion about the possible introduction of political science in the Soviet Union (January–February 1965), a rather liberal article by the then editor of *Pravda,* A. Rumyantsev, about the Party's relations with the Soviet intelligentsia,[200] the preparations for an at least partial rehabilitation of Bukharin[201]—all this and much else gave rise to the hope that de-Stalinization would be continued.

However, since the spring of 1965 there was increasing evidence that the dogmatic-conservative forces were on the advance—a fact that may have been connected with the beginning of the American bombing of North Vietnam in February. The first indication of a change of course was the attempt to rehabilitate Stalin and portray him more positively—at first by the publication of the memoirs of Marshal Bagramyan, Marshal Konev, and Admiral Kuznetsov,[202] and later in Brezhnev's speech on the twentieth anniversary of the Soviet victory in World War II. In this speech Brezhnev, for the first time, paid tribute to Stalin and avoided all criticism.[203] Articles about the Soviet secret police made hardly any mention of Stalin's crimes.[204] The change of course became even more obvious when, in September 1965, Rumyantsev was deposed and the conservative dogmatist Sergey Trapeznikov appointed head of the Central Committee Department for Science and Education. Trapeznikov complained in *Pravda,* in October 1965, that Soviet history had been "incorrectly" represented during the past few years. It was wrong to judge developments from the point of view of the "personality cult" and in doing so to miss the "heroic struggle" in the building of socialism.[205]

In autumn 1965 the Soviet writers Andrei Sinyavsky and Yuri Daniel were arrested and Solzhenitsyn's home was searched. In December 1965, the forty-eighth anniversary of the secret police received more emphasis than before, and without any mention whatever of Stalin's crimes. By the end of January 1966 *Pravda* was declaring that a number of mistakes had been made during the period of de-Stalinization, that the unmasking of the personality cult had gone too far, and that the concept of the "period of the personality cult" was an "erroneous, non-Marxist term."[206] A harder line became even more obvious in February 1966. The trial of Sinyavsky and Daniel was accompanied by a mud-slinging campaign strongly reminiscent of the Stalin era. In mid-February 1966 it was widely noticed that the tenth anniversary of the Twentieth Party Congress was being passed over in silence, although such anniversaries were normally played up a good deal. At the end of February, on the other hand, there came a marked tribute to, and indeed a glorification of, the Stalinist cultural dictator Zhdanov,[207] who had been condemned as the prototype of Stalinism in Lazurkina's speech at the Twenty-second Party Congress. At the beginning of March 1966 the Georgian Party Secretary Sturua actually asserted that the struggle against the Stalinist personality cult had given rise to "nihilism" and "cosmopolitanism" and other anti-Leninist ideas and movements.[208] The attempt by some particularly extreme neo-Stalinist Party circles to rehabilitate Stalin fully was so obvious that twenty-nine well-known Soviet intellectuals opposed any such attempts in a letter of protest.[209]

The Twenty-third Party Congress (March 29–April 8, 1966) did not officially rehabilitate Stalin, but the extraordinarily violent attacks on pro-reform writers, including Alexander Solzhenitsyn, Ilya Ehrenburg, and even Ambassador Maisky for the publication of books that had appeared legally under Khrushchev, and indeed with his approval; the change of the name of the Party Praesidium to "Politburo" and of the First Secretary to "General Secretary" (Stalin alone had borne this title), and the abolition of the system of rotation introduced by Khrushchev in 1961 (providing for a regular change of personnel in the Party and state hierarchy)—all testified that a harder line was being officially sanctioned at the Party Congress. The doctrines proclaimed under Khrushchev, including "socialist legality," the "state of the entire people," the "Party of the entire people," and the possibility of peaceful socialist transformation were either relegated to the background or no longer mentioned at all. The doctrine of coexistence, emphasized by Khrushchev as the general line of Soviet foreign policy, was now seen merely as part of the struggle against imperialism and linked with the demand for the unmasking of the aggressive policy of imperialism. The principal objective of Soviet foreign policy was defined by Brezhnev as the attainment of favorable international conditions for the building of socialism and Communism. In this connection he mentioned (in this order) the strengthening of the unity of the socialist countries, support for the national liberation movements and co-operation with the developing countries, peaceful coexistence with states with a different social order, and the struggle against the aggressive forces of imperialism.[210]

Simultaneously with its dissociation from Khrushchev's de-Stalinization doctrines the Twenty-third Party Congress confirmed a retreat from his optimistic visions of the future. Ever since 1965 the Soviet press had been noticeably silent about the future Communist society and avoided all statements that Communism would be attained shortly. "Lenin repeatedly warned against any leap forward. He taught us never to represent wishful thinking as reality, and he resolutely opposed the irresponsible use of the term 'Communism,' " an authoritative ideological article stated in August 1965. "Communism is such an exalted concept that we must not interpret some ordinary everyday event as the evolution of new 'Communist relationships.' "[211] Immediately before the Party Congress the well-known Soviet ideologist A. S. Fedoseyev warned against "excessive haste" in the matter of transition to Communism and hinted that the period of socialism would last for a good while yet before Communism was attained.[212] Similarly, at the Twenty-third Party Congress the Communist society was not defined either in the speeches of the Party leaders or in the final resolution; no one mentioned the promise in the Party Program of October 1961 that the phase of Communism would be embarked upon in 1980. Khrushchev's phrase, "the all-round building of the Communist society," was supplanted by the cautious formula of "transition to Communism." A few months after the Party Congress this was spelled out even more clearly: "The attempt to build Communism before socialism has been established, consolidated and developed is just as unthinkable as the attempt to build the roof of a house which has not yet got any foundations or wall."[213]

The Twenty-third Party Congress thus confirmed the changes since Khrushchev's fall. Instead of Khrushchev's over-optimistic visions of the future, the new leadership concentrated on the tasks of the present. Instead of dissociation from Stalinism and a multiplicity of de-Stalinization reforms, the new leadership was interested in consolidating its own power and authority. No experiments, keeping reforms down to a minimum, no criticism of Stalin but continuity of the Stalinist tradition in the sense of a harder line—these were its objectives. Censorship was intensified, the number of arrests and trials increased, conditions in the camps—most of the political detainees were in the camps of the Mordovian Autonomous Republic—deteriorated. In July 1966 the Ministry of the Interior (dissolved by Khrushchev in January 1960) was re-established under the name "Ministry for the Protection of the Social Order" and subsequently (just as under Stalin) renamed "Ministry of the Interior" with the notorious abbreviation MVD; new penalties were introduced for the "deliberate spreading of lies" insulting the Soviet state and the Soviet order, as well as for reviling the Union's coat of arms or the national flag.[214]

Ideologically this process was reflected by a further return to Stalinist tradition. Soviet writers were repeatedly attacked for insulting "our heroic history." The literature of the Stalin era, it was stated, must not be assessed negatively as "literature of the personality cult," since it must never be forgotten that Stalin had been Supreme Commander-in-Chief during World War II.[215] Criticism of Stalin was now replaced by the glorification of military feats of heroism during World War II—in Soviet terminology the "Great Patriotic War"—and much stress was laid on the military-patriotic education of the younger generation.[216] During the preparations for the fiftieth anniversary celebrations of the October Revolution, which dominated Soviet public life for several months, all criticism of Stalin and the Stalin era was avoided,[217] and in connection with the twenty-fifth anniversary celebrations of the Battle of Moscow (October 1966), Stalin was, in fact, extravagantly praised. The observances of the fiftieth anniversaries of the October Revolution (November 1967), of the secret police (December 1967), and of the Soviet armed forces (February 1968) were similarly characterized by a resumption of the Stalinist tradition. Soviet ideologists, especially historians, were now being reproved for "failing to correct with sufficient consistency"[218] the mistakes of the recent past, i.e., those committed during de-Stalinization. Stalin's resolutions concerning the study of history, dating back to the early 1930's, were praised as "a profoundly progressive matter," in contrast to the "negative phenomena" that were said to have emerged in Soviet historiography in the late 1950's and early 1960's. Earlier views had been too hastily revised and there had been relapses into a "nihilist relationship" with the past.[219]

The inspiring hopes of reforms and visions of the future were now replaced by a conservative attachment to the defense of bureaucratic positions of power against all liberalizing influences from within the country and from without. In August 1967 the Central Committee declared that steadfastness "in the struggle against imperialist ideology and the bourgeois and reformist falsifiers of Marxism-Leninism" was "one of the most important obligations" of Soviet social science.[220] The emphasis was no longer on the propagation of one's own ideology but on resistance to "slanderous fabrications"; significantly enough, the main target of these Soviet attacks were not reactionary theories but the supporters of "convergence" and of the ideas of "bridge-building" between East and West— a clear indication of the fear the neo-Stalinist leadership had of the attractiveness of just these ideas. The study of Soviet Party history was now also to stand "in the forefront of the struggle against bourgeois ideology."[221] Sergei Trapeznikov, who was now playing a role similar to that of Zhdanov under Stalin, complained that many Soviet ideologists were still lacking in "offensive spirit" and "Party passion" in the struggle "against anti-Communism, reformism, and revisionism," and demanded "a thorough and convincing critique of anti-Communism, of the various opportunist currents." Above all, he warned against "pluralism" and "revisionistically colored ideas of a multiplicity of formulas of Marxism."[222]

However, the political and ideological change of course after Khrushchev's overthrow was reflected not only in topical ideological publications but above all in the textbook *Foundations of Scientific Communism,* which was published in 1967 and replaced the *Fundamentals of Marxism-Leninism* of 1959 and the Soviet Party Program of October 1961.

☐ **"The Foundations of Scientific Communism" of 1967**

*The Foundations of Scientific Communism,* which had reached two printings (1,100,000 copies) by the summer of 1968, was compulsory reading not only for the political training of Party members but also for students of all faculties at all universities and colleges in the U.S.S.R.

The ideological line of the new textbook emerged clearly in its attitude to the problems of war, peace, and coexistence. While the corresponding doctrine under Khrushchev was entitled "the danger of war and the struggle of the peoples for peace," it was now "the revolutionary process and the struggle for peace." The distinction between "just" and "unjust wars," which had been widely ignored during de-Stalinization, was reintroduced. The non-inevitability of wars, on the other hand, receded far into the background, and Khrushchev's doctrine that, even while capitalism continued to exist in part of the world, it was possible to banish war from the life of society, was no longer mentioned. Peaceful coexistence was no longer the "general line" of Soviet foreign policy; the struggle for peace and coexistence, in the new formulation, was inseparably bound up with the struggle against the "aggressive policy of imperialism."[223] The objectives of world revolution, on the other hand, were proclaimed with greater clarity and with greater emphasis: "The Communists proclaim their principal objective openly —the overthrow of the capitalist system throughout the world and its replacement by a Communist society."[224]

Proceeding from the concept of the "three revolutionary streams" (the countries of the world socialist system, the international workers' movement, and the national liberation movements) the world Communist movement was said to be similarly made up of three "main sections" which, according to the *Foundations,* each had their separate, different tasks in the struggle for the common goal. The Communist parties of the socialist countries were responsible for the "successful building of socialism and Communism" and were to "do their utmost to discharge their international duties in resolutely and actively supporting all forms of the liberation struggle against imperialism." The Communist parties of the developed capitalist countries had as their main aim "the overthrow of the capitalist system by a socialist revolution." The Communist parties of the countries liberated from colonialism must see their main task in "bringing the national liberation revolutions to their conclusion and insuring their countries' development along the non-capitalist road which creates the opportunity for building socialism."[225]

Khrushchev's concept of the possibility of a peaceful transition to socialism was once more replaced in the *Foundations* of 1967 by an emphasis on violent revolution:

The use of armed forms of struggle under conditions when the exploiting classes resort to armed force is necessary and logical. Without this means it would be impossible to break the opposition of reactionary circles. In a number of countries where the monopolies hold sway and militarism is strong the socialist revolutions will in all probability take place by force of arms.[226]

The concept of different roads to socialism was diminished so much that there might never have been a Twentieth Party Congress. Admittedly, it was now stated, each country had its "own peculiarities" on the road to socialism, but since "in its decisive features the economic structure of all countries during the period of transition is basically the same, the national peculiarities cannot affect the general laws of the building of socialism."

All ruling Communist parties in socialist countries had now, according to the new textbook, to follow the ten "general laws," which were clearly taken from Soviet experience: (1) Leadership of the working people "by the working class whose nucleus is the Marxist-Leninist Party"; (2) the "realization of the proletarian revolution in one form or another"; (3) the alliance of workers and peasants; (4) replacement of capitalist ownership by social ownership of the means of production; (5) the gradual socialist transformation of agriculture; (6) the "planned development of the economy"; (7) a "socialist revolution in the field of ideology and culture," including the "training of an intelligentsia" which would be "devoted . . . to the cause of socialism"; (8) solution of the nationalities problem; (9) "defense of the achievements of socialism against the plots of external and domestic enemies"; (10) proletarian internationalism—which in practice invariably meant subordination to the Soviet Union.

The "general laws" covered the fields of "politics, economics, and culture." True, "the concrete historical, economic, political, geographical, and cultural conditions of a particular country, as well as the international situation" were to be taken into account, but "the Soviet experience has international signifiance."[227]

In discussing the dictatorship of the proletariat, the *Foundations* of 1967, in much the same way as under Stalin, laid greater emphasis on the need for force. The use of force, it was asserted, was necessary because the establishment of the dictatorship of the proletariat "does not immediately remove the exploiting classes from their positions in society" and because the remnants of the former classes, supported by "help from outside," would try "to re-establish the power of the capitalists in the country; in this struggle they resort to the most varied methods, from sabotage to the organization of counterrevolutionary rebellions and the unleashing of civil wars." In this way they tried to attract the peasantry and the middle strata to their side and to undermine the working class's confidence in proletarian power. "Hence the suppression of opposition of hostile classes is an inseparable aspect of the dictatorship of the proletariat"; indeed, this was "a continuation of the class struggle in a new form."[228]

The passages about the socialist society make it clear that the system established in the Soviet Union was to be regarded as a model for all other countries. In various socialist countries, the textbook declared, certain differences in the social structure might occur as a result of different historical traditions and economic developments, but "the fundamental trends are the same in all socialist countries." The socialist society was characterized, in the Soviet view, by "social, political, and ideological unity," reflecting "not only the unity of interests and activity of the classes but also a unity of nature and character." Although disputes between classes had been liquidated under socialism, this did not mean that "the question of the class struggle had altogether become a thing of the past" since "the front of the class struggle against the capitalist world" must be kept up, as must also the struggle against its subversive activity and its influence in the socialist countries. "Hence the struggle against the survivals of capitalism must be continued."[229]

Under these circumstances it was not surprising that the new textbook contained no trace of the Khrushchev era's sharp criticism of the March 1937 Stalinist doctrine of the alleged exacerbation of the class struggle with the further development of socialism. Altogether the book contained no criticism of Stalin or of his rule. The *Foundations* conveyed the impression that there had never been any such things as a personality cult, or show trials, or mass arrests in the Soviet Union.

The doctrine of the transition to Communism no longer made any mention of the promises contained in the Party Program of 1961, including its detailed timetable for Soviet development up to 1980. Nor was the Communist society of the future described in a chapter of its own, as it had been in the *Fundamentals* of 1959; it was mentioned merely in connection with the transition to Communism. The new textbook made it clear that any detailed description of the Communist future was no longer opportune.

Thus the *Foundations of Scientific Communism,* as valid at this moment, is distinguished by three decisive characteristics. First, all criticism of Stalin and the Stalinist era has been expunged—a clear demonstration that the present leadership regards itself as the continuation, even though in a somewhat modernized form, of the Stalin era. Second, all the important de-Stalinization doctrines of the Khrushchev period have either been totally eliminated or reduced to a minimum —a clear ideological indication that the present leadership attaches chief importance not to reforms or changes but to the maintenance and consolidation of its own authority and power. Third, the ideas about an early attainment of the final Communist goal have been reduced to a minimum—a clear indication that the present Soviet leadership no longer believes it can reach these goals. The emphasis is no longer on the moral incentive of an early achievement of the final Communist goal, but on discipline and subordination to the decisions of the Party leadership in the solution of all topical political questions.

☐ **Brezhnev's Doctrine of "Limited Sovereignty"**

Hand in hand with the political and ideological re-Stalinization inside the Soviet Union, increasing emphasis was placed on the Soviet Union's leading role in relation to the other socialist countries. The *Foundations of Scientific Communism* had already set out ten "general laws" for the evolution of all socialist countries, in order to pin them down to the Soviet line, but that was only a beginning. In July 1968 Brezhnev announced that the Soviet Union would never be indifferent "to the fate of the building of socialism in other countries."[230] On August 21, 1968, there followed the occupation of Czechoslovakia. Within a short space of time the Soviet leadership announced three new doctrines—"silent counterrevolution," "limited sovereignty," and the "international dictatorship of the proletariat"—with the aim not only of justifying the occupation of Czechoslovakia in retrospect but also of curtailing the sovereignty of the other socialist countries in the future, and of reserving for the Soviet leadership the right of intervention.

The first step in this direction was the new doctrine of "silent" or "creeping" counterrevolution. According to this doctrine it was wrong to visualize "counterrevolution" exclusively "in the form of armed actions or direct military attacks," since "counterrevolution" could also take place in a "silent" and "peaceful" manner:

It is therefore the intention of "silent" counterrevolution at first "not to make much noise," to proceed only gradually, without publicly opposing the socialist accomplishments, while at the same time flinging mud at everything, falsifying, disrupting, and undermining everything. In this manner a "peaceful" gradual transformation of the socialist system into a capitalist order of society is to be prepared.

The methods of "peaceful counterrevolution," according to this doctrine, included also "statements about a 'democratization' of socialism" and "talk about the 'improvement' of the socialist order."[231]

The new doctrine provided the Soviet leadership with the chance of automatically labeling as "silent counterrevolution" any reforms in a socialist country beyond measures desired by Moscow, and thus of avoiding any serious discussion or examination of the problem. Above all, the concept of "silent counterrevolution" provided a prior justification for any Soviet pressure against any reforms in a socialist country.

Under the new doctrine of "limited sovereignty," proclaimed shortly afterward, the defense of the socialist system in a certain country was not just a matter for the country concerned but primarily a matter concerning the entire (Soviet-led) "world socialist system." The defense of the world socialist system, it was now declared, was an "internationalist duty." The socialist countries must not shirk this duty either for reasons of some "abstract sovereignty" or of some "formal observance of freedom of self-determination."[232]

All law, including international law, was subject under this doctrine to the "laws of the class struggle" (which automatically meant the interests of the Soviet leadership):

In the Marxist conception, the norms of law, including the norms governing relations among socialist countries, cannot be interpreted in a narrowly formal way, outside the general context of the class struggle in the present-day world. . . . Laws and the norms of law are subordinated to the laws of the class struggle and the laws of social development. These laws are clearly formulated in the documents jointly adopted by the Communist and Workers' parties.[233]

The Soviet Communists "take the view that national and state independence cannot be seen in the abstract," it was pointed out shortly afterward. "Marxist-Leninists have always invested the concept of sovereignty with a concrete class content. The world today is divided into two opposing systems; hence independence and sovereignty of a socialist state means above all independence from capitalism."[234]

Even questions of the domestic development of a socialist country —including the question whether its socialist order was in danger—was now to be decided not so much by the Communists of the country concerned as by the "socialist world system." Thus Brezhnev declared: "When internal and external forces hostile to socialism try to turn the development of any socialist country backward to a capitalist restoration, when a threat arises to the cause of socialism in that country, a threat to the security of the socialist community as a whole, that is no longer a problem only of the people of the country in question, but a general problem, the concern of all the socialist countries."[235]

Here was the official proclamation of the right of intervention on the part of the "socialist world system" (in effect the Soviet Union), which was also to be the sole judge of what represented "hostile forces" and when a "danger to socialism" existed. Since, however, under the doctrine of "silent counterrevolution," even any support for a democratization of socialism could be declared "counterrevolution" or "capitalist restoration," any Soviet intervention from outside was now a priori justified.

A further curtailment of the sovereignty of the socialist countries occurred late in the autumn of 1968 as a result of the new doctrine of the "international dictatorship of the proletariat." Referring to Lenin— though hardly in the sense in which he had understood it—the Soviet Politburo member K. T. Mazurov declared that the time had come for "transforming the dictatorship of the proletariat from a national into an internationalist one." The task now was "to strengthen the power and solidarity of the world socialist system," with particular emphasis on the co-operation of the countries of the socialist community in "strengthening their defense capabilities."[236]

The new doctrine of limited sovereignty made it clear that (1) the countries allied with the Soviet Union were to be sovereign only vis-à-vis the capitalist world but not vis-à-vis the (Soviet-led) "world socialist system"; (2) every socialist country had to subordinate itself to the interests of the "world socialist system"; (3) relations between socialist countries were to be governed not by the rules of international law, by some "abstract idea of sovereignty," or some "formal preservation of the principle of self-determination," but, instead, by the jointly (under Soviet leadership) agreed on political and ideological documents; (4) any threat to the socialist system in a socialist country was to be the problem not of the country concerned but primarily that of the "world socialist system" which must "deal" with it; (5) all-round co-operation of the socialist states was to be further intensified, with the aim of an "international dictatorship of the proletariat" (which in practice always meant the Soviet power system).

However, the Soviet doctrine of "limited sovereignty" was rejected by many Communist parties, above all by those of Yugoslavia and Rumania. Tito, speaking on behalf of the Yugoslav Communists, declared:

This doctrine, by referring to some allegedly higher stage of relations between the socialist countries, negates the sovereignty of these countries and attempts to legalize the right of one or more countries to impose its own will upon other socialist countries, according to its own judgment, even by means of military intervention. Of course we resolutely reject any such concept as running counter to the fundamental right of all peoples to independence and to the principles of international law. Moreover, such a concept also clashes with the interests of the struggle for socialism.[237]

Nicolai Ceausescu, the leader of the Rumanian Communists, made a similar statement on August 14, 1968, i.e., a week before the Soviet intervention in Czechoslovakia:

There can be no justification for allowing any kind of use of armed forces for an intervention in the internal affairs of any member state of the Warsaw Treaty. The regulation of internal affairs is the exclusive business of the parties and the peoples of those countries; any kind of intervention can only damage the cause of socialism, of friendship and co-operation of the socialist countries.[238]

After the occupation of Czechoslovakia Ceausescu formulated these views even more clearly:

There is no justification whatsoever, and there can be no excuse, for accepting even for a moment the idea of military intervention in the affairs of a fraternal socialist state. The problem of choosing the ways of socialist construction is a problem of each Party, each state, and of every people, and nobody can set himself up as an adviser or guide for the way in which socialism must be built. It is the affair of every people, and we deem that, in order to place the relations between socialist countries and Communist parties on a truly Marxist-Leninist basis, it is necessary to put an end once and for all to interference in the affairs of other states and other parties.[239]

The Soviet doctrines of "limited sovereignty" and the "international dictatorship of the proletariat" were opposed not only by Yugoslavia and Rumania but also—and with even far greater vehemence—by the Chinese Communists. They declared:

The theories of "limited sovereignty" and the "international dictatorship" flagrantly trample underfoot the universally acknowledged principle of state sovereignty. . . . According to the gangster logic of the Soviet revisionist renegades, other countries can only exercise "limited sovereignty" while Soviet revisionism itself assumes unlimited sovereignty. . . . Should any of these countries be disobedient or even resist, Soviet revisionism will take measures of "international dictatorship," armed intervention included, against that country.[240]

□ **Criticism and Reform Proposals**

Ever since Stalin's death there have been repeated endeavors in the Soviet Union—mostly among the Soviet intelligentsia—to formulate concepts of political reform. During the period of de-Stalinization these were mostly concerned with lending greater momentum to the half-hearted official de-Stalinization doctrines and reforms, and supplementing them by new, far-reaching proposals. Subsequently, since the beginning of neo-Stalinism, concepts of political reform emerged in direct opposition to the official ideology. Of the large number of such opinions only a few particularly typical ones can be listed here, opinions emphasizing reforms of the political system.

Hopes of a democratization in the Soviet Union were especially high after the Twentieth Party Congress in February 1956. An English visitor, who speaks Russian fluently, had long and extensive conversations with Soviet students in the autumn of 1956. He reported that they had expressed the following ideas: "We should have a real workers' democracy," one student had said. "All workers should be free to form their own political organizations." Another had proposed that the electoral system introduced in the Stalin era (and still in force), providing for only one candidate in each constituency, should be amended: "We need more than one candidate for each constituency. We want to be able to choose. All the different groups of workers should be able to put up their own candidates." The principle of collective leadership should not be confined to the Central Committee; the Supreme Soviet should meet regularly, and the leading functionaries of Party and government should "not live in a special quarter outside the city in luxury villas, heavily guarded. They should live among the people and be constantly in touch with them." Others wanted to replace the collective farms with a system of voluntary co-operatives: "If I were asked what I want, I would first advocate the abolition of the collective farm system . . . we want things to be as in Yugoslavia. In Yugoslavia there are no collective farms . . .

each works his own plot . . . or there are free co-operatives of a number of households . . . voluntary in fact and not pro forma."[241]

Even the possibility of a multi-party system in the U.S.S.R. was discussed at that time. "It is sometimes asked why there is only one party in the U.S.S.R.," *Pravda* wrote at the time—but immediately, as was to be expected, dispensed with this idea.[242] Demands were also voiced for workers' councils in the factories and for workers' self-administration in industry. The leading official Party periodical *Kommunist* reported demands "to replace the principle of appointing factory managements from above by the election of factory managements from below." Others had proposed a "social self-administration" of factories and entire industries, and suggested that factory managers should be elected from within the factories themselves since this was entirely in line with Lenin's ideas. *Kommunist* remarked that such proposals had been "isolated cases" and firmly rejected them, but the fact that a leading article was devoted to the subject indicates that they were not quite so isolated.[243]

During the so-called "people's discussion" of the draft Party Program in the summer and autumn of 1961, the Soviet press published a large number of readers' letters which contained, though sporadically and certainly in muted form, proposals for the democratization of the political and economic system. One reader, for instance, proposed that the administrative economic apparatus be replaced by elected economic bodies,[244] and that the state economic apparatus be supplanted by "councils of works managers," who would among themselves establish direct connections between individual factories.[245] A worker demanded that the economic leaders be elected by the factory staff.[246] In the political sphere there were suggestions that functionaries should "more frequently meet the people, listen more attentively to their wishes and troubles, and respond to them."[247] At least once every three months all functionaries should report back about their work to the workers who had elected them[248] and the state apparatus should be reduced by 50 per cent during the next two or three years.[249] All functionaries in the state and Party should be appointed in a democratic manner, for "it is not a rare occurrence that the appointment of a functionary to an important post takes place without participation by the public."[250] Within the Party, all Party members should have the opportunity "to voice their opinion freely" at meetings—which so far, unfortunately, is rarely the case.[251]

Following Khrushchev's fall, the emergence of a harder line, and neo-Stalinist tendencies, the rift between the regime and society was getting deeper, and serious reform proposals could no longer appear in the press. That was why illegally disseminated political letters, and indeed whole program memoranda—described by their own authors as "unofficial literature" or *samizdat* (meaning "self-published") —began to play an important part. Concepts of political reform were expounded and argued in greater detail. The numerous statements and protests by authors and artists are too well known to be repeated in this book. Less well known, but exceedingly important, is the fact that scientists, and even liberal Party functionaries have increasingly protested in recent years against the growing neo-Stalinism and championed a liberalization of the system.

A typical example is the letter the Party functionary and collective chairman Ivan A. Yakhimovich (from the Kraslava district in Latvia) addressed to Suslov at the beginning of 1968. Needless to say, it was not published in the Soviet Union. In this letter Yakhimovich protested against the writers' trials and contrasted the original ideas of the October Revolution with present-day neo-Stalinist policy: "We were clad in rags, hungry and powerless, but we came out victorious because we emphasized man's liberation from injustice, arbitrariness, and lawlessness. Yet all could be lost in spite of rockets and hydrogen bombs, if we were to forget the mainsprings of the Great Socialist October Revolution."

The protests of the intelligentsia and the increasing spread of "unofficial literature," Yakhimovich declared, could not be stopped by trials or oppressive measures but solely by "the unfolding of democratic rights," "observance of the Constitution," and the "practical realization of the Declaration of Human Rights" to which the Soviet Foreign Minister had also put his signature. Above all, Yakhimovich demanded a new relationship with protesting young people: "I believe that in a country where more than 50 per cent of the population is under thirty, the persecution of young opponents represents an extremely dangerous line, indeed adventurism." Not yes-men or mothers' darlings, "but just these young rebels, the most energetic, most courageous members of the younger generation, inspired by high principles, will determine the future of the Soviet Union. It is nonsense to see in them opponents of Soviet rule, and even greater nonsense to let them languish in prisons or to poke fun at them." It was necessary to come to an understanding with these young people. "They will inevitably create a new Party. Ideas cannot be destroyed with bullets, prison, or banishment. Anyone failing to understand this is no politician, no Marxist." Yakhimovich supported Togliatti's reform proposals as well as the Twentieth Congress of the CPSU and declared that the forces then liberated could never again be crushed by anyone, by any force, or by any pressure:

"Remember: Leninism—yes! Stalinism—no!" Yakhimovich called on the leading functionaries: "Have the courage to correct the mistakes committed before the workers and peasants take this matter into their own hands."[252]

While the collective farm chairman and Party official Yakhimovich addressed himself to the leadership as an individual and confined himself to a few political aspects, the views of the Soviet reformists were expressed a good deal more clearly in the memorandum of the nuclear scientist Sakharov. His memorandum "Reflections on Progress, Peaceful Coexistence, and Intellectual Freedom," drafted in June 1968, represents a kind of collective paper—Sakharov himself thanked a number of other persons for suggested improvements. The extensive memorandum, running to about sixty pages, was addressed not only to the leadership of the country but also to all Soviet citizens and "all men of good will in the world."

Sakharov proceeded from the demand to make socialism attractive.

The prospects of socialism now depend on whether socialism can be made attractive, whether the moral attractiveness of the ideals of socialism and the glorification of labor, compared with the egotistical ideas of private ownership and the glorification of capital, will be the decisive factors that people will bear in mind when comparing socialism with capitalism, or whether people will remember mainly the limitations of intellectual freedom under socialism or, even worse, the fascistic regime of the cult [of personality].

The future of Soviet society demanded liquidation of Stalinism, a merciless critique of the Stalinist past: "The exposure of Stalin must be carried through to the end, to the complete truth," Sakharov declared, "not just to the carefully weighed half-truth dictated by caste considerations." There must be no yielding to the attempts by Party *apparatchiki* to prevent this: "Lately we are often told not to 'rub salt into wounds.' This is usually being said by people who suffered no wounds. Actually only the most meticulous analysis of the past and of its consequences will now enable us to wash off the blood and dirt that befouled our banner."

Sakharov praised Khrushchev's "bold speech" at the Twentieth Party Congress, which "came as a surprise to Stalin's accomplices in crime," as well as the de-Stalinization measures including "the release of hundreds of thousands of political prisoners and their rehabilitation, steps toward the revival of the principles of peaceful coexistence and toward a revival of democracy." In view of these facts Khrushchev, "despite his regrettable mistakes of a voluntarist character in subsequent years and despite the fact that Khrushchev, while Stalin was alive, was one of his collaborators in crime," must on the whole be assessed positively; indeed, Sakharov spoke of the need to "value highly the historical role of Khrushchev."

However, the exposure of Stalinism must be carried through much more consistently. It was indispensable "to publish all authentic documents, including the archives of the NKVD, and conduct nationwide investigations." It would further be "highly useful for the international authority of the Soviet Communist Party and the ideals of socialism if, as was planned in 1964 but never carried out, the Party were to announce the 'symbolic' expulsion of Stalin, murderer of millions of Party members, and at the same time the political rehabilitation of the victims of Stalinism."

Such measures were the more urgent as neo-Stalinist attempts were being made "to publicly rehabilitate Stalin" and "his pseudosocialism of terroristic bureaucracy." The neo-Stalinist tendencies, including the Daniel-Sinyavsky trial, the persecution of progressive representatives of the Soviet intelligentsia, the dismissal of people on the strength of blacklists, the increasing hardening of the regime in the camps, and the tightening of the "crippling censorship of Soviet artistic and political literature" had greatly disquieted and outraged the Soviet public.

Among Sakharov's principal demands was, first of all, intellectual and political freedom: "Intellectual freedom of society will facilitate and smooth the way for this trend toward patience, flexibility, and a security from dogmatism, fear, and adventurism." The prerequisite for that was the abolition of censorship. "Liberalized" instructions would not do—at least not in the long run. "Major organizational and legislative measures are required, for example, adoption of a special law on press and information that would clearly and convincingly define what can and what cannot be printed and would place the responsibility on competent people who would be under public control." The international exchange of information (press, tourism) must be extended. Sociological, political, and economic research should "be conducted not only according to government-controlled programs, otherwise we might be tempted to avoid 'unpleasant' subjects and questions."

Simultaneously Sakharov proposed a number of measures that would eliminate arbitrariness and make socialist legality a reality. He said all unconstitutional laws and decrees that violate human rights must be rescinded. This should be linked with a revision of the penal system: "The restoration of Leninist principles of public control over places of imprisonment would undoubtedly be a healthy development. Equally important would be a complete amnesty of political prisoners, and not just the recent limited amnesty, which was proclaimed on the fiftieth anniversary of the October Revolution. . . . There should also be a review of all political trials that are still raising doubts among the progressive public." In the political and state sphere Sakharov, proceeding from Marx and Lenin, emphasized democratic control: "Both Marx and Lenin always stressed the viciousness of a bureaucratic system as the opposite of a democratic system." Especially under present-day conditions, when the complexity of social phenomena and the dangers threatening mankind had grown immeasurably, it was "the more important that mankind be protected against the danger of dogmatic and voluntaristic errors, which are inevitable when decisions are reached in a closed circle of secret advisers or shadow cabinets." Sakharov believed that the Soviet development would lead first to a multi-party system. Although he did not regard the multi-party system as "an essential stage in the development of the socialist system" or as "a panacea for all ills," he nevertheless assumed that "a multi-party system may be an inevitable consequence of the course of events when a ruling Communist Party refuses for one reason or another to rule by the scientific democratic method required by history."

In economic policy Sakharov called for an objective assessment of Soviet economic development. In any propaganda about catching up with and outstripping the U.S.A. it must always be remembered that

we are now catching up with the United States only in some of the old, traditional industries, which are no longer as important as they used to be for the United States (for example, coal and steel). In some of the newer fields, for example, automation, computers, petrochemicals, and especially in industrial research and development, we are not only lagging behind but are also growing more slowly, so that a complete victory of our economy in the next few decades is unlikely.

In his proposals for economic policy Sakharov stood for "the preservation of the basic present features of ownership of the means of production in the socialist countries." As a necessary prerequisite for further economic progress he saw "a greater role for economic and market factors accompanied by increased public control over the managerial group" and "the establishment of a correct system of market prices, proper allocation and rapid utilization of investment funds." The reform experiments of certain socialist countries, including Yugoslavia and Czechoslovakia, were "of great significance."

In the social sphere Sakharov urged the abolition of concealed privileges since they gave rise to the suspicion that "loyal servants of the existing system are being bribed." The correct way would be "not the setting of income ceilings for Party members or some such measure, but simply the prohibition of all privileges and the establishment of unified wage rates, based on the social value of labor and an economic market approach to the wage problem."

In the sphere of foreign policy Sakharov called for an objective assessment of the new trends in capitalism. "There are no grounds for asserting, as is often done in the dogmatic vein, that the capitalist mode of production leads the economy into a blind alley or that it is obviously inferior to the socialist mode in labor productivity, and there are certainly no grounds for asserting that capitalism always leads to absolute impoverishment of the working class." Indeed, the new trends in capitalism should be "a fact of great theoretical significance for any non-dogmatic Marxist." He supported a peaceful coexistence and a possible rapprochement of the two systems. "Both capitalism and socialism are capable of long-term development, borrowing positive elements from each other, and actually coming closer to each other in a number of essential aspects." The propaganda confrontation of capitalism and socialism, Sakharov maintained, disregarded the fact that the development of modern society both in the Soviet Union and in the United States was marked by "increasing complexity of structure and of industrial management, giving rise in both countries to managerial groups that are similar in social character." More important was the fact "that on any other course except ever-increasing coexistence and collaboration between the two systems"—including an ironing out of their antagonisms and mutual aid—"annihilation awaits mankind." However, a rapprochement between the two systems must "not be an unprincipled, antipopular plot between ruling groups, as happened in the extreme case [of the Soviet-Nazi rapprochement] of 1939–41. Such a rapprochement must rest not only on a socialist, but on a popular, democratic foundation, under the control of public opinion, as expressed through publicity, elections, and so forth." Sakharov stated that he was taking over the term "convergence" from Western literature but was giving it "a socialist and democratic meaning." Convergence presupposed both (the already mentioned) reforms in the Soviet Union and "wide social reforms in the capitalist countries," including "substantial changes in the structure of ownership, with a greater role played by government and co-operative ownership."

Sakharov's reform proposals were all on the line of a humanist socialism of the kind (the memorandum was drafted in June 1968, at the time of the "Prague Spring") that was being attempted in Czechoslovkia. "Today the key to a progressive restructuring of the system of government in the interest of mankind lies in intellectual freedom. This has been understood, in particular, by the Czechoslovaks and there can be no doubt that we should support their bold initiative, which is so valuable for the future of socialism and all mankind. That support should be political and, in the early stages, include increased economic aid."[253]

The demands of the Soviet reformers, disseminated only illegally within the Soviet Union, agree very largely with the political concepts of humanist Marxism as voiced in Yugoslavia since 1948 and by individuals and groups in Eastern Europe, and also in Western European Communist parties during the past decade. We shall deal with these concepts in a later chapter. Meanwhile we must cast a glance at another political-ideological current of present-day Communism—that of Maoism, described by its own followers and champions as "the great thought of Mao Tse-tung."

# 5

## The Political Concepts of Maoism

The Chinese Communists claim to have developed a Communist ideology of their own. They describe themselves as followers of "the
thought of Mao Tse-tung," or sometimes "the great thought of Mao
Tse-tung." The Peking leadership maintains that this is not simply a
Chinese interpretation of Marxism but that "Marxism has developed to
a completely new stage—the stage of Mao Tse-tung's thought."[1]

Whether or not one accepts this somewhat extravagant claim—and
it is disputed by the majority even within the world Communist movement—one thing is certain: Maoism had its origin in the endeavor to
transfer the political tenets of Marxism and Leninism to China's totally
different conditions. This "Sinification of Marxism" led, step by step
over four decades, to the emergence of a specifically Chinese political
theory of Communism.

This was not entirely surprising. Over a hundred years ago, in
1850, Karl Marx had prophesied that the application of socialist principles to China would result in considerable changes. "Chinese socialism
may stand in the same relation to the European variety as Chinese
philosophy stands to the Hegelian."[2] Lenin, too, had repeatedly pointed
out that Communism in China would show a multitude of peculiarities.
The Communists of the "awakening peoples of the East," Lenin declared at the end of 1919, were faced with the task of applying "Com-

munist theory and practice to conditions in which the bulk of the population are peasants, and in which the task is to wage a struggle against medieval survivals and not against capitalism."[3] The importance of the Chinese tradition and the different nature of class forces and objectives had thus been recognized by Marx and Lenin, even though only in passing.

These were problems the Communist Party of China, founded in 1921, had to deal with from the start. In China neither the conditions existed for a social revolution in the sense of Marx and Engels, nor even those for a socialist revolution in the sense of Lenin. The Chinese Communists were operating in a vast semi-colonial, semi-feudal country, economically even more backward than the czarist Russia of 1917, a country where the working class did not even account for 1 per cent of the population. Moreover, China was largely controlled by foreign powers, and the country's national liberation, therefore, played a decisive role. Finally, the many centuries of isolation, the Confucian tradition, the ethnocentric idea of the "middle kingdom"—China invariably saw herself as the center of the world—were bound to have their effect on the development and character of the Chinese Revolution and on Chinese Communism. Instead of a socialist revolution, what China needed first of all was an anti-feudal revolution and the overcoming of its medievalism. Under these circumstances, it was not the working class but the peasantry that had to represent the main force of the revolution—a revolution inseparably linked with China's national liberation struggle against foreign powers.

These peculiarities were reflected in Chinese Communism, both in its practice and in its theory. The "Sinification of Marxism" took place in the 1930's and 1940's. Following the victory of the Chinese Revolution in October 1949, the concepts evolved by Mao were raised to the status of an official state doctrine—described as "the great thought of Mao Tse-tung"—and since the early 1960's held up as a universally valid theory for Communists in all countries.

Maoism, officially called the "great thought of Mao Tse-tung," is—according to *Peking Review*—based on four theories:

It is Chairman Mao who has taught us that the new democratic revolution is the necessary preparation for the socialist revolution and that the socialist revolution is the inevitable sequel to the new democratic revolution. Following the victory of the new democratic revolution, it was necessary, without interruption, for the revolution to move on to the stage of socialism.

It is Chairman Mao who has taught us that political power grows out of the barrel of a gun and that only with guns can the old world under the rule of imperialism and all reaction be transformed.

It is Chairman Mao who has taught us that after seizing political power, the proletariat must persist in and consolidate the dictatorship of the proletariat and keep to the socialist road. No matter how many things we may have to do, we must never forget the dictatorship of the proletariat.

It is Chairman Mao who personally initiated the great and unprecedented proletarian cultural revolution, and who has taught us that classes and class struggle continue to exist throughout the historical period of socialist society, and that under the dictatorship of the proletariat, the revolution must be carried through to the end.[4]

In contrast to Soviet ideology, Maoism—at least so far—has not summed up its concepts either in a Party Program or in any systematic textbook. The principal work is the four-volume edition of *Selected Works of Mao Tse-tung,* an edition that is continually quoted. Special emphasis is placed on Mao Tse-tung's "three constantly to be read articles": "In Memory of Norman Bethune" (December 21, 1939), "Serve the People" (September 8, 1944), and "The Foolish Old Man Who Removed the Mountains" (June 11, 1935).[5] Sometimes reference is made to the "five constantly to be read articles," in which case Mao's articles "On Correcting Mistaken Ideas in the Party" (December 1929) and "Combat Liberalism" (September 1937) have to be added.[6]

The key position in ideological writings and mass propaganda, however, is held by those remarks of Mao Tse-tung that are contained in the "Quotations from Chairman Mao Tse-tung," published in 1967. "Mao Tse-tung's thought is the guiding principle for all the work of the Party, the army and the country," it says in the foreword to this book.[7]

Maoism is regarded as a universally valid higher development of Marxism. The "great thought of Mao Tse-tung" is "the acme of Marxism-Leninism in the present era,"[8] the "acme of Marxism-Leninism of our epoch,"[9] and "Marxism-Leninism at its highest level."[10] In Peking's view Mao Tse-tung has "developed Marxism-Leninism and raised it to an entirely new peak," and Mao Tse-tung's teaching therefore is "Marxism-Leninism at its highest in the present era."[11]

All of this is by no means confined only to China or the developing countries, but, in the official Chinese view, is valid for the whole world. "Our country has become the base of the world revolution. Our Party has become the standard bearer of the world revolution. Mao Tse-tung's thought is the beacon of the world revolution."[12] Mao Tse-tung's teaching is "the beacon light of mankind, the sharpest weapon of world revolution and the universally valid truth applying to the whole world."[13]

## ☐ The Origins of Maoism

Influenced by the Russian October Revolution of 1917, a multitude of revolutionary democratic organizations sprang up in China, whose objectives, however, were frequently vague and contradictory. Marxism, nationalism, peasant socialism, and other ideologies were often intermingled. This was reflected also in the first "Marxist study circles," in which a most important part was played by Li Ta-shao (1888–1927) and Chen Tu-hsiu (1880–1942). Marxist writings were virtually unknown in China at that time—even the *Communist Manifesto* did not appear in Chinese translation until the end of 1919. Nevertheless, evidently in view of the upsurge of the national revolutionary movement—known as the "May 4 Movement"—the Communist Party of China was founded, somewhat precipitately, in July 1921. Two Comintern emissaries, Grigory Voytinsky and Henryk Sneevliet, played important parts. From the outset they called for collaboration with the exceedingly heterogeneous national-revolutionary Kuomintang led by Sun Yat-sen, and toward the end of 1922 they even demanded that the Chinese Communists join the Kuomintang.

The Chinese Communist Party, concentrating (at the request of the Comintern emissaries) on political activity in the cities, made only slow headway. In that vast country it had only 200 members in 1922; by 1925, despite the revolutionary upswing, the total was still only about 1,000. All attention in China (including that of the Soviet emissaries) was concentrated on the Kuomintang, which had its main strongholds in the south, in Canton, and which, after Sun Yat-sen's death in March 1925, was led by Chiang Kai-shek. In 1926 Chiang Kai-shek began his famous March to the North. The greater his military successes, the clearer became the differentiation within the Kuomintang between national-bourgeois forces on the one hand and the revolutionary wing (including the Communists) on the other. By April 1926 Chiang Kai-shek began to remove the Soviet advisers and the Chinese Communists from important positions. In April 1927 came the complete break between the Kuomintang and the Communists, the former allies who were suddenly turned into outlaws. Thousands of Communists were arrested and many executed. Nevertheless, the Chinese Communists—again on the basis of directives from Moscow—did not entirely abandon co-operation with the Kuomintang. However, their hopes of being able to continue co-operation with the so-called "Left Kuomintang," which was based in Wuhan, foundered within a few months. In the summer of 1927 the Left Kuomintang also turned against the Communists, and on August 7, 1927, an extraordinary conference of the Central Committee of the Communist Party of China proclaimed a new line: the struggle against the Kuomintang.

Shortly afterward Soviet emissaries and Comintern trustees, including Besso Lominadze and the German Communists Heinz Neumann and Gerhard Eisler, began to prepare a Communist *coup d'état* in Canton (referred to in Soviet literature as the "Canton commune")—an action that served not so much the interests of the Chinese revolution as Stalin's power struggle against Trotsky in Moscow. The ruthless crushing of the Canton commune in December 1927 marked the end of attempts at staging artificial rebellions in the cities. It seems likely that these events led many Chinese Communists, including Mao Tse-tung, to conclude that the Chinese Communist movement should not be guided by Comintern emissaries but should be based on China's own revolutionary forces, principally on the peasantry.

Mao Tse-tung was born in December 1893, the son of a peasant in Hunan Province. As a youth of eighteen he took part in the Chinese Revolution of 1911 as a member of an army unit; he subsequently participated in the student movement in Changsha, the capital of Hunan Province, and in 1918 went to Peking. He became an assistant librarian, and attended one of the Marxist study circles. Mao Tse-tung later claimed that ever since 1920 he had regarded himself as a politically conscious Marxist. After taking part in the Founding Congress of the Chinese Communist Party in July 1921, he returned to Changsha, as secretary of the newly founded Communist Party of Hunan Province. At the Third Congress of the Communist Party of China in June 1923 Mao moved up into the Central Committee and was entrusted with heading the Organizational Department. In view of the close collaboration between the Chinese CP and the Kuomintang at that time, there was nothing unusual in Mao's being elected also as a candidate of the Kuomintang Central Executive Committee in January 1924. In his political work Mao concentrated from the outset on the rapidly developing revolutionary peasant movement. In the winter of 1924 he took a leading part in the peasant movement in Hunan; in 1925 he conducted courses for the peasant functionaries in Canton, and in the Central Committee he was responsible for the peasant movement from 1926 on.

Having studied the peasant movement of his native province and organized the Peasant Congress of Hunan Province in late 1926, Mao in March 1927, in an article, "Report on an Investigation of the Peasant Movement in Hunan," which attracted little notice at the time but has since become famous, proclaimed the leading role of the peasantry in the Chinese Revolution: "In a very short time, in China's central, southern, and northern provinces, hundreds of millions of peasants will rise like a mighty storm, like a hurricane, a force so swift and violent that no power, however great, will be able to hold it back. They will smash all the trammels that bind them and rush forward along the road to liberation."[14] If, Mao pointed out even then, ten points had to be given for the realization of the Chinese revolution, then seven went to the peasantry and no more than three to the urban population.[15]

For the first time in the history of Marxism the peasantry was being declared the main force of revolution, in direct contradiction to Marxist theory. This declaration was to become the creed of Maoism. In the autumn of 1927 Mao took part in the direction of revolutionary peasant risings in the provinces of Hunan and Kiangsi (the "rising of the autumn harvest") and in October 1927 he led armed peasant detachments into the pathless and remote Chingkang mountains (in the eastern part of Hunan Province, southeast of Changsha). After Mao (together with revolutionary units led by Chu Te) had created the first revolutionary bases, Peng Teh-huai arrived in 1928 at the head of further military detachments.

By the end of 1928 the "Soviet" territories in the south of Kiangsi Province and in the western part of Fukien Province had grown rapidly. This fast spread of Chinese Soviet territories, with Hsutsin as their capital, and the increasing strength of the Chinese Red Revolutionary Units (called the "Red Army" at the time) made it possible to call an All-Chinese Soviet Congress at Hsutsin in November 1931.

On November 7, 1931—the fourteenth anniversary of the Russian October Revolution—the Congress proclaimed the Chinese Soviet Republic. Mao Tse-tung was appointed Chairman of the Republic, but he was not the Party leader—he did not even enter the Politburo until January 1933. The Central Committee of the Chinese CP, which had until then been working illegally in Shanghai, was transferred to the Chinese Soviet territories in 1932. Once more Soviet Russian emissaries and "returned students"—i.e., graduates of the Sun Yat-sen University in Moscow—arrived in China. The period from 1930 to 1933 was marked both by operations against the Kuomintang (which, in four successive campaigns, tried in vain to conquer the Soviet territories) and by disputes within the Party between Mao and his adherents on the one hand and the Soviet emissaries, supported by a few "returned students," on the other.

In the autumn of 1933 the Kuomintang, with the help of German military experts (von Seeckt and von Falkenhausen), mounted a huge offensive against the Chinese Soviet territories, surpassing anything that had gone before. There was only one course left for the Chinese Communist leaders: to escape annihilation by a breakout, to evacuate the Soviet territories of Kiangsi, and to try to set up a new revolutionary base in other parts of China. Mid-October 1934 saw the breakout of the Red Chinese forces and the beginning of the famous "Long March." Under indescribable difficulties and in battle against a militarily superior enemy, the Chinese Red Army crossed eleven Chinese provinces—a distance of more than 7,500 miles—until in December 1935 it reached the northern province of Shensi. Here a new revolutionary center was set up, with Yenan as its capital, and before long the Chinese Communists were controlling a territory with 40 million inhabitants.

The Long March was of decisive importance for the evolution of Maoism. It was there that the Chinese Communists' confidence in their own strength and the inseparable, typically Maoist, fusion of political and military problems had their origin. It was, moreover, during the Long March, at Tsungyi in Kweichow Province in January 1935, that the Party leadership held its famous extended Conference (glorified ever since by the Chinese Communists, and during the last few years discredited by the Soviet Communists as an illegal coup) at which Mao Tse-tung rose to be the leader of the Chinese Communist Party.

Only then, in 1935–36, when Mao had become the Party leader and the Chinese Communists had independently and without external help set up a new revolutionary center in Yenan, the real history of Chinese Communism began. Only then did Mao have both the opportunity and the power to embark on a "Sinification" of Marxism.

The decade 1935–45 saw the adaptation of Marxism-Leninism, as taken over from the Soviet Union, to the conditions of the Chinese Revolution. Mao Tse-tung was developing new political and military concepts for the Chinese Revolution under the conditions of the anti-Japanese national liberation war, which had begun in the summer of 1937.

Mao defined the class forces and the objectives of the Chinese Revolution and proclaimed the aim of creating a "new democracy" that would differ both from the democracies of the Western industrial countries and from the Soviet system. Again and again Mao reminded the Chinese Communists of China's special conditions and urged them to abandon the "Soviet model." According to Mao, the revolutionary forces should first of all rely on rural bases and only then go over to an offensive against the cities ("encirclement of the cities"). Revolutions, according to Mao, could be accomplished only by force of arms, and the armed struggle, the revolutionary war, was the highest form of political struggle ("omnipotence of the revolutionary war").

Mao's most important writings during the period of the "Sinification" (1935–45) are: *On Tactics Against Japanese Imperialism* (December 1935), *The Tasks of the Chinese Communist Party in the Period of Resistance to Japan* (May 1937), *On Practice* (July 1937), *On Contradiction* (August 1937), *On Protracted War* (May 1938), *The Role of the Chinese Communist Party in the National War* (October 1938), *Problems of War and Strategy* (November 1938), *The Chinese Revolution and the Chinese Communist Party* (December 1939), *On New Democracy* (January 1940), *Reform Our Study* (May 1941), *Rectify the Party's Style of Work* (February 1942), and *Talks at the Yenan Forum on Literature and Art* (May 1942).

☐ **The "New Democratic Revolution" and the "Three-thirds System"**

"It is Chairman Mao who has taught us that the new democratic revolution is the necessary preparation for the socialist revolution and the socialist revolution is the inevitable sequel to the new democratic revolution. Following the victory of the new democratic revolution, it was necessary, without interruption, for the revolution to move on to the stage of socialism."[16]

Immediately upon his appointment to the chairmanship of the Party in January 1935, Mao began to reformulate the class relationships, the driving forces, and the objectives of the Chinese Revolution. In the conditions prevailing in China at the time there could be no question of a socialist revolution under the leadership of the working class. In Mao's view it was necessary, first of all, to aim at a people's republic, representing the interests of all anti-imperialist and anti-feudal forces. In addition to workers, peasants, and the urban petty bourgeoisie, the government should "include also the members of all other classes who are willing to take part in the national revolution."[17] By 1937 Mao formulated the objective of the revolution as the creation of a "new democratic republic." At the same time, the Party was not to depend only on the support of workers, peasants, and the urban petty bourgeoisie, but should also "welcome [the bourgeoisie] and revive its alliance with them for the common struggle, so as to help the Chinese Revolution forward."[18]

Mao defined two main tasks of the Chinese Revolution: first, "to carry out a national revolution to overthrow foreign imperialist oppression," and, second, "a democratic revolution to overthrow feudal landlord oppression." Of the two, the national revolution was "the primary and foremost task." The Chinese new democratic revolution, according to Mao, differed both "from the democratic revolutions of Europe and America" and "from a socialist revolution in that it overthrows the rule of the imperialists, traitors and reactionaries in China but does not destroy any section of capitalism which is capable of contributing to the anti-imperialist, anti-feudal struggle."[19]

For the realization of these aims Mao demanded the formation of a broad "national united front" which would embrace all classes wishing to take part in the revolution. The Communists, he urged, must uphold the program of the united front and in doing so invariably would set an example in the discharge of political and military tasks. Communists must be "free from arrogance and sincere in consulting and co-operating with the friendly parties and armies. . . . It must be realized that Communists form only a small section of the nation, and that there are large numbers of progressives and activists outside the Party with whom we must work. It is entirely wrong to think that we alone are good and that no one else is any good."[20] At the same time, "every party and group in the united front must preserve its ideological, political, and organizational independence."[21] Mao warned against a complete surrender of independence since, in that case, "collaboration will turn into amalgamation." He proclaimed the directive: "We must not split the united front, but neither should we allow ourselves to be bound hand and foot."[22]

How, then, did Mao visualize that intermediate stage which he described first as a people's republic (December 1935), then as a new democratic republic (May 1937), and eventually as a new democracy (January 1940)? The new democracy is "the transitional form of state to be adopted in the revolutions of the colonial and semi-colonial countries." It differed, on the one hand, from the "old democratic states" and, on the other, from the Soviet system. Economically, the "new democracy" was characterized by the nationalization of the great banks and major industrial and commercial enterprises; the state sector was to "constitute the leading force in the whole national economy" but, at the same time, "the republic will neither confiscate capitalist private property in general nor forbid the development of . . . capitalist production." In agriculture, the land of the great landlords would be confiscated and redistributed among landless and poor peasants; at the same time, large agricultural units would be permitted. Hand in hand with the new political order and the new economic system a cultural revolution was to sweep away reactionary culture and create a "new democratic culture."[23] Politically, the "new democracy" was marked neither by a "bourgeois dictatorship" nor by a "dictatorship of the proletariat" but by a "joint dictatorship of all the revolutionary classes."[24] "All who stand for resistance to Japan and for democracy are entitled to share in this political power, regardless of their party affiliation."[25]

After the beginning of 1940, Mao repeatedly declared that, in connection with the new democratic revolution, a three-thirds system was to be instituted in the organs of power to be set up. Under this three-thirds system one-third of the seats was to go to the Communists and the remaining two-thirds to "the non-Party Left progressives [and] the intermediate sections who are neither Left nor Right."[26] Mao explained that the Communists represented the working class and the poorest peasants, the Left-wing progressive elements represented the petty bourgeoisie, while the remaining third would be made up of representatives of the middle bourgeoisie and of progressive landowners. This, however, was a "broad rule" to be realized not mechanically but "according to the specific conditions."[27]

The three-thirds system, according to Mao Tse-tung, was needed on the one hand to win over the petty bourgeoisie and the middle bourgeoisie, and thus to isolate the ultra-reactionaries, and also in order to "educate the Party members who work in the organs of political power, overcome the narrowness manifested in their reluctance and uneasiness in co-operating with non-Communists. . . ."[28] In a later article Mao Tse-tung combined support for the three-thirds system with the rejection of one-party rule: "We do not favor one-party dictatorship either by the Communist Party or by any other party."[29] In isolated instances, "the proportion of Communists may be even less than one-third," since "on no account should our Party monopolize everything. We are not destroying the dictatorship of the big comprador bourgeoisie and the big landlord class in order to replace it with a one-party dictatorship of the Communist Party."[30]

Mao's theses on the new democratic revolution, including his proposal for the three-thirds system, played an important role far beyond the boundaries of China. Though the three-thirds system was never officially mentioned in the Communist Party schools of other countries during the Stalin era, it was secretly approved by independent-minded Communists searching for alternatives to Stalinism. (To quote a typical example, the well-known Marxist theoretician Hermann Duncker, in telling the author in East Berlin in 1947 about the three-thirds system of the Chinese Communists, added: "If only we had something of this kind in East Germany!")

The new democratic revolution was visualized by Mao Tse-tung as a protracted transitional period. The democratic revolution would "inevitably be transformed into a socialist revolution." But this would be "in the future" and would "take quite a long time."[31] In May 1937

Mao added: "We are exponents of the theory of the transition of the revolution and we are for the motion of the democratic revolution in the direction of socialism." In this transition the democratic republic would "develop through several stages."[32] Later Mao also repeatedly emphasized that the revolutionary development in China must pass through two stages. Only when the first stage of the new democratic revolution was accomplished could the second stage, that of the socialist revolution, begin.[33] The first phase of the revolution would take "quite a long time," but the two phases were linked: "For the present period, new democracy, and for the future, socialism; these are two parts of an organic whole."[34] But even at that time Mao never left any doubt about the ultimate political objective: the establishment of socialism and Communism in China. "China will certainly go over to socialism in the future; that is an irresistible law,"[35] Mao declared in May 1939, at a time when many people in the West were still describing the Chinese Communists as "agrarian reformers." A few months later Mao again stated: "The ultimate aim for which all Communists strive is to bring about a socialist and Communist society."[36] In April 1945 Mao once more pointed out that "our future or maximum program is to carry China forward to socialism and Communism."[37]

Mao Tse-tung's theory of the new democratic revolution, based on a broad united front and envisaging the intermediate stage of the new democracy, the establishment of new power organs in accordance with the three-thirds system and the gradual organic development into a socialist revolution was developed not in times of peace but in the midst of China's national revolutionary war. It was no accident, therefore, that this concept was closely linked with a number of new military and political objectives known in Maoism under the slogan "power grows out of the barrel of a gun."

☐   **"Power Grows Out of the Barrel of a Gun"**

"It is Chairman Mao who has taught us that political power grows out of the barrel of a gun and that only with guns can the old world under the rule of imperialism and all reaction be transformed."[38]

The thesis that "power grows out of the barrel of a gun" represents a number of experiences and conclusions drawn by Mao from the Chinese Revolution in the 1930's and 1940's and is now being proclaimed, in the present-day "great thought of Mao Tse-tung," as a universally valid theory for all countries and periods.

In contrast to Marx, Engels, and Lenin, Mao declared as early as 1936 that revolutionary wars represented not just one but the highest form of struggle: "War is the highest form of struggle for resolving contradictions when they have developed to a certain stage, between classes, nations, states, or political groups, and it has existed ever since the emergence of private property and of classes."[39] In August 1937 Mao added that "revolutions and revolutionary wars are inevitable in class society [since] without them, it is impossible to accomplish any leap in social development and to overthrow the reactionary ruling classes and therefore impossible for the people to win political power."[40]

This view led in November 1938 to the concept of the "omnipotence" of revolutionary war:

The seizure of power by armed force, the settlement of the issue by war, is the central task and the highest form of revolution. This Marxist-Leninist principle of revolution holds good universally, for China and for all other countries. . . . Every Communist must grasp the truth, "political power grows out of the barrel of a gun." Our principle is that the Party commands the gun, and the gun must never be allowed to command the Party. . . . According to the Marxist theory of the state, the army is the chief component of state power. Whoever wants to seize and retain state power must have a strong army. Some people ridicule us as advocates of the "omnipotence of war." Yes, we are advocates of the omnipotence of revolutionary war; that is good not bad; it is Marxist. . . . Experience in the class struggle in the era of imperialism teaches us that it is only by the power of the gun that the working class and the laboring masses can defeat the armed bourgeoisie and landlords; in this sense we may say that only with guns can the whole world be transformed.[41]

The new concept of the omnipotence of revolutionary war was inseparably linked with the thesis that the outcome of a war was decided not by weapons but by people, by the popular masses. This thesis, first proclaimed in May 1938,[42] was maintained by Mao even after the advent of the nuclear age: "Of course, the atom bomb is a weapon of mass slaughter, but the outcome of a war is decided by the people, not by one or two new types of weapons," Mao declared in August 1946.[43]

A particularly important military-political concept of Mao, developed at that time and subsequently to play an important part in the Moscow-Peking conflict, is the thesis of the encirclement of the cities. In 1939 (developing more fully an idea first mooted in 1927) Mao pointed out that the peasants "are the main force in the revolution," and that "victory in the Chinese Revolution can be won first in the rural areas." He described the villages as the "bastions of revolution" and demanded that "rural districts be utilized as revolutionary base areas."[44]

On subsequent occasions Mao repeated that "the vast rural areas inhabited by the broad masses of the peasantry represent important and indispensable positions of the Chinese Revolution," and proclaimed the formula: "The revolutionary village can encircle the cities."[45]

☐  **The Party and the "Divinity of the People's Masses"**

Mao's marked concentration on the general problems of revolution, above all on military and political problems, is reflected in a further peculiarity of Maoism—the problem of the Party is mentioned only marginally. Even Mao's infrequent observations on the subject are markedly different from anything said in Marxist literature about the problem of the Party. Marx and Engels saw the Party as the representative of the interests of the working class, Lenin saw it as an elite organization of professional revolutionaries, Stalin repeatedly likened the Party to an army, and present-day Soviet Marxism-Leninism stresses "democratic centralism" and the "leading role" of the Party in all spheres of social life.

By way of contrast, Maoism is characterized by a profound faith in the creative force of the people—Mao himself has referred to the "divinity of the people"—and from this view it follows that the main task of the Party is to work in closest connection with the people. To achieve this aim, Party members and Party officials must distinguish themselves primarily by close ties with the people and modesty toward the masses of the population.

Communists must proceed "from the real needs of the masses." All measures of the Party would fail unless the masses "are conscious and willing,"[46] since the people's masses "have boundless creative power."[47] Typical of this attitude is Mao's famous allegory: "We Communists are like seeds and the people are like the soil. Wherever we go, we must unite with the people, take root and blossom among them."[48]

Such a close connection with the people's masses, however, could only be achieved if Party functionaries behaved with modesty—and it is no accident, therefore, that this demand stands right at the head of all Maoist demands. A Chinese Communist, Mao stated in October 1938, must not "slight or despise" backward people but must "befriend them, unite with them, convince them and encourage them to go forward." Communists must work by "persuasion . . . and not . . . exclusion." At work they must "set an example in being practical as well as far-sighted" and also "set an example in study."[49] In one of the "three constantly to be read articles" Mao particularly emphasized the spirit of "utter devotion to others without any thought of self."[50] "A Communist must never be opinionated or domineering, or think that he is good in everything while others are good in nothing; he must never shut himself up in his little room, or brag and boast and lord it over others!"[51] Mao did not exclude himself from these duties. "It is my wish to go on being a pupil, learning from the masses, together with all other Party comrades."[52]

Modesty and the closest possible ties with the popular masses have been emphasized by the Peking leadership during the past few years—no doubt also in order to prevent the emergence of a closed caste of officials and of a socially privileged stratum. Thus the Peking leaders insist on a "system of cadre participation in collective productive labor." The functionaries "are ordinary workers and not overlords sitting on the backs of the people. By taking part in collective productive labor, the cadres maintain extensive, constant and close ties with the working people." This was "of fundamental importance" in order to "overcome bureaucracy." Differentials of income between functionaries and the public "should be rationally and gradually narrowed and not widened. All working personnel must be prevented from abusing their power and enjoying special privileges."[53]

In his famous article "The Foolish Old Man Who Removed the Mountains," written in June 1945—one of the "three constantly to be read articles"—Mao likens the people to a deity and explains the role of the Communist Party by means of an old Chinese parable:

In ancient times an old man known as the Foolish Old Man of North Mountain lived in the north of China. The road from his front door to the south was blocked by two big mountains. The Foolish Old Man decided to remove the mountains with pickaxes, with the help of his sons. Another old man, known as the Wise Old Man, laughed at him: "It is quite impossible for you few to dig up these two huge mountains." But the Foolish Old Man replied: "When I die, my sons will carry on; when they die, there will be my grandsons, and then their sons and grandsons, and so on to infinity. High as they are, the mountains cannot grow any higher and with every bit we dig, they will be that much lower. Why can't we clear them away?" Without the least hesitation the Foolish Old Man set to work, hacking away at the mountains day after day. This so moved God that he sent two of his angels down to earth to carry the two mountains away on their backs.

"Today, two big mountains lie like a dead weight on the Chinese people," Mao explained. "One is imperialism, the other is feudalism. The Chinese Communist Party has long made up its mind to dig them up. We must persevere and work unceasingly, and we, too, will touch God's heart. Our God is none other than the masses of the Chinese people."[54]

## ☐ The Emphasis on Chinese Traditions

By the middle of the 1930's Mao was urging the Party members with increasing frequency and growing insistence to free themselves from the "Soviet model," to concentrate on China's peculiarities, and to base themselves on Chinese experience and Chinese tradition.

Again and again he called on the Chinese Communists to take account of China's historical tradition, to study the development of China, and not to apply Soviet experience to China. In the summer of 1936 he said in an interview with Edgar Snow: "We are certainly not fighting for an emancipated China in order to turn the country over to Moscow!"[55] At the end of 1936 Mao turned against the "wrong view, which we . . . refuted long ago. They say that it is enough merely to study the experience of revolutionary war in Russia . . . that it is enough merely to follow . . . the military manuals published by Soviet military organizations." To do that, he suggested, was like "cutting the feet to fit the shoes," and such a fallacy would lead to defeat.[56]

In October 1938 Mao called on the Chinese Communists to study not only Marx and Lenin but also "our historical heritage and use the Marxist method to sum it up critically."

Our national history goes back several thousand years and has its own characteristics and innumerable treasures. But in these matters we are mere schoolboys. Contemporary China has grown out of the China of the past. . . . We must not lop off our history. We should sum up our history from Confucius to Sun Yat-sen and take over this valuable legacy. . . . For the Communists who are part of the great Chinese people, flesh of its flesh and blood of its blood, any talk about Marxism in isolation from China's characteristics is merely Marxism in the abstract, Marxism in a vacuum. Hence to apply Marxism concretely in China so that its every manifestation has an indubitably Chinese character . . . becomes a problem which it is urgent for the whole Party to understand and solve. . . . Foreign stereotypes must be abolished . . . dogmatism must be laid to rest; they must be replaced by the fresh, lively Chinese style and spirit which the common people of China love.[57]

About the same time a number of foreign policy moves by the Soviet Union did not escape Mao's criticism—notably the Hitler-Stalin Pact (August 23, 1939) and the entry of Soviet troops into Poland (September 1939). Mao openly revealed that "some people" in the Chinese CP—in Party jargon this invariably means a large body of opinion—believed that "the present war was precipitated by the Soviet Union's conclusion of a non-aggression treaty with Germany instead of a treaty of mutual assistance with Britain and France." There were also "some people" who regarded the Soviet Union's agreement with Hitler Germany as an indication that the Soviet Red Army was "on the point of joining the German imperialist front." Nor was it possible to miss Mao's criticism of the Soviet Union in the remark: "Many people in China are bewildered by the fact that Soviet troops have entered Poland."[58]

In January 1940 Mao criticized the concept of a "wholesale westernization" of China and declared: "China has suffered a great deal from the mechanical absorption of foreign material." Chinese Communists must "fully and properly integrate the universal truth of Marxism with the concrete practice of the Chinese revolution, or in other words, the universal truth of Marxism must be combined with specific national characteristics and acquire a definite national form." Marxism must never be applied formulistically: "Marxists who make a fetish of formulas are simply playing the fool with Marxism and the Chinese Revolution, and there is no room for them in the ranks of the Chinese Revolution."[59] In May 1941 Mao spoke with scorn of those who were returning to China from Europe, America, or Japan—he did not mention the Soviet Union but everybody understood it to be included. These "returned students" could "only parrot things foreign. They become gramophones and forget their duty to understand and create new things. This malady has also infected the Communist Party." Mao Tse-tung complained that very few cadres "really know the history of the Communist Party of China and the history of China in the hundred years since the Opium War. Hardly anyone has seriously taken up the study of the economic, political, military, and cultural history of the last hundred years," and the Party should "direct its cadres to investigate and study these matters."[60]

In February 1942 Mao again demanded a "serious study of China's economics, politics, military affairs, and culture." Marxism-Leninism must not be viewed as "a religious dogma"; what mattered was "serious research into the realities of China's history and revolution, to do creative theoretical work to meet China's needs in different spheres."[61]

A few days later Mao urged that the "foreign stereotypes" (patterns) in Party literature should be "destroyed." It was necessary "to oppose all empty talk about Marxism, and Communists living in China must study Marxism by linking it with the realities of the Chinese Revolution."[62]

Mao again and again warned against foreign patterns, the "patterns from across the seas," and against the transfer of Soviet experience to China. In 1943 he observed, not without a touch of pride, that the Chinese Revolution was "even more complex than the Russian Revolution" and that since 1935 the Chinese Communists had received neither help nor advice from the Communist International residing in Moscow.[63] In the spring of 1945 he officially announced that the Chinese Communists did not intend to "follow Russia's example and establish the dictatorship of the proletariat and a one-party system." Instead, there would arise in China "a special form of state and political power," which would differ "from the Russian system."[64]

This new, independent line was reflected ideologically by an emphasis on Mao Tse-tung's ideas. Thus, an official publication of the Chinese Communist Party stated in 1945: "Mao Tse-tung has brilliantly developed Lenin's and Stalin's teachings on the revolutionary movement in the colonial and semi-colonial countries"; elsewhere they referred to "Marxist-Leninist ideology as represented by Comrade Mao Tse-tung."[65] No other Communist Party would have then dared to use such formulas, in the lifetime of Stalin. The Party statute adopted in 1945 went even further: "The CCP takes the theories of Marxism-Leninism and . . . the ideas of Mao Tse-tung—as the guiding principles of all its work."[66]

Liu Shao-chi, then still number two after Mao in the Party leadership, had therefore every reason to state in 1946:

> Mao Tse-tung's great accomplishment has been to change Marxism from a European to an Asiatic form. . . . Marx and Lenin were Europeans; they wrote in European languages about European histories and problems, seldom discussing Asia or China. The basic principles of Marxism are undoubtedly adaptable to all countries, but to apply their general truth to concrete revolutionary practice in China is a difficult task. Mao Tse-tung . . . uses Marxist-Leninist principles to explain Chinese history and the practical problems of China. He is the first who has succeeded in doing so. . . . On every kind of problem—the nation, the peasants, strategy, the construction of the Party, literature and culture, military affairs, finance and economy, methods of work, philosophy—Mao has not only applied Marxism to new conditions but has given it a new development. He has created a Chinese or Asiatic form of Marxism.[67]

## ☐ Ideological Polemics Against Moscow

The above outline of the Sinification of Marxism from 1935 to 1945 shows the extent to which the Communist Party of China had dissociated itself from Moscow's official line even during the Stalin era, developed its own political concepts, and emphasized its independence. It was, of course, during that decade that the Chinese Communists became an important and indeed a decisive factor. Between 1937 and 1945 the membership of the Chinese Communist Party rose from 40,-000 to 1,200,000. The troops under Mao Tse-tung's command, subsequently renamed the "People's Liberation Army," increased from 90,000 in 1937 to 1,300,000 in 1945. The territory controlled by the Chinese Communists in 1945 had grown to 370,000 square miles with a population of 100 million.[68]

The increasing power and independence of Chinese Communism was viewed by the Stalinist leadership in Moscow with anything but unalloyed joy—even in the 1940's. The conflict of interests was too obvious. To Stalin's leadership the Chinese Communists were important chiefly as auxiliary forces in the war against Japan; to the Chinese Communists, on the other hand, the struggle against Japanese aggression was merely one aspect—albeit an important one—of the Chinese Revolution. In September 1941, as the Soviet press has revealed in recent years, a serious controversy arose. Moscow at that time instructed Mao "that the struggle against Japan be intensified so as to prevent it from striking at the Soviet Union from the rear." Mao is said to have disregarded this instruction.[69] Although this is certainly a one-sided account, it nevertheless reflects the conflicting objectives of Moscow and Yenan. During the 1940's, according to Soviet publications, there were repeated ideological differences between Mao and the Soviet emissaries in Yenan—principally on the question whether, and to what extent, the Soviet type of Marxism-Leninism was applicable to China. The Soviet representatives had demanded strict acceptance, while Mao had doubted the applicability of Soviet-type Marxism-Leninism to China and had emphasized the peculiarities of the Chinese Revolution.[70]

The clash between Soviet interests and the aims of the Chinese Communists emerged with particular clarity in 1945. Stalin at that time (as he himself later revealed in a conversation with Yugoslav Communists) advised the Chinese Communists to find a *modus vivendi* with Chiang Kai-shek, to join his government, and to dissolve their own People's Liberation Army.[71] The Chinese Communists (as on some previous occasions) agreed to this while in Moscow, but upon their return did the very opposite. This victorious campaign, which, on October 1, 1949, resulted in the proclamation of the Chinese People's Republic, was very largely mounted by China's own forces and in open disregard of Stalin's directive. There is every justification for the statement made in a pamphlet published in Peking in 1963 that "in the late 1920's, the 1930's, and the early and middle 1940's the Chinese Communists had "resisted the influence of Stalin's mistakes" had gradually succeeded in "overcoming them and finally led the Chinese Revolution to victory."[72]

In spite of the frequent protestations of Soviet-Chinese friendship at that time, it was no secret in Comintern circles in the early 1940's that, from Moscow's point of view, the Chinese Communists were "not entirely in line." I know from my personal recollection—I was in the Comintern school in 1942–43—that, for instance, Mao Tse-tung's famous speech on literature and art, made in Yenan in May 1942, was not published in the mimeographed bulletins customary for the "fraternal parties," but in the white bulletins containing "bourgeois views." When Chou En-lai's daughter, who lived at the Comintern's Lux Hotel in Moscow in 1943–44, talked about her experiences under the Chinese Communists in Yenan, a good many of the younger Comintern functionaries from various countries drew their own conclusions from her comparison of life in Yenan and Moscow, and these were by no means in favor of Stalin's capital.

Certainly, in the 1940's the Stalin leadership feared a possible spread of Maoism to the Communist parties of other countries, which might regard the revolutionary-egalitarian model of Chinese Communism as an attractive alternative to Stalinism with its bureaucracy and terror. These fears were not unfounded. Among thoughtful Communists it was quite customary at that time to start critical "private conversations" with a reference to China. If one's partner went along, one knew that one could go further; if not, it was always easy to withdraw, since the Chinese Communists had not yet been officially condemned or even openly criticized. Mao's "three-thirds system" was being talked about in whispers but with patent approval among thoughtful Communists.

When the Cominform conflict between Moscow and Yugoslavia broke out in the summer of 1948, many people were hoping that the Chinese Communists would not participate in Moscow's anti-Yugoslav campaign. It was also noticeable that the Soviet press in 1948 and 1949 referred only very reservedly and sparsely to Mao's victorious campaign that culminated in the proclamation of the Chinese People's Republic. The editor of the official central Party paper of a Western Communist Party in 1950 informed this author that he had received instructions to publish as little as possible about the successes of the Chinese Communists.

The greater Stalin's reserve, the higher were the hopes of some Communists that China might produce an alternative to Stalinism. "While in all zones, sectors, provinces and regions of our country the henchmen of the victors are anxiously watching lest some spiritual spark burst into flame, it seems as if over there, in the Far East, a light is beginning to shine for 500 million. *Ex oriente lux?"* the author Alfred Kantorowicz wrote in his diary in East Berlin in January 1949. "Mao and his people have captured the masses with the theory of social justice and national emancipation. They have become the exponents of ideas—something Party bureaucrats can never be. That is the secret of their victory."[73] Such ideas—the differentiation between the bureaucratic-dictatorial Stalinist Party officials and the revolutionary Communist fighters of China—were typical of many Communists in many different countries at the time.

The Yugoslav *Borba,* in a full-page article, declared on May 1, 1949, that the Yugoslav Communists were experiencing particular joy at the victory of the Chinese people's revolution because China's and Yugoslavia's revolutionary liberation struggles were similar—both in the concrete application of Marxism to their countries' specific conditions, and in the strategy, tactics, and forms of the struggle that eventually led to victory. Both revolutions had shown that what mattered was "to find one's own road to socialism." The victory of both revolutions had been a triumph over all attempts to turn the ideas of Marxism-Leninism into dead letters and dogmas.[74]

True enough, after their victory in October 1949, the Chinese Communists initially confined themselves to realizing the measures envisaged in the Soviet version of Marxism-Leninism—nationalization, land reform, planned economy, and collectivization—with certain Chinese amendments, but without emphasizing Chinese ideological or political peculiarities. Yet behind the facade of protestations of Soviet-Chinese friendship, the differences were not to be missed. From 1950 on there was much discussion and argument in the Indian and Korean Communist parties about the "Soviet" and "Chinese" roads. From 1951 on the Chinese Communists began to translate some of their articles into foreign languages and to disseminate them, and these often showed considerable discrepancies with the "official" Soviet version of Chinese Communist Party papers. The publication of certain writings of Mao, including his speech to the writers and artists, was banned in East Berlin in 1951. The ideological differences were reflected also at the international Party school founded in Peking in June 1951 for the training of Communist Party functionaries from Burma, Thailand, Vietnam, Indonesia, Japan, and Australia. An Australian participant reported that the Soviet lecturers, who would quote everything verbatim from Soviet textbooks, met with no response. The Chinese Communist Party lecturers, on the other hand, had made a profound impression on the foreign participants, many of whom tried, after their return home, to reshape their own Party life on the "Chinese model."[75]

It was against this background that Peking's ideological polemics against Moscow began. The turning point was the Twentieth Congress of the Soviet Communist Party in February 1956. By April 1956 Mao had complained to Mikoyan not only about the new theses proclaimed at the Twentieth Soviet Party Congress (non-inevitability of wars, co-existence, possibility of a peaceful transition to socialism, and criticism of Stalin) but chiefly about the fact that the Chinese Communists had not been given advance notice of the proclamation of these general directives for the entire world movement. After a number of such complaints by Peking,[76] the leadership of the Communist Party of China began to dissociate itself more clearly from Moscow's political practice and ideology. Mao's new concepts of the contradictions in socialism and his thesis "Let a hundred flowers bloom" (1956–57), his criticism of the Soviet concept of the non-inevitability of wars, and his concept "The East Wind prevails over the West Wind," put forward at the Moscow International Conference (November 1957), the "great leap forward" (early 1958), the establishment of people's communes (August 1958), and the publication of China's own ideological periodical *Hung Chi* (*Red Flag*) in the autumn of 1958 all marked the opening of a new stage of ideological and political independence on the part of the Chinese Communist Party.

The ideological polemics against Moscow began with the Program document *Long Live Leninism!* (April 1960)—aimed, to begin with, against the concept of the non-inevitability of wars, the possibility of peaceful socialist transformation, and coexistence. From 1961 to 1964 the ideological polemics grew in scope and attacked also the Soviet doctrine of the "state of the entire people," the "Party of the entire people," the "world socialist system," the "international socialist division of labor," and Moscow's concept of the unity of the world Communist movement. Especially important for this period were the polemical pamphlets (immediately translated by Peking into many languages): *The Differences Between Comrade Togliatti and Us* (December 31, 1962), *Whence the Differences?* (February 27, 1963), and *More on the Differences Between Comrade Togliatti and Us* (March 4, 1963), and, above all, *A Proposal Concerning the General*

*Line of the International Communist Movement,* known as the "Twenty-five Point Program" (June 14, 1963), which for the first time summed up the entire political concept of Maoism.

In the subsequent "nine commentaries," especially in *On the Question of Stalin* (September 13, 1963), *Apologists of Neo-Colonialism* (October 22, 1963), *Two Different Lines on the Question of War and Peace* (November 19, 1963), *Peaceful Coexistence—Two Diametrically Opposed Policies* (December 12, 1963), and *The Proletarian Revolution and Khrushchev's Revisionism* (March 31, 1964), the Chinese Communists quite outspokenly confronted the Soviet ideology with their own political concepts.

In these pamphlets the Peking leadership supported the concept of the inevitability of wars (as against the Soviet thesis of their non-inevitability), and the violent character of revolution (against the Soviet thesis of the possibility of peaceful transformation). The Chinese Communists declared that wars continued to be decided by people and that atomic weapons were mere "paper tigers" (against the Soviet thesis of a new situation in the nuclear age), and they supported the concept of proletarian internationalism as a general foreign policy line (as against the Soviet doctrine of coexistence). Peking stressed the preservation of the dictatorship of the proletariat until the full attainment of Communism (as against the Soviet thesis of the dictatorship of the proletariat developing into the "state of the entire people") and demanded the economic and political independence of each separate socialist country (as against the Soviet theses of the "socialist camp" and the "international socialist division of labor"). These polemics began in the spring of 1960, and as they progressed the Chinese Communists proclaimed their own experience more and more outspokenly as valid for all countries and nations; they described themselves as the "true Marxist-Leninists" and attacked the Soviet Communists and their followers as "revisionists"—indirectly at first, but soon more openly and sharply.

The polemics against Moscow were further intensified with the publication of the pamphlet *On Khrushchev's Phony Communism and Its Historical Lessons for the World* (July 1964). In this "ninth commentary" the Chinese Communists for the first time accused the Soviet leadership of restoring capitalism in the Soviet Union, of transforming the Soviet Union into a capitalist state, and of being exponents of a new privileged bourgeois stratum in the U.S.S.R. From that moment on Peking considered the Soviet Communists no longer mere "revisionists" —people with whom one had to dispute ideologically—but class enemies, representatives of a capitalist state that must be opposed. The break was complete, there was no more common ground, and the sole task then was to prevent a similar restoration of capitalism in China. In practical politics this led to the "cultural revolution"; on the ideological plane it led to the new Peking theses of the class struggle, which would continue even after the victory of socialism, extend throughout many generations, and necessitate a continuous effort to prevent the restoration of capitalism.

## ☐   The "Hundred Flowers" Campaign

Maoism differs from Soviet ideology in its totally different concept of a socialist society. Whereas the Soviet ideologists claim that a socialist society is characterized economically by planning, politically by its "moral-political unity" and the "leading role of the Party," as well as, in the intellectual and cultural sphere, by "Party-mindedness" and "socialist realism," all these characteristics remain virtually unmentioned in Maoism. Instead, the emphasis is on something else: on the contradictions and conflicts in the socialist society.

Mao's pamphlet *On Contradiction,* published in August 1937, already emphasized this point far more than had ever been done by Soviet ideologists. Proceeding from this fundamental concept, Mao, in 1956 and 1957, proclaimed his new concept of conflicts under socialism, expressed by his formula "Let a hundred flowers bloom, let a hundred schools of thought contend." Even assuming—as one is justified in doing—that Mao was thinking of the Revolution in Hungary which had occurred a short time before, and that he saw his concept as a "safety valve," his tenets of 1957 (still much quoted in Peking) express a number of basic Maoist ideas on socialism. Thus Mao declared that even during the "period of building socialism" a multitude of conflicts would exist, including "the contradictions between the working class and the peasantry, the contradictions between the workers and peasants on the one hand and the intellectuals on the other, the contradictions between the working class and other sections of the working people on the one hand and the national bourgeoisie on the other, the contradictions within the national bourgeoisie, and so on." Moreover, "there are still certain contradictions between the government and the people." These included "contradictions among the interests of the state, the interests of the collective, and the interests of the individual; between democracy and centralism; between the leadership and the led; and the contradictions arising from the bureaucratic style of work of certain government workers in their relations with the masses."[77] Mao Tse-tung here made a distinction between two kinds of conflicts—"those between ourselves and the enemy and those among the people themselves." The two kinds of conflicts were "totally different in their nature."[78]

Proceeding from this distinction, Mao proclaimed the slogan of "Let a hundred flowers bloom, let a hundred schools of thought contend," which he described as a "good method for revealing and resolving the conflicts." What mattered, Mao declared, was that "all people express their opinions freely, so that they dare to speak, dare to criticize and dare to debate; it means not being afraid of wrong views or anything poisonous; it means to encourage argument and criticism among people holding different views, allowing freedom both for criticism and for countercriticism; it means not suppressing wrong views but convincing people by reasoning with them."[79]

In addition to revealing conflicts, the new directive was to promote the upsurge of the arts, science, and culture:

Different forms and styles in art should develop freely and different schools in science should contend freely. We think that it is harmful to the growth of art and science if administrative measures are used to impose one particular style of art or school of thought and to ban another. Questions of right and wrong in the arts and sciences should be settled through free discussion in artistic and scientific circles and through practical work in these fields.

Finally, the slogan of "Let a hundred flowers bloom" was to facilitate the emergence of new knowledge:

Throughout history, new and correct things have often failed at the outset to win recognition from the majority of people and have had to develop by twists and turns in struggle. . . . The growth of new things can be hindered in the absence of deliberate suppression simply through lack of discernment. It is therefore necessary to be careful about questions of right and wrong in the arts and sciences, to encourage free discussion and avoid hasty conclusions.

Even Marxism itself, Mao promised in 1956–57, was to be a permitted subject for open criticism:

Marxists should not be afraid of criticism from any quarter. Quite on the contrary they need to temper and develop themselves and win new positions in the teeth of criticism and in the storm and stress of struggle. Fighting against wrong ideas is like being vaccinated—a man develops greater immunity from disease as a result of vaccination. Plants raised in hothouses are unlikely to be sturdy. Carrying out the policy of letting a hundred flowers bloom and a hundred schools of thought contend will not weaken but strengthen the leading position of Marxism in the ideological field.[80]

This exceedingly far-reaching statement on freedom of discussion under socialism was made by Mao Tse-tung at the Eleventh Session of the Supreme State Conference on February 27, 1957. Similar to Khrushchev's secret report on Stalin, it was subsequently spread by word of mouth at conferences and meetings throughout the country. Its effect on the public, however, was far stronger than Mao had expected; very soon public criticism turned to the fundamental questions of Party dictatorship. Not until June 19, 1957, did Mao have his speech published. Meanwhile, however, he had considerably restricted all criticism of mistakes of his own policies as well as limiting free discussion. This was done chiefly by the new "six criteria." According to these, criticism was to be permitted only if it contributed (1) toward uniting the people of various nationalities, (2) toward promoting the socialist transformation and socialist construction, (3) toward consolidating the people's democratic dictatorship, (4) toward strengthening democratic centralism, (5) toward strengthening the leadership of the Communist Party, and (6) toward promoting the international socialist unity and the unity of all peace-loving peoples.[81]

The great flood of critical observations throughout China during the short-lived "hundred flowers" period, from March to June 1957, soon led not only to a sharp turnabout of political practice—the campaign against the "Right-wing deviation," the proclamation of the "great leap forward," and the establishment of people's communes (in the summer and autumn of 1958)—but also to the emergence of new doctrines in Mao's political theory.

## ☐ War, Peace, and Coexistence

The questions of war, peace, and coexistence played a particularly important role in the ideological dispute between Moscow and Peking. While the Soviet leadership, albeit halfheartedly and belatedly, had adjusted to the new conditions of the nuclear age and, at the Twentieth Party Congress, had proclaimed the theses of the non-inevitability of wars and defined coexistence as its general line, Mao Tse-tung not only stuck to his earlier theses of "the omnipotence of revolutionary war," and "power comes from the barrel of a gun," but actually supported them with even greater emphasis. Thus Maoism declared that Lenin's thesis of 1915–17 about the inevitability of wars continued to be valid: "We believe in the absolute correctness of Lenin's thinking: war is an inevitable outcome of systems of exploitation and the source of modern wars is the imperialist system. Until the imperialist system and the exploiting classes come to an end, wars of one kind or another will always occur."[82]

Second, Maoism supports the view that the outcome of a war depends not on weapons but on people, on the people's masses. This thesis, first proclaimed by Mao in May 1938,[83] was restated in the political Program of *Long Live Leninism!* in April 1960: "Marxist-Leninists have always maintained that in world history it is not technique but man, the masses of people, that determine the fate of mankind. . . . An awakened people will always find new ways to counteract a reactionary superiority in arms and win victory for itself. This was so in past history, it is so at present, and it will be so in the future."[84] In their "Twenty-five Point Program" the Chinese Communists also stated that the emergence of nuclear weapons had not in effect changed anything: "Marxist-Leninists attach importance to the role of technological change, but it is wrong to belittle the role of man and exaggerate the role of technology. The emergence of nuclear weapons can neither arrest the progress of human history nor save the imperialist system from its doom."[85]

But the Chinese Communists went even further. In an official statement they attempted to depict the consequences of an atomic war as harmless. A nuclear war, they said, would with certainty lead to "the very speedy destruction of these monsters encircled by the peoples of the world, and the result will certainly not be the annihilation of mankind. . . . On the debris of a dead imperialism, the victorious people would create very swiftly a civilization thousands of times higher than the capitalist system and a truly beautiful future for themselves."[86] This statement was criticized particularly often and strongly by Communists in other countries. Thus the Soviet Central Committee pointed out that "the nuclear bomb does not adhere to the class principle— it destroys everybody within the range of its devastating force. . . . It is permissible to ask the Chinese comrades if they realize what sort of 'ruins' a nuclear rocket world war would leave behind."[87]

In addition to the inevitability of wars and the thesis that nuclear weapons are "paper tigers," Maoism also declares that the present ratio of forces in the world is marked not by an equilibrium but by a clear superiority of revolutionary forces. Again and again the Chinese Communists have quoted Mao's statement of August 1946: "All reactionaries are paper tigers. In appearance, the reactionaries are terrifying, but in reality they are not so powerful."[88] In the late autumn of 1957 Mao expressed the superiority of revolutionary forces in the world even more clearly:

It is my opinion that the international situation has now reached a new turning point. There are two winds in the world today, the East Wind and the West Wind. There is a Chinese saying, 'Either the East Wind prevails over the West Wind or the West Wind prevails over the East Wind.' I believe it is characteristic of the situation today that the East Wind is prevailing over the West Wind. That is to say, the forces of socialism have become overwhelmingly superior to the forces of imperialism.[89]

In subsequent publications the Peking Government explained that "the East Wind symbolizes the anti-imperialist forces of the proletariat and of the oppressed peoples of Asia, Africa, and Latin America," while the West Wind represents "the decadent forces of imperialism and reaction in all countries." In the 1960's it was accepted as a "scientific thesis" in Maoism that "the forces of socialism are prevailing over the forces of imperialism."[90]

Proceeding from the assumption that the revolutionary forces are stronger than reaction, Maoism rejects the doctrine of coexistence and in particular the Soviet thesis, endorsed in the Khrushchev era, that coexistence must be the "general line of the foreign policy of the socialist countries." In the Maoist view it was "wrong to make peaceful coexistence the general line of the foreign policy of the socialist countries." Coexistence was to be used by the socialist countries for achieving a peaceful international environment and for "exposing the imperialist policies of aggression and war and for isolating the imperialist forces."[91]

Maoism regarded the Soviet concept of coexistence as an ideological justification by the Soviet leadership for subordinating the revolutionary struggle of the oppressed peoples to the foreign-political objectives of the Soviet Union.[92] The Chinese Communists accused the Soviet leadership of propagating the doctrine of coexistence for no other reason than to "demand that all the socialist countries and the Communist parties must submit to their long-cherished dream of Soviet-U.S. collaboration. The heart and soul of the general line of peaceful coexistence pursued by the leaders of the CPSU is Soviet-U.S. collaboration for the domination of the world."[93] Coexistence should be replaced as "the guide for the foreign policy of socialist countries"[94] by proletarian internationalism, i.e., the alliance of socialist countries with the revolutionaries and all oppressed peoples.

For the first time in the political theory of Marxism, Mao thereby declared that wars represented the highest form of political struggle (contrary to all the ideas of Marx, Engels, Lenin, and the present-day Soviet ideology which demands that Communists must master both peaceful and violent forms of struggle), that wars continue to be inevitable (contrary to the Soviet thesis of the non-inevitability of wars), that nuclear weapons have changed nothing fundamentally and that wars continue to be decided by people (contrary to the Soviet thesis of a new situation in the nuclear age), that the revolutionary forces in the world are stronger than the forces of reaction and imperialism (contrary to the Soviet assumption of a balance of power in the world), and, as the conclusion drawn from all this, that the foreign policy of the socialist states should be based on the principle of "proletarian internationalism" (contrary to the Soviet doctrine of coexistence).

## ☐ World Revolution

In the mid-1960's Maoism came out openly and unequivocally in favor of world revolution. "The proletariat is sure to win the whole world and Communism is sure to achieve complete and final victory on earth."[95] For this, Mao Tse-tung's teaching must be the directive: "Once the world's people have mastered Mao Tse-tung's thought, which is living Marxism-Leninism, they are sure to win their emancipation, bury imperialism, modern revisionism and all reactionaries, lock, stock and barrel, and realize Communism throughout the world step by step."[96] In October 1967, on the fiftieth anniversary of the October Revolution, Peking declared: "Once Marxism-Leninism, Mao Tse-tung's thought, is integrated with the revolutionary practice of the people of all countries, the entire old world will be shattered to smithereens."[97]

The Maoist concept of world revolution, however, differs very considerably from all other ideas previously expressed by Marxists on this issue. Marx and Engels had referred to a simultaneous revolution of industrial workers in the highly developed Western countries, thinking chiefly of Britain, Germany, France, and the United States. Lenin supported the concept of the "merger" of socialist revolutions in Europe with national liberation revolutions in Asia. In the mid-1920's Stalin proclaimed the thesis of the "two centers" (the "socialist" and the "capitalist" centers, the conflict between which would be the subject of world revolution) and later he described world revolution as a "tragi-comic misunderstanding." Present-day Soviet Marxism-Leninism speaks of a world-wide transition from capitalism to socialism, to be accomplished by the merging of three currents (the "socialist camp," the working-class movement in the industrially developed capitalist countries, and the non-capitalist road of development in the countries of Asia, Africa, and Latin America).

Maoism has developed a fifth concept of world revolution, rather at variance with the other four. Mao's concept is based on the premise that the national liberation movements represent the main force of revolution:

The various types of contradictions in the contemporary world are concentrated in the vast areas of Asia, Africa, and Latin America; these are the most vulnerable areas under imperialist rule and the storm-centers of world revolution dealing direct blows at imperialism. . . . In a sense, therefore, the whole cause of the international proletarian revolution hinges on the outcome of the revolutionary struggles of the people of these areas, who constitute the overwhelming majority of the world's population. Therefore, the anti-imperialist revolutionary struggles of the people in Asia, Africa, and Latin America are definitely not merely a matter of regional significance but one of over-all importance for the whole cause of proletarian world revolution.[98]

The Chinese Communists state that "an extremely favorable revolutionary situation now exists in Asia, Africa, and Latin America," that the liberation revolutions in Asia, Africa, and Latin America "are the most important forces dealing imperialism direct blows," and it was there that "the contradictions of the world" were concentrated. The socialist countries must therefore support the "revolution of the oppressed nations" and "carry the proletarian world revolution through to completion."[99]

The Maoist doctrine of world revolution differs from Soviet ideology not only in its assessment of the main force but also on the subject of the methods to be used for the transformation of the world. While Soviet ideology emphasizes both the methods of armed struggle and the possibility of a peaceful accomplishment of a socialist revolution, the Chinese Communists declare that "there is no historical precedent for peaceful transition from capitalism to socialism."[100] Maoism regards violent revolution as the only road: "Marxism has always proclaimed the inevitability of violent revolution. It points out that violent revolution is the midwife to socialist society, the only road to the replacement of the dictatorship of the bourgeoisie by the dictatorship of the proletariat and a universal law of proletarian revolution."[101]

Any possibility of a peaceful transition to socialism by gaining a majority in parliament is denied by Maoism: "So long as the bourgeoisie controls the military-bureaucratic apparatus, either the acquisition of a 'stable majority in parliament' by the proletariat through elections is impossible or this 'stable majority' is undependable. To realize socialism through the 'parliamentary road' is utterly impossible and is mere deceptive talk."[102] By way of explanation the Chinese Communists add:

To obtain a majority in Parliament is not the same as smashing the old state machinery (chiefly the armed forces) and establishing new state machinery (chiefly armed forces). Unless the military-bureaucratic state machinery of the bourgeoisie is smashed, a parliamentary majority for the proletariat and its reliable allies will either be impossible (because the bourgeoisie will amend the constitution whenever necessary in order to facilitate the consolidation of its dictatorship) or undependable (for instance, elections may be declared null and void, the Communist Party may be outlawed, Parliament may be dissolved, etc.).[103]

In February 1964 the Peking Party leadership declared authoritatively: "Communists are makers of revolutions. If they refuse to make revolutions, they cease to be Marxist-Leninists."[104]

But how is this armed revolution to be accomplished? As with their other concepts, the Chinese Communists proclaim their own experience in the Civil War to be universally valid for all nations.

Proceeding from Mao's concepts of the "encirclement of the cities" and the village as the "base of the revolution," Lin Piao in September 1965 proclaimed this idea as a universally valid directive for the world revolution. In Peking's view the nations of Asia, Africa, and Latin America are in a situation similar to China before the revolution:

As in China, the peasant problem is exceptionally important in those territories. The peasant represents the main force in the national democratic revolution against the imperialists and their lackeys. The imperialists as a rule start their aggression against such countries by capturing the great cities and the main lines of communication, but they are unable to bring the vast rural areas fully under their control. The rural areas, and only these, provide the vast spaces in which the revolutionaries may maneuver unimpeded. The rural areas, and only these, provide the revolutionary strongpoints from which the revolutionaries can mount their advance toward final victory.

But Lin Piao went further than that. Not only were the revolutionaries of the highly developed countries expected to adopt the Chinese tactics, but the entire world revolution was to be accomplished according to the formula that "the revolutionary village can encircle the cities":

Taking the entire globe, if North America and Western Europe can be called "the cities of the world," then Asia, Africa, and Latin America constitute "the rural areas of the world." Since World War II, the proletarian revolutionary movement has for various reasons been temporarily held back in the North American and West European capitalist countries, while the people's revolutionary movement in Asia, Africa, and Latin America has been growing vigorously. In a sense, the contemporary world revolution also presents a picture of the encirclement of cities by the rural areas.[105]

With this concept of world revolution, the tendency of Maoism to present its own experience of the Chinese Revolution as a universally valid directive for the rest of the world reached its climax. Marx, of course, was turned upside down in the process. Marx and Engels had seen the industrial workers as the main source of social transformation; Mao, on the other hand, describes the peasantry as the main revolutionary force and the rural areas as bases of revolution. While Marx and Engels regarded both violent revolution and the peaceful transformation to a classless society as possible, Mao proclaims violent revolution as the only road and indeed as the touchstone of loyalty to Marxism. Marx and Engels believed the social revolution to be possible only in industrially developed countries, while Mao proclaims the victory of the revolution first in the developing countries which would then "encircle" the more highly developed industrial states.

## ☐ Independence and Equal Rights

Unlike the Maoist concept of war, peace, and world revolution (a concept rejected by most of the world's Communist parties), the Maoist concept of independence and equal rights has met with a strong echo in the world Communist movement.

In the Maoist view the Communist Party of each country must be independent and autonomous: a party "that parrots the words of others, copies foreign experience without analysis, runs hither and thither in response to the baton of certain persons abroad," would never be able to "lead the proletariat and the broad masses of the people" or to win "a thorough victory in the national democratic revolution." What was needed was a party "that can use its brains to think for itself and acquire an accurate knowledge of the trends of the different classes in its own country through serious investigation and study, and knows how to apply the universal truth of Marxism-Leninism and integrate it with the concrete practice of its own country."[106]

Independence and autonomy, however, are possible only under conditions of equal rights within the world Communist movement. In relations between fraternal parties there must be no superior and no inferior Party, and it is therefore "not admissible for one Party to proclaim its own Program, its own decisions, and its own line as a joint Program for the international Communist movement or to foist it upon other fraternal parties." Nor should too much importance be attached to who is in the majority and who in the minority. Relations within the world movement must be based on "equal rights of all Communist and workers' parties in all socialist countries" since "any claim to leadership on the part of any one Party or the emergence of any kind of hegemony would prove entirely negative and bring nothing positive to the international Communist and working-class movement."[107]

In the autumn of 1963 the Chinese Communists added:

According to this principle, the relations among fraternal parties should under no circumstances be like the relations between a leading Party and the led, and much less like the relations between a partriarchal father and his son. We have always opposed any one Party commanding other fraternal parties. . . . Our criticism of the leadership of the Communist Party of the Soviet Union concerns its attempt to lord it over fraternal parties and to impose its line of revisionism and splittism on them. What we desire is merely the independent and equal status of the fraternal parties.[108]

Maoism claimed these equal rights also for relations among socialist countries. While Soviet ideology supports the closest possible collaboration of all socialist countries ("socialist camp," "world socialist system," "international socialist division of labor"), Maoism knows neither a socialist camp nor a world socialist system but merely socialist countries whose relations "are based on the principles of fully equal rights, respect for territorial integrity, sovereignty, and independence, and mutual non-interference in internal affairs."

Maoism, moreover, champions the independence of each socialist country: "Every socialist country must rely first of all on the diligent labor and talents of its own people, utilize all its available resources fully and in a planned way bring all its potential into play in socialist construction. Only thus can it build socialism effectively and develop its economy speedily."

The Chinese Communists reject the Soviet ideologists' proposal of an international socialist division of labor because, they maintain, this would lead to a stronger socialist country "putting economic pressure on other fraternal countries" and using this as a pretext "to impose [its] own will on others, infringe on the independence and sovereignty of fraternal countries," and would be a "manifestation of national egoism" and of "great-power chauvinism."[109]

## ☐ The "Capitalist Restoration" in the Soviet Union

Maoism has not only developed its own political theories on all decisive political problems, theories that diverge widely from Soviet ideology, but has also subjected the Soviet system itself to a close and merciless criticism. With their ninth commentary, *On Khrushchev's Phony Communism and Its Historical Lessons for the World* of July 1964, the Chinese Communists first proceeded to a general critical analysis of Soviet developments.

Whereas most critical Communists see the degeneration of the Soviet Union as a result of Stalinism—indeed, some believe it had already begun under Lenin—Maoism places the crucial turning point in Soviet development after Stalin's death. The Soviet Union, according to Peking, on the whole developed in a positive manner until Stalin's death. By nationalizing industry and collectivizing agriculture, and in its building of socialism generally, the Soviet Union had scored "great achievements" under Lenin's and Stalin's leadership.

True, some negative trends had emerged even during the first few years after the October Revolution of 1917. The ideology of the bourgeoisie and the petty bourgeoisie had demoralized certain strata of the working classes, and this had led "to the emergence from among the Soviet officials and functionaries both of bureaucrats alienated from the masses" and of "new bourgeois elements." These negative trends, however, had been opposed by Lenin, for instance, by keeping the salaries of responsible Party, state, and economic officials at a level no higher than the workers' wages, so as "to prevent leading cadres . . . from abusing their powers or degenerating morally or politically." Stalin, in Peking's view, had "held fast to the dictatorship of the proletariat and the socialist course," and had foiled all attempts by the bourgeoisie to restore capitalism in the Soviet Union. However, Stalin had been "premature" in proclaiming the victory of socialism in the mid-1930's following the collectivization of agriculture in the Soviet Union, and in claiming "that there 'were no longer antagonistic classes' in the Soviet Union and that it was 'free of class conflicts.'" In consequence, Stalin had one-sidedly stressed the unity within the socialist society while neglecting its antagonisms. He "failed to rely upon the working class and the masses in the struggle against the forces of capitalism." More-over, "it cannot be denied that before Stalin's death high salaries were already being paid to certain groups and that some cadres had already degenerated and become bourgeois elements." Nevertheless, Stalin had been "a great Marxist-Leninist" because he had "pursued a Marxist-Leninist line and ensured the Soviet Union's victorious advance along the road of socialism."[110]

The turning point in the Soviet system, according to the view of the Chinese Communists, did not occur until after Stalin's death, when the revisionists led by Khrushchev had staged a "palace revolution" and usurped power in the state, the Party, and the army. This turning point had been marked by "Khrushchev's revisionist policies," which had accelerated the development of capitalist forces in the Soviet Union. Khrushchev's struggle against the personality cult had "defamed the dictatorship of the proletariat and the socialist system." By emphasizing material incentives in the economy and by increasing differentials be-tween incomes, he had "accelerated the polarization of classes in Soviet society" and he "undermined socialist ownership by the entire people." With the slogans of "bourgeois liberty, equality, fraternity and humanity" the Khrushchev leadership had infected the Soviet people with the "re-actionary ideas of bourgeois individualism, humanism and pacifism" and had wrecked socialist morale.

As a result of Khrushchev's policy, the Chinese Communists main-tained, "the rotten bourgeois culture of the West is now fashionable in the Soviet Union" and "new bourgeois elements have appeared in large numbers among the leading cadres of the Soviet Party and govern-ment." These "new bourgeois elements" in the Soviet Union had

not only increased in number as never before, but their social status has changed. Before Khrushchev came to power they did not occupy the ruling position in Soviet society. Their activities were restricted in many ways and they were subject to attacks. But since Khrushchev took over, usurping the leadership of the Party and the state step by step, these new bourgeois elements have gradually risen to the ruling positions in the Party and gov-ernment and in the economic cultural and other departments, and formed a privileged stratum in Soviet society.

The members of the new Soviet privileged stratum "appropriate the fruits of the Soviet people's labor and pocket incomes that are dozens or even a hundred times those of the average Soviet worker and peasant." In its mode of life this privileged stratum is "completely divorced from the working people of the Soviet Union" and lives "the parasitic and decadent life of the bourgeoisie." Its members have "completely departed from the revolutionary traditions of the Bolshevik Party and discarded the lofty ideals of the Soviet working class. . . . Their sole concern is to consolidate their economic position and political rule. All their activities revolve around the private interests of their own privileged stratum."

The Soviet Party leadership, the Chinese charges continued, was "the political representative of the Soviet bourgeoisie, and particularly of its privileged stratum."[111] Khrushchev, therefore, had "abolished the dictatorship of the proletariat in the Soviet Union and established a dictatorship of the revisionist clique headed by himself, that is, a dictatorship of a privileged stratum of the Soviet bourgeoisie." The U.S.S.R. is "not a state of the dictatorship of the proletariat but a state where his [Khrushchev's] small revisionist clique wields its dictatorship over the masses of the workers, the peasants, and the revolutionary intellectuals."[112]

Under these conditions the Soviet slogan of "building Communism" was nothing but "fraud." Instead of developing public ownership of the means of production, the publicly owned enterprises in the U.S.S.R. are degenerating "into capitalist enterprises, and the farms under the system of collective ownership are gradually degenerating into units of a kulak economy." Instead of realizing the principle "from each according to his ability, to each according to his work," a small "handful of people are leading a luxurious life while the broad masses of people are living in misery." The present situation in the Soviet Union is characterized by people "appropriating the fruits of the Soviet people's labor and living the life of bourgeois lords." By propagating material incentives the Soviet leadership is turning "all human relations into money relations and encouraging individualism and selfishness." Instead of introducing a course of development that would lead to the withering away of the state, the dictatorship of the proletariat is being converted into an instrument "whereby a handful of privileged bourgeois elements exercise dictatorship over the mass of Soviet workers, peasants and intellectuals."[113]

After Khrushchev's fall (October 1964) the restoration of capitalism in the Soviet Union had, according to Peking, progressed even more rapidly. The new leadership under Brezhnev and Kosygin had continued Khrushchev's policy of restoration. They were leading Soviet agriculture "on to the capitalist road of free competition, the free market and profit-seeking."[114] With the Soviet economic reform "socialist ownership has been replaced by the ownership of a privileged bourgeois stratum and the masses of workers have been reduced to the status of wage slaves."[115] The Soviet state has been turned into a "bourgeois state" and the Soviet people were "again under oppression and enslavement by a group of despicable scabs—a new privileged bourgeois stratum." Communist morality was "being submerged in the icy water of egoism."[116] The Communist Party founded by Lenin had been turned "into a bourgeois political party and an instrument of the privileged stratum to exercise the dictatorship of the bourgeoisie" including an "ever tighter thought control over the broad Party membership" in order to "indoctrinate [it] with its revisionist lines and policies."[117] The Soviet trade unions had "betrayed" Lenin's teaching and had "degenerated into an instrument for the total restoration of capitalism and the enforcement of its fascist rule."[118]

The Peking concept of the accomplished "restoration of capitalism in the Soviet Union" implies logically that the Chinese Communists see the Soviet leaders no longer merely as "revisionists" with whom one must have ideological disputes, but as the exponents of a capitalist system, i.e., as class enemies, who must be fought politically with all possible means—including an open appeal to revolution in the Soviet Union: "Sooner or later the great Soviet people will rise in rebellion and put the revisionist renegades in the dock for the crimes they have committed."[119] The Soviet people will "finally topple the Soviet revisionist ruling clique and stamp out the parasites and bloodsuckers. The red banner of Leninism will fly over the Kremlin once again."[120] The Soviet leadership will be placed "in the dock of history" and "tried by Marxist-Leninists and the hundreds of millions of revolutionary people all over the world."[121]

Since the autumn of 1967 Peking has been calling even more clearly for revolution in the Soviet Union: "The day will come when the storm of a new 'October Revolution' will eventually throw this pack of renegades off the stage of history!"[122] By December 1967 it was said: "A mighty storm of proletarian revolution . . . is sure to sweep the Soviet land someday [and] will undoubtedly overthrow the Soviet revisionist renegades."[123] At the end of April 1968, Peking proclaimed: "Where there is oppression, there is revolt. The persecution of the Soviet people by the new czars in the Kremlin will only serve to speed up the people's revolution on a broader and more intense scale."[124]

For the first time in the history of Communism one Communist Party was thus calling upon the population of another Communist-governed country to rise in revolution. Moreover, hand in hand with the intensified criticism of the Soviet Union, Maoism was beginning to develop its own ideas about the socialist society.

## ☐ The Cultural Revolution

"It is Chairman Mao who personally initiated the great and un-precedented proletarian cultural revolution, and who has taught us that classes and class struggle continue to exist throughout the historical period of socialist society, and that under the dictatorship of the proletariat, the revolution must be carried through to the end."[125]

This frequently quoted observation shows that the "great socialist cultural revolution" (sometimes described by Peking as the "great proletarian cultural revolution") is not merely an important phenomenon of practical politics but has already become an important and inseparable part of Maoist political theory.

Mao Tse-tung's doctrine of the "cultural revolution" proceeds from the argument that a socialist revolution cannot content itself with transferring the means of production into the hands of society but that there must also be "a thoroughgoing socialist revolution" on the ideological and political fronts. It would take a very long time, "decades or even centuries will be required to decide the issue of which will win in the struggle in the political and ideological fields, socialism or capitalism."[126] Under these circumstances the class struggle must be continued even during the period of socialism. This is described as "the theory concerning classes and class contradictions in socialist society,"[127] and represents "a new development of Marxism-Leninism" and "an irrefutable teaching of the proletarian revolution."[128]

According to this new doctrine the socialist society passes through "a very very long historical stage," during which "the question of 'who will win' between the roads of capitalism and socialism remains, as does the danger of the restoration of capitalism."[129] As Stalin had done in March 1937, the Chinese Communists have been arguing since the mid-1960's that "throughout the stage of socialism" the class struggle would continue

in the political, economic, ideological, and cultural and educational fields. . . . It is a protracted, repeated, tortuous, and complex struggle. Like the waves of the sea it sometimes rises high and sometimes subsides, is now fairly calm and now very turbulent . . . whether a socialist society will advance to Communism or revert to capitalism depends upon the outcome of this protracted struggle. The class struggle in socialist society is inevitably reflected in the Communist Party.[130]

But how long was this class struggle under socialism to continue? Evidently until the final stage of Communism was reached. On this important question, however, Maoism made a sudden turnabout. In the autumn of 1958, during the tempestuous people's commune campaign in China, the Peking Party leadership still declared that China would now "actively make preparations for transition to Communism" and that "the realization of Communism in our country is no longer a thing of the distant future."[131]

After the beginning of the 1960's, however, this statement was no longer mentioned since the realization even of socialism had been postponed to the remote future: "The complete victory of socialism cannot be brought about in one or two generations; to resolve this question thoroughly requires five generations or even longer."[132] The final victory of socialism requires "a very prolonged period of time. . . . Several decades won't do it; success requires anywhere from one to several centuries."[133]

The long spans of time envisaged by the Chinese Communists for a socialist development have resulted in particular attention being given to the problems of the future generation. While Soviet ideology dismisses the generation conflict as a "bourgeois invention," the generation problem, the problem of the successors of the revolution, plays a key role in Maoism. The question is

whether or not there will be people who can carry on the Marxist-Leninist revolutionary cause started by the older generation of proletarian revolutionaries, whether or not the leadership of our Party and state will remain in the hands of the proletarian revolutionaries, whether or not our descendants will continue to march along the correct road laid down by Marxism-Leninism.

This was "a question of fundamental importance to the proletarian revolutionary cause for a hundred, a thousand, nay ten thousand years."[134]

What, then, are the qualities with which these successors, the people of the next generation, are to be equipped? Proceeding from a few observations by Mao Tse-tung in May 1939,[135] which are still frequently quoted today,[136] the Chinese Communists over the past years developed a concept described as "Mao Tse-tung's five conditions for worthy successors to the revolutionary cause of the proletariat." According to these, the successors should be "revolutionaries" who "wholeheartedly serve the majority of the people of China and the whole world" and who would be "capable of uniting and working together with the overwhelming majority." They must "master the method of leadership based on the principle of 'from the masses, to the masses,' " they must be modest, they must not be overbearing, and they must "have the courage to correct mistakes and shortcomings in their work."[137]

Again and again the Chinese Communists stress the importance of the generation problem for the future: "In order to guarantee that our Party and state do not change their color, we must train and bring up millions of successors who will carry on the cause of proletarian revolution."[138] The problem of the succession of the revolution is a "matter of life and death for our Party and our country."[139]

The continuation of the class struggle, especially in the political and ideological fields, during the period of socialism was necessary, in the Maoist view, in order to avert the danger of a counterrevolution, of a restoration of capitalism. "If we were to forget about the class struggle and drop our guard in these circumstances, we should be in danger of losing state power and allowing capitalism to make a comeback."[140] If vigilance were relaxed and the ideological struggle not consistently continued, "then it would not take long, perhaps only a decade, or several decades at most, before counterrevolutionary restoration on a national scale would inevitably occur, the Marxist-Leninist Party would undoubtedly become a revisionist party, a fascist party, and the whole of China would change its color."[141]

Thus, for the first time in Marxist political theory since Stalin's statement of March 1937, the doctrine was put forward that after the socialist revolution, after the overthrow of big landowners and capitalist enterprises, and after the complete transformation of social conditions, the danger of a restoration of capitalism (or counterrevolution) was still "inevitable."

But from where was this danger to come? From whom? In what way? In the opinion of the Chinese Communists the danger of capitalist restoration existed primarily because "the remnant forces of the bourgeoisie in our country are still fairly large, since there are still a fairly large number of bourgeois intellectuals, since the influence of bourgeois ideology is still fairly strong."[142] Second, there was a danger of a restoration of capitalism because it was not easy "to eradicate the idea of private ownership formed in thousands of years of class society and the forces of habit and the ideological and cultural influence of the exploiting classes associated with private ownership." The spontaneous forces of the petty bourgeoisie "constantly give rise to new bourgeois elements," and even among the ranks of the working class there was an influx of "some elements of complex background." Moreover, "a number of people in the ranks of the Party and state organizations degenerate following the conquest of state power and as a result of living in peaceful surroundings."[143] The danger of capitalist restoration, finally, was particularly serious because the enemies were using insidious methods, because they were double-tongued, supporting revolution in words but in fact opposing it.

They feign compliance while acting in opposition. They appear to be men but are demons at heart. They speak human language to your face but talk devil's language behind your back. They are wolves in sheep's clothing and man-eating tigers with smiling faces. They often use phrases of Marxism-Leninism and Mao Tse-tung's thought as a cover while greatly publicizing diametrically opposed views behind the word "but," and smuggling in bourgeois and revisionist stuff.

This was said to be particularly dangerous because the enemies were succeeding in infiltrating the Communist Party:

Enemies holding a false red banner are ten times more vicious than enemies holding a white banner. Wolves in sheep's clothing are ten times more sinister than ordinary wolves. Tigers with smiling faces are ten times more ferocious than tigers with their fangs bared and their claws sticking out. Sugar-coated bullets are ten times more destructive than real bullets. A fortress is most vulnerable when attacked from within. Enemies who have wormed their way into our ranks are far more dangerous than enemies operating in the open.[144]

Counterrevolution, in the Maoist view, invariably starts "in the realm of the mind—including ideology, superstructure, theoretical and academic work, literature and art—so as to mold public opinion." The Soviet development under Khrushchev (the Peking view is that this was prepared by the dissemination of revisionist theses) and the Hungarian intellectuals of the Petőfi Circle, who acted as the "shock troops" of the Hungarian Revolution (in Maoist terminology "counterrevolution") in the autumn of 1956 are quoted by the Chinese Communists as deterrent examples.[145] In addition to the Petőfi Circle and Khrushchev's revisionist group, the Chinese Communists also cite the Yugoslav development (in Maoist terminology the "Tito clique") as a warning example.[146]

The action of ideas inherited from class societies, bourgeois and petty-bourgeois influences, the emergence of new bourgeois forces and the degeneration of some Party officials, as well as the cunning methods used by the enemy all represent, in the Maoist view, a constant danger to the socialist society. These forces would first make their appearance in the cultural sphere and in ideology, but could, unless opposed resolutely and in good time, lead to a total transformation of the system, to counterrevolution and to the restoration of capitalism. For this reason the continuation of the class struggle was necessary primarily in the ideological and political fields; this struggle was described as "cultural revolution."

Three tasks of the cultural revolution were of particular importance:

First, opposition to and overthrow of people in positions of power who follow the capitalist road; second, criticism and repudiation of reactionary bourgeois academic "authorities" and the ideology of the bourgeoisie and all other exploiting classes; third, reshaping of education, literature and art and all other parts of the superstructure which do not conform with the socialist economic foundations.[147]

Elsewhere the objectives of the cultural revolution were defined as follows:

The great proletarian cultural revolution is a great revolution that touches people to their very souls. This revolution is intended to topple the handful of Party persons in authority taking the capitalist road, destroy bourgeois ideology, foster Mao Tse-tung's thought, change people's world outlook and dig out the roots of revisionism so as to consolidate and strengthen the dictatorship of the proletariat in our country and consolidate and develop the socialist system.[148]

Particular emphasis is placed by the Chinese Communists on the liquidation of the old culture, of old ideas, customs, and usages: "The Communist revolution is the most radical rupture with traditional property relations; no wonder that its development involves the most radical rupture with traditional ideas."[149] Proceeding from this allusion to Marx and Engels—though hardly in their sense—the Chinese Communists proclaimed the objective of the cultural revolution was "to demolish all the old ideology and culture and old customs and habits which have been fostered by the exploiting classes and poisoned the minds of the people for thousands of years, but also to create and cultivate among the masses an entirely new proletarian ideology and culture and entirely new proletarian customs and habits."[150] That is why the cultural revolution is a "great revolution to sweep away all monsters and a great revolution that remolds the ideology of people and touches their souls,"[151] a revolution which "reaches into the very souls of people,"[152] and "grips man's soul."[153]

But how was the cultural revolution to be accomplished? In addition to a multitude of practical political measures one point received particular emphasis—study of "Mao Tse-tung's great thought." It was during the cultural revolution that the "great thought of Mao Tse-tung" was more emphatically glorified than ever before.

This glorification came under three headings: first, Mao Tse-tung's ideas were to serve as a directive for the political struggle. Thus Mao's teaching was described as "a political telescope and a political microscope . . . to distinguish right from wrong," as a "magic mirror [in which] all monsters will be revealed for what they are,"[154] as a "compass for avoiding the countless dangerous shallows and reefs and, in spite of storms and big waves, advancing victoriously along the revolutionary course of Marxism-Leninism,"[155] and as a "detector" for uncovering "sinister elements" and unmasking "their true features."[156]

Second, the Peking pamphlets emphasized the strength and power, the infallibility and eternal validity of the "great thought of Mao Tse-tung." The leadership declared that the Chinese people, armed with Mao Tse-tung's ideas, were unconquerable.[157] Mao Tse-tung's ideas were "a moral atom bomb of colossal power"[158] since "every sentence by Chairman Mao is the truth, and carries more weight than ten thousand ordinary sentences. As the Chinese people master Mao Tse-tung's thought, China will be prosperous and ever-victorious."[159] Mao Tse-tung's ideas were likened to a "sun" and "none of the sinister powers can ultimately escape from the brilliant splendor of the ideas of Mao Tse-tung and the Party."[160] Mao's ideas were credited even with quasi-miraculous powers: "a quotation from Chairman Mao is as powerful as a pillar supporting the heavens,"[161] and "with Mao Tse-tung's thought which is an infinitely powerful spiritual atom bomb in our possession, there is no stronghold we cannot storm and we can create all kinds of miracles."[162] On the validity of Mao Tse-tung's ideas it was said: "There is a limit to the depth of the Pacific Ocean, but no limit to the profundity of Mao Tse-tung's thought; there is a limit to the height of Mt. Jolmo Lungma, but there is no limit to the height of Mao Tse-tung's thought; the physical atom bomb has limited power, but Mao Tse-tung's thought has unlimited power."[163]

Third, the Peking Party leadership saw Mao Tse-tung's thought as an instrument for the creation of ideological and political unity. Party members were to prove by their deeds "that they really regard the teachings of Comrade Mao Tse-tung as supreme directives for all their actions."[164] The leadership called upon the Chinese Communists to "build up the absolute authority of Mao Tse-tung's thought in their own minds,"[165] and to "establish the absolute authority"[166] of the "great thought of Mao Tse-tung." The idea was expressed even more clearly by Lin Piao, at that time Mao's official heir: "China is a great socialist state under the dictatorship of the proletariat, with a population of 700 million people. It needs unified, revolutionary, concrete thinking. The ideas of Mao Tse-tung are just that."[167]

The cultural revolution is seen by leaders of the Chinese Communist Party not as a once-only political campaign, but as an exceedingly protracted struggle:

Chairman Mao teaches us: the present great cultural revolution is only the first, and there will inevitably be many more in future. The issue of who will win in the revolution can only be settled over a long historical period. . . . It should not be thought by any Party member or any one of the people in our country that everything will be all right after one or two great cultural revolutions, or even in the socialist society.[168]

Contradictions will not be overcome even in the socialist society, for even "after a thousand, or ten thousand, or even a hundred million years there will be contradictions."[169]

□ **Soviet Critique of Maoism**

Maoism has thus become considerably more than a modification or adaptation of Marxism to Chinese conditions. The "great thought of Mao Tse-tung" is characterized by a multitude of new concepts, including a new model of the revolution, new military and political tenets, a totally changed concept of the Party, a new model of world revolution objectives, new international and foreign policy directives, and finally, a totally new concept of the development of the socialist society.

Maoism is far removed from the original ideas of Marx and Engels, and even from the concepts of Lenin. The political theory of the Chinese Communists is based almost exclusively on Mao Tse-tung's formulations of the experiences of the Chinese Revolution, and thus reflects the specific situation and tasks of the Chinese People's Republic—just as Leninism had reflected the peculiarities of the Russian Revolution, and Stalinism and present-day Soviet ideology those of Soviet developments and the interests of the leading forces of the Soviet Union.

Another parallel is also worth noting. Just as the Soviet ideology had generalized the Soviet experience and made it a mandatory general line for the international Communist movement, so the Chinese Communists in recent years have declared their ideological conclusions, based on their own development, to be universally valid for Communists in all countries. The inevitable result was an ideological conflict between the Soviet and Chinese Communists. It is hardly surprising, therefore, that Maoism is most sharply criticized and attacked by the Soviet Communists and their followers—often far more violently than by non-Communists.

During the first few years of the Sino-Soviet conflict Soviet criticism of Maoism remained confined to day-to-day polemics, which frequently degenerated into abuse, accusations, and insults. Gradually, however, the Soviet ideologists found themselves compelled to deal with the phenomenon of Maoism; they had to explain why and how Maoism had emerged, and what it meant politically and ideologically. Soviet ideologists had been using an argument similar to that used against the Soviet Union by the Chinese Communists ever since 1964. Just as the Chinese Communists explained the Soviet leadership's "revisionist" policy by the "restoration of capitalism in the Soviet Union," emphasizing in this connection Khrushchev's seizure of power and "palace revolution," so the Soviet ideologists viewed Mao's "usurpation of power" in January 1935 as a key point in the emergence of Maoism.

According to the official Soviet view,[170] China's backward social structure is reflected in its Communist Party, founded in 1921. Although the officials and leaders of the Chinese Communist Party had often been courageous and revolutionary people, they were, in the present Soviet view, far removed from Marxism and the labor movement.

Even in the 1920's the Chinese Communist Party had, in the Soviet view, "failed to give proper attention to work among the proletariat." More decisive had been the defeat of the revolution in 1925–27. Many of the best Party members and functionaries, especially in the cities and industrial centers, had lost their lives. In consequence, the view had gained ground in the Chinese Communist Party that the working class was not able to assume the leading role in the Chinese Revolution. The role of the peasantry had been made absolute. In the spring of 1927 Mao had published his pamphlet *Report on an Investigation of the Peasant Movement in Hunan,* which bore the mark of "a petty-bourgeois revolutionarism." In this pamphlet he had glorified the spontaneous actions of the peasantry, supported the mistaken thesis of the village as the basis of revolution, and denied the role of the working class and of the world Communist movement.

With the formation of Soviet territories in China in the late 1920's and early 1930's the center of gravity of the revolutionary movement had shifted to the countryside. The army, composed as it was of peasants, had become the principal force. The army began to undertake "substantive political tasks and became a tool for political upbringing of the population and even for administrative rule and Party construction."

During the Long March of 1934–36 the Party's activity had concentrated almost entirely on units of the People's Liberation Army, far from the centers of the Chinese working class. Non-proletarian strata of the population—peasants, petty-bourgeois elements, persons of the exploiting classes, and intelligentsia—had then joined the Party in large numbers. The pressure of petty-bourgeois nationalist elements had grown stronger. In January 1935, according to the Soviet view, these elements were able to strike a decisive blow. During the Long March Mao Tse-tung had used "the absence of contact with the Comintern" in order to seize "the leadership of the army and the Party" in January 1935. This had taken place at the Tsunyi Conference, officially described in China as "an enlarged session of the Politburo," but, according to the Soviet version, a meeting attended by only thirty to thirty-five military commanders who made many decisions without any vote whatever. It was there that Mao—under the pretext of transforming the Central Secretariat—had assumed the leadership of the Party.

The next decade—the period from 1935 to 1945—had been used by Mao and his followers "to establish complete control over the Communist Party." By means of "terrorism and repression, especially during the so-called campaign to organize the style of work (1941–44), they imposed 'Mao Tse-tung's ideas' on the Party as its theoretical foundation."

Between the spring of 1942 and the spring of 1943 Mao had conducted a campaign for the "ideological screening of cadres." In fact, according to Soviet opinion, this had been a "cruel squaring of accounts with unwelcome Party officials." By means of "psychological terror and physical violence Mao Tse-tung and his group dealt with everybody who voiced even the slightest objections to their policy or views." Among the victims had been primarily "exponents of the Marxist-Leninist view, internationalist Communists" (in Soviet usage a term meaning pro-Soviet Communists).

By that time Mao was supporting the view of the "inapplicability of Marxism to China." By the early 1940's, still according to Soviet opinion, Mao had declared that "the Marxist-Leninist doctrine is not applicable to Chinese conditions in view of the peculiarities of China." In conversation with Soviet representatives present in Yenan at the time, he had even observed that "knowledge of the theory of Marxism-Leninism is not absolutely necessary for the leadership of China."

During the first few years after the establishment of the People's Republic (October 1, 1949) even Mao and his group had aligned themselves with the experience of world socialism. In doing so, "Mao and his supporters, as has now become clear, were guided primarily by nationalist considerations. They counted on making use of the gigantic progress associated with development along the socialist path in alliance with the U.S.S.R. and the other fraternal states in order to carry out their great-power, hegemonic schemes."

Nevertheless, during those first few years considerable successes had been achieved in the country's economic and political development, successes which testified "that China was moving along the right path." In particular the Eighth Party Congress of the Chinese Communist Party in September 1956 had been positive, and had strengthened the "healthy Marxist-Leninist forces in the Party ranks." The realization of the resolutions of this Party Congress, however, "ran sharply counter to Mao Tse-tung's political conceptions and created a real threat to his absolute rule." Mao and his group had succeeded in preventing their realization and had once more seized the initiative. In 1958 the Mao leadership had proclaimed the "adventurous policy" of the "great leap" and the establishment of the people's communes. It had "ignored the friendly advice of the Marxist-Leninist parties, which were disturbed by the Chinese experiment and warned of its grave consequences." By this "great leap," the Mao leadership had wanted to force the pace of economic development artificially, to catch up with and overtake the other socialist countries and perform a "leap" into Communism.

The collapse of the "great leap" and China's economic difficulties, the Soviet analysis continued, had resulted in a marked intensification of the struggle within the Chinese Communist Party. While one trend supported rational methods of promoting the economy, with full use of the experience of other socialist countries, the other group, led by Mao Tse-tung, had insisted on the continuation of "voluntarist methods" and had categorically rejected international experience in the building of socialism. The disputes between these two trends continued, chiefly at the Ninth Plenary Session of the Central Committee in January 1961; only later, in the middle 1960's, was Mao Tse-tung able to proclaim the cultural revolution. "Under the flag of the 'great cultural revolution' the Maoists are at present engaged in a ruthless struggle against all those who do not agree with Mao Tse-tung's adventurous course, against all sound political forces in the Party, for the consolidation of his already unlimited autocratic rule."

The Maoist ideology had not emerged suddenly, but in the course of a "long evolution, with elements alien to Marxism-Leninism, accumulating and growing in strength at each stage." The Soviet periodical *Kommunist* summarized the ideological emergence of Maoism as follows:

While Mao Tse-tung at first combined the need of Chinese experience with the experience of the U.S.S.R. and the world Communist movement, with particular emphasis on the statement that "the revolution in China and the Chinese Red Army show many special peculiarities of their own," the Chinese experience was subsequently separated from the experience of world revolution, placed into opposition to it, and turned into a dogma. Mao Tse-tung justified the thesis of a special road for the revolution in China. . . . In doing so Mao Tse-tung in effect revised Marxist principles, including the tenet of the leading role of the proletariat in the socialist revolution and about the alliance of the working class with the peasantry. This revision of a "Sinified Marxism" he proclaimed as a "universal truth." . . . In this way, by the early 1930's, the ideological and organizational prerequisites were created in the Chinese Communist Party for replacing Marxism-Leninism by "Sinified Marxism." The road was now clear for converting "Mao's ideas" into the ruling ideology of the Communist Party of China and for transforming Chairman Mao "into a living Buddha."

In the Soviet view, Maoism was characterized mainly by "an underrating of the objective situation," and by a "voluntarist mode of thinking and a far-reaching over-estimation of the role of the subjective factor." Maoism consisted of a collection of views taken from various sources and subsequently adapted to its own political intentions and aims:

Along with elements of Marxism one can find here echoes of various currents of utopian socialism (clearly pronounced egalitarian tendencies, to the point of extolling primitive leveling); anarchism (an apology for violence and destruction, the absence of a creative, constructive foundation); Trotskyite conceptions (a reliance on artificial acceleration of history, on historical leaps and permanent revolution); populism (exaggeration of the role of the peasantry in the transformation of the old society), etc.

Finally, the Soviet ideologists also criticized the ultimate objective, the social order aspired to by Maoism:

A society built upon Mao's recipes would look like this: in the *economic sphere* there would be virtual forced labor organized on a military pattern (labor battalions and regiments, etc.); a supply situation which would barely satisfy even the most elementary requirements; and a concentration of all available means on the state's military power in the interests of great-power politics. In the sphere of *social relationships* there would be an administrative compulsory leveling of the classes, the degradation of the human personality to a minute cog in the state machine. In the sphere of *intellectual life* there would be a negation of the entire wealth of national and international culture, an emphasis on "Mao's ideas" as the only spiritual force of the nation, an idealization of unselfishness, a renunciation of natural human requirements and feelings. In the sphere of *politics* there would be total liquidation of democratic institutions, a dictatorial regime of personal rule, total disregard of legality and of any constitutional rights.

The above is a short outline of the Soviet version of the emergence of Maoism and the Soviet assessment of the "great thought of Mao Tse-tung." One is unwittingly reminded of the Maoist presentation of the "restoration of capitalism" in the Soviet Union.

Thus the development of Communist political theory in the 1960's has resulted in a curious situation in which the two strongest Communist parties in the world movement are accusing one another of having totally deviated from fundamental Marxist principles. The Soviet ideologists are charging the leadership of the Chinese Communist Party with having usurped power by a maneuver, with having silenced the true Communists by terror, with having replaced Marxism by the teaching of Mao Tse-tung, and with working toward a social order that no longer has anything in common with fundamental Marxist principles. The Chinese Communists in turn accuse the Soviet leadership of having usurped power by a "palace revolution," of having subsequently accomplished a restoration of capitalism in the U.S.S.R., and of exploiting and oppressing the population as the exponents of a new bourgeois caste in the Soviet Union.

The Sino-Soviet conflict, which manifested itself ideologically in the polemics between Soviet ideology and Peking's "great thought of Mao Tse-tung," continues to stand at the center of dispute in the world Communist movement today. But this is not the only dispute. At the same time as this ideological battle was (and is) being fought by the two most powerful Communist countries, a third political-theoretical current emerged and developed in world Communism, a current that questions both concepts and that has arrived at totally new conclusions: humanist Marxism.

# 6

## The Challenge of Humanist Marxism

Over the past two decades a third political-ideological development has emerged in world Communism, alongside the Soviet and the Chinese trends; this is usually referred to in Europe as "reform Communism."[1] The supporters, exponents, and champions of this viewpoint have themselves used a great variety of terms in order to differentiate themselves from Stalinism and neo-Stalinism: "humane socialism," "self-management socialism," "humanist socialism," "critical Marxism," "intellectual Marxism," "socialist humanism," "associationist socialism," "pluralist socialism," and, finally, in Czechoslovakia in the spring and summer of 1968, "socialism with a human face." In Western writings this trend has sometimes been described as "Titoism" or more frequently as "national Communism," but these terms are not only not used by the followers and exponents of this movement, they are in fact rejected by them. The term "revisionism" (used in Western writings as often as in Moscow or Peking, though not in the same derogatory sense) is likewise rejected by the movement's followers, who, on the contrary, are anxious to link up with Marx's and Engels' original concepts and to apply them to the problems of our present age and world.

The humanist Marxists have differed a good deal in the way in which they have championed their ideas in various countries and at various times. Some tried (and are still trying) to keep their views as much as possible within the framework of the official Party line, while others—often at considerable risk—deliberately placed themselves in opposition to their own Party establishment.

In spite of these differences, there are a number of fundamental concepts of humanist Marxism that distinguish it clearly from Stalinism, from present-day Soviet ideology, and from Maoism. These common basic concepts may be summed up as follows:

The humanist Marxists see their main objective in consistently and completely eliminating Stalinism from the world Communist movement —both in theory and in practice. They call for a return to the original sources of Marxism, and for a new emphasis on their fundamental concepts, especially their concern with the humanist ideal. They want to develop Marxism creatively, independent of the centers in Moscow and Peking, and in closest connection with an objective analysis of the new problems of the contemporary world. This the humanist Marxists regard as the crucial prerequisite for drawing the necessary conclusions for their political practice.

To realize these objectives the humanist Marxists demand equal rights in the international Communist movement, and the autonomy and independence of each Marxist movement. They champion an independent, autonomous road to socialism in accordance with the traditions and the economic, political, and cultural peculiarities of each country. They reject any mechanical transfer of Soviet experience to other countries, including the dictatorship of the proletariat in its Stalinist and sometimes also its Leninist form. This rejection means that humanist Marxists must not only find new roads to socialism but also develop new models of a socialist society.

The humanist Marxists reject the Soviet idea that a socialist society must be based on a planned state economy and be characterized by "moral and political unity" under the leadership of an all-powerful Party and its apparatus. Instead, they visualize socialism as a living, free, pluralist society, based economically on the self-management of producers (entailing workers' councils in the factories), and characterized politically by legally secured democratic liberties for its citizens and by free discussion among different groups. In such a socialist society a Communist Party must not practice a dictatorship over all spheres of life, but must gain its political influence by persuasion, through the voluntary support of the working people.

The Soviet view of a conflict between a "socialist" and a "capitalist" bloc—a conflict in which the one side must be supported and the other opposed—is rejected by the humanist Marxists. Instead, they emphasize the significant change and new trends in the Western industrial countries on the one hand, and the bureaucratic and "statist" features of the socialist countries on the other. It follows, therefore, that humanist Marxists in both systems come out in support of changes and reforms, though these may differ in detail. They see coexistence not as a temporary arrangement between the two superpowers and the power blocs led by them, but want to see the abolition of the blocs altogether, in favor of increasing independence for all countries.

The humanist Marxists, finally, do not view the present state of Marxist theory as optimistically or complacently as the centers in Moscow and Peking. Indeed, they believe that over the past few decades Marxism has often failed to explain or correctly analyze the social changes in the world. Marxism, they believe, is faced with a multitude of new tasks and problems, many of which were deliberately covered up during the Stalin era. They claim that it is necessary to abolish dogmatism, a one-sided approach, and backwardness, and to return to many forgotten or discredited Marxist theoreticians of the past. New critical analyses and theories must be worked out both about developments in the West and, more important, about the experience of the socialist countries. These problems, however, cannot be solved by shutting oneself off or repeating old slogans, but only by objective analysis and a frank and free dialogue with representatives of other political and philosophical trends. Such a dialogue would make it possible to acquaint oneself with different views, to review critically one's own point of view and enrich it with new conclusions.

In line with the above brief definition of humanist Marxism the following discussion will deal solely with concepts developed by Marxists within the framework of the present-day world Communist movement (although some of them have been expelled from their parties for their views). Reform concepts touching on only one aspect of life in the socialist countries (as, for instance, Soviet economic reformers of the Liberman type), however interesting and important they may be, will not be dealt with in this book nor will concepts developed outside the world Communist movement (such as Sartre, the New Left, or Djilas after 1953).

Humanist Marxism differs not only in content from the political and ideological currents described earlier in this book but also in other important aspects. While both the Soviet ideology and Maoism are decreed from above, from a Party center, humanist Marxism represents a current from below, developed by independently thinking Marxists (or groups) who, over the past two decades, have been publishing, discussing, and trying to realize their ideas, chiefly in Europe, and mostly in opposition to their official Party establishments.

This is reflected also in the way these ideas are disseminated. Whereas the Soviet leadership and Peking will publish their new political doctrines in their own "competent" press—such as *Kommunist,*

*Pravda,* and *World Marxist Review* (also called *Problems of Peace and Socialism*) for the Soviet course, and *Jenmin Jih Pao* (*Peking People's Daily*), *Hung Chi* (*Red Flag*), and *Peking Review* for Maoism—the followers of humanist Marxism have no official mouthpiece. They publish their views wherever circumstances permit, principally in Yugoslavia (e.g., in *Socialist Thought and Practice, Questions actuelles du Socialisme, Reviews of International Affairs,* as well as in the international edition of the Yugoslav philosophical periodical *Praxis*).

The humanist Marxists of other East European countries were (and are) able to publish their views only during periods of relative liberalization: in Poland during 1956–58, in Hungary from 1955 until the crushing of the uprising in 1956, and in Czechoslovakia during the "Prague Spring" of 1968. In recent years, humanist Marxists have expressed their views in their own journals (such as *Wiener Tagebuch*) and sometimes in the press of certain Western Communist parties, such as the Italian CP periodical *Rinascità.* Many humanist Marxist pamphlets and programs, especially in the Soviet Union, in Poland, and in East Germany, continue to be disseminated secretly—as was Wolfgang Harich's *Platform* in East Berlin late in 1956, the extensive program document of Jacek Kuron and Karol Modzelewski in Poland at the end of 1964, and the memorandum of the Soviet atomic scientist Sakharov in the summer of 1968.

The character and objectives of humanist Marxism are reflected also in the form of its representation. Whereas present-day Soviet ideology and Maoism both codify their own doctrines and (in spite of the frequent change of the Party line) invariably represent them as "correct," the humanist Marxists—much as Marx and Engels had done—proceed from a critique of the existing situation, in particular a critical analysis of the socialist countries. They do not codify their views but argue; they are concerned not with the disciplined observance of new doctrines but with critical thought. This is reflected also in their style, which is much closer to that of Marx and Engels than to that of Soviet ideological textbooks or the *Quotations of Chairman Mao.*

## ☐ The Marxist Alternative to Stalinism

The origins of present-day humanist Marxism go back to the 1920's, when opposition groups sprang up in many Communist parties —including the Soviet Communist Party—which adopted a critical attitude to the increasing centralization, bureaucratization, and dictatorial features of the Soviet system and championed greater democratic rights for the working people, freedom of discussion, democratization within the Party, and self-management for producers. Even during the 1930's and 1940's, under Stalin's dictatorship of terror, critical and thoughtful Communists, in spite of the continuous danger of police spies and arrest, would secretly discuss the question of how and why it was possible for Stalinism to arise, whether Stalinism could be assessed as socialism at all, and how a socialist society based on Marxist principles could be realized.

Behind the official facade of uniform "monolithic" world Communism a differentiation emerged even during the Stalin era—and, what is more, in nearly all Communist parties of the world. On the one side stood the hard-line dogmatic Stalinist Party *apparatchiks,* who saw power, discipline, and organization as aims in themselves and showed little interest in theoretical, ideological questions of Marxism but instead were concerned with ruthlessly and unscrupulously executing the orders of the Moscow Stalinist leadership. On the other side stood the thoughtful, searching, critical Communists, who were concerned with the fundamental humanist concepts of Marxism, with man's liberation from exploitation and oppression, and who viewed critically the turn that Stalinism had taken in the Soviet Union (the fashionable term at the time was "political colliwobbles") and were searching for an alternative to Stalinism. After the end of the war these circles were hoping that the popular-democratic countries of Eastern and Southeastern Europe would choose their own independent road to socialism, which would differ considerably from Stalinism. Independence and sovereignty for their own Communist parties and support for an independent road to socialism were not aims in themselves for the humanist Marxists, but rather an indispensable prerequisite for freeing themselves from Stalinism, both in theory and in practice, and for the realization of a Marxist alternative to Stalinism.

The discussions and hopes at that time were increasingly centered on Yugoslavia. The Yugoslav people's revolution, the courageous liberation struggle of the Yugoslav Communists, had made a considerable impression on many Communist Party members in different countries during World War II. This struggle was symbolized by the name of Tito. In 1937 Tito had been appointed Secretary-General of the Yugoslav Communist Party. Immediately after his appointment he moved the Party leadership, which had until then worked in exile, back to Yugoslavia, refused all subsidies from Moscow, relied on new forces active inside Yugoslavia, and thus—under conditions of strict illegality—laid the foundation for the subsequent people's revolution. Even though

Tito had been appointed during the Stalin era he was far more a Leninist type of international revolutionary than a Stalinist party official. In 1910, at the age of eighteen, he had joined the Social Democratic Party of Croatia and Slovenia and for a number of years had worked in various factories in Moravia, Bohemia, Germany, and Austria. Drafted into the Austro-Hungarian Army in 1913, he was taken prisoner by the Russians in April 1915, spent some years in a prisoner-of-war camp in the Urals, and was liberated by the Russian Revolution of 1917. He spent another three years in Russia; in June 1917 he participated in the Bolshevik demonstration against the Kerensky government, was arrested and banished, escaped, joined the Red Guards in Omsk for a short time, and was subsequently forced to go into hiding in the White Russian-controlled area of Kirghizia.

When Tito returned to Yugoslavia in September 1920 he had not only gathered much valuable revolutionary experience but had acquired, in addition to his native Croatian, a command of Czech, German, Slovenian, Russian, and Kirghizian. He immediately joined the Yugoslav Communist Party and was active as a metalworker in the Croatian metalworkers' union. Secretary of the metalworkers' union following 1927 (first for Zagreb and later for the whole of Croatia), he was sentenced to a long term of detention in a famous trial in November 1928. He spent over five years in Yugoslav prisons, some of the time together with the leading Marxist theoretician Mosha Pijade.

Within a few months of his release in March 1934, Tito moved up into the Central Committee and Politburo and was a delegate to the Seventh Comintern Congress in Moscow in the summer of 1935. During his almost two-year stay in the Soviet Union he worked in the Comintern's "Balkan Secretariat," which was under the direction of Wilhelm Pieck, and (together with Edvard Kardelj, who was then also living in Moscow) lectured at the Lenin School. Toward the end of 1936, Tito returned illegally to Yugoslavia, in order to reorganize the Yugoslav Communist Party. After this reorganization the Party gained ground rapidly, and by October 1940 it had 12,000 members; the Communist Youth League numbered 30,000.

Following Yugoslavia's occupation by Hitler Germany in April 1941, the Yugoslav Communists began an active resistance, and by June 1941 called upon the population of the country to rise against the occupiers. Very soon the Yugoslav Communists succeeded in setting up their own liberated territories—the first resistance movement in Europe to do so—gaining a firm basis for the people's revolution. From the outset they emphasized the revolutionary as much as the national character of their struggle: "Death to fascism, liberty for the people!" was their key slogan. Within the framework of the partisan movement they organized "proletarian brigades," with the hammer-and-sickle emblem, and in the liberated territories set up elected People's Liberation Committees as the new organs of power. The country's national liberation from the foreign occupiers was, therefore, from the very outset inseparably linked for the Yugoslav Communists with their struggle for a new Yugoslavia and its future socialist development.

## ☐ Yugoslavia's Break with Moscow

The first successes of the Yugoslav partisans led to conflicts with the Stalinist leadership in Moscow (just as in the case of China). Whereas the Yugoslav Communists had always linked the struggle for their country's national liberation with a revolutionary transformation of their society, Stalin used every means at his disposal to obstruct any independent (even though socialist) direction taken by the Yugoslav Revolution. He did so partly for foreign policy reasons (his alliance with Britain and the U.S.A.) but largely from fear that a victorious independent revolutionary movement in Yugoslavia might slip out of his control. The help promised by Moscow to the Yugoslav Communists in the spring of 1942 was withdrawn. Stalin repeatedly complained about the revolutionary socialist character of the Yugoslav partisan movement (for instance, about the proletarian brigades and the newly elected People's Committees) and instead suggested to the Yugoslav Communists that they should collaborate with Draža Mihajlović, the representative of the Yugoslav government-in-exile. Not even the communiqués of Tito's partisan government were published in the Soviet press at that time.

In the most difficult operations against a superior enemy and under indescribable privations and sacrifices the partisan movement grew to 150,000 men by the autumn of 1942. In November 1942 the "Antifascist Council of the People's Liberation of Yugoslavia" was convened in Bihac. But its original intention to proclaim a provisional government was vetoed by Moscow. Reluctantly, the Yugoslav Communists submitted. When a National Committee was formed a year later, at the Second Session of the Anti-fascist Council in Jajce in November 1943, as the nucleus of a new government, Stalin promptly described this as a "stab in the back for the Soviet Union." Important decisions by the National Committee, including the abrogation of the monarchy, were again not published in the Soviet press. Not until February 1944, when the U.S.A. and Britain had long been represented by a military mission, did Stalin agree to send a Soviet military mission to the Yugoslav partisans. At the end of September 1944, when the Yugoslav People's Liberation Army had virtually liberated the whole country by its own efforts, Soviet troops finally arrived.

The Red Army's excesses during its entry into Yugoslavia, including the numerous cases of rape and looting, were a further disappointment to the Yugoslav Communists. More were to follow after victory in May 1945. No sooner had victory been won than the Soviet leadership attempted to gain control of Yugoslavia's army, her economy, and her cultural life. Soviet "advisers"—in fact, controllers—were appointed to all key positions, and "joint companies" were set up to enable the U.S.S.R. to gain economic control of the country. Time and again Moscow demanded that Yugoslavia follow the "Soviet example" in every way. The Soviet secret police, moreover, tried again and again to enlist Yugoslav citizens, especially Party members and officials. But the Soviet *apparatchiks* found this far more difficult in Yugoslavia than in other East European countries. The close sense of community that had been born during the partisan war led the Yugoslav Communists to appear to accept these propositions, while in fact they immediately reported them to their own Party leadership, to whom they felt a far greater loyalty.

Between 1945 and 1948, all this led to an ever more pronounced conflict between the Soviet leadership's claim to hegemony and the Yugoslav Communists' endeavors to preserve their country's independence, which had cost them such sacrifices. The conflict was the more striking in that it represented a confrontation between two forms of Communism: the young, revolutionary Communism, newly born of a revolutionary liberation struggle versus Stalinism, which had long ago ossified into a bureaucratic hierarchy. Although, during the first few postwar years, the Yugoslav Communists followed the Soviet model in many respects, they began to show even then features of their own. Both the personalities and the policies of the Yugoslav Communists—in spite of their quite sincere admiration of Stalin—resembled the Leninist type of Communism far more than Stalinism. The Yugoslav Communists who visited other Communist parties after 1945 were characterized by far greater understanding, by a much more marked international approach to problems, and by sounder Marxist knowledge than was to be found among the dogmatic and bureaucratic—and frequently nationalistic—representatives of Moscow.

The enthusiasm with which Tito was received on his visits to the East European capitals in 1946–47 clearly reflected the popularity and mesmeric power of Yugoslav Communism—and this enthusiasm was watched with suspicion by the Stalinist leadership in Moscow. The founding of the Cominform, the Communist Information Bureau, in September 1947, provided Stalin with an instrument for a stricter control of the major Communist parties—an instrument he intended to use against Yugoslavia when the time came. Within a few months, by February 1948, an organized "whispering campaign" against the Yugoslav Communists was started in Moscow, to the effect that "there is something wrong with Yugoslavia." When in the spring of 1948 Tito's portraits were removed, when Yugoslavia was no longer invited to the Leipzig Spring Fair, and when travel to Yugoslavia was stopped, it became obvious that Stalin had launched a campaign against Yugoslav Communism. Toward the end of March 1948 Moscow began to put the Yugoslav Party leadership under pressure in confidential letters. In these the Stalin leadership did not confine itself to libelous accusations but likened the Yugoslav Party leaders to Trotsky and Bukharin, a threat that—in view of Trotsky's assassination by an NKVD agent and Bukharin's execution—was not to be misunderstood.

On April 12, 1948, a Plenary Meeting of the Central Committee of the Communist Party of Yugoslavia was held in the library of the Alexander Palace at Dedinje, on the outskirts of Belgrade, which marked not only a turning point in Yugoslavia's development, but also the emergence of humanist Marxism as an active political force. At this dramatic meeting, vividly described by Vladimir Dedijer,[2] the members of the Central Committee discussed the Soviet accusations. More than twenty Central Committee members—including Edvard Kardelj, Mosha Pijade, Milovan Djilas, and Boris Kidrić—indignantly rejected the Soviet attacks, and only one single Central Committee member, Sreten Zujović, attempted to defend Stalin. The Yugoslav reply confronted Stalin for the first time with the solid opposition of an entire Communist Party. A further and increasingly sharp exchange of letters followed; at the same time, Stalin mobilized a number of other Communist parties for his anti-Yugoslav campaign and called a Cominform meeting in Bucharest at the end of June 1948. The Yugoslav Communists—not surprisingly, in view of the threats in the Soviet letters—boycotted the meeting, at which several Communist Party leaders, in spite of all Party discipline, were at first reluctant to agree to a condemnation of Yugoslavia. Then Zhdanov said the Soviet leadership had in its possession information alleging that Tito was an "imperialist agent." Thus the Cominform resolution against Yugoslavia was adopted on June 28, 1948. It called on the Yugoslav Communist Party to submit to Moscow. If it did not, the Yugoslav Communists were to elect a new "internationalist Communist Party leadership"—in other words, a Soviet satellite leadership.

However, on June 30, 1948, the Yugoslav Communists repudiated the Cominform resolution—an action evidently not expected by Stalin. The existence of an independent socialist Yugoslavia represented an important turning point. For the first time it was possible, both in theory and in practice, to follow a new road and to realize the alternative to Stalinism that thousands of Communists had long hoped for. The consequences were immediate and far-reaching for the entire international Communist movement. In most Communist parties throughout the world quite a few Party members secretly sided with the Yugoslavs. In Poland, Gomulka at first refused to endorse the anti-Yugoslav Cominform resolution. In Bulgaria, Georgi Dimitrov, by then an old, sick, and broken man, endorsed the resolution officially but made it clear to the Yugoslav Communists that he sided with them. When the "Yugoslav question" was voted on by the Party leadership in East Berlin, two of the sixteen members of the Central Secretariat (Erich W. Gniffke and August Karsten) voted against the Cominform resolution.[3]

## ☐ Yugoslav Concepts (1948–55)

Immediately after the Cominform resolution Moscow began to step up its pressure against Yugoslavia. A unilateral breach of treaties and agreements, an almost total economic blockade, a massive anti-Yugoslav propaganda campaign, border incidents, mass arrests of real and putative "Titoists" in the Eastern bloc countries—all this led the Yugoslav Communists to realize very soon that the Cominform conflict was not some kind of "misunderstanding" but represented a fundamental issue of Soviet policy. At first Yugoslav Communists tried to deny the false reports spread by Moscow and to demonstrate the true state of affairs, but the emphasis soon shifted to arguments about fundamental political and ideological issues. The Yugoslav criticism of Stalinist domestic and foreign policy was linked with the proclamation of their own political concepts. The three main demands were: equality among Communist parties in the world movement and rejection of any "leading center"; economic and political equality of all socialist countries; and the right to an independent road to socialism in accordance with the specific traditions and the cultural, political, and economic conditions of the country in question.[4]

The fullest exposition of these concepts was supplied by Milovan

Djilas in his pamphlet *Lenin on the Relations Between Socialist States* (autumn 1949). In a careful analysis Djilas examined Lenin's ideas on this set of problems, including his attitude toward the possibility of an independent socialist Ukraine, and rejected any attempt to foist particular forms of socialism upon a country by pressure or compulsion from abroad.

Lenin indeed saw with extraordinary clarity that various individual countries, in marching to the same goal—to socialism, Communism—will inevitably advance toward it by following different paths, by moving forward at different rhythms and in different forms. . . . Every pressure, every artificial enforcement of forms which are not suitable, every imposition of forms from outside, and every other endeavor to "drive people into paradise by means of beating them" can only hinder . . . the progress of socialism. . . . In advancing toward socialism peoples are coming nearer to a constantly more consistent and increasing freedom and democracy. To imagine that they will all advance toward socialism in one and the same way, according to one and the same pattern, would be just as senseless as to figure socialism as some barracks where all peoples are to be lined up equally and uniformly.[5]

Kardelj similarly declared that any attempt by "the pseudo-Marxists of the Cominform to force upon the whole world" the specific pattern of Soviet development "as a universal recipe for a socialist development" must be firmly resisted.[6]

The rejection of the "barracks model" and of the Cominform recipe was invariably linked to the endeavor to develop an alternative to Stalinism. In his New Year's address of 1949 Tito stressed the need to dissociate oneself from Stalinist methods:

Those who are appeasing their conscience with the reflection that "the end hallows the means" should remember that this dictum was particularly current among the Jesuits at the time of the Inquisition. Great things cannot be accomplished by dirty means or in a dishonest manner. Great things can only be created by honest means and in an honest manner—this is what we shall always believe.

Of particular importance for the emergence of a new model of socialism was Edvard Kardelj's report to the Yugoslav Parliament on May 28, 1949—a mere eleven months after Yugoslavia's break with Moscow—which was later issued in pamphlet form under the title *On People's Democracy in Yugoslavia*. Although Kardelj was dealing chiefly with the problem of a people's democracy, his report—similar to Rosa Luxemburg's pamphlet *The Russian Revolution*—for the first time made a clear distinction between a bureaucratic deformation of socialism on the one side and the development of socialist democracy on the other:

It must never be forgotten that even the most perfect bureaucratic apparatus, with no matter how able leadership at its head, is incapable of building socialism. Socialism can grow only out of the initiative of the broad masses. . . . Failure to follow these principles inevitably leads to bureaucracy, to aloofness of the bureaucratic apparatus from the masses of the people, to subordination of these masses to the bureaucratic apparatus.

Such a bureaucratic development inevitably

leads to a whole series of negative phenomena, such as the mania of doing things by formulas, conservatism in methods and organizational forms, strangling of creative initiative from below, education of bureaucrats without backbones, stagnation of ideas, deviations from Marxism-Leninism on the nationalities question. . . . The characteristic trait of the champions of the bureaucratic line in socialist lands is what Marx and Engels called superstitious awe of the state.

"Bureaucratic centralism" thus represented the greatest danger to a socialist development: "Even the vision of genius cannot foresee what creative triumphs millions of builders of socialism may achieve in the course of their daily work if they are unfettered by bureaucratic centralism." The development of socialism could not be assured by "a centralized administrative apparatus"; such an apparatus, on the contrary, must become a "stumbling block on the road to socialist democracy," especially when the bureaucrats believed themselves "to be above making mistakes and that only actions sanctioned by them are permissible."

To prevent a bureaucratic degeneration Kardelj demanded "the steady deepening of socialist democracy in an ever-expanding self-government of the masses of the people" and "a ceaseless struggle against bureaucratic destruction of the basic principles of a socialist democracy." The objective was self-administration through "combining more and more the apparatus of the state with the activities of the masses," and through realizing the principle "of direct participation of the producers in the management of the economy." As an important step along these lines Kardelj proposed the setting up of workers' councils in industrial enterprises.[7]

The publication of these concepts in Yugoslavia was accompanied by the first practical steps toward the realization of an alternative to Stalinism. In the spring of 1949 the state-controlled economy was decentralized and debureaucratized. The functions of the central economic ministries were increasingly delegated to the people's republics, districts, and municipalities. Factories and other enterprises were given greater independence, and the first workers' councils were set up experimentally in several factories. Even these first practical measures—a kind of "de-Stalinization in Stalin's lifetime"—were accompanied by new theoretical ideas, by a rethinking of Marxist problems, and by an accelerated dissociation from Stalinist doctrines and patterns. "The Marxists, and progressive people in our country generally, have a feeling as though a crust of ice had been broken which, without their being aware of it, had enclosed their intellect"—that is how Djilas described the situation in Yugoslavia at the end of 1949.[8] Tito similarly declared in the summer of 1950 that the Communist Party of Yugoslavia had "had too many illusions" before the Cominform conflict and had accepted too uncritically the policy of the Soviet Union, "even those things which were not in harmony with our specific conditions, or in the spirit of the science of Marxism-Leninism." The Yugoslav Communists, however, were strong enough to free themselves of these illusions: "Whoever wants to understand it and is capable of perceiving its spirit needs no other authorities, no other instructors, no ersatz Marxist science."[9]

The frequently heard view that the Yugoslav Communists embarked on their reforms only when subjected to Soviet pressure, and only subsequently worked out an ideology for them, is not shared by this author. On the contrary, the inseparable interaction between increasing disillusionment with the Soviet Union and the choice of a specific road to socialism, the independent rethinking of Marxist problems and the drawing of new conclusions for the country's political practice appear to him to be typical of the Yugoslav development after 1948. By the end of June 1950, two years after the Cominform resolution, this process had led to a decisive transformation: the introduction of secretly elected workers' councils in all Yugoslav enterprises, and hence the first step toward the transformation of state ownership into social ownership, the replacement of a bureaucratic and centralized planned economy by socialist self-management practiced by society.

In his speech introducing the workers' councils, Tito referred to the danger of bureaucratization and to the bureaucratic degeneration in the Soviet Union. The growing bureaucratic centralization in the U.S.S.R., he said, had resulted in the concentration of all economic, political, and cultural functions in the hands of a huge centralized apparatus, in a continuous intensification of the terror system, in a coalescence of the Party with the bureaucratic state apparatus which had lost all contact with the people. Such a tendency of bureaucratization, Tito said, was the greatest danger to any socialist development, since the bureaucracy "like a polyp with thousands of tentacles obstructs and impedes the correct and rapid process of development. Bureaucracy is among the biggest enemies of socialism, precisely because it insinuates itself unnoticed into all the pores of social activity and people are not conscious of it in the beginning."

State ownership of the means of production, Tito further declared, "is the lowest form of social ownership, and not the highest, as the leaders of the U.S.S.R. consider it to be." Referring to Marx's formula of the "association of free producers" Tito pointed out that "social production must be managed by the producers themselves." Management of factories by elected workers' councils was "the only right road as regards the withering away of state functions in the economy."[10] The decisive point for a socialist development, Kardelj added in April 1952, was that the "factories and social production are wrested not only from the hands of private capitalists, but from bureaucracy, and the management of all forms of production is placed in the hands of the producers themselves." For Yugoslavia Kardelj proposed that, in addition to the workers' councils in the factories, there should also be elected producers' councils which would participate in the decisions made by local authorities on all economic and social issues.[11]

This concept of the self-management of producers, which, incidentally, was entirely in line with Marx and Engels, led the Yugoslav Communists to new conclusions concerning the role of the Party in a socialist society. As early as June 1950, Tito, as mentioned before, had criticized the bureaucratization of the Party in the Soviet Union. Here, too, criticism was immediately accompanied by practical conclusions. The Yugoslav Communist Party gradually withdrew from practical state administration, and above all from the cultural sphere. "Socialist realism" and "party-mindedness" in the arts and in science—a favorite doctrine of the Soviet ideologists—was described as incompatible with Marxist principles. At the Fourth Plenum, in June 1951, the Central Committee decided that statements and articles by members of the Party leadership were no longer binding upon Party members. Only official Party resolutions (which were less and less frequent) would continue to be binding.[12] Instead of the "uniform" associations of artists and writers, set up until then on the Soviet model, independent organizations now began to spring up and to compete and argue with one another.

The role of the Party in a socialist society was set out by Kardelj in a small but important pamphlet, *Socialist Democracy*. Proceeding from the critique of Stalinism (mentioned earlier, in the chapter on Soviet ideology) Kardelj declared: "The Party must in no case be led into the danger of merging with the apparatus of state executive authority, of becoming its instrument, or vice versa. That way its bureaucratization would be inevitable." Indeed, it was the task of the Party to "enlist ever broader sections of the working people for a conscious and direct management of society." Both "social self-management" and "free socialist political and scientific criticism" were indispensable to socialism.[13]

A socialist development, Kardelj said in June 1951, would result not only in the withering away of the state but also in that of the Party. The Yugoslav Communists did not wish "to arrive at a multi-party dictatorship but at a state without parties. The entire existence of the Party is linked with that of the state. Thus the dissolution of the state in the life of society must mean also the eventual end of the Party."[14] "The future free socialist society will certainly require neither a state machine nor parties—neither one Party nor many, at least not in the sense in which we refer to them today."[15]

Both the practical experiences and the new theoretical political concepts of the first four years following Yugoslavia's break with Moscow were reflected in the Sixth Congress of the Yugoslav Communists (November 2–7, 1952, in Zagreb). The Congress emphasized that "management of economic enterprises by the workers" and self-management of producers "are of vital importance for the further development and strengthening of socialist democracy and socialism." The rights of the immediate producers must be "extended and deepened" and bureaucratic centralism further "forced back."

The Yugoslav Communist Party was renamed at that Congress the "League of Communists of Yugoslavia" because it wanted to differentiate itself from the Communist parties of the Stalinist type, and in order to recall Marx's original concept of the *Communist Manifesto,* according to which the Communists were not a special Party leading the working class, but part of the working class itself. The number of full-time officials was drastically reduced, the autonomy and independence of lower-level organizations greatly enlarged, and the "closed" Party meeting, customary until then, abolished, so that all questions could be discussed and decided in the presence of non-Party people. "The League of Communists"—the Congress resolution stated—"does not operate as a direct leader or commander, either in economic or in political and social life—nor can it operate that way." Instead, it concentrates on "political and ideological work." The League of Communists would operate "in its political and ideological work primarily by the power of persuasion."[16]

In the spring of 1953, shortly after Stalin's death, the Yugoslav Communists decided also to abandon the collectivization of argiculture, effected under Stalinist influence. The members of all agricultural production co-operatives were now free to choose whether they wished to continue to belong to them or whether they wanted to leave them. The majority chose to leave them; the remaining co-operatives were based on the free will of their members. Simultaneously a limit was laid down for privately owned land. Instead of a collectivization forced upon them, the farmers were now given the chance to develop whichever form of co-operative they preferred and to decide whether, or to what extent, they wished to participate in various co-operative organizations—an attitude undoubtedly much closer to Marx's and Engels' original concept than to Stalin's policy of compulsory collectivization.

Thus, between the summer of 1948 and the mid-1950's, the Yugoslav Communists had laid the foundation for a new type of socialist society, combined with new political concepts: support for different roads toward socialism and for equality among socialist countries and Communist parties; abandonment of centralized bureaucratic planning and its replacement by the self-management of producers, including freely elected workers' councils in the factories; abandonment of forcible collectivization and realization of the farmers' right to decide for themselves on their forms of production; the transformation of the Party from a commanding organization into a league for ideological education functioning in closest co-operation with the public; and, finally, the abandonment of "socialist realism" and "party-mindedness" in the arts and in science.

However, the Stalin leadership in the U.S.S.R. was still strong enough to prevent the spreading of the Yugoslav model to other countries. Show trials and purges, mass arrests of real and presumptive "Titoists" stifled all attempts even to discuss this problem in public. Only in secret conversations was it possible, in the Soviet Union and the countries of Eastern Europe, to exchange ideas about these Yugoslav concepts, which probably aroused a far stronger echo among thoughtful Communists in other countries than the official Party documents of the time would suggest.

Between 1948 and the end of 1952 about 8,500 people escaped to Yugoslavia from the Stalinist countries of Eastern Europe; they included many Party members and even officials.[17] In some West European countries Party members who had either been expelled or had resigned from the Party formed their own cliques and organizations, such as the *Accion Socialista* of the former Spanish Communists, the *Unione Socialista Indipendente* in Italy, the *Unabhängige Arbeiterpartei* in West Germany, and the *Gnistan* group in Sweden—all of which, stimulated by Yugoslav writings, were discussing similar problems and arriving at similar conclusions. Certainly, in the beginning, these small groups were of little political importance. But it soon became obvious that the views they represented were typical of thousands of Communists in many countries. The Twentieth Soviet Party Congress (February 1956) suddenly revealed the extent to which thinking Communists in other countries—including many who had never read the Yugoslav writings—had arrived at similar conclusions.

□   **"The Explosion of Truth"**

The Twentieth Party Congress of the Soviet Union produced a tremendous echo throughout the world Communist movement. The proclamation of the concept of different roads to socialism, the possibility of peaceful socialist transformation, and especially the dissociation from Stalin—cautiously in the public sessions but far more extensively in Khrushchev's secret report—gave rise once more to open discussions in all Communist parties. After nearly thirty years of Stalinist "freeze," the Communist parties were once more able to discuss problems that until recently would have been branded as most dangerous heresies. Reactions among Communists varied. Those Party members who had until then looked up to Stalin with unquestioning faith were so horrified and disillusioned that many of them left the Party. The dogmatic Party *apparatchiks* accepted the new anti-Stalin line with the greatest reluctance, especially those who had participated in crimes either inside or outside the "socialist camp."

But the majority of Communists welcomed the Twentieth Congress. To them the criticism of Stalin and the proclamation of new concepts meant that the past could be totally abandoned and new roads embarked upon, roads leading toward the democratization of the Communist parties, toward freeing themselves from lies, and toward an open discussion on all subjects. Some of them called this period "the explosion of truth." In Poland and Hungary, in the Communist parties of Italy, Britain, and the U.S.A., the critique of Stalinism soon went beyond the limits laid down by the Soviet leadership. The point at issue, a Polish paper declared toward the end of March 1956, was not the cult of Stalin's personality but the fact that during the Stalin era "the features of human degeneration and a degeneration of Party life ran parallel."[18] The official daily of the Polish Party wrote about the "conflict of conscience" of Communists during the Stalin era: "Today we seek an answer to many tormenting questions. To many of them we have no answer ready yet, to many—who knows—we may never be able to find one. But if asked where lies the truth and where the lie, if asked what guarantee we have that the Twentieth Party Congress was not a new error, we can reply: the liquidation of this conflict and the restoration of harmony between a Communist's conscience, word, and deed mean a return to the truth."[19]

While the Soviet leadership at the Twentieth Party Congress confined the problem of Stalinism to the "personality cult"—in other words, to the glorification of Stalin and his methods of leadership—the leader of the Italian Communist Party, Palmiro Togliatti, went a great deal further in June 1956. While he welcomed the Soviet statement about Stalin, Togliatti regretted that the Soviet comrades had so far omitted "to tackle the thorny subject of an over-all political and historical judgment." The Soviet thesis that Stalin's personal characteristics were the cause of the Soviet development could not, according to Togliatti, be considered satisfactory, since such a judgment was not based on Marxist criteria. The real problem was how and why Soviet society "was able to deviate to the point of degeneration and in fact so deviated." Stalin's errors were closely linked "with an excessive growth of the bureaucratic apparatus in the Soviet Union's economic and political life, and perhaps primarily in the life of the Party." One could not but arrive at the conclusion "that the Party was the point of origin of the harmful curtailments of democracy and the gradual all-stifling growth of bureaucratic forms of organization."

It was against this background that Stalin's role must be seen. Stalin had proved an "organizer and conductor of the bureaucratic apparatus," but only from the moment when the apparatus had begun to "displace the forms of democratic life." That had been the basis of "the one-man rule which eventually declined to the point of degeneration"—a situation which "persisted to his death and which may possibly still linger to a certain extent." A continuation of Stalinist policies, Togliatti said, might even "possibly have led to a violent change" in the Soviet Union. The criticism of Stalin had raised the general problem of "the danger of bureaucratic degeneration" and the "stifling of democratic life" in the socialist countries. The Soviet Union must now "define precisely the extent of the old mistakes" and "the rectification must be carried out with courage and without hesitation." Only thus could the socialist society recover its impetus and develop "on a broad healthy democratic basis, rich in new lively impulses."

From this analysis of Soviet domestic developments Togliatti drew a number of conclusions for the international labor movement. The situation had changed so extensively that the Soviet model "can and must no longer be obligatory." Current developments had given rise to "a wish for an ever increasing autonomy" and this could "only be of advantage to our movement." Communists in all countries must proceed from their own national traditions and conditions, remembering that in some countries a development to socialism was possible "without the Communists acting as the leading Party." Within the international labor movement a "polycentric" system was emerging, and even within the world Communist movement one could "no longer speak of a single leadership."[20]

Shortly after the publication of Togliatti's analysis the Communist parties of France, Belgium, Britain, Norway, and the U.S.A. declared that they could not regard the Soviet explanations of Stalin's mistakes as adequate and demanded a thorough Marxist analysis of the general development that had led to Stalinism.[21]

At the same time as Togliatti in Rome, the well-known Marxist philosopher Georg Lukács in Budapest also called for a human socialism and an open dialogue with those holding different views. The Stalinist development, he said, had produced a situation in which the workers in the West "shy away from the present-day form of socialism." It was important now to realize a human socialism: "The more human the socialism we develop, the more human it is for ourselves, the more to our own advantage, and seen from the point of view of our own develop-ment, the better we shall serve the ultimate victory of socialism on an international scale." Lukács urged that "the stunting, the dogmatic restriction" of Marxism should be liquidated; he expressed the hope that in future "serious international conversations will start among Communists and that these will also be extended to the bourgeoisie and to social democracy." Lukács also supported a dialogue with the Catholic Church, since it was "desirable to make contact and enter into free discussion with the representatives of opposing views." For that, however, the "worn-out clichés about religion in our press" were no longer adequate; what was needed was thorough knowledge. The Twentieth Party Congress had posed one task: "A radical sweeping away of sectarianism and dogmatism. . . . It is our duty to make a vigorous break with the epoch that has come to an end."[22]

A few days later Robert Havemann, a member of the German

Communist Party since 1932 and an active resistance fighter under the Third Reich, raised his voice in East Berlin:

The original wealth of ideas has rigidified into lifeless dogma and doctrines which, with blinkered narrow-mindedness, endeavor to force the infinite variety of life and nature onto their Procrustean bed. . . . While the dogmatists are isolated, aloof from the world, and sectarian, we must be open to new ideas, receptive, and open-minded. . . . We want to examine all views and, whenever possible, extract from all ideas and opinions whatever correct and valuable features they may contain, and make them our property.[23]

In Belgrade Edvard Kardelj championed a free socialist development: "It is time we made our fundamental break with the Stalinist theses according to which the development of socialism merely requires a Communist Party to be in power so that it can then 'build socialism' by means of a state-political and planning apparatus, in other words, set up factories, collectivize economic production and fix wages—and all that in the name of its leading role." So long as the state remained the principal factor in the development there could be "no question of a socialist system, let alone of Communism."

Stalinism had "not only piled up a mass of social antagonism but also left behind desolation in the heads of the fighters for socialism." Although Party officials had to "know by heart at any time all sorts of data about the state of economy, data which is often of very little value," they had no idea of "what was happening among the people, what social processes were going on, what new social forces were born, what forces were dying, what antagonisms appeared and in what forms they appeared, where the tendencies of degeneration appeared." Under Stalinism the "people knew much more about chickens and about varieties of potatoes and corn than they knew about relations among men." But it could not be the task of the state and the political organs of a socialist country "to prescribe to the people how to feed cattle." The main task of socialism, instead, consisted in guaranteeing to each individual such an independence "that he will be able to develop his creative energies and initiatives in all fields," since the socialist system of society was based "on the free action of socialist working people and not on state power."[24]

The views expressed by Togliatti in Rome, by Lukács in Budapest, by Havemann in East Berlin, and by Kardelj in Belgrade were typical, in the summer and autumn of 1956, of increasingly outspoken criticisms of Stalinist degeneration, of a search for new roads, of a polycentrism, of a replacement of bureaucracy by social self-management, of a liquidation of dogmatic isolation, and of a frank dialogue with people of different views.

## ☐ Anti-Stalinist Concepts of Polish Marxists

In the development of the ideas of humanist Marxism an important role was played by the Polish Marxists who, at the time of the "Polish October"—roughly from the summer of 1956 to the summer of 1957—were able to publish their views relatively freely and without restriction. After the workers' uprising in Poznan in June 1956 the need for internal reform was realized—at least temporarily—even in leading Party circles. The Soviet leadership's attempt to halt this reformist course failed, and at the famous Eighth Plenum of the Polish Central Committee (October 20–21, 1956) it really seemed that, at long last, under Gomulka's leadership, the Stalinists had suffered final defeat and that the reform course in Poland was safe.

The hopes of the Polish reformers at the time were strikingly expressed by Edda Werfel, a well-known Communist from prewar days and the wife of the editor of the ideological periodical *Nowe Drogi*:

These days we have once more found our faith in socialism. We have been given, or we have achieved, the last great chance of building socialism in our lifetime. . . . We are now experiencing a reawakening of the peoples or, if one will, another 1917. A specter is haunting at least Eastern Europe: the specter of humanist socialism, and it frightens not only the capitalists but also the Stalinists. The Stalinist labor movement is nearing its end and must reach its end.

The alternative between Stalinism and capitalism was false because "there is a third way—socialism." The sooner Stalinism was liquidated the more rapidly and effectively would any possibility of a restoration of capitalism be averted. "If socialism is at stake one must finally put an end to Stalinism."[25]

The Polish Marxists criticized above all the relations within the world Communist movement, the subordination of foreign Communists to the Soviet Union: "In mutual relations between the Communist parties," Jadwiga Siekierska wrote, "blind faith reigned, an unconditional obedience of all parties toward one party which had the power of decision and which enjoyed the right to criticize the others. In public, on the other hand, mutual compliments were exchanged and diplomatic bows made to each other."[26] At the same time, Moscow's claim to a monopoly had resulted in a sense of superiority and in overbearing on the part of the Soviet Communists. Under Stalinism, as Jerzy Lovell wrote, "significant changes have taken place in the psyche of the Soviet Communists." Stalin's policy had "undoubtedly allowed a feeling of being the 'elect Communists' to emerge among the Soviet people, so that they would regard themselves as the only orthodox people and the only ones called upon to accomplish world revolution."[27]

Not only the relations between the Communist parties of different countries, but the entire Soviet concept of the Party was subjected to rigorous criticism. Thus Stanislaw Brodzki opposed the concept of a "monolithic Party." The metaphor of the "monolith," borrowed from dead nature, was not applicable to a living Party. "The concept of the monolithic Party supplied the theoretical foundations for the hierarchization of all internal Party life," Brodzki declared. In practice the principle was

that *"nachalstvo luche znayet"* ("the leadership knows better"), and that is why it should think for us, and when it has thought something up then it should give us our orders and we will carry them out. . . . With such a near-military hierarchy, based on a rigid ladder of rank from top to bottom, the so-called Party infantry was not used to thinking independently, to reporting new phenomena they might encounter, or to participating in ideological polemics so as to eliminate clashes of opinion by way of discussion— in short, to taking a part in the shaping of the general line of the Party. . . . Such a hierarchically structured Party—similar to a military detachment— well may heroically defend a beleaguered fortress, or take a fortress by storm, but it must find it difficult, indeed very difficult, to conduct a flexible long-term policy, either in order to win over the majority of the people for the establishment of the people's power or to perform the socialist transformation of society.[28]

The Marxist philosopher Elena Eilstein, well known for her writings on the relationship between philosophy and the natural sciences, pointed to the moral degradation of the Party under Stalinism:

It leads to an alienation of the Party from the people, and of the leadership from the Party masses; to a growing importance of the Party "apparatus" as the main pillar of a government resorting to administrative methods; to the withering away of the authentic political life of the Party. The Party is filled with elements that have nothing in common with the moral and intellectual vanguard of the masses, with careerists, politically immature and negative elements, etc. It leads to the emergence of a magic circle of the initiated, to a veil of secrecy being spread over public life, and hence to the paralysis of the people's creative potentialities, to the progressive narrowing of the horizon of the supreme organs of power which, at their own instigation, are fed with one-sided and specially doctored information.[29]

The Polish Marxists did not confine themselves to a critique of the Party's degeneration under Stalinism but also began to dissociate themselves from Lenin's doctrine of the Party. The well-known Marxist sociologist Zygmunt Bauman pointed out early in 1957 that "the structural model of the Party developed by Lenin in the past was tailored to its objectives at the time." Under the conditions of czarist terror and the need for strictly conspiratorial work the total centralization of political decision making was understandable. After the seizure of power, however, this had led the Party into becoming an "undemocratic institution," and in "the emergence of a leadership group beyond the control of society."[30] Wladislaw Bienkowski, then Polish Minister of Education, declared that Lenin's thesis about Party unity, proclaimed at the Tenth Congress of the Bolshevik Party in March 1921, had "not laid down any absolute or prominently valid concept of discipline. It sprang from the current political situation and from the Party's need at a time when it was faced with extraordinarily difficult tasks." Since then the Communists had gathered much experience and had lived to see how "with the aid of 'Party discipline' not only its ideological life but also the Party's ability to think had been liquidated."[31]

The criticism of Stalinist theory and practice was linked with a demand for a new model of socialism. "Over the past few months we have spent much energy and passion criticizing bureaucratic socialism à la Stalin," the most outspoken paper, *Po prostu,* said in the autumn of 1956; "the most pressing task now is to expound openly the ideas, endeavors, and projects that are being spontaneously born among the working masses and to speed their realization in every possible way." There was above all a need for a "real democracy in the economic sector"—in fact, "a real workers' democracy." The introduction of "workers' self-management" was "the prerequisite and the first condition for the establishment of such a socialist democracy," and such a development would also have a lasting "influence on the final shape of the model, on the structure of political power."[32]

The close interconnection between workers' self-management and a new political model of socialism was emphasized also by Artur Hajnicz, a well-known expert on international questions. Hajnicz pointed out that in Yugoslavia "a different social and economic model" had been "realized even while the political and social basis of socialism has been preserved." Whereas the Stalinist system could not be identified with socialism, the Yugoslav experience had met with "widespread popularity" in Poland. The Yugoslav development should be an incentive for "separating the grain from the chaff, in other words, separating the just principles of socialism from the compromising methods of their realization." Hajnicz urged that, "on the Yugoslav model, workers' self-management should be established and the personnel of enterprises enabled to participate in their management and revenues."[33] *Po prostu,* at the beginning of 1957, supported the view that "workers' councils are among the most important elements of the new socialist production relationships in our country. This is the aim to be pursued; it requires the breaking of the resistance not only of individual wicked bureaucrats but of the bureaucracy as a social stratum."[34]

A few weeks later the Polish Marxist philosopher Leszek Kolakowski summed up the political objectives of the humanist Marxists (described by him as the "Left") in the following points: abolition of all forms of privileges in social life; recognition of the principle of equality in relations among nations; abolition of all forms of anti-Semitism; freedom of speech and discussion; abolition of dogmas, of narrow-minded insistence on principles, and of magic thinking in political life; legality in public life; maximum participation of the working class in government; abolition of police arbitrariness; and victory of socialist democracy.

Kolakowski outlined some of the principal international objectives of the Left as follows:

In capitalist countries the fight of the Left is to abolish all social privilege. In non-capitalist countries it is to remove privileges that have grown out of non-capitalist conditions. In capitalist countries the Left fights all forms of colonial oppression. In non-capitalist ones it demands the abolition of inequalities, discrimination, and the exploitation of certain countries by others. In capitalist countries the Left struggles against limitations of freedom of speech and expression. It does so also in non-capitalist lands. In one and the other the Left fights all the contradictions of freedom. . . . Everywhere the Left fights against the encroachment of any type of obscurantism in social life; it fights for the victory of rational thought, which is by no means a luxury reserved for the intellectuals, but an integral component of social progress in this century.[35]

☐   **Imre Nagy and the Petöfi Circle**

Not only in Poland but also in Hungary, 1956 was a year of great hopes—especially during the short-lived period from the Twentieth Party Congress in February to the crushing of the Hungarian uprising by Soviet troops at the beginning of November. An account of these initially so promising and subsequently tragic developments in Hungary would go beyond the scope of this book. What does seem important, however, is the effect these events had on the political concepts of humanist Marxism. In this connection we must mention first of all a detailed analysis by Imre Nagy, which he submitted to the Central Committee as a memorandum.

Imre Nagy had been a member of the Hungarian Communist Party since 1918 and had worked for many years as an agricultural expert and university professor in the Soviet Union. In July 1953 he was for a short time Hungarian Premier and proclaimed a far-reaching program of reforms, including the abolition of prison camps, the protection of personal freedom and safety, the development of the consumer goods industry, the freedom for farmers to leave collective farms, and a tolerant policy toward the intelligentsia.[36] However, the opposition of dogmatic *apparatchiks* continued to grow, and in March 1955 Matyas Rákosi succeeded in halting the Nagy program of reforms, in deposing Nagy, and subsequently expelling him from the Central Committee. Shortly afterward Nagy also lost his seat in Parliament and his chair at the Agricultural University. Rákosi finally demanded from Imre Nagy a public self-criticism, but Nagy refused. Instead, he spent the time from the summer of 1955 to the beginning of 1956 in drafting a detailed memorandum to the Central Committee, which he intended to have discussed by the Party membership. Although this memorandum[37] is concerned predominantly with practical reform proposals, it also contains observations on a number of fundamental issues.

The further development of Marxism, according to Imre Nagy, was obstructed by two continually growing obstacles: first, "dogmatism, 'exegetic Talmudism,' that rigid adherence to the old theories and their mechanical application," and, second, the "monopolization . . . of explaining Marxism-Leninism . . . the crippling of courageous and pioneering theoretical work, the disregarding of the particular characteristics of the various countries—and the applying of the old, sometimes antiquated scholastic theories." This led to the negative phenomenon that any view or thesis that diverges ever so slightly from the pattern, and any method that is not an exact copy in time and space of the Soviet model, is assessed as "an anti-Marxist, anti-Leninist, anti-Party deviation."

Imre Nagy saw the future of socialism threatened by "the degeneration of power": "Power is increasingly being torn away from the people and turned sharply against them." The people's democracy "is obviously being replaced by a Party dictatorship, which does not rely on Party membership, but relies on a personal dictatorship and attempts to make the Party apparatus, and through it the Party membership, into a mere tool of this dictatorship. Its power is not permeated by the spirit of socialism or democratism, but by a Bonapartist spirit of minority dictatorship. Its aims are not determined by Marxism, the teachings of scientific socialism, but by autocratic views that are maintained at any cost and by any means."

As Kardelj had done before him, Imre Nagy defined two possible roads of development. One was "Bonapartism, individual dictatorship, and the employment of force; this had brought about a situation where the standard of social and Party morals and ethics has slumped lower than ever before." As an alternative Nagy demanded a socialism based on a "constitutional, legal system of the people's democracy, with its legislature and government, with the democracy of our entire state and social life," since socialism could be established only on the foundation of a "constitutional law and order and legality." The sharp clash between these two roads of development, Imre Nagy prophesied, would inevitably lead to struggle because the objectives of socialism can be accomplished only by the "destruction of Bonapartism and individual dictatorship."[38]

After the Twentieth Party Congress the Hungarian reformers, though still engaged in fierce arguments with the Stalinists, gradually regained the dominant position. From March 1956 on the Petöfi Circle began its work under the leadership of Gábor Tánczos, Balázs Nagy, and Pál Jónás. The original purpose of this circle was to hold meetings to discuss the lessons for Hungary of the Twentieth Party Congress. At first this plan was favored even by the Party leadership, in the hope that it would provide a kind of safety valve. Very soon, however, the events organized by the Petöfi Circle, marked as they were by free discussion, went far beyond the limits desired by the Party leadership. The influence of the Petöfi Circle grew rapidly. Its first meeting of economists, to discuss the Five-Year Plan, was attended by 300 people; the next discussion, by philosophers (who, among other things, demanded the rehabilitation of Georg Lukács), already had an audience of over 1,000. A particularly dramatic meeting of old Party activists with young intellectuals (at which one of the speakers was Julia Rajk, the widow of the murdered László Rajk) was attended by 1,500 people. On June 27, 1956, finally, when the Petöfi Circle billed a discussion of the problem of the press, 6,000 people turned up and the discussion went on throughout the night.[39]

The political and ideological demands of the Petöfi Circle were expressed in this discussion by Tibor Déry:

As long as we direct our criticism against individuals instead of investigating whether the mistakes spring from the very system, from the very ideology, we can achieve nothing more than to exchange evil for a lesser evil. I trust we will get rid of our present leaders. All I fear is that the limping race-horses will be followed by limping donkeys. . . . We must seek in our social-ist system the mistakes which not only permit our leaders to misuse their power, but which also render us incapable of dealing with each other with the humanity we deserve. The mistakes in question are structural mistakes that curtail, to an entirely unnecessary degree, the individual's rights and that, again unnecessarily, increase his burdens.[40]

Rákosi's replacement by Ernö Gerö (mid-July 1956) proved a belated and inadequate concession by the leadership. By then the reform movement was no longer to be halted by changes of personnel in the bureaucracy. The reformers were able to speak out freely. Among the many demands, that by the writer Gyula Hay for literary freedom was typical:

Well, let us get it over quickly. We are talking about the *full freedom* of literature. . . . The writer, like anybody else, should be allowed to tell the truth without restrictions; to criticize everybody and everything; to be sad, to be in love, to think of death . . . to believe or disbelieve in the omnipo-tence of God; to doubt the accuracy of certain statistics; to think in a non-Marxist way; to dislike certain leaders; to consider low the living stan-dard of people.[41]

During the second half of October the Eighth Plenum of the Central Committee was held in Poland. That Plenum seemed to mark the liquidation of Stalinism and the breakthrough to a socialist democ-racy. The news from Poland swept through Hungary. On October 22, sympathy demonstrations for Poland were held in many Hungarian towns. On October 23, several hundreds of thousands of people from all segments of the population demonstrated in Budapest, demanding independence, democratization, freedom of the press, withdrawal of Soviet troops, condemnation of Rákosi, and reappointment of Imre Nagy. That same evening the Hungarian Party leader Gerö called for help from the Soviet troops and proclaimed a state of emergency, and Hungarian state security officers ordered fire to be opened against the demonstrators. It was then that the originally peaceful demonstrations abruptly turned into a popular revolution. Mass strikes by workers and uprisings in the towns marked the beginning of a popular revolution whose aim was the transformation of a bureaucratic dictatorship de-pendent on Moscow into an independent socialist democracy.

Under these circumstances, there was scarcely time for theoretical discussions. Instead—a vital point for our examination—the theoretical concepts of humanist Marxism were for the first time summed up in the form of concrete demands for political action. The most important action program—including the 16-point program of the students, the resolution of the Petöfi Circle, the 14-point program of the trade unions, and the appeal of the Revolutionary Committee of Intellectuals—were all characterized by a common basic tendency: the demand for independence and sovereignty was inseparably linked with a general democratization of political, economic, and social life, especially a democratization of the Party.

The independence of the country was to be ensured by the immediate withdrawal of all Soviet troops and a change in Hungarian-Soviet relations, to be based on complete equality and non-interference in each other's internal affairs. Hungary's equality was to extend to economic relations with the Soviet Union and the public was to be informed about it.

To achieve the democratization of the system, secret general elections were demanded for a new National Assembly, with several parties participating and with all criminal leaders from the Stalin-Rákosi era dismissed from their posts. All political trials were to be re-examined by independent courts; the innocent were to be released and rehabilitated. This demand applied also to prisoners of war and to those deported to the Soviet Union. Freedom of opinion, freedom of the press and radio were to be guaranteed by law, and information hitherto accessible only to senior officials was to be made public. Secret elections were to be held for all Party bodies, including the leadership.

In the economic sphere the demand was for a radical transformation of planning and the enlistment of experts. The economy was to be adapted to the requirements of Hungarian conditions, and the management of enterprises to be assumed by freely elected workers' councils. In agriculture the delivery system was to be put on a new basis; in industry minimum wages were to be introduced for workers, and a gradual leveling of wages and salaries was to be achieved. The statue of Stalin, a symbol of tyranny and political oppression, was to be removed and replaced by a memorial to the freedom fighters and martyrs of the 1848–49 Revolution; the traditional Kossuth coat of arms was to be reintroduced.[42]

These demands were implemented almost immediately upon their proclamation. Revolutionary committees sprang up everywhere, throughout Hungary enterprises were taken over by workers' councils, the Hungarian Army went over to the revolutionaries, press and radio reflected the aims of the Hungarian revolution, and socialist parties and organizations of various types came into being.

The spontaneously formed revolutionary councils, as well as the workers' councils in the factories, were recognized by the coalition government formed on October 30, 1956, under the premiership of Imre Nagy; it consisted of three Communists, two representatives of the Small Farmers' Party, and one representative each of the Peasant Party and the Social Democrats. Both the socialist objectives and the mass character of the revolution were obvious. Nevertheless, the Soviet press referred to a "counterrevolutionary underground" in Hungary and to *"coups* by a few counterrevolutionary enemy agents,"[43] without the slightest attempt at explaining how "a handful of counterrevolutionary instigators" had managed to trigger off a universal popular revolution.

The central organ of the Hungarian Communist Party, *Szabad Nép,* now openly joined issue with the Soviet *Pravda.* The point at stake, it said, was "the workers' demand to become genuine masters of the factories." The peasants wanted to be "freed from the constant material uncertainty of existence and unwarranted vexations, and to be able to live their lives as individual or co-operative peasants according to their inclination or desires." This was a struggle for the "moral purity of our system," with the aim of leading the country "toward socialism on a Hungarian and democratic path." It was a struggle "for socialist democratism and for ensuring national independence."[44]

Georg Lukács summed up the aims of the Hungarian revolution as follows: "Our state, social, economic and cultural life must be renewed in the spirit of true democracy. True democracy can liquidate all remnants of Stalinism. The creation of democratic freedom and the people's autonomy in all spheres are for us the true foundations for finding the Hungarian road to socialism and pursuing it successfully in every respect."[45]

The Soviet invasion of November 4, 1956, the brutal crushing of the Hungarian Revolution, and the subsequent arrest of the leading Hungarian reformers, including Imre Nagy, Georg Lukács, and Géza Losonczi meant that the breakthrough toward socialist democracy in Hungary had been, at least for the time being, drowned in blood. The military intervention in Hungary, Roman Zimand wrote in Poland at the time, "created a situation of which only the most inveterate enemies of Communism could have dreamed—the army of a country which thirty-nine years ago was the first to accomplish a victorious revolution opened fire upon a people calling for the implementation of the most democratic demands." The Hungarian tragedy had proved "that Stalinism is the grave of Communism."[46]

## ☐  National or International?

Both the "Polish October" and the Hungarian Revolution of 1956 have mostly been seen from the point of view of national traditions and the political development in the countries concerned. Important as these factors are, certain common features in the objectives of the two movements emerge clearly. The events in Poland and Hungary in 1956 pursued the principal aim, even though under different conditions and with specific national features, of those in Yugoslavia after 1948: the transformation of a bureaucratic centralized dictatorship of Stalinist type into a socialist democracy.

The events of 1956 in Poland and Hungary demonstrated, therefore, that what had been going on in Yugoslavia ever since 1948 was not just a "Yugoslav deviation" but the beginning of an international current. This was now being stated openly by humanist Marxists in various countries. Edda Werfel wrote in the autumn of 1956: "Whoever does not understand that what happened in Poland is not just Poland's affair but a turning point, the beginning of a new epoch in the whole international labor movement, understands nothing at all."[47]

Roman Zimand similarly underlined the international character of the dispute:

If Stalinism had an international character, then the struggle against it must not be confined to the business of one country or one Party, for it is the indispensable condition of an effective struggle against Stalinism that this struggle should be conducted not just in one country or in one Party but within the framework of the international labor movement.[48]

A similar remark was made by Tito immediately after the Soviet intervention in Hungary: "What is actually involved is whether the new trend will triumph in the Communist parties, the trend which really began in Yugoslavia and was supported by a considerable number of factors originally in the decisions of the Twentieth Congress of the Communist Party of the Soviet Union. Now the question is: will this course be victorious or will the Stalinist course again prevail?"[49]

The tragic events in Hungary had a far-reaching effect on the entire world Communist movement. "Once one's attitude to the Paris Commune was decisive," a leading Polish paper wrote at the time. "Then it was one's attitude to the land of the Soviets. But tell me now what you think about Hungary and I will tell you who you are."[50] Disillusioned and embittered by the Soviet intervention, hundreds of tested Party members and officials left the Communist parties of many countries.

Among the many who left the Communist Party of France was the Marxist theoretician Henri Lefebvre. Many founded independent Marxist periodicals, groups, and organizations. In the Communist Party of the U.S.A. there were sharp disputes between reformers (including John Gates, Joseph Clark, and Joseph Starobin) and the Moscow wing under William Z. Foster.[51] In New Zealand even the Party's founder and for many years Secretary-General, Sidney Scott, left in protest against the Soviet intervention in Hungary, together with a large number of followers. There were Party crises also in Canada and in Holland. In Denmark the Communist Party split in two when the chairman, Larsen, with a large number of old Communists, most of them resistance fighters, left the Party and subsequently formed the "Socialist People's Party" which numerically far outstripped the official pro-Soviet Communist Party.

An increasingly noticeable differentiation between pro-Soviet Communists on the one hand and humanist Marxists searching for new roads on the other emerged even within the Soviet sphere of power. Typical of the emerging concepts was the platform of Wolfgang Harich in East Germany. Harich—a lecturer in philosophy at Humboldt University in Berlin and later at the High Party School "Karl Marx," as well as editor of the East Berlin *Deutsche Zeitschrift für Philosophie*—in cooperation with humanist Marxist journalists and authors in Berlin and Leipzig (including Bertolt Brecht) drafted a political proposal for the reform of the system: "We do not intend to repudiate Marxism-Leninism," Harich wrote, "but liberate it from Stalinism and dogmatism and restore its basis of humanist non-dogmatic thought." Marxist-Leninist theory had to be supplemented by new knowledge. The Soviet form of socialism "cannot be a model for every other country," and indeed, in its present shape had become "an impediment to further socialist progress."

Khrushchev's critique of Stalin was "not a Marxist analysis: it did not touch on the basic reasons for the degeneration of the Soviet system. Neither did it touch the basic questions of the relations between the U.S.S.R. and the people's democracies. . . . The resistance of the people's democracies against the hegemony of the U.S.S.R. is part and parcel of the revolutionary class struggle of the popular masses against the Stalinist Party and government apparatus and its methods." Harich warned against the danger of a Soviet relapse into Stalinism. Attempts at reform in Eastern Europe might lead the Soviet bureaucracy "to react with Stalinist and indeed fascist methods."

In East-West relations Harich hoped for a gradual, mutual permeation of the two systems, especially if de-Stalinization proceeded success-fully in the East.

Given radical de-Stalinization, both the U.S.S.R. and the people's democra-cies will gradually influence economic developments in Western Europe by their example. Simultaneously Western conceptions of liberal democracy will influence the East and step by step enforce a retreat from political totalitarianism. In this mutual influence and interpenetration we see the true meaning of coexistence, which should end up by giving the East political liberty and the West structural economic changes which at least in the basic industries, will prove indispensable.

For East Germany Wolfgang Harich proposed internal re-forms: "We want to reform the party from inside. We stick to Marxism-Leninism. We reject Stalinism." In detail Harich demanded the radical abolition of the rule of the Party apparatus over the Party members, the expulsion of Stalinists from the Party, the establishment of un-fettered intellectual freedom, an end to the struggle against the churches, autonomy for the universities, absolute legal security, and the dissolu-tion of the secret police (SSD) and of secret courts. "Workers' councils on the Yugoslav model" were to be introduced in all factories. Com-pulsory collectivization in agriculture was to be stopped and economic policy reshaped with a view to higher living standards. Moreover, there were to be "no more privileges for leading functionaries." In the political field Wolfgang Harich further demanded the "restoration of the supreme power of Parliament," elections "with more candidates and seats," and a "thorough de-bureaucratization of the administration from top to bot-tom." In foreign policy, East Germany was to adhere to its alliance with the socialist camp, but with "full independence and equality."

Harich hoped to see his program realized by way of a legal op-position rather than by a popular rising: "We intend to conduct an open and legal opposition. But we are ready also to use the method of faction and conspiracy if forced to it. We are taking up contact with oppositional forces in the people's democracies and comparing notes."[52]

While Harich was developing an over-all program of reform, two Marxist academic economists in East Germany—Fritz Behrens and Arne Benary—called for the transformation of the centralized bureau-cratic economic system into a self-management of producers. Behrens was then Vice-Chairman of the State Planning Commission, head of the Central Statistical Office and lecturer in statistics at Humboldt University in East Berlin; Benary was the head of the Department for Socialist Economics at the Institute of Economic Studies and also a teacher at Humboldt University. Both these men went far beyond what is generally understood as economic reform: "Socialist planned economy is in its essence a democratic economy. No central economic direction, however clever, can possibly guide the economic and social development in all its details." With biting sarcasm Behrens castigated the bureaucratic-dogmatic concept of a socialist economy:

The idea that the state can do everything and that all affairs, including the most private ones, must be directed and controlled by the state is not socialist but "Prussian"—in other words, an idea of Junker monopoly. The socialist idea, i.e., the Marxist-Leninist idea, is the withering away of the state to the extent to which the socialist production relations are consolidated. . . . Socialism demands self-management of the economy by the workers because the socialization of the means of production requires, as its supplement, the socialization of management.[53]

No serious discussion of Harich's, Behrens', or Benary's reform proposals ever took place. The reply of the Ulbricht regime was "administrative." Behrens and Benary were dismissed from their posts, Benary being degraded to a job "on probation" in the Oberspree Cable Works in East Berlin. Harich was arrested on November 29, 1956, and sentenced to ten years' imprisonment on March 9, 1957, for "forming a conspiratorial anti-state group." Some of his collaborators and followers were also sentenced to long terms of imprisonment.[54]

However, views similar to those represented by Harich were being discussed almost simultaneously in the top echelons of the Italian Communist Party. In the spring of 1957, as the Italian Communist Cesare Luporini later reported, a "highly dramatic meeting" took place in the leadership of the Italian Communist Party, at which Togliatti openly called for dissociation from the Soviet model:

We had a steel-like link with Soviet Russia, with the Communist Party of the Soviet Union. This position was correct in its historical period. But that historical period is now coming to an end. We are beginning to live in another era of history in which we need other models. We need other models for the countries of the West, just as other models again are needed for the underdeveloped countries of Asia and Africa. Wherever the models have not been adapted to the situation, the Communists have lost their position at the head of the revolution.[55]

This search for new models in 1956–57 was successfully halted and largely crushed by the Soviet leadership. The military intervention against the revolution in Hungary, the arrest of the Hungarian Communists and the murder of Imre Nagy (June 17, 1958), the gradual isolation and suppression of the reformers in Poland, the arrests in East Germany, and the expulsion of independently thinking Marxists from the Communist parties of many countries—all these were effective weapons in Moscow's hand. Nevertheless, opposition by then was stronger than it had been after Yugoslavia's break with Moscow in 1948. The tremendous impetus could no longer be missed, even though for the next few years, roughly from the end of 1957 to the end of 1961, the mainstream was once more to be found in Yugoslavia.

☐   **The Program of the Yugoslav Communists (1958)**

During the latter half of March 1958 the Yugoslav Communists published the draft of their new program, which contained their theoretical conclusions, drawn not only from Yugoslavia's own development after 1948, but also from the experiences of other countries. The draft program (running to over 300 printed pages) was sent out to all Communist countries together with an invitation to participate in the Seventh Congress of the League of Communists of Yugoslavia, to be held in Ljubljana, the Slovenian capital, beginning April 22, 1958.

By then Moscow had launched its ideological campaign against "revisionism." "Revisionism, just like national Communism, must be refuted and annihilated ideologically," a Soviet periodical wrote at the beginning of 1958. "Either we bury revisionism or revisionism will mean our death. There is no third solution."[56] The dissemination of the program of the Yugoslav Communists led to a sharpening of the dispute between dictatorial-bureaucratic forces and humanist Marxists in the world Communist movement. Leading Soviet ideologists in the spring and summer of 1958 ceaselessly attacked "revisionism," and especially the Yugoslav draft program.[57] The anti-Yugoslav articles by Soviet and foreign dogmatic ideologists were almost immediately afterward collected in book form and published under the revealing titles *Against Modern Revisionism* and *Revisionism—the Main Danger.*[58]

Under these circumstances, it was understandable that not only the Soviet Union but nearly all Communist parties of the world boycotted the Yugoslav congress. Only the Communists of Norway and Denmark sent Party delegations; the Communist parties of Italy, Tunisia, and Indonesia were represented by observers. The Eastern bloc states—contrary to normal practice—merely sent their ambassadors to the Yugoslav congress. But even these, with the exception of the Polish diplomats, walked out of the congress the following day.

After several days of deliberations the congress adopted the new program, which was subsequently translated into sixteen languages. The importance of the March 1958 program of the Yugoslav Communists rests chiefly in the fact that the various concepts of humanist Marxism are here comprehensively set out for the first time.

The first striking feature is a new assessment of modern capitalism. In contrast to the Soviet ideologists, who had so far omitted to analyze objectively the social changes in modern capitalism, the Yugoslav Communists declared in their program: The political events of the last few decades had resulted in big changes in capitalist society. These changes were reflected in the "increased role of the state" in the economic system. By means of various measures of control the state can "partially restrict the right of private management of capitalist property." Among the new features the Yugoslav Communists listed "nationalizing whole branches of industry," "large state investments," "restricting the right of management of private capital," "controlling the distribution of profits," and the increasing importance of "regional and still broader international economic organizations" which had emerged in the place of "the formerly exclusive activity of private monopolies."

The Yugoslav Party program also contained a critical analysis of Stalinist developments in the Soviet Union. In contrast to the Soviet theses of "Stalin's mistakes," the Yugoslav Communists pointed out that developments in the Soviet Union, under favorable conditions, had led to concentration of power in the state apparatus, to "bureau-cratic-state tendencies," to "deformities in the development of the political system of the state," and finally to "the rule by one man." The Soviet development was characterized by the "merging of the Party and state apparatus" and "lopsided centralism." Stalin had become the "political and ideological champion" of these trends.

The Yugoslav Communists professed the fundamental concept of different roads to socialism; they rejected any common fundamental features claimed to exist by Soviet ideologists: "Men build socialism consciously, but in different countries they do it under very different conditions." The objectives of socialism are realized by the peoples "for most diverse objective and subjective reasons"—along different roads and by different means. Under present-day conditions the most varied forces—trade unions, national revolutionary movements, social democratic parties, etc.—could all act as exponents of a development of socialism. "The conception that the Communist parties have a monopoly on every aspect of the movement toward socialism and that socialism is expressed only in them is theoretically incorrect and very harmful in practice." Indeed, serious shortcomings had appeared in the work of the Communist parties. They had failed to realize "that the conditions of the struggle of the working class had changed con-

siderably," and that had led to isolation and sectarianism. It was un-
acceptable "that any particular means or forms of struggle should be
made into a principle, into a dogma."

Closely linked with this was the demand for equality in the international labor movement. The forms of international co-operation in
the labor movement "cannot be figured out or prescribed in advance
by any central body." All international labor collaboration, and collaboration among various political parties as well, must be based "on
full equality, with no imposition of attitudes and no interference in the
internal relations of the parties." No working class or party could
claim "a monopoly position in the labor movement, least of all in
ideology," since any "cooperation in the labor movement is possible
only among equals."

The forms of the socialist system in the various countries would
differ from one another in view of the "different historical development
of the various nations"; "different economic, political and cultural conditions," and the "different political—especially different democratic
—conditions." The dictatorship of the proletariat in its Soviet interpretation was by no means an indispensable transitional stage. The concept of the dictatorship of the proletariat must not be understood either
as this or that external political form or a particular method of organization of the political system, but simply as such a set of relations
as would enable the working people "to change social relations in
conformity with their socio-economic interests." The forms, methods,
and organizations by which this process was to be accomplished could
be very different in different countries and at different times, and might
even take the form of parliamentary government under a decisive influence of the working class.

Of particular importance were the Yugoslav views on the socialist
society. In contrast to the Soviet thesis of the alleged need for a "socialist state," which indeed would be further consolidated during the
socialist development, the Yugoslav Communists declared in their
program: "Prolonged and excessive use of revolutionary-administrative
measures would of necessity create tension in internal relations . . . and
lead to the assertion of bureaucratism." Instead, the socialist society
must in its character and its forms develop more and more into a
direct democracy, based on the most varied forms of social self-management. The state administration must gradually turn into an expert
apparatus subordinated to the self-managing, elected social organizations. Any kind of administrative pressure or bureaucratic issuing of
orders in the field of socialist relations must be rejected. Instead, society
must be based on the mechanism of socialist democracy, on electors'

meetings, on the organs of social self-management, and on the social and political organizations.

The Soviet view that state ownership and economic planning were indispensable prerequisites of socialism was likewise rejected by the Yugoslav Communists. In their program they pointed out— in complete agreement with Marx and Engels—that nationalization could only be a transitional phenomenon since socialism was characterized by the self-management of the producers. The socialist economy was characterized by "workers' self-management, represented in workers' councils and other self-governing producers' organs." A socialist economy did not mean that the whole of society must be turned into a mechanism which prescribes in detail and concretely to each individual what he has to do, a state of affairs in which "man ceases to be a creator." Even the most perfect economic plan could never exhaust the countless possibilities, forms, and initiatives "afforded by the spontaneous development of economic forces." Socialist economic planning must therefore confine itself to "establishing the basic proportions between production and distribution" and "a few regulating measures by the state" but must guarantee "within these proportions, free initiative of economic enterprises under market conditions."

Proceeding from this criticism the Yugoslav Communists also rejected the Soviet thesis on the "leading role" of the Communist Party. The proclamation of the Communist Party's absolute monopoly to political power as a universal "eternal" principle of the dictatorship of the proletariat and of the building of socialism was described as "an untenable dogma." The Party could not replace the overall initiative of the masses or all those various social movements manifested by the creative activity of the new society.

The Party must not take any decisions that fall within the competence of organs elected by all citizens, since this would result in the significance and role of these representative organs being restricted. The relationship between the Communist Party and the public must be neither a relationship "between governing Party and governed, nor that between teacher and pupil," but instead a relationship between equals. The Communist Party must not act the part of a superior elite, separate from the people, but the role of an equal part of the working masses. The Yugoslav Communists also rejected any attempt to transform science and the arts into an instrument of political, day-to-day interests. Communists must not arrogate to themselves the role of a dogmatic judge in matters of trends, schools, and styles in science and the arts.

One of the key objectives of socialism was the realization of personal freedom. In contrast to the Soviet thesis that the individual must be subordinated to the collective and to the "higher aims" of the struggle for Communism, the Yugoslav Communists declared that socialism cannot subordinate the personal happiness of man to some "higher aims" since the highest aim of socialism is just that personal happiness of man. During the socialist phase man must be guaranteed, on an ever-increasing scale, "independence and freedom in expressing his opinions and religious and other convictions," as well as "the inviolability and integrity of human dignity, and his personality." The realization of man's personal rights "cannot be postponed until the arrival of some 'higher stage' of socialist development."

Finally, the Yugoslav Communists subjected Marxist theory to an objective and critical examination. In their view, Marxism was "not a doctrine established forever or a system of dogmas," but a "theory of social process." Under the conditions of Stalinism, Marxist theory had lagged behind the contemporary development of society. In the Marxist exposition of modern social problems there were numerous gaps. Stalinism had transformed Marxist theory into a static collection of stale dogmas and abstract truths adapted to certain pragmatic and temporary requirements. Particularly disastrous had been the fact that Stalin, over several decades, "passed authoritarian, uncontradicted judgments within the Communist movement on all evolutionary processes of our age." This had led to a dogmatization of Marxism and Leninism.

Under these circumstances, the Yugoslav Communists supported "the further independent development of Marxism" without, however, making any kind of claim to a "monopoly in this field." They did not regard themselves as "arbiters in the field of Marxism-Leninism or of individual social sciences." The Yugoslav Communists rejected altogether any claim to infallibility. Their program was not a body of dogmas and final truths. Future development would overtake, correct, or perhaps even refute certain points of view, because—as the program significantly concluded—"nothing that has been created must be so sacred for us that it cannot be surpassed to cede its place to what is still more progressive, more free, more humane."[59]

This program laid the foundations not only for further reforms in Yugoslavia itself, but also for further theoretical studies of various problems of Marxism. Above all, the problems of self-management and of contradictions in a socialist society were discussed in a great number of writings; philosophical problems of Marxism were examined from a new point of view; the historical development of Marxism was re-examined (as, for instance, in Predrag Vranicki's work *The History of Marxism*), as was also, proceeding from the policies of the Chinese Communists, the attitude of Marxism to war (especially in Edvard

Kardelj's book *Socialism and War*).[60] A number of Yugoslav studies on the problem of coexistence and proletarian internationalism were important for the international development of humanist Marxism.

## ☐ Coexistence and Proletarian Internationalism

At first sight it might appear that the Yugoslav Communists do not differ greatly in this field from Soviet ideology. Moscow speaks of peaceful coexistence, Belgrade speaks of active coexistence, and both support proletarian internationalism. A closer examination, however, reveals far-reaching differences.

The Soviet doctrine of coexistence, as mentioned above, proceeds from the existence of two camps, the "imperialist camp" and the "socialist camp." Between these two "camps," according to the Soviet view, there should be peaceful coexistence in the diplomatic sphere and economic competition, while the ideological struggle must be continued and indeed stepped up.

The Yugoslav Communists reject the limitation of coexistence to relations between two power blocs. Coexistence, according to Tito, does not aim at establishing an equilibrium between two power blocs but at "working actively against the rigid division of the world into two hostile camps."[61] The Soviet doctrine of coexistence, Ales Bebler declared, was restricted "to the coexistence of blocs—to the coexistence of great powers. For small countries there is no coexistence—they must join or be exposed to pressure."[62] Radoslav Ratković, in his article "Two Fundamentally Different Views of Coexistence," criticized the Soviet bloc view of coexistence because this regarded coexistence merely "as a passive toleration between the two contemporary big power blocs." The bloc concept proceeded from a relative equilibrium of forces between the power blocs. "As long as this balance exists, coexistence will exist too. According to this conception the prospects are that one of the blocs, upon realizing its supremacy and its advantage, will turn the relative balance in international relations into its own complete domination." But this would mean limiting coexistence to "a temporary solution, a tactical stage in international relations."[63]

Proceeding from this criticism the Yugoslav Communists support the kind of coexistence "which must not degenerate into a temporary coexistence of antagonistic groups of states but must preserve the form of a more thorough going and lasting coexistence—and this can be achieved only by a policy of gradual bridging of the present division in the world."[64] Vladimir Bakarić also pointed out that "the problem of coexistence does not only concern the ability of the two superpowers—America and Russia—to come to an understanding with each other but, even more important, their attitudes toward all other countries."[65]

Coexistence, in the Yugoslav view, must aim, therefore, not at preserving the existing power blocs, but at ultimately abolishing them in their entirety. The aim of coexistence is "consistent and full respect for the principles of independence, for self-determination, for non-interference in internal affairs and for equal rights," the widest international co-operation in all fields, the introduction of new methods and relations into international practice, and the rapprochement of peoples through better acquaintance with each other. Active coexistence, therefore, is "not a temporary, tactical slogan but has lasting significance."[66]

The economic competition between the two systems, as propogated by Soviet ideology, was also regarded as too "narrow" by the humanist Marxists. Thus a Polish author pointed out, as early as October 1956, that peaceful competition with capitalism must not remain limited to the economic sphere but must also be a competition "in the sphere of culture, in the sphere of social and constitutional institutions, and finally also in the sphere of the moral climate in relations between human beings."[67] In Yugoslavia, Bebler criticized the Soviet concept of economic competition which, he said, was confined to the production of material goods, whereas "no other social categories were mentioned . . . nor any other categories of the social superstructure. The producing capacity of the community as a whole comes first and man, as consumer of material goods, comes second. And man as a citizen and man as a being with non-material needs is absent. It is as if the two systems were not competing in their care for him." Even economic competition was seen almost exclusively as a "competition between two states—the U.S.S.R. and U.S.A. . . . One gains the impression that the competition between the systems actually narrows down to competition between those two states. Thus conceived, the competition obviously runs counter to the principle of peaceful coexistence of countries" and "its practical implication is a continuation of the Cold War."[68]

Similar profound differences of opinion between humanist Marxists and Soviet ideology exist also on the subject of proletarian internationalism. Originally this concept had meant the international solidarity and co-operation of the labor movements of different countries. In present-day Soviet ideology, however, "proletarian internationalism" is understood to mean the existence of alleged "general regular patterns in the development toward socialism" (patterns taken from Soviet developments), the subordination of each Marxist party to a "united world movement" (under Soviet leadership), and the observance of an "international general line" (determined by the Soviet leadership).

The humanist Marxists have always opposed this doctrine. Thus Velko Vlahović pointed out that proletarian internationalism could "develop and consolidate only among equal and independent workers' movements." Both "bourgeois-nationalist independence" and "an internationalism on the basis of military discipline" must equally be rejected. True proletarian internationalism meant "deliberate voluntary proletarian solidarity among equal revolutionary parties and movements enjoying equal rights." A unitary world movement with one center, on the other hand, must inevitably lead to an ideological and political monopoly, and hence to "phenomena of abuse of this privileged position." Such a monopoly "is the expression of an unhealthy situation, a phenomenon alien to the workers' movement."[69] Vlahović even called the different roads to socialism "a law of socialist development."[70]

Puniša Perović, in a detailed analysis in the spring of 1962, pointed out that championship of a different road to socialism was not some kind of "nationalism" or "deviation" but something stemming logically from the present situation. Different roads to socialism, according to Puniša Perović, were necessary above all for three reasons. First, almost one billion people had "chosen the road of building a socialist society in one way or another." All these people had their peculiar social development and their specific national problems, their own parties, organizations, and institutions, and could not therefore be forced into the same mold. Second, there was the awakening of the colonial nations, the emergence of independent national communities that were choosing roads of development "which will not and cannot be identical with the roads of other nations, for instance, the Europeans." Third, the conditions of the struggle for socialism in the highly developed civilizations of the West had greatly changed. In these conditions socialism was "no longer a matter only of the Communist parties" but had "become a matter for entire nations, for the broadest political forces." All this must lead "to the clear realization that it is impossible to reduce all these movements, all these specific national situations, to one common denominator and to believe that only one strategy and tactic is applicable to all socialist forces and movements."

The Soviet claim that Marxism-Leninism demanded a uniform general line for all Marxist parties is rejected by the humanist Marxists. "What does it mean, who is entitled to interpret Marxism-Leninism in such a way that it can serve as the basis for unity or as an 'instruction for action'?" Perović wrote. The interpretation of Marxism must be left to each individual Party. True, other parties might help in this,

but this too involves a risk. Help can suddenly become the imposition of one's own point of view. . . . Any absolute generalization of an opinion and any claim to a monopoly in the interpretation of Marxism-Leninism is not only an endeavor which is theoretically in conflict with Marxism and Leninism but moreover contains within itself a tendency toward political monopoly—an even more dangerous and even less acceptable endeavor.

The Soviet thesis of an alleged "general regular pattern in the development toward socialism" was similarly described by Perović as "clearly a schematical view." General laws and common elements, he claimed, appeared in different forms in different situations:

differently in a country with a highly developed social structure and differently in a backward society. And any attempt to enforce any experience, to prescribe any "general regular patterns" in the development of socialism, is not only contrary to the spirit of Marxism but also harms the general cause of socialism. Such attempts are the more harmful and the less acceptable when the experiences of a backward country in the building of socialism are recommended and forced upon countries and movements with a developed social structure.[71]

These views were shared also by the Italian Communists. As early as 1956, in his famous interview mentioned earlier, Togliatti supported the concept of polycentrism in the international labor movement and the autonomy of each Communist Party. Later the Italian Communist Party preferred the concept of "unity in variety" but clung to the fundamental idea. Thus the Italian Communists declared in November 1961 that "nowadays there can be neither a leading Party nor a leading state, nor a single center laying down the direction and organization of the world Communist movement."[72] In his memorandum of September 1964 Togliatti again expressed his "doubts and reservations on the opportuneness of the international conference." The unity of the international labor movement was best accomplished by contacts and exchanges of experience between the parties of different countries, and by public discussion "in an objective and persuasive manner, and always with a certain respect for the adversary."

The proclamation and acceptance of "universally valid rigid formulas" for the international Communist movement were "an obstacle" because "the forms and concrete conditions of the advance and victory of socialism today and in the immediate future will differ substantially from those in the past. At the same time, the differences between one country and another are very great. For that reason each Party must know how to act in an autonomous manner."[73]

The above quotations reveal the differences in the interpretation of "coexistence" and "proletarian internationalism." Soviet ideology views coexistence in terms of relations between the two power blocs led by the two superpowers, the U.S.A. and the U.S.S.R. Relations between the two blocs are characterized, in the Soviet view, by peaceful coexistence of the two different systems in the political sphere, by economic competition, and by ideological struggle. The humanist Marxists, on the other hand, do not want to restrict coexistence to the two powers but, on the contrary, want to overcome the present division into two blocs and eventually eliminate it altogether; their aim is international cooperation among all countries on the principles of independence, sovereignty, non-interference, and equality. Competition between states with different social orders should not be confined to the economy but extend to the sphere of culture, to social relations, human relations, and the well-being of the individual.

Proletarian internationalism, in the view of the humanist Marxists, must not be seen as a monopoly leadership of the world Communist movement, prescribing some general compulsory pattern or international general line for the entire world movement, but must be given its original meaning: equality within the international labor movement, rejection of any center, voluntary co-operation, and each country's right to its own road to socialism.

☐ **The Transition to Socialism and the Dictatorship of the Proletariat**

Equality in the international labor movement and the right to a different road to socialism are of particular importance to the West European Communists because the conflict between Soviet dogmas and reality is particularly striking in the highly industrialized countries. The new conditions of a modern industrial society, the changes in social structure—including that of the industrial working class—and the changed political conditions urgently demanded a new assessment of the situation. In October 1954 Edvard Kardelj, referring to the new circumstances, declared that "for a whole series of countries the evolutionary road to socialism through the political mechanism of classical European bourgeois democracy is not only possible but has become a fact."[74] In such a transition a "leading role" by the Communist Party was neither necessary nor likely, since it could equally well be performed by other political forces. In East Berlin, Wolfgang Harich in his *Plattform* emphasized: "we think Western European socialism will take over from capitalism in a peaceful manner" and that "the transformation process from capitalism to socialism in Western Europe will not everywhere take place under the auspices of the Communist Party, but that in many countries the Communists will have no part whatever in its direction."[75]

In Yugoslavia, Puniša Perović pointed out that in the highly industrialized countries of the West "the classical socialist revolutions which had at one time been expected have not materialized and there is little prospect that they will materialize." A socialist development was "no longer the affair of the Communist parties," since "in some developed countries of the West it is the social-democratically oriented wing that represents the strongest force."[76] Palmiro Togliatti likewise called for a "thorough rethinking" of the possibility "of a peaceful approach to socialism," including such questions as how, under present conditions "one can extend the limits of liberty and of democratic institutions and what are the most effective forms of participation for the working masses and the workers in economic and political life."[77]

At almost the same time Luciano Gruppi, the head of the ideological department of the Central Committee of the Italian Communist Party, challenged the idea that Lenin's theory of the state and his concept of the dictatorship of the proletariat were sacrosanct or universally valid. When Lenin had written *State and Revolution* in the summer and autumn of 1917, Gruppi declared, he had been thinking of the Russian state of his day. This had resulted in the "one-sided character of Lenin's analysis of the nature of the state"; in addition to the class character of the state and its aspect of a repressive power, the element of consent must also be taken into consideration. Such institutions as Parliament and regional, municipal, and provincial administrations could, under present conditions, be used for "renewing the social and state order from its very foundations." In this way, "the transition to socialism can be performed without a break in constitutional continuity, without suspension of democratic legality or of its institutions and processes."[78]

While Luciano Gruppi emphasized the changed position of state power, the Austrian Communist Ernst Fischer in an important article, "Marxism and Ideology," in May 1965 pointed to the "changed role of labor" in a modern society:

The modern worker is no longer the totally impoverished person he was in Marx's day; he has become qualified, he has gained social rights, he has more to lose than his chains and he has become a confident personality. A new nucleus of the labor movement has emerged—the highly qualified worker who works with scientific methods and does not differ essentially from the technician, a worker in alliance with large sections of the technical intelligentsia and with the intellectual generally.[79]

A few months later Franz Marek, then editor of *Weg und Ziel,* the theoretical periodical of the Austrian Communist Party, called for an objective examination of the conditions in the highly developed industrial countries. "We must acknowledge the fact, without dodging it any longer, that the three most powerful industrial states of the world— the United States, Britain, and West Germany—are the very states where the revolutionary workers' movement is not very strong—and not only because of discrimination, persecution, and prohibitions." These problems had been "shirked too much" by Communists in the past. Franz Marek, on much the same lines as Ernst Fischer, referred to the changed role of industrial labor. The present situation, he said, could not be compared with the world-wide economic slump of the 1930's. True, there are crisis features in it, there is uncertainty of employment in certain industries, there are difficult structural problems, there is increased work intensity and fear of the consequences of automation,

but there is no mass unemployment of the kind that existed during the great economic crisis; there is no growing misery; there is no intolerable situation for large sections of the working people . . . the car parks outside the factories have grown bigger . . . and in most countries of Western Europe the standard of living and also the workers' real wages—especially the family wages—have risen perceptibly since the war.

Foremost among the new political conditions were "fundamental democratic reforms." The struggle for socialism in the West European countries is mainly "a struggle for democratization, for a revival and renewal of democracy, for real co-determination of the working people in political and economic life, for an unfolding of democracy in municipalities and enterprises." This meant acknowledging "respect for parliamentary traditions, for the multi-party system." The concept of the dictatorship of the proletariat was no longer applicable under present-day conditions because "since the revelations of the crimes of Stalin's time" it had been totally discredited among the working people and "identified also by the young people with the rule of terror and police arbitrariness." Adoption of "the peaceful road to socialism entails endorsement of the multi-party system."[80]

In Yugoslavia Branko Pribičević criticized the outdated dogmatic assessment of Western capitalism and drew attention to the crucial changes it had undergone: over the past ten years the capitalist countries had reached a higher average economic growth rate than at any time before. Working conditions had substantially improved, and this included a rise in real wages. The accelerated economic development and technological progress had resulted in substantial changes in the social and class structure, in particular the structure of the working class. The state's influence on the economy had greatly increased; there can be no question of the state being a mere tool of the big monopolies in the sense of the Soviet formula of "state monopoly capitalism." The economic integration processes could not be countered by a "frontal opposition." The increase in planning in the Western countries moreover raised the question of "whether the workers' parties and the trade unions should take part in the work of various economic programming agencies," since it was "clear that the revolutionary forces cannot hold themselves apart from these processes."[81]

Zorica Priklmajer-Tomanović, of the Belgrade Research Institute for the Working Class Movement, listed several reasons why a peaceful transition to socialism by way of a parliamentary multi-party system was not only desirable but necessary in the West European countries. First, the complicated political structure of those countries and their strong tradition of the multi-party system; second, the pluralist character of the socialist workers' movement, which consists of various Leftist parties, groups, and organizations; third, the concept of democracy in Western Europe is closely tied to the parliamentary system, and it is therefore expected that a socialist democracy could be achieved by way of that system; fourth, a peaceful road to socialism means a continuity of methods and forms in the socialist movement. The rejection of the dictatorship of the proletariat is both understandable and necessary, since "the shadow of Stalinism" had fallen over this concept and it was natural that attempts should be made "to free oneself from all connections with Stalinist practice."[82]

Not only the Italian Communist Party, but other Communist parties of Western Europe, including those of Great Britain, Sweden, and even Denmark, began in 1964 to depart from Soviet political concepts. The West European Communists' increasing autonomy was not confined to theory but also extended to practical politics. The overthrow of Khrushchev in mid-October 1964—above all, the manner in which this change of leadership was brought about—met with open criticism from the leading Communist parties of Western Europe. The autonomous critical attitude of the West European Communist parties became even clearer in February 1966, in connection with the sentences passed on the Soviet writers Sinyavsky and Daniel. Exceedingly sharp protests came not only from the Italian Communist Party but also from the French writer Louis

Aragon, until then invariably loyal to the U.S.S.R.; from John Gollan, the General Secretary of the Communist Party of Great Britain; from C. H. Hermansson, the Chairman of the Swedish Communist Party; and even from the Communist Party of Denmark.[83]

The humanist Marxist ideas on the transition to socialism were supported with particular clarity by the Swedish Communist Party. Its new Party program, proclaimed at the beginning of 1967, for the first time lacked all reference to Lenin and Leninism. The doctrine of the dictatorship of the proletariat and the Soviet-glorified Party principle of "democratic centralism" were also missing. The multi-party system was regarded as necessary and correct not only for the transition to socialism but also for the socialist society itself.[84]

## ☐ The New Model of Pluralist Socialism

The lessons of bureaucratic degeneration in the Soviet Union on the one hand, and of Yugoslav developments and reformist endeavors in Poland and Hungary on the other, brought the humanist Marxists face to face with an entirely new problem in Marxism—the point that there can be and indeed must be different models of a socialist society. The humanist Marxists came to the conclusion that not only the road to socialism but the socialist society itself would not show the same forms everywhere. Reformers (including Kardelj and Djilas in 1949, Harich in 1956, and Togliatti at the closed session of the Central Committee of the Italian Communist Party in the spring of 1957) insisted that the Soviet model could not be obligatory for other countries.

This raised the question of new models of a socialist society. In 1958 the French Marxist theorist Henri Lefebvre (shortly after having been expelled from the Communist Party) wrote: "We now have before us two 'models' of socialism that differ very considerably from each other"; the one (Soviet) model is "administrative or state socialism," the other (Yugoslav) model "consists of a complex group of local, decentralized, and democratically elected organs: workers' and management councils in the factories, and various levels of producers' councils (commune, district, federal republic, federation)." A new model of a socialist society should now be developed for France, proceeding from her specific conditions.[85] In Austria, Ernst Fischer pointed out that "there will be no monolithic socialism, uniform for all parts of the world. . . . There is no final model of socialism that would be transferable to all countries and nations."[86]

In November 1965, at a Yugoslav-Czechoslovak symposium in Zadar, the Czechoslovak humanist Marxist Julius Strinka, a lecturer at the Philosophical Institute of the Slovak Academy of Sciences, also urged that the present model of socialism should be viewed as a "historically transient form of socialism," to be replaced "by a new, more adequate model." Present-day socialism could no longer be regarded as a permanent form "but as one of the possible forms, as one of the possible variants, as the first stage of greater and more far-reaching social transformations in the future, and as the starting point of a great social experiment which must be continually controlled and improved in every respect."[87]

The humanist Marxists of different countries all agreed that neither the economic model of the Soviet Union (State ownership of the means of production, economic management by central, hierarchically structured planning), nor the political structure of the Soviet Union (dictatorial rule by the Party apparatus over all spheres of social life) was compatible with a socialist society. In the view of the reformers, socialist society must be characterized by a combination of self-management of producers in the economic sphere with a pluralist political system of a socialist type.

In the economic field, the socialist society rested upon self-management by producers, including workers' councils in the factories. Its basis was not state ownership, but social ownership. Thus, in Yugoslavia Branko Horvat pointed out that the economic foundations of socialism had frequently been defined in the past as the negation and antithesis of capitalism. This had resulted in a general rejection of the market, of autonomous enterprises and of personal initiative. "Today we know from practical experience how naïve and false these antinomies are. The market must not be anarchic; planning must not be centralized or conducted by the administration; personal initiative is not necessarily bad and state initiative is not the only alternative; besides state and private ownership there can be a third way—social ownership."[88]

The humanist Marxists justify workers' self-management both by the negative experience of a rigid, bureaucratically planned economy and by Marx's original concept of the association of free producers. Rudi Supek, Professor of Sociology at Zagreb University, in an extensive analysis showed that workers' self-management was necessary not only for economic reasons but chiefly for political reasons, since statist bureaucracy could be avoided only in this way. Finally, workers' self-management also had a humanist foundation—the elimination of the alienation of man from production.[89]

In the political sphere, according to the humanist Marxists, a socialist society was unthinkable without the direct active participation of the population in all public affairs—this presupposed comprehensive information and also the development of all democratic freedoms. The nationalization of the means of production, according to the Polish reformer Mieczyslaw Maneli, was merely the prerequisite of a new society. More crucial for a socialist society was the need to "develop socialist democracy, continually extend the scope of fundamental democratic freedoms, and to guarantee the freedom of thought, speech, and criticism, as well as personal integrity, etc."[90]

Robert Havemann in his series of lectures at Humboldt University in 1963–64 (which later led to his dismissal and "other administrative measures") warned against regarding the development of socialism as a purely economic and technological process, since "socialism is not a matter that can be carried out just according to program," but a movement whose progress depends "on the measure in which an increasing number of people will gain an understanding of social interrelations and hence decide to co-operate actively in the transformation of society." A socialist society, Havemann declared, must ensure the "ever more comprehensive information of all members of society" so that "all members of society can participate as consciously as possible in the real processes and are as fully informed about them as possible."

Freedom of opinion and information was, therefore, vital to socialism:

Any restriction or limitation of information or the exchange of information impedes the work of the members of society and hence also the development of social relationships; it only retards the development. . . . People must not be subjected to mass-produced and officially authorized views because this leads them to purely mechanical and superficial thinking. We must improve the public's qualifications by comprehensive information, enabling it to understand reasoned connections. . . . Those who fear the consequences of universal unrestricted information, and therefore obstruct it, are creating the very conditions for a disastrous development. This proves the truth of an ancient thesis of Greek tragedy that man draws upon himself his fate by attempting to avert it.[91]

Palmiro Togliatti similarly demanded a libertarian model of socialism. In the socialist countries, he wrote in his memorandum, there should be "open debates on current problems, the leaders also taking part," since socialism must be understood as a system "in which there is the widest freedom for the workers, that they in fact participate in an organized manner in the direction of the entire social life."[92]

The first attempt (in the 1960's) at working out a new model of socialism in somewhat greater detail was made in Poland. In the autumn of 1964 Jacek Kuron and Karol Modzelewski, both Party members and lecturers at the Institute of History at Warsaw University, drafted a 128-page manuscript under the title *List otwarty do Partii* (*Open Letter to the Party*) in which they subjected the ruling system in Poland to a thorough Marxist critique and arrived at the conclusion that it was not a socialist system at all but a monopolistic, bureaucratic one. The two authors also criticized the parliamentary system of the West because, among other things, after an election the parties were largely independent of their own election programs, and because the deputies in Parliament felt an obligation not to their electors but to their own party leadership and could not be recalled by the electors. The electorate was subdivided into territorial constituencies on totally formal criteria and consequently "atomized." Participation by the citizens in political life, in the view of the two authors, was confined to reading statements by politicians in the newspapers, to hearing politicians on the radio or seeing them on television, and to electing a different party every four or five years to take over the government. The real power, therefore, was not in Parliament but in the executive apparatus. The parliamentary regime could not, therefore, be described as a real people's government; moreover, developments over the past few decades had shown that the parliamentary system was no guarantee against the establishment of a dictatorship.

Proceeding from this critique of the Eastern and Western systems, Kuron and Modzelewski championed a model of socialism based on a system of workers' councils and associated with the existence of several workers' parties. In their view, a simple liberation of factories and enterprises from centralized bureaucratic management (as demanded by many economic reformers) was not sufficient, since this would favor only the technocratic forces. What was important was the establishment of workers' councils in the factories, linked with one another by delegations. These elected councils of workers' deputies were to be set up throughout the country, with a central council at their head. The councils at all levels were to be responsible for all economic and political problems and would moreover practice legislative and executive functions. The delegates, elected on a production basis, were to be subject to recall by their electors at any time. In order to guarantee that this system of councils was absolutely democratic and expressed the will of the workers, Kuron and Modzelewski favored the existence of several workers' parties; each political trend or party was to have the right to its own newspaper, its own program, and its own political activity. This, in turn, entailed freedom of speech and the press, and the abolition of any kind of censorship.

A further characteristic of a workers' democracy, according to the two authors, was complete independence of the trade unions from the state (including the right to strike), and, above all, the abolition of the political police. The army (which might be turned into a tool of counter-revolution) was to be replaced by workers' militias subordinated to the various workers' councils. The interests of the peasantry were to be represented in this system by "councils of peasant producers."

Kuron and Modzelewski summed up their proposals under a few headings:

In liberating itself the working class liberates all of society. In order to liberate itself

- it must do away with the political police thereby liberating society from dictatorship and fear;
- it must do away with the regular army, thereby liberating soldiers from the brutalization of barrack life;
- it must introduce the plurality of parties thereby giving political freedom to all society;
- it must eliminate preventive censorship, introduce total freedom of the press, of scientific and cultural creation, of the creation of diverse currents of social thought, thereby liberating the writer, the artist, and the journalist and creating the conditions under which the intelligentsia can realize in the fullest way its proper social function.[93]

The two authors of this manifesto—which contained nothing beyond Marx's original ideas in a somewhat modernized form—were expelled from the Party and arrested on November 14, 1964. In mid-July 1965 they were sentenced to three and a half years' imprisonment for "preparing and disseminating materials damaging to the interests of the Polish state."[94]

While Kuron and Modzelewski were imprisoned in Poland, humanist Marxists in Western Europe publicized similar ideas without hindrance. The new model of socialism was now frequently described by the term "pluralist socialism."[95] At a meeting of the Paulus Society in Salzburg in April 1965, under the motto "Marxism and Christianity," the Italian reformers, above all, championed a pluralist socialism independent of ideology. The model of a socialist society, declared Cesare Luporini, Professor of Philosophy at Florence University and a researcher at the Gramsci Institute in Rome, was that of "a pluralist society, of real groups able also to group themselves ideologically." A socialist society must be characterized by "real freedom for groups with different ideologies provided they are determined to work together on political and social tasks."

At the same meeting Lucio Lombardo-Radice, Professor of Mathematics at Rome University and a member of the Communist Party for nearly thirty years, stressed that "the socialist society must be the objective of various trends, the common 'dialogue' composed of several ideological components." Socialists must not "acknowledge any distinction between citizens on grounds of ideology"; in this connection, "a Marxist 'restoration' of the liberal concept of a non-confessional (lay) state would be most fruitful." Luciano Gruppi also referred to socialism as "a pluralist society in which groups and forces of different political and ideological conviction co-operate." In such a society the state became "independent of ideologies of all kinds, and not committed to any ideology either formally or in practice. It will enable all views to compete with one another."[96]

The Yugoslav Marxist Gajo Petrović, Professor of Philosophy at Zagreb University, called socialism "a self-critical society." In a socialist society the right to criticism was a matter of course and need not be granted from outside. "Free personalities in a socialist society can and should practice and realize a much more ruthless and consistent critical attitude toward themselves and toward society as a whole than was ever possible for anyone in any earlier society."[97]

Support for pluralist socialism—and on this point the humanist Marxists of different countries were all agreed—meant the rejection of the Soviet concept of the "leading role of the Party," not only in its Stalinist but also in its Leninist form. Thus the Yugoslav Marxist Ivan Perić stated that "the day of the Leninist-type Party is gone," since such a Party bore "the stamp of a relatively backward phase, necessitating the tie-up of the Party with political power."[98] Ernst Fischer also demanded that the Party should give up its claim to infallibility. "We must at long last do away with the idea of the Party's infallibility, the slogan that the Party is always right. There is no Party that can claim for itself the whole truth, and we shall be very happy if we are able, all of us together, to approach the truth. There is no class truth, there is no Party truth—there is only the truth which we are all striving to attain."[99]

☐   **A Multi-party System Under Socialism?**

While the humanist Marxists agree on rejecting the "leading role of the Party" and endorsing a pluralist socialism, a number of different views exist on the details of its practical realization, including the issue of a possible multi-party system under socialism.

Most Yugoslav Communists support a further development of social self-management, the transformation of the Party into a League with new tasks, the promotion of socio-political mass organizations and of democratic freedoms, with the aim of the gradual emergence of a "non-party" direct democracy operated by the socialist society.

Not the creation of new political parties but the total transformation of the character, the function, and the internal organization of the Communist Party is seen as the main task. Thus Svetozar Stojanović of Belgrade University declared that, having won the revolution and seized power, a Communist Party must completely transform itself in order to make a socialist development possible. After the seizure of power every Communist Party was confronted by a fundamental dilemma—whether to promote a development in the direction of "social self-management" or to consolidate "the political rule of the Communist Party." The first road would lead to "socialism," the second to statism, to state ownership of the means of production, to the gradual emergence of a new ruling class as the collective proprietor of the means of production, to a statist system in the form of Stalinism. Whenever a Communist Party is organized as the type of Party "in which such principles as centralism, hierarchy, discipline, monolithic unity, and duty predominate," there is always a tendency to turn in the direction of "statism of the oligarchical type" after the seizure of power.

To prevent such a development the Communist Party, having seized power, must transform itself into a League. Such a transformation would be characterized, first of all, by a change of function and tasks. While a Communist Party developed into "the backbone of state authority," a League of Communists was characterized by the fact that "it should initiate and develop social self-management, i.e., gradually let state power out of its own hands." The second difference was in the social composition. As soon as a Communist Party assumed universal authority in the state it was inevitable that officials, public employees, etc., should wish to join it in order to participate in its authority. The backbone of the League of Communists, on the other hand, was represented by "workers and other direct producers of material and intellectual values." Third, there was the organizational structure: the Communist Party was marked by its "monopoly of leadership" and "a high centralization in political and personal matters." A League of Communists, on the other hand, was characterized by "the transparency of all levels of the organization and the visibility of all conceptions, actions and their promoters"; in consequence, its "members not only participate en masse in the realization but also in the making of decisions." Fourth, there was its position in society. The Communist Party enjoyed a position of monopolistic exclusiveness: all functionaries in social and state life were not elected but "appointed by the Communist organization and its transmission organs." A League of Communists, on the other hand, renounced all monopoly positions and placed itself under the continuous criticism of the public, including that of other social organizations. "Under socialist pluralism I do not mean a multi-party system, but socialist socio-political mass organizations which should become increasingly equal to and more and more autonomous toward the League of Communists."[100]

In the same spirit, Predrag Vranicki stresses the further development of social self-management. In this process the Party will have to be transformed from a power apparatus into an ideological and organizational guiding force of a self-managed society in which all socialist opinion can be expressed without reservation.

The development of a multi-party system might appear "plausible at first sight" but in Yugoslavia, at least, it was "not applicable for a number of reasons," since it would lead to power struggles between certain groups, as well as to "the danger of nationalist deformations." Above all, a multi-party system was to be rejected on grounds of principle: "In a society that introduces self-management the issue is not the rule of this or that political party but really the withering away of such a rule, the elimination of the predominance of the political sphere of society. Any 'augmentation' of politics and politicians is not in the interests of a self-managing community."[101]

Other humanist Marxists, on the other hand—principally in Italy and Sweden—have repeatedly come out in recent years in favor of a multi-party system under socialism. Thus the Italian Communist Cesare Luporini at the Salzburg meeting in April 1965 pointed out that a pluralist socialism was "not thinkable without the dialectics between government and opposition."[102] Quoting Luigi Longo, the General Secretary of the Italian Communist Party, another participant at the meeting, Lombardo-Radice, declared that "in a socialist society the existence of several parties and the free clash of opinion are a vital necessity."[103]

The farthest-reaching endorsement of a multi-party system under socialism came from the Chairman of the Swedish Communist Party, C. H. Hermansson, who stated in July 1966: "One cannot be a supporter of political democracy under capitalism and reject it under socialism." If one adopted such an attitude one would lose the confidence of the people. A victory of the bourgeois parties in an election during the transition to socialism, or even under socialism, would certainly entail serious problems, but they must on no account lead to anti-democratic measures such as, for instance, the suppression of parliamentary government or the multi-party system.[104]

A few months later a Yugoslav, Stevan Vračar of Belgrade University, also supported a two-party system under socialism. Unlike Hermansson he drew his justification from the negative experiences of the Soviet Union and many other East European countries. In those countries, he pointed out, there had repeatedly been political crises and "a brutal squaring of accounts between Party leaders," who had often been physically liquidated. In fact, these people had by no means been "enemies of socialism" but had merely had "natural differences concerning the most important political issues." These events "had led everywhere to an exceedingly painful and unpleasant image of the one-party system." In view of these experiences Vračar proposed a two-party system, with both parties standing on the basis of socialism:

Would it not be more natural to have two parties, both of which struggle for socialism? Naturally these two parties might differ in their structure and in their following, and also in their ideological attitude toward certain questions of building socialism. In such a situation the majority party would see itself as the ruling party, faced by an organized opposition. However, each party would have to acknowledge the fact that it cannot perpetuate itself or its structure. . . . In this way the worst aspects of the one-party system would disappear without socialism as such being jeopardized.[105]

According to Gert Petersen of the Socialist People's Party of Denmark, the question whether a pluralist socialism with emphasis on social self-management requires a multi-party system or not must depend on the situation and position of the country in question: "each country must develop her own form of socialist democracy." These forms might differ a good deal: "not the number of parties is decisive, but the degree of the actual rights of all citizens to co-decide their affairs and those of the state."[106]

The model of a pluralist socialism in the form of a multi-party system was most clearly set out in the new program of the Communist Party of Sweden. The Swedish Communists described as their objective the establishment of a socialist society in which

the people, in free co-operation, by way of discussion and democratically reached decisions, decide their own living conditions and their country's development. . . . This does not mean the emergence of a stagnating, conflict-free situation. Under socialism the social organization must be such that, following the elimination of power relationships in the class society, the conflicts between individuals, groups, ideas, and interests may be freely discussed and rationally solved.

Socialism, according to this program, was characterized by a "multi-party system and parliamentarianism," as well as "freedom of organization, assembly, and the press." Within the framework of co-ordinated planning, "the employees themselves manage their enterprises." The press, radio, and television are likewise "to be managed by the employees themselves." The socialist society was characterized by "broad and public discussion" and "free and fearless criticism."[107]

The view of the Italian Communist Party on the pluralist character of the hoped-for society of the future was similarly defined by Luigi Longo in the spring of 1968—at the time of the "Prague Spring." Under socialism "the forces will proceed from their own views, endeavors, and objectives." This applied to all "who profess socialist motivation—not necessarily a Marxist view—hence also those Catholic and democratic currents which are not tied to the interests of monopolies, speculators, or big landowners." Longo called for "the broadest democracy also for those parties which, during the building of socialism, disagree not just with some measure or other but even with fundamental issues," since the socialist society was characterized above all by "broad freedom—this is a vital element in our views—for political discussion, for scientific argument, for cultural debate, for an exchange of opinion between various schools, none of which can claim a privileged position in a state with a socialist government, let alone exclusive rights for itself."[108]

The discussions about the new model of a pluralist socialism did not take place in a vacuum, in isolation from political reality. While these discussions were going on, a great reform process began in Czechoslovakia known as the "Prague Spring."

## ☐ The "Prague Spring" of 1968

In Czechoslovakia a peaceful transformation of vast importance had been taking place since January 1968. This reform process was concerned with transforming a centralized bureaucratic, dictatorial system into a socialist democracy. For the first time this process was taking place in a country in the heart of Europe, which possessed all the prerequisites that Marx and Engels had regarded as necessary for a socialist society: a high level of economic development, an industrial working class that played a dominant role, a country with a deeply rooted democratic tradition, a country where the absolute majority of the population supported the realization of socialism.

The crisis of the Novotný regime in Czechoslovakia had reached its climax at the turn of 1967–68. The ossified bureaucratic and dictatorial system of government was in sharp conflict with the requirements of economic reform and of an overdue democratization. Tensions between Czechs and Slovaks had been aggravated. The ruling Party had isolated itself more and more from the public. The Action Program of April 1968 described the situation before the "Prague Spring" as follows: typical of Czechoslovakia had been a "mechanical acceptance and spreading of ideas, customs, and political conceptions which were at variance with Czechoslovak conditions and traditions." This had led to "a bureaucratic system," to the "suppression of the democratic rights and freedoms of the people," to "violation of laws" and the abuse of power and had also "undermined the initiative of the people."

Economic policy had been "enforced through directive administrative methods that no longer corresponded to the economic requirements and possibilities of the country" and led to the exhaustion of its material and human resources. Unrealistic tasks were allotted to the economy, "illusory promises were made to the workers." The result had been a marked "technical retardation" and in many cases even a "reduction in the living standard of the people." In the economic life of the country there was no recognition of "independence, diligence, expertise, and initiative"; instead there was "subservience, obedience, and even kowtowing to higher ups."

The causes of the economic difficulties were to be found in the "deformations in the political system." The revolutionary dictatorship had not developed into a socialist democracy but into "bureaucracy," and a "mechanism created which resulted in helplessness, in conflict between theory and practice." On the basis of the "false thesis that the Party is the instrument of the dictatorship of the proletariat" the leading role of the Party had been "conceived as a monopolistic concentration of power in the hands of Party bodies." The Party organs had assumed the tasks of state and economic authorities, with the result that there had been "an incorrect merging of the Party and state management, the emergence of monopolized power positions of some sections." This had led "to unqualified interference, the undermining of initiative at all levels, indifference, a cult of mediocrity, and unhealthy anonymity."

The "deformations of socialist life" had had their effect especially on young people; in particular, "contradictions between words and deeds, a lack of frankness, a phrase-mongering bureaucracy, attempts to settle everything from a position of power." The violations of legality had "done serious damage to Communists and non-Communists" and caused "irreparable losses" to the socialist movement. There had been "serious faults and fundamental deformations" in the nationalities policy, in relations between Czechs and Slovaks. The trade unions had "only inadequately looked after the interests of the working people." The Party's cultural policy had been "deformed"; "certain representatives of culture were discriminated against; some were subjected to unjustified political repression."[109]

That is how the Action Program of the Communist Party described the situation in Czechoslovakia at the beginning of 1968. A description of the reform movement itself lies outside the scope of this book. It is sufficient to say here that the opposition to the Novotný regime comprised the most varied forces: authors and artists demanding cultural freedom and the democratization of the system; factory managers, economists, and planners demanding a consistent economic reform; Slovak Communists and non-Communists calling for greater autonomy for Slovakia; functionaries of the state, and especially of the Party, who regarded the abolishing of dogmatism and the introduction of more modern working methods as indispensable; and finally humanist Marxists who consciously and clearly supported a fundamental transformation, a transition from a bureaucratic system to a socialist democracy.

"The cause of our political crisis," the Marxist philosopher Karel Kosík wrote at the time,

lies in the fact that the citizens of this country no longer want to live as a Party or non-Party mass without rights, or with inadequate rights, and that the exponents of power are no longer able to assert their leading role in a police-type bureaucratic dictatorship. . . . A radical solution of this crisis is possible only when the system of police-bureaucratic or bureaucratic dictatorship is replaced by a system of socialist democracy. The difference between the two systems is fundamental. The basis of the one system is denial of political rights to the mass of Party members and non-Party people; the basis of the other system is political equality for all citizens of the socialist state.[110]

By the end of 1967 the opposition to the Novotný regime had not only engulfed very considerable sections of the public, but even among the country's leadership the realization was gaining ground that a change was needed. At the January meeting of the Central Committee there were sharp clashes between conservative Stalinists and progressive reformers. After stormy discussions, with altogether 150 speakers participating, the reformers gained the upper hand. Novotný was forced to resign as First Secretary (although, for the time being, he remained in the Party Praesidium and retained the office of State President) and Alexander Dubček, the spokesman of the reformers, was elected to his post.[111]

Novotný's dismissal was far more than a change of leaders.

Throughout the country there was new hope of a democratization and liberalization of the system. "Even at the time of the January Plenum," the Czechoslovak reformer Radovan Richta wrote, "it had become obvious that the progressive forces of our Party were aiming at much more than some change or other in the leading organs, and that the issue was a new policy of the Party and new roads to socialism."[112]

The situation in Czechoslovakia changed virtually overnight. Censorship ceased to exist. The press, television, and radio, until then the boring mass media of a ruling bureaucracy, now voiced the ideas and hopes of the public. Apathy and lack of political interest abruptly changed into an activity unknown for many years, into a burning general interest in political issues. Here, too, the principal issue was an analysis of the Stalinist past, the crimes of the Novotný era. Josef Smrkovský, one of the leaders of the reform movement (and himself a victim of the Novotný regime), in early February described the rehabilitation of Communists and non-Communists as a top-ranking demand of socialist morality: "We Communists must be able to look everyone, including ourselves, straight in the face, and that is why we must support full rehabilitation of all innocent victims."[113]

This critical analysis of the past clearly was inseparably linked with the conclusion that this state of affairs must never again be permitted in Czechoslovakia, so it led inevitably to humanist Marxist ideas. The more the reformist forces crystallized within the Party and gained importance in it, the more the relations between the Party and the public began to change. The Party, until recently isolated as an instrument of bureaucratic power, was now regaining increasing support from the public. And the more positive the public's judgment was of the Party and the more interest it showed in the Party's problems, the more did the new ideas of the reformist trend within the Party gain strength.

By mid-February the reformers called for a transformation of the system. Zdeněk Mlynář, who had an active part in the preparation of the Action Program, pointed out that the former system in Czechoslovakia could not be explained "merely by the personal characteristics of an individual" and that a change of personnel could not therefore be seen as "a fundamental solution of the problem." The task was not to "perfect" the old political system but to "ensure its qualitative transformation." The "rights and freedoms of each citizen" must be guaranteed by the legal order and a mechanism built up "which provides for a timely correction of errors and mistakes before they have accumulated." What was needed was a political system "by no means aiming at the implementation of directives which must be viewed as correct from the outset, but at a formation of opinion and making of decisions which would express the objective requirements of the whole of society." This meant that in the political organizations, especially in the party, "the minority must also have a chance to put forward opinions." This process would undoubtedly be full of conflict, "but there is no other way unless we wish to stifle the inner dynamics of socialism."[114]

A few days later Milan Lakatoš of the Institute for Constitutional Law of the Czechoslovak Academy of Sciences also supported a pluralist political system. Lakatoš demanded that the National Front, degraded over the previous two decades to the position of a bureaucratic executive center, must be fundamentally transformed. The parties and organizations belonging to the National Front must "not become empty vessels, serving merely decorative purposes" nor must they be "understood as levers or tools, as transmission belts of other institutions," but must be able to develop "freely without interference from outside" and "to publish their own dailies and periodicals as their own mouthpieces." "No ready-made line of state policy must be carried" into the social organizations. The leading role of the Communist Party must "be based on totally different prerequisites." The Communist Party could play a leading role only if it fulfilled "the function of understanding [the social and economic development] better than anyone else" and if it proved able, on the basis of this function, to co-ordinate the interests of society, "on the common platform of all non-state social organizations, within the framework of the National Front."[115]

The problems of a pluralistic socialism were subsequently also discussed in *Literární Listy,* the weekly of the Writers' Union, published under its new name after February 1. In the course of this discussion Alexandr Kliment supported a "new type of socialist democracy." This required "first of all a platform for discussion within the ruling Party" and secondly "open and serious discussion" between Communists and non-Communists. This "presupposes an open system in which no one is excluded from participating in common affairs but where all may engage in accordance with their convictions and their conscience." The concept of an "opposition," regarded as an "anti-state phenomenon" in the Stalinist past, must be seen in a new light in a socialist democracy: "An opposition need not invariably mean the destruction of a state and the seizure of power—the image attributed to it in the Stalinist era." Under certain conditions an opposition can, on the contrary, "strengthen state authority and delineate its power." Under the socialist conditions of Czechoslovakia an opposition could "champion the democratic character of the state and concern itself with correcting its power and increasing its prestige, both at home and abroad, with defining the responsibility of the elected organs, from local people's committees all the way up to the government.[116]

The economist Ota Sïk called not only for an economic reform but also for public criticism to put an end to mismanagement. "This is no criticism of socialism; this is an attempt to lend socialism greater dynamism and to see to it that it really becomes universally attractive."[117] The Marxist philosopher Ivan Sviták summed up the aims of the "Prague Spring": "Replacement of totalitarian dictatorship by socialist democracy, in other words, a change in the manner of the exercise of power without giving up our socialist achievements—in particular, the communal ownership of the means of production—that is the basic problem of today."[118]

While this discussion proceeded, a tempestuous process of democratization was sweeping the country. The Czechoslovak Writers' Union elected Eduard Goldstücker as its chairman; he promptly called for the release of prisoners and for a number of reforms. Writers and journalists demanded that the freedom of the press and the abolition of censorship be guaranteed by legislation. At a meeting of the Ideological Commission of the Central Committee, the conservative dogmatist Iri Hendrych was replaced by the reformer Josef Špaček.

The conservative dogmatists around Novotný tried to regain power by means of the army and the secret police. The failure of this attempted palace revolution and General Šejna's escape at the end of February 1968 led to a further moral discrediting of the Novotný regime. In the press, on the radio, and on television, as well as at nearly all the sixty regional conferences of the Party, Novotný's resignation was being demanded with increasing persistence.

Under this growing pressure Novotný resigned on March 21, and a wave of resignations of Stalinist officials followed. For the election of a new President there were put forward, for the first time, several candidates: Ludvík Svoboda (the former commander of the Czechoslovak Brigade in the Soviet Union, who had been in disgrace under the Novotný regime), the reformers Josef Smrkovský and Laco Novomeský (the Slovak resistance fighter and poet), both of whom had been in prison under Novotný, and Čestmír Císař, the former Minister of Education demoted under Novotný. At a meeting of the National Assembly on March 30, General Svoboda was elected President of the Republic, and Josef Smrkovský Chairman of the National Assembly. "The National Assembly is faced with the task of establishing a socialist parliamentarianism by its entire legislative practice," Smrkovský declared in his inaugural speech. "Parliament must create safeguards to make sure that the Czechoslovak Socialist Republic becomes a law-abiding state in the best sense of the word."[119]

At the April Plenum of the Central Committee (April 1–5) the reformers scored a further victory. Novotný and six of his followers lost their seats in the Party Praesidium. Five new members took over their posts—including the reformers František Kriegel and Josef Smrkovský. Zdeněk Mlynár was included in the Secretariat of the Central Committee. The earlier expulsions of certain humanist Marxist authors from the Party, including Vaculík, Klíma, and Antonin Liehm, were revoked and in the final resolution of the Plenum it was stated: "The Central Committee emphatically supports the development of socialist democracy and will not allow the road it has now chosen to lead us back once more to the state of affairs that prevailed before January."[120]

## ☐ The Czechoslovak Action Program

A few days later, on April 10, 1968, the Central Committee published the new Action Program of the Party. In roughly sixty printed pages it summed up the vital measures for the transformation of a centralized, bureaucratic dictatorship into a socialist democracy.

In the economic sphere the Action Program proceeded from the statement "that the past methods of managing and organizing the national economy are outdated" and that a "new economic system" was necessary in order to prepare "the country . . . to join the world scientific-technical revolution." The "democratization program of the economy" demanded above all "the independence of enterprises and enterprise groups and their relative independence from state bodies." The drafting of the economic plan must be "subject to democratic control of the National Assembly and specialized control of scientific institutions"; the "positive functions of the market" must not be underrated. The aim should be a "regulated utilization" of a socialist market. Labor collectives "should be allowed to influence the management of the enterprise." This was to be done through democratically elected organs in the enterprises, consisting on the one hand of delegates of working teams and, on the other, of representatives outside the enterprise, "thereby ensuring the influence of the interests of the entire society and an expert and qualified level of decision making."

The task of the trade unions was "to defend the professional interests of the workers and the working people and act as an important partner in solving all questions of economic management." In agriculture, administrative centralization must be abolished and the individual co-operatives made "independent economic and social organizations with full rights." "Small-scale individual enterprises" had their justification even in a socialist economy and it was therefore necessary "to work out legal provisions concerning small-scale enterprises." The consumer must be protected "against the abuse of the monopoly position and the economic power of production and trading enterprises."

The focus of the Action Program, however, was on the political transformation of the system. The Action Program proceeded from the statement that "wide scope for social initiative, a frank exchange of opinion, and the democratization of the entire socio-political system are literally the prerequisites of a dynamic socialist society." This required the development of a political system that "corresponds to the needs of the country." It was important "to reform the whole political system so that it permits the dynamic development of socialist social relations, combines broad democracy with scientific, highly qualified management, strengthens the social order, stabilizes socialist relations, and maintains social discipline. The basic structure of the political system must at the same time provide firm guarantees against a return to the old methods of subjectivism and highhandedness from positions of power."

This required above all a change in the function, tasks, and internal structure of the Communist Party: "Substitution and interchanging of state bodies and agencies of economic and social organization by Party bodies must be stopped. Party resolutions are binding for the Communists working in these bodies, but the policy, managerial activities, and responsibility of the state, economic, and social organizations are independent."

Much like the humanist Marxists in other countries, above all in Yugoslavia, the Czechoslovak Communists now declared that "the Party's goal is not to become a universal 'caretaker' of the society, to bind all organizations and every step taken in life by its directives." Within the Party, each Party member had "not only the right, but the duty to act according to his conscience, with initiative, criticism, and different views on the matter in question, to oppose any functionary." Admittedly, the Party could not "abandon the principle of requiring that resolutions be put into practice once they are approved," but it was inadmissible to curtail the rights of Communists or "to create an atmosphere of distrust and suspicion of those who voiced different opinions, to persecute the minority under any pretext—as has happened in the past."

The Action Program rejected a multi-party system but supported the independence of parties and organizations within a—totally transformed—National Front. The parties and organizations of the National Front were "partners" which must solve "possible disputes concerning state policy" on the basis of their "common socialist concept" by way of "political agreement." Each member organization of the National Front "must be granted independent rights and its own responsibility for the management of our country and society." All that was possible only through a total turning away from the monopolistic structure of the system and through the broadest possible participation of the working people in all decisions:

Socialist state power cannot be monopolized either by a single party, or by a coalition of parties. It must be open to all political organizations of the people. The Communist Party of Czechoslovakia will use every means at its disposal to develop such forms of political life that will ensure the expression of the direct voice and will of the working class and all working people in political decision making in our country.

A vital role in this would be played by social organizations "based on truly voluntary membership and activity" and entitled "to choose their own officials and representatives, who must not be appointed from outside." To that end

constitutional freedoms of assembly and association must be ensured this year so that the possibility of setting up voluntary organizations, special-interest associations, societies, etc., is guaranteed by law and the present interests and needs of various strata and categories of our citizens are taken care of without bureaucratic interference and without a monopoly by any individual organization.

Restrictions could only be imposed by law. These "freedoms guaranteed by law" must "apply fully to citizens of various creeds and religious denominations."

The growing importance of social organizations was to be reflected also in the electoral system. Elections were to be held in accordance with "the principles of an advanced socialist democracy" and the electoral system was to take into account "the changes in our political life." In Parliament (the National Assembly) "it is necessary to overcome formalism in negotiations and the unconvincing unanimity concealing factual differences in opinions and attitudes of the deputies" so that the National Assembly "actually decides on laws and important political issues and not only approves proposals submitted." Measures must be passed "that will put into actual practice the constitutional status of the National Assembly as the supreme organ of state power in the Czechoslovak Socialist Republic," for "the Party regards the National Assembly as a socialist Parliament with all the scope for activities the Parliament of a democratic republic must have."

In the political and administrative sphere all monopoly practices must be eliminated: "The Party policy is based on the principle that no undue concentration of power must occur throughout the state machinery, in one sector, one body, or in a single individual." Socialist pluralism was to be guaranteed by "a division of power and a system of mutual supervision that can rectify the faults or encroachments of any of its links with the activities of another link." The system of mutual checks was to apply similarly to relations between elected and executive organs, as also to relations within the state executive and administration and to the position and function of courts of law.

The privileged position of the secret police was to be abolished. Its task was to be confined exclusively to "defending the state from the activities of enemy centers abroad." On no account must the State Security Service be "directed toward or used to solve internal political questions and controversies in socialist society. . . . Every citizen who has not been culpable must know with certainty that his political convictions and opinions, his personal beliefs and activities, cannot be the object of attention of the bodies of the State Security Service."

The fundamental rights of courts of law were to be accurately defined in order to guarantee legal security. "The legal policy of the Party is based on the principle that in a dispute over rights (including administrative decisions of state bodies) the basic guarantee of legality is proceedings in court which are independent of political factors and are bound only by law." This required "a strengthening of the whole social and political role and importance of courts of law in our society," and that "the full independence of lawyers from state bodies" be guaranteed.

The secret police was to be purged of all those who, because of their own past, might have an interest in preventing rehabilitation and restitution.

The Party realizes that people unlawfully condemned and persecuted cannot regain the lost years of their life. It will, however, do its best to remove any shadow of the mistrust and humiliation to which the families and relatives of those affected were often subjected, and will resolutely ensure that such persecuted people have every opportunity of showing their worth in work, in public life, and in political activities.

Rehabilitation was to be regulated by a special law.

The rectification of past injustices must cover also the issue of nationalities policy. Constitutional relations between Czechs and Slovaks would have to be resolved in the form of "a socialist federal arrangement" and a "coexistence of two equal nations in a common socialist state." For the remaining nationalities in the Czechoslovak Socialist Republic—Hungarians, Ukrainians, Poles, and Germans—a statute was foreseen that would ensure for them "the future of their national life and the development of their national individuality." The participation of the nationalities in public life must be based on the principle "that the nationalities have the right to independence and self-administration in provinces that concern them."

Of particular importance for the further development in Czechoslovakia were the passages in the Action Program dealing with the statutory basis of democratic freedoms:

The effective influence of views and opinions of the working people on all policies and a firm opposition to all tendencies to suppress the criticism of the people cannot be guaranteed if we do not ensure constitution-based freedom of speech and political and personal rights to all citizens systematically and consistently, by all legal means available. Socialism cannot mean only liberation of the working people from the domination of exploiting class relations, but must provide for a greater degree of self-fulfillment than any bourgeois democracy. The working people, who are no longer ordered about by a class of exploiters, can no longer be dictated to by an arbitrary interpretation from a position of power as to what information they may or may not be given, which of their opinions can or cannot be expressed publicly, where public opinion may play a role and where it may not. . . . The Central Committee of the Communist Party of Czechoslovakia considers it urgently necessary to define in a press law and more exactly than hitherto in the shortest possible time when a state body can forbid the propagation of certain information (in the press, radio, television, etc.), and exclude the possibility of preliminary factual censorship. It is necessary to overcome the holding-up, distortion, and incompleteness of information, to remove any unwarranted secrecy of political and economic facts, to publish the annual balance sheets of enterprises, to publish even alternatives to various suggestions and measures, and to increase the import and sale of foreign newspapers and periodicals. . . . In the press, it is necessary to make a distinction between official standpoints of the state, Party organs, and journalists. The Party press especially must express the Party's life and development along with criticisms of various opinions among the Communists, etc., and cannot be made to coincide fully with the official viewpoints of the state. . . . It is necessary to guarantee the freedom of opinion, including minority interests and minority views, by juridical norms.

True, "the ideological antagonists of socialism may try to abuse the process of democratization" but "bourgeois ideology can be challenged only in open ideological struggle before all of the people." The more the Communists conducted a policy "for the benefit of the people," based on "truthful and complete information, and on scientific analysis," the more they would win the public over "to the ideas and the policy of the Party."

The proclaimed freedoms also included the freedom of movement, including the right to foreign travel: "The constitutional freedom of movement, particularly that of travel abroad for our citizens must be guaranteed. In particular, this means that the citizen should have the legal right to long-term or permanent sojourn abroad, and that people should not be groundlessly placed in the position of emigrants."

The Action Program finally supported complete cultural and artistic freedom: "We reject administrative and bureaucratic methods of implementing cultural policy, we dissociate ourselves from them, and we shall oppose them. Artistic work must not be subjected to censorship. We have full confidence in men of culture and we expect their responsibility, understanding, and support." In contrast to the Soviet doctrines of "party-mindedness" and "socialist realism," the Action Program stated: "It is necessary to overcome a narrow understanding of the social and human function of culture and art, overestimation of their ideological and political role and underestimation of their basic general cultural and aesthetic tasks in the transformation of man and his world."

The basic orientation of foreign policy was "alliance and co-operation with the Soviet Union and the other socialist states." Friendly relations with "the countries of the world socialist community" were to be strengthened "on the basis of mutual respect," and the aim was "to intensify sovereignty and equality, and international solidarity." The Communist Party of Czechoslovakia would "continue to take an active part in the struggle for the unity of the international Communist movement" and in doing so would "take full advantage of its specific possibilities of establishing contacts with the socialist, peaceful, and democratic forces in the capitalist and developing countries."

In conclusion, the Czechoslovak Communists expressed their hope that these measures would "give the socialist development a new look." They would reactivate "the efficiency of the socialist idea, the attractiveness of the socialist example," which had been blunted and paralyzed by bureaucratic deformations in the past, and would in consequence allow "a fuller application of the advantages of socialism."[121]

The Action Program not only played a tremendous role in the main

Czechoslovak developments but—more important for our considerations—it also represents a vital document in the history of Marxism. Admittedly, it took over many important concepts from humanist Marxists of other countries, yet it displayed a number of new ideas of its own. A comparison between the Czechoslovak Action Program of April 1968 and the program of the League of Communists of Yugoslavia of March 1958 reveals a large measure of agreement on all central issues: the rejection of a dictatorial centralized system of the Stalinist type, including the concept of the leading role of the Party, of central economic planning, of control over culture and the arts, of a centralized, bureaucratic regulation of all spheres of life. Both programs support a pluralist society, the democratic management of enterprises by workers' collectives, a new relationship between the Party and social mass organizations, internal democratization of the Party, the right to freedom of opinion and criticism, the unimpeded development of the arts and sciences, as well as relations between socialist countries on the basis of sovereignty and equality.

Nevertheless, certain nuances and differences are not to be missed. The Yugoslav program of 1958 puts greater emphasis on the self-management of producers through workers' councils and the gradual withering away of the state. The Czechoslovak program of 1968 lays greater emphasis on statutory guarantees of democratic freedoms (freedom of assembly, of association, and of information, as well as the right to unimpeded travel abroad). The Yugoslav program supports a policy of non-alignment, whereas the Czechoslovak program (proceeding from different conditions) confines itself to certain specific possibilities within the framework of the world Communist movement.

More important than these nuances between the two humanist Marxist programs, however, was the pronounced difference and indeed conflict between the Czechoslovak humanist Marxist concepts on the one hand, and the bureaucratic conservative ideas of the Soviet leaders on the other. As early as March 23, 1968, at the Dresden Conference of East European Communist Leaders, they had expressed to Dubček their "anxiety" that the process "might be exploited by anti-socialist forces."[122] From that moment on all developments in Czechoslovakia not in line with the Soviet system were automatically branded "anti-socialist." Thus *Pravda* complained that the April Plenum in Prague had reflected "the influence of non-Marxist and non-socialist views."[123] *Pravda* printed a totally distorted version of the Action Program,[124] and by the end of April was talking about "anti-Communist hysteria and anarchy" in Czechoslovakia.[125]

## ☐ Socialism with a Human Face

The development of Czechoslovak reforms in the spring and summer of 1968 received increasing support from the Czechoslovak public under increasing disapproval from Moscow.

Following the publication of the Action Program, the road was now clear inside Czechoslovakia for the realization of a humanist socialism in the heart of Europe. The Central Committee called for a public discussion of the Action Program: "This Program, unlike past documents of its kind, is not a directive, not a categorical prescription for the activity of all organizations and every individual," declared Čestmír Císař, the new Central Committee Secretary for Education and Culture. "It is instead, for the moment, an open platform to which everyone can contribute, not only Party organizations and members, but also people outside the Party who have ideas they want to express. The program should therefore open wide the doors to an all-national discussion, so that it can be developed and perfected."[126] In the ensuing discussion about the model of a pluralistic socialism the humanist Marxists—who were now able to discuss these matters quite freely—all agreed on the fundamental issues of the Action Program. But there were divergent views whether a multi-party system and the existence of an opposition party would be desirable, or whether a socialist democracy must find other, new forms of political systems. A number of participants in the discussion, including the Marxist philosopher Ivan Sviták and the author and playwright Václav Havel, championed a two-party system on a socialist basis: "One can talk about democracy seriously only when people occasionally have an opportunity to elect freely those who are to govern them. This again assumes the existence of at least *two comparable alternatives*. That is to say, two equal and mutually independent political forces, both of which have the same chance of becoming the leading force in the country if the people so decide." The only consistent and effective road "to reach the ideal of democratic socialism is a regenerated and socialist social structure patterned on the two-party model."[127]

The majority of those who took part in the discussion, however, rejected these ideas. Thus the humanist Marxist Eduard Goldstücker, the Prorector of Charles University in Prague, declared that a two-party or multi-party system was by no means the only method of an effective check on power. Moreover, it was impossible "to transpose a ready-made model from one country to another." Such a system might "satisfy a class society" but the point in Czechoslovakia at the moment was the "creation and realization of a political system in line with the present phase of social development."[128]

Radoslav Selucky, a Czech specialist in political economy, said that the debate on the Action Program did not evade discussion of a plurality of political parties "on the theoretical level," but that "we realized that the only political force capable of bringing the democratization policy to a conclusion was the Communist Party, and we were therefore resolved to reform the political system under the Party's leadership."[129]

Other humanist Marxists declared that the transfer of a Western parliamentary system to the Czechoslovak Socialist Republic would be particularly anachronistic at a moment when in the West the great traditional political parties were losing their political features "and offering the electors not the alternative of different political programs, but merely different personalities or sets of leaders." Besides, the parliamentary system provided no guarantee against a new dictatorship. What mattered in a socialist democracy, therefore, was the "development of another political mechanism" that would offer "adequate guarantees" for "minority rights and human rights, for effective public control, for the political subject status of all parties, organizations, and individual citizens."[130]

The Marxist theoretician Karel Kosík, Professor of Philosophy at Charles University, saw the decisive feature of a socialist democracy in a combination of self-management of the producers with political democracy of the citizens: "Socialist democracy is an integral democracy or none at all. Its foundations include both the self-management of socialist producers and the political democracy of the socialist citizens of the state: the one degenerates without the other."[131]

The humanist Marxist Robert Kalivoda, member of the Philosophical Institute of the Academy of Sciences, proceeding from an extensive analysis of Stalinism and the problems of abolishing it, likewise championed a synthesis between political democracy and the self-management of producers. The abandonment of Stalinism in Czechoslovakia did not mean "a return to some 'pre-Stalinist' past," but "the inauguration of a higher phase in the development of socialism." The relations between parties and organizations in a socialist democracy differed, on the one hand, from Stalinism in that they stressed "the autonomy of parties and their specific character" and, on the other, they differed from the political systems of Western countries in that the relations of the parties under socialism were based on partnership and cooperation and not on those "antagonistic relations common in the bourgeois political system."

In the political sphere socialist democracy meant "the establishment of absolute freedom for various ideological and cultural concepts, provided they respect the socialist organization of society." Socialist democracy led "to the rebirth of the parliamentary system, to a new separation of legislative and executive power, to the restoration of the independence of judges, and to a real safeguarding of the citizens' constitutional rights."

But this, according to Robert Kalivoda, "does not by any means exhaust socialist democracy," since it was itself only "a certain stage in the development toward socialist self-management." In consequence, further "elements of direct democracy" had to be added, "representing the gradual emergence of the prerequisites of socialist self-management, of the gradual withering away of the state." Among the key elements of direct democracy Kalivoda listed, first, the mass communications media, i.e., the freedom of the press and of opinion, which on the basis of socialist relations were far more effective than in a bourgeois-liberal system, since under socialism it was much more difficult to avoid their impact, and since they had to be respected a great deal more. The second form of direct democracy was "an entirely new concept of the trade unions as direct organizations of the working people"—what Kalivoda described as "germ cells of a socialist syndicalism." This was of "enormous importance for the development of our socialist model," since "without direct influence by the primary organizations of the working people upon the institutions of the socialist state the higher forms of socialist democracy cannot be realized."

The realization "of direct control and management of our socialist enterprises by workers' collectives" was the most badly neglected but at the same time the most important question of socialism. Without a "system of enterprise self-administration, without a system of works' councils and workers' councils" there would be a danger of the socialist economy turning into a "manager system" and into "an economic and political dominion of technocrats." For that very reason it was necessary to realize workers' self-management as speedily as possible.

The Marxist model of socialism thus consisted of the political system of "co-operative partnership of political parties on the basis of a socialist program" and a "system of socialist parliamentarianism" that "is quite essentially linked with the development of direct democracy." A thus structured "political model of socialist democracy, if filled with a living content, can indeed be the beginning of the road to the highest aim, to the socialist self-management of the socialist society."[132]

In the hoped-for new model of a socialist democracy Marxism was not to be an official state doctrine but was to be opposed, in a free confrontation, by other ideologies. "In the future, Marxism-Leninism will not be a state ideology, although our state and our society are socialist and our democracy has socialist features. However, we must realize that, along with Marxism, non-Marxist views also exist in our society," declared Čestmír Císař, at the time of the Prague Spring the Central Committee Secretary for Education and Culture. "I think it is also important to stress that Marxism is not a Party monopoly."[133] Robert Kalivoda similarly stressed that Marxism could "be realized in a socialist society only in free confrontation with other cultural, ideological, and philosophical concepts."[134]

These discussions were inseparably linked with the country's political life. They were not abstract dissertations but reflected what the majority of the people felt and were trying to put into effect. From March to May the Stalinists were losing more and more ground while the reform trend was gaining growing support not only among the public but also among Party members. By the end of March, about 73 per cent of the public supported the Party's reform line, as shown by a public opinion poll,[135] and elected workers' councils were introduced in the factories.[136]

The process of democratization in Czechoslovakia was also hailed by the Communist parties of other countries. In addition to sympathy demonstrations in Yugoslavia, the Communist parties of Austria, France, Spain, Japan, and Italy all declared their support for the new model of socialism in Czechoslovakia which they regarded as an encouragement in their own struggle.[137] On April 12, Luigi Longo had this to say about Czechoslovak developments: "The realization of a more advanced socialist democracy is not only a great contribution to the struggle of the working class and of Left-wing forces in the capitalist countries, but also represents a stimulus for all socialist countries to overcome more boldly the obstacles obstructing the full development of socialist democracy.[138]

At the beginning of May, at the end of his visit to Czechoslovakia, Longo promised the Czechoslovak Communist Party "the full support and solidarity of the Italian Communists,"[139] and after his return he told his audience at the Gramsci Institute in Rome that "we assess their course of action positively, not only for their country but for all socialist countries and for the entire international workers' movement."[140]

Not only the West European Communists but, even more so, the humanist Marxists in East Germany, Poland, Hungary, and the Soviet Union saw the democratization process in Czechoslovakia as a hopeful example and model. Typical of the views of the humanist Marxists of those countries was a statement by Robert Havemann, which, admittedly, he was not allowed to publish in East Berlin:

Socialists and Communists throughout the world today follow the political development in Czechoslovakia with the warmest sympathy and with great hopes. What is happening there will be of decisive importance not only for the future of that country but will produce world-wide repercussions and indeed is already doing so. For the first time the attempt is here being made to harmonize socialism and democracy. There have indeed been a number of attempts in the socialist countries to break through the diabolical circle of Stalinism by some kind of creeping democratization. But the leaden weight of the Party bureaucracy has time and again paralyzed and halted the few hopeful attempts.

In Czechoslovakia we are witnessing today the magnificent attempt of a radical and uncompromising breakthrough toward socialist democracy. If this attempt succeeds, then this success will be of such far-reaching historic importance that it can be compared only with the Russian October Revolution. One of the main obstacles for the further transformation from capitalism to socialism will have been removed—the deeply discouraging experience of the past stage of world revolution, the realization that democracy is possible only under the conditions of bourgeois capitalism but is incompatible with the socialist system. . . . Socialism is democracy—this great dictum must be made true. In view of the exciting development in Czechoslovakia this is today our passionate hope. . . . Nothing has paralyzed and impeded the struggle of socialists and Communists in the capitalist countries more than the forms of Stalinist and bureaucratic socialism in the socialist countries. This fatal contradiction between possibility and reality has discredited the cause of socialism. But if it is proved in Czechoslovakia that socialism and democracy are not only compatible but identical, if it is proved that true democracy can be fully accomplished only under socialism, then this paralyzing disillusionment will vanish. The world's revolutionary youth will once more have before their eyes an aim that is free from dark shadows.[141]

☐ **Moscow's Answer to the "Prague Spring"**

But the more the Czechoslovak model of liberal socialism was being realized, and the greater the attraction of the Czechoslovak development became to the world Communist movement—especially in the East European countries—the greater grew the fear of the neo-Stalinist leaders in Moscow, Warsaw, and East Berlin. After the "summit meeting" in Moscow (May 8, 1968), attended by Brezhnev, Gomulka, Ulbricht, Kadar, and Zhivkov, the press campaign against the Czechoslovak course was abruptly stepped up. Soviet papers declared that the whole concept of socialist democracy was wrong and unscientific, since surely it had been proved that "the dictatorship of the proletariat"—by which the Soviet ideologists automatically understand the system in the Soviet Union—was "the highest form of democracy."[142] But matters did not stop at press polemics. On May 17, a military delegation arrived in Prague under Marshal Grechko's leadership. A few days later military exercises began in Czechoslovakia, clearly intended to provide moral support for conservatives and Stalinists in the country. The East German press prominently featured a false report about the alleged presence of American tanks in Prague, broadcasts of the Czechoslovak radio were jammed, and the sale of the German-language *Prager Volkszeitung* was prohibited.[143]

Under growing pressure from the Soviet Union a Plenary Meeting of the Central Committee of the Communist Party of Czechoslovakia (the May Plenum) was held May 29–31. At this meeting many questions were discussed in a more reserved and cautious manner. The leading role of the Party was again more strongly emphasized, and Dubček stated that criticism of past deformations must not lead to the moral condemnation of the whole Party. Workers and the mass media were asked to assure the Party's positive political influence and not to jeopardize Czechoslovakia's state interests in their foreign news reporting, especially in their reports about other socialist countries. On the other hand, Antonín Novotný and six of his most prominent followers, who had been involved in the political show trials of the 1950's, were suspended from Party membership. The Central Committee decided to convene the Fourteenth Party Congress September 9; at that congress the new Party statute was to be adopted and a new Party leadership elected. The rules for the election of delegates to the Party Congress were announced.[144]

Large sections of the public regarded the May Plenum as a setback and feared that democratization might be halted. These fears were reflected in an article by the humanist Marxist Ludvík Vaculík, entitled *Two Thousand Words,* which was signed by sixty-seven prominent figures and thus bore the character of a manifesto. Vaculík declared that it was of course impossible "to accomplish any kind of democratic renewal without the communists," but it was important now to consolidate democracy in factories and enterprises, in districts and regions. By way of public criticism, resolution, demonstrations, and collections of money ("to provide retirement pensions for them") the "resignation of those people who abused their power" must be accomplished. Democratization was to be supported by public meetings of national committees, the foundation of newspapers, and the formation of committees for the "defense of the freedom of speech." In the face of steadily increasing foreign interference it was best to "decently hold our own and not start anything. We can assure our government that we will back it—with weapons if necessary—as long as it does what we give it the mandate to do."[145]

The Vaculík manifesto met with a critical reception among the Party leaders,[146] but among the public it received an enthusiastic response. Within a few days 40,000 people had expressed their approval in letters and signature campaigns. Democratization was being increasingly supported and promoted "from below." The number of spontaneously formed "committees for the protection of the freedom of the press" in factories and institutions rose dramatically, and many enterprises threatened a general strike in case the reform process was halted or reversed.[147] Above all, the process was no longer to be checked within the Party. At meetings of local Party organizations (June 10–23, 1968) held in connection with preparations for the Party Congress and at regional Party conferences (July 4–7, 1968) the progressive reformers received an overwhelming majority. By the end of June the National Assembly adopted the Rehabilitation Law for persons innocently sentenced, and the new Press Law, which involved the abolition of censorship. Moreover, it was officially announced that any citizen of Czechoslovakia enjoyed the right to travel abroad without any special visa.[148]

The more striking the successes of the reformers, the sharper grew the attacks from Moscow. About mid-June the Soviet ideologist Fedor Konstantinov accused the Secretary of the Czechoslovak Central Committee Císař of being a "revisionist" and likened him to Bernstein, Kautsky, and "the Right-wing Social Democrats."[149] The Soviet propaganda chief Piotr Demichev called for an ideological campaign against revisionist fabrications,[150] and the Czechoslovak Marxist philosopher Sviták was described in the Soviet press as writing "with violence bordering on the maniacal."[151] At the beginning of July the Ukrainian Party Secretary Piotr Shelest joined in the campaign, attacking "far-fetched and unviable 'models of socialism' " which "cannot be permitted."[152] By July 11, *Pravda* reported that "rightist, anti-socialist forces" in Czechoslovakia, "allied with imperialist reaction," were planning on "overthrowing the existing system and restoring capitalism." An "unstable situation" had arisen in Czechoslovakia, but its "healthy forces" could always "rely on the understanding and full support of the people of the Soviet land."[153]

On July 14 and 15, the Warsaw Conference of the Party chiefs of the Soviet Union, Poland, East Germany, Hungary, and Bulgaria took place. In an open letter they accused the Czechoslovak Communist

Party leadership of failing to "check counterrevolutionary tendencies." In Czechoslovakia, they alleged, "hostile forces" were at work, trying to divert the country from socialism. The Communist Party of Czechoslovakia was no longer playing the leading role, the slogan of democratization was being used for a campaign against the Party, hostile forces had gained control of the mass communications media, and a situation had arisen in which "the common vital interests of the rest of the socialist countries" were being jeopardized. In an unmistakable manner, even though disguised in ideological formulas, the leaders assembled in Warsaw demanded a halt to democratization, the revocation of democratic freedoms (especially the freedoms of assembly and of the press), and the reintroduction of the centralized, bureaucratic principle of subordination to the Party. In much the same way as had happened in Yugoslavia in 1948, the leaders addressed themselves to certain "forces" inside Czechoslovakia and assured them that, provided they took the "necessary measures," they could always count on "the solidarity and comprehensive assistance from the fraternal socialist countries."[154]

The Warsaw declaration about an alleged "threat to socialism" in Czechoslovakia was to serve as a pretext for justifying the growing political (as well as the already planned military) intervention from outside. The lack of substance in the accusations was patent, since even the leaders in Moscow, Warsaw, and East Berlin must have known that both the influence of the Czechoslovak Communist Party and the attraction of socialism in Czechoslovakia were now stronger than ever before. Thus a public opinion poll in mid-July disclosed that 89 per cent of the Czechoslovak public was in favor of a further development of socialism, that 87 per cent was satisfied with the work of the government, and that 86 per cent welcomed the recent law abolishing censorship.[155] Encouraged by the support of its own public and of many Communist parties abroad, the leadership of the Czechoslovak Communist Party was able to reject the accusation of the "Warsaw five" politely but firmly. In its letter of reply the Czechoslovak Party leadership thanked them for their "no doubt sincerely intended advice," but observed that the Warsaw letter had not taken sufficient account of "the entire intricacy of the dynamic social movement." True, there were transitional difficulties, but these were due mainly to the fact that "for many long years the old Party leadership governed according to the principle of bureaucratic centralism and suppressed internal Party democracy." The Czechoslovak Communists, however, did not see "any realistic reasons" for the assertion that the situation in Czechoslovakia was "counterrevolutionary," that the socialist order was "directly threatened," or that

Czechoslovakia might move away from the socialist community. The leading role of the Communist Party at present was stronger than ever before because it was based "on the voluntary support of the people" and no longer "ruled over society." The abolition of censorship and the legalization of the freedoms of speech and the press were far better than the former whispering propaganda and had enhanced the "authority of the new democratic policy of the Party" among the entire population. Any attempt to revert to the old methods would "evoke the resistance of the overwhelming majority of Party members, the resistance of the working class." The Communist Party of Czechoslovakia did not wish in the future to practice its leading role by means of "discredited bureaucratic police methods," but instead "by the strength of its Marxist-Leninist ideas, by the strength of its program, its just policy supported by the majority of the people."[156]

After the Czechoslovak rejection of the Warsaw letter the Soviet Union resorted to stronger means. On July 19, 1968, *Pravda* spread the false report that near the frontier with West Germany a cache of weapons of American origin had been discovered; these were to have served the preparation of an armed coup.[157] The CIA had worked out a secret operational plan to "undermine the unity of the socialist countries" under which American armed forces would effect the "liberation of East Germany and Czechoslovakia" in conjunction with an early coup d'état in Czechoslovakia."[158] In accordance with the principle of "stop thief," *Pravda* carried reports about alleged interference by West Germany.[159]

The ideological argument was also continued. Konstantinov, in a polemic against the Czechoslovak Central Committee Secretary Čestmír Císař, declared that Leninism was the only interpretation of Marxism in our day and any attempt to develop new interpretations must be rejected.[160] *Pravda* bitterly opposed the concept of "democratic socialism"[161] and declared categorically: "We cannot agree with the attempts to work out new variants of Marxism."[162] On July 25, army maneuvers began throughout the western territories of the Soviet Union on a scale not observed for many years.

In the setting of this propaganda war of nerves the Soviet-Czechoslovak negotiations at Čierna took place from July 29 to 31, 1968,[163] followed by a conference of the leaders of the eastern bloc states (with the exception of Rumania) in Bratislava on August 3, 1968.[164] These represented another attempt to force the Czechoslovak Party and state leaders to adhere to the Soviet political line. Following the negotiations in Čierna and Bratislava, most Czechoslovak Communists believed that they could now continue and further consolidate their reform activities, whereas in fact the Soviet leaders were preparing a military invasion. In Czechoslovakia attention was now focused on preparations for the Party Congress and on the discussion of the new Party statute, on the attempt to redefine the Party's role in a pluralistic socialist society. The aim of the statute, according to Josef Špaček, was to transform the Party again "into a real Party of Communists, whose internal life will be a true realization of democracy and no longer of administrative-bureaucratic centralism, a Party whose policy is shaped and put into effect with the truly active participation of everybody."[165]

In the new Party statute the function, objective, structure, and organization of the Party were adapted to the new model of socialism. While the old Party statute had stated that the Party, "heading the working people," had led them to "the victory of socialism," the new statute said that the Party's strength was based upon a "close communication with the people, with their lives and needs." For that reason the Party, "by its activity," was "continually soliciting their trust and voluntary support, and is subordinate to their control." The final objective of the Party was "the development of a socialist democracy and the realization of the program of Communist humanism." The Party saw its mission "in the service of the people" and "in the struggle of our nations for socialism, democracy, human justice, freedom, and the humanistic ideals of Communism."

These aims were reflected also in the extensive changes in the Party structure. In contrast to the old rules, the new statute expressly stated that all organs of the Party were elected by secret ballot (Article 8). In order to prevent any abuse of power, the statute forbade leading functionaries to hold several Party, state, or public positions since this "could lead to the privileged position of an individual and would weaken control over this individual" (Article 13a). With the exception of primary organizations, officials could be elected "no more than three times in succession for a two-year election period and twice in succession for a four-year election period" (Article 13c).

The concept of privileged information was abolished and free access to information, as well as an obligation to publish information about all processes within the Party, laid down in the statute (Article 11). Every Party member had the right "to be informed on all basic questions of Party policy and any sort of information and documents on the activity of the organizations and organs of which he is a member" (Article 19c). Freedom of opinion and protection of minorities were guaranteed in the Party statute. Every member was given the right "to express openly and critically at Party meetings and in the Party press his opinion on the activity of the Party and all of its organs and members irrespective of the office they hold" (Article 19d). Any minority was entitled to "formulate its standpoint, and request that they be recorded," as well as "to persist in its view and to request from the relevant Party organization or organ a reevaluation of its standpoint, on the basis of new information" (Article 3). Control and revision commissions were instructed, among other things, "to provide effective protection of the rights of members, organizations, or minority groups" (Article 55b). Against those holding minority views, provided these were not in fundamental conflict with the program and statute, only "ideological means are admissible (Article 3b) and "it is not permissible to impose Party punishment for differences of views" (Article 60).[166]

The draft of the new Party statute was published on August 10, 1968. It met with an extraordinarily positive reception from Party members and functionaries—an opinion poll showed that 89 per cent of all Party members was in favor of the Party's leading role through persuasion and on the basis of confidence of the public.[167] The Soviet press, on the other hand, was highly indignant about the new concepts of the Party.[168] A few days after the publication of the Party statute, *Rude Právo,* the official daily of the Czechoslovak Communist Party, pointed out that the old Party structure had been taken over from the Russian Bolsheviks. "But that system is totally unsuitable for a Party" which "in its internal structure should also be a model of democracy for the rest of the state structure." The new Party statute would consolidate "an integral system of democratic principles" and make possible "a progressive adaptation of the political role of the Party to the present pluralistic political system."[169]

These lines were written in mid-August. On September 9, the Fourteenth Congress of the Czechoslovak Communist Party was due to open; this congress was to adopt the new Party statute, elect a new political leadership, and define the future line of a socialist democracy. There can be no doubt that this Party Congress would have sanctioned the new socialist model and represented the final defeat of the Stalinists. As a result, a tolerant humanist socialist society would have emerged in the heart of Europe, with freedom of opinion, genuine secret elections, security before the law, freedom of the press, freedom for all citizens to travel abroad, and direct participation of the public in all economic and political issues of the country—under the leadership of a Communist Party enjoying public confidence.

The realization of humanist Marxism in Czechoslovakia would have acted as a tremendous magnet—not only for all progressive socialists in the West, but even more so for the public of the East European countries and the Soviet Union.

During the night of August 20–21, 1968, Czechoslovakia was occupied by Soviet troops, supported by troops of East Germany, Poland, Hungary, and Bulgaria. Never had there been an action of the Soviet leaders that met with such extensive hostility and such protest from the entire world Communist movement. Not only the humanist Marxists, but a large number of Communists in many countries, who had until then kept their faith in Moscow, began to be critical and mistrustful and to think independently. The invasion and occupation of Czechoslovakia abruptly widened and deepened the chasm between the bureaucratic, dogmatic forces and the humanistic Marxists.

## ☐   From Dogmatic to Living Marxism

The humanist Marxist concepts described above—insistence on one's own road to socialism, equality and sovereignty within the world Communist movement, and above all a new liberal model of a socialist society—have always been closely linked with problems of Marxist theory. The humanist Marxists are demanding that Marxism, which in its Stalinist and post-Stalinist forms had become an ideological weapon for the manipulation of power, should once more be given its original liberating character and should be independently and creatively developed, in line with the problems of the present-day world.

Unlike the Party headquarters in Moscow and Peking, the humanist Marxists are far from taking an optimistic or complacent view of the development of Marxist theory; on the contrary, they are concerned about the neglect of Marxism during the past few decades: "Escape from real life, escape from an examination of reality into scholastic quotation mongering from the classical writers of Marxism-Leninism and the creation of 'quotological' dry and dogmatic catechisms—these are the characteristics of the Cominform 'ideology' of our day," Kardelj said in the spring of 1951. Stalinism had turned Marxist theory "into a worn-out dogma without blood or life, a dogma designed solely to discharge the task of a thought police against human reason and human thinking."[170]

A few months later Milovan Djilas, then still a member of the Yugoslav Communist leadership, complained that in the Soviet Union practical measures were forever being "accepted as final theoretical and scholarly conclusions and as the foundation of scientific theory itself." This had led "to a pragmatist vulgarization of Marxism."[171] Marxist theory was lagging behind the requirements of the day: "Often socialist thinking revolves within the framework of enclosed and ossified categories," Kardelj said in 1956. Often new "factors of socio-political development in the present-day world" were either underrated or not discussed at all.[172]

In addition to this lagging behind the new factors in the life of society, the humanist Marxists also criticized the arbitrariness and one-sidedness with which the official Party headquarters were viewing the history of Marxism and "further developing" the doctrine. The history of Marxism was "the most neglected field of our scholarship," the Polish humanist Marxist Jerzy Szacki declared in the autumn of 1956. "People concerned with it prefer to use scissors and razor blades rather than the pen. . . . Certain essential parts of Marxist theory (especially some ideas of the young Marx), such as the theory of alienation, were either belittled or passed over in silence." The ideological publications of the Stalin era "may one day be a useful historical source for studying the period of the great bluff." Stalinist ideologists considered even Marx and Lenin to be dangerous. "The Stalinist inquisition could not tolerate within the Party such an enemy as the authentic Marx or the authentic Lenin might well be." The creative development of Marxism-Leninism was a highly one-sided business. Ideological amendments conceived by the Central Committee were automatically regarded as "creative," whereas the same thing done by anybody else was immediately labeled "revisionism."[173]

The monopolization of Marxist theory and its degradation into an instrument for the justification of practical measures had led also, according to Leszek Kolakowski, to a loss of intellectual function, to a lack of precision, to ambiguity:

It was said that "on the one hand" the masses create history and "on the other" an individual who understands the trends of history can influence its course, and so forth. This statement is so nebulous that it can both justify and attack the deification of an autocrat. "On the one hand" one should overcome nationalism, and one should combat cosmopolitanism "on the other hand"; on the basis of such generalities one can easily tolerate chauvinist escapades now, then condemn them loudly as the need arises. The examples are innumerable. An all-purpose theory based on such vague formulations as "yes and no" or "on the one hand and on the other" defends itself scrupulously against any precision since its strength lies in its blurredness."[174]

Mihailo Marković, Professor of Philosophy at Belgrade University, similarly criticized the "sorry stagnation of the social sciences in the countries building socialism." Short-term, day-to-day politics were "predominating over scholarship" and this had led "to a disastrous neglect of the scientific foundations of Marxism."[175]

These shortcomings in the development of Marxism—the escape from an investigation of reality, an underrating of new problems and factors, the falsification of its own history, the arbitrary changes, and the lack of precision—were not accidental, in the view of the humanist Marxists, but were connected with the change in the function of Marxism from a revolutionary doctrine of liberation into the official state doctrine of the Soviet Union, and, in its further course, into an ideology to justify the existence of a small leading group. Marxism, "a doctrine that proclaimed the end of injustice," Henri Lefebvre declared, had been misused under Stalinism "to justify injustices that are among the most crying in history." This had become particularly obvious when Marxism became the state doctrine, and this "renunciation of living Marxism was officially named Marxism-Leninism."[176]

Kolakowski also pointed to the curious fact that Marxism, which seeks to unmask social consciousness, has itself, while proclaiming its liberation from myths, become the victim of just such mythmaking.[177]

A few years later Miroslav Kuzý, Professor of Philosophy at Comenius University in Bratislava and during the reform period head of the Ideological Department of the Central Committee of the Communist Party of Slovakia, emphasized the changed function of Marxism and its consequences. From the ideology of the oppressed and exploited, Marxism after the October Revolution had been "elevated to the ideology of the ruling class, to a ruling power ideology." The political dictatorship had soon been extended into an ideological dictatorship, and this ideological dictatorship had elevated

the Marxist teaching to a system of established truths which, following the victory of the Revolution, need no longer be tested as to its accuracy, or developed any further, or perfected. The clash of opinion was replaced by the forcible suppression of any other point of view; the place of serious analysis, of expert argument, and of patient demonstration was taken by an authoritarian, forcibly imposed, and "exclusively correct" official point of view.

Instead of serious investigation and discussion of various alternatives, people were fed "slogans, simple and universally applicable axioms, and 'easily understood formulas.' "[178] Franz Marek similarly criticized the schematic formalization of Marxism, which had led "to a canonization of basic ideas until eventually its textbooks, in their layout, in their summing up, in their self-assured judgments on what is and what is not Marxist, assumed the form of prayer books."[179]

This critique by the humanist Marxists is closely linked with their proposals and ideas for a revival and renewal of Marxism. Time and again the humanist Marxists in various countries had demanded that Marxist theory be cleansed of Stalinist deformations, one-sidedness, and outdated primitive slogans. Thus the Polish reformer Zbigniew Florczak proposed in October 1956 "that the ancient weapons of the revolution in its first stage, the intellectual simplifications that have the effect of blunt instruments, be consigned to the museums." It was time "to do away with slogans" and to produce once more "intellectually defensible—in short, sensible—ideas. We must start to think again and must not turn Marxism into a kind of Talmud."[180]

That required first of all the liquidation of the "monolithic character"; the emergence of different "schools" of Marxism was regarded as probable and indeed desirable. "Marxism must lose its monolithic character," Henri Lefebvre declared, and consequently "different schools may emerge within Marxism." Living Marxism must proceed from an objective analysis of present-day historical and social conditions and contradictions. It must critically examine all excrescences and exaggerations.[181]

Even Adam Schaff, who would not as a rule dissociate himself too much from the official Party line, objected in 1961 to a "black-and-white view" of Marxism, the idea that only one trend possessed the monopoly of truth:

The fact that one proceeds from a common theoretical and methodological Marxist basis does not mean that one invariably arrives at the same solutions. This must depend on many factors. Two Marxists starting from the same premises may well represent two not only different but even contradictory views. . . . All attempts to "forcibly align" Marxist views must end in failure and be proved wrong by life itself.[182]

Marxist thinking was "not tied to a Party card," Franz Marek declared, because "no Party has an exclusive lease on wisdom or progress." Marxism was "manifested in the most various forms and colors—the realization of this fact is also the prerequisite of an understanding between Marxists and Marx-inspired thinkers."[183]

In the autumn of 1956 Kolakowski—still in the official theoretical periodical of the Polish Party—examined the necessary prerequisites of a creative upsurge of Marxist theory:

In the present condition of Marxist theory one might well wish that Karl Marx could be resurrected. But since that is highly unlikely, the theoretical work that is supposed to create for the Communist movement a scientific basis for political activity adequate to the needs of our times can only be a collective effort on the part of Communist intellectuals who are trained in various fields of knowledge about society, and who are capable of utilizing the everyday experiences of the masses and are attuned to the voice of public opinion.

The realization of this task required a definite end to the following malpractices: first, "any political restriction on the subject matter of scientific research," second, announcing "that certain truths are 'politically correct' and demanding that they be disseminated without resorting to scientific discussion"; third "laying down certain directions for research in scientific circles," and fourth, establishing "a 'sphere of untouchable truths' that are excluded from discussion." Any activity within the sphere of Marxist theory "led by the real interests of Communism depends on the maximum amount of freedom from all non-scientific motivation in establishing the content of knowledge and on the formation of the most resolutely objective and critical attitude."[184]

Liberation from monolithic one-sidedness, the development of different schools within Marxism, and unimpeded Marxist theoretical research—these, in the view of the humanist Marxists, were the crucial conditions for overcoming the neglect of many years. But beyond these general observations the humanist Marxists pointed to a few specific areas of particular importance to the further development of Marxist theory.

First of all, they would reject the view common among Soviet ideologists that Marxism must be restricted to its "three classical authors," Marx, Engels, and Lenin. They would champion an "opening up" of Marxism in order to supplement it by the findings of other Marxist theoreticians who had been neglected by Soviet ideologists. Thus Jerzy Szacki called for solid research into and for scholarly editions of the writings of Franz Mehring, Paul Lafargue, August Bebel, Arturo Labriola, Karl Kautsky, Plekhanov, and Bukharin (in particular his *Theory of Historical Materialism*), and he recommended the study of Lassalle, Bakunin, and Sorel.[185] Wolfgang Harich suggested that Marxist theory be supplemented by the findings of Trotsky, Bukharin, Rosa Luxemburg, and, in part, also of Karl Kautsky, Fritz Sternberg, and other social-democratic theoreticians, and especially by "the experience gathered in Yugoslavia."[186]

In Poland Julian Hochfeld also called for greater attention to the writings of Rosa Luxemburg, in particular her ideas "of the inevitable degeneration of the socialist revolution if, in the course of its progress, justice, freedom, and democratic guarantees are destroyed or even seriously curtailed," and her warnings to the international working class not to accept the lessons of the Russian Revolution as a model of revolutionary strategy and tactics, since that "Revolution was carried out under the particular conditions of a backward and isolated country suffering from specific difficulties."[187]

Franz Marek pointed out that Antonio Gramsci, Arturo Labriola, Karl Korsch, Rosa Luxemburg, and Georg Lukács should be studied much more attentively[188] and—just as Julian Hochfeld had done—urged an intensified study of Rosa Luxemburg, who fascinated "the Marxist by the wealth of her knowledge, the beauty of her style, and the compelling logic of her argument."[189] Similarly, "such important figures as Th.W. Adorno, Claude Levi-Strauss, Ernst Bloch, Herbert Marcuse, and Erich Fromm" must no longer remain "in a hidden corner of Communist writings."[190]

Roger Garaudy, then a member of the Politburo of the French Communist Party and director of the *Centre d'Études et de Recherches Marxiste* in Paris, went even further; admittedly, he was concerned not only with political theory but with Marxism in general. It was the task of Marxism, he said, "to discover everywhere the minutest grain of truth, even if it lies hidden below a thousand distortions to acquire this minute grain, to strip it of its mystical or idealist husk and—in its proper perspective—to fit it into the living thought of Marxism-Leninism. . . . Marxism would be the poorer if Plato or St. Augustine, Pascal or Kafka were to be strangers to us."[191]

At the meeting of the Paulus Society in Salzburg in 1965 Garaudy reiterated his thesis: "Marxism, as a matter of principle, integrates whatever values of culture and civilization man has ever created in his history. Christianity, too, is an inheritance of humanity."[192] Lucio Lombardo-Radice similarly demanded that "Marxism can and must supplement itself and develop with the aid of other truths which may be one-sided in their way but nevertheless, in a sense, are 'complementary' to it." As an example, he referred to the epoch-making discoveries of Sigmund Freud.[193]

In addition to "opening up" Marxist theory, the humanist Marxists also called for a serious investigation of the new developments in modern capitalism, the new problems of Western industrial countries, in order to do away with Stalinist dogmatism in this field. "The dogmatic classification of the Stalin era resulted in a very one-sided and simplified picture and understanding of life in the capitalist countries."

Any objective study had been branded as a deviation. The result had been a "distorted and frequently totally untrue propaganda picture of capitalism. Our knowledge of contemporary capitalism is very superficial, and we very often replace thorough study by slogans." Such problems as the Marshall Plan, the impoverishment of the working class, the so-called workers' aristocracy, and the role of the state in the capitalist economy must be rethought on the basis of available factual information.[194] The Polish Marxist Zygmunt Bauman criticized "the scantiness of the knowledge of Marxists about the modern political parties" in the Western countries and proposed that the methodological thesis of Marxism, according to which a political party expresses certain class interests, be re-examined and redefined against the background of the complex stratification of modern capitalist society: "Our knowledge of the present-day world is so backward that whatever field we examine we encounter, right at the start of our work, a great many more questions than ready-made answers."[195]

Henri Lefebvre pointed out that during the period of Stalinism, Marxists had lost the ability "to analyze concretely the bourgeois state." In this field, "political analysis was reduced to mere polemics."[196] Georg Lukács was even more outspoken: "Because of the Stalin era we have missed fifty years of capitalist development." During that time there had been no "systematic analysis of the contradictions of capitalism by Marxist-Leninist methods." Lukács demanded: "We must be fully informed about the West."[197]

An even more important task of Marxism was the critical analysis of developments in the socialist countries. Thus Henri Lefebvre regretted that under Stalinism Marxists had "abandoned the critical analysis of the socialist state." Marxism had "neglected the analysis of contradictions in the socialist society, in particular the contradictions in that society between the individual and the social aspects." It was an urgent task to examine critically the development of the socialist countries, including developments "in the economic field (planning), in social and cultural life (reduction of culture to a certain form of political awareness and state ideology), and in the field of history (distortions and even falsifications of history)."[198] In Belgrade, at the end of 1960, Mičunović pointed out that the authors of the Moscow Declaration of Eighty-one Communist Parties of December 5, 1960, "were not prepared to tackle the real problems of the socialist world." Accusations against capitalism were insufficient: "It would be far more important and more useful for the development of socialism to elucidate and avert those phenomena which are impeding the development of the socialist world."[199] In the opinion of Svetozar Stojanović,

Marxism at present must "develop primarily as a criticism of socialist or quasi-socialist movement and of society."[200]

The humanist Marxists did not confine themselves to making these demands but soon began to publish a number of extensive analyses of the trends of Soviet development, of the character of Stalinism, and of the present socio-political system of the Soviet Union and a few East European countries particularly closely linked with her. Apart from Kardelj's analysis in the spring of 1952, particular interest attaches to the concepts of "monopolistic bureaucratism" (Kuron and Modzelewski) and "oligarchic etatism" (Svetozar Stojanović). Only a very short outline of these theories can be given here.

In 1964 Kuron and Modzelewski subjected the system in Poland to a Marxist analysis which, they claimed, was valid also "for all industrialized, bureaucratically ruled countries, for Czechoslovakia, for East Germany, for Hungary, and for the Soviet Union." The official claim that Poland was a socialist country, the authors explained, was based on an equation of state ownership. Such an equation, however, was wrong, since under state ownership the producers were also alienated from their product. State-owned property belonged to those who held state power. Power in the state, however, belonged to "one single monolithic and monopolistic Party," which, in consequence, was also "the true owner of the means of production." But that Party was hierarchically organized: "information circulates from the bottom up, orders from the top down." The Party elite, by "exercising power in the state also controls the state-owned means of production, determines the amount of accumulation and consumption, the trend of investments, the share of the various social groups in the national product—in short, it determines the distribution and application of all goods produced by the social production process"; hence, it was also "the true owner of the means of production."

Kuron and Modzelewski described this power elite as a political monopolistic bureaucracy which was performing the functions of a "ruling class": "It has exclusive control over the basic means of production; it buys the labor power of the workers; it takes their surplus product from them by naked force and economic coercion and uses it for purposes alien or hostile to the workers, namely, to reinforce and extend its own control over production and society." The difference between it and a capitalist class consisted merely in the fact that "bureaucratic ownership is not of an individual nature but is the collective ownership by an elite identifying itself with the state."

With increasing industrialization the negative features of the system were becoming more pronounced and the system itself developed into a brake on economic development. This very process made the oppressive character of the system emerge ever more clearly. Propaganda and enthusiasm were replaced by economic punishment, administrative compulsion and—in the event of open rebellion—by the police. Since it was impossible to abolish the economic and political contradictions within the framework of the monopolistic bureaucratic system, it was necessary to stage an anti-bureaucratic revolution, overthrow the monopolistic bureaucracy, and replace it by a workers' democracy. "The only road to progress is through revolution."[201]

Unlike Kuron and Modzelewski, Svetozar Stojanović views the system in the Soviet Union and the East European countries more from the point of view of historical development and, chiefly on the basis of Yugoslav developments, regards an evolutionary elimination and transformation of the system as possible under certain conditions. Stojanović sees the starting point of the Soviet development in the fact that Marx's expectation had not come true that socialist revolutions would take place in the most highly developed industrial countries with a strong and politically aware working class. The fact that the first socialist revolutions took place in underdeveloped countries had turned further developments in a totally different direction. "The absence of a large and developed industrial proletariat has been one of the decisive causes of the statist distortion of the socialist revolution."

Yet this is by no means an inevitable process, and, as has been shown in Yugoslavia, a victory of statist trends could be prevented "by a long and persistent struggle of consistently revolutionary, socialist forces." But this has not been the case in Soviet Russia. Faced with the country's backwardness, the revolutionary elite has been confronted with the fundamental dilemma of "whether to develop social self-management initiated by the soviets of workers', soldiers', and peasants' deputies, or to replace it by the state rule of the Communist Party."

The clash between Lenin (who had preferred state economic planning and in March 1921 proclaimed the "unity of the party") and the "workers' opposition" (who had supported self-management by producers and the democratization of the Party) was, in Stojanović's view, the crucial turning point.

Under the difficult conditions of Soviet Russia, the "expropriated feudal and bourgeois property" became "the basis of statist ownership" and in the course of the further development, under Stalinism, the broad masses became "the object of exploitation by a new ruling class." This process had taken place against the opposition of consistently revolutionary forces within the Communist Party, but these had been suppressed and later physically liquidated. Subsequently,

Soviet statism had spread to other countries which had come to be dependent on "the parent and most powerful statist country."

The process of statist distortions and the emergence of a new class system had been disguised by the fact that the statist system described itself as "socialism." Of course the statist system was not capitalist, but "it does not follow that it must be socialist." Socialism is a system "based on social ownership and social self-management." Statism, on the other hand, is a system "based on state ownership of the means of production and state control over production and other social activities. The state apparatus represents a new ruling class. As the collective owner of the means of production it employs labor and exploits it." Both Stalinism and Maoism reflect these features of a statist system ruled by a statist class. Just because the members of the ruling class could not individually appropriate any part of the state property, some people believed that it was common property, whereas in fact, rather like feudal church property, it was collective class property. Statism was further disguised by the fact that the new statist ruling class was partially recruited from working people; the crucial point, however, was that the working class was totally subjected to the statist system. "Nominal workers' organizations are in practice statized and made [transmission belts] of the statist class and its party."

The new class clung "to Marxism as its ideology, although it is a greatly modified Marxism." It tried—as Marx once observed of the bourgeoisie—to represent its own interests as the common interests of society, of lending to its own ideas a semblance of universality. Statism, according to Stojanović, appears in different forms: in countries with a mature bourgeois tradition—multi-party system, parliamentary government, political liberalism—it is marked by a trend toward a kind of "democratic statism" that takes on the form of a welfare state. In the Soviet Union and certain East European countries, on the other hand—because of their underdeveloped working class, their low economic and cultural standards, and the absence of democratic traditions—an "oligarchic" statism has emerged, centrally and hierarchically organized, with an all-embracing economic, political, cultural, and moral monopoly of the ruling class.

Under these conditions an entirely new situation has arisen. Marxists in all countries are now faced with the crucial question: statism or socialism? The dilemma of the epoch is "statism or socialism, rather than capitalism or socialism."[202]

Predrag Vranicki sees bureaucratic statism as the main threat to a socialist development. In Vranicki's view, past experience testifies to the existence and antagonism between three trends and concepts in the emergence of socialist relations. The first trend is bureaucratic statism; its "most striking instance is Stalinism." The second trend is self-managing humanism; this had emerged in Yugoslavia as "a sharp negation of the Stalinist concept of socialism." It involved the "realization of those ideas that had already been so clearly formulated by Marx and Engels, such as the withering away of the state and the realization of an association of free producers." This was by no means merely "a specific Yugoslav road to socialism" but concerned, though perhaps in different forms, the "realization of production and social relations in which man will increasingly become the real subject of history, ruling and not ruled, planning and not planned, eliminating alienation instead of being alienated."

The third trend of development "which is becoming increasingly patent in socialism" is the technocratic. As a result of the tremendous development of science and technology the need for co-ordination and planning, for complete information, has become an integral part of social development, and this has led, in the realization and development of social self-management, not only to conflicts with political-administrative bureaucratism but also with technocratic concepts and trends. There is a danger that the first (bureaucratic, statist) and the third (technocratic) trends "might very easily find themselves on the same track within socialism" as a result of an alliance "between the technocratic intelligentsia and the political administrative bureaucracy." Under these circumstances Marxists are faced with the task of

avoiding such a development, of preventing the formation of a technocratic society that would see society as a machine and individuals as definite quantities in certain cybernetic calculations; a society that, carried away by enthusiasm for planetary and interplanetary technical achievements, would forget the broad and rich field of human creativity, that by its many technological accomplishments would largely turn man into the passive and compliant user (instead of the creator) of tempting inventions.[203]

Like Stojanović and Vranicki, Robert Kalivoda also distinguishes between the "bureaucratic" and the "Marxist" model of socialism. Stalinism had enjoyed the optimum conditions for its development during its first phase, during the period of Soviet industrialization, but had tried "artificially to extend and inflate that period in the interest of maintaining its own power." The turning point had come when Soviet Stalinism "brutally interfered in the affairs of the other European socialist states." That had been the decisive cause of the eruption of the conflict and had led to "a complex, dramatic, and often also tragic process of de-Stalinization." Yugoslavia's break with Moscow had been the first sign; the Yugoslav road of "a communalistic concept of socialist democracy" has been of "enormous importance as an inspiration for the further de-Stalinization process."

After the Twentieth Party Congress "an ever larger proportion of Communists" had realized the conflict between "the bureaucratic and the Marxist models of socialism." The tragic events in Hungary (1956) and the further developments in Poland, however, have shown "that the process of de-Stalinization does not take place automatically, that Stalinism will not leave the stage voluntarily." Nevertheless, in spite of many reverses, the "process of de-Stalinization in the socialist part of the European continent can no longer be reversed." Stalinism must "yield ground to the Marxist concept of socialism." The dispute is about "the fundamental Marxist idea of the meaning of socialism and its relation to the emancipation of man; the issue is the fundamental Marxist idea of the social transformation of socio-economic social relations, its function and dynamics."[204]

The humanist Marxist critique of Stalinism and neo-Stalinism is inseparably linked with a positive definition of the concept of socialism. Thus the Czechoslovak humanist Marxist Karel Kosík points to the urgent need for an explanation of "what socialism really is" by way of a clear "differentiation between assumed and real socialism." The (Soviet) explanation that the foundation of socialism is "social ownership of the means of production" and that "socialism is the scientific direction of society" is patently insufficient.

Modern socialism is unthinkable without a highly developed technology (technical progress) and without socially owned means of production. But these two chief characteristics and all further principal features may turn against socialism—i.e., they can degenerate and play a totally opposite part if socialism loses its historical meaning. . . . The historical meaning of socialism is the liberation of man, and socialism has its historical justification only insofar as it represents a revolutionary and liberating alternative—an alternative to misery, to exploitation, to oppression, to injustice, to lies and mystification, to unfreedom, to loss of human dignity, and to humiliation.[205]

These few quotations make it clear that the humanist Marxists are once more linking the realization of socialism—as Marx and Engels had done—with the liberation of man. "In the socialist system the human being must not become the slave of a state machine in the name of some kind of higher interests," Kardelj had declared at the end of 1956. The transformation of the worker into a free creator, the realization of Marx's demands for a fully developed individual, is a central task of socialism. "It seems to me that many people in various socialist movements, who are otherwise so fond of quoting Marx as their authority, have forgotten his ideas."[206]

Jadwiga Siekierska expressed the hope "that the moral and humanist meaning of Communism will not be obscured" or once more shunted onto some dead siding in the name of tactics or political expediency. "Communism becomes empty twaddle and Marxism a dead doctrine if our movement is stripped of its moral instincts and our doctrine of its humanist meaning."[207]

The "Polish October" brought the first open statement that socialism of the Stalinist type had not eliminated alienation but had led to new forms of alienation. "Admittedly, private ownership of the means of production was abolished," but the new stratum of political rulers, who held in their hands both economic and political power, became, "as it were, the administrators of people." On the basis of a centralized, bureaucratic state economy the producer was being alienated from his work in the classical sense,

and, just as in the past, the fruits of his work continued to be withdrawn from his control. The formal owners were neither able to dispose of nor guide the object that belonged to them, and the workers had no other influence on the factory or on production than the "influence" of plan fulfillers. . . . The producers had no kind of influence on the fate of their products, which meant that through their work entire areas of their lives and their existence were also alienated. . . . Shop floor and office workers were wholly and totally enmeshed in this widely ramified system of dependence.[208]

In view of this alienation—even in the countries calling themselves socialist—the humanist Marxists consider it necessary to move the human problem once more into the foreground of Marxist theory. "Emphasis on man as the starting and finishing point, as the ultimate objective of the entire practical and theoretical work of Marxism," Pawel Beylin said in Poland, "does not run counter to Marx's theoretical principles, as various quarters often try to make us believe. If we regard Marx's legacy from this point of view we are merely taking the ideology of the working class back to the foundations and objectives that once belonged to it and are eliminating the alienation that has arisen since. Marxism is returning to itself."[209] The Polish Marxist philosopher Adam Schaff, in the autumn of 1962, complained that Marxism did not yet possess a fully developed philosophy of the human being. "Because for a long time there was no interest in this set of problems, Marxism has failed to pose many theoretical questions altogether or failed to show any interest in them, as for instance the problem of conflict situations which is so important to the individual."[210]

These were also the main problems of a theoretical conference held at Liblice Castle near Prague in May 1963. Originally this meeting had been called on the occasion of the eightieth anniversary of Franz Kafka's birth, to present the author, until then "in disgrace," in a new light and to "rehabilitate" him. The participants included, apart from its convenor, Eduard Goldstücker, Roman Karst (Poland), Roger Garaudy, and Ernst Fischer. The discussion very soon went beyond Kafka's writings and embraced the problem of alienation under socialism. "The Marxist analysis of alienation," Garaudy declared in an argument with an East German dogmatist, "proves that objective roots for alienation continue to exist throughout the entire period of the building of socialism."[211] The Prague Conference, Ernst Fischer was to write later, "had the result that many of the younger people in the socialist countries for the first time heard the word 'alienation,' that they began to concern themselves more with the young Marx, and that the discussion about alienation was no longer to be halted."[212]

Robert Havemann, in his lectures on the "Scientific Aspects of Philosophical Problems" (1963–64) pointed out that the development toward socialism by no means suddenly eliminated man's alienation. Indeed, it is only then that "an active confrontation with man's alienation begins, with the concealment of reality, both the old and the new reality. Moreover, a confrontation begins with *new forms* of the concealment of reality."[213] Altogether, he claimed, Marxist anthropology was insufficiently developed. Throughout the period of dogmatic ossification of Stalinism there had been a "positively hectic denial of anthropology and sociology," which had been regarded as "bourgeois-imperialist pseudo-sciences." Marxist theory in the past had "presented man too one-sidedly, undialectically, only as the product and object of society."[214] Julius Strinka similarly urged "the revival of the suppressed humanist ethos of Marxist studies and politics."[215]

At the Salzburg meeting of the Paulus Society Roger Garaudy declared that it was the aim of the struggle for a new society "to create those social conditions which the human being needs in order to be a truly human being, a creative human being."[216] These theses were supported with particular emphasis by the Yugoslav Marxist philosophers in their periodical *Praxis*. Gajo Petrović defines socialist society as a "humanist, truly human society." Svetozar Stojanović regards socialism "as a socio-political system the *main* task of which is not to develop the national economy but to try to realize the humanistic ideals of de-alienation, liberation of man, and participatory democracy." The development so far has shown that socialism is not in a position to solve the problem of alienation and that, moreover, new forms of alienation have emerged. "What should be the job of a Marxist in a socialist country other than to try to expose them?"[217]

Ivan Sviták during the "Prague Spring" similarly dealt with this problem:

The central question of socialism remains the elimination of the problem of man's alienation in modern industrial society, and not merely the attainment of the Western level of consumer goods. Socialism is not primarily about forms of ownership, but about the measure of human freedom. We do not have to be ashamed that we only have half the national income of the Western countries, but should be ashamed that we possess less than half their civil rights.[218]

The renewal of Marxist theory, therefore, in the view of the humanist Marxists, requires the abolishment of one-sidedness and monolithic character, the development of several schools of Marxism, the supplementation of Marxism by the findings of hitherto neglected Marxist theoreticians, an objective study of recent developments in modern capitalism, a critical analysis of the experiences of the socialist countries (with a clear differentiation between etatism and socialism), and greater emphasis on the problem of man and the problem of alienation.

The multiplicity of these tasks, needless to say, cannot be solved by encapsulation and isolation but only by means of a dialogue with people of the most varied political and philosophical views. In contrast to the Soviet ideologists, who reject any kind of ideological coexistence and invariably speak of the ideological struggle, Georg Lukács in Hungary and Robert Havemann in East Berlin demanded an ideological dialogue as early as 1956—and this demand has been raised increasingly by humanist Marxists of various countries since the beginning of the 1960's.

Togliatti in his memorandum urged that "we do not counterpose in an abstract manner our conceptions to trends and currents of a different nature. But let us initiate a discussion with these currents."[219] Robert Havemann called for intensive contacts between the socialist and the capitalist parts of the world. The deeper meaning of peaceful coexistence, he said, was not in isolation or separation but in continuous mutual influence.

Never was a world transformed when the revolutionaries cut themselves off or isolated themselves from the rest of the world. Truly revolutionary ideas do not stop at frontiers. . . . The revolutionaries of our day must always learn anew. They must rid themselves of the illusion that their experiences and traditions will retain unshakable validity throughout the entire process of transformation of the world.[220]

The problem of the dialogue was discussed at the meeting of the Paulus Society. The "free confrontation" of Marxism with other philosophies was necessary, according to Lombardo-Radice, "because there are also partial truths in theories that are wrong in other respects, and finally because an absolute negative is just as improbable as an absolute positive."[221] Roger Garaudy underlined "the absolute necessity of dialogue and co-operation for Christians and Marxists" and welcomed "the first genuinely major international conversation between Christianity and Marxism."[222] A few weeks later Ernst Fischer also demanded an ideological dialogue:

We must finally overcome that fear of old-fashioned ideological fortress commanders to venture forth into the open. We must "coexist ideologically," i.e., we must know the real ideas of those holding different views and not just doctored quotations, we must put ourselves in their position in order not to dispute obstinately from outside but "immanently," and we must beware of regarding condemnations such as "bourgeois, decadent, anti-Marxist, revisionist, dogmatic," etc., as proof of truth. Let us return to the simple categories of "correct" and "false," because there are no "bourgeois" or "proletarian," "capitalist" or "socialist" results of science but only correct and false results (or half-correct, doubtful ones, etc.). What we need in order to be Marxists is not isolation in an "ideology" but comprehensive acquaintance with the modern world and its new intellectual aspects.[223]

This dialogue did not remain a theoretical demand but was in fact realized by the humanist Marxists. In contrast to Soviet ideological meetings at which prepared texts are read, usually in the presence of Party leaders, with any kind of "discussion" being limited from the outset by the prevailing "Party line," humanist Marxists have been meeting at unofficial symposia, seminars, and conferences with genuinely free and uninhibited discussions. The Kafka Conference at Liblice was followed by a Yugoslav symposium on "Marx and Our Time" in Belgrade (December 1963),[224] by a Yugoslav-Czechoslovak symposium in Zadar, Yugoslavia (November 1965), and by an international symposium called "Marx and the Western World," at which both Western Marxist experts and humanist Marxist theoreticians participated at Notre Dame University in Indiana, in April 1966.[225]

Best known internationally were the symposia organized by the Paulus Society in Salzburg in April 1965, at Herrenchiemsee in April 1966, and in Mariánske Lázně in April 1967,[226] at which humanist Marxists from Yugoslavia and several East European countries participated, as well as Marxist theoreticians from the Italian Communist Party (including Lombardo-Radice, Cesare Luporini, and Luciano

Gruppi) and the French Communist Party (Roger Garaudy). At a conference in Vienna in May 1967 the problems of socialism in Europe were discussed jointly by West European Social Democrats and humanist Marxists, including Rudi Supek (Professor of Sociology at the Philosophical Faculty in Zagreb and editor of *Praxis*), Andras Hegedüs (Director of the Institute of Sociology at the Hungarian Academy of Sciences), and Franz Marek.[227] For a number of years, moreover, regular seminars have been taking place every summer on the Yugoslav island of Korčula, at which Marxist and non-Marxist philosophers and sociologists from various countries have been discussing problems of Marxism.

The free, undogmatic development of Marxist theory—in the view of the humanist Marxists—is to consist in a return to original Marxism (i.e., the ridding of Marxism of later distortions and falsifications) and in the deduction of new theoretical conclusions for the world's present-day problems. As early as 1957 Zygmunt Bauman demanded:

The labor movement needs a theory that is tailored to the new age. From the period during which science was blunted we have inherited theoretical backwardness and helplessness in the face of many new phenomena. There is no more urgent task in the labor movement than to provide itself once more with a scientific theory that would tackle present-day phenomena with the same scientific equipment as Marx's theory did those of his own day.[228]

Julius Strinka observed: "One of the most urgent tasks of Marxism today is the development of a critical-revolutionary theory of present-day socialism, a theory that could positively contribute to the greatest possible release of the latent potentialities of socialism and lend it attractive new perspectives."[229]

This is what Georg Lukács called the "restoration of Marxism." In an interview with a Czechoslovak journalist he urged Communists

to return to genuine Marxist theory, and in doing so apply the results of the new discoveries of technology and modern research. Marx and Engels invariably incorporated into Marxism the newest scientific and technological discoveries. This came to an end with Lenin's death, and we must now restore the Marxist method in order to make Marxism truly alive. We must adopt all the new and scientifically progressive elements that have emerged in the West since Lenin's death.[230]

The humanist Marxists hope that by overcoming Marxism's one-sidedness and dogmatism, by its humanization and renewal, it will once more become a powerful magnet. "My ingrained optimism makes me see Stalinism as a closed period," Jerzy Szacki wrote in October 1956, "and I believe that after a happily brief medieval period a true renaissance of Marxism now lies ahead of us."[231] Roger Garaudy similarly remarked in April 1965: "We are certain that we are witnessing today the beginning of an event, the beginning of something historic that concerns the future of us all."[232]

Franz Marek spoke of a "renaissance of Marxist thinking."[233] Ernst Fischer declared that Marxism "since it began to crack the ice of Stalinism and to become a stream once more" had been gaining "new attractive force."[234] A similar observation was made by Svetozar Stojanović: "After several decades of grave crisis, we may today speak with assurance of a renaissance of Marxism. It rises like a phoenix from the ashes even though it has repeatedly been subjected to an autopsy."[235]

# A Few Conclusions

In this book I have attempted to present the political concepts of Marxism from the *Communist Manifesto* to the present day. Attention was focused on two aspects: first, the transformation of the political concepts of original Marxism through Leninism to Stalinism; and, second, an examination of the three main trends in present-day Marxism —Soviet Marxism-Leninism, Maoism, and (found mainly in Europe) humanist Marxism.

The focus of this book is primarily informative, based on original sources whenever possible. I feel, however, that a few conclusions are in order, as well as some personal thoughts on the future development of socialism.

First of all, the preceding study has shown that there is no such thing as uniform Marxism-Leninism, nor an unbroken line of development from Marx to the present-day Soviet ideological textbooks. Instead, there are clear and obvious differences between Marxism and Leninism, between Leninism and Stalinism, and among the various concepts that have prevailed since Stalin's death.

Both in the East and in the West, though for different reasons, the continuity of thought from Marx to the present is overestimated. The Soviet leadership tries to convey the impression that there is an unbroken line, a "creative development" of Marxism, from Marx and Engels through Lenin to present-day Soviet political concepts. Contemporary Soviet "scientific Communism" is claimed to be the only legitimate interpretation of this Marxism-Leninism, and thus to possess international validity. All other interpretations of Marxism are branded as "deviations" to be opposed—by means of ideology, whenever possible, but if necessary with tanks.

In the West, too, one frequently encounters attempts to lump together, under the heading of Marxism, the most varied and contradictory concepts ever proclaimed or defined by any Communist Party— even if they have hardly anything to do with real Marxism. This is partly due to a wish, which is entirely understandable, to refer all current Soviet declarations and actions back to earlier concepts of Marx, Engels, and Lenin in order to reveal their origins. Sometimes, however, the alleged continuity is deliberately emphasized in order to represent the horrors of the Stalin era and the actions of a neo-Stalinist leadership (such as the crushing of the Hungarian Revolution or the occupation of Czechoslovakia) as allegedly logical consequences of Marxism and in this way to discredit Marxism itself.

To overestimate the continuity of Marxist political concepts, from whatever motive, is to hinder an understanding of the changed function of Marxist theory. The four periods of (original) Marxism, Leninism, Stalinism, and post-Stalinism are related in contradictory ways. To begin with, certain ideological theories of the past period were invariably taken over; however, a great many theories were changed or adapted to the new conditions, whereas others were relegated to the background or totally taken out of circulation; finally, new doctrines and theories were fitted in wherever needed. All this was done under the heading of "creative development," a phrase designed to imply that the appropriate changes or reformulations were carried out "officially" by the leadership. Other formulations and adaptations (which were embarrassing to the leadership even though they were often more in line with the original theories and the new realities) were labeled "deviations," "falsifications," and "distortions."

It is of course true that since the death of Marx and Engels a multitude of new situations and problems required those who wished to remain true to the spirit of Marxism to vary from the letter of Marxism. From this, however, it does not follow that the line from Marxism through Leninism to Stalinism is the only logical and consistent development, if it is one at all. Even the transformation to Leninism included certain adjustments to Russian conditions; furthermore, after Lenin's death Marxism in the world Communist movement changed more and more into an "ideology of justification" that was incompatible with both the spirit and the letter, the inner logic and the objective, of original Marxism.

Leninism itself is a controversial development of Marxism. Although the Soviet concept of Marxism-Leninism is designed to convey the impression that Marxism and Leninism represent an inseparable unity, Leninism is still an adaptation of Marxist ideas to Soviet conditions and an ideological generalization of the lessons of the Russian Revolution.

Admittedly, Marxism does form the basis of Leninism. The central political concepts of Marx were also the fundamental directives for the thought and action of Lenin. They included the overthrow of capitalism by means of a social revolution of the oppressed classes; the international character of this struggle for emancipation; the right of the Marxist labor movement in each country to pursue this aim on the basis of the country's own traditions and economic and social conditions; the concepts of different roads to socialism and of equality among the working class movements of different countries; and, finally, the ultimate objective of a classless Communist society.

At the same time, significant differences may be discerned between Marxism and Leninism. Marx and Engels, in spite of their political activity, were primarily revolutionary theoreticians; Lenin, in spite of several theoretical essays, was primarily the strategist and tactician of revolution. Marxism is a social doctrine, a theory of social processes with definite political conclusions; Leninism, on the other hand, is primarily a revolutionary ideology (even though founded on theory) in which problems of political tactics occupy the most important position, while Marx's humanist interests recede into the background.

Most important of all, Lenin adapted the basic political concepts of Marxism, conceived primarily for the industrialized countries of Western Europe, to the totally different conditions of czarist Russia, i.e., a country where industrial labor accounted for only a small part of the population and where the revolutionary struggle was directed not against capitalism, but first and foremost against czarism.

This adaptation of Marxism to Russian conditions resulted in four crucial changes:

1. The original concept of a workers' party as the representative of the interests of a living working-class movement was replaced by Lenin with the new principle of the Party as an organization of professional revolutionaries, designed to "lead" the working class, a disciplined elite organization based on ideological unity.

2. Marx's idea of a social revolution in industrially developed countries, where the working class would represent the majority of the population, was replaced by Lenin with a two-phase model of revolution. The democratic revolution against czarism was to change gradually into a socialist revolution, with emphasis on an alliance between workers

and peasants, on the leadership of the revolution by a vigorous revolutionary party, and on flexible political tactics. The economic and social prerequisites of revolution, invariably stressed by Marx and Engels, were replaced by Lenin with favorable political conditions ("the revolutionary situation"), with the possibility of a peaceful transition to socialism being progressively replaced by Lenin with violent revolution in the form of an armed uprising.

3. The victory over the October Revolution in an economically backward country, the upheavals of World War I and of nearly four years of Civil War were reflected also in a marked shift of accent in the concept of the dictatorship of the proletariat. Thus Lenin, proceeding from adverse conditions in Russia, emphasized the application of dictatorial, forceful measures for the suppression of opponents of the Bolshevik Party.

4. Unfavorable conditions in Soviet Russia and the failure of the world revolution to materialize also resulted in certain changes in the ideas about the new society (ideas which Lenin, after 1917, did not expound in any major work but merely touched upon in articles and speeches in connection with practical measures). The first point is that, in contrast to Marx, the economic foundations of the new society were not to be established until after the victory of the revolution. ("Communism is Soviet power plus electrification.") The attainment of the ultimate Communist objective was moved by Lenin into a more distant future and the new society—much more clearly and outspokenly than in Marx's writings—was subdivided into two periods ("socialism" and "Communism"), the withering away of the state was put off to the later phase, i.e., Communism, and Marx's idea of the association of free producers was replaced by Lenin with centralized state planning.

It is true that Lenin repeatedly warned the Communists of other countries against a slavish acceptance of Russian experience and that he stressed their right and indeed their duty to conduct matters differently and better in other countries. However, the inconsistency of his remarks—especially about the dictatorship of the proletariat in the new society—made it possible for his successors to emphasize different and contradictory aspects of Leninism. Further development would therefore depend on whether the international or the Russian aspect of Leninism, the revolutionary or the dictatorial-bureaucratic aspect, gained the upper hand.

The development that occurred after Lenin's death—Stalinism—does not by any means represent the logical or consistent continuation of Leninism. It developed into an ideology for the justification of a bureaucratic, centralized, dictatorial system.

Present-day Soviet ideology denies the existence of Stalinism. Even during the period of de-Stalinization, Soviet criticism was confined to Stalin's character, to his methods of governing, and to certain of his theses without subjecting Stalinism as a system to any analysis. Many Western writers similarly regard Stalinism as a logical consequence of Leninism, differing from Leninism merely in certain quantitative changes, such as an increasing use of coercive methods, the transition from internationalism to nationalism, and in certain differences in the characters of the two Soviet leaders.

It is true that some of the roots of the degeneration of the revolutionary Soviet regime into a totalitarian police state could already be discerned during the Lenin era, but that does not mean that Soviet rule was bound by some iron law to develop into that centralized, bureaucratic reign of terror we call Stalinism. Although Stalinism stems from Leninism, it represents the negation of many of Lenin's key principles.

The transition from Leninism to Stalinism took place during the decline of the revolution, the weakening of revolutionary enthusiasm, the disappointment over the failure of world revolution to occur, and the steady advance of bureaucratic forces rallied around Stalin's secretariat. The victory of Stalinism was achieved because of a successful struggle against internationalist revolutionaries of Lenin's type, a struggle which Stalin conducted with intrigues and slanders, and which began ideologically with the proclamation of the slogan "socialism in one country."

The Stalin era (1929–53) was the time of industrialization and collectivization, of the transformation of a largely backward agrarian country into a powerful industrial state. Hand in hand with the growing economic potential, the power positions of the ruling caste were greatly consolidated, the dictatorial coercive apparatus further developed, and oppression and terror made inseparable parts of the system. The political objectives of Leninism were largely amended and frequently turned into their very opposite. Lenin's revolutionary elite Party was replaced by a bureaucratic power apparatus, world revolution by Soviet patriotism and (later) by Great-Russian chauvinism, the ideal of equality by increasing social differentiation leading to the emergence of a new ruling caste. Lenin's plan for a slow, cautious evolutionary development of agricultural co-operatives was replaced by compulsory collectivization ordered from above and ruthlessly implemented. The revolutionary comradeship-in-arms of the Leninists was replaced by vigilance campaigns and mutual mistrust, and Lenin's personal modesty gave way to an excessive cult of Stalin's personality.

The proclamation of the "victory of socialism" in the Soviet Union at the end of 1936 equated this system with a socialist society and socialism was defined by Stalin as a system based economically on a state-controlled, planned economy and politically on "political-moral unity" and the "leading role of the party." Stalin's concepts of the "capitalist encirclement," the strengthening of the socialist state (replacing Marx's idea of the withering away of the state), and his doctrine of the intensification of the class struggle with the further development of socialism all served the object of justifying terror, vigilance campaigns, purges, and the vast network of forced labor camps.

Leninism had been a revolutionary doctrine aimed at international revolutionary transformation of society; Stalinism was an ideology hinging upon the strength, the power, and the authority of the Soviet state and on the "wisdom of the leader." Stalinism was an ideology whose goal was the justification of the bureaucratic, dictatorial, centralized system of the U.S.S.R., of the dictatorship of the new ruling caste which, in the name of Marxism-Leninism, was now directing and controlling the entire political, economic, and intellectual life of the country. The ideology of Stalinism further served the aim of subjecting the entire world Communist movement to the Soviet leadership and placing all other Communists in the service of Soviet power interests.

Even during the Stalin era it became clear that the ideology and organizational form of international Communism under Soviet leadership, as molded by Stalin, was at variance with changing realities. The only successful Communist-led revolutions—in Yugoslavia and in China—were victorious just because they did not subordinate themselves to the Soviet Union, because they did not follow Stalinist recipes and directives, but instead acted independently and developed their own concepts of the revolution. The victory of these revolutions marked the beginning of the end of Stalinism and the beginning of differentiation in world Communism. The Soviet Union was no longer able to maintain its leading role in the old way. Yugoslavia's break with the Stalin leadership in 1948 was the crucial turning point. The monolithic character of world Communism in the Stalinist mold had been broken, and the Stalinist interpretation of Marxism-Leninism was no longer sacrosanct.

The Soviet leadership was finding it increasingly difficult to ascribe a common denominator or to apply its own general line—either in theory or in practice—to the various socialist states which had come into being under totally different conditions, which were marked by their own traditions, and which stood at different stages of development —thus demanding from their ruling Communist parties different objectives, measures, and working methods.

After Stalin's death in March 1953, and in particular after the

Twentieth Congress of the Communist Party of the Soviet Union in February 1956, that process of differentiation in world Communism gained further momentum, finding expression in the "Polish October," in the Hungarian Revolution, in the steadily sharpening conflict between Moscow and Peking, in Rumania's increasingly independent line, and in the tremendous reform process in Czechoslovakia in the spring and summer of 1968. These and many other processes (such as Castroism in Cuba and the stirrings of independence among West European Communists) are manifestations of an extensive process of political and ideological differentiation, which is by no means confined to practical politics or national differences but which touches the very foundations of Marxism.

These processes were not confined to the world Communist movement as a whole; within the Communist parties of many countries there have been worsening disputes not only between the followers of the Soviet and Chinese trends, but also between reactionary and progressive Communists, between dogmatic bureaucrats and humanist Marxists.

The present situation differs both quantitatively and qualitatively from earlier disputes in the Marxist movement, such as those among the German Social Democrats in the 1890's or those within the Bolshevik Party or the Comintern in the 1920's: quantitatively, because it is a dispute in a world movement comprising ninety-four Communist parties, including fourteen Communist parties in power; qualitatively, because this is not a dispute about one or two issues, but disagreements touching on the most fundamental concepts of Marxist political, social, and economic theory. The road to socialism, the forms and methods of socialist revolution, the transitional measures after the victory of the revolution, the assessment of national revolutionary liberation movements, attitudes to the problem of war, peace, and coexistence, and above all the fundamental characteristics of a socialist society—on all these issues there are profound differences of opinion and divergent and contradictory views current in present-day world Communism. At the center of the problem are three main currents of Marxism: Soviet Marxism-Leninism, Maoism, and humanist Marxism.

The first of these three main currents, Soviet Marxism-Leninism, reflects the Soviet leadership's endeavor to maintain the existing centralized, bureaucratic system under the conditions of an emerging Soviet industrial society, while in the international sphere, ideologically justifying and supporting the U.S.S.R.'s leading role vis-à-vis other socialist countries and the world Communist movement.

The profound contradiction between the system of political rule inherited from Stalin and the new conditions and requirements of the emerging Soviet industrial society is reflected in the political concepts of Soviet ideology ("scientific Communism").

During the de-Stalinization period (1953–64) the Soviet leadership tried, by means of partial reforms, to adapt Stalin's terrorist dictatorship to the new conditions without, however, basically altering the power structure. Curtailment of the power of the secret police, release of prisoners, amnesties and rehabilitations, a somewhat more liberal cultural policy, reforms and reorganizations in the system of economic management, a certain decentralization in the state and economic spheres—all these served the purpose, while remaining within the framework of the system inherited from Stalin, of replacing pressure and terror by initiative and material incentives, and making the system's forms of government more modern and more elastic.

The fact that these were partial reforms decreed from above was reflected also in the ideological changes. Although Stalin's methods of rule and some of his doctrines were criticized, the problem of Stalinism as a system was excluded from all discussion. The doctrine of coexistence was proclaimed the general line of foreign policy but at the same time restricted by the thesis of the ideological struggle; the right to different roads to socialism was effectively limited by the alleged existence of "common basic features" of socialist development. The emphasis on "socialist legality" and "collective leadership," the concept of the "state of the entire people," and of the "Party of the entire people" certainly represented a partial departure from Stalinism but could hardly be seen as serious concepts marking a transition toward socialist democracy.

Important as de-Stalinization was, both in theory and in practice (especially if compared with Stalinism), the partial reforms decreed from above and the new political concepts were insufficient to eliminate the centralized, bureaucratic power structure or to provide for a breakthrough toward socialist democracy. The conservative and bureaucratic forces proved stronger, and following the overthrow of Khrushchev (October 1964) the reforms of de-Stalinization were either watered down or totally rescinded. Instead of reforms, the emphasis is once more on power and authority, and a tougher line has been adopted in all spheres of life, reflected in the present-day version of scientific Communism.

Soviet "scientific Communism," in Moscow's opinion, is the only legitimate and internationally valid interpretation of Marxism-Leninism, and therefore serves the purpose of ideologically justifying and confirming the leading role of the Soviet Union over the other socialist countries and the world Communist movement. This subordination is seen both in the U.S.S.R.'s political practice (the most important and most tragic instance of which was the occupation of Czechoslovakia in August 1968) and also in the doctrines of the "world socialist system," the "international socialist division of labor," the alleged existence of "common basic features" in the development toward socialism (all of which have been taken from Soviet experience), and finally the new doctrine of limited sovereignty. However, the Soviet claim to the leading role in world Communism and her ideological monopoly in the interpretation of Marxism are no longer accepted without opposition.

The second modern current of Marxism, Maoism ("the great thought of Mao Tse-tung"), represents an ideological generalization of the experiences of the Chinese Revolution and contains a number of ideological-political concepts for the development after the victory of the Revolution with particular emphasis on the transformation of the human consciousness.

Just as Leninism clearly reflects an adaptation of Marxism to Russian conditions, so Maoism—sometimes even to a higher degree—represents an attempt to combine certain Marxist and Leninist concepts with Chinese tradition (Sinification of Marxism) and to transfer them to a country that lacked both the pre-conditions for a social revolution as defined by Marx and Engels and for a socialist revolution as defined by Lenin.

The country's century-old isolation, the Confucian tradition, the ethnocentric idea that China was the center of the world, the country's economic backwardness, the fact that industrial workers accounted for only 1 per cent of the population, as well as China's semi-colonial status and extensive control by foreign powers—all these and other peculiarities demanded a totally new theory of revolution which inevitably differed extensively from Marxist and even from Leninist concepts. When the transposition of Soviet ideas and doctrines to the revolutionary movement in China had led to disastrous defeats and enormous sacrifices for the Chinese Communists, Mao developed a new set of concepts corresponding to Chinese conditions. Of particular importance was his new model of the Revolution—the combination of the national liberation struggle with an anti-feudal revolution ("new democratic revolution"), the proclamation of the leading role of the peasantry in such a revolution ("the village is the base of the Revolution"), and an intermediate phase envisaged as a short-term objective ("the new democracy"). Since the Revolution was inseparably linked with a war for national liberation, military-political concepts acquired vital importance in Maoism (the "omnipotence of revolutionary war"), with the military struggle proclaimed as the central issue of the Revolution ("power grows out of the barrel of a gun"). Along with success came the wish to be free from the Soviet example and—after the victory of the Revolution and the proclamation of the People's Republic of China —to embark on an independent road (the "great leap forward," introduction of people's communes).

The peculiar characteristics of China, the independent development of the Chinese Revolution, the difference in the conditions and tasks faced by the Russians on the one hand and the Chinese on the other, gave rise to different political conclusions and to increasingly pronounced differences of opinion, which found their expression in the conflict between Moscow and Peking. In the course of this conflict the Chinese Communists proclaimed their own experiences to be generally valid findings of Marxism, applicable to all countries and all nations: the inevitability of war, violent revolution as the only method of socialist transformation, armed people's war as the supreme form of struggle, the "great thought of Mao Tse-tung" as the culmination of Marxism-Leninism. The Soviet Communists were first branded as "revisionists," and since 1964 Peking has been arguing that a restoration of capitalism has taken place in the Soviet Union and that the Soviet leaders are the exponents of a new ruling class. By means of the cultural revolution, finally, the Chinese Communists tried to establish the priority of revolutionary consciousness over rational and economic thought, to perform a transformation of the human mind and soul, to transmit revolutionary enthusiasm to the younger generation, to prevent a Soviet-type bureaucratic development in China, and to fight in the Party, the state, the economy, and the army all forces that might oppose such a trend.

The third main current, humanist Marxism, was born in the struggle against Stalin's terrorist dictatorship; it tries to rid Marxism of subsequent deformations, to place Marx's humanist ideas once more at the center of attention, and, in theory and practice, to support the realization of a libertarian model of humane socialism.

Humanist Marxism, created as an opposition to Stalinism, represents an attempt to explain the phenomenon of Stalinist dictatorship and to develop a Marxist alternative. The independent character of the Yugoslav Revolution and Yugoslavia's break with Moscow provided the first opportunity for realizing a new concept of the road to socialism and a new model of a socialist society.

It has become obvious since 1948—but more particularly over the past decade—that this trend is far from being a special Yugoslav phenomenon but is, in fact, an international current that has its source in Europe. Humanist Marxists—in complete agreement with Marx and

Engels—champion equality within the international workers' movement and the autonomy and independence of the workers' movement of each country. They therefore oppose the establishment of a leading center and the monopoly position of any one party. They support—again in full agreement with the original concepts of Marxism—an independent road to socialism, in line with each country's historical traditions and economic, political, and cultural conditions. They reject the transposition of the dictatorship of the proletariat, as it emerged under Soviet conditions, to other countries. Marx's and Engels' fundamental principle of the association of free producers (all but forgotten in the course of the further development of Marxism) is again at the center of the humanist Marxists' ideas on socialism, albeit in a modernized form corresponding to present-day conditions.

The humanist Marxists see socialism as a living, free, pluralistic society, based economically on the self-management of producers (including workers' councils in the factories) and characterized politically by legally insured democratic freedoms for its citizens, and by free discussion between various groups.

Among the key features of the new model of socialism are the separation of the legislative, executive, and judicial powers, democratization and freedom of discussion within the Party, abandonment of centralized bureaucratic planning of the economy and a transition to a socialist market economy, the independence of trade unions from state and Party, freedom of the press and of association, personal security guaranteed under the law, and freedom for all citizens to travel abroad. They believe that the Party must be transformed from the dictatorial instrument of power of a bureaucratic ruling caste into a political organization based on the voluntary support of the population. It cannot realize its leading role by dominating all spheres of society, by tying down all institutions and organizations by directives, or by enforcing its policy by decree. It must stimulate socialist initiative and win the public over by persuasion and personal example.

For humanist Marxists, Marxist theory, which had been an ideological weapon for the manipulation of power since the period of Stalinism, must once more be given its original liberating character. Marxism must rid itself of dogma and one-sidedness; it must not limit itself to its "three classics" (Marx, Engels, and Lenin) but also must absorb the concepts of other Marxist thinkers. The further development of Marxism requires new critical analyses—both of the development of Western industrial societies and of the lessons of the socialist countries. Instead of shutting themselves off from the outside and isolating themselves, as

Communists have done in the past, the humanist Marxists demand an open and free dialogue with the exponents of other philosophical and political trends.

These conclusions derive from a study of the original sources of the political theory of Marxism, from Marx until today. It remains to say a few words—naturally open to debate—on the possible future development of Marxism. Naturally, this discussion reflects the personal view of the author, and is open to debate.

Opinions on the future prospects of Marxism diverge greatly. Official statements from Moscow and Peking keep talking of the victorious and triumphal advance of Marxism. In the West, on the other hand, the view is frequently heard that Marxism is nearing its end and has already lost all importance. Diametrically opposite as these views are, they have one point in common: they refer to Marxism in general and abstract terms without taking account of the various interpretations of Marxism.

Yet the future development of Marxism will very probably depend on which of the three present-day currents will dominate in the future. Indeed, it is entirely possible that other new interpretations of Marxism may emerge, both in the highly industrialized Western countries and in the countries of Africa, Asia, and Latin America. What influence these new interpretations will have in the future is, of course, impossible to predict. Any forecast of the future of Marxism must therefore confine itself to its three main contemporary currents.

Soviet Marxism-Leninism, the official state doctrine throughout the Soviet sphere of power, serves to legitimize and justify the country's bureaucratic and dictatorial system and the Soviet Union's hegemony in the world Communist movement. In foreign policy it emphasizes the struggle between two systems—the "socialist camp" on the one hand and the "camp of capitalism and imperialism" on the other—this struggle being largely identified with the two existing power blocs. Although Marxism-Leninism has a tremendous potential, it is losing more and more of its influence for the very reason that it is an attempted justification of Soviet policy and has shown itself incapable of developing Marxism to embrace the problems of our present-day world.

Even within the Soviet leadership's own sphere of power, Soviet ideological concepts succeed only rarely in inspiring politically interested people. The soporific bureaucratic style, the obvious fact that Soviet political theory lags behind many new phenomena, the profound contradiction between theoretical declarations and reality, the exclusion of all real problems from discussion, the all-pervading censorship restricting the importation and dissemination even of foreign Marxist literature if it diverges ever so slightly from the Soviet line, and the ban on the free and untrammeled discussion of political and theoretical problems even from a platform of Marxism—all these have resulted in "scientific Communism" becoming no more than a ritual performance in the obligatory classes of "Marxism-Leninism" in colleges, universities, and Party instruction courses even within the Soviets' own sphere of power.

These weaknesses have had their effect also on the Communist movement outside the Soviet sphere. It may be expected that more and more Communist parties, especially in the industrialized countries, will move away from the Soviet Union for these and other reasons and develop their own divergent ideas and concepts of Marxism. A gradual rapprochement toward the ideas of humanist Marxism seems therefore quite possible. Needless to say, Soviet Marxism-Leninism will continue to be of importance in the future, but more and more as the instrument and expression of Soviet policy and less and less as a source of intellectual or political inspiration.

Of the three contemporary currents, Maoism is most obviously tied to a living person. Its future prospects, therefore, will largely depend on whether China's political development continues on present lines after Mao's death or makes an abrupt change of course. To what extent the millions of Chinese citizens who now study Mao Tse-tung's Little Red Book, read it to each other, and triumphantly wave it at demonstrations are truly permeated by Maoism is very difficult to assess. But there seems to be some indication that the hold of Maoism on present-day China is considerably stronger than that of Soviet Marxism-Leninism on the Soviet population. The question, of course, remains whether, with a probable decline of revolutionary enthusiasm and an increasing influence of state interests and economic considerations resulting from China's further industrialization, Maoism can retain its inspiring force.

Added to this is the contradictory aspect of Maoism which, on the one hand, is rooted in Chinese tradition and ideologically generalizes the experiences of Chinese Communism, and, on the other, demands to be seen as the only legitimate, internationally valid interpretation of Marxism. In the long run these two aspects will scarcely be compatible. For the highly industrialized Western countries Maoism offers hardly the answer to the new problems—which does not, of course, prevent Mao from being glorified as a symbol of protest among certain circles of the revolutionary Left. Even Maoism's claim to represent the revolutionary ideology of the liberation movements of Asia, Africa, and Latin America will be difficult to uphold, since Maoism is much too deeply rooted in the experiences of the Chinese Revolution.

The third main current, humanist Marxism, is, from the point of view of power politics, in the least favorable position. Outside Yugoslavia all attempts so far to put humanist-Marxist ideas into effect have been suppressed. The "Polish October" of 1956 was pushed back step by step by bureaucratic and dictatorial forces and eventually annulled altogether; the Hungarian Revolution of 1956 was crushed by Soviet military intervention; and the most important and probably most significant attempt so far—in Czechoslovakia in 1968—to create a model of "socialism with a human face," was stopped by the Soviet occupation of August 21, 1968. Throughout the Soviet sphere of power the dissemination of humanist-Marxist literature is banned. Humanist Marxism is brutally suppressed; its exponents and followers are shot (Imre Nagy), sentenced to long terms of imprisonment (Wolfgang Harich in East Germany, Jacek Kuron and Karol Modzelewski in Poland, and Ivan Yakhimovich in the U.S.S.R.), punished by "administrative measures" (Fritz Behrens, Arne Benary, and Robert Havemann in East Germany), or forced to emigrate (Ernst Bloch, Zygmunt Bauman, Eduard Goldstücker, Radoslav Selucky); others, like many humanist Marxists in Czechoslovakia, are denied all chance to work except as manual laborers of the lowest grade.

In view of these serious setbacks the opinion is often heard in the West that humanist-Marxist attempts to establish humane socialism are doomed to failure in the face of the Soviet Union's vast power potential. This assumption, in my opinion, overlooks three factors.

First, humanist-Marxist ideas are concepts stemming from existing contradictions and antagonisms within the system of the Soviet Union and most East European countries. The present bureaucratic, dictatorial power system dates back to the period of Stalin's industrialization and is profoundly at variance with the reality of the emerging modern industrial society. Even the economic objectives of the leadership of the U.S.S.R. and certain East European countries are incapable of being realized within the framework of the present economic and political system. The need for far-reaching economic reforms is therefore acknowledged even in ruling circles of the Party apparatus of those countries. Yet their attempt to confine the reforms to the management of the economy, while maintaining and indeed consolidating their centralized, bureaucratic dictatorship over all other spheres of life, will prove impossible in the long run. Hence the view of the humanist Marxists that reforms in the management of the economy are not enough and that an appropriate change must also be brought about in the political system: replacement of the centralized, bureaucratic form of government by a pluralistic socialism thus appears as the only chance of resolving the present antagonisms within the framework of socialist social relations.

The concepts of the humanist Marxists are therefore not abstract ideas but an attempt to create the social and political prerequisites for any further development in the Soviet Union and its allies in Eastern Europe.

Second, in spite of the above-mentioned setbacks and defeats, the past two decades have repeatedly shown that the humanist concepts of humanist Marxism are theoretically far superior to Soviet-type "scientific Communism" and, above all, have a far greater power of attraction and inspiration. While the bureaucratic rulers in the Soviet sphere of power fear the views of the reformers and fight them with "administrative measures," the humanist Marxists accept the dissemination of Soviet concepts calmly, unperturbed and with ironic amusement. In the few periods when humanist Marxist ideas were freely disseminated in the East European countries—as in Poland and Hungary in 1956 and in Czechoslovakia in 1968—their echo was enormous. The same public that until then had accepted the official Soviet-type Party declarations with apathy and boredom, if not indeed with distaste, suddenly awoke to a new political life the moment the ideas and concepts of a humane socialism were propagated.

Third, the past twenty years testify to a growing influence of humanist-Marxist ideas, not only in Eastern Europe but also among the Communists of Western Europe. After Yugoslavia's break with Moscow, when the first steps were being taken to realize a new model of socialism, there was indeed some sympathy among Communists in other countries, but the effect was still relatively limited. A mere eight years later—in the summer and autumn of 1956—the "Polish October" and the Hungarian liberation struggle were followed with sympathy by thousands of Communists in other countries, and the crushing of the Hungarian Revolution by Soviet troops aroused vigorous opposition in many Communist parties. Another twelve years later the Czechoslovak reform movement was being hailed by the majority of Communists in the industrialized countries (including many leading Party members), and the Soviet occupation of Czechoslovakia unleashed an unprecedented storm of protest throughout the world Communist movement. The invasion and occupation of Czechoslovakia dramatically widened and deepened the gulf, which nothing since that time has narrowed, between the bureaucratic and dogmatic forces in world Communism on the one hand, and the humanist Marxists' striving for independence and a freer development, on the other.

The future of Marxism will, in my opinion, be determined largely by the present struggle within the world Communist movement, by which of the three currents will prevail in the future. The outcome of this struggle, which depends on a multitude of factors, is impossible to predict. Certainly—and this will probably be true for some time to come—the Soviet trend now predominates in world Communism. But Soviet Marxism-Leninism, being an ideology for the justification of a bureaucratic and dictatorial system, has already lost much of its attraction. A rebirth of Marxism caused by official Soviet bureaucratic ideologists is scarcely conceivable.

It is possible, on the other hand, that Marxism may experience a new upsurge as the revolutionary ideology of the liberation movements in the countries of Asia, Africa, and Latin America—either in the form of Maoism, Castroism, or some new doctrines yet to emerge—but in that case it would become the national liberation ideology of oppressed nations and the doctrine of industrialization for economically underdeveloped countries. It would, in fact, be a "Marxism" which, like Soviet Marxism-Leninism and Maoism, has relatively little in common with the original concepts and ideas of Marx and Engels.

We are left, therefore, with the conclusion that Marxist theory today is most effectively represented by the humanist Marxists—branded by the Soviet leadership as "deviationists" and "renegades." The fundamental concepts of the humanist Marxists are not only closest to the spirit and to the writings of Marx but, more important, the humanist Marxists are willing and able to apply these concepts independently and open-mindedly to the new problems in our times and our world—including a critical analysis of the developments in the Soviet Union and in Eastern Europe. Only in this form and interpretation could Marxism again play a significant role in the future, that is, only if it places its humanist, liberating aims and its critical method once more at the center of its teaching, if it learns its lesson from the tragic deformities of Stalinism and post-Stalinism in the Soviet Union and certain East European countries, if it rises above dogmatism and one-sidedness, if it faces boldly and with an open mind the new problems of our age, and if it champions a new model of a socialist society that is not confined to the nationalization of the means of production but characterized above all by social self-management, democratic freedom, and respect for human dignity.

# Notes

## ☐ Chapter 1

Wherever possible, quotations are from official translations of the works of Marx and Engels, otherwise they have been translated from the new German edition of the Collected Works of Marx and Engels (*Werke*) published by Dietz Verlag in East Berlin, 1961–68.

1. Karl Marx, "Debatte über die Pressefreiheit," in *Rheinische Zeitung*, May 5, 1842. *Werke*, I, 54.
2. Marx, Preface to *A Contribution to the Critique of Political Economy*. Marx and Engels, *Selected Works* (Moscow: Progress Publishers, 1969), I, 502.
3. *Loc. cit.*
4. Marx, "Der Kommunismus und die Augsburger," *Allgemeine Zeitung*, October 16, 1842. *Werke*, I, 108.
5. Marx to Arnold Ruge, Cologne, January 25, 1843. *Werke*, XVII, 415.
6. Marx, *Letter from the Deutsch-Französische Jahrbücher*, September 1843. *Werke*, I, 344–45.
7. Friedrich Engels, "On the History of the Communist League," 1885. Marx and Engels, *Selected Works* (New York: International Publishers, 1969), 442.
8. *Ibid.*
9. *Ibid.*, 443.
10. *Ibid.*
11. *Ibid.*, 445.
12. *Ibid.*, 446.
13. Engels to Marx, November 23–24, 1847. Marx and Engels, *Selected Correspondence* (New York: International Publishers, 1942), 20.
14. Engels, Preface to the German edition of 1883 of the *Manifesto of the Communist Party*. Marx and Engels, *Selected Works* (Moscow), I, 101.
15. Marx and Engels, Preface to the German edition of 1872 of *Manifesto of the Communist Party, Selected Works* (Moscow), I, 98.
16. Engels, "Marx und die *Neue Rheinische Zeitung*" in *Der Sozialdemokrat*, No. 11 (March 13, 1884). *Werke*, XXI, 18.
17. Engels to Marx, November 27, 1851. *Werke*, XXVII, 373.
18. Marx to Engels, March 31, 1851. *Werke*, XXVII, 226–27.
19. Marx to Engels, February 27, 1852. *Werke*, XXVIII, 30.
20. Marx to Engels, April 12, 1855. *Werke*, XXVIII, 444.

21. Marx to Engels, January 21, 1859. *Werke,* XXIX, 358.
22. Marx, Preface to *A Contribution to the Critique of Political Economy,* January 1859. Marx and Engels, *Selected Works* (Moscow), I, 503.
23. Marx, "General Rules of the International Workingmen's Association," 1871. *Selected Works* (Moscow), II, 19.
24. Marx, "Vierter jährlicher Bericht des Generalrates der Internationalen Arbeiter-Assoziation," London, September 1, 1868. *Werke,* XVI, 322.
25. Marx to Engels, July 29, 1868. *Werke,* XXXII, 128.
26. Marx to Engels, March 13, 1865. *Werke,* XXXI, 100.
27. Marx, Interview in *The World* (New York), July 18, 1871.
28. Marx to Friedrich Bolte, London, February 12, 1873. *Werke,* XXXIII, 565.
29. Notes for a speech by Marx on the secret societies, September 22, 1871. *Werke,* XVII, 655.
30. Marx to Engels, May 7, 1867. *Werke,* XXXI, 296.
31. Marx to Engels, June 22, 1867. *Selected Correspondence* (New York), 221.
32. Marx to Ludwig Kugelmann, April 12, 1871. Karl Marx, *Letters to Doctor Kugelmann* (New York: International Publishers, 1934), 123.
33. Marx to Ludwig Kugelmann, April 17, 1871. *Ibid.,* 125.
34. Notes for a speech by Marx on the political action of the working class, September 20, 1871. *Werke,* XVII, 650–51.
35. Marx to Friedrich Adolf Sorge, September 27, 1873. Marx and Engels, *Selected Correspondence* (Moscow: Progress Publishers, 1965), 286.
36. Marx to Engels, April 8, 1882. *Werke,* XXXV, 54.
37. Engels, "Speech at the Graveside of Karl Marx." *Selected Works* (New York), 453.
38. *Ibid.,* 435–36.
39. Marx, *Nationalökonomie und Philosophie* (Cologne: Kiepenheuer und Witsch, 1950), 146, 148–49.
40. Marx, "Speech at the Anniversary of the *People's Paper,*" April 14, 1856. *Selected Works* (Moscow), I, 500.
41. Marx and Engels, *Die Heilige Familie,* Ch. IV, 1845. *Werke,* II, 37.
42. Marx, "Zur Kritik der Hegelschen Rechtsphilosophie, Einleitung." *Werke,* I, 385.
43. *Manifesto of the Communist Party. Selected Works* (Moscow), I, 119.
44. "Speech at the Anniversary of the *People's Paper.*" *Selected Works* (Moscow), I, 501.
45. Engels, footnote to the English edition of the *Manifesto of the Communist Party,* 1888. *Selected Works* (Moscow), I, 108.
46. *Manifesto of the Communist Party. Selected Works* (Moscow), I, 117.
47. *Ibid.,* 118.
48. Engels, "Das Fest der Nationen in London 1845–1846." *Werke,* II, 614.

49. Engels, "Den tschechischen Genossen zu ihrer Maifeier," April 8, 1893. *Werke,* XXII, 403.

50. *Manifesto of the Communist Party. Selected Works* (Moscow), I, 118.

51. Marx, *The Eighteenth Brumaire of Louis Bonaparte. Selected Works* (Moscow), I, 202.

52. Marx to Engels, April 16, 1856. *Selected Correspondence* (New York), 87.

53. Engels, "Die europäischen Arbeiter im Jahre 1877," March 1878. *Werke,* XIX, 132.

54. Engels, *The Peasant Question in France and Germany. Selected Works* (New York), 634.

55. Marx and Engels, *Die Heilige Familie,* Ch. IV, 1842–43. *Werke,* II, 38.

56. Engels, *On the History of the Communist League. Selected Works* (New York), 443.

57. Marx and Engels, "Address of the Central Committee to the Communist League." *Selected Works* (Moscow), I, 179.

58. *Manifesto of the Communist Party. Selected Works* (Moscow), I, 119–20.

59. Karl Marx to Ferdinand Freiligrath, February 29, 1860. *Werke,* XXX, 490, 495.

60. Karl Marx to Friedrich Bolte, November 23, 1871. *Selected Works* (Moscow), II, 423–24.

61. Karl Marx to Wilhelm Blos, November 10, 1877. *Selected Correspondence* (Moscow), XXXIV, 310.

62. Engels, "An den Sängerverein des Kommunistischen Arbeiterbildungsvereins," November 28, 1891. *Selected Correspondence* (Moscow), XXII, 264.

63. Engels to J. P. Becker, April 1, 1880. *Selected Correspondence* (New York), 381.

64. "Die europäischen Arbeiter im Jahre 1877," March 1878. *Werke,* XIX, 124.

65. Marx and Engels, "Ein Komplott gegen die Internationale Arbeiter-Assoziation," April–July 1873. *Werke,* XVIII, 346.

66. *On the History of the Communist League. Selected Works* (New York), 446.

67. Engels to Karl Kautsky, February 1891. Included after the *Critique of the Gotha Program* (East Berlin: Verlag Neuer Weg, 1945), Supplement, 54.

68. Engels to Friedrich Adolf Sorge, August 9, 1890. *Werke,* XXXVII, 440.

69. Engels to August Bebel, November 19, 1892. *Werke,* XXXVIII, 517.

70. Engels to August Bebel, May 1–2, 1891. *Werke,* XXXVIII, 94.

71. Engels to Minna Kautsky, November 26, 1885. *Selected Correspondence* (Moscow), 390.

Notes

72. Engels to Margaret Harkness, early April 1888. *Selected Correspondence* (Moscow), 401.
73. Engels to Marx, February 13, 1851. *Werke*, XXVII, 189–90.
74. *Manifesto of the Communist Party*. *Selected Works* (Moscow), I, 137.
75. "Address of the Central Committee to the Communist League," 1850. *Selected Works* (Moscow), I, 177–78.
76. Engels, Supplement to the Preface of 1870 for the third edition of *The Peasant War in Germany*, 1874. *Selected Works* (Moscow), II, 170.
77. Marx, "Inaugural Address of the International Workingmen's Association," 1864. *Selected Works* (Moscow), II, 18.
78. Marx, "First Address of the General Council of the International Workingmen's Association on the Franco-Prussian War," July 23, 1870. *Selected Works* (Moscow), II, 193.
79. Engels, *Anti-Dühring* (Moscow: Foreign Languages Publishing House, 1959), 239.
80. Engels, "Die auswärtige Politik des russischen Zarentums," December 1889–February 1890. *Werke*, XXII, 45, 47.
81. Engels, "Kann Europa abrüsten?" February 1893. *Werke*, XXII, 371, 373.
82. Marx, "Instructions for the Delegates of the Provisional Central Council," 1867. *Selected Works* (Moscow), II, 78.
83. Engels, Supplement to the Preface of 1870 for the third edition of *The Peasant War in Germany*, 1874. *Selected Works* (Moscow), II, 170.
84. Engels to Marx, April 29, 1870. *Werke*, XXXII, 498.
85. Engels, Supplement to the Preface of 1870 for the third edition of *The Peasant War in Germany*, 1874. *Selected Works* (Moscow), II, 170.
86. *Manifesto of the Communist Party*. *Selected Works* (Moscow), I, 124.
87. Engels, "Eine polnische Proklamation," 1875. *Werke*, XVIII, 527.
88. Engels, "Reden über Polen," November 29, 1847. *Werke*, IV, 417.
89. Engels to Vera Ivanovna Zasulitch, April 3, 1890. *Werke*, XXXVII, 374.
90. Engels, "Über den Antisemitismus," *Arbeiter-Zeitung*, May 9, 1890. *Werke*, XXII, 49–50.
91. Engels, *The Role of Force in History* (New York: International Publishers, 1968), 30.
92. Engels, Preface to the Polish edition of the *Manifesto of the Communist Party of 1892*. *Selected Works* (Moscow), I, 105.
93. See, for example, Karl Marx, "Konfidentielle Mitteilung," March 28, 1870. *Werke*, XVI, 416–17.
94. See, for example, "Reden über Polen," November 29, 1847. *Werke*, IV, 416–18.
95. Marx, Review from *Neue Rheinische Zeitung*, January–February

1850. Marx and Engels, *On Colonialism* (Moscow: Foreign Languages Publishing House, no date), 14.

96. Marx, "Future Results of British Rule in India." *Selected Works* (Moscow), I, 498.

97. Engels to Minna Kautsky, September 12, 1882. *Selected Correspondence* (New York), 399.

98. Engels, "On Social Relations in Russia," 1894. *Selected Works* (Moscow), II, 387.

99. Marx, "Comments on Bakunin's Book *Statehood and Anarchy.*" *Selected Works* (Moscow), II, 411–12.

100. Marx, Preface to *The Critique of Political Economy,* 1859. *Selected Works* (Moscow), I, 504.

101. Engels, *The Housing Question: III. Selected Works* (Moscow), II, 278.

102. Engels, *Socialism: Utopian and Scientific. Selected Works* (New York), 431.

103. Marx and Engels, *The German Ideology* (New York: International Publishers, 1947), 24.

104. "On Social Relations in Russia." *Selected Works* (Moscow), 11, 389.

105. Marx and Engels, Reviews from the *Neue Rheinische Zeitung; Politisch-Ökonomische Revue,* No. 4, April 1850. *Werke,* VII, 273.

106. Engels, "Program of the Blanquist Commune Emigrants" (Article II from *Flüchtlingsliteratur*). *Selected Works* (Moscow), II, 381.

107. *The German Ideology,* p. 25.

108. *Manifesto of the Communist Party. Selected Works* (Moscow), I, 125.

109. Engels, *Principles of Communism,* 1847. *Selected Works* (Moscow), I, 91–92.

110. Marx, *The Class Struggles in France, 1848–1850. Selected Works* (Moscow), I, 213, 237.

111. "Speech at the Anniversary of the *People's Paper.*" *Selected Works* (Moscow), I, 501.

112. "Inaugural Address of the International Workingmen's Association," 1864. *Selected Works* (Moscow), II, 18.

113. Marx, "The Hague Congress," 1872. *Selected Works* (Moscow), II, 293–94.

114. Engels to Minna Kautsky, September 12, 1882. *Selected Correspondence* (New York), 399.

115. *Principles of Communism. Selected Works* (Moscow), I, 92.

116. "The Hague Congress." *Selected Works* (Moscow), II, 292–93.

117. *Principles of Communism. Selected Works* (Moscow), I, 89.

118. *Manifesto of the Communist Party. Selected Works* (Moscow), 118, 137.

119. *Anti-Dühring,* 234.

120. *Loc. cit.*
121. Marx to Ludwig Kugelmann, April 12, 1871. *Selected Correspondence* (New York), 309.
122. "The Hague Congress." *Selected Works* (Moscow), II, 293.
123. *Loc. cit.*
124. Marx, "Konspekt der Reichstagsdebatte über das Sozialistengesetz, 1878." *Werke,* XXXIV, 498.
125. Only Germany, where "the government is practically omnipotent, and the Parliament and all other representative bodies are without real power," was excluded from this possibility. See also Engels, *Zur Kritik des sozialdemokratischen Programmentwurfs,* 1891. *Werke,* XXII, 234.
126. Engels, Interview with a correspondent of the newspaper *Le Figaro,* May 8, 1893. *Werke,* XXII, 542–43.
127. *Manifesto of the Communist Party. Selected Works* (Moscow), I, 120.
128. *The Class Struggles in France, 1848–1850. Selected Works* (Moscow), I, 281.
129. Marx to Joseph Weydemeyer, March 5, 1882. *Selected Correspondence* (New York), 57.
130. *The Housing Question: III. Selected Works* (Moscow), II, 355.
131. Marx, *Critique of the Gotha Program* (New York: International Publishers, 1966), 18.
132. Engels, "Die Kommunisten und Karl Heinzen," second article in *Deutsche Brüssler-Zeitung,* No. 80, October 7, 1847. *Werke,* IV, 317.
133. *Principles of Communism. Selected Works* (Moscow), I, 90.
134. Engels, in *The Democratic Review,* March 1850.
135. Marx in the New York *Daily Tribune,* August 25, 1852.
136. Marx, *The Civil War in France. Selected Works* (Moscow), II, 223.
137. Engels, Introduction to Karl Marx, *The Civil War in France. Selected Works* (Moscow), II, 189.
138. *The Civil War in France. Ibid.,* II, 220.
139. Introduction to Karl Marx, *The Civil War in France. Ibid.,* II, 187.
140. *Ibid.,* 187–88.
141. *Manifesto of the Communist Party. Selected Works* (Moscow), I, 126.
142. *The Housing Question: III. Selected Works* (Moscow), II, 373.
143. *Principles of Communism. Selected Works* (Moscow), I, 91. A similar though shorter form of the transitional measures, which includes the elimination of child labor and the introduction of polytechnic education, is found in the *Manifesto of the Communist Party. Selected Works* (Moscow), I, 127. ("Combination of education with industrial production.")
144. Engels, Afterword to *On Social Relations in Russia. Selected Works* (Moscow), II, 401.
145. *The Housing Question: III. Selected Works* (Moscow), II, 370.

146. *The Peasant Question in France and Germany. Selected Works* (New York), 649.
147. *Ibid.*, 644–45.
148. *Manifesto of the Communist Party. Selected Works* (Moscow), I, 127.
149. *Principles of Communism. Ibid.*, I, 90.
150. Engels, Introduction to Karl Marx, *Wage Labor and Capital,* 1891. *Ibid.*, I, 149.
151. Engels, *Program of the Blanquist Commune Emigrants. Ibid.*, II, 385.
152. Engels, *Karl Marx. Selected Works* (New York), 376–77.
153. Engels, "Über die Assoziation der Zukunft," 1884. *Werke,* XXI, 391.
154. *Principles of Communism. Selected Works* (Moscow), I, 94.
155. *Anti-Dühring,* 384.
156. *Critique of the Gotha Program. Selected Works* (New York), 323.
157. Karl Marx, *Capital* (Chicago: Charles H. Kerr and Co., 1909), III, Ch. XXVII, 520.
158. *Ibid.*, III, Ch. XLVIII, 954.
159. Marx, *The Nationalization of the Land. Selected Works* (Moscow), II, 290.
160. Engels, *The Origin of the Family, Private Property, and the State. Selected Works* (New York), 589.
161. Introduction to Karl Marx, *The Civil War in France. Selected Works* (Moscow), II, 186.
162. *Capital,* III, Ch. VI, 144.
163. *The Nationalization of the Land. Selected Works* (Moscow), II, 288, 290.
164. Engels to August Bebel, January 1886. *Briefe an Bebel* (East Berlin: Dietz Verlag, 1958), 123.
165. *Socialism: Utopian and Scientific. Selected Works* (New York), 429.
166. *Anti-Dühring,* 409.
167. *Socialism: Utopian and Scientific. Selected Works* (New York), 432.
168. Engels, *Zur Kritik des sozialdemokratischen Programmentwurfs,* 1891. *Werke,* XXII, 232.
169. *Capital,* III, Ch. XLIX, 992.
170. Engels, "An den Internationalen Kongress sozialistischer Studenten," December 1893. *Werke,* XXII, 415. See also Engels' Interview with a correspondent of *Le Figaro,* May 8, 1893. *Werke,* XXII, 543.
171. *The German Ideology,* 190. See also Karl Marx, *Selected Works* (New York), 376; also *Critique of the Gotha Program, Selected Works* (New York), 324–25.
172. *Principles of Communism. Selected Works* (Moscow), I, 92.
173. Marx, "The Poverty of Philosophy," in Selsam, Goldway, and Martel, eds., *Dynamics of Social Change* (New York: International Publishers, 1970), 333.

174. *Manifesto of the Communist Party. Selected Works* (Moscow), I, 127.
175. Engels to August Bebel, March 18–28, 1875. *Selected Correspondence* (New York), 336–37.
176. *Socialism: Utopian and Scientific. Selected Works* (New York), 430.
177. Marx and Engels, "Fictitious Splits in the International." *Selected Works* (Moscow), II, 285.
178. Engels, "Zum Tode von Karl Marx," March 1883. *Werke,* XIX, 344.
179. *The Origin of the Family, Private Property, and the State. Selected Works* (New York), 589.
180. Introduction to Karl Marx, *The Civil War in France,* 1891. *Selected Works* (Moscow), II, 189. For further reading on the "withering away of the state" see Engels, "On Authority." *Selected Works* (Moscow), II, 379, and *Anti-Dühring,* 387.
181. *Principles of Communism. Selected Works* (Moscow), I, 93.
182. *The Housing Question: I. Ibid.,* II, 317.
183. *Anti-Dühring,* 409–10.
184. *The Housing Question: III. Selected Works* (Moscow), II, 368.
185. *The German Ideology,* 44.
186. "Debatte über die Pressefreiheit," in *Rheinische Zeitung,* May 14, 1842. *Werke,* I, 60.
187. *The German Ideology,* 22.
188. *Capital,* I, 534. "Machinery and Modern Industry."
189. *Principles of Communism. Selected Works* (Moscow), I, 93.
190. *Capital,* I, 534.
191. *Ibid.,* I, 529–30.
192. *Ibid.,* I, 534.
193. Engels, *The Condition of the Working Class in England* (Stanford, Calif.: Stanford University Press, 1968), 133.
194. *Anti-Dühring,* 406.
195. *Principles of Communism. Selected Works* (Moscow), I, 94.
196. *Manifesto of the Communist Party. Ibid.,* I, 124.
197. *The Origin of the Family, Private Property, and the State. Selected Works* (New York), 511.
198. *Anti-Dühring,* 436–37.
199. Engels, *Program of the Blanquist Commune Emigrants. Selected Works* (Moscow), II, 384.
200. *Critique of the Gotha Program. Selected Works* (New York), 324–25.
201. *The Civil War in France. Selected Works* (Moscow), II, 224.
202. *The Housing Question: I. Ibid.,* II, 317.
203. *The Housing Question: III. Ibid.,* II, 373.
204. *The Origin of the Family, Private Property, and the State. Selected Works* (New York), 517.
205. "Reden über Polen," November 29, 1847. *Werke,* IV, 416.
206. *Manifesto of the Communist Party. Selected Works* (Moscow), I, 125.
207. Marx, "First Address on the Franco-Prussian War." *Ibid.,* II, 193–94.

208. "Den tschechischen Genossen zu ihrer Maifeier," April 1893. *Werke,* XXII, 403.
209. Engels, "An den Nationalrat der französischen Arbeiterpartei zum 23. Jahrestag der Pariser Kommune," March 25, 1894. *Werke,* XXII, 443.
210. Engels, *The New Moral World,* November 4, 1843. *Werke,* I, 487.
211. Letters from the *Deutsch-Französische Jahrbücher* (to Arnold Ruge), 1843. *Werke,* I, 344–45. Also in Selsam, Goldway, and Martel, eds., *Dynamics of Social Change,* title page.
212. Engels, "Die Kommunisten und Karl Heinzen," second article, *Deutsche Brüssler-Zeitung,* October 7, 1847. *Werke,* IV, 321.
213. Engels to Florence Kelley Wischnewetsky, December 28, 1886. *Selected Correspondence* (New York), 453.
214. Marx, *Bekenntnisse. Werke,* XXXI, 597.
215. Engels refers to this statement of Marx; see his reply to the *Sächsische Arbeiter-Zeitung,* September 13, 1890. *Werke,* XXII, 69.
216. See the references in the letters of Engels to Eduard Bernstein, November 2–3, 1882 (*Werke,* XXXIII, 388), and to Paul Lafargue, August 27, 1890 (*Werke,* XXXVII, 450).
217. Engels to Florence Kelley Wischnewetsky, December 28, 1886. *Selected Correspondence* (New York), 453.
218. Engels to Paul Lafargue, August 27, 1890. *Werke,* XXXVII, 383.
219. Engels to Conrad Schmidt, April 12, 1890. *Ibid.,* XXXVII, 383.
220. Engels to J. Bloch, September 12, 1890. *Selected Correspondence* (New York), 477.
221. Engels to Friedrich Adolph Sorge, March 15, 1883. *Ibid.,* 413.

☐ **Chapter 2**

All quotations from Lenin are taken from the English edition of Lenin's *Collected Works* (in 44 volumes), published by Foreign Languages Publishing House and Progress Publishers, Moscow. The translation is from the fourth Russian complete edition, published by the State Publishing House for Political Literature, Moscow, 1960–66.

1. V. I. Lenin, "Lecture on the 1905 Revolution," January 9 (22), 1917, *Collected Works,* XXII, 253.
2. Lenin, "The Bolsheviks Must Assume Power," September 12–14 (25–27), 1917, XXVI, 21.
3. Lenin, "Letter to the Central Committee, the Moscow and Petrograd Committees, and the Bolshevik Members of the Petrograd and Moscow Soviets," October 1 (14), 1917, XXVI, 141.
4. John Reed, *Ten Days That Shook the World* (New York: Boni and Liveright, 1919), 125–26. In a newer edition of the book (New York:

International Publishers, 1967), the reference to Lenin's shabby clothes and too-long trousers is deleted.

5. Friedrich Engels, *The Peasant War in Germany* (London: George Allen & Unwin, 1926), Ch. VI, 135.
6. Lenin, *What Is to Be Done?* 1901–2, V, 422.
7. *Ibid.*, 446.
8. *Ibid.*, 464.
9. *Ibid.*, 452.
10. *Ibid.*, 472.
11. *Ibid.*, 464.
12. *Ibid.*, 466.
13. *Ibid.*, 469.
14. *Ibid.*, 467.
15. Lenin, "Second Speech in the Discussion on the Party Rules" to the Second Congress of the RSDLP, August 2 (15), 1903, XI, 504.
16. Lenin, "Party Organization and Party Literature," November 13 (26), 1905, X, 46.
17. *Ibid.*, 47.
18. Lenin, "Freedom to Criticize and Unity of Action," May 20 (June 2), 1906, X, 443.
19. Lenin, "Terms of Admission into the Communist International," July 1920, XXXI, 210.
20. Lenin, *State and Revolution,* 1917 (New York: Vanguard Press, 1929), 133.
21. Lenin, " 'Left-Wing' Communism—An Infantile Disorder," April–May 1920, XXXI, 23.
22. Lenin, "Preliminary Draft Resolution of the Tenth Congress of the RCP on Party Unity," March 1921, XXXII, 243.
23. Lenin, "Two Tactics of Social Democracy in the Democratic Revolution," June–July 1905, V, 362.
24. *What Is to Be Done?* 1901–2, V, 362.
25. " 'Left-Wing' Communism—An Infantile Disorder," XXXI, 70–71.
26. Lenin, "Political Report of the Central Committee" to the Extraordinary Seventh Congress of the RCP(B), March 7, 1918, XXVII, 101.
27. Lenin, "On Compromises," September 17 (30), 1917. XXV.
28. " 'Left-Wing' Communism—An Infantile Disorder," XXXI, 95.
29. *Ibid.*, 37–38.
30. *Ibid.*, 28.
31. *Ibid.*, 53.
32. *Ibid.*, 55.
33. *Ibid.*, 59.
34. Lenin, "We Have Paid Too Much," April 9, 1922, XXXIII, 333.
35. " 'Left-Wing' Communism—An Infantile Disorder," XXXI, 96.
36. *Ibid.*, 28.

37. Lenin, "Speech on the Agrarian Question" to the First Congress of Peasants' Deputies, May 22 (June 4), 1917, XXIV, 173.
38. Lenin, "Speech to the Second All-Russia Conference of Organizers Responsible for Rural Work," May 22 (June 4), 1917, XXIV, 173.
39. Lenin, "The Immediate Tasks of the Soviet Government," March–April 1918, XXVII, 274.
40. " 'Left-Wing' Communism—An Infantile Disorder," XXXI, 92.
41. *Ibid.*, 103.
42. Lenin, "Inflammable Material in World Politics," July 23 (August 5), 1908, XV, 182–88.
43. Lenin, "Events in the Balkans and in Persia," October 16 (29), 1908, XV, 220–30.
44. Lenin, "The Awakening of Asia," May 7 (20), 1913, XIX, 86.
45. Lenin, "The Historical Destiny of the Doctrine of Karl Marx," March 1 (14), 1913, XVIII, 585.
46. Lenin, "The Right of Nations to Self-Determination," February–May 1914, XX, 406.
47. *Ibid.*, 397.
48. Lenin, "The Revolutionary Proletariat and the Right of Nations to Self-Determination," October 16 (29), 1915, XXI, 413.
49. Lenin, "The Socialist Revolution and the Right of Nations to Self-Determination," January–February 1916, XXII, 149.
50. Lenin, "A Caricature of Marxism and Imperialist Economism," August–October 1916, XXIII, 60.
51. "The Socialist Revolution and the Right of Nations to Self-Determination," XXII, 149.
52. Lenin, "Preliminary Draft Theses for the National and the Colonial Questions" for the Second Congress of the Communist International, June 1920, XXXI, 149–51.
53. Lenin, "Report of the Commission on the National and the Colonial Questions" to the Second Congress of the Communist International, July 26, 1920, XXXI, 241–43.
54. *Ibid.*, 244.
55. Lenin, "Speech Delivered at a Meeting of Activists of the Moscow Organization of the RCP(B)," December 6, 1920, XXXI, 453.
56. Lenin, "On the Slogan for a United States of Europe," August 23 (September 5), 1915, XXI, 341.
57. Lenin, "The Conference of the RSDLP Groups Ahead," February 19 (March 4), 1915, XXI, 159.
58. Lenin, "A Caricature of Marxism and Imperialist Economism," August–October 1916, XXIII, 33.
59. *Ibid.*
60. Lenin, "The Proletarian Revolution and the Renegade Kautsky," October–November 1918, XXVIII, 286.

61. Lenin, "Revision of the Party Program," October 6–8 (19–21), 1917, XXVI, 162.
62. Lenin, "Socialism and War," July–August 1915, XXI, 299. Lenin wrote this work with Zinoviev, who was shot during Stalin's regime. Zinoviev's co-authorship is not acknowledged in the Soviet Union today.
63. Lenin, "Speech in the Polytechnical Museum," August 23, 1918, XXVIII, 69.
64. "Socialism and War," XXI, 299–300.
65. Lenin, "Letter to American Workers," August 20, 1918, XXVIII, 69.
66. "Socialism and War," XXI, 300–301.
67. "Revision of the Party Program," XXVI, 162.
68. *Ibid.*
69. Lenin, "The Junius Pamphlet," July 1916, XXII, 310.
70. "Letter to American Workers," XXVIII, 63.
71. "Revision of the Party Program," XXVI, 162.
72. "The Junius Pamphlet," XXII, 309.
73. Lenin, "Imperialism, the Highest Stage of Capitalism," January–June 1916, XXII, 191.
74. *Ibid.,* 269.
75. *Ibid.,* 191.
76. Lenin, "The Military Program of the Proletarian Revolution," September 1916, XXIII, 78.
77. *Ibid.*
78. *Ibid.,* 80.
79. "Political Report of the Central Committee" to the Extraordinary Seventh Congress of the RCP(B), March 7, 1918, XXVII, 95.
80. "Letter to American Workers," XXVIII, 75.
81. Lenin, "Report on the Tactics of the RCP" to the Third Congress of the Communist International, July 5, 1921, XXXII, 479–80.
82. "Speech Delivered at a Meeting of Activists of the Moscow Organization of the RCP(B)," December 6, 1920, XXXI, 439–43.
83. Lenin, "Report on Concessions Delivered to the RCP(B) Group at the Eighth Congress of Soviets," December 21, 1920, XXXI, 466.
84. Lenin, "Report of the Central Committee" to the Eighth Congress of the RCP(B), XXIX, 457.
85. "Speech Delivered at a Meeting of Activists of the Moscow Organization of the RCP(B)," XXXI, 457.
86. Lenin, "Answers to Questions Put by a Chicago *Daily News* Correspondent," October 27, 1919, XXX, 51.
87. Lenin, "In Reply to Questions Put by Karl Weigard, Berlin Correspondent of Universal Service," February 18, 1920, XXX, 365.
88. "Speech Delivered at a Meeting of Activists of the Moscow Organization of the RCP(B)," XXXI, 447.
89. Lenin, "To the American Workers," September 23, 1919, XXX, 39.

90. Lenin, "Report to the Party Groups at the Eighth Congress of Soviets," December 21, 1920, XXXI, 470.
91. Lenin, "The Home and Foreign Policy of the Republic," Report to the Ninth All-Russia Congress of Soviets, December 23, 1921, XXXIII, 150.
92. Lenin, "On the Slogan for a United States of Europe," XXI, 342.
93. "The Military Program of the Proletarian Revolution," September 1916, XXIII, 79.
94. Lenin, *Two Tactics of Social Democracy in the Democratic Revolution,* especially Chs. V and VI, IX, 44–61.
95. Lenin, "Social Democracy's Attitude Toward the Peasant Movement," September 1 (14), 1905, IX, 327.
96. Lenin, "The Collapse of the Second International," May–June 1915, XXI, 213–14.
97. *Ibid.,* 214.
98. " 'Left-Wing' Communism—An Infantile Disorder," XXXI, 84–85.
99. Lenin, "A Retrograde Trend in Russian Social Democracy," 1899, IV, 276.
100. *State and Revolution,* 129.
101. Lenin, "The Tasks of the Revolution," September 26–27 (October 9–10), 1917, XXV, 67–68.
102. Lenin, "Advice of an Onlooker," October 8 (21), 1917, XXVI, 179.
103. Lenin, "Marxism and Insurrection," September 13–14 (26–27), 1917, XXVI, 23–24.
104. "Advice of an Onlooker," October 8 (21), 1917, XXVI, 180.
105. Lenin, "The Immediate Tasks of the Soviet Government," March–April 1918, XXVII, 49.
106. Lenin, "Letters on Tactics," April 8–13 (21–26), 1917, XXIV, 49.
107. *State and Revolution,* 141.
108. Lenin, "A Caricature of Marxism and Imperialist Economism," August–October 1916, XXIII, 69.
109. *State and Revolution,* 193.
110. *Ibid.,* 133.
111. Lenin, "The Immediate Tasks of the Soviet Government," XXVII, 263–68.
112. Lenin, "Six Theses on the Immediate Tasks of the Soviet Government," April 30–May 3, 1918, XXVII, 316.
113. "The Proletarian Revolution and the Renegade Kautsky," XXVIII, 236.
114. Lenin, "Foreword to the Published Speech 'Deception of the People With Slogans of Freedom and Equality,' " June 23, 1919, XXIX, 381.
115. "The Immediate Tasks of the Soviet Government," XXVII, 265.
116. Lenin, "Report on the Work of the All-Russia Central Executive Committee and the Council of People's Commissars," February 2, 1920, XXX, 328.

117. Lenin, "Greetings to the Hungarian Workers," May 27, 1919, XXIX, 391.
118. Lenin, "Speech to the Third All-Russia Trade Union Congress," April 7, 1920, XXIX, 391.
119. *State and Revolution,* 133.
120. " 'Left-Wing' Communism—An Infantile Disorder," XXXI, 44–45.
121. *Ibid.,* 47–48.
122. Lenin, "Economics and Politics in the Era of the Dictatorship of the Proletariat," October 30, 1919, XXX, 107.
123. *Ibid.,* 115.
124. The well-known Russian phrase, "Kto kovo?" is sometimes translated as "Who will come out on top?" See Lenin, "The New Economic Policy and the Tasks of the Political Education Departments," October 17, 1921, XXXIII, 66.
125. "Greetings to the Hungarian Workers," XXIX, 388.
126. "The Proletarian Revolution and the Renegade Kautsky," XXVIII, 254.
127. Lenin, "Speech Against Bukharin's Amendment to the Resolution on the Party Program" at the Seventh Congress of the RCP(B), March 8, 1918, XXVII, 148.
128. Lenin, "Speech to the Third All-Russia Trade Union Congress," April 7, 1920, XXX, 513.
129. *Ibid.,* 508.
130. Lenin, "Speech Delivered at the First Congress of Agricultural Communes and Agricultural Artels," December 4, 1919, XXX, 202.
131. Lenin, "The Chief Task of Our Day," March 11, 1918, XXVII, 161.
132. Lenin, "Our Foreign and Domestic Position and the Tasks of the Party," November 21, 1920, XXXI, 419.
133. "Report on the Work of the Council of People's Commissars" to the Eighth All-Russia Congress of Soviets, XXXI, 516.
134. Lenin, "Speech at the First Congress of Economic Councils," May 26, 1918, XXVII, 412.
135. Lenin, "The Achievements and Difficulties of the Soviet Government," March–April 1919, XXIX, 74.
136. Lenin, "Speech Delivered at the First All-Russia Conference on Party Work in the Countryside," November 18, 1919, XXX, 147.
137. Lenin, "Speech to the Third All-Russia Congress of Water Transport Workers," March 15, 1920, XXX, 429–31.
138. Lenin, "The Role and Functions of the Trade Unions Under the New Economic Policy," January 12, 1922, XXXIII, 194.
139. Lenin, "Report on the Activities of the Council of People's Commissars" to the Third All-Russia Congress of Soviets, January 11 (24), 1918, XXVI, 458.
140. Lenin, "Reply to a Peasant's Question," February 14, 1919, XXXVI, 501.

141. Lenin, "Speech at the Eighth Congress of the RCP(B) on Work in the Countryside," March 23, 1919, XXIX, 210–12.
142. "Speech Delivered at the First All-Russia Conference on Party Work in the Countryside," XXX, 146, 148, 150.
143. "Speech Delivered at the First Congress of Agricultural Communes and Agricultural Artels," XXX, 198.
144. Lenin, "Draft Resolution of the Central Committee, RCP(B), on Soviet Rule in the Ukraine," November 1919, XXX, 165.
145. Lenin, "Speech Closing the Debate on the Party Program" at the Eighth Congress of the RCP(B), March 19, 1919, XXIX, 194–95.
146. Lenin, "To the Communists of Turkestan," November 1919, XXX, 138.
147. "Draft Resolution of the Central Committee, RCP(B), on Soviet Rule in the Ukraine," XXX, 164.
148. Lenin, "The Constituent Assembly Elections and the Dictatorship of the Proletariat," December 16, 1919, XXX, 270–71.
149. Lenin, "Letter to the Workers and Peasants of the Ukraine à propos of the Victories over Denikin," December 28, 1919, XXX, 293, 296.
150. Telegram from Lenin to G. K. Orjonikidze, April 2, 1920, XXX, 494.
151. Lenin, "The Question of Nationalities and Autonomization," December 31, 1922, XXXVI, 608–9.
152. Lenin, "Memo to the Political Bureau on Combating Dominant Nation Chauvinism," October 6, 1922, XXXIII, 372.
153. *State and Revolution,* 201, 204–5.
154. Lenin, "Can the Bolsheviks Retain State Power?" October 1917, XXVI, 118.
155. Lenin, "The Immediate Tasks of the Soviet Government," March–April 1918, XXVII, 268–69.
156. Lenin, "Political Report of the Central Committee of the RCP(B)" to the Eleventh Congress of the RCP(B), March 27, 1922, XXXIII, 308.
157. Lenin, "Speech at the Fourth Session of the All-Russia Central Executive Committee, Ninth Convocation," October 31, 1922, XXXIII, 393.
158. Lenin, "Report on the Work of the All-Russia Central Executive Committee and the Council of People's Commissars, Delivered at the First Session of the All-Russia Central Executive Committee, Seventh Convocation," February 2, 1920, XXX, 328–29.
159. Lenin, "On Co-operation," January 6, 1923, XXXIII, 467–69.
160. Lenin, "Fourth Anniversary of the October Revolution," October 14, 1921, XXXIII, 58.
161. "The New Economic Policy and the Tasks of the Political Education Departments," XXXIII, 70.
162. "The Role and Functions of the Trade Unions Under the New Economic Policy," XXXIII, 188, 190, 193.
163. Lenin to G. Myasnikov, August 5, 1921, XXXII, 506.

164. Lenin, "How to Ensure the Success of the Constituent Assembly," XXV, 377–78.
165. Lenin, "Speech at a Rally and Concert for the All-Russia Extraordinary Commission Staff," November 7, 1918, XXVIII, 170.
166. Lenin, "Concluding Speech on the Report of the All-Russia Central Executive Committee and the Council of People's Commissars" at the Seventh All-Russia Congress of Soviets, December 6, 1919, XXX, 234.
167. Lenin, "Speech to Activists of the Extraordinary Commission," November 7, 1918, XXVIII, 179.
168. Lenin, "Report on the Work of the All-Russia Central Executive Committee and the Council of People's Commissars Delivered at the First Session of the All-Russia Central Executive Committee, Seventh Convocation," February 2, 1920, XXX, 327–28.
169. Lenin, "The Home and Foreign Policy of the Republic," Report to the Ninth All-Russia Congress of Soviets, December 23, 1921, XXXIII, 176.
170. Lenin, "Closing Speech on the Political Report of the Central Committee of the RCP(B)," March 28, 1922, XXXIII, 313.
171. "Can the Bolsheviks Retain State Power?" XXVI, 111.
172. Lenin, "Speeches Concerning the Left Socialist-Revolutionaries' Questions" at the Meeting of the All-Russia Central Executive Committee, November 4 (17), 1917, XXVI, 289.
173. Lenin, "Report on the Right of Recall at a Meeting of the All-Russia Central Executive Committee," November 21 (December 4), 1917, XXVI, 339–40.
174. Lenin, "Reply to a Question from the Left Socialist-Revolutionaries" at the Meeting of the All-Russia Central Executive Committee, November 4 (17), XXVI, 288.
175. Lenin, "Speech Delivered at the Third All-Russia Trade Union Congress," April 7, 1920, XXX, 514–15.
176. Lenin, "Speech Delivered at a Meeting of Activists of the Moscow Organization of the RCP(B)," December 6, 1920, XXXI, 457.
177. Lenin, "Closing Speech on the Political Report of the Central Committee, RCP(B)" at the Eleventh Congress of the RCP(B), March 28, 1922, XXXIII, 310–24.
178. Lenin, "Report on the Review of the Program and on Changing the Name of the Party" to the Seventh Extraordinary Congress of the RCP(B), March 8, 1918, XXVII, 135.
179. Lenin, "Political Report of the Central Committee of the RCP(B), to the Eleventh Congress of the RCP(B)," March 27, 1922, XXXIII, 290.
180. Lenin, "The Tasks of the Proletariat in Our Revolution," April 10 (23), 1917, XXIV, 84.
181. Lenin, "Speech Delivered at the Third All-Russia Trade Union Congress," April 7, 1920, XXX, 506.
182. "Greetings to the Hungarian Workers," XXIX, 388.

183. "The Tasks of the Proletariat in Our Revolution," XXIV, 84–85.
184. Lenin, "A Great Beginning: Heroism of the Workers in the Rear, Communist Subbotniks," July 1919, XXIX, 420.
185. Lenin, "Report on Subbotniks," delivered to a Moscow City Conference of the RCP(B), December 20, 1919, XXX, 284–85.
186. *State and Revolution,* 200.
187. *Ibid.,* 206.
188. *Ibid.,* 200.
189. Lenin, "From the Destruction of the Old Social System to the Creation of the New," April 8, 1920, XXX, 517.
190. Lenin, "The Importance of Gold Now and After the Complete Victory of Socialism," November 5, 1921, XXXIII, 113.
191. Lenin, "Concluding Speech on the Report of the All-Russia Central Committee and the Council of People's Commissars" to the Seventh All-Russia Congress of Soviets, December 6, 1919, XXX, 240.
192. Lenin, "Report of the Central Committee" to the Ninth Congress of the RCP(B), March 29, 1920, XXX, 459.
193. "Fourth Anniversary of the October Revolution," XXXIII, 56–57.
194. Friedrich Engels, "Program of the Blanquist Commune Emigrants," June 1874. Marx and Engels, *Selected Works* (Moscow: Progress Publishers, 1969), II, 385.
195. Lenin, "Speech Closing the Debate on the Party Program" at the Eighth Congress of the RCP(B), March 19, 1919, XXIX, 192.
196. Lenin, "Speech Delivered at a Meeting Organized by the Moscow Committee of the RCP(B) in Honor of Lenin's Fiftieth Birthday," April 23, 1920, XXX, 526.
197. "The Importance of Gold Now and After the Complete Victory of Socialism," XXXIII, 109.
198. "The Home and Foreign Policy of the Republic," Report to the Ninth All-Russia Congress of Soviets, XXXIII, 166.
199. *Ibid.,* 175.
200. Lenin, "The International and Domestic Situation of the Soviet Republics," Speech at the All-Russia Congress of Metalworkers, March 6, 1922, XXXIII, 223.
201. "Political Report of the Central Committee of the RCP(B)" to the Eleventh Congress of the RCP(B), XXXIII, 291.
202. *Ibid.,* 308.
203. Lenin, "Five Years of the Russian Revolution and the Prospects of the World Revolution." Report to the Fourth Congress of the Communist International, November 13, 1922, XXXIII, 429.
204. "Report on the Review of the Program and on Changing the Name of the Party" to the Seventh Extraordinary Congress of the RCP(B), XXVII, 132, 135.
205. Lenin, "Alliance Between the Workers and the Working and Exploited Peasants," November 18 (December 1), 1917, XXVI, 334.

206. Lenin, "Report on the Activities of the Council of People's Commissars" to the Third All-Russia Congress of Soviets, January 11 (24), 1918, XXVI, 457.
207. Lenin, "To the Comrade Communists of Azerbaijan, Georgia, Armenia, Daghestan, and the Mountaineer Republic," April 14, 1921, XXVI, 457.
208. Lenin, "Our Revolution (à propos of N. Sukhanov's Notes)," Part II, January 17, 1923, XXXIII, 480.
209. "Report on the Party Program" to the Eighth Congress of the RCP(B), March 19, 1919, XXIX, 175.
210. Lenin, "The Third International and Its Place in History," April 15, 1919, XXIX, 311.
211. Lenin, "The Fight Against Kolchak," speech at a Conference of Moscow Factory Committees and Trade Unions, April 17, 1919 (newspaper report), XXIX, 322–23.
212. " 'Left-Wing' Communism—An Infantile Disorder," XXXI, 21.
213. Lenin, "Speech on the Italian Question" to the Third Congress of the Communist International, June 28, 1921, XXXII, 430–31.
214. Lenin, "Five Years of the Russian Revolution and the Prospects of the World Revolution," Report to the Fourth Congress of the Communist International, November 13, 1922, XXXIII, 430–31.
215. Rosa Luxemburg, "Organizational Questions of Russian Social Democracy," originally published in *Neue Zeit,* 1904, No. 2, 484–92, 529–35; in D. Howard, ed., *Selected Political Writings* (New York and London: Monthly Review Press, 1971), 295, 306.
216. Leon Trotsky, *Our Political Tasks* (Geneva, 1904), quoted in R. V. Daniels, ed., *A Documentary History of Communism* (New York: Vintage Books, 1960), I, 31.
217. R. V. Daniels, *The Conscience of the Revolution* (Cambridge, Mass.: Harvard University Press, 1960), 45.
218. *Ibid.,* 60.
219. *Ibid.,* 66.
220. Karl Kautsky, *Terrorism and Communism,* trans. W. H. Kerridge (London: George Allen and Unwin, 1920), 209.
221. Rosa Luxemburg, "The Russian Revolution," in *Rosa Luxemburg Speaks* (New York: Pathfinder Press, 1970), 389.
222. *Ibid.,* 390–91.
223. *Ibid.*
224. *Ibid.*
225. *Ibid.,* 393–94.
226. Leon Trotsky, *My Life* (New York: Pathfinder Press, 1970), 503–4.
227. Quoted in R. V. Daniels, *The Conscience of the Revolution,* 85–86.
228. *Ibid.,* 114.
229. *Das Manifest der Arbeitergruppe der Russischen kommunistischen Partei* (Moscow: no publishing house given, February 1923), 9.

230. *Ibid.*, 20–21, 27.
231. Lenin, "The Trade Unions, the Present Situation, and Trotsky's Mistakes," December 30, 1920, XXXII, 24.
232. See many such references in Lenin, "The Work of the People's Commissariat for Education," February 7, 1921, XXXII, 123–32.
233. Lenin, "Speech at a Plenary Meeting of the Moscow Soviet Workers' and Peasants' Deputies," February 28, 1921, XXXII, 156.
234. Lenin, "Report on the Political Work of the Central Committee of the RCP(B)," March 8, 1921, XXXII, 190.
235. Lenin, "Summing-Up Speech on the Report of the Central Committee of the RCP(B)" to the Tenth Congress of the RCP(B), March 9, 1921, XXXII, 195.
236. *Ibid.*, 203.
237. Lenin, "The Question of Nationalities or 'Autonomization,'" December 30, 1922, XXXVI, 605–6.
238. Lenin, "The Conditions for Admitting New Members to the Party," Part II, March 26, 1922, XXXIII, 257.
239. Lenin, "Addition to the Letter of December 24, 1922," January 4, 1923, XXXVI, 596.

☐ **Chapter 3**

Quotations from Stalin's *Works* refer to the English edition (in 13 volumes), published by Foreign Languages Publishing House, Moscow, 1952–55. The translation is from the complete Russian edition published by the State Publishing House for Political Literature from 1946 to 1951.

1. J. V. Stalin, "On the Death of Lenin," January 26, 1924, *Works*, VI, 47.
2. Robert V. Daniels, *The Conscience of the Revolution* (Cambridge, Mass.: Harvard University Press, 1960), 268
3. V. I. Lenin, "Letter to the Congress," Part II, December 24, 1922, *Collected Works*, XXXVI, 595.
4. Stalin used this definition in a conversation with a group of Soviet writers in Maxim Gorky's apartment on October 26, 1932. It appears in no work of Stalin's but in a diary of his activities included in his collected works. See *Works*, XIII, 419.
5. Stalin, *The October Revolution and the Tactics of the Russian Communists*, December 17, 1924, *Works*, VI, 387.
6. *Ibid.*, 391.
7. Stalin, "Questions and Answers," speech delivered at Sverdlov University, June 9, 1925, *Works*, VII, 168.
8. Stalin, *Concerning Questions of Leninism*, January 25, 1926, *Works*, VIII, 69–70.

9. Stalin, *The Possibility of Building Socialism in Our Country,* February 10, 1926, *Works,* VIII, 103.
10. Stalin, *The Social-Democratic Deviation in Our Party,* November 1, 1926, *Works,* VIII, 261.
11. *Ibid.,* 293.
12. *Concerning Questions of Leninism, Works,* VIII, 79–80.
13. Stalin, "Once More on the Social-Democratic Deviation in Our Party." Report to the Seventh enlarged Plenum of the ECCI, December 7, 1926, *Works,* IX, 25.
14. *Concerning Questions of Leninism, Works,* VIII, 33.
15. Stalin, "Political Report of the Central Committee" to the Fourteenth Congress of the CPSU(B), December 18, 1925, *Works,* VII, 352. See also Stalin, *The Economic Situation of the Soviet Union and the Policy of the Party,* April 13, 1926, *Works,* VIII, 128.
16. Stalin, "Reply to the Discussion on the Political Report of the Central Committee" to the Fourteenth Congress of the CPSU(B), December 23, 1925, *Works,* VII, 386–87.
17. Stalin, "New Conditions—New Tasks in Economic Construction," June 23, 1931, *Works,* XIII, 59.
18. *Ibid.,* 62.
19. Stalin, "Talk with the German Author Emil Ludwig," December 13, 1931, *Works,* XIII, 120. Compare Stalin, "Report to the Seventeenth Party Congress on the Work of the Central Committee of the CPSU(B)," January 26, 1934, *Works,* XIII, 362.
20. Stalin, "To the First All-Union Conference of Proletarian Students," April 15, 1925, *Works,* VII, 86–87.
21. Stalin, "Concerning Questions of Agrarian Policy in the U.S.S.R.," December 27, 1929, *Works,* XIII, 152.
22. *Ibid.,* 173.
23. *Ibid.,* 177.
24. Stalin, "Concerning the Policy of Eliminating the Kulaks as a Class," January 21, 1930, *Works,* XII, 189.
25. *History of the Communist Party of the Soviet Union (Bolsheviks) —Short Course* (New York: International Publishers, 1939), 305.
26. Stalin, "The Right Deviation in the CPSU(B)," April 1929, *Works,* XII, 87–89.
27. Stalin, "The Results of the First Five-Year Plan." Report delivered to the Joint Plenum of the CC and CCC, CPSU(B), January 7, 1933, *Works,* XIII, 215.
28. Stalin, "Political Report of the Central Committee to the Sixteenth Congress of the CPSU(B)," June 27, 1930, *Works,* XII, 381.
29. "Talk with the German Author Emil Ludwig," *Works,* XIII, 107.
30. "The Results of the First Five-Year Plan," *Works,* XIII, 215.
31. Stalin, *The Foundations of Leninism,* April–May 1924, *Works,* VI, 177–84.

32. *Concerning Questions of Leninism, Works,* VIII, 34.
33. *The Foundations of Leninism, Works,* VI, 189–92.
34. "Political Report of the Central Committee" to the Fourteenth Congress of the CPSU(B), *Works,* VII, 352.
35. Stalin, "Interview with the First American Labor Delegation," September 9, 1927, *Works,* X, 106.
36. *Ibid.,* 120.
37. "The Right Deviation in the CPSU(B)," *Works,* XII, 69.
38. "Speech Delivered on August 5 [1927]" to the Joint Plenum of the CC and CCC of the CPSU(B), *Works,* X, 82.
39. "The Right Deviation in the CPSU(B)," *Works,* XII, 14.
40. *Ibid.,* 110.
41. "Against Vulgarizing the Slogan of Self-criticism," June 26, 1928, *Works,* XI, 133.
42. *Ibid.,* 134.
43. *Ibid.,* 139.
44. "The Right Deviation in the CPSU(B)," *Works,* XII, 13.
45. Stalin, "Report on the Work of the Central Committee to the Seventeenth Congress of the CPSU(B)," January 26, 1934, in *Leninism: Selected Writings* (New York: International Publishers, 1942), 349.
46. *Ibid.,* 358.
47. Stalin, *Mastering Bolshevism.* Report to the Plenum of the CC of the CPSU(B) on March 3, 1937 (New York: New Century Publishers, 1946), 27–28.
48. *The Foundations of Leninism, Works* VI, 157–60.
49. *Ibid.,* 163–66.
50. *Ibid.,* 161.
51. *Ibid.,* 167.
52. *Ibid.,* 167, 170.
53. Stalin, "On the Draft Constitution of the U.S.S.R.," November 25, 1936, in *Leninism: Selected Writings,* 386.
54. *Ibid.,* 381–82.
55. *Ibid.,* 384.
56. *Ibid.,* 395.
57. *From Socialism to Communism,* Report on the Work of the Central Committee to the Eighteenth Congress of the CPSU(B) on March 10, 1939 (New York: International Publishers, n.d.), 35.
58. Stalin, *Economic Problems of Socialism in the U.S.S.R.* (New York: International Publishers, 1952), 33.
59. *Mastering Bolshevism,* 22.
60. "On the Draft Constitution of the U.S.S.R.," in *Leninism: Selected Writings,* 387.
61. *From Socialism to Communism,* 57.
62. *Ibid.,* 23.
63. *Ibid.,* 25.

64. *Ibid.,* 57.
65. Stalin, "Reply to A. Kholopov," July 28, 1950, in *Marxism and Linguistics* (New York: International Publishers, 1951), 43.
66. Stalin, "Concerning the Errors of L. D. Yaroshenko," in *Economic Problems of Socialism in the U.S.S.R.* (New York: International Publishers, 1952), 51–53.
67. "Interview with the First American Labor Delegation," *Works,* X, 139–40.
68. "Talk with the German Author Emil Ludwig," *Works,* XIII, 120.
69. *Economic Problems of Socialism in the U.S.S.R.,* 25.
70. *The October Revolution and the Tactics of the Russian Communists, Works,* VI, 419.
71. "Political Report of the Central Committee" to the Fourteenth Congress of the CPSU(B), *Works,* VII, 291.
72. Stalin, "The International Situation and the Defense of the U.S.S.R.," speech to the Joint Plenum of the Central Committee and Central Control Commission of the CPSU(B), August 1, 1927, *Works,* X, 53–54.
73. Stalin, "The International Character of the October Revolution," November 6–7, 1927, *Works,* X, 245.
74. Stalin, "The Program of the Comintern," speech to the Plenum of the CC, CPSU(B), July 5, 1928, *Works,* XI, 157.
75. Stalin, "To Comrade Demyan Bedny," December 12, 1930, *Works,* XIII, 25–26.
76. Stalin, "The Tasks of Business Executives," February 4, 1931, *Works,* XIII, 40–41.
77. *Pravda,* March 21, 1936; *The New York Times,* March 7, 1936; compare also with the sharp critical commentary by Leon Trotsky, in *Revolution Betrayed* (New York: Merit Publishers, 1965).
78. "The Tasks of Business Executives," *Works,* XIII, 41.
79. Stalin, "Speech on the Twenty-fourth Anniversary of the October Revolution," November 6, 1941, in *War Speeches* (London: Hutchinson & Co., n.d.,), 20.
80. Stalin, "Toast to the Russian People," May 24, 1945, in *War Speeches,* 138–39.
81. Stalin, Victory Address, September 2, 1945, quoted in *The New York Times,* September 3, 1945, 5.
82. "Political Report of the Central Committee" to the Fourteenth Congress of the CPSU(B), *Works,* VII, 268.
83. *Ibid.,* 294.
84. "Interview with the First American Labor Delegation," *Works,* X, 128–30.
85. Stalin, "Political Report of the Central Committee" to the Fifteenth Congress of the CPSU(B), December 3, 1927, *Works,* X, 296.
86. Interview with American newspaper editor Roy Howard, March 5,

1936, *The New York Times,* March 7, 1936; *Pravda,* March 21, 1936.

87. Interview with London *Sunday Times* correspondent Alexander Werth, *The New York Times,* September 24, 1946.

88. Interview with Elliott Roosevelt, December 21, 1946, in Stalin, *Über den Kampf um den Frieden* (East Berlin: Dietz Verlag, 1954), 292.

89. *Pravda,* May 8, 1947.

90. *Pravda,* May 18, 1948.

91. *Pravda,* April 2, 1952.

92. "Political Report of the Central Committee" to the Fifteenth Congress of the CPSU(B), *Works,* X, 287.

93. *Economic Problems of Socialism in the U.S.S.R.,* 27–28.

94. *Ibid.,* 30.

95. See the resolution of the Central Committee of November 4, 1938, on the publication of the *Short Course* on the history of the CPSU in *The CPSU in Resolutions,* in Russian (Moscow: Gospolitizdat, 1954), III, 317.

96. Leon Trotsky, *The Revolution Betrayed* (New York: Merit Publishers, 1965), 97–99.

97. *Ibid.,* 51–52.

98. Trotsky, *Stalins Verbrechen* (Zurich: Jean-Christophe Verlag, 1937), 366–67.

99. *The Revolution Betrayed,* 133.

100. *Ibid.,* 249.

101. *Ibid.,* 183.

102. Edvard Kardelj, *On People's Democracy in Yugoslavia* (New York: Yugoslav Information Center, 1949), 44–49.

103. Milovan Djilas, "On New Roads of Socialism," speech at a pre-election rally of Belgrade students, March 1950 (Belgrade: Jugoslovenska Knjiga, 1950).

104. *Ibid.*

105. Kardelj, *Socialist Democracy* (Belgrade: Federation of Yugoslav Jurists' Association, 1952), 24, 13, 14.

107. J. B. Tito, "Speech to the Sixth Congress of the Communist Party Of Yugoslavia" (Belgrade, 1952).

108. *Ibid.*

109. *Socialist Democracy,* 23.

110. *Ibid.,* 19.

111. Trotsky, "Stalins Verbrechen" (Zürich: Jean-Christophe Verlag, 1937), 369–71.

☐ **Chapter 4**

*CDSP* refers to the *Current Digest of the Soviet Press,* published by the American Association for the Advancement of Slavic Studies, Ohio State University, Columbus, Ohio, Leo Gruliow, editor.

1. L. Slepov, "Collectivity is the Highest Principle of Party Leadership," *Pravda,* April 16, 1953, *CDSP,* V, No. 13 (May 9, 1953), 3.
2. *Pravda,* March 27, 1953.
3. "Soviet Socialist Law Is Inviolable," *Pravda* editorial, April 6, 1953, *CDSP,* V, No. 11 (April 25, 1953), 3.
4. "In the U.S.S.R. Supreme Court," *Pravda* and *Izvestia,* December 24, 1954, *CDSP,* VI, No. 49 (January 19, 1955), 12.
5. "On Eliminating Waste in Design and Construction," *Pravda* and *Izvestia,* November 10, 1955, *CDSP,* VII, No. 43 (December 7, 1955), 16.
6. A. Chistyakov, "Development of Economic Co-operation in Countries of the Socialist Camp," *Kommunist,* No. 15, 1954, *CDSP,* VI, No. 49 (January 19, 1955), 3–8.
7. K. Ostrovityanov, "What Political Economy Teaches Us," *Pravda,* September 27, 1954, *CDSP,* VI, No. 37 (October 27, 1954), 4.
8. *Pravda,* May 8, 1955.
9. *The New York Times,* May 27, 1955.
10. *Ibid.,* June 2, 1955.
11. "Fifty Years of the Communist Party of the Soviet Union," *Pravda,* July 26, 1953, *CDSP,* V, No. 26 (August 8, 1953), 3–7.
12. See "Documents of Struggle and Victories," *Pravda,* January 15, 1954, *CDSP,* VI, No. 2 (February 24, 1954), 3–5.
13. "On Studying Modern and Recent History of Capitalist Countries," *Voprosi Istorii* (Problems of History), No. 7, July (published in August) 1954, *CDSP,* VI, No. 38 (November 3, 1954), 5.
14. "For Increasing Co-operation Among Historians of All Countries," *Voprosi Istorii,* 1955, No. 8.
15. V. Diachenko, "Tasks of Research in the Economic Field," *Voprosi Ekonomiki* (*Problems of Economics*), 1955, No. 10.
16. "The Interrelation Between Theory and Practice and Party Propaganda," *Kommunist,* 1955, No. 14.
17. "On Studying Modern and Recent History of Capitalist Countries," 6.
18. "For Thorough All-Round Research on the History of Soviet Society," *Voprosi Istorii,* 1954, No. 9.
19. "Tasks of Research in the Economic Field."
20. S. V. Zhitomirskaya, I. M. Kudryavtsev, and B. A. Shlikhter, "On the Correct Use of Soviet Archive Materials," *Voprosi Istorii,* September 1954, No. 9, *CDSP,* VI, No. 44 (December 15, 1954), 16.

21. M. Kim and G. Golokov, "Some Questions on the Study of the History of Soviet Society," *Kommunist,* 1954, No. 5.
22. I. B. Berkhin and M. P. Kim, "On Periodization of the History of Soviet Society," *Voprosi Istorii,* 1954, No. 10.
23. "Resolution of the Central Committee on the CPSU on Lenin Day," January 4, 1955, *Pravda,* January 11, 1955.
24. "The Interrelation Between Theory and Practice and Party Propaganda," *Kommunist,* 1955, No. 14.
25. *Voprosi Istorii,* 1956, No. 2.
26. A. I. Mikoyan, "Speech to the Twentieth Congress of the CPSU," *Pravda* and *Izvestia,* February 18, 1956, *CDSP,* VIII, No. 8 (April 4, 1956), 11.
27. G. M. Malenkov, "Speech to the Twentieth Congress of the CPSU," *Pravda* and *Izvestia,* February 19, 1956, *CDSP,* VIII, No. 9 (April 11, 1956), 10.
28. M. A. Suslov, "Speech to the Twentieth Congress of the CPSU," *Pravda,* February 17, 1956, *CDSP,* VIII, No. 8 (April 4, 1956), 32.
29. N. S. Khrushchev, "Report to the Twentieth Congress of the CPSU," *Pravda,* February 15, 1956, *CDSP,* VIII, No. 5 (March 14, 1956), 14.
30. *Ibid., CDSP,* VIII, No. 6 (March 21, 1956), 7–8.
31. A. I. Mikoyan, "Speech to the Twentieth Congress of the CPSU," *Pravda* and *Izvestia,* February 18, 1956, *CDSP,* VIII, No. 8 (April 4, 1956), 3–11.
32. N. S. Khrushchev, "Report to the Twentieth Congress of the CPSU," *Pravda,* February 15, 1956, *CDSP,* VIII, No. 4 (March 7, 1956), 11.
33. *Ibid.,* 10–11.
34. *Ibid.,* 11.
35. O. V. Kuusinen, "Speech to the Twentieth Congress of the CPSU," *Pravda,* February 20, 1956, *CDSP,* VIII, No. 10 (April 18, 1956), 23.
36. Khrushchev, "Report to the Twentieth Congress of the CPSU," *Pravda,* February 15, 1956, *CDSP,* VIII, No. 4 (March 7, 1956), 11.
37. Khrushchev, *The Crimes of the Stalin Era,* in Boris I. Nikolaevsky, *The New Leader,* 1962, 12–13.
38. *Ibid.*
39. Tosa Popovski, "Report from Moscow," *Borba,* Belgrade, March 26, 1956.
40. Olga Bergholz, in *Literaturnaya Gazeta,* Moscow, April 21, 1956.
41. See "The Twentieth Party Congress and Problems of Research on Party History," editorial in *Voprosi Istorii,* No. 3, March (published in April) 1956, *CDSP,* VIII, No. 19 (June 20, 1956), 6–9.
42. *Pravda,* April 22, 1956.
43. See E. N. Burdzhalov, "Tactics of the Bolsheviks in March and April, 1917," *Voprosi Istorii,* April 1956, No. 4, *CDSP,* VIII, No. 39 (November 7, 1956), 3–5.

44. "The Twentieth Congress and Problems of Research on Party History," 9.
45. M. Sidorov, "On the Philosophical Heritage of Plekhanov," *Kommunist,* 1956, No. 6.
46. "Discussion on the Question of the Genesis of Feudalism in Russia and the Emergence of an All-Russian State," *Voprosi Istorii,* 1956, No. 3.
47. "The Twentieth Party Congress and the Objectives of Soviet Legal Science," *Sovetskoe Gosudarstvo i Pravo* (*Soviet State and Law*), April 1956, No. 2, *CDSP,* VIII, No. 17 (June 6, 1956), 13.
48. See A. Bolgov, "On the Expanded Socialist Reproduction on the Collective Farms," *Kommunist,* 1956, No. 6.
49. Colonel I. Shashnikov, "An Important Question in Military History," *Krasnaya Zvezda* (*Red Star*), April 3, 1956.
50. "Large and Honorable Tasks of the Soviet Press," editorial in *Pravda,* May 5, 1956, partly translated in *CDSP,* VIII, No. 18 (June 13, 1956), 31–32.
51. J. Lazebnik, "Against Monotony and Clichés in Newspapers," *Kommunist,* 1956, No. 4.
52. "Under the Banner of Leninism," editorial in *Kommunist,* 1956, No. 5.
53. "The Party Congress of the CPSU and Tasks in Research on Party History," *Voprosi Istorii,* 1966, No. 3.
54. "An Important Decision," editorial in *Pravda,* April 18, 1956, *CDSP,* VIII, No. 16 (May 30, 1956), 6.
55. Unpublished Documents of V. I. Lenin, *Kommunist,* 1956, No. 9.
56. *Pravda,* June 21, 1956; *The New York Times,* June 21, 1956, 10.
57. These statements are from the speeches by Khrushchev, Mikoyan, Furtseva, Polyansky, Suslov, and Ponomaryev at the Twenty-Second Congress of the CPSU, *Pravda,* October 18, 22, 23, 24, and 26, 1961, published in part in *CDSP,* XIII, Nos. 44–45 and 50–52, November 29, 1961–January 24, 1962.
58. *Pravda,* July 2, 1956; *Moscow News,* 1956, No. 53, 3–5.
59. *Pravda,* July 6, 1956.
60. "The Indestructible Unity of the Countries of the Socialist System," *Pravda,* July 24, 1956.
61. Y. Bugaev, "When the Scientific Approach is Lost," *Partiinaya Zhizn* (*Party Life*), July 1956, No. 14, *CDSP,* VIII, No. 41 (November 21, 1956), 16–19.
62. "The Unity of the International Communist Movement is Indestructible," *Kommunist,* 1956, No. 11.
63. *Pravda,* November 7, 1966.
64. "On Proletarian Internationalism," *Pravda,* December 23, 1956.
65. Khrushchev, "Speech at the Chinese Embassy in Moscow," *Pravda,* January 19, 1957, *CDSP,* IX, No. 3 (February 27, 1957), 24.
66. Khrushchev, "On Control Figures for Development of the U.S.S.R.

National Economy in 1959–65," Report to the Twenty-First Congress of the CPSU, *Pravda,* January 28, 1959, *CDSP,* XI, No. 4 (March 4, 1959), 20.

67. The anthology *For Victory in Peaceful Competition with Capitalism* (New York: Dutton, 1960) contains Khrushchev's speeches and interviews in 1958, with a special introduction by Khrushchev for the U.S. edition. The anthology *World Without Weapons, World Without War,* in 2 volumes (Moscow: Foreign Languages Publishing House, 1960), contains materials for 1959.

68. L. Ilyichev, "Peaceful Coexistence and the Struggle of Two Ideologies," *World Marxist Review,* II, No. 11 (November 1959), 14–16.

69. Khrushchev, "On Peaceful Coexistence," *Foreign Affairs,* XXXVIII, No. 1 (October 1959), 3.

70. Khrushchev, "Interview Given to the Editor-in-chief of *Al Ahram,*" Cairo, November 18, 1957, in N. S. Khrushchev, *Speeches and Interviews on World Problems, 1957* (Moscow: Foreign Languages Publishing House, 1958), 291.

71. Khrushchev, "Replies to Questions Put by Manuel Mejido, Correspondent of the Mexican Newspaper *Excelsior,*" February 21, 1958, in *For Victory in Peaceful Competition with Capitalism* (New York: Dutton, 1960), 108.

72. Khrushchev, "Speech at the Academy of Sciences of the Hungarian People's Republic," April 9, 1958, in *For Victory in Peaceful Competition with Capitalism,* 302.

73. Khrushchev, "Speech at a Reception in New Delhi," February 12, 1960, *Pravda,* February 14, 1960.

74. Khrushchev, "Speech During a Visit to Indonesia," *Pravda,* February 24, 1960.

75. Khrushchev, "Speech to the Delegates of the National Assembly," Paris, March 25, 1960, in *Freundschaft Frankreich-U.d.S.S.R. festigt Frieden in Europa* (East Berlin: Dietz Verlag, 1960), 58.

76. Khrushchev, "Replies to Questions of Union Leaders," Paris, March 31, 1960, in *ibid.,* 98.

77. Khrushchev, "Speech on the Fortieth Anniversary of the Great October Revolution," November 6, 1957, in *Für dauerhaften Frieden und friedliche Koexistenz* (East Berlin: Dietz Verlag, 1959), 257.

78. Khrushchev, "Service to the People Is the Lofty Mission of Soviet Writers," *Pravda,* May 24, 1959, *CDSP,* XI, No. 21 (June 24, 1959).

79. *Pravda,* November 2, 1959.

80. Ilyichev, "Peaceful Coexistence and the Struggle of Two Ideologies," 9.

81. Khrushchev, "Speech at the Embassy of the People's Republic of Albania," April 15, 1957, in Khrushchev, *Speeches and Interviews on World Problems* (Moscow: Foreign Languages Publishing House, 1958), 37.

82. Khrushchev, "Interview Given to I. McDonald, Foreign Editor of *The*

*Times,"* (London), January 31, 1958, in *For Victory in Peaceful Competition with Capitalism,* 88.

83. Khrushchev, "Interview Given to a Correspondent of *Le Figaro,"* March 19, 1958, *ibid.,* 209.
84. Khrushchev, "Speech at the Fifth Congress of the Socialist Unity Party of Germany," July 11, 1958, *ibid.,* 544.
85. Khrushchev, "Interview Given to CBS Correspondents," May 28, 1957, in Khrushchev, *Speeches and Interviews on World Problems, 1957,* 66.
86. Khrushchev, "Interview Given to the Editor-in-Chief of *Asahi Shimbon,"* June 18, 1957, *ibid.,* 112.
87. Khrushchev, "Interview Given to I. McDonald, Foreign Editor of *The Times,"* January 31, 1958, in *For Victory in Peaceful Competition with Capitalism,* 88.
88. Khrushchev, "Speech on Arrival in Berlin of the CPSU Delegation to the Fifth Congress of the Socialist Unity Party of Germany," July 8, 1958, *ibid.,* 522.
89. Khrushchev, "Speech at the Embassy of the People's Republic of Albania," April 15, 1957, in Khrushchev, *Speeches and Interviews on World Problems, 1957,* 35.
90. Khrushchev, "Interview Given to the Editor-in-chief of *Asahi Shimbon,"* June 18, 1957, *ibid.,* 112–13.
91. Khrushchev, "Speech at a Soviet-Czechoslovak Friendship Meeting in Ostrova, Czechoslovakia," July 13, 1957, *ibid.,* 132.
92. Khrushchev, "Speech at a Meeting of Electors of Kalinin Constituency, Moscow," March 14, 1958, in *For Victory in Peaceful Competition with Capitalism,* 190.
93. Khrushchev, July 8, 1958, *ibid.,* 373.
94. Khrushchev, "Replies to Questions Put by *Trybuna Ludu,"* March 10, 1958, *ibid.,* 142.
95. "Speech at Academy of Sciences of the Hungarian People's Republic," 312–13.
96. *Spravochnik Partiinogo Rabotnika (Handbook of Party Officials)* (Moscow: Gospolitizdat), I, 358–59.
97. "Statement of the Meeting of Representatives of the Communist and Workers Parties," *World Marxist Review,* III, No. 12 (December 1960), hereafter referred to as "Declaration of the Eighty-one Parties."
98. *Ibid.,* 7.
99. *Program of the CPSU* (New York: International Publishers, 1963), 46. The Program appeared originally in *Pravda,* July 13, 1961.
100. *Fundamentals of Marxism-Leninism,* 2nd revised edition (Moscow: Foreign Languages Publishing House, 1963), 334–35.
101. "Declaration of the Eighty-one Parties," 23–24.
102. *Ibid.,* 22–23.
103. *Fundamentals of Marxism-Leninism,* 103.
104. "Declaration of the Eighty-one Parties," 15.

105. *Ibid.*, 16.
106. *Program of the CPSU*, 55.
107. "Declaration of the Eighty-one Parties," 17.
108. *Program of the CPSU*, 56.
109. *Fundamentals of Marxism-Leninism*, 457.
110. "Declaration of the Eighty-one Parties," 12.
111. *Ibid.*, 13–14.
112. *Fundamentals of Marxism-Leninism*, 496.
113. *Ibid.*, 489.
114. "Declaration of the Eighty-one Parties," 21.
115. *Fundamentals of Marxism-Leninism*, 500, 504.
116. "Declaration of the Eighty-one Parties," 21.
117. *Fundamentals of Marxism-Leninism*, 555, 557.
118. *Ibid.*, 553, 555.
119. See *Fundamentals of Marxism-Leninism*, 1st edition, German translation (East Berlin: Dietz Verlag, 1960), 693.
120. *Fundamentals of Marxism-Leninism*, 621–33.
121. *Program of the CPSU*, 30.
122. "On Old Positions," *Kommunist*, Belgrade, September 28, 1968.
123. *Program of the CPSU*, 143.
124. *Ibid.*, 76, 97, 100.
125. *Ibid.*, 103.
126. *Ibid.*, 97.
127. *Ibid.*, 104–5.
128. *Pravda*, September 23, 1961.
129. *Program of the CPSU*, 112–13.
130. *Ibid.*, 115–16.
131. *Ibid.*, 137, 139–40.
132. *Ibid.*, 134.
133. *Ibid.*, 71.
134. *Fundamentals of Marxism-Leninism*, 703.
135. *Program of the CPSU*, 73.
136. *Fundamentals of Marxism-Leninism*, 704.
137. *Program of the CPSU*, 72.
138. *Fundamentals of Marxism-Leninism*, 706.
139. *Program of the CPSU*, 71, 73.
140. *Fundamentals of Marxism-Leninism*, 711–12.
141. G. Shakhnazarov, "From the State to Communist Self-government," *Politicheskoe Samoobrazovanie (Political Self-education)*, 1960, No. 8; see also A. I. Denisov, "On the Relationship of State and Society in the Period of Transition from Capitalism to Communism," *Sovetskoe Gosudarstvo i Pravo*, April 1960, No. 4, *CDSP*, XII, No. 22 (June 29, 1960), 17–20.
142. See P. Ramashkin, "The Socialist State and Communist Self-government," *Partiinaya Zhizn*, 1961, No. 9.

143. G. Zhitaryov, "The Party and the Construction of Communism," *Politicheskoe Samoobrazovanie,* 1960, No. 8. See also V. Nikolaev, "On the Development from Socialist Statehood to Communist Self-government," *Voprosi Filosofii (Problems of Philosophy),* 1960, No. 12.

144. *Fundamentals of Marxism-Leninism,* 716.

145. *Program of the CPSU,* 73.

146. *Fundamentals of Marxism-Leninism,* 709–10, 715.

147. S. Strumilin, "Communism and the Workers' Daily Life," *Novy Mir (New World),* 1960, No. 7, *Soviet Review,* II, No. 2 (February 1961), 26.

148. V. Tugarinov, "The Personality and Socialist Society," *Kommunist,* 1960, No. 18.

149. T. S. Stepanyan, "Stages and Periods," *Oktyabr,* 1960, No. 7, 150–62.

150. S. Popov, report at an academic conference at Moscow State University on the theme "The Full-Scale Construction of Communism and the All-Round Development of Personality," *Vestnik Moskovskogo Universiteta (Bulletin of Moscow University),* Economic-Philosophical Series, 1960, No. 5.

151. "Communism and the Workers' Daily Life," II, 16–17.

152. G. Gradov, "The City and Everyday Life," *Izvestia,* January 13, 1960, *CDSP,* XII, No. 2 (February 10, 1960), 36–37.

153. A. Kharchev, "The Family and Communism," *Kommunist,* May 1960, No. 7, *CDSP,* XII, No. 21 (June 22, 1960), 12.

154. "Communism and the Workers' Daily Life," II, 8.

155. *Ibid.*

156. "The Family and Communism," 12.

157. *Program of the CPSU,* 73.

158. *Fundamentals of Marxism-Leninism,* 713. Compare on the same subject Khrushchev, "Speech to the Ninth All-German Workers' Conference in Leipzig," March 7, 1959, *Pravda,* March 27, 1959, *CDSP,* XI, No. 13 (April 29, 1959), 3–7; Stepanyan, "Stages and Periods," *Kommunist,* 1960, No. 18; J. P. Frantser, *Kommunismus heute und morgen* (Vienna: Europa Verlag, 1965), 357.

159. V. I. Lenin, "Preliminary Draft Theses on the National and the Colonial Questions," June 1920, *Collected Works,* XXXI, 147.

160. *Program of the CPSU,* 136.

161. *Ibid.,* 132.

162. *Fundamentals of Marxism-Leninism,* 713–14.

163. Stalin, Reply to Discussion on "Political Report of the Central Committee to the Sixteenth Congress of the CPSU," June 27–July 2, 1930, in Joseph Stalin, *Marxism and Linguistics* (New York: International Publishers, 1951), Appendix 2, 55–56.

164. Stalin, "Reply to A. Kholopov" July 28, 1950, in *Marxism and Linguistics,* 46.

165. *Komsomolskaya Pravda,* April 13, 1960.

166. M. D. Kammari, "Fusion of the Peoples," *Voprosi Filosofii*, 1961, No. 9.
167. *Fundamentals of Marxism-Leninism*, 715.
168. Khrushchev, "On the Program of the Communist Party of the Soviet Union," Report to the Twenty-second Congress of the CPSU, *Pravda*, October 18, 1961, *CDSP*, XIII, No. 45 (December 6, 1961), 26.
169. Speeches of P. A. Satyukov and P. N. Pospelov to the Twenty-second Congress, *Pravda*, October 27 and 28, 1961, *CDSP*, XIV, No. 4, 27–29; No. 5, 19.
170. Speeches of N. A. Mukhitdinov and R. Y. Malinvosky to the Twenty-second Congress, *Pravda*, October 25, 1961, CDSP, XIV, No. 1, 19–22; No. 2, 14–17.
171. "Speech of N. V. Podgorny to the Twenty-second Congress," *Pravda*, October 20, 1961, *CDSP*, XIII, No. 48 (December 27, 1961), 16.
172. "Speech of L. Ilychev to the Twenty-second Congress," *Pravda*, October 26, 1961, *CDSP*, XIV, No. 2 (February 7, 1962), 21.
173. "Speech of N. M. Shvernik to the Twenty-second Congress," *Pravda*, October 26, 1961, *CDSP*, XIV, No. 2 (February 7, 1962), 21.
174. "Speech of A. N. Shelepin to the Twenty-second Congress," *Pravda*, October 27, 1961, *CDSP*, XIV, No. 4 (February 21, 1962), 36.
175. "Concluding Remarks by N. S. Khrushchev at the Twenty-second Party Congress," *Pravda*, October 29, 1961, *CDSP*, XIII, No. 46 (December 13, 1961), 28–29.
176. "Speech by I. V. Spiridonov to the Twenty-second Congress," *Pravda*, October 20, 1961, condensed text in *CDSP*, XIII, No. 48 (December 27, 1961), 17–18.
177. "Speech of D. A. Lazurkina to the Twenty-second Congress," *Pravda*, October 31, 1961.
178. *Pravda*, November 1, 1961.
179. See Tito's speech in Sofia, *Borba*, Belgrade, November 14, 1961; and the report of Togliatti about the Twenty-second Congress of the CPSU, in *L'Unitá*, Rome, November 11, 1961; both in *Diversity in International Communism*, Alexander Dallin, ed. (New York and London: Columbia University Press, 1963), 408–21, 584–87; see also the debate in the Italian Communist Party on de-Stalinization, 421–50.
180. Istvan L. Szabo, "The Lenin Mausoleum: A Report from Red Square," in *Elet es Irodalom*, Budapest, 1961, No. 46.
181. See M. A. Suslov, "The Twenty-second Party Congress and the Tasks of Social Science Departments," *Pravda*, February 4, 1962, *CDSP*, XIV, No. 5 (February 28, 1962), 12–16; M. P. Kim, "Tasks for the Study of the Historical Experiences in the Construction of Socialism in the U.S.S.R. in the Light of the Resolutions of the Twenty-second Congress of the CPSU," *Voprosi Istorii*, 1962, No. 2; and A. Borin, "Truth in the Administration of Justice," *Izvestia*, February 9, 1962, *CDSP*, XIV, No. 6 (March 7, 1962), 6–7.

182. G. L. Smirnov, N. P. Filomonov, and A. F. Yudenkov, "Marxism-Leninism as a United, Indivisible Teaching," *Voprosi Filosofii,* 1960, No. 1; G. J. Glesserman, "On the Subject of Historical Materialism, *Voprosi Istorii,* 1960, No. 3; L. N. Suvorov, "On the Question of the introduction of the Theory of Scientific Communism and Its Scientific Problems," *Filosofskie Nauki (Philosophical Sciences),* 1961, No. 2.

183. M. A. Suslov, "The Twenty-second Party Congress and the Tasks of Social Science Departments," *Pravda,* February 4, 1962, translated in part in *CDSP,* XIV, No. 5 (February 28, 1962), 12–16.

184. Z. A. Stepanyan, "On the Contents of the Course 'Foundations of Scientific Communism,'" *Voprosi Filosofii,* 1962, No. 6, 24–35. See also M. S. Dzhunusov, *Voprosi Filosofii,* 1963, No. 5, 118–23; V. P. Rozhin, *Voprosi Filosofii,* 1963, No. 5, 124–29; A. Kovalev, *Kommunist,* 1963, No. 15, 106–11; L. N. Suvorov, *Voprosi Filosofii,* 1964, No. 8, 139–42; and D. I. Chesnokov, *Voprosi Filosofii,* 1965, No. 3, 20–31.

185. *History of Socialist Ideas,* in Russian—not translated into foreign languages (Moscow: Publishing Office of the Academy of Sciences of the U.S.S.R., 1962).

186. *Kommunist,* March 1964, No. 5, 126.

187. *Spravochnik Partiinogo Rabotnika,* Moscow, Vol. 5 (1964), 258, 260.

188. F. Burlatsky, "Politics and Science," *Pravda,* January 10, 1965, *Soviet Review,* IV, No. 1 (Summer 1965), 52–55.

189. E. V. Tadevosyan, "Discussion on Political Science," *Voprosi Filosofii,* 1965, No. 10, 164–66.

190. *Voprosi Filosofii,* 1965, No. 5, 141–61; see also contributions by G. I. Kurbatova, F. I. Tamonov, B. A. Shabat, M. M. Suzhikov, and L. N. Suvorov, *Voprosi Filosofii,* 1965, No. 12, 15–23.

191. *Voprosi Filosofii,* 1965, No. 11, 150–54.

192. A. K. Kurilev and G. M. Shtraks, "Marxist Philosophy and Scientific Communism," *Voprosi Filosofii,* 1966, No. 6, 27–34; A. M. Kovelev, "Once More on the Sociology of Marxism and Scientific Communism," *Filosofskie Nauki,* 1967, No. 1, 110–20; V. A. Fomina, *Vestnik Moskovskogo Universiteta,* 1967, No. 3.

193. Compare the anthology Khrestomatiya, ed., *Po Nauchnomy Kommunizmu (On Scientific Communism)* (Moscow: Mysl, 1968), Vol. I: "From Utopia to Science."

194. V. Afanasyev, *Nauchny Kommunizm, Popularny Ocherk (Scientific Communism—A Popular Outline)* (Moscow: Politizdat, 1966).

195. V. Afanasyev, *Scientific Communism, A Popular Outline* (Moscow: Progress Publishers, 1967).

196. *Osnovy Nauchnogo Kommunizma (Foundations of Scientific Communism)* (Moscow: Politizdat, 1967). A textbook compiled on behalf of the Central Committee of the CPSU by a collective of authors, P. N. Fedoseev, J. I. Bugaev, F. M. Burlatsky, V. K. Gabuniya, L. M. Gotovsky, G. J. Glezevman, V. O. Evdokomov, A. M. Kovalev, J. I.

Kuskov, G. L. Smirnov, V. P. Stepanov, Z. A. Stepanyan, L. N. Tokunov, G. P. Frantzev, and A. N. Yakovlev.

197. Siderov, "Foundations of Scientific Communism," *Pravda,* December 27, 1960.
198. *Osnovy Nauchnogo Kommunizma,* 4, 6–7.
199. See "The Unshakable Leninist General Line of the CPSU," *Pravda,* October 17, 1964, *CDSP,* XVI, No. 40 (October 28, 1964), 3–6; "Exactingness Is an Important Feature of Party Guidance," *Partiinaya Zhizn,* No. 20 (October 1964), *CDSP,* XVI, No. 42 (November 11, 1964), 4–6; "We Follow the October Road," *Kommunist,* No. 15, 1964; "Great Banner of the Builders of Communism," *Pravda,* November 1, 1964, *CDSP,* XVI, No. 44 (November 25, 1964), 6–8; "The CPSU: Party of the Revolutionary," *Partiinaya Zhizn,* 1964, No. 21.
200. A. Rumyantsev, "The Party and the Intelligentsia," *Pravda,* February 21, 1965, *CDSP,* XVII, No. 7 (March 10, 1965), 3–5.
201. See Edward Crankshaw, "The Last Word of Bukharin," *Observer,* May 23, 1965, and Wolfgang Leonhard, "Bukharins letzter Brief," *Die Zeit,* May 21, 1965.
202. I. Bagramyan, "The Difficult Summer," *Literaturnaya Gazeta,* April 17, 1965, and P. Troyanovsky, "The Road to Berlin," conversation with I. S. Konev, *Sovetskaya Rossia,* April 16, 1965, both in *CDSP,* XVII, No. 17 (May 19, 1965), 19–23; *Neva,* 1965, No. 5.
203. L. I. Brezhnev, "Great Victory of the Soviet People," *Pravda,* May 9, 1965, *CDSP,* XVII, No. 18 (May 26, 1965), 3–12.
204. V. Semichastny, "Soviet Chekists in the Great Patriotic War," *Pravda,* May 7, 1965, *CDSP,* XVII, No. 18 (May 26, 1965), 13–14.
205. S. Trapeznikov, "Marxism-Leninism—Firm Foundation of Development of the Social Sciences," *Pravda,* October 8, 1965, *CDSP,* XVII, No. 40 (October 27, 1965), 17–19.
206. Y. Zhukov, V. Trukhanovsky, V. Shunkov, "The High Responsibility of Historians," *Pravda,* January 30, 1966, *CDSP,* XVIII, No. 5 (February 23, 1966), 28.
207. P. Lavrov, "An Outstanding Party Figure," *Pravda,* February 26, 1966, *CDSP,* XVIII, No. 8 (March 16, 1966), 32–33.
208. *Zarya Vostoka* (*Eastern Dawn*), Tbilisi, March 10, 1966.
209. *The New York Times,* March 21, 1966.
210. *The Twenty-third Congress of the CPSU* (Moscow: Novosti Press Agency Publishing House, 1966), 30.
211. J. Zazersky, "What We Want Is Still Not Reality," *Izvestia,* August 31, 1965.
212. P. Fedoseyev, "Dialectics of Life and Philosophical Science," *Pravda,* March 16, 1966, *CDSP,* XVIII, No. 11 (April 6, 1966), 4.
213. F. Burlatsky, "On the Construction of the Developed Socialist Society," *Pravda,* December 21, 1966.
214. "On Additions to the Russian Republic Criminal Code," *Vedomosti*

*Verkhovnovo Soveta RSFSR* (*Bulletin of the Supreme Soviet of the RSFSR*), No. 38 (September 22, 1966), *CDSP,* XVIII, No. 41 (November 2, 1966), 3.

215. M. Alekseyev in *Literaturnaya Rossia,* April 22, 1966.

216. See the speech by Major-General Yepishev, in *Krasnaya Zvezda,* May 25, 1966, and the account of a patriotic youth meeting in Moscow, "In the Shade of Banners of Glory," *Pravda,* September 12, 1966, *CDSP,* XVIII, No. 37 (October 5, 1966), 20–21.

217. "On Preparations for the Fiftieth Anniversary of the Great October Socialist Revolution," Resolution of the CPSU Central Committee, January 4, 1967, *Pravda,* January 8, 1967, *CDSP,* XIX, No. 1 (January 25, 1967), 11–14.

218. S. P. Trapeznikov, "The New Tasks of Social Science," *Voprosi Filosofii,* 1967, No. 11.

219. "Stages of Development of Soviet Historical Science: On the Question of the History of the Fatherland," *Voprosi Istorii,* 1967, No. 11.

220. "On Measures for Further Developing Social Sciences and Heightening Their Role in Communist Construction," Resolution of the CPSU Central Committee, *Pravda,* August 22, 1967, *CDSP,* XIX, No. 34 (September 13, 1967), 8.

221. "The Duty of Historians of the Party," *Pravda* editorial, November 18, 1967, *CDSP,* XIX, No. 46 (December 6, 1967), 20

222. S. P. Trapeznikov, "The New Tasks of Social Science," *Voprosi Filosofii,* 1967, No. 11.

223. *Osnovy Nauchnogo Kommunizma,* 211. Not translated into English. These comments do not appear with the same degree of harshness in the Afanasyev text, cited above, which was written a year earlier.

224. *Ibid.,* 280.

225. *Ibid.,* 235–8.

226. *Ibid.,* 239.

227. *Ibid.,* 259–60.

228. *Ibid.,* 265.

229. *Ibid.,* 302–3.

230. *Pravda,* July 4, 1968.

231. S. Kovalev, "On 'Peaceful' and Nonpeaceful Counterrevolution," *Pravda,* September 11, 1968, *CDSP,* XX, No. 37 (October 2, 1968), 11–12.

232. S. Kovalev, "Sovereignty and the Internationalist Obligations of Socialist Countries," *Pravda,* September 26, 1968, *CDSP,* XX, No. 39 (October 16, 1968), 11. The Kovalev statements have been harshly criticized by the Chinese Communists; see "Theories of 'Limited Sovereignty' and 'International Dictatorship' Are Soviet Revisionist Social-Imperialist Gangster Theories," *Peking Review,* No. 13 (March 28, 1969), 23–25.

233. S. Kovalev, "Sovereignty and the Internationalist Obligations of Socialist Countries," 11–12.
234. Colonel N. Chernyak, "Proletarian Internationalism—The Unshakable Principle of Socialist Mutual Friendship," *Krasnaya Zvezda,* December 1, 1968.
235. L. I. Brezhnev, "Speech at the Fifth Congress of the Polish United Workers' Party," November 12, 1968, *Pravda,* November 13, 1968; L. I. Brezhnev, *Following Lenin's Course* (Moscow: Progress Publishers, 1972), 145.
236. K. T. Mazurov, "The Fifty-first Anniversary of the Great October Socialist Revolution," November 6, 1968, *Pravda,* November 7, 1968, *CDSP,* XX, No. 45 (November 27, 1968), 6.
237. Tito, *Borba,* Belgrade, March 13, 1969, English version in *Ninth Congress of the League of Communists of Yugoslavia* (Belgrade: Socialist Thought and Practice, 1969), 63. Compare also the article by L. Erven, " 'Limited Sovereignty' and the Problem of International Competition," *Review of International Affairs,* Belgrade, No. 446, (November 5, 1968), 8–9.
238. N. Ceausescu, "Speech to Graduates of the Rumanian Military Academy," August 14, 1968, in Boris Meissner, *Die Breshnew-Doktrin* (Cologne: Verlag Wissenschaft und Politik, 1969), 146–47.
239. N. Ceausescu, "Balcony Speech on Czechoslovakia," August 21, 1968, in *Scînteia,* August 22, 1968. English translation in Robin A. Remington, *Winter in Prague* (Cambridge, Mass.: M.I.T. Press, 1969), 359–61.
240. "Theories of 'Limited Sovereignty' and 'International Dictatorship' Are Soviet Revisionist Social-Imperialist Gangster Theories," *Peking Review,* 23.
241. William C. Just, "The Young People of Russia—3," *The Observer,* London, October 7, 1956, 7–8. Earlier installments in the issues of September 23, 7 and September 30, 7.
242. "The Communist Party is the Inspirer and Leader of the Soviet People," *Pravda,* July 6, 1956, *CDSP,* VIII, No. 29 (August 29, 1956), 5.
243. *Kommunist* editorial, March 1957, No. 3.
244. *Pravda,* September 22, 1961.
245. *Pravda,* September 27, 1961.
246. *Partiinaya Zhizn,* 1961, No. 19, 48.
247. *Pravda,* August 20, 1961.
248. *Partiinaya Zhizn,* 1961, No. 19, 54.
249. *Pravda,* October 10, 1961.
250. *Partiinaya Zhizn,* 1961, No. 19, 41.
251. *Kommunist,* 1961, No. 13, 91.
252. Letter of Soviet collective-farm chairman protesting the trial of dissidents, *The New York Times,* March 8, 1968; see also Abraham Brum-

berg, ed., *In Quest of Justice* (New York: Praeger, 1970), "The Duty of a Communist," 129–32. After this letter, Yakhimovich was removed from his job. In July 1968 he declared his support for the "Prague Spring," protested after the Soviet occupation of Czechoslovakia, and was arrested on March 25, 1969.

253. Andrei D. Sakharov, *Progress, Coexistence, and Intellectual Freedom* (New York: Norton, 1968). Excerpts from the book were first published in *The New York Times,* July 22, 1968.

☐ **Chapter 5**

All quotations from Mao Tse-tung, unless otherwise specified, are from the *Selected Works of Mao Tse-tung,* English language edition (in 4 volumes), published by Foreign Languages Press, Peking, 1967.

1. "Mao Tse-tung's Thought Illuminates the Road for the Party's Victorious Advance," *Peking Review,* No. 28 (July 7, 1967), 12.
2. Karl Marx and Friedrich Engels, *On Colonialism* (Moscow: Foreign Languages Publishing House, n.d.), 14.
3. V. I. Lenin, "Address to the Second All-Russia Congress of Communist Organizations of the Peoples of the East," November 22, 1919, *Collected Works* (Moscow: Progress Publishers, 1965), XXX, 161.
4. Mao, "Along the Socialist or the Capitalist Road?" *Peking Review,* No. 34 (August 18, 1967), 17.
5. Mao Tse-tung, "Maxims for Revolutionaries—The 'Three Constantly Read Articles,'" *Peking Review,* No. 2 (January 6, 1967), 7.
6. Mao, "Sining Successfully Runs Classes for the Study of Mao Tse-tung's Thought," *Peking Review,* No. 43 (October 20, 1967), 23.
7. Mao, *Quotations from Chairman Mao Tse-tung* (Peking: Foreign Languages Press, 1966), ii.
8. Mao, *The Great Socialist Cultural Revolution in China,* No. 3 (Peking: Foreign Languages Press, 1966), 14.
9. Mao, *The Great Socialist Cultural Revolution in China,* No. 5 (Peking: Foreign Languages Press, 1966), 25.
10. Mao, "Basic Assurance for Consolidating the Proletarian Dictatorship," *Peking Review,* No. 35 (August 25, 1967), 10.
11. Mao, "Comrade Lin Piao's Speech at the Peking Rally Commemorating the Fiftieth Anniversary of the October Revolution," *Peking Review,* No. 46 (November 10, 1967), 6, 7.
12. *The Great Socialist Cultural Revolution in China,* No. 5, 17.
13. "Basic Assurance for Consolidating the Proletarian Dictatorship," 10.
14. Mao, "Report on an Investigation of the Peasant Movement in Hunan," March 1927, in *Quotations from Chairman Mao Tse-tung,* 119.

15. Mao himself removed this (at that time) highly "heretical" observation from his writing in 1951. However, he continued to maintain the basic thesis of the leading role of the peasantry. See Stuart Schram, *The Political Thought of Mao Tse-tung* (New York: Praeger, 1963), 181–82, 184.
16. "Along the Socialist or the Capitalist Road?" *Peking Review,* No. 34 (August 18, 1967), 17.
17. Mao, *On Tactics Against Japanese Imperialism,* December 27, 1935, in *Selected Works,* I, 165.
18. Mao, *The Tasks of the Chinese Communist Party in the Period of Resistance to Japan,* May 3, 1937, in *Selected Works,* I, 272.
19. Mao, *The Chinese Revolution and the Chinese Communist Party,* December 1939, in *Selected Works,* II, 318.
20. Mao, *The Role of the Chinese Communist Party in the National War,* October 1938, in *Selected Works,* II, 197–98.
21. *Ibid.,* 200.
22. Mao, "The Question of Independence and Initiative Within the United Front," November 5, 1938, in *Selected Works,* II, 214, 216.
23. Mao, *On New Democracy,* January 1940, in *Selected Works,* II, 350–51, 353–54, 369, 379–80.
24. *Ibid.,* 350.
25. Mao, *The Chinese Revolution and the Chinese Communist Party,* II, 327.
26. Mao, "On the Question of Political Power in the Anti-Japanese Base Areas," March 6, 1940, in *Selected Works,* II, 418.
27. Mao, "Current Problems of Tactics in the Anti-Japanese United Front," March 11, 1940, in *Selected Works,* II, 427–28.
28. Mao, "On the Question of Political Power in the Anti-Japanese Base Areas," II, 418.
29. Mao, "Unity to the Very End," July 1940, in *Selected Works,* II, 438.
30. Mao, "On Policy," December 25, 1940, in *Selected Works,* II, 445.
31. Mao, *On Tactics Against Japanese Imperialism,* I, 170.
32. Mao, "Win the Masses in Their Millions for the Anti-Japanese National United Front," May 7, 1937, in *Selected Works,* I, 290.
33. *The Chinese Revolution and the Chinese Communist Party,* II, 330–31.
34. *On New Democracy,* II, 358, 361.
35. Mao, "The Orientation of the Youth Movement," May 4, 1939, in *Selected Works,* II, 243.
36. *The Chinese Revolution and the Chinese Communist Party,* II, 331.
37. Mao, "On Coalition Government," April 24, 1945, in *Selected Works,* III, 232.
38. "Along the Socialist or the Capitalist Road?" 17.
39. Mao, *Problems of Strategy in China's Revolutionary War,* December 1936, in *Selected Works,* I, 180. Here quoted from *Quotations from Chairman Mao Tse-tung,* 58.

40. Mao, *On Contradiction,* August 1937, in *Selected Works,* I, 344.
41. Mao, *Problems of War and Strategy,* November 6, 1938, in *Selected Works,* II, 219, 224–25. Compare also *Quotations from Chairman Mao Tse-tung,* 61–63.
42. Mao, *On Protracted War,* May 1938, in *Quotations from Chairman Mao Tse-tung,* 139.
43. Mao, "Talk with the American Correspondent Anna Louise Strong," August 1946, in *Quotations from Chairman Mao Tse-tung,* 140.
44. *The Chinese Revolution and the Chinese Communist Party,* II, 317.
45. Mao, "Resolution on Some Questions in the History of Our Party," April 20, 1945, in *Selected Works,* IV.
46. Mao, "The United Front in Cultural Work," October 30, 1944, in *Quotations from Chairman Mao Tse-tung,* 124–25.
47. "Introductory note to 'Surplus Labor Has Found a Way Out,'" 1955, in *Quotations from Chairman Mao Tse-tung,* 118.
48. Mao, "On the Chungking Negotiations," October 17, 1945, in *Quotations from Chairman Mao Tse-tung,* 273.
49. *The Role of the Chinese Communist Party in the National War,* II, 198. See also, *Quotations from Chairman Mao Tse-tung,* 271–72.
50. Mao, "In Memory of Norman Bethune," December 21, 1939, in *Selected Works,* II, 337.
51. Mao, "Speech at the Assembly of Representatives of the Shensi-Kansu-Ningsia Border Region," November 21, 1941, in *Selected Works,* III, 33.
52. Mao, "Preface and Postscript to Rural Surveys," March and April 1941, in *Selected Works,* III, 13. See also Mao's self-critical statements in this respect: "Talks at the Yenan Forum on Literature and Art," May 1942, in *Selected Works,* III, 73–74.
53. *On Khrushchev's Phony Communism and Its Historical Lessons for the World,* July 14, 1964 (Peking: Foreign Languages Press, 1964), 68–69.
54. Mao, *The Foolish Old Man Who Removed the Mountains,* June 11, 1945, in *Selected Works,* III, 272. See also *Quotations from Chairman Mao Tse-tung,* 201–2.
55. *The Political Thought of Mao Tse-tung,* 286.
56. *Problems of Strategy in China's Revolutionary War,* I, 181.
57. *The Role of the Chinese Communist Party in the National War,* II, 209–10.
58. Mao, "The Identity of Interests Between the Soviet Union and All Mankind," September 28, 1939, in *Selected Works,* II, 275, 277–78.
59. *On New Democracy,* II, 380–81.
60. Mao, *Reform Our Study,* May 1941, in *Selected Works,* III, 19–20, 23–24.
61. Mao, "Rectify the Party's Style of Work," February 1, 1942, in *Selected Works,* III, 38, 43.

62. Mao, "Oppose Stereotyped Party Writing," February 8, 1942, in *Selected Works,* III, 63, 67.
63. Speech to cadres of the Chinese Party explaining the dissolution of the Communist International, May 26, 1943. Quoted in *The Political Thought of Mao Tse-tung,* 288–90.
64. *On Coalition Government,* III, 234–35.
65. "Resolution on Some Questions in the History of Our Party," 171–72, 218.
66. Quoted from *Einheit,* East Berlin, 1968, Nos. 4 and 5, 628; see also "Constitution of the Chinese Communist Party, June 11, 1945," in Conrad Brandt, Benjamin Schwartz, and John K. Fairbank, *A Documentary History of Chinese Communism* (Cambridge, Mass.: Harvard University Press, 1959), 422.
67. Anna Louise Strong, "The Thought of Mao Tse-tung," *Amerasia,* XI, No. 6 (June 1947), 161–62. Quoted in *The Political Thought of Mao Tse-tung,* 56.
68. The rapid rise of the Chinese Communist Party was acknowledged in the Soviet Union before the Sino-Soviet split. See *Bolshaya Sovetskaya Entsiklopedia (Large Soviet Encyclopedia),* 2nd edition (Moscow, 1953), entry for "China," XXI, 238.
69. See "The Roots of the Current Events in China," *Kommunist,* No. 6 (April 1968), in *Current Digest of the Soviet Press,* XX, No. 19 (May 29, 1968), 5.
70. See O. Vladimirov and V. Ryasentsev, "On Some Questions on the History of the Communist Party of China," *Kommunist,* No. 9 (June 1968), 93–108.
71. Vladimir Dedijer, *Tito* (New York: Simon and Schuster, 1953), 322.
72. Mao, *On the Question of Stalin,* September 13, 1963 (Peking: Foreign Languages Press, 1963), 7–8.
73. Alfred Kontorowicz, *Deutsches Tagebuch* (Munich: Kindler Verlag, 1959), 569, 575.
74. Peko Dapcevic, "China on the Eve of Victory," *Borba,* Belgrade, May 1, 1949, 3.
75. See Keith McEwan, *Once a Jolly Comrade* (Brisbane: The Jacaranda Press, 1966), 30–38.
76. Mao, "The Origin and Development of the Differences Between the Leadership of the CPSU and Ourselves," September 6, 1963, in *The Polemic on the General Line of the International Communist Movement* (Peking: Foreign Languages Press, 1965), 63.
77. Mao, "On the Correct Handling of Contradictions Among the People," February 27, 1957, in *Quotations from Chairman Mao Tse-tung,* 46–47.
78. *Ibid.,* 45.
79. Mao, "Speech at the Chinese Communist Party's National Conference on Propaganda Work," March 12, 1957, in *Selected Readings from*

*the Works of Mao Tse-tung* (Peking: Foreign Languages Press, 1971), 493.

80. "On the Correct Handling of Contradictions Among the People," February 27, 1957, in *Peking Review*, No. 26 (June 23, 1967), 20–22.
81. *Ibid.*, 22. See also *Quotations from Chairman Mao Tse-tung*, 48–49.
82. Mao, "Long Live Leninism!" April 16, 1960, in G. F. Hudson, Richard Lowenthal, and Roderick MacFarquhar, eds., *The Sino-Soviet Dispute* (New York: Praeger, 1961), 98.
83. Mao, *On Protracted War*, May 1938, in *Quotations from Chairman Mao Tse-tung*, 139.
84. "Long Live Leninism!" 92–93.
85. "A Proposal Concerning the General Line of the International Communist Movement," June 14, 1963 (Peking: Foreign Languages Press, 1963), 33.
86. "Long Live Leninism!" *op. cit.*, 93–94.
87. "Open Letter" of the CPSU Central Committee, July 14, 1963, in William E. Griffith, *The Sino-Soviet Rift* (Cambridge, Mass.: M.I.T. Press, 1964), 299.
88. "Talk with the American Correspondent Anna Louise Strong," 100.
89. Mao, "Speech at the Moscow Meeting of Communist and Workers' Parties," November 18, 1957, in *Quotations from Chairman Mao Tse-tung*, 80–81.
90. *The Great Socialist Cultural Revolution in China*, No. 2 (Peking: Foreign Languages Press, 1966), 14–15.
91. *A Proposal Concerning the General Line of the International Communist Movement*, June 14, 1963 (Peking: Foreign Languages Press, 1963), 35–36.
92. "The Origin and Development of the Differences Between the Leadership of the CPSU and Ourselves," 63.
93. *Peaceful Coexistence—Two Diametrically Opposed Policies*, December 12, 1963 (Peking: Foreign Languages Press, 1963), 41.
94. *Ibid.*, 26.
95. *On Khrushchev's Phony Communism and Its Historical Lessons for the World*, 75.
96. *The Great Socialist Cultural Revolution in China*, No. 3, 15.
97. "Comrade Lin Piao's Speech At the Peking Rally Commemorating the Fiftieth Anniversary of the October Revolution," 7.
98. "A Proposal Concerning the General Line of the International Communist Movement," 12–13.
99. "Apologists of Neo-Colonialism," in *The Polemic on the General Line of the International Communist Movement*, 202, 207.
100. "A Proposal Concerning the General Line of the International Communist Movement," 21.
101. *The Proletarian Revolution and Khrushchev's Revisionism*, March 31, 1964 (Peking: Foreign Languages Press, 1964), 8, 11.

102. *Ibid.*, 34.
103. "The Origin and Development of the Differences Between the Leadership of the CPSU and Ourselves," 73, 107.
104. *The Leaders of the CPSU Are the Greatest Splitters of Our Times,* February 4, 1964 (Peking: Foreign Languages Press, 1964), 50.
105. Lin Piao, "Long Live the Victory of People's War!" In Commemoration of the Twentieth Anniversary of Victory in the Chinese People's War of Resistance Against Japan, *Peking Review,* No. 36 (September 3, 1965), 24.
106. "A Proposal Concerning the General Line of the International Communist Movement," 55.
107. *Ibid.*, 47.
108. "The Origin and Development of the Differences Between the Leadership of the CPSU and Ourselves," 102–3.
109. *The Polemic on the General Line of the International Communist Movement,* June 14, 1963 (Peking: Foreign Languages Press, 1965), 41.
110. *On Khrushchev's Phony Communism and Its Historical Lessons for the World,* 14–16, 24–25.
111. *Ibid.*, 27–29, 30–31.
112. *Ibid.*, 42.
113. *Ibid.*, 52, 53–56.
114. "Soviet Union Under Revisionist Rule—Capitalist Restoration in Agriculture," *Peking Review,* No. 36 (September 1, 1967), 33.
115. "Soviet Union Under Revisionist Rule—New System Makes Wageslaves of Workers" in *Peking Review,* No. 24 (June 9, 1967), 35.
116. "Advance Along the Road Opened Up by the October Socialist Revolution," *Peking Review,* No. 46 (November 10, 1967), 10–11.
117. "CPSU Reduced to Instrument of Bourgeois Dictatorship in Name of 'Party of Entire People,' " *Peking Review,* No. 50 (December 8, 1967), 32–33.
118. "Trade Unions Under Soviet Revisionism—Tool for Capitalist Restoration," *Peking Review,* No. 18 (May 3, 1968), 28.
119. "Soviet Union Under Revisionist Rule—Capitalist Restoration in Agriculture," 34.
120. "Facts Speak Louder Than Slanders," *Peking Review,* No. 38 (September 15, 1967), 37.
121. "Advance Along the Road Opened Up by the October Socialist Revolution," 10.
122. "Big Force Put On by Renegades to October Revolution," *Peking Review,* No. 47 (November 17, 1967), 24.
123. "CPSU Reduced to Instrument of Bourgeois Dictatorship in Name of 'Party of Entire People,' " 34.
124. "Privileged Strata Brutally Oppress and Exploit Working People," *Peking Review,* No. 17 (April 26, 1968), 29.

125. "Along the Socialist or the Capitalist Road?" 17.

126. *The Great Socialist Cultural Revolution in China,* No. 5, 18.

127. *The Great Socialist Cultural Revolution in China,* No. 2, 51.

128. *The Great Socialist Cultural Revolution in China,* No. 6 (Peking: Foreign Languages Press, 1966), 10.

129. *On Khrushchev's Phony Communism and Its Historical Lessons for the World,* 5.

130. *Ibid.,* 8–9.

131. Resolution of the Central Committee of the Chinese Communist Party, "On the Establishment of People's Communes in the Rural Areas," August 29, 1958, in Robert V. Daniels, ed., *A Documentary History of Communism,* (New York: Vintage Books, 1960), II, 377.

132. *On Khrushchev's Phony Communism and Its Historical Lessons for the World,* p. 12.

133. *Ibid.,* 65.

134. *Ibid.,* 72–73.

135. "The Orientation of the Youth Movement," II, 246.

136. *Quotations from Chairman Mao Tse-tung,* 291–92.

137. *On Khrushchev's Phony Communism and Its Historical Lessons For the World,* 73–74.

138. "Basic Assurance for Consolidating the Proletarian Dictatorship," *Peking Review,* No. 35 (August 25, 1967), 11.

139. *On Khrushchev's Phony Communism and Its Historical Lessons For the World,* 72.

140. *The Great Socialist Cultural Revolution in China,* No. 5, 12.

141. *Ibid.,* 16.

142. *The Great Socialist Cultural Revolution in China,* No. 1 (Peking: Foreign Languages Press, 1966), 2 (small format).

143. *The Great Socialist Cultural Revolution in China,* No. 5, 12.

144. *The Great Socialist Cultural Revolution in China,* No. 3, 12–13.

145. *The Great Socialist Cultural Revolution in China,* No. 1, 47–48 (small format).

146. *The Great Socialist Cultural Revolution in China,* No. 5, 14.

147. *The Great Socialist Cultural Revolution in China,* No. 7, 2–3.

148. "A Great Revolution to Achieve the Complete Ascendancy of Mao Tse-tung's Thought," *Peking Review,* No. 42 (October 13, 1967), 11.

149. Marx and Engels, *Manifesto of the Communist Party,* 1848, in Marx and Engels, *Selected Works* (Moscow: Progress Publishers, 1969), 126. See also *The Great Socialist Cultural Revolution in China,* No. 7.

150. *The Great Socialist Cultural Revolution in China,* No. 3; see also No. 5, 23.

151. *The Great Socialist Cultural Revolution in China,* No. 3, 11.

152. *The Great Socialist Cultural Revolution in China,* No. 5, 23.

153. *The Great Socialist Cultural Revolution in China,* No. 7, 2.

154. *The Great Socialist Cultural Revolution in China,* No. 5, 25–26.
155. *The Great Socialist Cultural Revolution in China,* No. 7, 16–17.
156. *The Great Socialist Cultural Revolution in China,* No. 7, 25.
157. *The Great Socialist Cultural Revolution in China,* No. 2, 65.
158. *The Great Socialist Cultural Revolution in China,* No. 3, 5.
159. *Ibid.,* 15.
160. *The Great Socialist Cultural Revolution in China,* No. 6, 11.
161. "All China Studies 'Quotations from Chairman Mao Tse-tung,' " *Peking Review,* No. 2 (January 6, 1967), 14.
162. "Hail to Chairman Mao Leading Us from Victory to Victory," *Peking Review,* No. 2 (January 6, 1967), 17.
163. *Ibid.,* 18.
164. *The Great Socialist Cultural Revolution in China,* No. 6, 20.
165. "Use Mao Tse-tung's Thought to Remold Our World Outlook," *Peking Review,* No. 28 (July 7, 1967), 16.
166. "Thoroughly Establish the Absolute Authority of the Great Supreme Commander Chairman Mao and of His Great Thought," *Peking Review,* No. 46 (November 10, 1967), 17.
167. *The Great Socialist Cultural Revolution in China,* No. 7, 17.
168. "China's Great Revolution and the Soviet Union's Great Tragedy," *Peking Review,* No. 24 (June 9, 1967), 15.
169. *The Great Socialist Cultural Revolution in China,* No. 3, 8.
170. See "The Roots of the Current Events in China," *Kommunist,* Moscow, No. 6 (April 1968), 102–13; in *Current Digest of the Soviet Press,* XX, No. 19 (May 29, 1968), 3–7; and O. Vladimirov and V. Ryasantsev, "On Some Questions from the History of the Communist Party of China," *Kommunist,* No. 9 (June 1968), 93–108. All the following quotations in Chapter 5 are taken from these two articles.

☐ **Chapter 6**

1. The term "Reform Communism" was coined by Boris Meissner. See his essay "Die Auseinandersetzung zwischen dem Sowjet- und dem Reformkommunismus," Wirtschaftswissenschaftliche Südosteuropa-Forschung, *Südosteuropa-Schriften,* Munich, 1963, 75–100.
2. Vladimir Dedijer, *Tito* (New York: Simon and Schuster, 1953), 336–47.
3. Erich W. Gniffke, *Jahre mit Ulbricht* (Cologne: Verlag Wissenschaft und Politik, 1966, 1970), 325.
4. See Boris Ziherl, *Communism and Fatherland* (Belgrade: Jugoslovenska Knjiga, 1949); Tito's Speech to the Slovene Academy of Science, Ljubljana, November 16, 1948; "On Nationalism and Internationalism," Belgrade, 1949; and Mosha Pijade, "Speech on the Thirtieth

Anniversary of the Communist Party of Yugoslavia," April 30, 1949, *Borba*, Belgrade, May 1, 1949.

5. Milovan Djilas, *Lenin on the Relations Between Socialist States* (New York: Yugoslav Information Center, n.d.), 25, 47, 48.

6. Edvard Kardelj, *Über die prinzipiellen Grundlagen der Aussenpolitik Jugoslawiens* (Belgrade: Jugoslovenska Knjiga, 1950), 7.

7. Kardelj, *Über die Volksdemokratie in Jugoslawien* (Belgrade: Jugoslovenska Knjiga, 1950), 51–55, 73–74.

8. Djilas, Speech to the Third Plenary Session of the Central Committee of the Communist Party of Yugoslavia, December 29 and 30, 1949, in *Der Sozialismus und das Schulwesen im neuen Jugoslawien* (Belgrade: Jugoslovenska Knjiga, 1950).

9. Josip Broz Tito, *Workers Manage Factories in Yugoslavia* (Belgrade, 1950), 10–11.

10. *Ibid.*, 26, 29–30, 36, 38, 41. See also Pavle Kovac, "Workers' Management in Yugoslavia," Belgrade, Information Service, No. 1010 (June 1960).

11. Kardelj, "Socialist Democracy, in Its Effect on the Whole Development and Social Life of Yugoslavia" (Belgrade: Federation of Yugoslav Jurists' Association, 1952), 25.

12. *Tanjug-Wochenbericht*, Bad Godesberg, June 7, 1951.

13. Kardelj, *Socialist Democracy*, 25.

14. Kardelj, "Die Grundzüge des neuen Jugoslawiens," *Die Neue Zeitung*, Munich, June 28, 1951.

15. Kardelj, *Socialist Democracy*, 29.

16. *Der sechste Kongress der kommunistischen Partei Jugoslawiens 1952* (Mehlem: Press and Information Bureau of the Yugoslav Embassy, 1952), 139–40.

17. "Political Emigrants in Yugoslavia," *Review of International Affairs*, Belgrade, III, No. 23 (December 1, 1952), 21.

18. *Zycie Warszawy*, March 27, 1956.

19. Tribuna Ludu, Warsaw, March 29, 1956.

20. Interview with Togliatti in *L'Unità*, Rome, June 17, 1956; in *The Anti-Stalin Campaign and International Communism*, Russian Institute preface by Henry L. Roberts (New York: Columbia University Press, 1956), 103–4, 108, 112, 120–21, 138–39.

21. *L'Humanité*, June 19, 1956, *Daily Worker*, London, June 22, 1956; *Friheten*, June 19, 1956, *Drapeau Rouge*, June 19, 1956; see: *The Anti-Stalin Campaign and International Communism*, 167–79.

22. Georg Lukács in *Tarasdalmi Szemle* (*Red Flag*), Budapest, June–July 1956.

23. Robert Havemann, "Meinungsstreit fördert die Wissenschaften," *Neues Deutschland*, July 8, 1956.

24. Kardelj, "Speech to the Federal People's Assembly of Yugoslavia," December 6, 1956, in Robert Bass and Elizabeth Marbury, eds., *The*

*Soviet-Yugoslav Controversy, 1948–1958: A Documentary Record* (New York: Prospect Books, 1959), 99–100.

25. Edda Werfel, "To the Comrades of Our Brother Parties," *Przeglad Kulturalny*, Warsaw, 1956, No. 44. Hermann Axen, one of the leaders of the Socialist Unity Party in East Germany, attacked this view in *Neues Deutschland*, November 27, 1956.

26. Jadwiga Siekierska, "An Optimistic Tragedy?" *Po Prostu*, Warsaw, 1956, No. 49.

27. Jerzy Lovell, "In the Heart of Europe," *Zycie Literackie*, Cracow, November 25, 1956.

28. Stanislaw Brodzki, "Dead Words and a Living Party," *Trybuna Ludu*, October 8, 1956.

29. Helena Eilstein, "Revisionism and Dogmatism," *Nowa Kultura*, Warsaw, 1957, Nos. 17–19.

30. Zygmunt Bauman, "On the Necessity for a Sociology of Political Parties," *Mysl Filozoficzna*, Warsaw, 1957, No. 2.

31. Wladislaw Bienkowski, "And Yet It Moves," *Przeglad Kulturalny*, Warsaw, 1956, No. 44.

32. Jerzy Kossak, Ryszard Turski, and Witold Wirspsza, "Worker Self-management," *Po Prostu*, September 30, 1956.

33. Artur Hajnicz, "Poland and Yugoslavia," *Zycie Warszawy*, November 29, 1956.

34. "What Is Still Blocking Our Way?" editorial in *Po Prostu*, 1957, No. 4.

35. Leszek Kolakowski, "The Concept of the Left," *Po Prostu*, 1957, No. 8. English translation in *Toward a Marxist Humanism* (New York: Grove Press, 1968), 75–76, 78.

36. See Tamás Aczel, and Tibor Méray, *The Revolt of the Mind* (New York: Praeger, 1959).

37. Imre Nagy, *On Communism: In Defense of the New Course* (New York: Praeger, 1957).

38. *Ibid.*

39. For a description of the Petöfi Circle, see *The Revolt of the Mind*, 403–12.

40. *Ibid.*, 404.

41. Gyula Hay, in *Irodalmi Ujság*, September 8, 1956. English translation in *The Revolt of the Mind*, 428–29.

42. R. V. Daniels, ed., *A Documentary History of Communism* (New York: Vintage Books, 1960), II, 240–46.

43. "Collapse of the Anti-Popular Adventure in Hungary," editorial in *Pravda*, October 28, 1956. English translation in *Current Digest of the Soviet Press* (hereafter *CDSP*), VIII, No. 41 (November 21, 1956), 12–13.

44. "Faithful to the Truth," editorial in the Budapest newspaper *Szabad Nep*, October 28, 1956. In Paul E. Zinner, ed., *National Communism*

*and Popular Revolt in Eastern Europe* (New York: Columbia University Press, 1956), 424–25. The direct attack on *Pravda* occurred on October 29, 1956, *ibid.*, 449–51.

45. Quoted from *Ungarn, zehn Jahre danach, 1956–1966*, Werner Frauendienst, ed. (Mainz: Hase & Koehler Verlag, 1966), 258.

46. Roman Zimand, "The Task of the Workers of the Whole World," *Po Protsu*, 1956, No. 45.

47. Werfel, "To the Comrades of the Brother Parties."

48. Zimand, "The Task of the Workers of the Whole World."

49. Tito's Address to the Members of the League of Communists, November 11, 1956, in Zinner, ed., *National Communism and Popular Revolt in Eastern Europe*, 535.

50. "Instead of a Political Chronicle," *Zycie Gospodarcze*, Warsaw, November 26, 1956.

51. See Clark's letter to the *Daily Worker*, New York, in *A Documentary History of Communism*, II, 249–53.

52. Wolfgang Harich, "The Testament of a Party Rebel," *Observer*, London, March 17, 1957, 5.

53. Fritz Behrens, "On the Problem of the Use of Economic Laws in the Transition Period," *Wirtschaftwissenschaft*, 3rd special issue, 1957. Similar concepts were expounded by Arne Benary in his article "On the Fundamental Problems of the Political Economy of Socialism in the Transitional Period," in the same issue.

54. "Staatsfeindliche Gruppe unschädlich gemacht," *Neues Deutschland*, December 1, 1956.

55. See *Christentum und Marxismus heute* (*Christianity and Marxism Today*), Conference of the Paulus Society (Vienna: Europa-Verlag, 1966).

56. See the journal *Moskva*, Moscow, 1958, No. 1.

57. See "The Struggle Against Bourgeois and Reformist Ideologies Must Be Strengthened," editorial in *Kommunist*, Moscow, 1958, No. 2; and P. Fedoseev, I. Pomelov, and V. Shcheprakov, "On the Draft Program of the League of Communists of Yugoslavia," *Kommunist*, 1958, No. 6.

58. The anthology *Revisionism: The Main Danger*, in Russian (Moscow: Gospolitizdat, 1958) contains, in addition to Soviet articles on the question, articles by Walter Ulbricht, Gomulka, Ho Chi Minh, and even essays by Chinese Communists (primarily from the year 1957). In a second anthology, *Against Modern Revisionism* (Moscow, 1958), there also are articles by Chinese Communists. The ideological-philosophical struggle was the main topic of this volume, and it was directed principally against Ernst Bloch, Georg Lukács, and Henri Lefebvre.

59. All references concerning the Yugoslav conference are to *Yugoslavia's New Way: The Program of the League of Communists of Yugoslavia*,

Stoyan Pribechevich, trans. (New York: All-Nations Press, 1958), especially 5, 8–9, 24, 43–44, 53–54, 61–64, 106–7, 121, 152–53, 168, 181, 233–34, 263.

60. Kardelj, *Socialism and War: A Survey of Chinese Criticism of the Policy of Coexistence,* Alec Brown, trans. (New York: McGraw-Hill, 1960).

61. Tito's Speech to the Yugoslav National Assembly, *Borba,* Belgrade, March 8, 1955.

62. Ales Bebler, "The Twenty-first Congress of the Communist Party of the U.S.S.R. and Peaceful Coexistence," *Review of International Affairs,* Belgrade, X, No. 213 (February 16, 1959), 2.

63. Radoslav Ratković, "Coexistence and Contemporary Relations," *Review of International Affairs,* XI, Nos. 248–49 (August 1–16, 1960), 11.

64. "The Twenty-first Congress of the Communist Party of the U.S.S.R. and Peaceful Coexistence."

65. Vladimir Bakarić, "Peaceful Coexistence Is a Necessity for All Mankind," *Review of International Affairs,* XI, Nos. 242–43 (May 1–16, 1960), 14.

66. "Coexistence and Contemporary Relations," 10–11.

67. "About the West: Once Differently," *Zycie Warszawy,* October 17, 1956.

68. Bebler, " 'Economic' Competition Between the Two Systems," *Review of International Affairs,* X, No. 216 (April 1, 1959), 1–2.

69. Velko Vlahović, "The Content of the Term 'Proletarian Internationalism,' " *Socijalizam,* Belgrade, 1958, No. 1.

70. Vlahović, "On the Forms of Co-operation of Socialist Forces," *Komunist,* Belgrade, 1955, Nos. 6–7.

71. Puniša Perović, "On the Problems of the Leadership and Relations in the International Working-Class Movement," *Nasa Stvarnost,* Belgrade, 1962, No. 3.

72. Declaration of the Central Committee of the Communist Party of Italy on the Twenty-second Party Congress of the CPSU, *L'Unità,* Rome, November 28, 1961, in Alexander Dallin, ed., *Diversity in International Communism* (New York and London: Columbia University Press, 1963), 451–67.

73. Palmiro Togliatti's "Memorandum" first appeared in *L'Unità,* September 4, 1964, and in English on September 5, 1965, in *The New York Times.* Reprinted in full in W. E. Griffith, *Sino-Soviet Relations, 1964–1965* (Cambridge, Mass.: M.I.T. Press, 1967), 373–83. Also quoted in part in an article by Luigi Longo, "The Italian Communist Party and Problems of the International Communist Movement," *World Marxist Review,* VII, No. II (November 1964), 3–10.

74. Kardelj, Speech in Oslo, Norway, October 8, 1954.

75. Harich in *Observer,* London, March 17, 1957, 5.

76. "On the Problems of the Leadership and Relations in the International Working-Class Movement."
77. "Memorandum," 380.
78. Luciano Gruppi, "The Concepts of Lenin and Engels on the State," *Rinascità*, Rome, July 25, 1964.
79. Ernst Fischer, "Marxismus und Ideologie," *Weg und Ziel*, Vienna, May 1965, 356.
80. Franz Marek, "Probleme der kommunistischen Parteien Westeuropas," *Weg und Ziel*, Vienna, November 1965, 660–72.
81. Branko Pribičević, "Changes in European Capitalism and the Working-Class Movement," *Review of International Affairs*, XVII, No. 385 (April 20, 1966), 16.
82. See the two-part article by Zorica Priklmajer-Tomanovic, "Contemporary Socialist Thought," *Review of International Affairs*, XVII, No. 394 (September 5, 1966) and No. 395 (September 20, 1966).
83. On the case of Sinyavsky and Daniel, see *L'Unità*, Rome, February 16, 1966; "Une declaration d'Aragon à propos d'un procès," *L'Humanité*, Paris, February 16, 1966.
84. "A Socialist Alternative—The Pragmatic Declaration of the Communist Party of Sweden," *Norrskenens Flamman*, Lulea, February 4–11, 1967.
85. Henri Lefebvre, *Problèmes actuels du Marxisme* (Paris: Presses Universitaires de France, 1958), 32.
86. "Marxismus und Ideologie," 358.
87. Julius Strinka, "Two Opinions on Dialectics in Socialism," *Nase Teme*, 1965, No. 12.
88. Branko Horvat, "The Individual and Social Property in Socialism," *Gledista*, Belgrade, March 1967, 336; quoted from Stankovic, "The Crisis of the One-Party System in Yugoslavia," *Eastern Europe*, 1967, No. 7.
89. See Rudi Supek, "Die Selbstverwaltung in der sozialistischen Gesellschaft," in Jozsef Varga, ed., *Sozialismus in Europa* (Vienna: Europa-Verlag, 1967), 107–20.
90. Mieczyslaw Maneli, "State and History," *Zycie Warszawy*, November 21, 1961.
91. Havemann, *Dialektik ohne Dogma?* (Reinbek: Rowohlt Taschenbuch Verlag, 1964).
92. "Memorandum," 383.
93. Jacek Kuron and Karol Modzelewski, *Revolutionary Marxist Students in Poland Speak Out* (New York: Merit Publishers, 1968), 83.
94. *Ibid.*, 3.
95. This term was first used in the beginning of 1962 by Hungarian humanist socialists who, after the crushing of the Hungarian Revolution, escaped to the West. See "Pluralist Socialism," in *The Review*,

published by the Imre Nagy Institute for Political Research, 1962, No. 1.

96. See *Christianity and Marxism Today,* 232, 235, 258–59, 327. See also the article by Branko Bosnjak, "Christianity and Marxism Today," in German, *Praxis,* Zagreb, 1966, Nos. 1–2, 247–56.

97. "Kritik im Socialismus," *Praxis,* international edition, 1966, Nos. 1–2, 177–91.

98. Ivan Perić, "The Theory of the Party of the Working Class and the League of Communists of Yugoslavia," *Nase Teme,* Zagreb, December 1966, 2046, quoted from Stankovic, "The Crisis of the One-Party System in Yugoslavia."

99. From the interview of Ernst Fischer on the West German national television network, quoted in *Der Gewerkschafter,* organ of the metal industry trade union, No. 8 (August 1966).

100. Svetozar Stojanović, "The Statist Myth of Socialism," *Praxis,* 1967, III, No. 2, 184–85.

101. Predrag Vranicki, "State and Party in Socialism," in German, *Praxis,* international edition, 1967, No. 2.

102. *Christianity and Marxism Today,* 232.

103. Quoted from *Der Gewerkschafter,* No. 8 (August 1966).

104. C. H. Hermansson, "Tidsignal," July 15–21, 1966, quoted from *RFE-Bulletin,* Munich, November 4, 1966.

105. Stevan Vracar, *Gledista,* Nos. 8–9 (August-September 1967), 1053–66, quoted from "Jugoslawischer Theoretiker für Zweiparteiensystem," *Osteuropäische Rundschau,* No. 12 (December 1967).

106. Gert Petersen, "The Socialist People's Party in Denmark: Foundations and Perspectives," *Review of International Affairs,* XVII, No. 388 (June 5, 1966), p. 18.

107. "A Socialist Alternative: Draft Program of the Communist Party of Sweden," *Norrskenens Flamman,* Lulea, February 4–11, 1967. The draft program was positively greeted by the Communist Party of Italy. See Irma Trevi, "The Strategy of Swedish Communism," *Rinascità,* Rome, May 26, 1967.

108. "The Socialist Model of the Communist Party of Italy," press conference with Luigi Longo, *L'Unità,* April 10, 1968.

109. "The Action Program of the Communist Party of Czechoslovakia," April 5, 1968, printed in *Rudé Právo,* April 10, 1968. Reprinted in Robin A. Remington, ed., *Winter in Prague* (Cambridge, Mass., and London: M.I.T. Press, 1969), 88–137.

110. Karel Kosík, "The Crisis of Our Time," *Literarni Listy,* 1968, Nos. 7–12.

111. Communiqué of the Conference of the Central Committee, *Rudé Právo,* January 6, 1968; for a more detailed description of the January Plenum, see V. Mencl and F. Ourednik, "What Happened in January,"

*Winter in Prague,* 18–39, and Radio Free Europe, *Czechoslovak Press Survey,* No. 2133 (November 13, 1968).

112. Radovan Richta, "How the Action Program Was Prepared," *Rudé Právo,* Prague, April 1, 1968.

113. Josef Smrkovský, *Rudé Právo,* February 9, 1968.

114. Zdenek Mlynar, "Our Political System and the Division of Power," *Rudé Právo,* February 13, 1968, in *Winter in Prague,* 43–47.

115. Milan Lakatoš, "Die Bürgergesellschaft sucht ihren Platz," *Kulturni Noviny,* February 24, 1968; English translation in Radio Free Europe *Czechoslovak Press Survey,* No. 2063, May 2, 1968. See also "What Is to Be Done About the Representative Bodies?" *ibid.,* No. 2079 (May 29, 1968).

116. Alexandr Kliment, "The Activity of the Anonymous," *Literarni Listy,* No. 3 (March 14, 1968).

117. Ota Sik, *Pravda,* Bratislava, February 29, 1968.

118. Ivan Sviták, "Open Letter to the Workers and Technicians of the Dubrova Mines," March 29, 1968, *Literarni Listy,* No. 8 (April 18, 1968).

119. Smrkovský, *Pravda,* Bratislava, April 19, 1968.

120. "Resolution on the Political Situation Adopted by the Plenary Session of the Central Committee of the Communist Party of Czechoslovakia," *Rudé Právo,* April 6, 1968.

121. "The Action Program of the Communist Party of Czechoslovakia," April 5, 1968, *Rudé Právo,* April 10, 1968. Reprinted in *Winter in Prague,* 88–137.

122. Interview with Dubček, *Pravda,* March 28, 1968, *CDSP,* XX, No. 13 (April 17, 1968), 20.

123. "March-April Plenum of the Central Committee of the Communist Party of Czechoslovakia," *Pravda,* April 12, 1968.

124. "Plenary Session of the Central Committee of the Czechoslovak Communist Party's Action Program," *Pravda,* April 17, 1968, *CDSP,* XX, No. 16 (May 8, 1968), 13, 19.

125. "On the Party Conference in the CSSR," *Pravda,* April 13, 1968.

126. See Leopold Grünwald, ed., *CSSR im Umbruch* (Vienna: Europa-Verlag, 1968), 26.

127. Václav Havel, "On the Subject of Opposition," *Literarni Listy,* April 4, 1968, *Winter in Prague,* 67.

128. Eduard Goldstücker, "The National Front and the New Political System," interview on Austrian television, April 12, 1968, in *CSSR im Umbruch,* 39.

129. Radoslav Selucky, *Czechoslovakia: The Plan That Failed* (London: Thomas Nelson and Sons, 1970), 127.

130. See *CSSR im Umbruch,* 39.

131. "The Crisis in Our Time."

132. Robert Kalivoda, "Democracy and Critical Thought," *Literarni Listy,* Nos. 10–11 (May 2 and 9, 1968).

133. Čestmír Císař, Interview with the Hungarian newspaper *Elet es Irodalom,* May 4, 1968; English translation in *Hungarian Press Survey,* Radio Free Europe, Munich, No. 1294 (May 11, 1968), 4.

134. "Democracy and Critical Thought."

135. *Četeka,* March 26, 1968; see *Osteuropäische Rundschau,* No. 4 (April 1968), 13.

136. Radio Prague, May 20, 1968; *Osteuropäische Rundschau,* No. 6 (June 1968), 29.

137. See the statement of the chairman of the Communist Party of Austria, Franz Muhri, in *Volkstimme,* Vienna, April 18, 1968, and the statement of the Plenary Session of the Central Committee of the Communist Party of France, in *Informations-Bulletin (IB),* Vienna, 1968, Nos. 26–27, 64.

138. Luigi Longo in *Rinascità;* quoted from *IB,* Vienna, 26–27, 72.

139. Longo, Press Conference in Prague, May 7, 1968, *IB,* Vienna, Nos. 26–27, 72.

140. Longo, "Report on the CSSR at the Gramsci Institute in Rome," May 8, 1968, quoted from *Weg und Ziel,* Vienna, Nos. 7–8 (July-August 1968), 353.

141. Havemann, "Sozialismus und Demokratie-ein freisinniges Wort zu der Umwälzung in der Tschechoslowakei," *Die Zeit,* Hamburg, May 31, 1968.

142. V. Gorin, "In Whose Favor Is It?" in the Soviet trade union newspaper *Trud,* May 15, 1968. This article was directed against the article by L. Sohor "Marx and Our Times" in the Czech trade union paper *Prace,* May 5, 1968. See also Lev Onikov, "Socialist Democracy," *Pravda,* May 19, 1968.

143. "VZ verboten—in der DDR," *Prager Volkszeitung,* Prague, May 31, 1968.

144. "Resolution on the Present Situation and the Further Tasks of the Party," *Rudé Právo,* June 2, 1968, English translation in Paul Ello, *Czechoslovakia's Blueprint for "Freedom"* (Washington, D.C.: Acropolis Books, 1968), 53–80.

145. Ludvík Vaculík, "Two Thousand Words to Workers, Farmers, Scientists, Artists, and Everyone," *Literarni Listy,* June 27, 1968, *Winter in Prague,* 201.

146. "On the Declaration 'Two Thousand Words,' Statement of the Presidium of the Central Committee of the Communist Party of Czechoslovakia," *Rudé Právo,* June 28, 1968.

147. *Četeka,* May 27, 1968, *Osteuropäische Rundschau,* No. 6 (June 1968), 30.

148. See *Osteuropäische Rundschau,* 1968, No. 7.

149. Fedor Konstantinov, "Marxism-Leninism Is a Unified International Teaching," *Pravda*, June 14, 1968; *Studies in Comparative Communism*, July-October 1968, 204–6.

150. "The Lofty Responsibility of Social Scientists," *Pravda*, June 20, 1968, *CDSP*, XX, No. 25 (July 10, 1968), 8–10.

151. G. Ognev, "What Does 'The Student' Teach?—The Prague Weekly for the Young Intelligentsia and Its Concept of Democracy," *Komsomolskaya Pravda*, Moscow, June 21, 1968, *CDSP*, XX, No. 26 (July 17, 1968), 11–13.

152. Piotr Shelest, "The Strength of the Communists Lies in Unity," *Pravda*, July 5, 1968, *CDSP*, XX, No. 27 (July 24, 1968), 25.

153. I. Aleksandrov, "An Attack on the Socialist Foundations of Czechoslovakia," *Pravda*, July 11, 1968, *Studies in Comparative Communism*, 243–47.

154. "To the Czechoslovak Communist Party Central Committee," *Pravda*, July 18, 1968, *Winter in Prague*, 225–30.

155. Figures are given in *Vecerni Praha* and *Prace*, July 12 and 18, 1968, quoted from *Rissener Information*, July-October 1968, Haus Rissen, Institut für Politik und Wirtschaft, Hamburg.

156. Czech answer to the Warsaw Letter "Statement of the Presidium of the Central Committee of the Communist Party of Czechoslovakia to the Letter of the Five Communist and Workers' Parties," *Rudé Právo*, July 19, 1968, *Winter in Prague*, 234–43.

157. "Secret Arms Caches at the Border with FRG," *Pravda*, July 19, 1968, *CDSP*, XX, No. 29 (August 7, 1968), 7.

158. "Adventurist Plans of the Pentagon and the CIA," *Pravda*, July 19, 1968, *CDSP*, XX, No. 29 (August 7, 1968), 6–7.

159. "FRG Interference in Czechoslovakia," *Pravda*, July 20, 1968, *CDSP*, XX, No. 29 (August 7, 1968), 7–8.

160. Konstantinov, "Leninism is the Marxism of the Present Era," *Pravda*, July 24, 1968, *CDSP*, XX, No. 31 (August 21, 1968), 7–8.

161. Yuri Zhukov, "Concerning a False Slogan," *Pravda*, July 26, 1968, *CDSP*, XX, No. 31 (August 21, 1968), 8–9.

162. "Faithfulness to Marxism-Leninism," editorial in *Pravda*, July 13, 1968.

163. "Joint Communiqué of the Meeting of the Politburo of the Central Committee of the Communist Party of the Soviet Union and the Praesidium of the Central Committee of the Communist Party of Czechoslovakia" (Cierna Conference), *Pravda*, August 2, 1968, *CDSP*, XX, No. 31 (August 21, 1968), 3.

164. "Statement of the Communist and Workers' Parties of Socialist Countries" (Declaration of the Bratislava Conference), *Pravda*, August 4, 1968, *CDSP*, XX, No. 31 (August 21, 1968), 4–5.

165. Josef Špaček in *Nova Mysl*, 1968, No. 7, 807–14, here quoted from

Wolf Oschlies, "Zum Entwurf des neuen Statuts der KPC," *Berichte des Bundesinstituts für ostwissenschaftliche und internationale Studien,* Cologne, 1969, No. 12, 9.

166. "Draft Statute [Rules] of the Communist Party of Czechoslovakia," *Rudé Právo,* August 10, 1968, *Winter in Prague,* 265–87.

167. *Rudé Právo,* August 13, 15, 18, 20, 1968.

168. See S. Selyuk, "The Strength of Our Party Lies in Its Leninist Unity," *Pravda,* July 25, 1968; and P. Rodyonov, "The Immutable Principle of the Marxist-Leninist Party," *Pravda,* August 9, 1968, *CDSP,* XX, No. 32 (August 28, 1968), 8–10.

169. *Rudé Právo,* August 13, 1968.

170. Kardelj, in *Kommunist,* Belgrade, March–May 1951.

171. Djilas, "On Some Questions of Theoretical Work of the Party," Speech at the Fourth Plenary Session of the Central Committee of the Communist Party of Yugoslavia, June 3, 1951; German translation in *Tanjug Bulletin,* Bad Godesberg, June 7, 1951.

172. Kardelj, "Speech at the Regional Annual Conference of the League of Communists of Yugoslavia at Novi-Sad," *Borba,* March 3, 1956.

173. Jerzy Szacki, "Observations on the History of Marxism," *Po Prostu,* October 21, 1956.

174. Leszek Kolakowski, "The Intellectuals and the Communist Movement," *Nowe Drogi,* theoretical organ of the Polish United Workers' Party, September 1956. English translation in *Toward a Marxist Humanism,* 164.

175. Mihailo Marković, "Science and Ideology," *Nasa Stvarnost,* Belgrade, 1959, Nos. 7–8.

176. Lefebvre, *Problèmes actuels du Marxisme,* 9, 117.

177. Kolakowski, "Permanent vs. Transitory Aspects of Marxism," in *Toward a Marxist Humanism,* 173–87, especially 179 and 187.

178. Miroslav Kuzý, "The Social Roots of Dogmatism," *Pravda,* Bratislava, October 19, 1966.

179. Franz Marek, "Die Zukunft des Marxismus," in Varga, ed., *Sozialismus in Europa,* 158.

180. Zbigniew Florczak, "Dialogue with the West," *Nowa Kultura,* Warsaw, October 21, 1956.

181. *Problèmes actuels du Marxisme,* 3.

182. Adam Schaff, "The Situation and the Current Tasks of Political Philosophy," *Nowe Drogi,* Warsaw, 1961, No. 3.

183. "Die Zukunft des Marxismus."

184. "The Intellectuals and the Communist Movement." English translation in *Toward a Marxist Humanism,* 165–68.

185. "Observations on the History of Marxism."

186. Harich, in *Observer,* London, March 17, 1957, 5.

187. Julian Hochfeld, "About Forgotten Polemics," *Po Prostu,* 1957, No. 7.

188. "Die Zukunft des Marxismus," in *Sozialismus in Europa,* 167.
189. Marek, "Zur Luxemburg-Renaissance," *Weg und Ziel,* No. 1 (January 1969), 16–24.
190. Marek, "Prinzip-Diskussion," *Weg und Ziel,* No. 12 (December 1968), 580–583.
191. Roger Garaudy, "Communism and Catholics—After the Promulgation of the Encyclical 'Pacem in terris,' " *Cahiers du Communisme,* Paris, 1963, Nos. 7–8.
192. Garaudy, "Wertung der Religion im Marxismus," in *Christentum und Marxismus heute,* 77 ff.
193. Lucio Lombardo-Radice, "Pluralismus in einer sozialistischen Gesell-schaft," *Christentum und Marxismus heute,* 256 ff.
194. "About the West: Once Differently."
195. Zygmunt Bauman, "The Necessity of a Sociology of Political Parties," *Mysl Filozoficzna,* Warsaw, 1957, No. 2.
196. *Problèmes actuels du Marxisme,* 34.
197. Antonin Liehms' Interview with Georg Lukács, *Literarni Noviny,* 1964, No. 3.
198. *Problèmes actuels du Marxisme,* 34.
199. Vukasin Mičunović, "The Declaration of the Conference of the Com-munist and Workers' Parties," *Borba,* December 11, 1960.
200. "The Statist Myth of Socialism," 176.
201. *Revolutionary Marxist Students in Poland Speak Out,* especially 28 and 68.
202. "The Statist Myth of Socialism," 177–81, 187.
203. Predrag Vranicki, "Zum Thema der Befreiung des Menschen," *Praxis,* in German, international edition, 1967, No. 1, 84–97.
204. "Democratization and Critical Thought."
205. "The Crisis of Our Time."
206. Kardelj, "Speech to the Federal People's Assembly of Yugoslavia," December 6, 1956, *Borba,* December 8–9, 1956; see also an abridged version in Robert Bass and Elizabeth Marbury, eds., *The Soviet-Yugo-slav Controversy 1948–58* (New York: Prospect Books, 1959), 86–104, which, however, omits this quotation.
207. "An Optimistic Tragedy?"
208. Janusz Kucynski, "On the Search for Lost Wisdom."
209. Pawel Beylin, "Marx and the Problems of Humanism," *Przeglad Kulturalny,* Warsaw, 1961, No. 48.
210. Schaff, "On the Right to Existence of a Philosophy of Man," *Przeglad Kulturalny,* Warsaw, 1962, No. 40.
211. Quoted from Roman Karst, "Wide Views on Realism," *Polytika,* War-saw, 1964, No. 1.
212. Fischer, *Kunst und Koexistenz* (Reinbek: Rowohlt Taschenbuch-Verlag, 1966), 72–73.

213. Havemann, *Dialektik ohne Dogma?* (Reinbek: Rowohlt Taschenbuch-Verlag, 1964), esp. 104, 115.
214. Havemann, "Kommunismus—Utopie und Wirklichkeit," in *Christentum und Marxismus heute,* 241.
215. Julius Strinka, "Two Opinions on Dialectics in Socialism," *Nase Teme,* Zagreb, 1965, No. 12.
216. *Christentum und Marxismus heute,* 62.
217. Stojanović, "The Present State of Yugoslav Philosophy," *Ethics,* Chicago, LXXVI, No. 5 (July 1966).
218. Svitak, "Conflicts and Solutions," *Student,* Prague, No. 5, 1968.
219. "Memorandum," 373–83.
220. *Dialektik ohne Dogma?,* 11, 150.
221. See *Christentum und Marxismus heute,* 260.
222. *Ibid.,* 329.
223. "Marxismus und Ideologie," 335–56.
224. See "Marx and Our Times—A Scientific Gathering," *Socialist Thought and Practice,* Belgrade, January–March 1964, 119–29.
225. N. Lobkowicz, ed., *Marx and the Western World* (Bloomington, Ind.: University of Notre Dame Press, 1967). See also report by Gajo Petrovic, "Marx and the Western World," *Praxis,* 1966, No. 4, 498–503.
226. See *Christentum und Marxismus heute,* and the Report on the Conference of the Paulus Society by Branko Bosnjak in *Praxis,* 1966, Nos. 1–2, 247–56.
227. See *Sozialismus in Europa.*
228. "The Necessity of the Sociology of Political Parties."
229. From a lecture by Julius Strinka at the Yugoslav-Czechoslovak Symposium in Zadar, November 1967; see "Two Opinions on Dialectics and Socialism," *Nase Teme,* 1965, No. 12.
230. Interview with Georg Lukács, *Literarni Noviny,* 1964, No. 3. A criticism of this interview, because of Lukács' "revisionist" views, appeared in *Rude Právo,* April 3, 1964.
231. Szacki, in *Po Prostu,* October 21, 1956.
232. *Christentum und Marxismus heute,* 329.
233. "Die Zukunft des Marxismus," 158.
234. *Kunst und Koexistenz,* 42.
235. "The Statist Myth of Socialism."

# Selected Bibliography

The literature on Marxism, Leninism, Stalinism, and the political and ideological arguments in present-day world Communism is extremely voluminous. This selected bibliography is therefore confined mainly to publications concerned with political concepts. The emphasis is on English-language publications of the past decade because they are most readily accessible to the interested reader.

The selected bibliography follows the structure of the book:

☐ **The Political Concepts of Marx and Engels**

*Marx and Engels: Works, Selected Works, Anthologies*

Engels, Friedrich. *Anti-Dühring*. Moscow: Progress Publishers, 1969.

———. *The Origin of the Family, Private Property, and the State*. Moscow, 1968.

———. *The Peasant War in Germany*. Moscow, 1969.

———. *Selected Writings*. W.O. Henderson (ed.). Baltimore: Penguin, 1967.

———. *Socialism: Utopian and Scientific*. Moscow, 1968.

Marx, Karl. *Articles on India*. Bombay: People's Publishing House, 1951.

———. *Capital; A Critique of Political Economy*. New York: International Publishers, 1967.

———. *The Civil War in France*. Intro. by Friedrich Engels. New York: International Publishers, 1933.

———. *The Class Struggle in France, 1848–1850*. Moscow: Progress Publishers, 1952 (several editions).

———. *The Cologne Communist Trial*. London: Lawrence & Wishart, 1971.

————. *On Colonialism and Modernization.* Shlomo Avineri (ed.). Garden City, N.Y.: Doubleday, 1968.

————. *Early Texts.* D. McLellan (trans. and ed.). Oxford: Basil Blackwell; New York: Barnes & Noble, 1971.

————. *Early Writings.* T.B. Bottomore (ed.). New York: McGraw-Hill, 1964.

————. *The Eastern Question.* New York: Burt Franklin, 1968.

————. *Economic and Philosophical Manuscripts of 1844.* Dirk S. Struik (ed.). New York: International Publishers, 1964.

————. *The Eighteenth Brumaire of Louis Bonaparte.* New York: International Publishers, 1963.

————. *The Essential Marx.* Ernst Fischer (ed.). New York: Herder and Herder, 1970.

————. *Essential Writings of Karl Marx.* David Caute (ed.). New York: Macmillan, 1967.

————. *Letters to Dr. Kugelmann.* London: Martin Lawrence, 1934.

————. *Marx on China, 1853–1860.* Dona Torr (ed.). London: Lawrence Wishart, 1951.

————. *Karl Marx: Economy, Class, and Social Revolution.* London: Michael Joseph, 1971.

————. *The Karl Marx Library.* Vol. I, arranged and edited with intro. by Saul K. Padover. New York: McGraw-Hill, 1971.

————. *Marx vs. Russia* (Selected Writings). J.A. Doerig (ed.). New York: Frederick Ungar, 1962.

————. *The Paris Commune.* London: Sidgwick & Jackson, 1971.

————. *Selected Writings in Sociology and Social Philosophy.* T.B. Bottomore and Maximilien Rubel (eds.). London: Watts, 1956.

————. *Writings on the Paris Commune.* New York: Monthly Review Press, 1971.

————. *Writings of the Young Marx on Philosophy and Society.* Lloyd D. Easton and Kurt H. Guddat (eds.). Garden City, N.Y.: Doubleday, 1961.

Marx, Karl, and Engels, Friedrich. *The American Journalism of Marx and Engels.* Henry M. Christman (ed.). New York: New American Library, 1966.

————. *Basic Writings on Politics and Philosophy.* Lewis S. Feuer (ed.). Garden City, N.Y.: Doubleday, 1959.

————. *On Britain.* Moscow: Foreign Languages Publishing House, 1962.

————. *The Civil War in the United States.* New York: International Publishers, 1937.

————. *On Colonialism.* Moscow: Progress Publishers, 1968.

————. *The Communist Manifesto.* A.J.P. Taylor (ed.). Baltimore: Penguin Books, 1969.

————. *Correspondence 1846–1895.* New York: International Publishers, 1934.

————. *Essential Works of Marxism.* Arthur P. Mendel (ed.). New York: Bantam Books, 1965.

————. *The German Ideology.* Moscow: Progress Publishers, 1968.

————. *Letters to Americans, 1848–1895.* New York: International Publishers, 1963.

————. *On Literature and Art—Selections from Their Writings.* New York: International Publishers, 1947.

————. *The Marx-Engels Reader.* Robert C. Tucker (ed.). New York: Norton, 1972.

————. *Marxist Social Thought—Selections.* Robert Freedman (ed.). New York: Harcourt Brace Jovanovich, 1968.

————. *On the Paris Commune.* Moscow: Progress Publishers, 1971.

————. *On Religion.* Moscow: Progress Publishers, 1957.

————. *On Religion.* Intro. by Reinhold Niebuhr. New York: Schocken Books, 1964.

————. *The Russian Menace to Europe.* Paul W. Blackstock and Bert F. Hoselitz (eds.). Glencoe, Ill.: Free Press; London: Allen and Unwin, 1952.

————. *Selected Correspondence.* Moscow: Progress Publishers, 1965.

————. *Selected Works.* Moscow: Progress Publishers, n.d.

————. *Selected Works in One Volume.* London: Lawrence and Wishart; New York: International Publishers, 1968.

Marx, Karl, Engels, Friedrich, and Lenin, V.I. *On Scientific Communism.* Moscow: Progress Publishers, 1967.

Selsam, Howard. *Dynamics of Social Change: A Reader in Marxist Social Science.* New York: International Publishers, 1970.

## Marx and Engels: Biographies, Memoirs, Reminiscences

Alexander, Albert. *Karl Marx—The Father of Modern Socialism.* New York: Franklin Watts, 1969.

Banning, Willem. *Karl Marx, Leben, Lehre und Bedeutung.* München und Hamburg: Taschenbuch Verlag, 1966.

Beer, Max. *The Life and Teaching of Karl Marx.* London: L. Parsons, 1925.

Berlin, Isaiah. *Karl Marx; His Life and Environment.* 3rd ed. New York: Oxford University Press, 1963.

Blumenberg, Werner. *Karl Marx in Selbstzeugnissen und Bilddokumenten.* Reinbek: Rowohlt Taschenbuchverlag, 1962.

Bruhat, Jean. *Karl Marx—Friedrich Engels: Essai biographique.* Paris: Union Generale d'Editions, 1971.

Carmichael, Joel. *Karl Marx, The Passionate Logician.* New York: Scribner's, 1967.

Carr, E. H. *Karl Marx: A Study in Fanaticism.* London: J. M. Dent, 1938.

Cornu, August. *Karl Marx et Friedrich Engels: Leur vie et leur oeuvre.* Paris: Presses Universitaires de France, 1955.

Dornemann, Luise. *Jenny Marx, Der Lebensweg einer Sozialistin.* East Berlin: Dietz Verlag, 1968.

*Familie Marx in Briefen.* Zusammengestellt und eingeleitet von Manfred Müller. Institut für Marxismus-Leninismus beim ZK der SED. East Berlin: Dietz Verlag, 1966.

Hammer, Oscar J. *The Red 48ers: Karl Marx and Friedrich Engels.* New York: Scribner's, 1969.

Kettle, Arnold. *Karl Marx.* London: Weidenfeld & Nicolson, 1963.

Künzli, Arnold. *Karl Marx—Eine Psychographie.* Wien, Frankfurt, Zürich: Europa Verlag, 1966.

Lafargue, Paul. *The Right to Be Lazy, and Other Studies.* Chicago: C.H. Kerr & Co., 1907.

Lefebvre, Henri. *Marx: Sa vie, son oeuvre.* Paris: Presses Universitaires de France, 1964.

Liebknecht, Wilhelm. *Karl Marx, Biographical Memoirs.* Chicago: Charles H. Kerr & Co., 1906.

McLellan, David. *Marx Before Marxism.* London: Macmillan; New York: Harper & Row, 1970.

*Karl Marx–Eine Biographie.* Heinrich Gemkow (ed.). East Berlin: Dietz Verlag, 1968.

*Marx und Engels und die ersten proletarischen Revolutionäre.* East Berlin: Dietz Verlag, n.d.

*Karl Marx' englischer Alltag.* Richard Sperl (ed.). East Berlin: Dietz Verlag, 1962.

*Karl Marx und die Gründung der I. Internationale.* East Berlin: Dietz Verlag, 1964.

*Karl Marx heute.* Ein Erinnerungsbuch an den 70. Todestag. Hanover: J.H.W. Dietz Nachf., 1953.

Mayer, Gustav. *Friedrich Engels.* New York: Alfred A. Knopf, 1936.

Mehring, Franz. *Karl Marx, The Story of His Life.* London: Allen and Unwin, 1951.

Mende, Georg. *Karl Marx' Entwicklung vom revolutionären Demokraten zum Kommunisten.* East Berlin: Dietz Verlag, 1955.

Mohr und General. *Erinnerungen an Marx und Engels.* East Berlin: Dietz Verlag, 1964.

Mons, Heinz. *Karl Marx und Trier—Verhältnisse, Beziehungen, Einflüsse.* Trier: Druckerei und Verlag Neu, 1964.

Morgenthaler, Walter. *Der Mensch Karl Marx.* Bern: Schweizerisches Ostinstitut, 1962.

Nikolaevsky, Boris I., and Maenchen-Helfen, Otto. *Karl Marx, Man and Fighter.* Philadelphia and London: J.B. Lippincott, 1936.

Nova, Fritz. *Friedrich Engels: His Contribution to Political Theory.* New York: Philosophical Library, 1968.

Payne, Robert. *Marx.* London: W.H. Allen; New York: Simon and Schuster, 1968.

Postgate, Raymond W. *Karl Marx.* London: Hamish Hamilton, 1933.

*Reminiscences of Marx and Engels.* Moscow: Foreign Languages Publishing House, n.d.

Riazanov, D. *Karl Marx and Friedrich Engels.* New York: International Publishers, 1927.

Rubel, Maximilien. *Bibliographie des oeuvres de Karl Marx.* Paris: M. Rivière, 1956.

―――. *Karl Marx. Essai de biographie intellectuelle.* Paris: Editions Marcel Rivière, 1971.

Ruhle, Otto. *Karl Marx, His Life and Work.* New York: Viking Press, 1929.

Schwarzschild, Leopold. *The Red Prussian: The Life and Legend of Karl Marx.* Trans. from the German. New York: Scribner's; London: Hamish Hamilton, 1947.

Schwerbrock, Wolfgang. *Karl Marx privat.* Munich: Paul List Verlag, 1962.

Spargo, John. *Karl Marx: His Life and Work.* New York: B. W. Huebsch, 1910.

Sprigge, Cecil. *Karl Marx.* London: Duckworth, 1941; New York: Macmillan, Collier Books paperback, 1962.

Ullrich, Horst. *Der junge Engels.* 2 vols. East Berlin: VEB Deutscher Verlag der Wissenschaften, 1966.

## Marxism: Presentation, Analysis, Criticism

Acton, H. B. *What Marx Really Said.* New York: Schocken Books, 1967.

Althusser, Louis. *For Marx.* New York: Random House, 1969.

Avineri, Shlomo. *The Social and Political Thought of Karl Marx.* New York and London: Cambridge University Press, 1971.

Bloch, Ernst. *Karl Marx und die Menschlichkeit.* Reinbek: Rowohlt Taschenbuchverlag, 1969.

————. *On Karl Marx.* New York: Herder and Herder, 1971.

Bober, Mandell M. *Karl Marx's Interpretation of History.* 2nd ed. Cambridge, Mass.: Harvard University Press, 1948.

Böhm-Bawerk, Eugen. *Karl Marx and the Close of His System.* New York: Macmillan, 1898.

Browder, Earl. *Marx and America.* New York: Duell, Sloan & Pearce, 1958.

Burns, Emile (ed.). *A Handbook of Marxism.* London: Victor Gollancz, 1935.

Calvez, Jean Yves. *La pensée de Karl Marx.* Paris: Editions du Seuil, 1956.

Chang, Sherman. *The Marxian Theory of the State.* Philadelphia: no publisher, 1931.

Cole, G. D. H. *The Meaning of Marxism.* London: Chapman and Hall, 1935.

————. *What Marx Really Meant.* New York: Alfred Knopf, 1934.

Curtis, Michael. *Marxism.* New York: Atherton Press, 1970.

Dahrendorf, Ralf. *Marx in Perspektive.* Die Idee des Gerechten im Denken von Karl Marx. Berlin, Hannover: J.H.W. Dietz Nachf., 1957.

Demetz, Peter. *Marx, Engels and the Poets.* Chicago: University of Chicago Press, 1967.

Duncker, Hermann. *Einführungen in den Marxismus.* Ausgewählte Schriften und Reden. 2 vols. East Berlin: Verlag Tribüne, 1958, 1959.

Fetscher, Iring. *Marx and Marxism.* New York: Herder and Herder, 1971.

Feuer, Lewis S. *Marx and the Intellectuals.* Garden City, N.Y.: Doubleday, 1969.

Fischer, Ernst. *Marx in His Own Words.* Trans. from the German: *Was Marx wirklich sagte.* London: Allen & Sons, 1970. *The Essential Marx.* New York: Herder and Herder, 1970.

Fleischer, Helmut. *Marxismus und Geschichte.* Frankfurt/M.: Suhrkamp, 1969.

Fromm, Erich. *Marxist Concept of Man.* Selected Writings of Karl Marx. New York: Frederick Ungar, 1965.

Garaudy, Roger. *Karl Marx, The Evolution of His Thought.* New York: International Publishers, 1967.

Gay, Peter. *The Dilemma of Democratic Socialism: Eduard Bernstein's Challenge to Marx.* New York: Columbia University Press; London: Oxford University Press, 1952.

Gustafsson, Bo. *Marxismus und Revisionismus: Eduard Bernsteins Kritik des Marxismus und ihre ideengeschichtliche Voraussetzungen.* Frankfurt/M.: Europäische Verlagsanstalt, 1972.

Hook, Sidney. *From Hegel to Marx: Studies in the Intellectual Development of Karl Marx.* Ann Arbor: University of Michigan Press, 1962.

————. *Towards the Understanding of Karl Marx.* New York: John Day Co., 1933.

Jackson, J. Hampden. *Marx, Proudhon and European Socialism.* New York: Collier Books, 1966.

Kamenka, Eugene. *The Ethical Foundations of Marxism.* New York: Praeger, 1962.

Kautsky, Karl. *The Class Struggle (Erfurt Program).* Chicago: C.H. Kerr, 1910.

————. *The Road to Power.* Chicago: S.A. Bloch, 1909.

Koren, Henry J. *Marx and the Authentic Man.* Pittsburgh: Duquesne University Press, 1967.

Korsch, Karl. *Karl Marx.* New York: J. Wiley & Sons, 1938.

————. *Marxism and Philosophy.* London: NLB, 1970.

Laski, Harold. *Communist Manifesto, Socialist Landmark.* London: Allen and Unwin, 1948.

Lefebvre, Henri. *Marx, sa vie, son oeuvre.* Paris: Presses Universitaires de France, 1964.

————. *The Sociology of Marx.* New York: Pantheon Books, 1968.

Lewis, John. *The Life and Teachings of Karl Marx.* New York: International Publishers, 1965.

Lichtheim, George. *Marxism: An Historical and Critical Study.* London: Routledge & Kegan Paul; New York: Praeger, 1961.

Lukács, Georg. *Karl Marx und Friedrich Engels als Literaturhistoriker.* East Berlin: Aufbau Verlag, 1952.

MacIntyre, Alasdair C. *Marxism: An Interpretation.* London: Student Christian Movement Press, 1953.

McLellan, David. *The Thought of Karl Marx.* London: Macmillan, 1971.

Mann, Golo, et al. *Karl Marx, 1818–1968.* Bad Godesberg: Inter Nationes, 1968.

Mayo, Henry B. *Introduction to Marxist Theory.* New York: Oxford University Press, 1960.

Meyer, Alfred G. *Marxism, The Unity of Theory and Practice.* Ann Arbor: University of Michigan Press, 1966.

Mitrany, David. *Marx Against the Peasant: A Study in Social Dogmatism.* London: Weidenfeld & Nicolson, 1951.

Plekhanov, G.W. *Fundamental Problems of Marxism.* New York: International Publishers, 1969.

————. *The Materialist Conception of History.* New York: International Publishers, 1940.

Spratt, Philip. *A New Look at Marx.* London: Phoenix House, 1957.

Struik, Dirk Jan. *The Birth of the Communist Manifesto.* New York: International Publishers, 1971.

Theimer, Walter. *Der Marxismus. Lehre, Wirkung, Kritik.* Munich, Bern: Francke Verlag, 1960.

Thier, Erich. *Das Menschenbild des jungen Marx.* Göttingen: Vandenhoeck & Ruprecht, 1961.

Trotsky, Leon. *The Communist Manifesto Today.*

―――. *The Living Thoughts of Karl Marx.* New York: Longmans, 1939.

Tucker, Robert C. *Philosophy and Myth in Karl Marx.* Cambridge, Mass.: Harvard University Press, 1961.

Wolfe, Bertram D. *Marx and America.* New York: John Day, 1934.

☐ **The Political Concepts of Leninism**

*Lenin: Collected Works, Selected Works, Anthologies*

Lenin, V.I. *Collected Works.* New York: International Publishers, 1927–45.

―――. *Collected Works.* 44 vols. Moscow: Foreign Languages Publishing House, 1960–70.

―――. *Against Imperialist War.* Articles and Speeches. Moscow: Progress Publishers, 1968.

―――. *Alliance of the Working Class and the Peasants.* Moscow: Progress Publishers, 1959, 1965.

―――. *The April Theses.* Moscow: Foreign Languages Publishing House, 1951.

―――. *On Britain.* Moscow: Foreign Languages Publishing House, n.d.

―――. *Capitalism and Agriculture.* New York: International Publishers, 1946.

―――. *The Collapse of the Second International.* Moscow: Foreign Languages Publishing House, 1952.

―――. *Critical Remarks on the National Question.* Moscow: Foreign Languages Publishing House, 1951.

―――. *On Culture and Cultural Revolution.* Moscow: Progress Publishers, 1970.

―――. *The Development of Capitalism in Russia.* Moscow: Foreign Languages Publishing House, 1956.

―――. *The Emancipation of Women.* From the Writings of V.I. Lenin. Preface by Nadezhda Krupskaya, with an appendix "Lenin on the Woman Question" by Clara Zetkin. New York: International Publishers, 1934; rev. ed., 1966.

————. *On the Foreign Policy of the Soviet State.* Moscow: Progress Publishers, n.d.

————. *Imperialism, the Highest Stage of Capitalism.* Rev. trans. New York: International Publishers, 1969.

————. *"Left Wing" Communism: An Infantile Disorder.* New York: International Publishers, 1940.

————. *Lenin on Politics and Revolution.* Selections. James E. Connor (ed.). New York: Pegasus, 1968.

————. *The Lenin Reader.* Stephen T. Possony (ed.). Chicago: Regnery, 1960.

————. *V.I. Lenin: Selected Works.* London: Lawrence & Wishart, 1969.

————. *Lenin on the United States.* Selected Writings. New York: International Publishers, 1970.

————. *Lenin's Impact on the United States.* Daniel Mason and Jessica Smith (eds.). New York: New Publications, 1970.

————. *Letters from Afar.* London: Martin Lawrence, 1932.

————. *The Letters of Lenin.* Elizabeth Hill and Doris Mudie (eds. and trans.). New York: Harcourt, Brace, 1937.

————. *Marx, Engels, Marxism.* Moscow: Progress Publishers, 1968.

————. *The Paris Commune.* London: Martin Lawrence, 1931.

————. *On the Paris Commune.* Moscow: Progress Publishers, 1970.

————. *On Proletarian Internationalism.* Moscow: Progress Publishers, 1967.

————. *The Proletarian Revolution and the Renegade Kautsky.* Moscow: Foreign Languages Publishing House, 1952.

————. *Questions of National Policy and Proletarian Internationalism.* Moscow: Progress Publishers, 1970.

————. *The Right of Nations to Self-determination.* New York: International Publishers, 1951.

————. *On Socialist Economic Organization.* Collected Articles and Speeches. Moscow: Progress Publishers, 1967.

————. *On the State Apparatus.* Articles and Speeches. Moscow: Progress Publishers, 1969.

————. *State and Revolution.* New York: International Publishers, 1932.

————. *One Step Forward, Two Steps Back.* London: Lawrence & Wishart, 1941.

————. *The Teachings of Karl Marx.* New York: International Publishers, 1933.

————. *On Trade Unions.* Selected Speeches and Letters. Moscow: Progress Publishers, 1970.

————. *Two Tactics of Social Democracy in the Democratic Revolution.* New York: International Publishers, 1935.

————. *On the United States of America.* Moscow: Progress Publishers, 1967.

————. *On the Unity of the International Communist Movement.* Moscow: Progress Publishers, 1966.

————. *On Utopian and Scientific Socialism.* Articles and Speeches. Moscow: Progress Publishers, 1965.

————. *What Is to Be Done?* New York: International Publishers, 1929.

————. *What Is Soviet Power?* Moscow: Progress Publishers, 1969.

————. *Will the Bolsheviks Retain State Power?* London: Martin Lawrence; New York: International Publishers, 1932.

————. *On the Workers' Control and Nationalization of Industry.* Collected Articles and Speeches. Moscow: Progress Publishers, 1969.

Lenin, V.I., and Zinoviev, G. *Socialism and War.* London: Martin Lawrence, 1931.

## Lenin: Biographies, Memoirs, Reminiscences

Balabanoff, Angelica. *Impressions of Lenin.* Ann Arbor: University of Michigan Press, 1964.

Conquest, Robert. *V. I. Lenin.* New York: Viking Press, 1972.

Deutscher, Isaac. *Lenin's Childhood.* London: Oxford University Press, 1970.

Fischer, Louis. *The Life of Lenin.* New York: Harper & Row, 1964.

Fox, Ralph. *Lenin, A Biography.* New York: Harcourt Brace Jovanovich, 1934.

Gourfinkel, Nina. *Portrait of Lenin.* New York: Herder and Herder, 1972.

Hahlweg, Werner. *Lenins Rückkehr nach Russland 1917.* Die deutschen Akten. Leiden, 1957.

Hölzle, Erwin. *Lenin 1917.* Die Geburt der Revolution aus dem Kriege. Munich: Oldenbourg, 1957.

Krupskaya, Nadezhda Konstantinovna. *Memories of Lenin.* London: Martin Lawrence, 1930.

*V.I. Lenin—A Biography.* Moscow: Progress Publishers, n.d.

*Lenin Through the Eyes of the World.* Selected Letters and Comments from Foreigners. Moscow, 1969.

*Lenin. Leben und Werk.* Contributions by Bukharin, Kamenev, Lepeshinski, Radek, Rykov, Zinoviev, Stalin, Trotsky, Ulianov, et al. Vienna: Verlag für Literatur und Politik, 1924.

*Lenin's Comrades-in-Arms.* Moscow: Progress Publishers, 1969.

Lewin, Moshe. *Lenin's Last Struggle.* New York: Vintage Books, 1968.

Marcu, Valeriu. *Lenin.* London: Victor Gollancz, 1928.

Possony, Stefan T. *Lenin, the Compulsive Revolutionary.* Chicago: Regnery, 1964; London: Allen and Unwin, 1966.

Radek, Karl. *Lenin.* Berlin: Neuer Deutscher Verlag, 1924.

Rauch, Georg v. *Lenin—Grundlegung des Sowjetsystems.* Berlin, Frankfurt/M.: Musterschmidt Verlag, 1958.

Schapiro, Leonard, and Reddaway, Peter (eds.). *Lenin: The Man, the Theorist, the Leader; A Reappraisal.* New York: Praeger, 1964.

Shub, David. *Lenin: A Biography.* Garden City, N.Y.: Doubleday, 1948; Harmondsworth: Penguin Books, 1966.

Trotsky, Leon. *Lenin: Notes for a Biographer.* Rev. ed. Intro. by Bertram D. Wolfe, trans. by Tamara Deutscher. New York: Putnam's, 1971.

*Unvergesslicher Lenin.* Erinnerungen deutscher Genossen. East Berlin: Dietz Verlag, 1957.

Valentinov, Nikolai (Volsky, N.V.). *Encounters with Lenin.* New York and London: Oxford University Press, 1968.

Williams, Albert Rhys. *Lenin, The Man and His Work.* New York: Scott and Seltzer, 1919.

Zetkin, Clara. *Reminiscences of Lenin.* London: Modern Books, 1929.

Zinoviev, Grigory. *Nicolai Lenin, His Life and Work.* Cleveland: Toiler Publishing Assoc., 1919.

*The Lenin Era and Leninism: Presentation, Analysis, Criticism*

Abramovitch, Raphael R. *The Soviet Revolution.* New York: International Universities Press, 1962.

Anweiler, Oskar. *Die Rätebewegung in Russland 1905 bis 1921.* Leiden, Köln: Brill, 1958.

Avrich, Paul. *Kronstadt 1921.* Princeton, N.J.: Princeton University Press, 1970.

Azizian, A. *Lenin on Proletarian Internationalism.* Moscow, 1964.

Brahm, Heinz. *Trotzkis Kampf um die Nachfolge Lenins.* Die ideologische Auseinandersetzung 1923–1926. Cologne: Verlag Wissenschaft und Politik, 1964.

Bukharin, N. *Historical Materialism—A System of Sociology.* Ann Arbor: University of Michigan Press, 1969.

Bukharin, N., and Preobrazhensky, E. *The ABC of Communism.* Baltimore: Penguin Books, 1969.

Carr, Edward H. *The Bolshevik Revolution.* 3 vols. New York: Macmillan, 1951–53.

———. *The Interregnum, 1923–1924.* New York: Macmillan, 1954.

———. *Socialism in One Country, 1924–1926.* New York: Macmillan, 1958.

Chamberlin, William Henry. *The Russian Revolution, 1917–1921.* 2 vols. New York and London: Macmillan, 1935; reissued with new intro., 1952.

Chernov, Victor M. *The Great Russian Revolution.* New Haven: Yale University Press, 1936.

Curtiss, John S. *The Russian Revolution of 1917.* New York and London: Van Nostrand, 1962.

Dan, Theodore. *The Origins of Bolshevism.* London: Secker & Warburg, 1964; New York: Schocken Books, 1971.

Daniels, Robert V. *The Conscience of the Revolution: Communist Opposition in Soviet Russia.* Cambridge, Mass.: Harvard University Press, 1960.

———. *Red October: The Bolshevik Revolution of 1917.* New York: Scribner's, 1967.

Deutscher, Isaac. *The Prophet Armed: Trotsky, 1879–1921.* London and New York: Oxford University Press, 1954.

Ehrenburg, Ilya. *First Years of Revolution 1918–1921.* Trans. from the Russian. London: MacGibbon & Kee, 1962.

Footman, David. *Civil War in Russia.* London: Faber & Faber; New York: Praeger, 1961.

———. *The Russian Revolutions.* London: Faber & Faber, 1962.

Geyer, Dietrich. *Lenin in der russischen Sozialdemokratie.* Die Arbeiterbewegung im Zarenreich als Organisationsproblem der revolutionären Intelligenz 1890–1903. Cologne, 1962.

Goldman, Emma. *My Disillusionment in Russia.* New York: Thomas Y. Crowell, 1970.

Grottian, Walter. *Lenins Anleitung zum Handeln.* Theorie und Praxis sowjetischer Aussenpolitik. Cologne, Opladen: Westdeutscher Verlag, 1962.

Gruber, Helmut. *International Communism in the Era of Lenin. A Documentary History.* New York: Fawcett Publications, 1967.

Haimson, Leopold H. *The Russian Marxists and the Origins of Bolshevism.* Cambridge, Mass.: Harvard University Press; London: Oxford University Press, 1955.

Hillquit, Morris. *From Marx to Lenin.* New York: Hanford Press, 1921.

*History of the October Revolution.* U.S.S.R. Academy of Sciences. Moscow: Progress Publishers, 1966.

Kautsky, Karl. *Bolshevism at a Deadlock*. London: Allen and Unwin, 1931.

———. *The Dictatorship of the Proletariat*. Ann Arbor: University of Michigan Press, 1964.

———. *Social Democracy Versus Communism*. David Shub (ed.). Intro. by Sidney Hook. New York: Rand School Press, 1946.

———. *Terrorism and Communism*. London: Allen and Unwin, 1920.

Kindersley, Richard. *The First Russian Revisionists: A Study of "Legal Marxism" in Russia*. London and New York: Oxford University Press, 1962.

Lazitch, Branco. *Lénine et la IIIe International*. Neuchâtel, 1951.

*Lenin and the World Revolutionary Working Class Movement*. Moscow: Progress Publishers, 1971.

*Lenin's Ideas and Cause Are Immortal*. Moscow: Novosti Press, 1970.

Lerner, Warren. *Karl Radek, The Last Internationalist*. Stanford: Stanford University Press, 1970.

Liberman, Simon I. *Building Lenin's Russia*. Chicago: University of Chicago Press, 1945.

Löwy, A.G. *Die Weltgeschichte ist das Weltgericht*. Bukharin: Vision des Kommunismus. Wien, Frankfurt, Zürich: Europa Verlag, 1969.

Lukács, Georg. *History and Class Consciousness*. Cambridge, Mass.: M.I.T. Press, 1971.

———. *Lenin; A Study on the Unity of His Thought*. London: NLB, 1970; Cambridge, Mass.: M.I.T. Press, 1971.

Lunacharsky, A.V. *Revolutionary Silhouettes*. Trans. and ed. by Michael Glenny. Intro. by I. Deutscher. London: Penguin Press, 1967.

Luxemburg, Rosa. *The Russian Revolution*, and *Leninism or Marxism?* New intro. by Bertram D. Wolfe. Ann Arbor: University of Michigan Press, 1961.

Mason, Daniel, and Smith, Jessica (eds.) *Lenin's Impact on the United States*. New York: NWR Publications, 1970.

Meyer, Alfred G. *Leninism*. Cambridge, Mass.: Harvard University Press; London: Oxford University Press, 1957.

Nettl, J. Peter. *Rosa Luxemburg*. New York and London: Oxford University Press, 1966.

Nürnberger, Richard. *Lenins Revolutionstheorie*. Eine Studie über Staat und Revolution. In *Marxismusstudien* (Bd. 1). Tübingen, 1954.

Page, Stanley W. *Lenin and World Revolution*. New York: McGraw-Hill, 1952. Rev. ed., 1970.

Pannekoek, Anton. *Lenin as a Philosopher*. New York: New Essays, 1948.

Pethybridge, Roger. *Witnesses to the Russian Revolution*. New York: Citadel Press, 1964.

*Petrograd, October 1917.* Moscow: Foreign Languages Publishing House, 1957.

Pipes, Richard (ed.). *Revolutionary Russia: A Symposium.* Garden City, N.Y.: Doubleday, 1969.

———. *Social Democracy and the St. Petersburg Labor Movement, 1885–1897.* Cambridge, Mass.: Harvard University Press; London: Oxford University Press, 1962.

Pollack, Emmanuel. *The Kronstadt Rebellion.* New York: Philosophical Library, 1959.

Postgate, R.W. *The Bolshevik Theory.* London, 1920.

Ransome, Arthur. *Russia in 1919.* New York: B. W. Huebsch, 1919.

Reed, John. *Ten Days That Shook the World.* New York: International Publishers, 1967.

Roy, M.N. *The Russian Revolution.* Calcutta: Rennaissance Publishers, 1949.

Schapiro, Leonard B. *The Origin of the Communist Autocracy: Political Opposition in the Soviet State, First Phase 1917–1922.* Cambridge, Mass.: Harvard University Press; London: Bell, 1955.

Sukhanov, Nikolai Nikolaevitch. *The Russian Revolution, 1917. A Personal Record.* London and New York: Oxford University Press, 1955.

Sweezy, P.M. (ed.). *Lenin Today.* Eight Essays on the Hundredth Anniversary of Lenin's Birth. New York: Monthly Review Press, 1970.

Treadgold, Donald W. *Lenin and His Rivals: The Struggle for Russia's Future, 1898–1906.* New York: Praeger; London: Methuen, 1955.

Trotsky, Leon. *The Age of Permanent Revolution.* A Trotsky Anthology. Intro. and ed. by I. Deutscher. New York: Dell, 1964.

———. *The First Five Years of the Communist International.* 2 vols. New York: The Monad Press, 1965; rev. ed., 1972.

———. *The History of the Russian Revolution.* New York: Simon and Schuster, 1932.

———. *On Lenin's Testament.* With "The Testament of Lenin." New York: Pioneer Publishers, 1948.

———. *Lessons of October.* New York: Pioneer Publishers, 1937.

———. *Literature and Revolution.* New York: Russell & Russell, 1957.

———. *The New Course.* Ann Arbor: University of Michigan Press, 1965.

———. *The Permanent Revolution.* New York: Pioneer Publishers, 1931.

———. *Writings on Literature and Art.* New York: Pathfinder Press, 1969.

Ulam, Adam B. *The Bolsheviks: An Intellectual and Political History of the Triumph of Communism in Russia.* New York: Macmillan, 1965.

Voline. *Nineteen Seventeen: The Russian Revolution Betrayed.* London: Freedom Press; New York: Libertarian Book Club, 1954.

————. *The Unknown Revolution* (Kronstadt 1921. Ukraine 1918–21). New York: Libertarian Book Club; London: Freedom Press, 1955.

Wilde, Harry. *Trotzki—In Selbstzeugnissen und Bilddokumenten.* Reinbek: Rowohlt Taschenbuchverlag, 1969.

Wolfe, Bertram D. *Three Who Made a Revolution: A Biographical History.* New York: Dial Press, 1948; London: Thames & Hudson, 1956.

Zeman, Z.A.B. *Germany and the Revolution in Russia 1915–1918.* Documents from the Archives of the German Foreign Ministry. London and New York: Oxford University Press, 1958.

## ☐ The Political Concepts of Stalinism

*Stalin: Works, Anthologies, Articles, and Speeches*

Stalin, Joseph. *Works.* 13 vols. Moscow: Foreign Languages Publishing House, 1952–55.

————. *Anarchism or Socialism?* Moscow: Library of Marxist-Leninist Classics, 1952.

————. *Defects in Party Work and Measures for Liquidating Trotskyite and Other Double-Dealers.* Report and Speech March 3–5, 1937. Moscow: Cooperative Publishing Society of Foreign Workers in the U.S.S.R., 1937.

————. *Dialectical and Historical Materialism.* New York: International Publishers, 1940.

————. *The Draft New Constitution.* London: The Anglo-Russian Parliamentary Committee, 1936.

————. *Economic Problems of Socialism in the U.S.S.R.* Moscow: Foreign Languages Publishing House, 1952.

————. *The Essential Stalin: Major Theoretical Writings, 1905–1952.* Bruce Franklin (ed.). New York: Anchor Books, 1972.

————. *Foundations of Leninism.* New York: International Publishers, 1932.

————. *The Foundations of Leninism; On the Problem of Leninism.* Moscow: Foreign Languages Publishing House, 1950.

————. *The Great Patriotic War of the Soviet Union.* New York: International Publishers, 1945.

————. *Lenin.* Three Speeches About Lenin. New York: International Publishers, 1934.

————. *Marxism and Linguistics.* New York: International Publishers, 1951.

————. *Marxism and the National and Colonial Question.* Collected Articles and Speeches. New York: International Publishers, 1936.

————. *Marxism and the National Question.* New York: International Publishers, 1942.

————. *Selected Works.* Davis, Ca.: Cardinal Publishers, 1971.

————. "Speech at the Nineteenth Party Congress, October 14, 1952." Moscow, 1952.

————. *Stalin on China.* Collected Writings. Bombay: People's Publishing House, 1951.

## *Stalin: Biographies, Memoirs, Reminiscences*

Alliluyeva, Svetlana. *Twenty Letters to a Friend.* New York: Harper & Row, 1967.

Barbusse, Henri. *Stalin.* New York: Macmillan, 1935.

Basseches, Nikolaus. *Stalin.* New York: Dutton; London: Staples Press, 1952.

Benoit, Jean. *Staline.* Paris: Editions Resma, 1969.

Deutscher, Isaac. *Stalin: A Political Biography.* London and New York: Oxford University Press, 1949.

Djilas, Milovan. *Conversations with Stalin.* New York: Harcourt Brace Jovanovich; London: Rupert Hart-Davis, 1962.

Fischer, Louis. *The Life and Death of Stalin.* New York: Harper & Row, 1952.

Fishman, Jack, and Hutton, J. Bernard. *The Private Life of Josif Stalin.* London: W. H. Allen, 1962.

Hutton, J. Bernard. *Stalin—The Miraculous Georgian.* London: Spearman, 1961.

Lyons, Eugene. *Stalin: Czar of All the Russias.* New York: Lippincott, 1940.

Molotov, V. M., et al. *Stalin. Articles for the Occasion of His Sixtieth Birthday, December 21, 1939.* New York: Workers Library Publishers, 1940.

Murphy, J. T. *Stalin 1879–1944.* London: The Bodley Head, 1945.

Payne, Robert. *The Rise and Fall of Stalin.* New York: Simon and Schuster, 1965.

Smith, Edward Ellis. *The Young Stalin: The Early Years of an Elusive Revolutionary.* New York: Farrar, Straus & Giroux, 1967.

Souvarine, Boris. *Stalin: A Critical Survey of Bolshevism.* Trans. by C.L.R. James. London: Secker and Warburg, 1939.

Trotsky, Leon. *Stalin: An Appraisal of the Man and His Influence.* New York: Harper & Row; London: Hollis and Carter, 1946.

*The Stalin Era and Stalinism:*
*Presentation, Analysis, Criticism*

Achminow, Hermann. *Die Totengräber des Kommunismus—Eine Soziologie der bolschewistischen Revolutionen.* Stuttgart: Steingrüben Verlag, 1964.

Avtorkhanov, Abdurakhman. *Stalin and the Soviet Communist Party: A Study in the Technology of Power.* New York: Praeger; London: Stevens, 1959.

Barghoorn, Frederick C. *Soviet Russian Nationalism.* New York: Oxford University Press, 1956.

Beck, F., and Godin, W. (pseuds.) *Russian Purge and the Extraction of Confession.* New York: Viking Press; London: Hurst & Blackett, 1951.

Brzezinski, Zbigniew K. *The Permanent Purge: Politics in Soviet Totalitarianism.* Cambridge, Mass.: Harvard University Press; London: Oxford University Press, 1956.

Cliff, Tony. *Stalinist Russia, A Marxist Analysis.* London: M. Kidron, 1955.

Conquest, Robert. *The Great Terror—Stalin's Purge of the Thirties.* New York and London: Macmillan, 1968.

Daniels, Robert V. *The Conscience of the Revolution: Communist Opposition in Soviet Russia.* Cambridge, Mass.: Harvard University Press; London: Oxford University Press, 1961.

Daniels, Robert V. (ed.). *The Stalin Revolution—Fulfillment or Betrayal of Communism?* Boston: D. C. Heath, 1965.

Eastman, Max. *Stalin's Russia and the Crisis in Socialism.* New York: W. W. Norton, 1940.

Fischer, George. *Soviet Opposition to Stalin: A Case Study in World War II.* Cambridge, Mass.: Harvard University Press; London: Oxford University Press, 1952.

Gurian, Waldemar (ed.). *The Soviet Union: Background, Ideology, Reality.* Bloomington: University of Notre Dame Press, 1951.

Hazard, John N. *Law and Social Change in the U.S.S.R.* London: London Institute of World Affairs, 1953.

Hofmann, Werner. *Stalinismus und Antikommunismus—Zur Soziologie des Ost-West-Konflikts.* Frankfurt/M.: Suhrkamp Verlag, 1967.

Joravsky, David. *Soviet Marxism and Natural Science 1917–32.* New York: Columbia University Press, 1961.

Katkov, George. *The Trial of Bukharin.* London: B. T. Batsford, 1969.

Lewitzkyj, Borys. *Die rote Inquisition.* Frankfurt/M.: Societäts-Verlag, 1967.

Lyons, Eugene. *Workers' Paradise Lost.* New York: Paperback Library, 1967.

McKenzie, Kermit E. *Comintern and World Revolution, 1928–1943*. New York and London: Columbia University Press, 1964.

Marek, Franz. *Was Stalin Wirklich Sagte*. Vienna: Molden, 1970.

Medvedev, Roy A. *Let History Judge: The Origins and Consequences of Stalinism*. New York: Alfred A. Knopf, 1971.

Medvedev, Zhores A. *The Rise and Fall of T.D. Lysenko*. New York and London: Columbia University Press, 1969.

Mehnert, Klaus. *Stalin Versus Marx: The Stalinist Historical Doctrine*. New York: Macmillan; London: Allen and Unwin, 1952.

Milosz, Czeslaw. *The Captive Mind*. New York: Alfred A. Knopf, 1953.

Moore, Barrington. *Soviet Politics—The Dilemma of Power*. Cambridge, Mass.: Harvard University Press; London: Oxford University Press, 1950.

Rigby, Thomas H. (ed.). *Stalin*. Englewood Cliffs, N.J.: Prentice-Hall, 1966.

Rosenberg, Arthur. *A History of Bolshevism*. Garden City, N.Y.: Doubleday, 1967.

Schapiro, Leonard. *The Communist Party of the Soviet Union*. New York: Random House, 1959.

Scharndorff, Werner. *Moskaus permanente Säuberung*. Munich: Günter Olzog Verlag, 1961.

Schwarz, Solomon. *Labor in the Soviet Union*. New York: Praeger, 1952.

Seton-Watson, Hugh. *From Lenin to Khrushchev: The History of World Communism*. New York and London: Praeger, 1960.

Shachtman, Max. *Behind the Moscow Trials*. New York: Pioneer Publishers, 1936.

———. *The Bureaucratic Revolution: The Rise of the Stalinist State*. New York: Ronald Press, 1962.

*Stalin's Slave Camps: An Indictment of Modern Slavery*. Brussels: International Federation of Free Trade Unions; Boston: Beacon Press, 1951.

Sternberg, Fritz. *The End of a Revolution: Soviet Russia from Revolution to Reaction*. New York: John Day, 1953.

Towster, Julian. *Political Power in the U.S.S.R., 1917 to 1947*. The Theory and Structure of Government in the Soviet State. New York: Oxford University Press, 1948.

Trotsky, Leon. *The Class Nature of the Soviet State*. London: New Park Publications, 1968.

———. *In Defense of Marxism*. New York: Pioneer Publishers, 1942.

———. *The Revolution Betrayed*. New York: Merit Publishers, 1966.

———. *The Soviet Union and the Fourth International*. The Class Nature of the Soviet State. New York: Communist League of America, 1934.

————. *The Stalin School of Falsification.* New York: Pioneer Publishers, 1936.

————. *Stalinism and Bolshevism.* New York: Pioneer Publishers, 1937.

————. *Stalin's Frame-up System and the Moscow Trials.* New York: Pioneer Publishers, 1950.

————. *The Suppressed Testament of Lenin.* New York: Pioneer Publishers, 1935.

————. *Their Morals and Ours.* Merit Publishers, 1966.

————. *The Third International After Lenin.* New York: Pioneer Publishers, 1936.

————. *The Workers' State and the Question of Thermidor and Bonapartism.* London: New Park Publications, 1968.

Tucker, Robert C., and Cohen, Stephen F. (eds.). *The Great Purge Trial.* New York: Grosset and Dunlap, 1965.

Uralov, Alexander (pseud. of A. Avtorkhanov). *The Reign of Stalin.* Trans. from the French. London: The Bodley Head, 1953.

von Laue, Theodore H. *Why Lenin? Why Stalin?* Philadelphia: J.B. Lippincott, 1964.

von Rauch, Georg. *A History of Soviet Russia.* New York: Praeger; London: Thames & Hudson, 1957.

Webb, Beatrice and Sidney. *Soviet Communism: A New Civilization?* New York: Scribner's, 1936.

Werth, Alexander. *Russia at War: 1941–1945.* New York: Avon Books, 1964.

Wolfe, Bertram D. *Six Keys to the Soviet System.* Boston: Beacon Press, 1956.

## The Stalin Era: Memoirs and Eyewitness Accounts

Barmine, Alexander. *One Who Survived: The Life Story of a Russian Under the Soviets.* Intro. by Max Eastman. New York: Putnam's, 1945.

Bialer, Seweryn. *Stalin and His Generals: Soviet Military Memoirs of World War II.* New York: Pegasus, 1969.

Borodin, Nikolai M. *One Man in His Time.* London: Constable; New York: Macmillan, 1955.

Buber-Neumann, Margarete. *Under Two Dictators.* New York: Dodd, Mead, 1951.

Ciliga, Anton, *Au pays du grand mensonge.* Paris: Gallimard, 1938.

Crossman, R. H. S. (ed.). *The God That Failed: Six Studies in Communism.* London: Hamish Hamilton; New York: Harper and Row, 1950.

Derjabin, Peter, and Gibney, Frank. *The Secret World.* Garden City, N.Y.: Doubleday; London: Barker, 1959.

Ehrenburg, Ilya. *Memoirs: 1921–1941.* New York: Grosset & Dunlap, 1966.

Einsiedel, Heinrich von. *I Joined the Russians: A Captured German Flier's Diary of the Communist Temptation.* New Haven: Yale University Press, 1953.

Ginzburg, Eugenia Semenovna. *Journey into the Whirlwind.* New York: Harcourt Brace Jovanovich, 1967.

Giordano, Ralph. *Die Partei hat immer recht. . . .* Cologne: Kiepenheuer & Witsch, 1961.

Gliksman, Jerzy. *Tell the West.* New York: Gresham Press, 1948.

Gniffke, Erich W. *Jahre mit Ulbricht.* Cologne: Verlag Wissenschaft und Politik, 1970.

Gollwitzer, Helmut. *Unwilling Journey: A Diary from Russia.* Trans. from the German. London: Student Christian Movement Press, 1953.

Gonzalez, Valentin. *El Campesino: Life and Death in Soviet Russia.* New York: Putnam's; London: Heinemann, 1952.

Gorbatov, A. V. *Years of My Life: A Soviet General's Experiences of the Stalinist Purges* (abridged translation from Gorbatov's autobiography published in *Novy Mir,* Moscow, March–May 1964). London: Constable, 1964.

Gouzenko, Igor. *This Was My Choice.* London: Eyre & Spottiswoode, 1948.

Granovsky, Anatoli. *All Pity Choked: The Memoirs of a Soviet Secret Agent.* London: Kimber, 1955.

Haldane, Charlotte. *Truth Will Out.* London: Weidenfeld & Nicolson, 1949.

Herling, Gustav. *A World Apart.* Trans. from the Polish. Preface by Bertrand Russell. London: Heinemann; New York: Roy, 1951.

Hutton, Joseph B. *The Great Illusion.* London: David Bruce & Watson, 1970.

Hyde, Douglas. *I Believed.* London: Heinemann; New York: Putnam's, 1950.

Kantorowicz, Alfred. *Deutsches Tagebuch.* 2 vols. Munich: Kindler Verlag, 1959–61.

Kasenkina, Oksana S. *Leap to Freedom.* Philadelphia: Lippincott, 1949; London: Hurst & Blackett, 1950.

Kaznacheev, Aleksandr I. *Inside a Soviet Embassy; Experiences of a Russian Diplomat in Burma.* Philadelphia: Lippincott, 1962.

Khokhlov, Nikolai. *In the Name of Conscience.* New York: McKay; London: Muller, 1959.

Klimov, Gregory. *The Terror Machine: The Inside Story of the Soviet Administration in Germany.* New York: Praeger; London: Faber & Faber, 1953.

Koestler, Arthur. *Arrow in the Blue: An Autobiography.* London: Collins with Hamish Hamilton; New York: Macmillan, 1952.

——. *The Invisible Writing.* London: Collins with Hamish Hamilton; New York: Macmillan, 1954.

Kravchenko, Victor. *I Chose Freedom.* New York: Scribner's; London: Hale, 1946.

Krüger, Horst. *Das Ende einer Utopie. Hingabe und Selbstbefreiung früherer Kommunisten.* Olten und Freiburg: Walter Verlag, 1963.

Kuvsinen, Aino. *Der Gott stürzt seine Engel.* Vienna: Molden, 1972.

Leonhard, Susanne. *Gestohlenes Leben.* Schicksal einer politischen Emigrantin in der Sowjetunion. Herford: Nicolaische Verlagsbuchhandlung, 1967.

Leonhard, Wolfgang. *Child of the Revolution.* London: Collins; Chicago: Regnery, 1957.

Lipper, Elinor. *Eleven Years in Soviet Prison Camps.* London: Hollis & Carter; Chicago: Regnery, 1951.

London, Artur. *The Confession.* New York: Ballantine Books, 1970.

Ludovici, L.J. *Tomorrow Sometimes Comes: Ten Years Against Tyranny.* Foreword by Earl Attlee. London: Odhams, 1957.

Maisky, Ivan. *Memoirs of a Soviet Ambassador. The War: 1939–43.* New York: Scribner's, 1967.

Mandelshtam, Nadezhda. *Hope Against Hope.* New York: Atheneum, 1971.

Orlov, Alexander. *The Secret History of Stalin's Crimes.* New York: Random House; London: Jarrolds, 1953.

Parvilahti, Unto. *Beria's Gardens: Ten Years in Captivity in Russia and Siberia.* London: Hutchinson; New York: Dutton, 1959.

Petrov, Vladimir. *It Happens in Russia.* London: Eyre & Spottiswoode, 1951.

Petrov, Vladimir and Evdokia. *Empire of Fear.* London: Andre Deutsch; New York: Praeger, 1956.

Pirogov, Peter. *Why I Escaped.* New York: Duell, Sloan & Pearce; London: Harvill Press, 1950.

Pollak, Stephen. *Strange Land Behind Me.* London: Falcon Press, 1951.

Prauss, Herbert. *Doch es war nicht die Wahrheit.* Berlin: Morus Verlag, 1960.

Roeder, Bernhard. *Katorga: An Aspect of Modern Slavery.* London: Heinemann, 1958.

Savarius, Vincent, and Szasz, Bela Sandor. *Volontaires pour la potence.* Paris: Juilliard, 1963.

Schenk, Fritz. *Im Vorzimmer der Diktatur.* 12 Jahre Pankow. Cologne: Kiepenheuer & Witsch, 1962.

Scholmer, Joseph. *Vorkuta.* London: Weidenfeld & Nicolson; New York: Holt, Rinehart and Winston, 1954.

Serge, Victor. *From Lenin to Stalin*. New York: Monad Press, 1937; rev. ed., 1973.

————. *Memoirs of a Revolutionary, 1901–1941*. London and New York: Oxford University Press, 1963.

Sinko, Ervin. *Roman eines Romans*. Moskauer Tagebuch. Cologne: Verlag Wissenschaft und Politik, 1962.

Tokaev, G.A. *Betrayal of an Ideal*. London: Harvill Press; Bloomington: Indiana University Press, 1954.

————. *Comrade X*. London: Harvill Press, 1956.

Trotsky, Leon. *Diary in Exile*. Cambridge, Mass.: Harvard University Press, 1958.

————. *My Life*. New York: Merit Publishers, 1970.

Valtin, Jan (Krebs, Richard J.H.). *Out of the Night*. New York: Alliance Book Corp., 1941.

Weissberg, Alexander. *The Accused*. New York: Simon and Schuster, 1951.

## ☐ Soviet Political Concepts After Stalin

*Khrushchev: Speeches, Articles, Anthologies*

Khrushchev, N.S. *An Account of the Party of the People*. Moscow, 1961.

————. *The Anatomy of Terror: Khrushchev's Revelations About Stalin's Regime*. Washington, D.C.: Public Affairs Press, 1956.

————. *Collected Articles:* "Imperialism"; "The National Liberation Movement"; "The Revolutionary Working Class"; "Socialism and Communism"; "To Avert War—Our Prime Task."

————. *Conquest Without War*. An Analytical Anthology of Speeches, Interviews, Remarks. New York: Simon and Schuster, 1961.

————. "The Crimes of the Stalin Era: Special Report to the Twentieth Congress of the Communist Party of the Soviet Union." New York: *New Leader*.

————. *Disarmament and Colonial Freedom*. Speeches and Interviews at the United Nations, Sept.–Oct. 1960. London: Lawrence & Wishart, 1961.

————. *Freedom and Independence of All Colonial Peoples*. Moscow, 1960.

————. *General and Complete Disarmament Is a Guarantee of Peace and Security for All Nations*. Moscow, 1962.

————. *The Great Mission of Literature and Art*. Moscow: Progress Publishers, 1964.

————. *Khrushchev in America*. Full Text of His Speeches During the Tour of the United States. New York: Crossroads Press, 1960.

————. "Khrushchev on Culture." London: *Encounter,* 1963.

————. *Khrushchev Remembers.* Intro., commentary, and notes by E. Crankshaw. Trans. and ed. by Strobe Talbott. Boston: Little, Brown, 1970.

————. *Khrushchev Speaks.* Selected Speeches, etc., 1949–61. Ann Arbor: University of Michigan Press, 1963.

————. *The Land of Soviets.* Collected Articles. Moscow: Foreign Languages Press, 1957.

————. *Let Us Live in Peace and Friendship.* Visit to the United States, Sept. 15–27, 1959.

————. *The National Liberation Movement.* Moscow: Foreign Languages Publishing House, 1963.

————. *On Peaceful Coexistence.* Collection of Speeches and Articles. Moscow, 1961.

————. *For Peaceful Competition and Cooperation.* New York: International Arts and Sciences Press, 1959.

————. *Prevent War, Safeguard Peace.* Moscow: Progress Publishers, 1962.

————. *Report of the Central Committee of the Communist Party of the Soviet Union to the Twenty-second Congress of the CPSU.* 2 vols. New York: Crosscurrents Press, 1961.

————. *The Revolutionary Working Class and the Communist Movement.* Moscow: Foreign Languages Publishing House, 1963.

————. *Socialism and Communism.* Moscow: Foreign Languages Publishing House, 1963.

————. *For Victory in Peaceful Competition with Capitalism.* New York: Dutton, 1960.

————. *World Without Arms, World Without War.* Moscow: Foreign Languages Publishing House, 1960.

## Khrushchev: Biographies

Abbas, Khwaja Ahmad. *Face to Face with Khrushchev.* Delhi: Rajpal & Sons, 1960.

Frankland, Mark. *Khrushchev.* Harmondsworth: Penguin Books, 1966.

Hirschfeld, Burt. *Khrushchev.* New York: Hawthorn Books, 1968.

Kellen, Konrad. *Khrushchev: A Political Portrait.* New York: Praeger; London: Thames & Hudson, 1961.

Leonhard, Wolfgang. *Chruschtschow—Aufstieg und Fall eines Sowjetführers.* Luzern, Frankfurt/M.: Bucher, 1965.

Paloczi-Horvath, George. *Khrushchev: The Road to Power.* London: Secker & Warburg; Boston: Little, Brown, 1960.

Pineau, Christian. *Nikita Sergeevitch Khrouchtchev.* Paris: Librairie Academique Perrin, 1965.

Pistrak, Lazar. *The Grand Tactician: Khrushchev's Rise to Power.* New York: Praeger; London: Thames & Hudson, 1961.

Rush, Myron. *The Rise of Khrushchev.* Washington, D.C.: Public Affairs Press, 1958.


*Official Post-Stalin Soviet Ideological Publications (In English)*

Afanasyev, V. *Scientific Communism.* Moscow: Progress Publishers, 1967.

Afanasyev, V., Makarova, M., and Minayev, L. *Fundamentals of Scientific Socialism.* Moscow: Progress Publishers, 1969.

Arzumanyan, A.A., et al. *World Revolutionary Movement of the Working Class.* Moscow: Progress Publishers, 1967.

Brezhnev, L.I. *Following Lenin's Course.* Moscow: Progress Publishers, 1972.

———. *Great October, 1917–1967.* Speech Delivered Before the Central Committee of the Communist Party of the Soviet Union, the Supreme Soviet of the U.S.S.R., and the Supreme Soviet of the R.S.F.S.R. Moscow, 1967.

———. *The Great Victory of the Soviet People.* Speech Delivered on the Occasion of the Twentieth Anniversary of the Victory of World War II. Moscow, 1965.

———. *For Greater Unity of Communists, for a Fresh Upsurge of the Anti-imperialist Struggle.* Speech Delivered at the International Meeting of the Communist and Workers' Parties, June 7, 1969. Moscow, 1969.

———. *Socialism's First Half-century.* Sydney: Novosti Press Agency, 1968.

Burlatsky, F. *The State and Communism.* Moscow: Progress Publishers, n.d.

———. *World Liberation Movement and Socialism.* Moscow, 1966.

Butenko, A. *The Way to Socialism and the Dictatorship of the Proletariat.* Moscow, 1966.

Butsky, I. *Political Work in the Soviet Army.* Moscow: Progress Publishers, n.d.

Bykhovsky, B. *The New Man in the Making.* Moscow, 1967.

Chesnokov, D.I. *Historical Materialism.* Moscow: Progress Publishers, 1969.

Demichev, P.N., et al. *Against Modern Anti-Communism.* Prague: Peace and Socialism Publishers, 1970.

"Fiftieth Anniversary of the Great October Revolution." Thesis of the Central Committee of the Communist Party of the Soviet Union. Moscow, 1967.

*Fortieth Anniversary of the Great October Socialist Revolution.* Collected Speeches. Moscow, 1958.

Frantsev, Y. *Fifty Years of a New Era.* Moscow, 1967.

German, S. *Reflections on the Social Future of Mankind.* Moscow: Novosti Press Agency, 1968.

Grigoryan, L. *Soviet Society.* Moscow, 1968.

*Historical Materialism, Basic Problems.* Moscow, 1968.

*History of the Communist Party of the Soviet Union.* Moscow: Foreign Languages Publishing House, n.d.

International Conference of Communist and Workers' Parties. *Documents.* Moscow: Novosti Press Agency, 1969.

Ivanov, Y. *Caution: Zionism.* Moscow: Progress Publishers, 1970.

Kosolapov, R. *Communism and Freedom.* Moscow: Progress Publishers, 1970.

Lavrov, A. *Twenty-third Congress of the Communist Party of the Soviet Union: Results and Prospects of Political, Economic, and Cultural Development of the U.S.S.R.* Moscow, 1966.

Mshvenieradze, Vladimir. *Anti-Communism, Who Benefits by It?* Moscow: Novosti Press Agency, n.d.

Polyakov, Y., and Lelchuk, V. *A Short History of Soviet Society.* Moscow: Progress Publishers, 1971.

Ponomarev, B.N., et al. *A Short History of the Communist Party of the Soviet Union.* Moscow: Progress Publishers, 1970.

Pospelov, P.N., et al. *Development of Revolutionary Theory by the Communist Party of the Soviet Union.* Moscow: Progress Publishers, 1971.

"Program of the Communist Party of the Soviet Union." Adopted at the Twenty-second Congress of the Communist Party of the Soviet Union, Oct. 31, 1961. Moscow: Foreign Languages Publishing House, 1961.

Rabinovich, S. *Jews in the Soviet Union.* Moscow, 1967.

"Resolutions of the Twentieth Congress of the Communist Party of the Soviet Union." Moscow, 1956.

Rosenthal, E. *Man in Modern Society.* Moscow, 1969.

Shakhnazarov, G., Sukhodeyev, V., Krasin, Y., Pisarzhevsky, O., Bobrykin, A., and Lushnikov, A. *Man, Science, and Society.* Moscow: Progress Publishers, 1965.

Skvortsov, L. *The Ideology and Tactics of Anti-Communism.* Moscow: Progress Publishers, 1969.

*The Twenty-fourth Congress of the Communist Party of the Soviet Union, Mar. 30–Apr. 9, 1971: Documents.* Moscow: Novosti Press Agency, 1971.

*The Twenty-third Congress of the Communist Party of the Soviet Union.* Moscow: Novosti Press Agency, 1966.

Vladimirov, T. *The Twenty-third Congress of the Communist Party of the Soviet Union and the World Revolutionary Movement.* Moscow, 1966.


*Development in the U.S.S.R. After Stalin:*
*Political and Ideological Aspects*

Ahlberg, René. *Weltrevolution durch Koexistenz.* Berlin: Colloquium Verlag, 1962.

Amalrik, Andrei. *Involuntary Journey to Siberia.* New York: Harcourt Brace Jovanovich, 1970.

Barghoorn, Frederick C. *Politics in the U.S.S.R.* Boston: Little, Brown, 1966.

Behrens, Erwin. *Tagebuch aus Moskau.* Hamburg: Christian Wegner Verlag, 1964.

Boettcher, Lieber, and Meissner. *Bilanz der Ära Chruschtschow.* Stuttgart: W. Kohlhammer, 1966.

Boffa, Giuseppe. *Inside the Khrushchev Era.* New York: Marzini; London: Allen and Unwin, 1959.

Brant, Stefan. *The East German Rising, June 17, 1953.* London: Thames & Hudson; New York: Praeger, 1955.

Brumberg, Abraham (ed.). *Russia Under Khrushchev.* New York: Praeger; London: Methuen, 1962.

Brzezinski, Zbigniew. *Dilemmas of Change in Soviet Politics.* New York and London: Columbia University Press, 1969.

————. *Ideology and Power in Soviet Politics.* New York: Praeger; London: Thames & Hudson, 1962.

————. *The Soviet Bloc: Unity and Conflict.* Cambridge, Mass.: Harvard University Press, 1960.

Conquest, Robert. *Power and Policy in the U.S.S.R.* Rev. ed. New York: Harper & Row, 1967.

————. *Russia After Khrushchev.* New York: Praeger, 1965.

Crankshaw, Edward. *Khrushchev's Russia.* London and Baltimore: Penguin Books, 1959.

————. *Russia Without Stalin: The Emerging Pattern.* New York: Viking Press; London: Michael Joseph, 1956.

Dallin, Alexander, and Larson, Thomas B. (eds.). *Soviet Politics Since Khrushchev.* Englewood Cliffs, N.J.: Prentice-Hall, 1968.

Deutscher, Isaac. *Russia in Transition.* New York: Grove Press, 1960.

————. *Russia, What Next?* New York: Oxford University Press, 1953.

Dornberg, John. *The New Tsars: Russia Under Stalin's Heirs.* Garden City, N.Y.: Doubleday, 1971.

Fast, Howard. *The Naked God: The Writers and the Communist Party.* New York: Praeger, 1957.

Feron, Bernard. *L'U.R.S.S. sans Idole.* Paris: Casterman, 1966.

Fetscher, Iring. *Gesichtspunkte zur Kritik der Sowjetideologie.* Zeven: Heimat Verlag, 1961.

Fischer, Louis. *Russia Revisited: A New Look at Russia and Her Satellites.* New York: Doubleday; London: Cape, 1957.

Fischer, Ruth. *Die Umformung der Sowjetgesellschaft.* Chronik der Reformen 1953–1958. Düsseldorf, Köln: Diederichs, 1958.

Hildebrandt, Rainer. *The Explosion: The Uprising Behind the Iron Curtain.* New York: Duell, Sloan & Pearce, 1955.

Hindus, Maurice. *House Without a Roof: Russia After Forty-three Years of Revolution.* New York: Doubleday; London: Gollancz, 1961.

Hollander, Gayle D. *Soviet Political Indoctrination: Developments in Mass Media and Propaganda Since Stalin.* New York: Praeger, 1972.

Hyland, William, and Shryock, Richard Wallace. *The Fall of Khrushchev.* New York: Funk & Wagnalls, 1968.

Ingensand, Harald. *Die Ideologie des Sowjetkommunismus.* Hanover: Verlag für Literatur und Zeitgeschehen, 1962.

Jacoby, Susan. *Moscow Conversations.* New York: Coward, McCann and Geoghegan, 1972.

Kalnins, Bruno. *Der sowjetische Propagandastaat.* Das System und die Mittel der Massenbeeinflussung in der Sowjetunion. Stockholm: Tidens, 1956.

Kolasky, John. *Two Years in Soviet Ukraine (1963–65).* Toronto: Peter Martins Associates, 1970.

Labedz, Leopold. *International Communism After Khrushchev.* Cambridge, Mass.: M.I.T. Press, 1965.

Laqueur, Walter, and Labedz, Leopold (eds.). *The Future of Communist Society.* New York: Praeger, 1962.

Lazareff, Hélène and Pierre. *The Soviet Union After Stalin.* London: Odhams; New York: Philosophical Library, 1955.

Leonhard, Wolfgang. *The Kremlin Since Stalin.* London: Oxford University Press; New York: Praeger, 1962.

Lewytzky, Borys. *Porträt eines Ordens—Die kommunistische Partei der Sowjetunion.* Stuttgart: Klett, 1967.

Lieber, Hans-Joachim. *Individuum und Gesellschaft in der Sowjetideologie.* Hanover: Niedersächsische Landeszentrale für politische Bildung, 1964.

Linden, Carl A. *Khrushchev and the Soviet Leadership, 1957–1964.* Baltimore: The Johns Hopkins Press, 1966.

Little, D. Richard (ed.). *Liberalization in the U.S.S.R.: Facade or Reality?* Lexington, Mass.: D. C. Heath, 1968.

Löwenthal, Richard. *World Communism, The Disintegration of a Secular Faith.* New York: Oxford University Press, 1964.

Löwenthal, Richard, and Meissner, Boris (eds.). *Sowjetische Innenpolitik —Triebkräfte und Tendenzen.* Stuttgart: Kohlhammer, 1968.

Löwenthal, Richard, and Vogel, Heinrich (eds.). *Sowjetpolitik der 70er Jahre.* Stuttgart: Kohlhammer, 1972.

McLean, Hugh, and Vickery, Walter (eds.). *The Year of Protests: 1956.* New York: Vintage Books, 1961.

Marko, Kurt. *Evolution wider Willen.* Die Sowjetideologie zwischen Orthodoxie und Revision. Vienna, Cologne: Hermann Böhlau Nachf., 1968.

————. *Sic et Non—Kritisches Wörterbuch des sowjetrussischen Marxismus-Leninismus der Gegenwart.* Wiesbaden: Otto Harrassowitz, 1962.

————. *Sowjethistoriker zwischen Ideologie und Wissenschaft. Aspekte der* sowjetrussischen Wissenschaftspolitik seit Stalins Tod, 1953 bis 1963. Cologne: Verlag Wissenschaft und Politik, 1964.

Mayer, Peter. *Cohesion and Conflict in International Communism. A Study of Marxist-Leninist Concepts and Their Application.* The Hague: Martinus Nijhoff, 1968.

Medvedev, Zhores A. *The Medvedev Papers: The Plight of Soviet Science Today.* New York: St. Martin's Press, 1971.

Mehnert, Klaus. *The Anatomy of Soviet Man.* London: Weidenfeld & Nicolson, 1961.

————. *Soviet Man and His World.* New York: Praeger, 1962.

Meissner, Boris. *The Brezhnev Doctrine.* Kansas City, Mo.: Park College Press, 1971.

————. *Das Ende des Stalin-Mythos.* Die Ergebnisse des zwanzigsten Parteikongresses der kommunistischen Partei der Sowjetunion. Frankfurt/M.: Europäischer Austauschdienst, 1956.

————. *Das Parteiprogramm der KPdSU 1903 bis 1961.* Cologne: Verlag Wissenschaft und Politik, 1962.

————. *Russland unter Chruschtschow.* Munich: Oldenbourg, 1960.

————. *Sowjetrussland zwischen Revolution und Restauration.* Cologne: Verlag für Politik und Wirtschaft, 1956.

Mickiewicz, Ellen Propper. *Soviet Political Schools.* The Communist Party Adult Instruction System. New Haven: Yale University Press, 1967.

Mihajlov, Mihajlo. *Moscow Summer.* New York: Farrar, Straus & Giroux, 1965.

Müller-Markus, Siegfried. *Der Aufstand des Denkens.* Düsseldorf: Econ Verlag, 1968.

Nicolaevsky, Boris I. *The Crimes of the Stalin Era: Special Report to the*

*Twentieth Congress of the Communist Party of the Soviet Union.* New York: *New Leader,* 1956.

Nollau, Günther. *Zerfall des Weltkommunismus—Einheit oder Polyzentrismus?* Cologne: Kiepenheuer & Witsch, 1963.

Novak, Joseph. *The Future Is Ours, Comrade.* Garden City, N.Y.: Doubleday, 1960.

————. *No Third Path.* Garden City, N.Y.: Doubleday, 1962.

"Observer." *Message from Moscow.* New York: Alfred A. Knopf, 1969.

Paloczi-Horvath, George. *The Facts Rebel.* London: Secker & Warburg, 1964.

Pethybridge, Roger. *A Key to Soviet Politics: The Crisis of the Anti-Party Group.* New York: Praeger, 1962.

Pörzgen, Hermann. *So lebt man in Moskau.* Munich: List Verlag, 1958.

Revesz, Laszlo. *Ideologie und Praxis in der sowjetischen Innen- und Aussenpolitik.* Mainz: V. Hase und Koehler, 1966.

Ritvo, Herbert. *The New Soviet Society: Final Text of the Program of the Communist Party of the Soviet Union.* New York: *New Leader,* 1962.

Rothberg, Abraham. *The Heirs of Stalin: Dissidence and the Soviet Regime, 1953–1970.* Ithaca: Cornell University Press, 1972.

Schapiro, Leonard, and Boiter, Albert (eds.). *The U.S.S.R. and the Future: An Analysis of the New Programs of the Communist Party of the Soviet Union.* New York: Praeger; London: Pall Mall, 1963.

Schmiederer, Ursula. *Die sowjetische Theorie der friedlichen Koexistenz.* Probleme sozialistischer Kritik, 8. Frankfurt/M.: Verlag Neue Kritik, 1968.

Schwartz, Harry (ed.). *Russia Enters the 1960's: A Documentary Report on the Twenty-second Congress of the Communist Party of the Soviet Union.* Philadelphia: J.B. Lippincott, 1962.

Shub, Anatole. *The New Russian Tragedy.* New York: Norton, 1969.

Specovius, Günther. *Die Russen sind anders.* Mensch und Gesellschaft im Sowjetstaat. Düsseldorf: Econ Verlag, 1963.

Sulzberger, Cyrus L. *The Big Thaw: A Personal Exploration of the New Russia and the Orbit Countries.* New York: Harper & Row, 1956.

Swearer, Howard R. *The Politics of Succession in the U.S.S.R.: Materials on Khrushchev's Rise to Leadership.* Boston: Little, Brown, 1964.

Tatu, Michel. *Power in the Kremlin from Khrushchev to Kosygin.* New York: Viking, 1970.

Thomas, Stephen. *Perspektiven sowjetischer Macht.* Der XXIII Parteitag der KPdSU und das Parteiprogramm. Cologne: Kiepenheuer & Witsch, 1967.

Tucker, Robert C. *The Soviet Political Mind.* Studies in Stalinism and Post-Stalin Change. New York and London: Praeger, 1963.

Ulam, Adam B. *The New Face of Soviet Totalitarianism.* Cambridge, Mass.: Harvard University Press; London: Oxford University Press, 1963.

Vladimir, Leonid. *The Russians.* New York: Praeger, 1968.

Werth, Alexander. *The Khrushchev Phase: The Soviet Union Enters the "Decisive" Sixties.* London: Hale, 1961.

————. *Russia: Hopes and Fears.* New York: Simon and Schuster, 1969.

Wetter, Gustav A. *Soviet Ideology Today.* New York: Praeger, 1966.

Wolfe, Bertram D. *Khrushchev and Stalin's Ghost.* New York: Praeger, 1957.

## ☐ Political Concepts of Maoism

*Mao Tse-tung: Selected Works, Anthologies*

Mao Tse-tung. *Selected Readings from the Works of Mao Tse-tung.* Peking: Foreign Languages Press, 1971.

————. *Selected Works.* London: Lawrence & Wishart, 1954–56. New York: International Publishers. Volume I: The Period of the Revolutionary Civil Wars in China, from 1926 to 1936. Volume II: The First Two Years of the War of the Resistance Against Japanese Aggression, 1937 to 1938. Volume III: The War of Resistance from 1938 to 1941. Volume IV: The War of Resistance from 1941 to the Defeat of Japan in 1945. Volume V: The Third Revolutionary Civil War Period.

————. *Selected Works.* 4 vols. Peking: Foreign Languages Press, 1967.

————. *Six Essays on Military Affairs.* Peking: Foreign Languages Press, 1971.

————. *On Art and Literature.* Peking: Foreign Languages Press, 1960.

————. *The Chinese Revolution and the Chinese Communist Party.* Peking: Foreign Languages Press, 1954.

————. *On Coalition Government.* Peking: Foreign Languages Press, 1955.

————. *Concerning Practice.* London, 1951.

————. *On Contradiction.* New York: International Publishers, 1953.

————. *On the Correct Handling of Contradictions Among the People.* New York: *New Leader,* 1957. Special supplement.

————. *Five Articles by Chairman Mao Tse-tung.* Peking: Foreign Languages Press, 1968.

————. *On Guerrilla Warfare.* New York: Praeger, 1961.

————. *Let a Hundred Flowers Bloom.* The Complete Text of "On the

Correct Handling of Contradictions Among the People." New York: The Tamiment Institute, n.d.

————. *Mao Papers; Anthology and Bibliography.* Jerome Ch'en (ed.). London and New York: Oxford University Press, 1970.

————. *Mao Tse-tung; An Anthology of His Writings.* Updated and expanded. Anne Freemantle (ed.). New York: New American Library, 1971.

————. *Maoism, A Sourcebook.* Selections from the Writings of Mao Tse-tung. H. Arthur Steener (ed.). Los Angeles: UCLA Press, 1952.

————. *On New Democracy.* Peking: Foreign Languages Press, 1954, 1960.

————. *New Democracy;* Basis of Social, Political, and Economic Structure of New China. Shanghai: Rapid Current Publishing Co., 1949.

————. *Nineteen Poems.* Peking: Foreign Languages Press, 1958.

————. "On People's Democratic Dictatorship" and "Speech at the Preparatory Meeting of the New PCC." Peking: New China News Agency, 1949.

————. "On Practice; On the Relation Between Knowledge and Practice— Between Knowing and Doing." Peking, 1951.

————. "Problems of Art and Literature." Address to a Conference at Yenan, May 2–23, 1942. Bombay: People's Publishing House, 1952.

————. *On the Protracted War.* Peking: Foreign Languages Press, 1954.

————. *The Question of Agricultural Cooperation.* Peking: Foreign Languages Press, 1956.

————. *The Question of Independence and Autonomy Within the United Front.* Peking: Foreign Languages Press, 1954.

————. *Quotations from Chairman Mao Tse-tung.* Peking: Foreign Languages Press, 1966.

————. *On the Rectification of Incorrect Ideas in the Party.* Peking: Foreign Languages Press, 1953.

————. *Rectify the Party; Style in Work.* Peking: Foreign Languages Press, 1955.

————. *On Revolution and War.* M. Rejai (ed.). Garden City, N.Y.: Doubleday, 1969.

————. *The Role of the Chinese Communist Party in the National War.* Peking: Foreign Languages Press, 1956.

————. *Selected Military Writings.* Peking: Foreign Languages Press, 1963.

————. *On the Tactics of Fighting Japanese Imperialism.* Peking: Foreign Languages Press, 1953.

————. "Talk with the American Correspondent Anna Louise Strong." Peking: Foreign Languages Press, 1961.

————. *Talks at the Yenan Forum on Art and Literature.* Peking: Foreign Languages Press, 1956.

————. *The Thoughts of Chairman Mao Tse-tung.* London: Gibbs, 1967.


## Mao Tse-tung: Biographies, Memoirs, Reminiscences

Abegg, Lily. *De l'empire du milieu a Mao Tse-toung.* Lucerne: Editions Rencontre, 1966.

Archer, Jules. *Mao Tse-tung.* New York: Hawthorn, 1972.

Chen, Jerome. *Mao and the Chinese Revolution.* New York and London: Oxford University Press, 1965.

Chen, Jerome (ed.). *Mao.* Englewood Cliffs, N.J.: Prentice-Hall, 1969.

Devillers, Philippe. *Mao.* New York: Schocken Books, 1969.

Elegant, Robert S. *China's Red Masters.* New York: Twayne Publishers, 1951.

Grimm, Tilemann. *Mao Tse-tung in Selbstzeugnissen und Bilddokumenten.* Reinbek: Rowohlt, 1968.

Hsiao-Yu. *Mao Tse-tung and I Were Beggars.* Foreword by Lin Yutang. Syracuse: Syracuse University Press, 1959; London: Hutchinson, 1961.

Paloczi-Horvath, George. *Mao Tse-tung, Emperor of the Blue Ants.* London: Secker & Warburg, 1962.

Payne, Robert. *Mao Tse-tung, Ruler of Red China.* New York: Schuman; London: Secker & Warburg, 1950.

Schram, Stuart R. *Mao Tse-tung.* New York: Simon and Schuster, 1967.

Snow, Edgar. *The Other Side of the River: Red China Today.* New York: Random House, 1962.

————. *Red Star over China.* New York: Random House, 1938.

Wang, Anna. *Ich kämpfte für Mao.* Eine deutsche Frau erlebt die chinesische Revolution. Hamburg: Christian Wegner, 1964.


## Political and Ideological Development of Chinese Communism; The Sino-Soviet Conflict

Barcata, Louis. *China in the Throes of the Cultural Revolution.* New York: Hart Publishing Co., 1967.

Barnett, A. Doak. *China After Mao.* Princeton, N.J.: Princeton University Press, 1967.

————. *Chinese Communist Politics in Action.* Seattle: University of Washington Press, 1969.

————. *Communist China in Perspective*. New York: Praeger, 1962.

Bogush, Y. *Maoism and Its Policy of Splitting the National Liberation Movement*. Moscow: Progress Publishers, 1970.

Brahm, Heinz. *Pekings Griff nach der Vormacht*. Der chinesisch-sowjetische Konflikt von Juli 1963 bis März 1965. Cologne: Verlag Wissenschaft und Politik, 1966.

Brandt, Conrad. *Stalin's Failure in China 1924–1927*. New York: Norton, 1966.

*Commemorate the 50th Anniversary of the Communist Party of China, 1921–1971*. Peking: Foreign Languages Press, 1971.

Compton, Boyd (trans.). *Mao's China: Party Reform Documents, 1942–44*. Seattle: University of Washington Press, 1966.

Crankshaw, Edward. *The New Cold War. Moscow vs. Peking*. London and Baltimore: Penguin Books, 1963.

Dmitriev, F. *Whither China?* Moscow: Novosti Press Agency, 1968.

Floyd, David. *Mao Against Khrushchev*. New York: Praeger, 1964.

Griffith, W.E. *Sino-Soviet Relations, 1964–1965*. Cambridge, Mass.: M.I.T. Press.

————. *The Sino-Soviet Rift*. Cambridge, Mass.: M.I.T. Press, 1964.

Grigoryev, A. *U.S.S.R.: A Friend and Brother of the Chinese People*. Moscow: Novosti Press Agency, 1971.

Hamm, Harry, and Kun, Joseph. *Das rote Schisma*. Cologne: Verlag Wissenschaft und Politik, 1963.

Hudson, G.F., Löwenthal, Richard, and MacFarquhar, Roderick (eds.). *The Sino-Soviet Dispute*. New York: Praeger, 1961.

Jackson, W.A. Douglas. *Russo-Chinese Borderlands*. Princeton, N.J.: Van Nostrand, 1962.

Kyuzajhyan, L. *The Chinese Crisis: Causes and Character*. Moscow, 1968.

Liebson, Boris. *Petty Bourgeois Revolutionism*. Moscow: Progress Publishers, 1970.

London, Kurt. *Unity and Contradiction: Major Aspects of Sino-Soviet Relations*. New York: Praeger, 1962.

McLane, Charles B. *Soviet Policy and the Chinese Communists, 1931–1946*. New York: Columbia University Press; London: Oxford University Press, 1958.

Malukhin, A. *Militarism—Backbone of Maoism*. Moscow: Novosti Press Agency, 1970.

Mehnert, Klaus. *Peking and Moscow*. New York: Putnam's, 1962.

Quaroni, Pietro. *Russen und Chinesen*. Die Krise der kommunistischen Welt. Frankfurt/M.: Scheffler, 1968.

Schatten, Fritz. *Der Konflikt Moskau-Peking*. Dokumente und Analyse des roten Schismas. Munich: Piper, 1963.

Schwartz, Harry. *Tsars, Mandarins and Commisars: The History of Chinese-Russian Relations.* Philadelphia: Lippincott, 1964.

Selden, Mark. *The Yenan Way in Revolutionary China.* Cambridge, Mass.: Harvard University Press, 1973.

Swarup, Shanti. *A Study of the Chinese Communist Movement.* Oxford: Clarendon Press, 1966.

Tang, Sheng-hao. *The Twenty-second Congress of the Communist Party of the Soviet Union and Moscow-Tirana-Peking Relations.* Chestnut Hill, Mass.: Research Institute on the Sino-Soviet Bloc, 1963.

Thornton, Richard C. *The Comintern and the Chinese Communists, 1928–1931.* Seattle: University of Washington Press, 1969.

Treadgold, Donald W. (ed.). *Soviet and Chinese Communism, Similarities and Differences.* Seattle: University of Washington Press, 1967.

Walker, Richard L. *Letters from the Communes.* New York: New Leader, 1959.

Wang Ming. *China: Cultural Revolution or Counterrevolutionary Coup?* Moscow, 1969.

Weber, Hermann. *Konflikte im Weltkommunismus.* Munich: Kindler, 1964.

Wheelwright, Edward, and McFarlane, Bruce. *The Chinese Road to Socialism—Economics of the Cultural Revolution.* New York: Monthly Review Press, 1970.

Whiting, Allen S. *Soviet Policies in China, 1917–1924.* New York: Columbia University Press; London: Oxford University Press, 1954.

Wilson, Dick. *The Long March—The Epic of Chinese Communism's Survival.* New York: Viking, 1972.

Wint, Guy. *China, Grossmacht der Zukunft.* Cologne: Verlag Wissenschaft und Politik, 1961.

Yu, Frederick T.C. *Mass Persuasion in Communist China.* New York: Praeger, 1964.

Zagoria, Donald S. *The Sino-Soviet Conflict, 1956–1961.* New York: Atheneum, 1967.

Zanegin, B. *National Background of China's Foreign Policy.* Moscow: Novosti Press Agency, n.d.

☐ **Political Concepts of Humanist Marxism**

*Critiques of Soviet Communism, the Search for a New Model of Socialism: General Works*

Fromm, Erich. *Socialist Humanism: A Symposium.* Garden City, N.Y.: Doubleday, 1965.

Garaudy, Roger. *From Anathema to Dialogue*. New York: Herder and Herder, 1966.

———. *Pour un modèle français du socialisme*. Paris: Gallimard, 1968.

———. *Reconquête de l'espoir*. Paris: Grasset, 1971.

———. *The Turning Point of Socialism*. London: Fontana Books, 1970.

Hillmann, Günther. *Selbstkritik des Kommunismus*. Text der Oppositionen. Reinbek: Rowohlt, 1967.

Kersten, Heinz. *Aufstand der Intellektuellen*. Ein dokumentarischer Bericht. Stuttgart: Seewald Verlag, 1957.

Kolakowsky, Leszek. *Der Revolutionäre Geist*. Stuttgart: Kohlhammer, 1972.

———. *Toward a Marxist Humanism*. New York: Grove Press, 1969.

Labedz, Leopold (ed.). *Revisionism*. Essays on the History of Marxist Ideas. London: Allen and Unwin; New York: Praeger, 1962.

Laqueur, Walter, and Labedz, Leopold (eds.). *Polycentrism: The New Factor in International Communism*. New York: Praeger, 1962.

Lemberg, Eugen. *Reformation im Kommunismus?* Ideologische Wandlungen im Marxismus-Leninismus Ostmitteleuropas. Stuttgart: Klett Verlag, 1967.

Lombardo-Radice, Lucio. *Socialismo e Libertà*. Rome: Editori Riuniti, 1968.

Marek, Franz. *A Philosophy of World Revolution*. New York: International Publishers, 1969.

Meissner, Boris. "Die Auseinandersetzung zwischen dem Sowjet- und dem Reformkommunismus." *Südosteuropa-Schriften* (Munich), 1963, IV, 75–100.

Petkoff, Teodoro. *Checoeslovaquia: El Socialismo como Problema*. Caracas, 1969.

———. *Socialismo para Venezuela?* Caracas, 1970.

Petrovic, Gajo. *Marx in the Mid-twentieth Century*. Garden City, N.Y.: Doubleday, 1967.

Richta, Radovan. *Civilization at the Crossroads*. White Plains: International Arts and Science Press, 1968.

Schack, Herbert. *Die Revision des Marxismus-Leninismus*. Berlin: Duncker & Humblot, 1959.

Schaff, Adam. *Marxism and the Human Individual*. New York: McGraw-Hill, 1970.

———. *A Philosophy of Man*. New York: Dell, 1963.

Sik, Ota. *Der Dritte Weg*. Hamburg: Hoffman und Campe, 1972.

———. *Plan and Market Under Socialism*. White Plains: International Arts and Sciences Press, 1968.

Stojanovic, Svetozar. *Between Ideals and Reality—A Critique of Socialism and Its Future*. Gerson S. Sher (trans.). New York: Oxford University Press, 1973.

Ströhm, Carl-Gustav. *Zwischen Mao und Chruschtschow.* Wandlungen des Kommunismus in Südosteuropa. Stuttgart: Kohlhammer, 1964.

Supek, Rudi, and Bosnjak, Branko (eds.). *Jugoslawien denkt anders. Marxismus und Kritik des etatistischen Sozialismus.* Vienna and Frankfurt: Europa Verlag, 1971.

Vanek, Jaroslav. *The Participatory Economy. An Evolutionary Hypothesis and a Strategy for Development.* Ithaca, N.Y.: Cornell University Press, 1971.

Vranicki, Predrag. *Mensch und Geschichte.* Frankfurt/M.: Suhrkamp, 1969.

Weber, Hermann. *Demokratischer Kommunismus?* Zur Theorie, Politik und Geschichte der kommunistischen Bewegung. Hanover: Dietz Verlag, 1969.

Zinner, Paul E. (ed.). *National Communism and Popular Revolt in Eastern Europe.* Documents on the Events in Poland and Hungary, February–November 1956. New York: Columbia University Press; London: Oxford University Press, 1956.

Zöger, Heinz. *Revisionismus hinter dem eisernen Vorhang.* Düsseldorf: Arbeitsgemeinschaft Arbeit und Leben, 1962.

*Yugoslav Communism and Workers' Self-management: Sources*

Bilandzic, Dusan. *Management of Yugoslav Economy, 1945–1966.* Belgrade: Yugoslav Trade Unions, 1967.

———. *Social Self-government.* Belgrade: Medjunarodna Politika, 1965.

Bogosavljevic, Miliutin. *The Economy of Yugoslavia.* Belgrade: Publističko Izdavacki Zavod Jugoslavija, 1961.

Bogosavljevic, Miliutin, and Pesakovic, M. *Workers' Management of a Factory in Yugoslavia.* A monograph about "Rade Koncar" Works. Belgrade: Yugoslav Trade Unions, 1959.

The Constitution of the Socialist Federal Republic of Yugoslavia (and Constitutional Amendments), Secretariat of Information of the Federal Executive Council. Belgrade: Prosveta, 1969.

Djilas, Milovan. "Lenin on the Relations Between Socialist Countries." *The Communist,* September 1949.

———. *Memoirs of a Revolutionary.* New York: Harcourt Brace Jovanovich, 1973.

———. "On New Roads of Socialism." Address Delivered at the Preelection Rally of Belgrade Students, March 18, 1950. Belgrade, 1950.

Gerskovic, Leon. *Social and Economic System in Yugoslavia.* Belgrade: Publishing House Jugoslavija, n.d.

Gorupic, Ivan. *Workers' Self-management in Yugoslav Undertakings.* Zagreb: Ekonomski Institut, 1970.

Horvat, Branko. *An Essay on Yugoslav Society*. White Plains: International Arts and Sciences Press, 1969.

Jovanovic, Aleksander. *The Social and Political System in Yugoslavia*. Belgrade: Medjunarodna Politika, 1966.

Kardelj, Edvard. *After Five Years*. Socialist Movements and the U.S.S.R. Five Years After the Yugoslav-Cominform Split. New York: Yugoslav Information Center, 1953.

————. "The Communist Party of Yugoslavia in the Struggle for New Yugoslavia, for People's Authority, and for Socialism." Report Delivered at the Fifth Congress of the Communist Party of Yugoslavia. Belgrade, 1948.

————. *The International Scene and the Yugoslav Position*. New York: Yugoslav Information Center, 1951.

————. *Problems of Socialist Policy in the Countryside*. London: Lincolns-Praeger, 1962.

————. *Socialism and War: A Survey of the Chinese Criticism of the Policy of Coexistence*. New York: McGraw-Hill, 1960; London: Methuen, 1961.

————. *Socialist Democracy in Its Effect on the Whole Development and Social Life of Yugoslavia*. Belgrade: Federation of Yugoslav Jurists Associations, 1952.

Kmetić, Miladen. *Self-management in the Enterprise*. Belgrade: Medjunarodna Stampa Interpress, 1967.

Kovac, P. *Workers' Management in Yugoslavia*. Belgrade: Publishing Office Yugoslavia, 1958.

Markovic, Mihajlo. "The Concept of Revolution." *Praxis*, 1969, Nos. 1–2.

————. "Humanism and Dialectic." Fromm (ed.). *Socialist Humanism*.

————. "Personal Integrity in Socialist Society." *Praxis*, 1966, No. 4.

Pesakovic, Milentije. *Twenty Years of Self-management in Yugoslavia*. Belgrade: Medjunarodna Politika, 1970.

Pijade, Mosha. *About the Legend That the Yugoslav Uprising Owed Its Existence to Soviet Assistance*. London, 1950.

Popovich, Koča. *Revisionism of Marxism-Leninism on the Question of the Liberation War in Yugoslavia*. Belgrade: Jugoslovenska Knjiga, 1949.

Savez Sindikata Jugoslavije (Confederation of Trade Unions of Yugoslavia). *How Do the Working Collectives Distribute Creative Values?* Belgrade: no publisher, 1964.

Supek, Rudi. "Selbstverwaltung in der sozialistischen Gesellschaft." Jozsef Varga (ed.). *Sozialismus in Europa*. Vienna: Europa Verlag, 1967.

————. "Vom staatlichen Totalitarismus zur individuellen Totalität." Club Voltaire, Jahrbuch für kritische Aufklärung. Vol. III. Munich: Szczesny Verlag, 1967.

Tito, Josip Broz. *Selected Military Works.* Belgrade: Vojnoizdavački Zavod, 1966.

――――. *Selected Speeches and Articles, 1941–1961.* Zagreb: Naprijed, 1963.

――――. "Workers Manage Factories in Yugoslavia." Belgrade, 1950.

Vranicki, Predrag. "Der augenblickliche Stand der ideologischen Diskussion in Jugoslawien." *Marxismusstudien,* Series 5. Tübingen: J.C.B. Mohr Verlag, 1968.

――――. "Staat und Partei im Sozialismus." *Praxis,* 1967, Nos. 5–6.

――――. "Zum Thema der Befreiung des Menschen." *Praxis,* 1967, No. 1.

*Yugoslavia's Way: The Program of the League of Communists of Yugoslavia,* adopted at the Seventh Congress, March 1958. New York: All Nations' Press, 1958.

Ziherl, Boris. *Communism and Fatherland.* Belgrade, 1949.


*Yugoslav Communism and Workers' Self-management: Presentation and Analysis*


Adamic, L. *The Eagle and the Roots.* Garden City, N.Y.: Doubleday, 1952.

Adizes, Ichak. *Industrial Democracy: Yugoslav Style.* New York: Free Press, 1971.

Auty, Phyllis. *Tito: A Biography.* New York: McGraw-Hill, 1970.

Avakumovic, I. *History of the Communist Party of Yugoslavia.* Aberdeen: Aberdeen University Press, 1964.

Broekmeyer, M. J. *Yugoslav Workers' Self-management.* Dordrecht: D. Reidel, 1970.

Campbell, John C. *Tito's Separate Road.* New York: Harper & Row, 1967.

Dalmas, Louis. *Le Communisme Yougoslave depuis la rupture avec Moscou.* Paris, 1950.

Dedijer, Vladimir. *The Battle Stalin Lost: Memoirs of Yugoslavia, 1948–1953.* New York: Viking, 1971.

――――. *Tito Speaks.* His Self-portrait and Struggle with Stalin. London: Weidenfeld & Nicolson, 1953. Appeared in U.S.A. as: *Tito.* New York: Simon and Schuster, 1953.

Djilas, Milovan. *Anatomy of a Moral.* New York: Praeger; London: Thames & Hudson, 1959.

Farrell, Robert Barry. *Yugoslavia and the Soviet Union 1948–1956: An Analysis with Documents.* Hamden, Conn.: Shoe String Press, 1956.

Halperin, Ernst. *The Triumphant Heretic: Tito's Struggle Against Stalin.* London: Heinemann, 1958.

Hoffman, George W., and Neal, Fred W. *Yugoslavia and the New Communism.* New York: Twentieth Century Fund, 1962.

Hoffmann, Walter. *Marxismus oder Titoismus?* Titos Versuch zur Neuordnung gesellschaftlicher Beziehungen im Staate. Munich: Isar-Verlag, 1956.

International Labor Office. *Workers' Management in Yugoslavia.* Geneva, 1962.

Kolaja, Jiri. *Workers' Councils: The Yugoslav Experience.* New York: Praeger, 1966.

Leonhard, Wolfgang. *Kominform und Jugoslawien.* Über einige grundsätzliche Fragen des Kominform-Konflikts. Belgrade: Jugoslovenska Knjiga, 1949.

————. *Die Wahrheit über das sozialistische Jugoslawien.* Eine Antwort auf die Kominform-Verleumdungen. Belgrade: Jugoslovenska Knjiga, 1949.

MacLean, Fitzroy. *The Heretic.* Republished as *Tito: The Man Who Defied Hitler and Stalin.* New York: Ballantine Books, 1957.

McVicker, Charles P. *Titoism: Pattern for International Communism.* New York: St. Martin's Press; London: Macmillan, 1957.

Meier, Viktor. *Das neue jugoslawische Wirtschaftssystem.* Winterthur: P.G. Keller, 1956.

Meister, Albert. *Ou va l'Autogestion Yougoslave?* Paris: Editions Anthropos, 1971.

Milenkovitch, Deborah. *Plan and Market in Yugoslav Economic Thought.* New Haven: Yale University Press, 1971.

Neal, Fred W. *Titoism in Action.* The Reforms in Yugoslavia After 1948. Berkeley: University of California Press; London: Cambridge University Press, 1958.

Neuberger, E., and Estelle, J. *The Yugoslav Self-managed Enterprise: A Systematic Approach.* Stony Brook, N.Y.: Economics Research Bureau, 1971.

Pejov, M. *The Market-Planned Economy of Yugoslavia.* Minneapolis: University of Minnesota Press, 1966.

Popovic, N. D. *Yugoslavia: The New Class in Crisis.* Syracuse: Syracuse University Press, 1968.

Roggemann, Herwig. *Das Modell der Arbeiterselbstverwaltung in Jugoslawien.* Frankfurt/M.: Europäische Verlagsanstalt, 1970.

Ross Johnson, A. *The Transformation of Communist Ideology—The Yugoslav Case, 1945–1953.* Cambridge, Mass.: M.I.T. Press, 1972.

Schleicher, Harry. *Das System der betrieblichen Selbstverwaltung in Jugoslawien.* Berlin: Duncker & Humblot, 1961.

*The Second Soviet-Yugoslav Dispute.* Full Text of Main Documents April–June 1958. Vaclav L. Benes, Robert F. Byrnes, and Nicolas Spulber (eds.). Bloomington: Indiana University Press, 1959.

Singleton, Frederick, and Topham, Anthony. *Workers' Control in Yugoslavia.* London: Fabian Society, 1963.

*The Soviet-Yugoslav Controversy, 1948–1958: A Documentary Record.* Robert Bass and Elizabeth Marbury (eds.). New York: Prospect Books, 1959.

*The Soviet-Yugoslav Dispute.* Text of the Published Correspondence. London: Royal Institute of International Affairs, 1948.

Sturmthal, A. *Workers' Councils—A Study of Workplace Organization on Both Sides of the Iron Curtain.* Cambridge, Mass.: Harvard University Press, 1964.

Tornquist, David. *Look East, Look West: The Socialist Adventure in Yugoslavia.* New York: Macmillan, 1966.

Ulam, Adam B. *Titoism and the Cominform.* Cambridge, Mass.: Harvard University Press; London: Oxford University Press, 1952.

Vinterhalter, Vilka. *Der Weg des Josip Broz Tito.* Vienna: Europa Verlag, 1969.

Vucinich, W. S. (ed.). *Contemporary Yugoslavia: Twenty Years of Socialist Experiment.* Berkeley, Ca.: University of California Press, 1969.

Vukmanovic-Tempo, Svetozar. *The Ongoing Revolution.* London: McDonald, 1972.

*White Book.* Aggressive Activities by the Government of the U.S.S.R., Poland, Czechoslovakia, Hungary, Rumania, Bulgaria, and Albania Toward Yugoslavia. Belgrade: Ministry of Foreign Affairs of the Federal People's Republic of Yugoslavia, 1951.

Zalar, Charles. *Yugoslav Communism: A Critical Study.* Washington: U.S. Government Printing Office, 1961.

Zaninovich, M. George. *The Development of Socialist Yugoslavia.* Baltimore: The Johns Hopkins Press, 1968.

Zilliacus, Konni. *Tito of Yugoslavia.* London: Michael Joseph, 1952.

*Oppositional Tendencies and Humanist-Marxist Concepts in Poland, East Germany, and the U.S.S.R.*

Amalrik, Andrei. *Will the Soviet Union Survive Until 1984?* Rev. ed. New York: Harper & Row, 1971.

Boukovsky, V. *Une nouvelle maladie mentale en URSS: L'opposition.* Paris: Editions du Seuil, 1971.

Bronska-Pampuch, Wanda. *Polen zwischen Hoffnung und Verzweiflung.* Cologne: Verlag für Politik und Wirtschaft, 1958.

Browne, Michael (ed.). *Ferment in the Ukraine.* New York: Praeger, 1971.

Brumberg, Abraham (ed.). *In Quest of Justice: Protest and Dissent in the Soviet Union Today.* New York: Praeger, 1970.

Chornovil, Vyacheslav. *The Chornovil Papers.* New York: McGraw-Hill, 1968.

Dzyuba, Ivan. *Internationalism or Russification?* London: Weidenfeld & Nicolson, 1968.

Gerstenmaier, C. *Die Stimme der Stummen: Die demokratische Bewegung in der Sowjetunion.* Stuttgart: Seewald Verlag, 1971.

Ginsburg, Alexander (ed.). *Weissbuch in Sachen Sinjawskij-Daniel.* Frankfurt/M.: Possev Verlag, 1967.

Havemann, Robert. *Dialektik ohne Dogma?* Naturwissenschaft und Weltanschauung. Reinbek: Rowohlt, 1964.

————. *Fragen Antworten Fragen.* Munich: Piper, 1970.

————. "Kommunismus—Utopie und Wirklichkeit." *Christentum und Marxismus—heute.* Gespräche der Paulus-Gesellschaft. Vienna: Europa Verlag, 1966.

Hayward, Max (ed. and trans.). *On Trial: The Soviet State Versus "Abram Tertz" and "Nikolai Arzhak,"* New York: Harper & Row, 1966.

Jänicke, Martin. *Der Dritte Weg.* Cologne: Neuer Deutscher Verlag, 1964.

Jordan, Z.A. *Philosophy and Ideology.* The Development of Philosophy and Marxism-Leninism in Poland Since the Second World War. Dordrecht: D. Reidel, 1963.

Katz, Zev. *Soviet Dissenters and Social Structure in the U.S.S.R.* Cambridge, Mass.: Center for International Studies, M.I.T. Press, 1971.

Knötzsch, Dieter. *Interkommunistische Opposition.* Das Beispiel Robert Havemann. Opladen: C.W. Leske Verlag, 1968.

Kuron, Jacek. *Revolutionary Marxist Students in Poland Speak Out, 1964–1968.* New York: Merit Publishers, 1968.

Labedz, Leopold. *Solzhenitsyn: A Documentary Record.* New York: Harper & Row, 1970.

Lewytzky, Boris. *Politische Opposition in der UdSSR 1960–1972. Analyse und Dokumentation.* Munich: Deutscher Taschenbuch Verlag, 1972.

Litvinov, Pavel. *The Demonstration in Pushkin Square.* The Trial Records with Commentary and an Open Letter. Boston: Gambit, 1969.

————. *The Trial of the Four. A Collection of Materials on the Case of Galanskov, Ginzburg, Dobrovolsky, and Lashkova, 1967–1968.* New York: Viking Press, 1971.

Marchenko, Anatol. *My Testimony.* London: Pall Mall, 1969.

Marie, Jean Jacques, and Head, Carol. *L'Affaire Guinzbourg Galanskov.* Paris: Editions de Seuil, 1969.

Medvedev, Roy and Zhores. *A Question of Madness.* New York: Alfred A. Knopf, 1971.

Moroz, Valentyn. *A Chronicle of Resistance in the Ukraine.* Smoloskyp, 1970.

Parsons, Howard L. *Humanist Philosophy in Contemporary Poland and Yugoslavia.* New York: The American Institute for Marxist Studies, 1966.

Potichny, Peter J. (ed.). *Papers and Proceedings of the McMaster Conference on Dissent in the Soviet Union.* Hamilton, Ont.: 1972.

Raina, Peter K. *Die Krise der Intellektuellen.* Die Rebellion für die Freiheit in Polen. Olten: Walter Verlag, 1968.

Reddaway, Peter. *Uncensored Russia: Protest and Dissent in the Soviet Union.* New York: American Heritage Press, 1972.

Reve, Karel van Het (ed.). *Dear Comrade: Pavel Litvinov and the Voices of Soviet Citizens in Dissent.* New York: Pitman, 1969.

———. *Letters and Telegrams to Pavel M. Litvinov.* Dordrecht, Holland: D. Reidel, 1969.

Rothberg, Abraham. *The Heirs of Stalin; Dissidence and the Soviet Regime, 1953–1970.* Ithaca, N.Y.: Cornell University Press, 1972.

Sakharov, Andrei D. *Progress, Coexistence, and Intellectual Freedom.* New York: Norton, 1968.

Slavinsky, Michel. *La presse clandestine en URSS.* Paris: Nouvelle Editions Latines, 1970.

Tairow, Alexander von. *Demokratie in der Illegalität.* Stuttgart: Seewald Verlag, 1971.

Tertz, Abram. *On Socialist Realism.* New York: Pantheon, 1960.

## Oppositional Trends in Hungary: The Hungarian Revolution of 1956

Aczel, Tamás, and Meray, Tibor. *The Revolt of the Mind.* New York: Praeger; London: Thames & Hudson, 1959.

Arendt, Hannah. *Die ungarische Revolution und der totalitäre Imperialismus.* Munich: Piper, 1958.

Aron, Raymond. *The Meaning of Hungary.* New York: *New Leader,* 1958.

Bain, Leslie B. *The Reluctant Satellite.* An Eyewitness Report on Eastern Europe and the Hungarian Revolution. New York and London: Macmillan, 1960.

Beke, László. *A Student's Diary: Budapest, October 16–November 1, 1956.* New York: Viking; London: Hutchinson, 1957.

Darnoy, Paul. *Ungarn nach dem Volksaufstand.* Cologne: Kiepenheuer & Witsch, 1960.

Dewar, Hugo, and Norman, Daniel. *Revolution and Counterrevolution in Hungary.* London: Socialist Union of Central-Eastern Europe, 1957.

*Der Fall Imre Nagy.* Eine Dokumentation. Cologne: Kiepenheuer & Witsch, 1958.

Fejto, François. *Behind the Rape of Hungary.* New York: McKay, 1957.

*Four Days of Freedom: The Uprising in Hungary.* Brussels: International Confederation of Free Trade Unions, 1957.

Fryer, Peter. *Hungarian Tragedy.* London: Dobson, 1956.

Gosztony, Peter. *Der ungarische Volksaufstand in Augenzeugenberichten.* Düsseldorf: Karl Rauch Verlag, 1966.

Hegedüs, András. "Konfrontation mit der Wirklichkeit." *Club Voltaire. Jahrbuch für kritische Aufklärung.* Vol. III. Munich: Szczesny Verlag, 1967.

———. "Prinzipien der Gesellschraftskontrolle in der sozialistischen Wirtschaft." Varga (ed.). *Sozialismus in Europa.* Vienna: Europa Verlag, 1967.

———. "Die soziale Kontrolle in der sozialistischen Wirtschaft." *Club Voltaire.*

*The Hungarian Uprising.* An Abridgement of the Report of the United Nations Special Committee on the Problem of Hungary. London: Her Majesty's Stationery Office, 1957.

Kecskemeti, Paul. *The Unexpected Revolution: Social Forces in the Hungarian Uprising.* Stanford: Stanford University Press; London: Oxford University Press, 1961.

Lasky, Melvin J. (ed.). *The Hungarian Revolution.* Recorded in Documents, Dispatches, Eyewitness Accounts, and World-wide Reactions. New York: Praeger; London: Secker & Warburg, 1957.

Meray, Tibor. *Thirteen Days That Shook the Kremlin.* New York: Praeger; London: Thames & Hudson, 1959.

Mikes, George. *The Hungarian Revolution.* New York: Praeger; London: Andre Deutsch, 1957.

Nagy, Imre. *On Communism: In Defense of the New Course.* New York: Praeger; London: Thames & Hudson, 1957.

Paloczi-Horvath, George. *The Undefeated.* Boston: Little, Brown; London: Secker & Warburg, 1959.

*The Revolt in Hungary.* New York: Free Europe Committee, 1956.

*The Truth About the Nagy Affair.* Facts, Documents, Comments. New York: Praeger; London: Secker & Warburg, 1959.

Urban, George. *The Nineteen Days.* London: Heinemann, 1957.

Vali, Ferenc A. *Rift and Revolt in Hungary.* Cambridge, Mass.: Harvard University Press; London: Oxford University Press, 1961.

*Czechoslovakia: The "Prague Spring" and the Soviet Occupation*

Brahm, Heinz. *Der Kreml und die CSSR 1968–1969.* Stuttgart: Kohlhammer, 1970.

Chapman, Colin. *August 21—The Rape of Czechoslovakia*. Philadelphia: J.B. Lippincott, 1968.

Ello, Paul (ed.). *Czechoslovakia's Blueprint for "Freedom."* Washington, D.C.: Acropolis Books, 1968.

Golan, Galia. *The Czechoslovak Reform Movement: Communism in Crisis, 1962–1968*. New York: Cambridge University Press, 1971.

Hodnett, Grey, and Potichny, Peter J. *The Ukraine and the Czechoslovak Crisis*. Canberra: Australian National University, 1970.

Jownalist, M. *A Year Is Eight Months: Czechoslovakia 1968*. Garden City, N.Y.: Doubleday, 1970.

Littell, Robert (ed.). *The Czech Black Book*. New York: Praeger, 1969.

Löbl, Eugen. *Stalinism in Prague*. New York: Grove Press, 1969.

Löbl, Eugen, and Grünwald, Leopold. *Die intellektuelle Revolution*. Düsseldorf: Econ Verlag, 1968.

Remington, Robin Allison (ed.). *Winter in Prague. Documents on Czechoslovak Communism in Crisis*. Intro. by William E. Griffith. Cambridge, Mass.: M.I.T. Press, 1969.

Schwartz, Harry. *Prague's 200 Days: The Struggle for Democracy in Czechoslovakia*. New York: Praeger, 1969.

Selucky, Radoslav. *Czechoslovakia: The Plan That Failed*. New York: Thomas Nelson, 1970.

Shawcross, William. *Dubček*. New York: Simon and Schuster, 1971.

Svitak, Ivan. *The Czechoslovak Experiment 1968–1969*. New York: Columbia University Press, 1971.

Windsor, Philip, and Roberts, Adam. *Czechoslovakia 1968: Reform, Repression, and Resistance*. New York: Columbia University Press, 1969.

Zeman, Z.A.B. *Prague Spring*. A Report on Czechoslovakia, 1968. New York: Hill & Wang, 1969.

☐ **Other Works on Marxism—General Development and Particular Aspects**

Acton, H.B. *The Illusion of the Epoch*. Marxism-Leninism as a Philosophical Creed. London: Cohen & West, 1955; Boston: Beacon Press, 1957.

Almasi, M., Aptheker, H., et al. *Marxism and Alienation*. Collected Essays. New York: American Institute for Marxist Studies, 1965.

Almond, Gabriel A., et al. *The Appeals of Communism*. Princeton, N.J.: Princeton University Press; London: Oxford University Press, 1954.

Anderson, Thornton. *Russian Political Thought*. Ithaca: Cornell University Press, 1967.

Aptheker, H., Cohen, R.S., et al. *Marxism and Democracy*. Collected Essays. New York: American Institute for Marxist Studies, 1965.

Aron, Raymond. *The Opium of the Intellectuals*. London: Secker and Warburg, 1957; New York: Norton, 1962.

Banning, W. *Der Kommunismus als politisch-soziale Weltreligion*. Berlin: Lettner, 1953.

Bell, Daniel. *Marxian Socialism in the United States*. Princeton, N.J.: Princeton University Press, 1970.

Bernal, J. D. *Marxism and Science*. London: 1952.

Bernstein, Samuel (ed.). *A Centenary of Marxism*. New York: Science & Society, 1948.

Bochenski, Joseph M., and Niemeyer, Gerhart (eds.). *Handbook on Communism*. New York: Praeger, 1962.

Buber, Martin. *Paths in Utopia*. London: Routledge & Kegan Paul; New York: Macmillan, 1949.

Buchholz, Arnold. *Der Kampf um die bessere Welt*. Ansätze zum Durchdenken der geistigen Ost-West-Probleme. Stuttgart: Deutsche Verlags-Anstalt, 1962.

Bukharin, N.I., Deborin, A.M., et al. *Marxism and Modern Thought*. New York: Harcourt Brace Jovanovich, 1935.

Carew Hunt, R.N. *A Guide to Communist Jargon*. London: Bles; New York: Macmillan, 1957.

———. *Marxism, Past and Present*. London: Bles; New York: Macmillan, 1954.

———. *The Theory and Practice of Communism*. London: Bles; New York: Macmillan, 1950.

Carr, Edward Hallett. *Studies in Revolution*. London: Macmillan; New York: Macmillan, 1950.

Chambre, Henri. *Christianity and Communism*. New York: Hawthorn Books, 1960.

———. *De Karl Marx à Mao Tse-toung*. Introduction critique au marxisme-leninisme. Paris: Institut catholique de Paris, 1959.

———. *Le Marxisme en Union Sovietique, ideologie et institutions, leur évolution de 1917 à nos jours*. Paris: Editions du Seuil, 1955.

Cole, George Douglas Howard. *A History of Socialist Thought*. London: Macmillan, 1954. 4 vols. 1. Socialist Thought. The Forerunners, 1789–1850. 2. Marxism and Anarchism, 1850–1890. 3. The Second International, 1894–1914. 4. Communism and Social Democracy, 1914–1931.

———. *The Meaning of Marxism*. London: Gollancz, 1948.

Collinet, Michel. *Du Bolchevisme*. Evolution et variations du marxisme-leninisme. Paris: Amiot & Dumont, 1957.

*The Communist Blueprint for the Future.* The Complete Texts of All Four Communist Manifestos, 1848–1961. Intro. by Thomas P. Whitney. New York: Dutton, 1962.

Conquest, Robert. *Where Marx Went Wrong.* London: Tom Stacey, Ltd., 1970.

Cornforth, Maurice. *Historical Materialism.* New York: International Publishers, 1954.

Daniels, Robert V. (ed.). *A Documentary History of Communism from Lenin to Mao.* New York: Random House, 1960.

————. *The Nature of Communism.* New York: Random House, 1962.

Degras, Jane (ed.). *The Communist International 1919–1943. Documents.* London and New York: Oxford University Press, 1965.

Deutscher, Isaac. *Heretics and Renegades.* London: Hamish Hamilton, 1955; Indianapolis: Bobbs, Merrill, 1969.

————. *Marxism in Our Time.* Berkeley: Ramparts Press, 1971.

————. *The Unfinished Revolution, Russia 1917–1967.* New York and London: Oxford University Press, 1967.

Djilas, Milovan. *The New Class.* New York: Praeger; London: Thames & Hudson, 1957.

Dobb, Maurice. *On Marxism Today.* London: The Hogarth Press, 1952.

Drachkovitch, Milorad M. *Marxism in the Modern World.* Stanford: Stanford University Press, 1965.

————. *Marxist Ideology in the Contemporary World—Its Appeals and Paradoxes.* New York: Praeger, 1966.

Dunayevskaya, Raya. *Marxism and Freedom: From 1776 Until Today.* New York: Bookman Associates; London: Vision Press, 1958.

Eastman, Max. *Marxism: Is It a Science?* New York: Norton, 1940.

————. *Reflections on the Failure of Socialism.* New York: Devin-Adair, 1955.

Fetscher, Iring. *Die Freiheit im Lichte des Marxismus-Leninismus.* Bonn: Bundeszentrale für Heimatdienst, 1963.

————. *Karl Marx und der Marxismus.* Munich: Piper, 1967.

————. *Von Marx zur Sowjetideologie.* Frankfurt/M.: Diesterweg, 1961.

————. *Der Marxismus: Seine Geschichte in Dokumenten.* Munich: Piper, 1962–65. Bd. 1: Philosophie, Ideologie; Bd. 2: Okonomie, Soziologie; Bd. 3: Politik.

Feuer, Lewis S. *Marx and the Intellectuals: A Set of Post-ideological Essays.* Garden City, N.Y.: Doubleday, 1969.

Fisher, Harold H. *The Communist Revolution.* An Outline of Strategy and Tactics. Stanford: Stanford University Press; London: Oxford University Press, 1955.

Fisher, Marguerite J. *Communist Doctrine and the Free World.* The Ideology of Communism According to Marx, Engels, Lenin, and Stalin. Syracuse: Syracuse University Press, 1952.

Fougeyrollas, Pierre. *Le Marxisme en question.* Paris: Editions du Seuil, 1959.

Friedrich, Carl J., and Brzezinski, Zbigniew K. *Totalitarian Dictatorship and Autocracy.* Cambridge, Mass.: Harvard University Press; London: Oxford University Press, 1957.

Fromm, Erich. *Beyond the Chains of Illusion—My Encounter with Marx and Freud.* New York: Pocket Books, 1963.

Fulton, Robert B. *Original Marxism—Estranged Offspring.* A Study of Points of Contact and of Conflict Between Original Marxism and Christianity. Boston: Christopher, 1960.

Garaudy, Roger. *From Anathema to Dialogue.* New York: Herder and Herder, 1966.

————. *A Christian-Communist Dialogue.* Garden City, N.Y.: Doubleday, 1968.

————. *Marxism in the Twentieth Century.* New York: Scribner's, 1970.

Geiger, Theodor. *Die Klassengesellschaft im Schmelztiegel.* Cologne: Verlag Gustav Kiepenheuer, 1949.

George, Richard T. de. *Patterns of Soviet Thought.* Ann Arbor: University of Michigan Press, 1966.

Goodman, Elliot R. *The Soviet Design for a World State.* New York: Columbia University Press; London: Oxford University Press, 1960.

Graham, Loren R. *Science and Philosophy in the Soviet Union.* New York: Alfred A. Knopf, 1972.

Gramsci, Antonio. *The Modern Prince, and Other Writings.* London: Lawrence & Wishart, 1957; New York: International Publishers, 1957, 1967.

Gurian, Waldemar. *Bolshevism: A Study of Soviet Communism.* Notre Dame, Ind.: University of Notre Dame Press, 1952.

Hammond, Thomas T. (ed.). *The Anatomy of Communist Takeovers.* Munich: Institute for the Study of the U.S.S.R., 1971.

Hampsch, George H. *The Theory of Communism.* New York: Philosophical Library, 1965.

Hook, Sidney. *Marx and the Marxists.* Princeton, N.J.: Van Nostrand, 1955.

————. *Marxist Ideology in the Contemporary World.* Stanford: Stanford University Press, 1966.

Howe, Irving (ed.). *Essential Works of Socialism.* New York: Holt, Rinehart and Winston, 1970.

Jacobs, Dan N. (ed.). *The New Communist Manifesto and Related Documents.* Evanston, Ill.: Row, Peterson, 1961.

Jacobson, Julius. *Soviet Communism and the Socialist Vision.* New York: New Politics Publishing Co., 1972.

Kelsen, Hans. *The Political Theory of Bolshevism.* Berkeley: University of California Press; London: Cambridge University Press, 1948.

Künzli, Arnold. *Über Marx hinaus.* Beiträge zur Ideologiekritik. Freiburg i. Br.: Rombach, 1969.

Landy, A. *Marxism and the Democratic Tradition.* New York: International Publishers, 1946.

Lange, Max G. *Marxismus, Leninismus, Stalinismus.* Stuttgart: Klett, 1957.

Laski, Harold J. *Communist Manifesto: Socialist Landmark.* London: Allen and Unwin, 1948.

Lefebvre, Henri. *Probleme des Marxismus, heute.* Frankfurt/M.: Suhrkamp, 1965.

———. *Problèmes actuels du Marxisme.* Paris: Presses Universitaires de France, 1958.

Leites, Nathan C. *A Study of Bolshevism.* Glencoe, Ill.: Free Press, 1953.

Lepp, Ignace. *From Karl Marx to Jesus Christ.* London and New York: Sheed & Ward, 1958.

Le Rossignol, James E. *Background to Communist Thought—From Marx to Stalin.* New York: Thomas Y. Crowell, 1968.

Leser, Norbert. *Die Odyssee des Marxismus.* Vienna: Molden, 1971.

Lewis, John. *Marxism and the Open Mind.* London: Routledge & Kegan Paul; New York: Paine-Whitman, 1957.

Lichtheim, George. *Marxism in Modern France.* New York and London: Columbia University Press, 1966.

Lobkowicz, Nicholas (ed.). *Marx and the Western World.* Notre Dame, Ind.: Notre Dame University Press, 1967.

Macek, Josef. *An Essay on the Impact of Marxism.* Pittsburgh: University of Pittsburgh Press, 1956.

Marcuse, Herbert. *Soviet Marxism.* New York: Columbia University Press; London: Routledge & Kegan Paul, 1957.

Mayo, Harry B. *Introduction to Marxist Theory.* New York: Oxford University Press, 1960.

———. *Democracy and Marxism.* London and New York: Oxford University Press, 1955.

Merleau-Ponty, Maurice. *Humanism and Terror: An Essay on the Communist Problem.* Boston: Beacon Press, 1969.

Meyer, Alfred G. *Communism.* New York: Random House, 1960.

Meyer, Frank S. *The Molding of Communists.* New York: Harcourt Brace Jovanovich, 1961.

Monnerot, Jules. *Sociology and Psychology of Communism.* Boston: Beacon Press, 1953.

Moore, Stanley W. *The Critique of Capitalist Democracy*. An Introduction to the Theory of the State in Marx, Engels, and Lenin. New York: Paine-Whitman, 1957.

———. *Zur Theorie politischer Taktik des Marxismus*. Frankfurt/M.: Europäische Verlags-Anstalt, 1969.

Nollau, Günther. *International Communism and World Revolution*. London: Hollis & Charter; New York: Praeger, 1961.

Oelssner, Fred. *Der Marxismus der Gegenwart und seine Kritiker*. East Berlin: Dietz, 1952.

Parkes, Henry Bamford. *Marxism, an Autopsy*. Chicago: University of Chicago Press, 1964.

Parson, Howard L. *Humanism and Marx's Thought*. Springfield, Ill.: Charles C Thomas, 1971.

Pietromarchi, Luca. *The Soviet World*. London: Allen and Unwin, 1965.

Plamenatz, John. *German Marxism and Russian Communism*. London and New York: Longmans, Green, 1954.

Polin, Raymond. *Marxian Foundations of Communism—An Introduction to the Study of Communist Theory*. Chicago: Regnery, 1966.

Portus, G. W. *Marx and Modern Thought*. Sydney, Australia: Macmillan, 1921.

Rossiter, Clinton. *Marxism: The View from America*. New York: Harcourt Brace Jovanovich, 1960.

Savage, Katherine. *The Story of Marxism and Communism*. New York: New American Library, 1970.

Schack, Herbert. *Marx, Mao, Neomarxismus—Wandlungen einer Ideologie*. Frankfurt/M.: Akademische Verlagsgesellschaft Athenaion, 1969.

Schlesinger, Rudolf. *Marx: His Time and Ours*. London: Routledge & Kegan Paul, 1950.

Schumpeter, Joseph A. *Capitalism, Socialism, and Democracy*. New York: Harper & Row; London: Allen and Unwin, 1950.

Scott, Andrew MacKay. *The Anatomy of Communism*. New York: Philosophical Library, 1951.

Selsam, Howard. *Philosophy in Revolution*. New York: International Publishers; London: Lawrence & Wishart, 1957.

Seton-Watson, Hugh. *From Lenin to Khrushchev: The History of World Communism*. New York and London: Praeger, 1960.

Simirenko, Alex. *Social Thought in the Soviet Union*. Chicago: Quadrangle Press, 1967.

Sternberg, Fritz. *Anmerkungen zu Marx—heute*. Frankfurt/M.: Europäische Verlags-Anstalt, 1965.

———. *Marx und die Gegenwart*. Cologne: Verlag für Politik und Wirtschaft, 1955.

Sweezy, P.M., and Bettelheim, Charles. *On the Transition to Socialism*. New York and London: Monthly Review Press, 1971.

Talmon, J.L. *The Rise of Totalitarian Democracy*. Boston: Beacon Press, 1952.

Thier, Erich. *Etappen der Marxinterpretation. Marxismusstudien*. Schriften der Studiengemeinschaft der Evangelischen Akademien. Tübingen: J.C.B. Mohr, 1954.

Tucker, Robert C. *The Marxian Revolution Idea*. New York: Norton, 1969.

——. *Paths of Communist Revolution*. Princeton, N.J.: Princeton University Press, 1968.

——. *The Soviet Political Mind*. New York: Praeger, 1963.

Turner, John K. *Challenge to Karl Marx*. New York: Reynal and Hitchcock, 1941.

Ulam, Adam B. *The Unfinished Revolution*. An Essay on the Sources of Influence of Marxism and Communism. New York: Random House, 1960.

Vigor, P.H. *A Guide to Marxism and Its Effects on Soviet Development*. London: Faber and Faber, 1966.

Vranicki, Predrag. *Geschichte des Marxismus*. Vol. 1. Frankfurt/M.: Suhrkamp, 1972.

Wilson, Edmund. *To the Finland Station*. Garden City, N.Y.: Doubleday, 1953; London: Collins, 1956.

Wittfogel, Karl A. *Oriental Despotism*. New Haven: Yale University Press, 1959.

Wolfe, Bertram D. *Communist Totalitarianism: Keys to the Soviet System*. Boston: Beacon Press, 1961.

——. *An Ideology in Power*. New York: Stein & Day, 1969.

——. *Marxism, 100 Years in the Life of a Doctrine*. New York: Delta Books, 1967.

Wright, David McCord. *The Trouble with Marx*. New Rochelle, N.Y.: Arlington House, 1961.

Zeitlin, Irving M. *Marxism, A Re-examination*. Princeton, N.J.: Van Nostrand, 1967.

# Index